CIBSE GUIDE

Volume A

DESIGN DATA

CIBSE

© The Chartered Institution of Building Services Engineers
Delta House, 222 Balham High Road, London SW12 9BS

First published as a loose-leaf volume, 1940
Revised and published as a bound volume, 1955
Reprinted, 1957
2nd edition, 1959
Reprinted, 1961
3rd edition, 1965
4th edition, in three volumes, 1970
5th edition, in separate sections, 1974 onwards
Reprinted in three volumes, 1986

THE CHARTERED INSTITUTION OF BUILDING SERVICES ENGINEERS

LONDON

1986

(Reprinted 1988)

Vol. A ISBN 0 900953 29 2
Vol. B ISBN 0 900953 30 6
Vol. C ISBN 0 900953 31 4
Set ISBN 0 900953 28 4

Printed and bound by Staples Printers St Albans Ltd.

TECHNICAL PUBLICATIONS COMMITTEE

Chairman
R. J. OUGHTON

Elected Members
J. B. COLLINS
S. L. HODKINSON
A. J. MARRIOTT
N. O. MILBANK
D. J. STOKOE
G. WORTHINGTON
A. N. YOUNG

Co-opted Members
S. ASHLEY
J. BARNES
M. COREY

Ex-officio Member
D. M. LUSH

Secretary
S. P. HODGSON

Technical Secretary
K. J. BUTCHER

Members of Task Groups and other contributors to Volume A
N. S. BILLINGTON
G. W. BRUNDRETT
J. CAMPBELL
A. A. CORNELL
J. P. CORNISH
D. J. CROOME
S. C. EDWARDS
D. FITZGERALD
A. P. GAIT

J. HARRINGTON-LYNN
M. A. HUMPHREYS
R. H. L. JONES
R. E. LACY
A. G. LOUDON
N. O. MILBANK
D. R. OUGHTON
P. G. T. OWENS
J. PEACH

P. PETHERBRIDGE
D. A. RUSSELL
R. SCOTT
D. L. THORNLEY
D. TUDDENHAM
P. R. WARREN
J. D. WATTS
A. WILSON
D. W. WOOD

Coordinating Editor
S. P. HODGSON

Editors
K. J. BUTCHER
A. P. GAIT
D. J. ROWE

FOREWORD TO THE FIFTH EDITION

Views expressed by practicing members of the Institution in informal contacts with the Technical Publications Committee have reinforced the growing opinion that the reissue of the Guide in a three volume set would be popular with the membership. Since 1982, the Committee has pursued this aim.

This edition of Volume A, forming part of the reissue, has been revised completely since the 1970 bound Guide was published. In particular, Sections A4, A7, A8 and A10 of this bound volume are new editions. A further change has been the incorporation of Section A6, Solar Data, into Section A2, the numbering of the other Sections, however, has been left unchanged to provide consistency of reference.

In the Foreword to Book A of the 1970 Guide the then Chairman of the Guide Committee wrote that the contents were in advance of technology elsewhere in the world. Since then, further advances have been made in the technology presented, particularly in the Sections dealing with the Thermal Response of Buildings and the Estimation of Plant Capacity. The energy balances used in these Sections now take direct account of dry resultant temperature, considered to be the acceptable index of comfort. These more definitive calculation techniques bring with them, perhaps, a greater need for users of the Guide to understand and appreciate the design process if errors in application are to be avoided.

Additionally, since the 1970 bound Guide, Section A3, Thermal Properties of Building Structures, a comprehensive and very widely used Section, has been included as a reference document in the Building Regulations.

An important part is played in the continuing process of reviewing and revising the Guide by many individual members of the Institution and other practitioners in the profession and industry. Their names are listed an an expression of the Institution's gratitude for their contribution.

The Technical Publications Committee is keenly aware of the enormous challenge of maintaining the Guide as an up-to-date work of reference and design tool. There is also seen to be a need to continue to offer manual calculation techniques as well as developing more sophisticated and improved design methods. The Committee will try to continue to meet these needs and challenges. Comment or criticism from Members or other users of the Guide provides a useful measure of how these objectives are met and purposeful and constructive feedback will be welcomed.

R. J. Oughton

CONTENTS

Volume A: Design Data

Section A1 ENVIRONMENTAL CRITERIA FOR DESIGN

Thermal comfort. Ventilation. Relative humidity. Ionisation. Lighting. Sound.

Section A2 WEATHER AND SOLAR DATA

UK Cold weather data. Warm weather data. Annual weather data. Wind. Precipitation. Daylight availability. Atmospheric pollution. World weather data. Solar data. Intensity of solar radiation. Sol-air temperatures. Availability of solar radiation. Basic radiation data – world values.

Section A3 THERMAL PROPERTIES OF BUILDING STRUCTURES

Building Regulations. Steady state thermal characteristics. Non-steady state thermal characteristics. Tables of U and Y values. Properties of materials. Thermal conductivity testing.

Section A4 AIR INFILTRATION AND NATURAL VENTILATION

Calculation of infiltration and natural ventilation. Natural ventilation rates. Infiltration rates for design. Empirical values for air infiltration.

Section A5 THERMAL RESPONSE OF BUILDINGS

Temperatures. Steady state energy balances. Cyclic conditions. Energy inputs. Applications to heating. Air conditioning plant sizing. Summertime temperatures. Calculating annual energy consumption.

Section A7 INTERNAL HEAT GAINS

Human and animal bodies. Lighting. Electric motors. Computer and office equipment. Miscellaneous electrical appliances. Gas heated appliances.

Section A8 SUMMERTIME TEMPERATURES IN BUILDINGS

Calculation sequence. Data required. Mean heat gains. Mean internal temperature. Swing in heat gain. Swing in internal environmental temperature. Peak internal environmental temperature. Example calculations.

Section A9 ESTIMATION OF PLANT CAPACITY

Temperatures. Heating. Air conditioning. Assessment of reliability. Cooling load tables. Example calculations.

Section A10 MOISTURE TRANSFER AND CONDENSATION

Hygroscopic materials. Evaporation and condensation at surfaces. Vapour diffusion within materials. Vapour diffusion in composite structures. Prediction of moisture condensation. Sources of moisture. Controlling and eliminating condensation.

INDEX

To volume A.

CONTENTS

Volumes B and C

Volume B   INSTALLATION AND EQUIPMENT DATA

B1   Heating

B2   Ventilation and Air Conditioning (Requirements)

B3   Ventilation and Air Conditioning (Systems, Equipment and Control)

B4   Water Service Systems

B5   Fire Safety Engineering

B6   Miscellaneous Piped Services

B7   Corrosion Protection and Water Treatment

B8   Sanitation and Waste Disposal

B10 Electrical Power

B11 Automatic Control

B12 Sound Control

B13 Combustion Systems

B14 Refrigeration and Heat Rejection

B15 Vertical Transportation

B16 Miscellaneous Equipment

B18 Owning and Operating Costs

Index to Volumes A, B and C

Volume C   REFERENCE DATA

C1   Properties of Humid Air

C2   Properties of Water and Steam

C3   Heat Transfer

C4   Flow of Fluids in Pipes and Ducts

C5   Fuels and Combustion

C7   Metric Units and Miscellaneous Data

Index to Volume C

SECTION A1 ENVIRONMENTAL CRITERIA FOR DESIGN

Introduction.. *Page* A1–3

Thermal Comfort... A1–3

    Thermal Indices A1–4

    Criteria for Sedentary Occupations..................... A1–4

    Criteria for Active Occupations........................... A1–6

    Effect of Air Movement on Comfort A1–6

    Difference between Air Temperature and Mean Radiant Temperature A1–6

    Radiation A1–6

    Asymmetric Radiation and Discomfort................. A1–7

Ventilation.. A1–8

    Physiological Considerations............................... A1–8

    Odour Dilution A1–8

Relative Humidity A1–9

Ionisation A1–9

Lighting A1–10

    Lighting for Safety... A1–10

    Lighting for Performance A1–11

    Lighting for Pleasantness A1–13

Sound.. A1–15

    Response of the Human Ear................................. A1–15

    NR and NC Curves A1–16

    Background Conditions.. A1–16

    Vibration A1–17

    Effects of Vibration A1–18

Appendix A1–19

Bibliography... A1–20

This edition of Section A1 was first published: 1979
Reprinted with amendments: 1986

SECTION A1 ENVIRONMENTAL CRITERIA FOR DESIGN

INTRODUCTION

The indoor environment should be safe, appropriate for its purpose and pleasant to inhabit. There should be little to cause annoyance or distraction and work or pleasure activities should be unhindered physically or mentally. A suitable environment can contribute towards a person's health, well-being and productivity.

The environmental factors considered here include the thermal, visual and acoustic conditions. It is not practical to formulate a single index which quantifies the individual's response to all these factors. It is necessary, therefore, to treat each separately in this section. However, in design all aspects need to be considered together, since the means of providing some components may influence the design of another. For example, ventilation plant needs acoustic treatment, heat gain from lighting is an additional load on cooling plant and acoustic treatment of a building affects the thermal properties.

THERMAL COMFORT

An individual senses skin temperature rather than the room temperature. The environmental control system is therefore a means of achieving controlled personal cooling with appropriate skin temperatures.

Virtually all of the energy derived from a person's food is emitted in the form of heat. Under normal conditions, the physiological process liberates about 115W, of which 75% is lost from the body by convection and radiation and 25% by evaporation. Physical work entails production of further quantities of heat which must be dissipated to the environment. Table A1.1 gives data on the total heat production, with sensible and latent distribution, under various conditions of work output and indoor climate.[1,2]

By means of involuntary mechanisms (shivering, sweating, control of blood flow) together with judicious use of clothing and variation of physical activity, a person is capable of maintaining his temperature constant in a wide range of environmental conditions. However, an individual is truly comfortable only over a much narrower range of climates. Individuals differ in the temperature they require and furthermore the comfort zone varies with activity, clothing and with the degree of acclimatization. Comfort depends not merely on the global sensation of warmth but on the relationship between the several factors which can affect the heat exchange between the person and the environment.

Fig. A1.1 shows the percentages of people in thermal comfort at temperatures around the optimum for the group. The curves are based on the results of numerous field studies in air conditioned buildings.[3] Curve A includes people giving any of the three central descriptions on a seven point comfort scale. Typical descriptions are 'slightly cool, neutral/comfortable and slightly warm'. Curve B is for the 'neutral/comfortable' category alone.

There is no temperature at which everyone is in the 'neutral/comfortable' zone, but near the optimum for the group, all are free from actual discomfort.

Clothing, which acts as an insulating layer between the skin temperature sensors and the room, also has a powerful effect on the preferred temperature. It has been found that, while there is a wide range of clothing available for each sex, women wearing dresses cannot easily become well insulated and men wearing suits cannot easily become lightly insulated. A change of clothing, such as removing a jacket, would mean an increase of 2 or 3°C in the preferred temperature.

The extent to which extra clothing may be used to offset cooler room temperatures is rather limited. Extra clothing may keep the body warm enough but leave the extremities unprotected and uncomfortable.[4] Also, with heavy clothing, the range of activity which is possible without sweating or shivering is considerably reduced.[5]

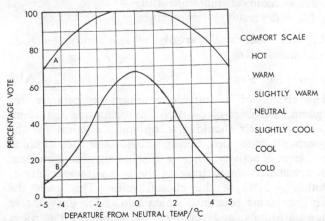

Fig. A1.1. Percentage comfort vote for people at around the neutral temperature.

Table A1.1. Heat emission from the human body (Adult Male, body surface area 2m²).

Application		Total	Sensible (s) and latent (1) heat emissions/W at the stated dry-bulb temperatures/°C									
			15		20		22		24		26	
Degree of activity	Typical		(s)	(l)	(s)	(l)	(s)	(l)	(s)	(l)	(s)	(l)
Seated at rest	Theatre, Hotel lounge	115	100	15	90	25	80	35	75	40	65	50
Light work	Office, Restaurant*	140	110	30	100	40	90	50	80	60	70	70
Walking slowly	Store, Bank	160	120	40	110	50	100	60	85	75	75	85
Light bench work	Factory	235	150	85	130	105	115	120	100	135	80	155
Medium work	Factory, Dance hall	265	160	105	140	125	125	140	105	160	90	175
Heavy work	Factory	440	200	220	190	250	165	275	135	305	105	335

*For restaurants serving hot meals, add 10 W sensible and 10 W latent for food.

Thermal Indices

Since a person's feeling of warmth depends on air temperature, radiant temperature, air movement and humidity, together with personal factors such as clothing and activity, many attempts have been made to devise indices which combine these variables. Dry bulb air temperature has long been used as a convenient measure of warmth but it can sometimes be misleading. Of the many indices, the most commonly encountered are equivalent temperature, effective temperature, globe temperature and resultant temperature. Four measurements are required to evaluate the thermal environment: the air temperature, mean radiant temperature, wet bulb temperature and air speed.

Resultant Temperature

The resultant temperature is the temperature recorded by a thermometer at the centre of a blackened globe 100 mm in diameter. This index is recommended for use in the UK and is given by:

$$t_{res} = \frac{t_r + t_{ai}\sqrt{10v}}{1 + \sqrt{10v}} \qquad .. \quad .. \quad .. \quad A1.1$$

where:

t_{ai} = inside air temperature .. .. .. °C
t_r = mean radiant temperature .. .. °C
t_{res} = dry resultant temperature .. .. °C

At 'still' indoor air speeds of $v=0.1$m/s, equation A1.1 simplifies to:

$$t_{res} = \tfrac{1}{2}t_r + \tfrac{1}{2}t_{ai} \quad .. \qquad .. \qquad .. \qquad .. \qquad A1.2$$

The choice of a suitable resultant temperature for system design resolves itself into choosing that temperature which should give optimum comfort for the occupants concerned, taking into account their clothing and level of activity. There will be no significant increase in dissatisfaction so long as the actual temperature is within ±1½°C of the chosen value. This gives the designer some tolerance which allows for unavoidable non-uniformity and temporal variations in the room temperature.

Criteria for Sedentary Occupations

A consideration of the data, the circumstances under which they were obtained and of current practice in the UK, Europe and USA leads to the suggestion that a majority of people will neither be warm nor cool in winter in rooms where the resultant temperature is between 19°C and 23°C when the air speed is less than 0.1 m/s, (i.e. nominally still air).

It can be assumed that the effect of humidity on warmth can be ignored when the resultant temperature is not much greater than the preferred value and the relative humidity lies between 40% and 70%.

Comparing results of field studies has shown a rather close relation between the preferred indoor temperature and the mean outdoor temperature for the location and the season of the year.[6] For occupants of buildings where no energy is being supplied for heating or cooling plant, there is a linear relationship between the preferred indoor temperature and the mean outdoor air temperature, such that the preferred temperature increases by approximately 0.5°C for every 1°C rise in the outdoor air temperature, see Fig. A1.2 Zone A. Where heating or cooling is in operation, a non-linear relationship exists, having a minimum when the outdoor mean is just below freezing and gradually rising for warmer or cooler conditions, see Fig. A1.2 Zone B. Fig. A1.2 thus provides a background of experience against which to view suggested indoor temperatures for any part of the world.

Table A1.2 gives recommended design criteria for various locations and Table A1.3 gives recommended values for internal resultant temperatures.

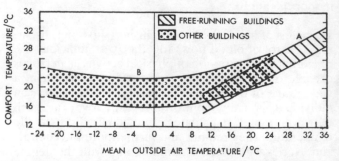

Fig. A1.2. Relationship between outside air temperature and comfort temperature.

Table A1.2. Design conditions.

Country	Season	Occupancy/category	Resultant temperature/°C	Relative humidity/%
UK	Summer	Continuous	20 to 22	50
		Transient	23	50
UK	Winter	Continuous	19 to 20	50
		Transient	16 to 18	50
Tropics	Summer	Continuous (optimum)	23	50
		Continuous (maximum)	25 / 26	60 / 45
		Transient (humid climate)	25 / 26	70 / 50
		Transient (arid climate)	27 / 28	45 / 40
Tropics	Winter	Short winter (as in humid climate)	Generally no heating required	
		Long winter (as in arid climate)	22	45

Table A1.3. Recommended design values for dry resultant temperature.

Type of building	t_{res}/°C	Type of building	t_{res}/°C
Art galleries and museums	20	Hotels:	
		Bedrooms (standard)	22
Assembly halls, lecture halls	18	Bedrooms (luxury)	24
		Public Rooms	21
Banking halls:		Staircases and corridors	18
Large (height > 4 m)	20	Entrance halls and foyers	18
Small (height < 4 m)	20		
		Laboratories	20
Bars	18		
		Law Courts	20
Canteens and dining rooms	20		
		Libraries:	
Churches and chapels:		Reading rooms (height > 4 m)	20
Up to 7000 m³	18	(height < 4 m)	20
> 7000 m³	18	Stack rooms	18
Vestries	20	Store rooms	15
Dining and banqueting halls	21	Offices:	
		General	20
Exhibition halls:		Private	20
Large (height > 4 m)	18	Stores	15
Small (height < 4 m)	18		
		Police stations:	
Factories:		Cells	18
Sedentary work	19		
Light work	16	Restaurants and tea shops..	18
Heavy work	13		
		Schools and colleges:	
Fire stations; ambulance stations:		Classrooms	18
Appliance rooms	15	Lecture rooms	18
Watch rooms	20	Studios	18
Recreation rooms	18		
		Shops and showrooms:	
Flats, residences, and hostels:		Small	18
Living rooms	21	Large	18
Bedrooms	18	Department store	18
Bed-sitting rooms	21	Fitting rooms	21
Bathrooms	22	Store rooms	15
Lavatories and cloakrooms	18		
Service rooms	16	Sports pavilions:	
Staircases and corridors	16	Dressing rooms	21
Entrance halls and foyers	16		
Public rooms	21	Swimming baths:	
		Changing rooms	22
Gymnasia	16	Bath hall	26
Hospitals:		Warehouses:	
Corridors	16	Working and packing spaces	16
Offices	20	Storage space	13
Operating theatre suite	18–21		
Stores	15		
Wards and patient areas	18		
Waiting rooms	18		

Criteria for Active Occupations

Comparatively little study has been made of the environmental conditions which are most acceptable to people engaged in physical work, although the tolerance to extreme conditions (usually of heat) has been investigated. In those cases where the process does not demand particular conditions of temperature and humidity, the resultant temperature in places where physical work is done should be from 3 to 5°C below that recommended for sedentary occupation, depending on the level of activity. It must also be remembered that when working hard, most people remove some of their normal clothing to a certain extent. Furthermore, hard work is usually carried out in short spells separated by rest pauses. Both these factors limit the reduction in resultant temperature which should be allowed.

At high rates of activity, particularly in a warm environment, sweating is an important mechanism for bodily heat loss. Reduced relative humidity is then a factor which can lead to improved comfort.

Some leisure activities (dancing, indoor games, etc.) involve a high degree of physical activity and the same considerations apply to them as to work activities. Warm conditions and low air movement are required in spaces such as swimming pools used by unclothed people. The resultant temperature should be between 25 and 30°C. If the body is wet, rapid air movement leads to chilling by evaporation and the air speed should be as low as possible.

Effect of Air Movement on Comfort

The cooling effect of air is well known and, if excessive, gives rise to complaints of draught. It should be noted that moving air temperature is not necessarily either the room air temperature or the inlet temperature of the ventilation air. It will generally lie between these values. The back of the neck is particularly sensitive to air movement and if the stream is directed onto this part of the body, the maximum allowable velocity is reduced. It is also worth noting that people are more tolerant of air movement where the direction varies.

Where air velocities in a room are greater than 0.1 m/s as may often be the case when mechanical ventilation systems are in use, the resultant temperature should be raised from its still air value to compensate for the cooling effects of the air movement. Fig. A1.3 gives suggested corrections. Velocities greater than 0.3 m/s are probably unacceptable except in summer.

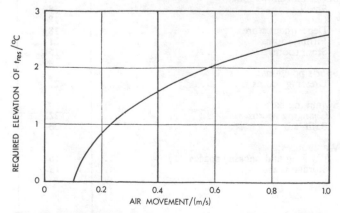

Fig. A1.3. Corrections to the dry resultant to take account of air movement.

Difference between Air Temperature and Mean Radiant Temperature

The experience from various field studies of occupied buildings is that the difference between the air temperature and mean radiant temperature is usually small.[7-11] For buildings of various kinds and in widely different climates, surveys during occupation have mean excesses of radiant temperature over air temperature ranging from 0 to 2°C. However, during cold weather in poorly insulated rooms having warm air heating, the air temperature may greatly exceed the mean radiant temperature. On sunny days in rooms with large areas of unshielded glass the reverse is true.

Radiation

Mean radiant temperature

People's thermal comfort depends significantly on the radiation exchange between them and their surroundings. To describe this balance the concept of mean radiant temperature is used. The mean radiant temperature at a point within an enclosure is a function of the areas, shapes, surface temperatures and emissivities of the enclosing elements viewed from that point. Mean radiant temperature is defined in terms of a small sphere placed at that point. It does not ideally represent the human body. For example, the body of a standing person presents a larger area to horizontal radiation than to vertical radiation, hence mean radiant temperature tends to overemphasise the effect of overhead radiation. However, for most purposes it is satisfactory to use mean radiant temperature.

Unless all the room surfaces are at the same temperature, mean radiant temperature varies throughout the enclosure. This variation will produce a change in resultant temperature and also introduce asymmetry where for example one side of the body is hot and the other side cold. This degree of asymmetry is not strong enough in most practical cases to create discomfort.[12] However, strong asymmetry can arise for example with radiant heating Practical considerations are given below. To quantify the degree of discomfort it is helpful to introduce the concepts of plane radiant and vector radiant temperature.[13]

Plane radiant temperature

The plane radiant temperature is the surface temperature inside a uniform hemisphere which would produce the same radiation on a small plane element at the test point as exists in the actual situation. If a room is considered to be divided by a plane through it the plane radiant temperature can be visualised as the radiant temperature resulting from the room surfaces to one side of the plane.

Vector radiant temperature

The vector radiant temperature is the maximum difference between two opposite plane radiant temperatures. It is a quantity having both magnitude and direction and obeys the laws of vector addition. It can be visualised as the average radiant temperature of one side of a room minus the other half in a direction such that it is a maximum.

Appendix 1 considers the three temperatures above in more detail.

Asymmetric Radiation and Discomfort

There are three cases of asymmetric radiation which may lead to discomfort:

(a) local cooling – radiation exchange with adjacent cold surfaces – such as single glazed windows;

(b) local heating – radiation with adjacent hot surfaces, such as overhead lighting;

(c) intrusion of short wavelength radiation such as solar radiation through glazing.

Local cooling

The most common occurrence is the discomfort which may be felt when near cold window surfaces. This experience, sometimes miscalled cold radiation, is due to the radiation exchange on one side of the body with the cold window surface. This effect both lowers the resultant temperature near to the window and also creates asymmetry. Discomfort will be experienced if the plane radiant temperature facing the cold surface is more than 8°C below the resultant temperature in a room containing normally clothed people and a low air speed.[12–14] Fig. A1.4[15] illustrates the position of the 13°C plane radiant temperature contour at 1m above the floor when the outside air temperature is −1°C and the resultant temperature is 21°C. Comfortable distances for other single glazed window sizes set in a cavity wall can be estimated from Fig. A1.5. This local cooling may be reduced by using double glazing or compensated by situating a radiator beneath the window.

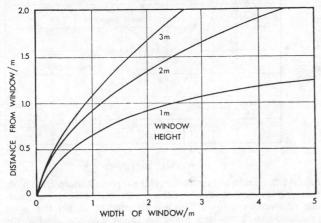

Fig. A1.4. Discomfort zone produced by local cooling.

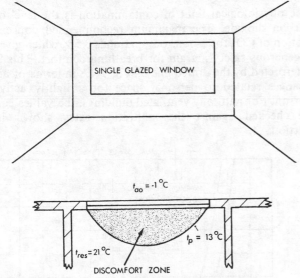

Fig. A1.5. Comfortable distances from centre of single glazed windows.

Radiant heating

Radiant heating systems are designed to provide the appropriate resultant temperature in that particular environment. However in producing the right degree of warmth the radiation may be strong enough to introduce uncomfortable asymmetric conditions.[16,17,18] Vector radiant temperatures up to 20°C do not increase discomfort but the directional effects may be noticeable and give rise to complaint. A maximum vector radiant temperature of 10°C is therefore recommended for ceiling heating applications. This criterion can be expressed as a relationship between downward emission from the ceiling and area of the heated panel. It is given for different distances between head and the ceiling in Fig. A1.6 for a square, low temperature panel. Fig. A1.6 can also be used in conjunction with the form factors of Fig. A1.17.

Criteria can be relaxed in exposed industrial situations where low air temperatures occur. High temperature emitters, such as bright gas-fired or electric heaters, may be based on the following criteria for buildings in which the air temperature is maintained around 15°C:

(a) the total irradiance on the floor due to the heaters should be approximately uniform and should not exceed 80 W/m²;

(b) the summed mean spherical irradiance 1.8m above the floor should not exceed 240 W/m²;

(c) the maximum irradiance from any one heater should not exceed 32 W/m² at floor level.

Another source of radiant heat is lighting. Fluorescent lighting raises the mean radiant temperature slightly and requires a lower air temperature to achieve a given resultant temperature. This reduction in air temperature is $\frac{1}{4}$–$\frac{1}{2}$°C under current office lighting standards, see Table A1.4. Tungsten lamps require a much larger reduction in air temperature to avoid overheating people and there is a risk of complaints of discomfort if the illuminances exceed 850 lx.

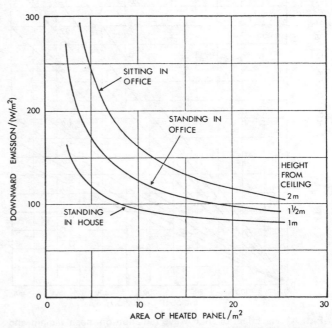

Fig. A1.6. Downward heat emission from centre of square low temperature radiant panel.

Table A1.4. Lamp data.

Lamp type	Radiation output (W/m² lx)	Elevation of t_r for 1 klx diffuse /°C	Reduction in design air temp for 1 klx diffuse /°C	Illuminance for t_v of 10°C /lx
Tungsten filament–Spot and GLS	0.07	6	2.6	850
Tungsten halogen	0.05	5	2.2	1200
Sodium LP – SOX	0.006	0.5	0.2	10000
Sodium HP – SON	0.009	0.8	0.4	6500
Mercury fluorescent – MBF	0.015	1.4	0.6	4000
Fluorescent – MCFE	0.008	0.7	0.3	7500

Short Wave Radiation

When solar radiation falls on a window the transmitted short wave radiation augments the mean radiant temperature as well as contributing to the cooling requirement from its absorption and subsequent convection from in-internal surfaces. In practice, the only significant part is the direct component of the radiation falling on occupants near the window and internally reflected radiation may be ignored.[19]

The amount of sunshine received depends on:

(a) the position of the sun;

(b) the transmittance of the window;

(c) the average absorptance of the clothing and skin of the person.

Fig. A1.7 shows the elevation of mean radiant temperature and of resultant temperature due to sunshine falling on a person in the direct rays of the sun. The graph will also work for all directional sources of radiation as well as solar radiation and may be used as an adjunct to the data given above.

Solar control glasses also absorb radiation which causes a rise in temperature when the sun falls on them. This elevation of temperature may be dealt with as given in the section on local heating, but the effect is not found to be troublesome in the UK.

VENTILATION

The object of introducing fresh air into a room is to dilute the level of contamination to one which is safe and acceptable. The contamination can be simply due to body odours in a crowded room or moisture build-up due to perspiration. Contamination in industrial situations may be gaseous or particulate and should be treated on the recommendations given in Sections B2 and B3 of the *Guide*.

Physiological Considerations

The physiological limit of contamination is the level of carbon dioxide. The maximum recommended concentration of CO_2 for 8-hour occupation is 0.5% which gives a generous safety margin for breathing comfort. This is interpreted by the dotted line on Fig. A1.8 in terms of air changes related to personal space for a lightly active person. For naturally ventilated buildings, the values can be checked against the infiltration rates shown in Section A4.

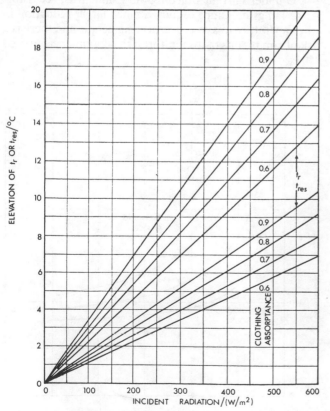

Fig. A1.7. Effect of short wave radiation on mean radiant and dry resultant temperatures.

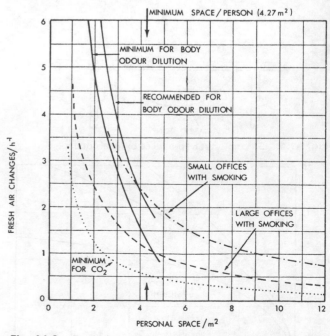

Fig. A1.8. Fresh air requirements for people in a room 2.7m high. Smoking is based on 26m³/h per smoker. Small offices may contain all smokers, large offices are assumed to reflect the adult population i.e. ½ smokers. Minimum space is as specified in the Offices, Shops and Railway Premises Act.[25]

Odour Dilution

Odours in living rooms come mostly from the occupants themselves. Healthy and clean people give off odours even immediately after a bath. This unpleasantness is related to the odour concentration, though adaptation occurs with prolonged exposure. A study of the factors influencing the generation of odours and the amount of dilution needed to bring the odour to a level acceptable to newcomers to the room showed there was no sex difference in odour generation providing perfume was not used.[20] Age became important below 14 years since younger children created more objectionable odours. Odour generation was also strongly related to the time which had elapsed since the last bath.

Sensitivity to odours was such that it took three times more fresh air to change an assessment from strong to moderate and a further factor of three to reduce it to definite. Crowding was very important with much more air being needed to dilute the odours created from a number of people. This quantity of fresh air needed to dilute odours to a moderate level which is neither pleasant nor disagreeable is shown in Fig. A1.8.

An extension of this study included cigarette smoking.[21] Three categories of observers were used: the smokers themselves, non-smokers sitting in the same room and observers making spot assessments and then retiring from the room. The smokers themselves were incapable of perceiving the smoke odour regardless of air flow. They were, however, more susceptible to irritation of eyes, nose and throat than the non-smokers or the observers, and this was related to the contamination level. The non-smokers were sensitive to the amount of fresh air and for acceptable odour conditions required some 20% more fresh air than the smokers required to prevent irritation of the eyes. The observers required 50% more fresh air for the same acceptability level. Fresh air recommendations for people working in rooms where smoking is permitted are also super-imposed on Fig. A1.8 and recommended outdoor air supply rates are shown in Table A1.5.

RELATIVE HUMIDITY

The nature of the role played by relative humidity in the environment is less well-defined than that for temperature. At higher air temperatures, when sweating occurs, the thermal balance is dependent on evaporation and so relative humidity becomes a critical factor. There is a trend for lower humidities being preferred at higher air temperatures. However, for most applications, relative humidity should be between 40% and 70%.[22]

Besides human comfort, a suitable relative humidity is important for the preservation of furniture, objets d'art and plants, remembering that plants provide decor in landscape offices.

Another problem often encountered in dry air is the build-up of static electricity. The incidence of electrostatic shocks depends upon the electrical resistance of the carpet. This electrical resistance is a function of the material, weave, backing and moisture content of the carpet. At low relative humidities the carpet becomes dry and highly resistive and people may experience electrostatic shocks after walking about on it. Typical relationships are displayed in Fig. A1.9 together with the extreme values reported in the literature. In general, shocks are unlikely above 40% r.h. Carpeted buildings with underfloor heating have particularly dry carpets and require 55% r.h. or greater to avoid electrostatic shocks.

IONISATION

It has been suggested that the nature of the ionisation of the air is an important factor of comfort in that negative ions tend to provide sensations of freshness and well-being and that positive ions tend to cause headache, nausea and general malaise. Present evidence on ionisation is inconclusive and no design criteria can be evaluated.[53]

Table A1.5. Recommended outdoor air supply rates for air conditioned spaces.

| Type of space | Smoking | Outdoor air supply (litre/s) | | |
		Recommended Per person	Minimum (Take greater of two) Per person	Per m² floor area
Factories*†	None			0·8
Offices (open plan)	Some			1·3
Shops, department stores and supermarkets	Some	8	5	3·0
Theatres*	Some			—
Dance Halls*	Some			—
Hotel bedrooms†	Heavy			1·7
Laboratories†	Some			—
Offices (private)	Heavy	12	8	1·3
Residences (average)	Heavy			—
Restaurants (cafeteria)†‡	Some			—
Cocktail bars	Heavy			—
Conference rooms (average)	Some			—
Residences (luxury)	Heavy	18	12	—
Restaurants (dining rooms)†	Heavy			—
Board rooms, executive offices and conference rooms	Very heavy	25	18	6·0
Corridors		A *per capita* basis is not appropriate to these spaces.		1·3
Kitchens (domestic)†				10·0
Kitchens (restaurant)†				20·0
Toilets*				10·0

* See statutory requirements and local bye-laws.

† Rate of extract may be over-riding factor.

‡ Where queuing occurs in the space, the seating capacity may not be the appropriate total occupancy.

Notes:

1 For hospital wards, operating theatres see Department of Health and Social Security Building Notes.

2 The outdoor air supply rates given take account of the likely density of occupation and the type and amount of smoking.

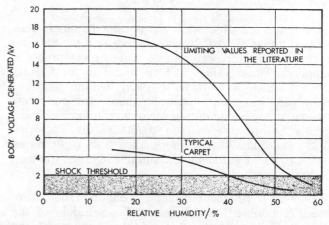

Fig. A1.9. Typical relationship between relative humidity and electrostatic shocks.

LIGHTING

Lighting in a building can be considered to have three purposes:

    (a) to enable the occupant to work and move about in safety;

    (b) to enable tasks to be performed;

    (c) to make an interior look pleasant.

Good lighting can aid the avoidance of hazards during normal use of a building or in emergency situations by clearly revealing obstacles and exits in the interior. It can make tasks easier to see and it can contribute to an interior that is considered satisfactory and perhaps even inspiring for its particular function by providing emphasis, colour and variety.

Lighting must always satisfy the requirements for safety, but in practice the three functions are not mutually exclusive. Any interior that is adequately lit for performing tasks usually meets the safety requirements for normal use although a separate lighting system for emergencies may be needed. A similar situation often applies for a pleasantly lit interior. The balance between lighting for performance and pleasantness is usually a matter of the primary purpose for which the interior is intended. For example, in an engineering workshop the lighting is required, first and foremost, so that the product can be made quickly, easily and accurately. Nevertheless a cheerful but non-distracting atmosphere produced by lighting can be an aid to productivity. An example at the other extreme is a restaurant where the prime purpose of the lighting is often to produce a particular impression of the interior but this must be achieved without making the meals invisible. Unless the lighting is matched to the context and the operational requirements it is unlikely to be successful.

Lighting for Safety

Quantity of light

There are two aspects of lighting for safety. The first refers to the conditions prevailing in an interior when the normal lighting system is in operation. The safety factors here are the ability to move about the interior without falling or colliding with people and objects, and the facility to operate machinery without danger due to poor visibility. The second becomes apparent when the normal lighting system fails and this aspect comes under the general heading of emergency lighting.

Illuminance for safety while the normal lighting system is operating is almost always satisfactory if the illuminance desirable for performance and/or pleasantness is supplied. These values will be found in the CIBSE Code[23] which is a guide to good lighting practice. However, in many instances there are minimum standards applicable during use of a building which are legally enforceable. Taken together, the Factories Act[24] and the Offices, Shops and Railway Premises Act,[25] demand 'sufficient and suitable lighting, whether natural or artificial'.

In 1969 the Department of Employment and Productivity issued a booklet[26] which included a schedule of the minimum illuminances that, in the opinion of the Department, satisfy the provisions of the Act[25] for various locations. It can be expected that in due course lighting standards will be required to meet the obligations of the Health and Safety at Work Act,[27] which will become similarly codified.

Although safety is a main pre-occupation of the legislators, there are situations where health and welfare become the prime considerations. For locations where food is prepared (other than in agriculture) the Food Hygiene (General) Regulations[28] require 'suitable and sufficient means of lighting' in order that proper cleanliness can be maintained, and the Local Authorities (who are responsible for enforcement) should be consulted for guidance on actual standards. Rather more demanding are the provisions of the Slaughterhouse (Hygiene) Regulations.[29]

Finally, mention must be made of schools and hospitals, for each of which the appropriate Ministries have specified minimum lighting standards. Relevant legislation for many applications is listed in the CIBSE Code schedule.

The above review of mandatory requirements does not claim to be comprehensive. It is only a selection of standards that concern the provision of lighting as obviously the range of standards governing the safe use of lighting equipment is far more extensive, and in many instances, more demanding. Even so, the advisability of discussing lighting standards at the design stage with Local Authorities and others, such as the Factory Inspectorate, who might become involved, should be apparent.

Emergency lighting can conveniently be divided into two classes;

    (a) standby lighting, which is intended to enable essential work to be carried out, e.g. in hospitals;

    (b) escape lighting which enables people to evacuate a building quickly and safely.

For general use an absolute minimum illuminance of 0.2 lx is recommended for escape route lighting. British Standard 5266[30] and CIBSE Technical Memoranda TM12[34] give extensive details of the design of emergency lighting.

Layout of lighting

There are a number of points which require specific attention in a normal lighting installation to avoid danger due to reduced visibility through glare or confusion. One of the most commonly occurring examples of bad lighting as regards safety is the location of a window at the end of an otherwise windowless corridor. This produces considerable disability glare during daylight hours that may result in someone tripping over an unseen obstruction. Another area requiring care is the lighting of staircases, particularly if there are changes of direction at short intervals. There can be no excuse for fashionable solutions that combine visual confusion with poor visibility. This is a zone of potential hazard, and the guiding principles should be to reveal clearly the stair treads (by locating sources so that each riser appears shadowed) and to make evident the location and direction of the stairways.

At workplaces, light reflections off shiny surfaces can make important objects or parts of machinery, controls or indicators difficult to see. This can be avoided if matt surfaces are used or the lighting is arranged to avoid specular reflections towards the worker. Another possible but rare hazard is the stroboscopic effect which can be produced in rotating machinery by discharge lamps operating off an AC supply. This can be alleviated by wiring adjacent luminaires on different electrical phases, thereby reducing the modulation of the light.

For emergency lighting systems, BS 5266 recommends that the ratio of maximum/minimum illuminances on an escape route should not exceed 40:1. For design to this 40:1 emergency lighting value, it becomes particularly important that luminaires are arranged to draw attention to changes of direction, level, and intersections. Apart from their use as sources of illuminance, the appearance of an organised installation of luminaires can serve to give a sense of orientation and direction. The last point is also relevant for normal lighting.

Lighting for Performance

Quantity of light

The exact relationship between task performance and illuminance has been the subject of many investigations.[31,32,33] One thing all the results agree about is that the relationship shows a law of diminishing returns, see Fig. A1.10. At low illuminances, say less than 100 lx, a change in illuminance of 200 lx will produce a large change in performance. At much higher illuminances, say greater than 1000 lx, the same change will produce only a small change in performance, if any at all. The exact relationship between task performance and illuminance depends on a number of factors, for example the visual difficulty of the task, including such factors as size, contrast, task movement, etc.; the age and eyesight of the workers and the significance of the visual component of the work. The CIBSE Code contains illuminance recommendations for many different working interiors.

Table A1.6. is a summary chart which specifies the standard service illuminances for a number of working situations. The CIBSE Code demonstrates, by means of a flow chart, the way these standard service illuminances should be modified if the assumptions made in drawing up the standards are violated in particular ways. It should be noted that these illuminances are intended to be measured on the appropriate working plane, be it horizontal, vertical or somewhere between. By service illuminance is meant the illuminance averaged over the maintenance cycle of the installation and over the relevant area. It is important to note that it is often more economic to improve performance by making the task easier through in-

creases in size (e.g. use optical aids) and contrast (e.g. select suitable task background) rather than by increasing illuminance.

These recommendations do not identify the source that is to produce these illuminances. It is possible to meet the recommendations with both natural and electric light. However it is only possible when using natural light to give the criteria in terms of daylight factors as daylight illuminance is continually varying. Recommendations for interiors in which natural lighting is to be the dominant lighting feature are given in the CIBSE Code and British Standard Draft for Development DD73[35]

Distribution of light

When considering the distribution of light in an interior there exists a basic decision that has to be made about the type of lighting to be used. Broadly the alternatives are between an installation which provides a uniform illuminance across the working plane and hence complete flexibility of work layout in the space, and a building lighting/task lighting approach where each task area has its own lighting and the general room lighting is used only as a background.

In the former type of installation, it is recommended that the ratio of the minimum to the average illuminance over the working plane should be not less than 0.8. Where the building/task lighting approach is used the illuminance of surrounding areas should be not less than one-third of the task illuminance.

Directional effects

Some directional effects of light make it easier to recognize the details of a task; others make recognition more difficult.

The contrasts perceived in a task depend on the reflection characteristics of its surface and on how the task is lit. Contrasts are reduced if the images of bright sources, such as luminaires or the sky, are seen in a glossy surface. This 'veiling' effect is often most apparent when a bright source is reflected in a glossy paper. Most printing inks are glossy and few papers are matt, so legibility of the print is sometimes seriously impaired by veiling reflections. Nevertheless, loss of contrast due to veiling reflections can be minimized by various means. For example, it is possible to prevent disturbing images from affecting visibility of the task by careful positioning of the viewer, the task and the source so as to avoid the arrangement shown in Fig. A1.11.

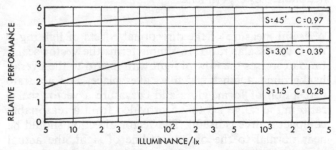

Fig. A1.10. Relation between illuminance and task performance for different values of apparent size (s) and contrast (c).

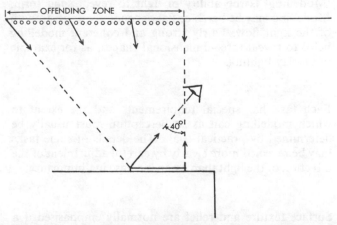

Fig. A1.11. Occurrence of veiling reflections

Table A1.6. Standard service illuminance for various activities/interiors.

Standard Service Illuminance (lx)	Characteristics of the activity/interior	Representative activities/interiors
50	Interiors visited rarely with visual tasks confined to movement and casual seeing without perception of detail.	Cable tunnels, indoor storage tanks, walkways.
100	Interiors visited occasionally with visual tasks confined to movement and casual seeing calling for only limited perception of detail.	Corridors, changing rooms, bulk stores.
150	Interiors visited occasionally with visual tasks requiring some perception of detail or involving some risk to people, plant or product.	Loading bays, medical stores, switchrooms.
200	Continuously occupied interiors, visual tasks not requiring any perception or detail.	Monitoring automatic processes in manufacture, casting concrete, turbine halls.
300	Continuously occupied interiors, visual tasks moderately easy, i.e. large details >10 min arc and/or high contrast.	Packing goods, rough core making in foundries, rough sawing.
500	Visual tasks moderately difficult, i.e. details to be seen are of moderate size (5-10 min arc) and may be of low contrast. Also colour judgement may be required.	General offices, engine assembly, painting and spraying.
750	Visual tasks difficult, i.e. details to be seen are small (3-5 min arc) and of low contrast, also good colour judgements may be required.	Drawing offices, ceramic decoration, meat inspection.
1000	Visual tasks very difficult, i.e. details to be seen are very small (2-3 min arc) and can be of very low contrast. Also accurate colour judgements may be required.	Electronic component assembly, gauge and tool rooms, retouching paintwork.
1500	Visual tasks extremely difficult, i.e. details to be seen extremely small (1-2 min arc) and of low contrast. Visual aids may be of advantage.	Inspection of graphic reproduction, hand tailoring, fine die sinking.
2000	Visual tasks exceptionally difficult, i.e. details to be seen exceptionally small (<1 min arc) with very low contrasts. Visual aids will be of advantage.	Assembly of minute mechanisms, finished fabric inspection.

Reproduced from CIBSE Code for Interior Lighting. [23]

'Modelling' is the ability of light to reveal solid form. Modelling may be harsh or flat depending on the strength of the light flow. Fairly strong and coherent modelling helps to reveal three-dimensional shapes, as for example in display lighting.

Each task has special requirements and the extent to which modelling can assist perception must usually be determined by practical trials. The details of some tasks may be revealed more clearly by careful adjustment of the direction of the light than by an increase in illuminance.

Surface texture and relief are normally emphasised if a strong flow of light is directed across the surface in a direction nearly parallel to it, and are subdued if the surface is lit mainly from the front. Particular tasks should be lit to provide the maximum relevant visual information, and the best arrangement must usually be determined by experiment.

A useful measure of the directional effects of lighting is the vector/scalar ratio. In simple terms the vector/scalar ratio expresses the flow of light with regard to the overall background against which it takes place. For accurate perception of form, gloss and curvature a vector/scalar ratio in the range 1.5 to 2.5 provided from a reasonably compact source is useful. The vector direction should be near normal to the observer's line of sight, the actual direction being chosen with regard to the form of the objects to be studied.

To achieve vector/scalar ratios close to 2.5 calls for a compact source and low reflections for the surrounding surfaces. Reflectances in the range 0.1 to 0.3 will be required for this purpose.

The above recommendations will be adequate for general viewing but for situations where a particular task requires a particular type of visual discrimination to be made, a special lighting solution that accentuates that aspect of appearance may be appropriate.

Disability Glare
Veiling reflections directly affect the visibility of the task by reflection from the task area. However, there is another form of veiling which can influence the task visibility without reflection from the task; disability glare. This effect is partly due to light from a light source entering the eye and being scattered so that it forms a veil over the retinal image of the task. Obviously the closer the source is to the line of sight of the observer seeing the task the greater will be its effect. For this reason, disability glare caused by the reflection of light sources in areas adjacent to the work is particularly troublesome.

This effective loss of contrast due to disability glare can readily be experienced by looking at some detail in the vicinity of a window or luminaire, and then using the hand to shield the eyes from the direct view of the source. There is only one way to eliminate disability glare. This is to separate all areas of high luminance from the immediate surround of the task. This is usually a matter of avoiding the use of glossy surfaces close to the task or moving the task. In practice, disability glare direct from luminaires is rare in interior lighting.

Colour of light
All sources of light, both natural and artificial, differ in their spectral composition. Since surface colour is produced by a combination of the wave-lengths incident on it and the spectral reflectance of the surface, differences between sources produce changes in colours. For most purposes these changes are modified by chromatic adaptation, a process whereby the observer adapts to the particular composition of the light. However for some tasks the perceived colour of the surface is important and hence the choice of light source for that task is important.

The Colour Rendering Index (CRI) adopted by the Commission Internationale de l'Eclairage (CIE) specifies the accuracy with which lamps reproduce colours relative to some standard source. CRI has values going up to a maximum of 100. The CIBSE Code contains a lamp table and makes recommendations as to which light sources are appropriate in various work situations. The lamp table uses the international classification of sources into groups according to their CRI and describes the effect of the source on a number of colour regions. Although this is useful information the advice of a manufacturer should be sought when selecting lamps for applications where colour judgement is particularly important.

Lighting for Pleasantness
Quantity of light
It has been fairly well established that working environments lit uniformly to less than 200 lx tend to be rated as unsatisfactory.[36] This value is recommended in the CIBSE Code as a minimum amenity level in continuously occupied spaces, even though it could not be justified on the grounds of performance for many occupations where visual tasks are not demanding.

Preference considerations also suggest maximum illuminances for amenity. Studies extending to high levels of task illuminance have indicated a general tendency for preference to decline above 2000 lx.[37]

Economics are behind another development which may have a large effect on the validity of specifying general preferred illuminance. It is possible to save energy by separating the task lighting from the building lighting. The functions of the building lighting are to provide for safety and to present the occupants with a pleasant overall appearance, while the task lighting function is achieved by a separate system. Although daylight has several shortcomings as a source of task lighting, even quite modest admission can provide satisfactory building lighting for much of the working day. In addition, to many people the provision of daylight is in itself a desirable source of amenity. Thus there is the possibility that in future recommendations will need to be made in terms of daylight factor and task illuminance, rather than simply illuminance on a horizontal plane. If the building lighting/task lighting approach is adopted, it is important to note that reactions to sunlight are less predictable. Although surveys in homes have found overwhelming preference for sunlight admission[38] people react differently when they are at work and there is a strong case for effective sunlight control for working environments.[39]

For many interiors there is no obvious visual task, and reference to an illuminance on a working plane is not appropriate. The CIBSE Code goes some way towards recognising this by making recommendations for circulation areas (e.g. hotel foyers) in terms of scalar (mean spherical) illuminance, as it has been found to relate better than planar illuminance to assessments of how well lit people and objects appear to be.[40]

Distribution of light
The division of lighting into separate systems of task and building lighting offers scope for variety in many types of working environments, but it is in locations where the designer is free from the need to provide for demanding visual tasks that the opportunities to manipulate light for effect may be fully realised. The increasing use in recent years of display lighting techniques to create contrast that attracts attention and arouses interest is a welcome relief from the all-too-common practice of maintaining a regular layout but merely changing to a 'decorative' luminaire in non-working areas.

Selective lighting is one of the ways in which the conspicuousness of an object may be enhanced. Studies of the effects of bright elements in the field of view are not sufficient to enable measured values to be related to their subjective influence, but this has not prevented shop window designers from exploiting the phenomena as an everyday part of their craft. In general it can be recognised that it is desirable that the brightest elements in the field of view should be ones to which people wish to direct their attention: if this is not so an uneasy conflict is caused, producing the sensation of discomfort.

For working situations, the CIBSE Code recommends that the ratio of wall/working plane illuminance should be within the range 0.5 to 0.8, and ceiling/working plane illuminance within the range 0.3 to 0.9. In addition it links these ratios to specific ranges of surface reflectances. The upper limits are directed by the expectation that a working plane should appear to be more strongly illuminated than either walls or ceiling, and the lower limits by the empirical finding that below these values, the surfaces are likely to be judged underlit. The provision of lighting that achieves these illuminance ratios will usually ensure an acceptable distribution of light onto the main room surfaces, but this will not necessarily ensure a satisfactory balance of lighting on objects within the room.

Directional Effects

The term 'flow of light' is sometimes used to describe the overall impression of the strength and the direction of lighting as it affects the appearance of all the objects in a space[41]. The illumination vector provides two convenient indices: the vector direction indicates the apparent direction of the flow of light and the vector/scalar ratio relates to its apparent strength. Studies of the appearance of the human face have indicated that a lateral flow of light is generally preferred, corresponding to a vector direction 15° to 45° above the horizontal, with the vector/scalar ratio in the range 1.2 to 1.8. The test situation was one of close contact and it seems probable that for more distant or more formal communication, values in the range 1.8 to 2.4 would be more appropriate.

Discomfort Glare

When luminances that are much higher than the average occur in an interior then people may experience visual discomfort. The phenomenon is known as discomfort glare. Such discomfort glare does not directly affect the visual difficulty of tasks, unlike disability glare. It merely produces discomfort. In Britain, the accepted measure of direct discomfort glare due to light sources is the CIBSE Glare Index.[42] This index is based upon a glare formula developed at the Building Research Station that allows the calculation of a glare value that relates to an assessment of the discomfort glare due to each bright element in a particular field of view. In order to use this formula to assess discomfort glare in a room a separate calculation is required for each source. A simpler calculation method is published in Interior Lighting Design.[43]

Assessments of the acceptabilities of actual lighting installations have provided the basis for the CIBSE Code schedule of limiting Glare Indices. These vary according to the situation and should not be exceeded.

The following selection of limiting values serves to give some indication of the practical range of the Glare Index.

Museums, Art Galleries, Lecture Theatres, Control Rooms, Industrial Inspection; Limiting Glare Index =16.

Classrooms, Libraries, Laboratories, General Offices, Fine Assembly Work; Limiting Glare Index=19.

Supermarkets, circulation areas, medium assembly work; Limiting Glare Index=22.

Boiler Houses, Rough Assembly Work; Limiting Glare Index=25.

Foundries, Works Store Areas; Limiting Glare Index =28.

If an installation is found to have a high Glare Index then there are a number of variables which can be adjusted to reduce it, the most frequently used being a change of luminaire.

Colour of light

Natural light sources, such as flame, sunlight and daylight, each have visible spectral power distributions that are matched fairly closely by a Planckian radiator at an appropriate temperature. The development of electric lamps that do not rely on incandescence has made available many sources having discontinuous spectral power distributions that are quite different from that of Planckian sources. At the extreme, there are monochromatic sources, such as the low-pressure sodium lamp widely used for street lighting. This has very poor colour properties, particularly colour rendering.

Light sources used in interiors have better colour rendering than this. However, colour rendering should not be considered in isolation since it does not completely characterise the colour properties of a light source. The Colour Rendering Index tells us something about the appearance of surfaces lit by the light source but the appearance of the room is also influenced by the colour appearance of the lamp. The colour appearance of the lamp refers to the apparent colour of the light it emits. It is possible for two lamps to have the same colour appearance but very different colour rendering properties. For almost all interiors the recommended light sources are nominally white in appearance with varying degrees of warmth. This degree of warmth is quantified by the Correlated Colour Temperature (CCT) of the lamp. This quantity is the temperature of a Planckian radiator that is nearest in colour appearance to the lamp. The commonly used light sources are classified in the IES Code as follows:

(a) Warm—CCT less than 3300 K,

(b) Intermediate—CCT 3300 to 5300 K,

(c) Cold—CCT greater than 5300 K.

Studies have shown that preferences for colour appearance vary with illuminance. There is a general preference for intermediate and warm sources at illuminances of less than 300 lx. In the case of fluorescent lighting, the designer has available a range of nominally white tubes of various correlated colour temperatures to choose from.

For daylight this variation is catered for naturally as bright blue sky conditions give way to the warm tints of sunset. A special case for consideration is the lighting installation where daylight and electric lighting are used in combination. A study of various types of fluorescent lighting has identified the 'Daylight' tube (4300 K) as the preferred source for this type of use.[44]

In the more general context, it would appear that just as high or low illuminances may be appropriate for certain activities, so a corresponding warm or cool source colour appearance also is appropriate. Advice on this is given in the CIBSE Code. Once the decision has been made to select a source from within a certain band of correlated colour temperatures, then satisfaction with the appearance of surface colours is likely to be increased by selecting a source of high Colour Rendering Index.

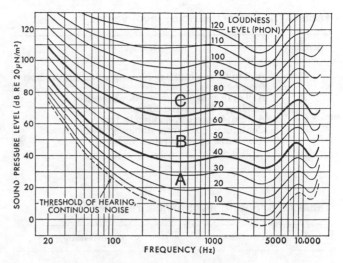

Fig. A1.12.   Equal loudness level contours.

SOUND

Like all the other environmental factors people react to sound in different ways. Care must be taken to protect people from the nervous tensions and the physiological damage which can be caused by noise; the acoustic environment must be designed so that it is not detrimental to human performance.

Response of the Human Ear

The ear responds to frequencies in the range 15 to 20 000 Hz. The precise range differs from person to person; acuteness to hearing high-frequency sound steadily falls off with age due to deterioration in the nerves and muscles operating the hearing system.

The response of the ear is non-linear. At low frequencies it is less sensitive; which is why, for instance, the low frequency body vibrations cannot be heard. The sensitivity of the ear is shown in Fig. A1.12. These curves of equal loudness level are derived by subjective experiments and show that the ear's response varies with loudness level and frequency. The unit of loudness level is the phon.

A 1000 Hz note may, for instance, have a sound pressure level of 60 dB; a 100 Hz note appears to be equally loud if the sound pressure level is 66 dB.

When sound levels are measured, the variation in the sensitivity of the ear can be taken into account by incorporating weighting networks in the meter; these are termed A, B and C. Their range of operation has been superimposed on the equal loudness level curves in Fig. A1.13.

In the Building Services Industry the dBA measure is normally used as the indicator which relates broadly to the subjective reactions.

Annoyance

The term 'annoyance' or 'disturbance' which is used to indicate when a stress becomes undesirable, is not confined to noise. It does not depend just on the event of the moment, it also depends on personality, so that it is diffi-

cult to find a reliable indicator of community response because attitudes to environment change. In general, annoyance depends on stimulus quality and information content; duration, past experience, expectancy and number of stimulus events; physical, emotional and arousal levels, and other personality attributes of the individual the activity of the individual, whether sleeping, working or relaxing and interactions with other factors.[52]

Unfortunately, no relationships are yet known which link all these parameters but criteria have been evolved which attempt to correlate subjective and objective measurements.

The simplest and most convenient indicator of subjective response is the dBA measure obtained using a sound level meter.

Noise fluctuates over time and human reactions depend on the amplitude and frequency of these fluctuations. It has become common practice to ignore the peak noise level and use the noise climate as a means of judging the acceptability of an environment.

The noise climate is defined as that zone between the L90 level (i.e. the noise level exceeded for 90% of the time) and the L10 level (the noise level exceeded for only 10% of the time). This rule has to be used with discretion as there might be applications particularly in an industrial context where the peak level might exceed the threshold of noise damage.

The level of noise emitted from industrial premises is currently assessed using the Corrected Noise Level (CNL in dBA) described in BS 4142. CNL consists of a basic level to which a correction has been added to allow for the tonal character (whine, hum, etc.) the impulsive character (bangs, clangs), the intermittency and the duration of the noise. Some values of CNL and the situations in which they are found are given in Table A1.7.[45]

Hearing Damage

Exposure to internal noise levels above 90 dBA can cause temporary or permanent hearing damage.[46] If the exposure is continued for 8 hours in any one day the sound level should not exceed 90 dBA. For lesser periods or fluctuating sound an equivalent sound level can be calculated and this value should not exceed 90 dBA, see Table A1.8.

Table A1.7. Corrected noise level values.[45]

CNL/dBA	Situation
85	At 9 m from a building housing an air stream drop forge hammer.
75	At 9 m from an air compressor housed in a building with louvred doors.
60	At 15 m from a can-making factory. Continuous noise from stamping machinery and from handling of thin sheet metal.

Table A1.8. Sound level exposure times.[46]

Sound level/dBA	Exposure time/h
90	8
92	5
94	3.2
96	2
98	1.3
100	0.8
102	0.5
104	0.32
106	0.20
108	0.13
110	0.08
112	0.05

The table is based on:
$$t = 8 \times 10^{-0.1(L-90)}$$

NR and NC Curves

Noise rating curves are a method of assessing the background noise level for annoyance and speech intelligibility in a given environment, and are attempts to express equal human tolerance in each frequency band. Beranek[47] and Kosten[48] have carried out experiments with office workers and home dwellers using broadband noise sources. They produced the well-known NC and NR curves, the latter being commonly used in Europe. NR curves, which are accepted throughout this *Guide*, give a slightly more stringent requirement than NC curves in the higher frequencies. For all practical purposes, NR and NC curves may be regarded as mutually interchangeable.

There is no constant relationship between the subjective noise assessments NR numbers and dBA. The relationship depends on the spectral characteristics of the noise but it can be said that for ordinary intrusive noise within the scope of building services the relationship usually lies between 4 and 8 units. Differences noted in the tabular data presented reflect the sources of the information rather than any conflict of technical material.

If in doubt both should be calculated for the specific noise spectrum under consideration.

The choice of an appropriate noise criterion is a compromise between system economics and achieving a large percentage acceptability. The corrections given in Table A1.9 should be applied to the NR value adopted.

The recommended noise ratings given in Table A1.10 apply to broadband continuous noise.

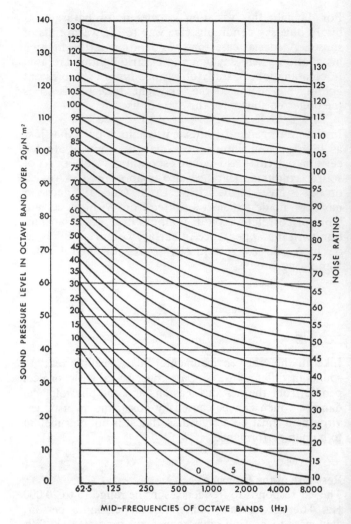

Fig. A1.13. NR curves.

Note to Fig. A1.13

Each curve is classified by a number corresponding to the speech interference level which was originally defined as the average of the sound pressure levels measured in the octave bands 600 to 1200, 1200 to 2400 and 2400 to 4800 Hz. The maximum permissible loudness level is taken to be 22 units more. Thus NR 30 has a speech interference level of 30 dB and a loudness level of 52 phons; this means that for effective speech communication the loudness level in a space designed to have a background level complying with NR 30 must not exceed 52 phons.

Table A1.9. Corrections to broadband continuous noise rating.

Reason	NR correction
Pure tone easily perceptible	−5
Impulsive and/or intermittent noise	−5

Background Conditions

The design criteria set out in Table A1.10 are those considered desirable for the applications described. However, in adopting a particular criterion, it is necessary to ensure that the background of noise is not so high as to render the criterion incapable of achievement or, conversely, so low as to make the equipment under consideration unduly audible. In considering

Table A1.10. Recommended noise ratings.

Situation	NR value
Concert halls, opera halls, studios for sound reproduction, live theatres (>500 seats) ..	20
Bedrooms in private homes, live theatres (<500 seats), cathedrals and large churches, television studios, large conference and lecture rooms (>50 people)	25
Living rooms in private homes, board rooms, top management offices, conference and lecture rooms (20–50 people), multi-purpose halls, churches (medium and small), libraries, bedrooms in hotels, etc., banqueting rooms, operating theatres, cinemas, hospital private rooms, large courtrooms	30
Public rooms in hotels, etc., ballrooms, hospital open wards, middle management and small offices, small conference and lecture rooms (<20 people), school classrooms, small courtrooms, museums, libraries, banking halls, small restaurants, cocktail bars, quality shops	35
Toilets and washrooms, drawing offices, reception areas (offices), halls, corridors, lobbies in hotels, etc., laboratories, recreation rooms, post offices, large restaurants, bars and night clubs, department stores, shops, gymnasia	40
Kitchens in hotels, hospitals, etc., laundry rooms, computer rooms, accounting machine rooms, cafeteria, canteens, supermarkets, swimming pools, covered garages in hotels, offices, etc., bowling alleys, landscaped offices	45

NR50 and above
NR50 will generally be regarded as very noisy by sedentary workers but most of the classifications listed under NR45 could just accept NR50. Higher noise levels than NR50 will be justified in certain manufacturing areas; such cases must be judged on their own merits.

Notes
1. The ratings listed above will give general guidance for total services noise but limited adjustment of certain of these criteria may be appropriate in some applications.

2. The intrusion of high external noise levels may, if continuous during occupation, permit relaxation of the standards but services noise should be not less than 5 dB below the minimum intruding noise in any octave band to avoid adding a significant new noise source to the area.

3. Where more than one noise source is present it is the aggregate noise which should meet the criterion.

4. NR $\approx$ dBA value – 6.

adverse background conditions it is important to realize that an installation will be judged in the quietest circumstances, not the noisiest, and thus relaxation of otherwise normal standards is only possible in respect of background noise which is effectively continuous during the hours of occupation.

In specifying noise design goals for an air conditioned space, a balance between air conditioning noise and activity noise should be sought, for the acceptability of the air conditioning noise does not depend upon its absolute level and frequency content but rather on its relationship with other noise involved. This shows the designer the importance of finding out the expected level and frequency content of the activity noise at the feasibility stage of design. In particular, if the background noise is expected to be NR45, then the design value of the air conditioning should not exceed NR40, in order to limit the percentage of people aware of noise from the air conditioning to within about 15%.[49]

The noise level within a room will vary from place to place with a given noise input. Higher levels are experienced nearer the noise sources decreasing approximately with the inverse square of distance from the source. The background level depends on the reverberations within the room.

The calculations of noise levels within a space due to individual noise sources is discussed in Section B12[52].

Speech Intelligibility
Speech intelligibility is dependent on the background noise and the distance from the speaker. Table A1.11[50] gives an indication of the distance at which normal speech will be intelligible for various background noise levels.

The background noise may also interfere with the intelligibility of telephone conversations. Table A1.12[51] shows with what background levels one might expect to have difficulty with hearing a conversation on the telephone.

Table A1.11. Sound levels for speech intelligibility.

Background sound level/dBA	Background NR	Maximum distance* for intelligibility/m
48	40	7
53	45	4
58	50	2.2
63	55	1.2
68	60	0.7
73	65	0.4
77	70	0.2
Over 77	Over 70	Too noisy for speech

*Distances are for normal speech. The distance is increased by raising the voice and is approximately doubled by raising the voice 5 to 6 dB.

Table A1.12. Speech levels for telephone conversations.

Quality of conversation	Sound level/dBA	NR
Satisfactory	58	50
Slightly difficult	68	60
Difficult	82	75
Unsatisfactory	Over 82	Over 75

Vibration

Frequency of Vibration
The frequency of vibration f (Hz) is the number of times the vibration repeats itself in one second. The angular frequency ω (rad/s) is $2\pi f$.

Magnitude of Vibration
The magnitude of a vibration is quantitatively defined by displacement, velocity or acceleration:

(a) *Displacement.* This is the distance of the vibrating surface from its mean or rest position. The maximum displacement is referred to as the displacement amplitude.

(b) *Velocity.* This is the rate of change of the displacement of the vibrating surface. In simple harmonic motion the vibration velocity is at its maximum when the displacement is zero.

(c) *Acceleration*. This is the rate of change of the velocity of the vibrating surface. In simple harmonic motion the vibration acceleration reaches a peak value when the amplitude is a maximum and the velocity is zero. The maximum acceleration is sometimes expressed relative to gravitational acceleration ($g = 9\cdot81$ m/s²).

The numerical relationships between these parameters for simple harmonic vibrations are:

$$v = y\omega = 2\pi f y \quad \dots \quad \dots \quad \dots \quad \dots \quad A1.3$$

$$a = y\omega^2 = 4\pi^2 f^2 y \quad \dots \quad \dots \quad \dots \quad A1.4$$

where:

a = acceleration	..	..	m/s²
f = frequency	..	..	Hz
v = velocity	..	..	m/s
y = amplitude	..	..	m
ω = angular frequency	..	..	rad/s

Effects of Vibration

Human Body Response

Vibrating motion of the human body can produce both physical and biological effects. The physical effects are the excitation of parts of the body and under extreme conditions physical damage can result. Of more direct relevance to building vibrations are the biological effects, both physiological and psychological. These can give rise to a degree of discomfort that is a function of the magnitude, frequency and direction of the vibratory motion and the individual response to it. Human sensitivity to vibration was studied in Germany by Reiher and Meister[51] and it was found that for frequencies up to about 50 Hz, sensitivity was proportional to the maximum vibration velocity. The results of this investigation are summarized in Fig. A1.14, the division between the 'just perceptible' and 'clearly perceptible' zones corresponding to a maximum velocity ($2\pi f y$) of approximately 10^{-3} m/s.

Effect on Structures

Vibration can damage a building structure, the degree of damage depending on the magnitude and frequency of vibration. The level of vibration likely to produce some cracking is well above the 'clearly perceptible' zone of the human sensitivity scale so that a clear warning of an excessive vibration intensity is given. An indication of the possible consequences of vibration on a structure are shown in Fig. A1.15.

In the field of building services engineering vibrations usually arise from imperfectly balanced rotating machines or from reciprocating machines. The vibration is often most noticeable during machine start-up (i.e. low frequency movement), when some machines have to pass through a critical (resonant) speed before reaching the normal operating condition. Vibration associated with start-up may not be important if the machine operates for long periods so that the condition occurs only infrequently: machines which switch in and out, perhaps under thermostat control, may require special precautions.

Vibrations transmitted from machines through their bases to the building structure may be felt at considerable distances from the plant—in extreme cases, even in neighbouring buildings. Adequate isolation is therefore important in those cases where vibration is expected.

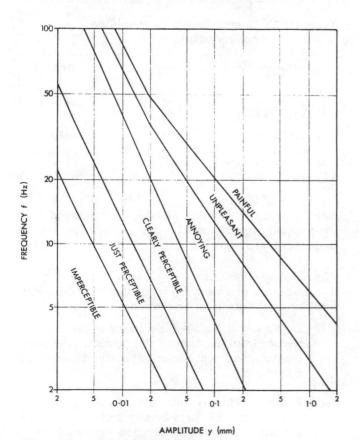

Fig. A1.14. Human reaction to vibration.

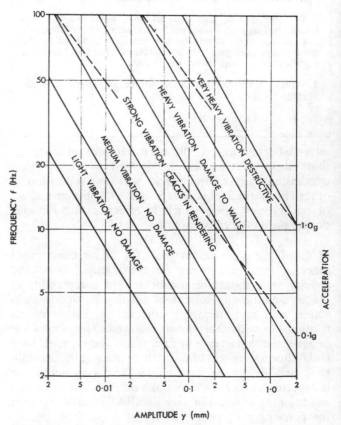

Fig. A1.15. Vibration intensity and possible damage.

APPENDIX I

Mean, plane and vector radiant temperatures

The derivation of these temperatures requires the use of absolute temperatures since it involves radiation exchanges and the Stephan-Boltzmann constant.

In the absence of short-wave radiation, mean radiant temperature is defined as:

$$T_r{}^4 = \frac{1}{4\pi} \int_0^{4\pi} T_s{}^4 \, d\psi \qquad .. \qquad .. \qquad A1.6$$

where:

T_r = mean radiant temperature .. .. K

T_s = absolute surface temperature .. .. K

ψ = solid angle .. .. sr

Where short-wave radiation is considered, equation A1.6 is modified:

$$T_r{}^4 = \frac{I_{sw}}{4\sigma} + \frac{1}{4\pi} \int_0^{4\pi} T_s{}^4 \, d\psi \quad .. \quad .. \quad A1.7$$

where:

I_{sw} = short-wave radiation .. .. .. W/m²

σ = Stephan-Boltzmann constant .. W/m² K⁴

By introducing angle factors, which for a surface subtending a solid angle ψ are defined by:

$$F_a = \frac{1}{4\pi} \int_0^{\psi} d\psi \quad .. \quad .. \quad .. \quad .. \quad A1.8$$

where:

F_a = angle factor referred to an elemental sphere, see Fig. A1.16.

equation A1.6 can be rewritten as:

$$T_r{}^4 = \Sigma(F_a T_s^4) \quad .. \quad .. \quad .. \quad .. \quad A1.9$$

So long as the individual surfaces do not differ by more than about 20°C from the ambient, equation A1.9 can be approximated by:

$$T_r = \Sigma(F_a T_s) \qquad .. \qquad .. \qquad .. \qquad A1.10$$

In terms of irradiance, a source such as a radiant heater will cause an increase in radiant temperature of:

$$\Delta T_r = \frac{I}{16\sigma T_r^3} \quad .. \quad .. \quad .. \quad .. \quad A1.11$$

where:

I = irradiance .. .. W/m²

At room temperatures and for small changes in T_r, equation A1.11 becomes:

$$\Delta T_r = 0.044 \, I \quad .. \quad .. \quad .. \quad .. \quad A1.12$$

The plane radiant temperature is given by:

$$T_p^4 = \Sigma(F_f T_s^4) \quad .. \quad .. \quad .. \quad .. \quad A1.13$$

where:

T_p = plane radiant temperature .. .. K

F_f = form factor referred to an elemental plane

As with mean radiant temperature, however, this equation can be simplified so long as the individual surfaces do not differ too much from the ambient and it becomes:

$$T_p = \Sigma(F_f T_s) \quad .. \quad .. \quad .. \quad .. \quad A1.14$$

Form factors are given in Fig. A1.17 and also in Section C3 of the *Guide*. Plane radiant temperature is simply related to the irradiance by:

$$T_p = \left(\frac{I}{\sigma}\right)^{0.25} \quad .. \quad .. \quad .. \quad .. \quad A1.15$$

$$= 64.8 \, I^{0.25} \quad .. \quad .. \quad .. \quad .. \quad A1.16$$

Unless all the surfaces are at the same temperature, the plane element referred to in the definition of plane radiant temperature will sense one plane radiant temperature on its front and another on its back. If the plane element is pointed in such a way that this difference is a maximum, this value of the difference is called the vector radiant temperature. The corresponding difference between the irradiances on either side of the plane element is called the radiation vector which is related to the vector radiant temperature by:

$$T_v = \frac{R}{4\sigma T_r^3} \quad .. \quad .. \quad .. \quad .. \quad A1.17$$

At room temperatures, equation A1.17 becomes:

$$T_v = 0.175 \, R \quad .. \quad .. \quad .. \quad .. \quad A1.18$$

where:

T_v = vector radiant temperature .. .. K

R = radiation vector .. .. W/m²

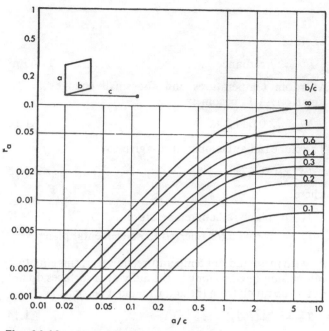

Fig. A1.16. Angle factors.

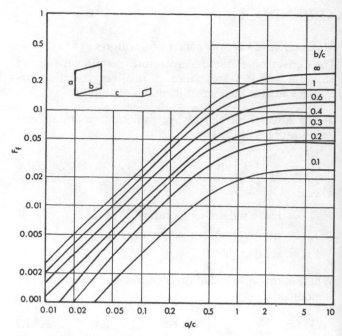

Fig. A1.17. Form factors.

REFERENCES

[1] McNall, P. E. et al, Metabolic rates at four levels and their relation to thermal comfort, *Trans. ASHRAE*, 1968, **74(i)**, 1V.3.20

[2] Fanger, P. O., Thermal Comfort, McGraw-Hill 1972.

[3] Humphreys, M. A., Field studies of thermal comfort, *BSE*, April 1976, **44**, 5–27.

[4] McIntyre, D. A. and Griffiths, I. D., The effects of added clothing on warmth and comfort in cool conditions, *Ergonomics*, 1975, **18(2)**, 205–211.

[5] Humphreys, M. A., A simple theoretical derivation of thermal comfort conditions, *BSE*, Aug 1970, **38**, 95–98.

[6] Humphreys, M. A., Outdoor temperatures and comfort indoors, *Building Research and Practice*, March/April 1978, 92–105.

[7] Bedford, T., The warmth factor in comfort at work, Industrial Health Board—Report No. 76, HMSO 1936.

[8] Webb, C. G., An analysis of some observations of thermal comfort in an equatorial climate, *BJIM*, 1959, **16**, 297–310.

[9] Humphreys, M. A. and Nicol, J. F., An investigation into thermal comfort of office workers, *BSE*, Nov 1970, **38**, 181–189.

[10] Nicol, J. F., An analysis of some observations of thermal comfort in Roorkee, India and Baghdad, Iraq, *Ann Hum Biol*, 1974, **1(4)**, 411–426.

[11] Grandjean, E., Ergonomics of the Home (p 188), Taylor and Francis, 1973.

[12] McIntyre, D. A., Overhead radiation and comfort, *BSE*, January 1977, **44**, 226–234.

[13] McIntyre, D. A., The thermal radiation field, *Build Sci*, 1974, **9**, 247–262.

[14] Anquez, J. and Croiset, M., Thermal comfort requirements adjacent to cold walls, *CSTB*, Jan/Feb 1969, **96**, 833.

[15] Jennings, R. and Wilberforce, R. R., Thermal comfort and space utilisation, *Insulation*, March 1973.

[16] McNall, P. E. and Biddison, R. E., Thermal comfort and comfort sensations of sedentary persons exposed to asymmetric radiation fields, *Trans. ASHRAE*, 1970, **76(1)**, 123–136.

[17] Griffiths, I. D. and McIntyre, D. A., Subjective responses to overhead thermal radiation, *Human Factors*, 1974, **16(4)**, 415–422.

[18] Schroder, G. and Steck, B. The subjective evaluation of the total radiation intensity of fluorescent lighting installations, *Lichttechnik*, 1973, **25(1)**, 17–21.

[19] Owens, P. G. T., Air conditioned comfort and sunshine, *JIHVE*, July 1969, **37**, 92–96.

[20] Yaglou, C. P., Riley, B. C. and Coggins, D. J., Ventilation requirements, *Trans. ASHVE*, 1936, **42**, 133.

[21] Yaglou, C. P., Ventilation requirements for cigarette smoke, *Trans. ASHVE*, 1955, **51**, 25–32.

[22] Nevins, R. G., Rohles, F. H., Springer, W., and Feyerherm, A. M., Temperature humidity chart for thermal comfort of seated persons, *Trans. ASHRAE*, 1966, **72**, 283.

[23] CIBSE Code for Interior Lighting 1984.

[24] Factories Act, HMSO.

[25] Office, Shops and Railway Premises Act, HMSO.

[26] Lighting in Offices, Shops and Railway Premises, HMSO

[27] Health and Safety at Work etc. Act, HMSO.

[28] Food Hygiene (General) Regulations, HMSO.

[29] Slaughterhouse (Hygiene) Regulations, HMSO.

[30] BS 5266—The Emergency Lighting of Premises, 1975.]

[31] Weston, H. C., The relation between illumination and visual performance. *Industrial Health Research Board Report No.* 87, HMSO, 1945.

[32] Stenzel, A. G. and Sommer, J., The effect of illumination on tasks which are independent of vision, *Lichttechnik*, 1969, **21**, 143–146.

[33] Boyce, P. R., Age, illuminance, visual performance and preference, *LRT*, 1973, **5**, 125–144.

[34] CIBSE Technical Memoranda TM12, Emergency Lighting, 1986.

[35] BS DD73, Basic data for the design of buildings: daylight, 1982.

[36] Saunders, J. E., The role of the level and diversity of horizontal illumination in an appraisal of a simple office task, *LRT*, 1969, **1**, 37–46.

[37] Fischer, D., The European approach to the integration of lighting and air-conditioning, *LRT*, 1970, **2**, 174–185.

[38] Bitter, C. and Van Ireland, J. F. A. A., Appreciation of sunlight in the home in 'Sunlight in Buildings' — Proceedings of the CIE International Conference, Newcastle-on-Tyne, April 1965.

[39] Ne'eman, E., Visual aspects of sunlight in buildings, *LRT*, 1974, **6**, 159–164.

[40] Cuttle, C. C., Valentine, W. B., Lynes, J. A. and Burt, W., Beyond the working plane, *CIE Washington, Compte Rendu*, Vol. B, 471–482, 1967.

[41] Cuttle, C. C., Lighting patterns and the flow of light, *LRT*, 1971, **3**, 171–189.

[42] CIBSE Technical Memoranda TM10, Calculation of Glare Indices, 1985.

[43] Lighting Industry Federation and Electricity Council, Interior lighting design, 1977.

[44] Cockram, A. H., Collins, J. B. and Langdon, F. J., A study of user preference for fluorescent lamp colours for daytime and night-time lighting, *LRT*, 1970, **2**, 249–256.

[45] A guide to noise units, *Noise Advisory Council*, 1973

[46] Code of Practice for Reducing the Exposure of Employed Persons to Noise, HMSO, 1972.

[47] Beranek, L. L., Criteria for office quieting based on questionnaire studies, *YJASA*, **28**, 833–52. September 1956.

[48] Kosten, C. W. and Van Os, G. J., Community & reaction criteria for external noises, Proc. NPL. Symp. No. 12 on Control of noise, 1962, HMSO.

[49] Hay, B., Design guide-lines for noise in landscaped offices, *BSE*, August 1972, **40**, 105–106.

[50] Handbook of Noise and Vibration Control, Trade and Technical Press.

[51] Reiher, H. J. and Meister, F. J., Human sensitivity to vibration, *Forsch. auf dem Geb. der Ing*, 1931, **2**, 11, 381–6. (*Transl.* Rep. F–TS–616–RE. Wright Field 1946).

[52] Croome, D. J., Noise, Buildings and People, Pergamon, 1977.

[53] Croome, D. J. and Roberts, B. M., Air conditioning and ventilation of buildings, Pergamon, 1975.

SECTION A2   WEATHER AND SOLAR DATA

Introduction .... *Page*   A2—3

Notation...   A2—3

U.K. Cold Weather Data.............................   A2—4

  External Design Dry-bulb Temperatures ....   A2—4

  Energy Consumption Calculations...................   A2—7

  Typical Winter Weather Situations.................   A2—7

  Coincidence of Wind Speed and Low
    Temperature...   A2—9

  Occurrence of Condensation............................   A2—9

  Degree Days...   A2—11

  Town Climate ....   A2—12

U.K. Warm Weather Data ....   A2—12

  General ....   A2—12

  Some Warm Weather Records ....   A2—12

  Dry-bulb and Wet-bulb Temperatures.............   A2—14

  Design Temperatures—Approximate Method   A2—18

U.K. Annual Weather Data..............................   A2—21

  Banded Weather Data ....   A2—21

  Example Weather Year..................................   A2—29

Wind ....   A2—30

Precipitation ....   A2—35

Daylight Availability......................................   A2—36

Atmospheric Pollution ....   A2—38

  Measurements of Atmospheric Pollution ....   A2—38

  Pollution from Motor Vehicle Exhausts...........   A2—39

World Weather Data ....   A2—39

Solar Data..   A2—53

  General..   A2—53

  Sun Position...   A2—53

  Sunpath Diagram ....   A2—57

Intensity of Solar Radiation.............................   A2—58

  General..   A2—58

  Basic Radiation Data ....   A2—59

  Design Radiation Data..................................   A2—60

  Overheating Design......................................   A2—65

  Simulation of Solar Irradiances........................   A2—65

  Design Total Irradiances................................   A2—66

Sol-Air Temperature and Long-Wave Loss........   A2—69

Availability of Solar Energy.............................   A2—74

Basic Radiation Data—World Values ....   A2—79

References..   A2—93

This edition of Section A2 first published: 1982

SECTION A2   WEATHER AND SOLAR DATA

INTRODUCTION

A fundamental pre-requisite to system design is the selection of meteorological information using appropriate criteria; absolute maxima or minima are unsuitable since they would lead to an uneconomic design. Consideration must be given, therefore, not only to extreme values of temperature, humidity and wind speed, etc., but also to their frequency, duration, co-incidence and to the order of diurnal variations. A number of published papers have made reference to these subjects[1,2,3] and these should be consulted in instances where detailed analysis is necessary.

Climatological data reported in the present section have been largely derived from information provided by the Meteorological Office, while the Building Research Establishment was responsible for some of the analysis of this information. The assistance given by both of these organisations is acknowledged.

The Meteorological Office* can, for a small fee, provide detailed information from its records of data collected at stations in this country and overseas in response to specific enquiries. In some cases this detailed information includes magnetic data tapes of particular climatological parameters. For the ten-year period 1959-68, the Meteorological Office can also provide magnetic tapes of coincident weather data (solar radiation, temperature, wind, etc.,) for Kew, Eskdalemuir, Lerwick and Aberporth.

Climatological data for the UK are referred to mean time, i.e. Greenwich Mean Time (GMT), except solar radiation data which are referred to sun time, i.e. Local Apparent Time (LAT), on which scale the sun is due south at noon. The difference between the two scales leads to GMT being slow on sun time by a maximum of 16 minutes in early November and fast on sun time by a maximum of 14 minutes in mid-February. At longitudes in the UK other than 0° (the reference longitude for GMT), there is a further difference, GMT being slow/fast on sun time by 4 minutes for every degree east/west of 0° longitude. For most building purposes, these differences are of no practical importance.

In other countries, Local Mean Time (LMT) is that given by the corresponding time zone, which usually differs by a whole number of hours from GMT. LAT in these other countries differs from LMT in the same manner as LAT differs from GMT in the UK.

---

* The Director General, Meteorological Office (Met 0 1), London Road, Bracknell, Berkshire RG12 2SZ.

NOTATION

C	= cloudiness	
Diff (cldy)	= diffuse (cloudy sky) irradiance	W/m²
Diff (clr)	= diffuse (clear sky) irradiance ..	W/m²
E	= wind energy	GJ
E_m	= wind energy at 10m over open level terrain	GJ
F_1	= sloping roof factor	
F_2	= sloping roof factor	
H	= horizontal surface (also N, NE, etc. for vertical surfaces)	
I	= overall radiation factor	
I_D	= basic direct solar irradiance ..	W/m²
I_{Dd}	= design direct solar irradiance ..	W/m²
I_d	= basic diffuse (sky) irradiance ..	W/m²
I_{dd}	= design diffuse (sky) irradiance..	W/m²
I_{DH}	= basic direct solar irradiance on horizontal surface	W/m²
I_{DHd}	= design direct solar irradiance on horizontal surface	W/m²
I_{dH}	= basic diffuse (sky) irradiance on horizontal surface	W/m²
I_{dHd}	= design diffuse (sky) irradiance on horizontal surface	W/m²
I_{DN}	= basic direct normal solar irradiance	W/m²
I_{DV}	= basic direct solar irradiance on vertical surface	W/m²
I_{DVd}	= design direct solar irradiance on vertical surface facing same direction as a sloping roof ..	W/m²
I'_{DVd}	= design direct solar irradiance on vertical surface facing opposite direction to a sloping roof ..	W/m²
I_{DSd}	= design direct solar irradiance on sloping surface	W/m²
I_l	= net long-wave radiation loss ..	W/m²

I_{TH} = total (global) irradiance on horizontal surface .. .. W/m^2

I_{THd} = design total (global) irradiance on horizontal surface .. .. W/m^2

I_{TSd} = design total (global) irradiance on sloping surface .. .. W/m^2

I_{TVd} = design total (global) irradiance on vertical surface .. .. W/m^2

K_e = parameter relating wind energy to nature of terrain

K_s = parameter relating wind speed to nature of terrain

R_{so} = outside surface resistance .. m^2K/W

a = exponent relating wind speed to height above ground

b = exponent relating wind energy to height above ground

f_1 = temperature interpolation factor

f_2 = temperature interpolation factor

h = solar altitude .. .. .. degree

i = angle of incidence .. .. degree

k_a = height correction factor

k_c = direct radiation (sky clarity) correction factor

k_D = direct radiation factor

k_d = diffuse radiation factor

k_r = ground reflection factor

t = temperature .. .. .. °C

t_{ao} = outdoor dry-bulb temperature °C

t_{base} = base temperature for degree days .. .. °C

$t_{d(\theta)}$ = required dry-bulb temperature at time θ .. .. °C

t_{eo} = sol-air temperature .. .. °C

t_{max} = daily maximum outdoor temperature .. .. °C

t_{min} = daily minimum outdoor temperature .. .. °C

t_{mean} = daily mean outdoor temperature .. .. °C

t_{sd} = screen dry-bulb temperature .. °C

t_{sw} = screen wet-bulb temperature .. °C

$t_{w(\theta)}$ = required wet-bulb temperature at time θ .. .. °C

u = mean wind speed.. .. .. m/s

u_m = mean wind speed at height 10 m over open level terrain .. m/s

z = height above ground level .. m

z_r = general roof top level .. .. m

α = solar absorptance .. ..

γ = wall azimuth .. .. .. degree

γ_s = wall-solar azimuth .. .. degree

ϵ = emissivity

θ = time of day .. .. .. h

θ_{max} = time of day at which outdoor temperature is maximum .. h

θ_{min} = time of day at which outdoor temperature is minimum .. h

σ_H = horizontal shadow angle .. degree

σ_V = vertical shadow angle .. .. degree

ϕ = solar azimuth .. .. .. degree

UK COLD WEATHER DATA

External Design Dry-Bulb Temperatures

An analysis of cold weather data is required to establish the external design temperatures to be used in sizing a heating plant and its associated distribution system, and in assessing the seasonal heating energy consumption using simplified calculation procedures.

The winter external design temperatures for the United Kingdom may be derived from the method contained in Post-War Building Studies No. 33,[4] as explained by Jamieson,[1] but using weather data for a more recent period.

Table A2.1 gives the values below which the mean temperature falls on given numbers of occasions per heating season for day-time, night-time, 24-hour and 48-hour periods. The table gives the basic external temperatures for eight locations in the UK from which design values can be selected for given design risks. These temperatures should be reduced by 0.6 °C for every complete 100 m by which the height of the site in question exceeds the height of the comparison location in the table.

For the purposes of selecting the external design temperature, buildings may be classified according to their thermal inertia:

Low thermal inertia — typically, single storey buildings
High thermal inertia — typically, multi-storey buildings with solid intermediate floors and partitions.

The adopted design temperature for buildings with low thermal inertia is such that on average only one day in each heating season has a lower mean temperature. Similarly, for buildings with high thermal inertia, the design temperature is selected such that, on average, only one two-day spell in each heating season has a lower mean temperature.

The values in Table A2.1 given in **bold type** are the external design temperatures determined by this method, which will allow internal design conditions to be maintained during the cold spells which occur during the average winter, when heat loss calculations are based upon the external temperatures thus indicated, and the following conditions are satisfied:

(a) The building thermal inertia is taken into account.

Heating systems in buildings with a low thermal inertia should be designed based on values given in the column headed "24 hour".

Heating systems in buildings with a high thermal inertia should be designed based on values given in the column headed "48 hour".

(b) The heating system overload capacity is taken into account.

In this context, overload capacity is the capability of the heating system, considered as a whole and including plant distribution and emitters as appropriate, to provide heat output in the space in excess of the calculated heating requirement based upon the selected design temperature.

The temperatures given in the table normally can be safely used with systems having 20% overload capacity. When overload capacities differ from this, adjustment should be made to the outside design temperature.

From a reappraisal of the temperature data used by Jamieson[1] it has been concluded that for systems with no overload capacity the design temperature should be approximately $2\frac{1}{2}°C$ lower than that for systems with overload capacity, regardless of building thermal inertia.

(c) The heating system can, if necessary, be operated continuously in severe weather.

When considering system overload capacity, careful consideration should be given to the effect on initial cost and energy consumption under full and part load operation. This matter is discussed more fully in Section A9 of the *Guide*.

Table A2.1 Number of occasions, per heating season, that the mean temperature over the stated period falls below the values indicated.

(a) Belfast (Aldergrove Airport).
Station height 68 m above sea-level. Period 1957-76.

Average number of occasions	Period*			
	Day	Night	24 hour	48 hour
	Mean Temperature / °C			
0.1	−4.6	−6.8	−5.1	−4.5
0.2	−4.2	−5.9	−4.4	−3.9
0.33	−3.8	−5.2	−4.3	−3.3
0.5	−3.3	−4.8	−3.8	−3.2
1.0	−2.5	−3.8	**−2.7**	−2.4
2.0	−1.5	−2.7	−1.9	**−1.5**
3.0	−0.8	−2.1	−1.3	−0.9
5.0	−0.2	−1.2	−0.4	−0.3
10.0	0.8	−0.2	0.4	0.7
15.0	1.5	0.3	1.1	1.2
20.0	2.0	0.9	1.6	1.7
25.0	2.4	1.3	2.0	2.1
30.0	2.8	1.7	2.4	2.5
40.0	3.4	2.4	3.0	3.2
50.0	4.0	3.0	3.6	3.7

(b) Birmingham (Elmdon Airport)
Station height 96 m above sea-level. Period 1957-76.

Average number of occasions	Period*			
	Day	Night	24 hour	48 hour
	Mean Temperature / °C			
0.1	−7.7	−11.5	−8.4	−9.6
0.2	−6.6	−9.0	−6.9	−6.5
0.33	−5.6	−8.0	−5.8	−5.6
0.5	−5.3	−7.3	−5.6	−5.2
1.0	−4.3	−6.1	**−5.0**	−4.4
2.0	−3.2	−4.9	−3.5	**−3.2**
3.0	−2.4	−4.1	−2.9	−2.5
5.0	−1.7	−3.1	−2.2	−1.8
10.0	−0.3	−1.6	−0.7	−0.6
15.0	0.3	−0.8	0.0	0.0
20.0	1.0	−0.1	0.5	0.6
25.0	1.4	0.3	1.0	1.2
30.0	1.9	0.7	1.3	1.6
40.0	2.7	1.4	2.2	2.4
50.0	3.5	2.1	2.9	3.0

(c) Cardiff (Rhoose Airport)
Station height 67 m above sea-level. Period 1957-76.

Average number of occasions	Period*			
	Day	Night	24 hour	48 hour
	Mean Temperature / °C			
0.1	−5.5	−8.8	−5.2	−5.3
0.2	−4.8	−5.8	−5.1	−4.9
0.33	−4.3	−5.4	−4.6	−4.2
0.5	−3.9	−5.0	−4.2	−4.0
1.0	−2.8	−4.1	**−2.9**	−2.7
2.0	−1.7	−3.1	−2.0	**−1.7**
3.0	−1.1	−2.4	−1.4	−1.3
5.0	−0.4	−1.4	−0.7	−0.4
10.0	0.7	−0.3	0.4	0.5
15.0	1.4	0.3	1.1	1.2
20.0	2.1	0.8	1.6	1.8
25.0	2.7	1.3	2.1	2.3
30.0	3.1	1.8	2.6	2.8
40.0	3.9	2.7	3.4	3.5
50.0	4.7	3.4	4.2	4.2

(d) Edinburgh (Turnhouse Airport)
Station height 35 m above sea-level. Period 1957-76.

Average number of occasions	Period*			
	Day	Night	24 hour	48 hour
	Mean Temperature / °C			
0.1	−7.0	−10.3	−8.4	−6.7
0.2	−6.7	−9.6	−6.9	−6.1
0.33	−5.6	−9.0	−6.3	−5.8
0.5	−5.3	−8.1	−5.8	−4.7
1.0	−4.0	−6.7	**−4.7**	−4.2
2.0	−3.1	−5.3	−3.8	**−3.4**
3.0	−2.3	−4.5	−2.9	−2.5
5.0	−1.4	−3.3	−2.0	−1.7
10.0	−0.2	−1.7	−0.7	−0.4
15.0	0.5	−0.7	0.0	0.2
20.0	1.2	−0.1	0.6	0.8
25.0	1.6	0.3	1.1	1.3
30.0	2.0	0.8	1.5	1.7
40.0	2.7	1.5	2.2	2.3
50.0	3.4	2.1	2.8	2.9

Table A2.1—*continued*

(e) Glasgow (Abbotsinch Airport)
   Station height 5 m above sea-level. Period 1966-76.

Average number of occasions	Period*			
	Day	Night	24 hour	48 hour
	Mean Temperature / °C			
0.1	−7.3	−8.2	−7.4	−6.1
0.2	−6.9	−6.8	−6.0	−5.8
0.33	−5.6	−5.8	−5.4	−4.0
0.5	−5.1	−5.7	−5.0	−3.9
1.0	−3.6	−4.7	**−3.8**	−3.3
2.0	−2.4	−3.2	−2.4	**−2.2**
3.0	−1.4	−2.6	−1.7	−1.3
5.0	−0.5	−1.4	−0.7	−0.3
10.0	1.0	0.0	0.5	0.7
15.0	1.9	1.0	1.4	1.6
20.0	2.8	1.8	2.3	2.4
25.0	3.5	2.5	3.2	3.1
30.0	4.1	3.1	3.8	3.8
40.0	5.4	4.3	4.9	4.9
50.0	6.5	5.8	5.9	5.8

(f) London (Heathrow Airport)
   Station height 25 m above sea-level. Period 1957-76.

Average number of occasions	Period*			
	Day	Night	24 hour	48 hour
	Mean Temperature / °C			
0.1	−7.6	−7.5	−7.6	−7.1
0.2	−6.1	−6.8	−6.5	−5.8
0.33	−4.6	−6.2	−4.8	−4.3
0.5	−4.1	−5.1	−4.2	−3.7
1.0	−2.9	−4.1	**−3.0**	−2.8
2.0	−1.9	−3.0	−2.2	**−1.8**
3.0	−1.3	−2.3	−1.6	−1.4
5.0	−0.6	−1.5	−0.9	−0.7
10.0	0.6	−0.4	0.2	0.3
15.0	1.3	0.3	0.9	1.0
20.0	1.9	0.8	1.6	1.8
25.0	2.5	1.3	2.1	2.3
30.0	2.9	1.7	2.5	2.6
40.0	3.8	2.5	3.3	3.3
50.0	4.5	3.2	3.9	4.0

(g) Manchester (Ringway Airport)
   Station height 75 m above sea-level. Period 1957-76.

Average number of occasions	Period*			
	Day	Night	24 hour	48 hour
	Mean Temperature / °C			
0.1	−7.5	−8.7	−7.2	−6.2
0.2	−5.5	−7.7	−6.7	−5.8
0.33	−4.7	−7.0	−5.2	−4.9
0.5	−4.3	−6.6	−4.9	−4.4
1.0	−3.4	−4.5	**−3.7**	−3.4
2.0	−2.4	−3.8	−2.9	**−2.3**
3.0	−1.9	−3.0	−2.2	−1.9
5.0	−1.1	−1.9	−1.4	−1.1
10.0	0.0	−0.8	−0.2	0.0
15.0	0.8	0.0	0.5	0.6
20.0	1.4	0.6	1.2	1.3
25.0	2.0	1.0	1.6	1.8
30.0	2.4	1.4	2.0	2.2
40.0	3.2	2.1	2.7	2.9
50.0	3.8	2.8	3.4	3.5

(h) Plymouth (Mount Batten)
   Station height 27 m above sea-level. Period 1957-76.

Average number of occasions	Period*			
	Day	Night	24 hour	48 hour
	Mean Temperature / °C			
0.1	−3.1	−4.2	−3.4	−3.1
0.2	−3.0	−4.2	−2.7	−2.7
0.33	−1.9	−2.8	−2.6	−2.1
0.5	−1.6	−2.5	−1.8	−1.5
1.0	−0.8	−2.0	**−1.0**	−0.7
2.0	0.0	−0.9	0.0	**0.0**
3.0	0.6	−0.4	0.3	0.5
5.0	1.2	0.1	1.0	1.1
10.0	2.3	1.2	1.9	2.1
15.0	3.1	1.9	2.7	2.9
20.0	3.7	2.5	3.3	3.4
25.0	4.2	3.1	3.8	4.0
30.0	4.7	3.5	4.3	4.5
40.0	5.5	4.4	5.1	5.3
50.0	6.3	5.1	5.8	5.9

* Day temperature is mean of hours 06 – 17 inclusive: night temperature is mean of hours 18 – 05 inclusive: 24 hour temperature is mean of hours 00 – 23 inclusive: 48 hour temperature is mean of hours 00 – 23 inclusive on two consecutive days.

Note that 0.1 occasions per heating season is equivalent to one occasion in ten years.

Table A2.2 Summary of winter external design temperatures.

Location	External Design Temperature / °C			
	Low Thermal Inertia		High Thermal Inertia	
	With overload capacity	Without overload capacity	With overload capacity	Without overload capacity
Belfast	−2.5	−5.0	−1.5	−4.0
Birmingham	−5.0	−7.5	−3.0	−5.5
Cardiff	−3.0	−5.5	−1.5	−4.0
Edinburgh	−4.5	−7.0	−3.5	−6.0
Glasgow	−4.0	−6.5	−2.0	−4.5
London	−3.0	−5.5	−2.0	−4.5
Manchester	−3.5	−6.0	−2.5	−5.0
Plymouth	−1.0	−3.5	0.0	−2.5

Table A2.2 summarises the recommended external design temperatures based on the above conditions, for the eight locations for which detailed data are provided in Table A2.1.

The following example serves to indicate how the foregoing information should be applied.

Example
Calculate the winter design temperature for a building with a high thermal inertia situated in Clee Hill, such that internal temperatures can be maintained during an average winter by a heating system with 20% overload capacity.

The village of Clee Hill lies at about 350 metres above sea-level. The 48h winter design temperature for Birmingham (Elmdon Airport), the nearest site in Table A2.2, is –3.0° C. Clee Hill lies approximately 260 metres higher than Elmdon, so the design temperature should be reduced by 1.2° C to –4.2° C.

If the heating system has no overload capacity, the design temperature should be –6.7° C.

When humidification is required, as may be the case in ventilation and air conditioning systems, the wet-bulb temperature associated with the selected dry-bulb temperature can be established by reference to Meteorological Office Climatological Memoranda, as discussed under the heading *Warm Weather Data*.

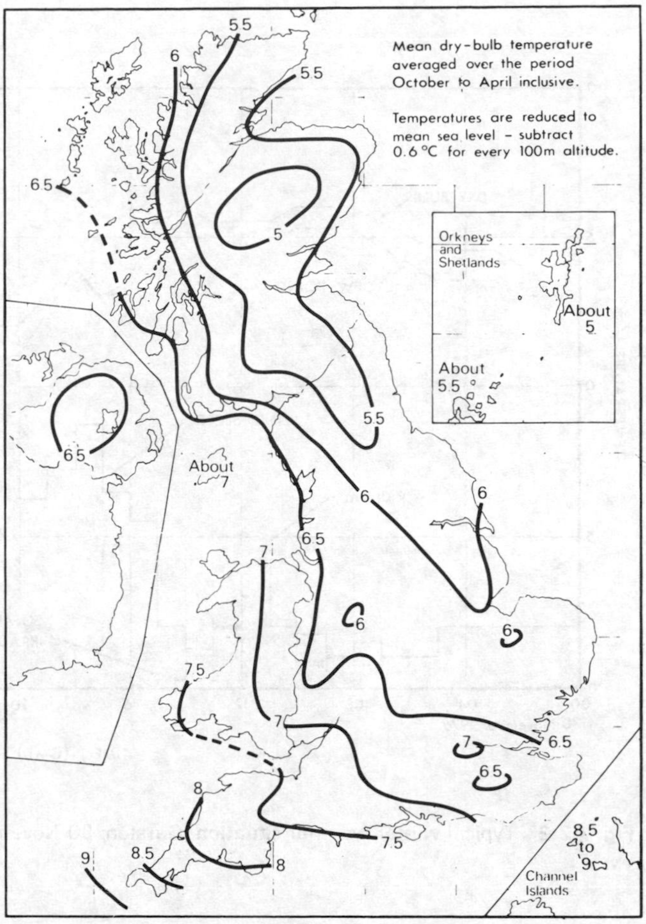

Energy Consumption Calculations

Simplified procedures for calculating the seasonal heating energy consumption, such as the method described in the CIBS Building Energy Code, Part 2(a),[5] require a knowledge of the daily mean outdoor temperature averaged over the heating season. Such information is given in Fig. A2.1, which shows the distribution over the UK of the daily mean outdoor temperature, averaged for the months October to April, for the thirty-year period 1941-70.

Temperatures relate to mean sea-level in open country. Corrections for height of the locality above sea-level and for the proximity of large towns are given on the figure. In the London area, the value indicated should be used without correction.

Mean dry-bulb temperature averaged over the period October to April inclusive.

Temperatures are reduced to mean sea level – subtract 0.6 °C for every 100m altitude.

For areas within a radius of one mile of the centre of large towns (population in excess of 500,000) 0.5 °C should be added, except for London, for which the value indicated should be used, without modification.

Fig. A2.1. Seasonal mean dry-bulb temperatures.

Typical Winter Weather Situations

Figures A2.2 and A2.3 illustrate the weather on certain winter days in the UK by showing how the principal weather elements varied during the selected periods. They were prepared using data obtained during normal measurements at meteorological sites and so do not represent the most extreme conditions which can occur. Each shows hourly values of dry-bulb and dew-point temperatures, global solar irradiance, wind speed and rainfall amount. Obviously these figures show only a small section of the many sorts of weather which can be experienced.

30 November 1976 (Fig. A2.2) began with a densely overcast sky, with moderate rain from 07 to 17 GMT, when rain changed to sleet before ceasing at about 19 GMT. The clouds then broke to give a cloudless night, and as the strong winds eased dry-bulb temperature fell, dropping to 0 °C by 04 GMT on 1 December. Ventilation heat losses from buildings will have been considerably increased during the evening by the wind, which averaged about 7 m/s at Garston, Hertfordshire, for about 7 hours, but in the hours before sunrise with a light wind and temperature around 0 °C, most heat loss will have been by conduction through the structure. Masonry walls exposed to the driving rain in the storm may have taken up enough water to increase their thermal conductance appreciably. Systems have greatest difficulty in coping with heating loads when strong wind is combined with low temperatures of 0 °C or less. Fortunately, such conditions are fairly uncommon at the lower altitudes in the UK, as is shown by Fig. A2.4.

Figure A2.3 illustrates how a cold spell in November 1947 ended as a moist, warm airstream moved over the country, giving an exceptionally prolonged and rapid increase in atmospheric dew-point temperature, amounting to some 10 °C in 13 hours at Kew Observatory, London. Unheated and poorly-heated masonry structures which had been chilled in the cold spell suffered severe condensation because the rate at which their surface temperatures rose was considerably less than the rate of rise in dew point. Fortunately such severe conditions occur only rarely, probably not more than once in 10 or 20 years on average.

An exceptionally rapid fall in temperature is often the result of large heat losses from the ground to a clear night sky with calm or light wind. Lightweight elements of buildings, especially roofs, respond rapidly to such a change in weather, which gives a great risk of condensation of atmospheric moisture on the underside of sheeted roofs. A single cold night will not necessarily give condensation problems with heavyweight structures, but it could, of course, be the first night of an extended spell of cold weather which will in time chill a heavyweight building. More information on the likely frequency of occurrence of condensation is given later in *Occurrence of Condensation*.

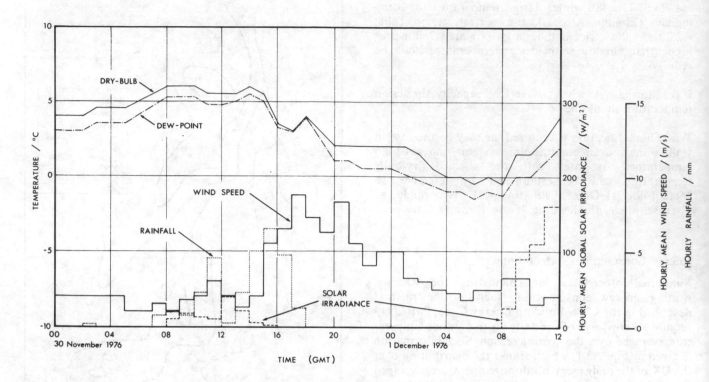

Fig. A2.2   Typical winter weather situation (Garston: 30 November – 1 December 1976)

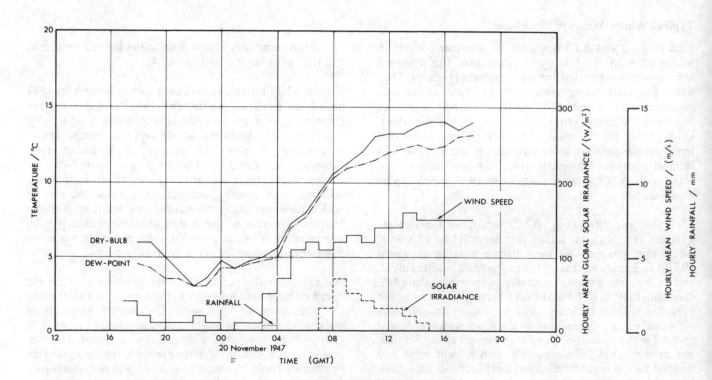

Fig. A2.3   Severe winter weather situation (Kew: 19–20 November 1947)

Coincidence of Wind Speed and Low Temperature

Figure A2.4 shows the frequency with which various simultaneous conditions of wind and temperature were recorded at London (Heathrow Airport) during the ten winters from December 1948 to February 1958,[6] winter being taken as December, January and February. The method of presentation shows the direction from which the wind came and clearly illustrates the greater frequency of cold winds from the northern quarters.

The upper set of curves on the left hand side of the figure shows the frequency when, for periods of 6 to 11 consecutive hours duration, the wind speed reached or exceeded 2.5 m/s and the temperature was below thresholds of –2.2 °C, 0 °C and +2.2 °C. The sets of curves below these show the frequency of similar conditions persisting for periods of 12 to 23, 18 to 35 and 24 to 47 consecutive hours duration. The right hand side of the figure shows similar information but refers to wind speeds in excess of 5.0 and 7.5 m/s.

Occurrence of Condensation

Condensation of atmospheric moisture on a surface can only occur when the dew-point temperature of the air in contact with the surface exceeds the temperature of the surface itself. Usually there is more moisture in the air in rooms than there is in the outside air, and condensation on surfaces in buildings occurs because there is inadequate ventilation and hence a build-up of moisture in rooms, or because there is insufficient heating to keep the wall temperatures above the dew-point temperature of the air in the rooms. Both conditions may occur together, thus aggravating the trouble. In these circumstances the condensation is normally most severe during continuously cold weather, when the outer parts of the building are cold.

Condensation may also occur as a result of the change of weather at the end of a cold spell, when a cold air-mass is replaced within a few hours by a warm, moist air-mass (e.g. Fig. A2.3). In these circumstances the atmospheric dew-point temperature may rise more rapidly than the surface temperature of heavyweight masonry structures, so that for a more or less prolonged period the dew point exceeds the surface temperature and condensation occurs on all such surfaces exposed to the outside air. This is particularly likely to occur in poorly heated or completely unheated buildings such as stores, and on their contents.

Table A2.3 lists, for eight locations in the UK, the frequency with which such conditions occurred in a 20-year period. The statistics are based on the difference between the dew-point temperature in the middle of the day (mean of values at 09, 12 and 15 GMT) and the mean dry-bulb temperature of the preceding day (mean of hourly values from 00 to 23 GMT). For example, at Edinburgh there were 25 occasions when the daytime dew point was in the range 5.0 to 5.9 °C higher than the mean dry-bulb of the preceding calendar day. The greatest difference ranged from about 8 °C to about 11 °C at the eight places considered. Almost all days with risk of condensation occur in the cold half of the year.

If it is assumed that the surface temperature of a heavyweight building during the preceding 24 hours is the same as the mean outside air temperature, the statistics in the table give a guide as to the likely frequency of occurrence of condensation following a rapid rise in atmospheric dew-point. Calculations based on a typical structure with brick walls 220 mm thick and normal timber floors and plasterboard ceilings, and a ventilation rate of one air-change per hour, show that if the outside dry-bulb temperature, following a period of steady temperature, rises at a constant rate, the temperature of the inside surface of the walls will, after 12 hours, have increased by less than one-quarter of the rise in outside air temperature. Condensation will occur on the walls, but at only about 20% of the possible rate because the low rate of ventilation limits the amount of water vapour available. Increasing the rate of ventilation will cause a corresponding increase in condensation.

Obviously the thermal characteristics of each building will determine just how quickly it responds to change in meteorological conditions so that different buildings may not behave in exactly the same way. However, it is probably reasonable to say that any unheated heavyweight building is liable to suffer more or less severe condensation from this cause at least once a year.

Table A2.3 Number of occasions in 20 years when dew-point temperature exceeds the preceding day's dry-bulb temperature by the amount indicated. Period 1957-76.

Temperature Difference /°C	Number of occasions in 20 years							
	Belfast	Birmingham	Cardiff	Edinburgh	Glasgow	London	Manchester	Plymouth
0.0 – 0.9	446	431	520	400	151	355	289	654
1.0 – 1.9	296	259	355	248	108	261	206	359
2.0 – 2.9	139	159	154	140	59	159	118	153
3.0 – 3.9	88	76	89	72	43	52	54	57
4.0 – 4.9	45	40	40	34	21	45	19	36
5.0 – 5.9	27	29	17	25	14	18	14	13
6.0 – 6.9	8	10	6	5	6	11	5	7
7.0 – 7.9	5	6	2	9	2	3	1	2
8.0 – 8.9	2	0	1	0	1	3	2	0
9.0 – 9.9	0	0	0	0	2	1	0	1
10.0 – 10.9	1	2	0	0	0	1	0	0
11.0 – 11.9	0	0	0	1	0	0	0	0
Total Frequency	1057	1012	1164	934	407	909	708	1282
Annual Average Frequency	53	51	58	47	20	45	35	64

Notes: Dew-point temperature is the mean of observations at 09, 12 and 15 GMT.
Dry-bulb temperature is the mean of hourly observations from 00 to 23 GMT on the preceding day.

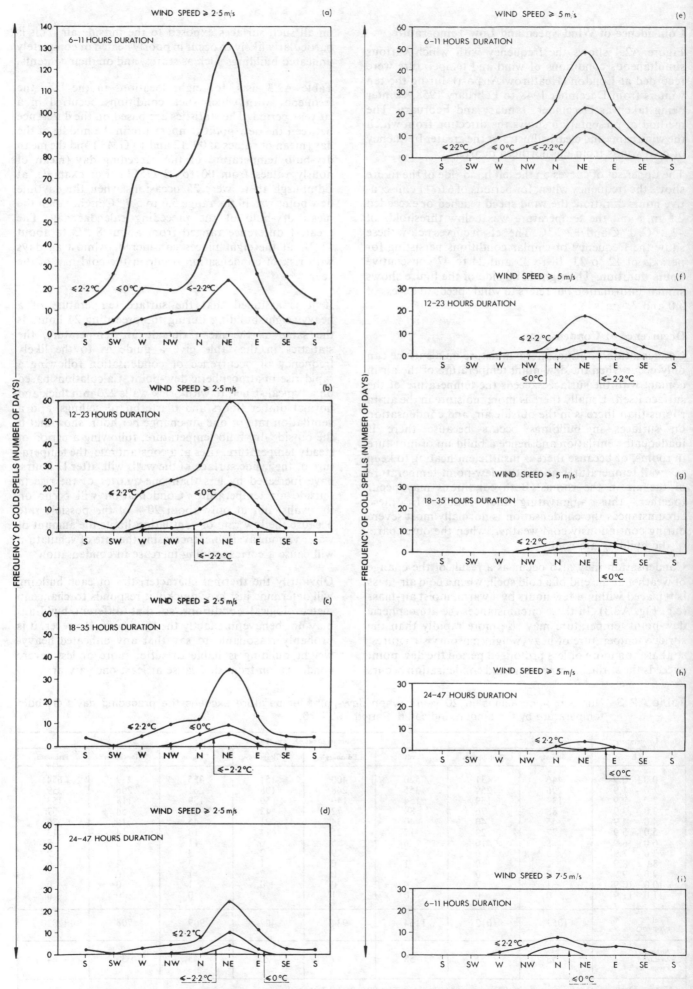

Fig. A2.4 Coincidence of wind speed and low temperature at London (Heathrow Airport) showing frequency of cold spells of specified durations.

If the building is initially at a steady temperature other than that of the outside air, the statistics of Table A2.3 may be used by adopting a "false zero" as follows; for a building in Glasgow at an initial temperature 3.0 °C above the mean outside dry-bulb temperature, there were two occasions when the difference between the day-time dew-point temperature and the preceding day's mean dry-bulb temperature was in the range 6.0 to 6.9 °C, (i.e. a temperature difference of 6.0 to 6.9 °C above a "zero" of 3.0 °C which corresponds to a true temperature difference of 9.0 to 9.9 °C in the table).

Clearly when such conditions occur, unheated buildings should as far as possible be closed to exclude the humid air. It is possible to obtain from the Meteorological Office weather forecasts warning when such occurrence is expected, so that stores or other buildings can be heated or otherwise protected to reduce the risk of condensation.

Degree days

To estimate the seasonal or annual energy consumption for space heating or to monitor the heating plant performance, information will be required to ensure that the influence of weather variations is taken into account. The seasonal mean dry-bulb temperatures given in Fig. A2.1 meet part of this requirement. Alternatively, the degree-day concept provides such information by giving a measure of the temperature difference between inside and outside as related to the period of time under consideration.

The degree days corresponding to a particular day are calculated as the difference between a base temperature and the mean dry-bulb temperature for that day. For this purpose, the mean dry-bulb temperature is defined as the mean of the daily maximum and minimum temperatures:

$$\text{Degree days} = t_{base} - \tfrac{1}{2}(t_{max} + t_{min}) \qquad \text{A2.1}$$

Monthly degree-day totals are obtained by summing these daily temperature differences, i.e.,

$$\text{Monthly degree days} = \sum_{month} \left[t_{base} - \tfrac{1}{2}(t_{max} + t_{min}) \right] \qquad \text{A2.2}$$

Summations of monthly degree-day totals may be performed to give a degree-day total for the heating season or for the whole year.

Equations A2.1 and A2.2 only apply when the outside temperature is less than the base temperature, i.e. $t_{max} < t_{base}$. The following alternative equations are used in the UK in situations where t_{max} exceeds t_{base}:

(i) If $t_{base} > \tfrac{1}{2}(t_{max} + t_{min})$,

$$\text{Degree days} = \tfrac{1}{2}(t_{base} - t_{min}) - \tfrac{1}{4}(t_{max} - t_{base})$$

$$\text{A2.3}$$

(ii) If $t_{base} < \tfrac{1}{2}(t_{max} + t_{min})$,

$$\text{Degree days} = \tfrac{1}{4}(t_{base} - t_{min}) \qquad \text{A2.4}$$

Since January 1977, data for 17 areas in the UK have been published monthly by the Department of Energy,[7]

the figures including monthly values for the most recent two heating seasons, together with monthly and seasonal values averaged over the latest twenty year period. Table A2.4 lists the seasonal and annual degree days for each area averaged over the twenty year period 1959-78, and Fig. A2.5 shows the present sub-division of the country for this purpose. Figure A2.6 gives seasonal average degree-day contours for the UK for the twenty year period 1957-76. Both Table A2.4 and Fig. A2.6 refer to a base temperature of 15.5 °C.

Table A2.4 Degree-day totals, to base temperature 15.5 °C, averaged over 20 years. Period 1959-78.

Area	September to May inclusive	Annual Total
Thames Valley	2019	2120
South Eastern	2258	2427
Southern	2110	2265
South Western	1825	1949
Severn Valley	2088	2211
Midland	2329	2507
West Pennines	2209	2362
North Western	2335	2532
Borders	2453	2709
North Eastern	2331	2510
East Pennines	2221	2373
East Anglia	2289	2451
West Scotland	2374	2585
East Scotland	2474	2719
North East Scotland	2602	2886
Wales	2066	2244
Northern Ireland	2310	2522

Degree day areas
1 Thames Valley
2 South Eastern
3 Southern
4 South Western
5 Severn Valley
6 Midland
7 West Pennines
8 North Western
9 Borders
10 North Eastern
11 East Pennines
12 East Anglia
13 West Scotland
14 East Scotland
15 North East Scotland
16 Wales
17 Northern Ireland

Fig. A2.5 Degree-day areas (from Fuel Efficiency Booklet 7, published by the Department of Energy and reproduced by permission of the Controller of H.M. Stationery Office).

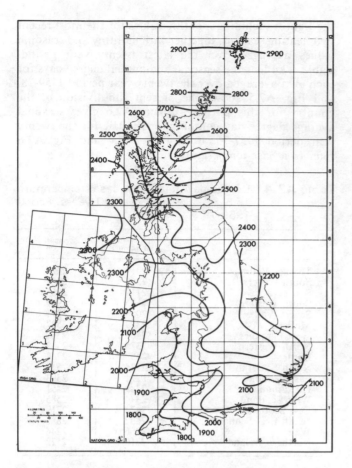

Fig. A2.6 Degree days (base temperature 15.5 °C) for the UK, September to May, reduced to mean sea level. Period 1957-76.

Town Climate

More solar radiation is absorbed by the fabric of a town than by the ground in the country. In the summer the extra heat absorbed keeps the average air temperature in the town a degree or two higher than that in the surrounding country. This so-called 'heat-island' effect is only noticeable on clear calm nights, when the centre of a town the size of London may be as much a 6 or 7 °C warmer than the country[9], for the maximum daytime temperature in London is little different from that in the country. In winter, the heat-island effect persists, but in the UK is probably caused mainly by the emission of heat from buildings, industrial plants and vehicles.

The result of this is that heat requirements for buildings, as measured by degree days, are some 10 per cent lower in central London than in open country at the same altitude. It should be remarked here that Kew Observatory, which supplied degree-day data for the London area, is itself in a suburb of London, and degree days for Kew amount to some 5 per cent less than in the country and 5 per cent more than for central London.

UK WARM WEATHER DATA

General

Analyses of warm weather data are required to establish design values for sizing air conditioning plant, assessing the likelihood of summer overheating and estimating the temperatures reached by outdoor surfaces exposed to the sun. The methods employed in weather data analyses are described by Knight[2] and Harrison[3].

Design values given by such analyses are generally less than the extremes which may occur, that is, a small but acceptable 'design risk' has been incorporated into the values. In normal air conditioning practice, however, the time lag of the structure makes it unnecessary to design for more severe conditions, but buildings of very light construction may require special consideration. Where a building or plant is required to cope with the most severe weather conditions, higher values than those proposed for routine design should be used.

This section gives some information on dry-bulb, wet-bulb and dew-point temperatures for the design of air conditioning systems and describes a method for their derivation for localities where such detailed information is not readily available. Coincident solar radiation and dry-bulb temperature data for summer overheating and outdoor surface temperature estimates are dealt with elsewhere—see *Overheating Design* and *Sol-Air Temperature and Long-Wave Loss*.

All wet-bulb temperatures quoted in this section are 'screen' values measured using a standard meteorological naturally-ventilated thermometer screen rather than the 'sling' values used in the standard CIBSE psychrometric chart.

Some Warm Weather Records

'Design' warm weather conditions occur on relatively few days in summer when the sky is cloudless for most or all of the day. However, almost invariably the hottest days are not those with the greatest amounts of solar radiation. This is illustrated in Figs. A2.7 and A2.8.

The base temperature to be adopted in calculations will depend upon the temperature maintained in the building, on the thermal insulation properties of the building and on the level of miscellaneous gains. Reference should be made to Section B18 of the *Guide* to establish the appropriate base temperature to be applied.

Monthly fuel consumption can be related to the degree-day values for the same period, corrected to the appropriate base temperature either by calculation or by graphical methods, to monitor trends in operating efficiency. Deviation from a constant relationship will indicate a change in the plant performance, or will reflect changes in thermal insulation standards or methods of working.

Annual and seasonal values should be increased by 2 degree days for every 1 metre of altitude above sea level. It is believed that for a given altitude, variations in local topography do not affect average seasonal heat losses by a significant amount.[8] The map does not take account of the rather warmer conditions which prevail in towns. An analysis of data for London[9] suggests that there could be a reduction in annual degree days of about 10% in the centre of cities and towns compared with places of similar altitude outside. This effect diminishes with distance from the centre.

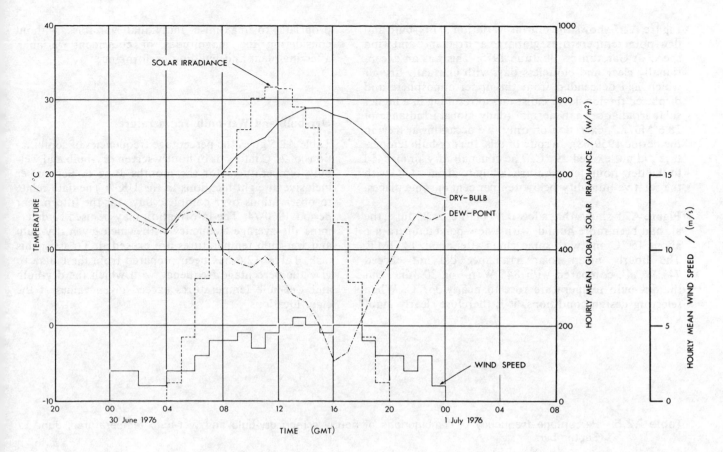

Fig. A2.7   Warm weather record (Garston: 30 June 1976).

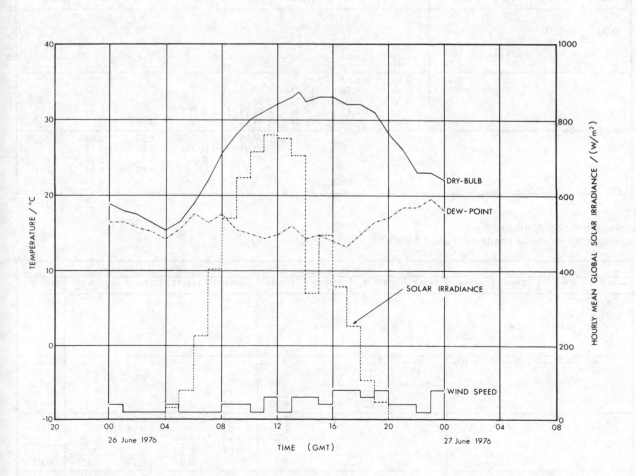

Fig. A2.8   Warm weather record (Garston: 26 June 1976).

Figure A2.7 shows the diurnal variation of dry-bulb and dew-point temperatures, global solar irradiance and wind speed at Garston on 30 June 1976. This was an exceptionally clear and cloudless day, with unusually dry air which had descended from the upper atmosphere and displaced the low-level moist air, so resulting in a higher solar irradiance than normal (daily global irradiance of 28.6 MJ/m², exceeded on only five occasions at Kew in the period 1959-68). In spite of this, the dry-bulb temperature did not exceed 29 °C. The unusually dry air also led to the dew-point temperature falling to about –4 °C with the relative humidity below ten per cent in some places.

Figure A2.8 shows that a few days before, on 26 June, the air had been more humid, with a dew-point temperature about 15 °C and with some cloud after about 14 GMT. The hourly mean solar irradiance did not exceed 745 W/m², compared with 845 W/m² on 30 June, but the dry-bulb temperature rose to nearly 34 °C. When selecting design conditions, it is therefore clearly inappropriate to maximise individual variables without considering the magnitudes of coincident variables affecting plant and building performance.

Dry-bulb and Wet-bulb Temperatures

Table A2.5 gives the percentage frequencies of combinations of 2 °C intervals of hourly screen dry-bulb and wet-bulb temperatures for the months June to September inclusive at eight locations in the UK[10]. The data relate to observations over complete days for the fifteen year period 1960-74. The information may be used to determine the average frequency with which given dry-bulb and wet-bulb temperatures are exceeded. To assist this task, Table A2.6 has been prepared from these data to give the percentage frequency with which the dry-bulb and wet-bulb temperatures exceed given values at the eight locations.

Table A2.5 Percentage frequency of combinations of hourly screen dry-bulb and wet-bulb temperatures, June to September.

(a) Belfast (Aldergrove Airport)
Station height 68 m above sea level. Period 1960-74.

Dry-bulb temperature / °C	Wet-bulb temperature / °C											
	-2 to 0	0 to 2	2 to 4	4 to 6	6 to 8	8 to 10	10 to 12	12 to 14	14 to 16	16 to 18	18 to 20	20 to 22
-2 to 0												
0 to 2	0.01	0.03										
2 to 4		0.01	0.16									
4 to 6			0.07	0.65								
6 to 8				0.69	2.44							
8 to 10				0.02	2.83	5.83						
10 to 12					0.30	9.56	10.95					
12 to 14					0.06	2.02	15.11	10.22				
14 to 16						0.15	4.30	12.28	4.75			
16 to 18							0.47	4.13	5.70	0.62		
18 to 20							0.01	0.55	2.22	1.58	0.02	
20 to 22								0.04	0.39	0.98	0.13	
22 to 24									0.08	0.31	0.19	
24 to 26										0.01	0.11	0.01
26 to 28											0.01	

(b) Birmingham (Elmdon Airport)
Station height 96 m above sea level. Period 1960-74.

Dry-bulb temperature / °C	Wet-bulb temperature / °C											
	-2 to 0	0 to 2	2 to 4	4 to 6	6 to 8	8 to 10	10 to 12	12 to 14	14 to 16	16 to 18	18 to 20	20 to 22	22 to 24
-2 to 0	0.01												
0 to 2	0.01	0.07											
2 to 4		0.01	0.43										
4 to 6			0.11	1.06									
6 to 8				0.48	2.53								
8 to 10				0.02	2.08	5.03							
10 to 12					0.33	6.75	8.05						
12 to 14					0.01	2.24	11.44	8.46					
14 to 16						0.50	4.99	10.26	4.53				
16 to 18						0.02	1.78	6.00	6.15	1.07			
18 to 20							0.08	2.31	4.04	2.07	0.07		
20 to 22								0.33	1.98	1.67	0.21		
22 to 24								0.05	0.43	0.97	0.36	0.01	
24 to 26									0.04	0.28	0.37	0.03	
26 to 28										0.04	0.14	0.05	0.01
28 to 30											0.02	0.02	

Table A2.5—*continued*

(c) Cardiff (Rhoose Airport)
Station height 67 m above sea level. Period 1960-74.

Dry-bulb temperature / °C	Wet-bulb temperature / °C											
	0 to 2	2 to 4	4 to 6	6 to 8	8 to 10	10 to 12	12 to 14	14 to 16	16 to 18	18 to 20	20 to 22	22 to 24
0 to 2	0.0+											
2 to 4	0.01	0.06										
4 to 6		0.10	0.35									
6 to 8			0.37	1.39								
8 to 10			0.01	1.50	3.52							
10 to 12				0.13	4.67	7.39						
12 to 14				0.01	0.92	11.30	11.81					
14 to 16					0.11	3.02	15.52	9.47				
16 to 18						0.41	4.84	9.73	2.54			
18 to 20						0.03	0.77	3.14	2.84	0.08		
20 to 22						0.01	0.07	0.75	1.35	0.40		
22 to 24							0.02	0.05	0.46	0.35	0.02	0.01
24 to 26									0.08	0.23	0.08	
26 to 28									0.01	0.04	0.03	0.0+

(d) Edinburgh (Turnhouse Airport)
Station height 35 m above sea level. Period 1960-74.

Dry-bulb temperature / °C	Wet-bulb temperature / °C											
	–2 to 0	0 to 2	2 to 4	4 to 6	6 to 8	8 to 10	10 to 12	12 to 14	14 to 16	16 to 18	18 to 20	20 to 22
–2 to 0	0.03											
0 to 2	0.01	0.13										
2 to 4		0.05	0.47									
4 to 6			0.23	1.27								
6 to 8				0.91	2.98							
8 to 10				0.07	3.66	6.40						
10 to 12					0.64	10.14	10.54					
12 to 14					0.04	2.71	14.46	8.53				
14 to 16						0.40	5.87	10.75	2.66			
16 to 18						0.01	1.27	5.03	4.09	0.28		
18 to 20							0.04	1.09	2.17	0.93	0.01	
20 to 22								0.09	0.53	0.71	0.05	
22 to 24								0.03	0.17	0.26	0.12	
24 to 26									0.01	0.05	0.07	
26 to 28										0.01	0.03	

(e) Glasgow (Abbotsinch Airport)
Station height 5 m above sea level. Period 1960-74.

Dry-bulb temperature / °C	Wet-bulb temperature / °C												
	–4 to –2	–2 to 0	0 to 2	2 to 4	4 to 6	6 to 8	8 to 10	10 to 12	12 to 14	14 to 16	16 to 18	18 to 20	20 to 22
–4 to –2	0.01												
–2 to 0		0.07											
0 to 2		0.01	0.13										
2 to 4			0.03	0.38									
4 to 6				0.21	1.11								
6 to 8				0.01	0.66	2.42							
8 to 10					0.01	2.95	5.03						
10 to 12						0.39	9.36	9.67					
12 to 14						0.04	2.33	15.65	9.47				
14 to 16							0.30	5.62	11.99	3.92			
16 to 18							0.02	0.89	4.89	4.71	0.42		
18 to 20								0.03	1.09	2.36	0.99	0.02	
20 to 22									0.11	0.65	0.82	0.07	
22 to 24										0.17	0.45	0.20	0.01
24 to 26										0.01	0.14	0.13	0.02
26 to 28											0.01	0.01	0.01

Table A2.5—*continued*

(f) London (Heathrow Airport)
Station height 25 m above sea level. Period 1960-74.

Dry-bulb temperature / °C	Wet-bulb temperature / °C											
	0 to 2	2 to 4	4 to 6	6 to 8	8 to 10	10 to 12	12 to 14	14 to 16	16 to 18	18 to 20	20 to 22	22 to 24
0 to 2	0.0+											
2 to 4	0.0+	0.05										
4 to 6		0.03	0.20									
6 to 8			0.21	1.01								
8 to 10			0.02	1.19	2.73							
10 to 12				0.15	4.45	5.02						
12 to 14				0.03	1.22	9.35	7.40					
14 to 16					0.28	3.82	12.06	5.43				
16 to 18					0.04	1.53	6.83	8.96	1.77			
18 to 20						0.23	3.19	5.57	3.27	0.13		
20 to 22						0.02	0.64	2.99	3.19	0.51	0.0+	
22 to 24							0.08	0.89	2.13	0.78	0.06	
24 to 26								0.13	0.73	0.73	0.11	
26 to 28								0.01	0.09	0.35	0.12	0.01
28 to 30									0.0+	0.11	0.08	0.01
30 to 32										0.0+	0.05	0.0+
32 to 34											0.01	

(g) Manchester (Ringway Airport)
Station height 75 m above sea level. Period 1960-74.

Dry-bulb temperature / °C	Wet-bulb temperature / °C											
	0 to 2	2 to 4	4 to 6	6 to 8	8 to 10	10 to 12	12 to 14	14 to 16	16 to 18	18 to 20	20 to 22	22 to 24
0 to 2	0.01											
2 to 4	0.01	0.07										
4 to 6		0.04	0.31									
6 to 8			0.48	1.41								
8 to 10			0.06	2.46	3.89							
10 to 12				0.46	8.14	6.85						
12 to 14				0.05	2.91	14.14	7.04					
14 to 16					0.57	6.25	11.94	4.01				
16 to 18					0.03	2.03	6.11	6.29	0.84			
18 to 20					0.01	0.18	1.96	3.68	1.67	0.03		
20 to 22						0.01	0.39	1.61	1.26	0.16		
22 to 24							0.04	0.53	0.88	0.29	0.01	
24 to 26								0.11	0.26	0.22	0.06	
26 to 28								0.01	0.07	0.06	0.07	
28 to 30									0.01	0.01	0.02	

(h) Plymouth (Mount Batten)
Station height 27 m above sea level. Period 1960-74.

Dry-bulb temperature / °C	Wet-bulb temperature / °C											
	0 to 2	2 to 4	4 to 6	6 to 8	8 to 10	10 to 12	12 to 14	14 to 16	16 to 18	18 to 20	20 to 22	22 to 24
0 to 2												
2 to 4		0.02										
4 to 6		0.02	0.17									
6 to 8		0.0+	0.11	0.92								
8 to 10			0.01	0.70	2.68							
10 to 12				0.05	2.95	5.92						
12 to 14					0.59	9.31	13.29					
14 to 16					0.05	2.73	16.08	14.04				
16 to 18						0.28	4.51	11.82	3.76			
18 to 20							0.49	2.85	3.24	0.13		
20 to 22							0.04	0.54	1.21	0.48		
22 to 24								0.05	0.28	0.42	0.03	
24 to 26									0.01	0.14	0.05	
26 to 28											0.03	

Note:
0.0+ indicates a value greater than 0.0 but less than 0.005%.
The range of temperature 0 to 2 represents measurements between 0.1 and 2.0 °C, 2 to 4 represents measurements between 2.1 and 4.0 °C, and so on.

Table A2.6 Percentage frequency for which the hourly screen dry-bulb and wet-bulb temperatures exceed the stated values in the period June to September (1960-74).

Dry-bulb		Wet-bulb		Dry-bulb		Wet-bulb	
Temperature / °C	Frequency / %	Temperature / °C	Frequency / %	Temperature / °C	Frequency / %	Temperature / °C	Frequency / %
(a) Belfast (Aldergrove Airport)				*(e)* Glasgow (Abbotsinch Airport)			
15	26.8	13	29.0	15	27.6	12	42.7
16	17.4	14	17.1	16	18.2	13	27.1
17	10.7	15	8.7	17	11.5	14	15.1
18	6.5	16	4.0	18	7.3	15	7.3
19	3.9	17	1.6	19	4.5	16	3.3
20	2.2	18	0.5	20	2.8	17	1.3
21	1.2	19	0.1	21	1.9	18	0.4
22	0.6	20	0.0+	22	1.1	19	0.1
23	0.3			23	0.7	20	0.0+
24	0.1			24	0.3		
25	0.1			25	0.1		
26	0.0+			26	0.0+		
(b) Birmingham (Elmdon Airport)				*(f)* London (Heathrow Airport)			
16	30.6	13	37.1	18	26.2	14	38.2
17	22.2	14	24.6	19	18.7	15	24.0
18	15.6	15	14.5	20	13.8	16	14.2
19	10.5	16	7.4	21	10.0	17	7.5
20	6.9	17	3.2	22	6.5	18	3.1
21	4.4	18	1.3	23	4.0	19	2.5
22	2.7	19	0.5	24	2.5	20	0.5
23	1.6	20	0.1	25	1.3	21	0.2
24	0.9	21	0.0+	26	0.8	22	0.0+
25	0.5			27	0.6		
26	0.2			28	0.3		
27	0.1			29	0.2		
28	0.0+			30	0.1		
				31	0.0+		
				32	0.0+		
(c) Cardiff (Rhoose Airport)				*(g)* Manchester (Ringway Airport)			
16	28.3	13	48.1	16	28.9	13	34.9
17	17.7	14	31.7	17	20.0	14	22.1
18	10.8	15	17.8	18	13.6	15	12.2
19	6.5	16	8.5	19	9.2	16	5.9
20	3.9	17	3.4	20	6.1	17	2.5
21	2.3	18	1.2	21	4.1	18	0.9
22	1.4	19	0.4	22	2.6	19	0.3
23	0.8	20	0.1	23	1.6	20	0.1
24	0.4	21	0.0+	24	0.9		
25	0.1			25	0.5		
26	0.1			26	0.2		
27	0.0+			27	0.0+		
(d) Edinburgh (Turnhouse Airport)				*(h)* Plymouth (Mount Batten)			
15	25.5	12	37.6	16	30.4	14	39.0
16	16.9	13	22.9	17	17.7	15	21.9
17	10.4	14	12.1	18	10.0	16	9.7
18	6.3	15	5.7	19	5.6	17	3.4
19	3.7	16	2.5	20	3.3	18	1.3
20	2.0	17	0.9	21	1.9	19	0.4
21	1.3	18	0.3	22	1.0	20	0.1
22	0.7	19	0.1	23	0.5	21	0.0+
23	0.3			24	0.2	22	0.0+
24	0.1			25	0.1		
25	0.1			26	0.0+		
26	0.0+						
27	0.0+						
28	0.0+						

Note: 0.0+ indicates a value greater than 0.0 but less than 0.05%.

The data in Table A2.5 may be used to plot the percentage frequencies of combinations of hourly dry-bulb and wet-bulb temperatures on a psychometric chart, which enables the frequency with which the specific enthalpy exceeds given values to be established. As an example, the data for London (Heathrow Airport) are used to produce Fig. A2.9. Additionally, the data for London (Heathrow Airport) contained in Table A2.6 have been used to plot the curves shown as Fig. A2.10.

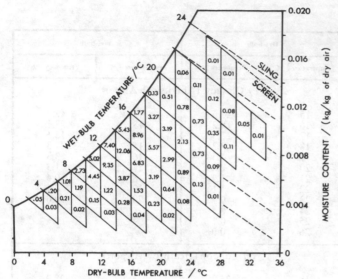

Fig. A2.9 Percentage frequencies of combinations of hourly screen dry-bulb and wet-bulb temperatures in June to September for London (Heathrow Airport).

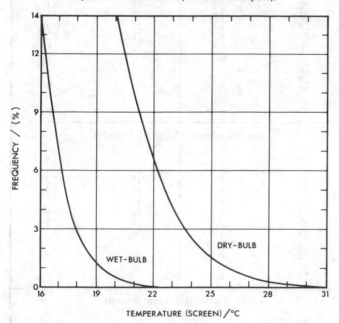

Fig. A2.10 Percentage frequencies with which hourly screen dry-bulb and wet-bulb temperatures exceed stated values in June to September for London (Heathrow Airport).

The Meteorological Office Climatological Memoranda[11] provide data of coincidence of screen dry-bulb and wet-bulb temperatures for other localities which enable similar analyses to be carried out. The Memoranda contain data for each month, quarter and year, thereby allowing analysis for winter conditions as well as summer.

Similar analyses for other localities in the United Kingdom enable the isotherms shown in Fig. A2.11 to be

plotted. These give design dry-bulb and wet-bulb temperatures which are reached or exceeded for only 1% and 2½% of all hours from June to September inclusive (i.e. 29 hours for 1% and 73 hours for 2½% values). These values relate to mean sea level and both dry-bulb and wet-bulb temperatures should be corrected by deducting 0.6 °C for each complete 100 m of height above sea level.

It is recommended that the data presented in Tables A2.5 and A2.6, transferred to a psychrometric chart where appropriate, or corresponding tables developed from other Climatological Memoranda be used to establish design conditions. Alternatively, when either a 1% or 2½% level of design risk is to be applied to independent dry-bulb and wet-bulb temperatures, reference may be made to Fig. A2.11, but this would be less accurate than when specific data for the locality are used.

Design Temperatures—Approximate Method

Where available dry-bulb and wet-bulb temperatures for a particular locality are not sufficiently comprehensive to enable analyses similar to those of Tables A2.5 and A2.6 and Fig. A2.9 to be performed or when selection of design values from Fig. A2.11 may be inappropriate or uncertain, then the following approximate method, which uses only general information available from the Meteorological Office[12], can be employed. The method requires for each month of the year, a knowledge of:—

Average monthly maximum dry-bulb temperature (where for July, say, this is the average over a period of years of the highest temperature in each July in that period).

Average daily maximum dry-bulb temperature (where for July, say, this is the average of the highest temperature for each July day in that period; e.g. over a period of 30 years, it is the average of the maximum temperature on all 930 days in that period).

Average daily minimum relative humidity (where for July, say, this is the average of the lowest relative humidity for each July day in that period).

The method is then as follows:—

(i)   The month is selected which has the highest average *monthly* maximum dry-bulb temperature.

(ii) This highest average *monthly* maximum dry-bulb temperature is chosen as the **design dry-bulb temperature.**

(iii) For the month selected in (i), a moisture content (from CIBSE psychrometric chart or *Guide* Section C1), dew-point temperature (from Meteorological Office Humidity Slide Rule) or vapour pressure is derived from the average *daily* maximum dry-bulb temperature and the average *daily* minimum relative humidity.

(iv) This moisture content, dew-point temperature or vapour pressure is combined with the highest average *monthly* maximum dry-bulb temperature (i) to give a **design wet-bulb temperature.**

This method has been used to obtain the world values given in Table A2.22, as shown in the following example.

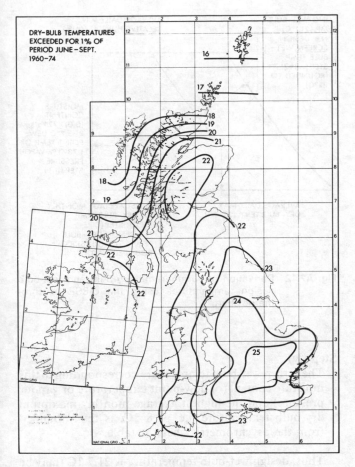

(*a*) Dry-bulb temperatures exceeded for 1% of hours.

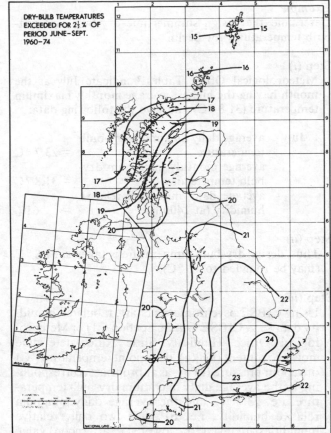

(*b*) Dry-bulb temperatures exceeded for 2½% of hours.

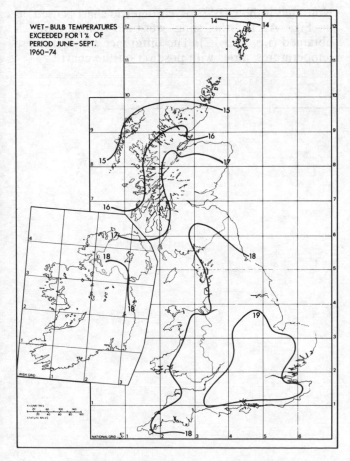

(*c*) Wet-bulb temperatures exceeded for 1% of hours.

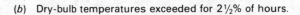

(*d*) Wet-bulb temperatures exceeded for 2½% of hours.

Fig. A2.11 Screen dry-bulb and wet-bulb isotherms for the UK for temperatures exceeded for the stated percentage of hours during
June to September. Period 1964-70.

Example

Determine the design summertime dry-bulb and wet-bulb temperatures for Berlin.

Step (*i*)

Meteorological Office Tables[12] indicate July as the month having the highest average monthly maximum temperature (31.8 °C) and give the following data:

July :	average daily maximum dry-bulb temperature	= 23.7 °C
	average monthly maximum dry-bulb temperature	= 31.8 °C
	average daily minimum relative humidity (at 1400 h)	= 61%

Step (*ii*)

Thus, design dry-bulb temperature is taken as 31.8 °C (may be rounded to 32 °C).

Step (*iii*)

Using CIBSE psychrometric chart, tabulated humidity data (e.g. CIBSE *Guide*, Section C1) or Meteorological Office Humidity Slide Rule, determine moisture content (kg/kg), dew-point temperature (°C) or vapour pressure (kPa), as appropriate, corresponding to the average daily maximum dry-bulb temperature, i.e. 23.7 °C, and the average daily minimum relative humidity, i.e. 61%. If two daily relative humidities are given, the lower (i.e. afternoon) value is taken.

This procedure is illustrated, using a psychrometric chart, in Fig. A2.12, with the following result:—

moisture content	= 0.01122 kg/kg
dew-point temperature	= 15.7 °C
vapour pressure	= 1.787 kPa

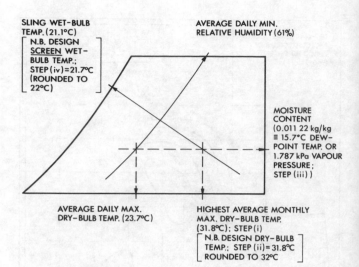

Fig. A2.12 Derivation of summertime dry-bulb and wet-bulb design temperatures using the CIBSE psychrometric chart.

Step (iv)

The screen wet-bulb temperature corresponding to this moisture content (or dew-point temperature or vapour pressure) and the highest average monthly maximum dry-bulb temperature, i.e. 31.8 °C, is then obtained from the psychrometric chart or table.

Thus, design wet-bulb temperature is 21.7 °C (may be rounded to 22 °C).

Note that if the CIBSE psychrometric chart is used, as in Fig. A2.12, the sling wet-bulb temperature is obtained (i.e. 21.1 °C). The difference between these temperatures varies with position on the chart.

UK ANNUAL WEATHER DATA

Banded Weather Data

To assess the energy requirements for the heating or cooling of buildings, information is required on one or more measures of the outdoor climate (dry-bulb temperature, solar irradiation, etc.). A single value, representing a relevant climatological parameter averaged over a complete year, may suffice (e.g. annual mean dry-bulb temperature of 10.5 °C for Kew, SE England).

In practice, it is likely that weather data will be required in greater detail than this; averaged for example, over the winter (heating) and summer (cooling) seasons or over individual months throughout the year. Inherent in this approach is the assumption that all days in the period have the same weather as the period average. A disadvantage is that, by disregarding the spread in daily values, the average weather data could lead to misleading results by indicating, for instance, that no heating was needed during the period, whereas, in fact, some heating would have been required on days with weather more severe than the period average.

To overcome this, the weather occurring on individual days in the period under consideration has, ideally, to be analysed separately. This requires access to a suitable bank of weather data (e.g. magnetic tape for an Example Weather Year or for, say, a 10-year period) and to an environmental computer program capable of handling weather data in this degree of detail.

The compromise adopted here has been to divide the weather in individual months into groups of days corresponding to ten equal intervals (bands) of a given climatological parameter (global solar radiation or dry-bulb temperature). Each band within each month is treated as a separate block of weather data when running an environmental computer program and the results obtained are weighted by the proportion of the month within each band.

The banded weather data are intended primarily for use in the context of a building, where:

(a) a number of coincident climatological parameters influence the indoor environment; these are allowed for by analysing coincident values of global and diffuse solar radiation, screen dry-bulb and wet-bulb temperatures and wind speed, and

(b) there is generally a thermal lag; this is allowed for by averaging the climatological data for pairs of consecutive days (e.g. the 24 hourly values of global solar irradiance on 7 Sept. 1961 with the corresponding 24 hourly values on 8 Sept. 1961, etc.)* before performing the banded data analysis.

At the same time, this analysis results in weather data which more nearly meet the requirements of 'steady cyclic' conditions inherent in the admittance method of estimating energy consumption (see CIBSE *Guide*, Section A5).

The banded weather data given in Tables A2.7 and A2.8 relate to Kew and are based on an analysis of measurements over the 10-year period 1959-68. Similar banded data could be prepared for those other localities (Eskdalemuir, Lerwick and Aberporth) for which magnetic tapes of coincident weather data have been compiled by the Meteorological Office. The data give, for each month of the year, the coincident climatological parameters listed above, averaged both for all days in the month and for groups of days banded on the magnitudes of both the measured global solar radiation (Table A2.7) and dry-bulb temperature (Table A2.8).

For example, Table A2.7(a) shows that in March, the global solar irradiation for the 310 days of the 10-year period varied between 0.80 and 18.23 MJ/m², giving 10 equal 'band widths' of approx. 1.74 MJ/m². (If the daily measurements had been analysed, rather than the consecutive-day averaged data, the span of global solar irradiation would have been between 0.47 and 18.68 MJ/m² with a 'band width' of approx. 1.82 MJ/m²). In the first band, the measured global irradiation occurring for 0.013 of the sample (i.e. for 4 of the 310 days) is seen to lie within the limits of 18.23 and 16.49 MJ/m², with an average of 17.58 MJ/m², while in the sixth band, the measured global irradiation occurring for 0.184 of the sample (i.e. for 57 of the 310 days) is seen to lie within the limits of 9.52 and 7.77 MJ/m² with an average of 8.64 MJ/m². The average global irradiation for all March days is seen to be 7.80 MJ/m². The daily diffuse irradiation, daily max., min. and mean of both dry-bulb and wet-bulb temperatures and daily mean of wind speed averaged over the days when the global irradiation lay within the corresponding band can be readily identified.

Similarly, Table A2.8(a) shows that in the same month, the dry-bulb temperature varied between −1.2 and 13.2 °C, giving equal 'band widths' of approx. 1.5 °C. The choice of banding, whether by global solar radiation or by dry-bulb temperature, depends on the relative importance of these parameters in relation to the particular energy requirement application. The data of Tables A2.7 and A2.8 can be used to simulate hourly values of solar irradiance and dry-bulb and wet-bulb temperatures corresponding to either average or banded days in a given month. The procedure for simulating solar irradiances is described later in *Simulation from Banded Weather Data* and uses the direct and diffuse radiation factors k_D and k_d listed in these tables.

---

* For convenience, the averaged data are identified by the date of the second of the pair of consecutive days, that is, by 8 Sept. 1961 in the above example. In the discussion on banded data that follows, the term 'day' implies a 24-hour period defined in this way. One result of consecutive-day averaging is to compress the range of data, as indicated below. Monthly averaged data are unaffected.

Table A2.7　Weather data banded on global solar radiation for Kew. Period 1959-68.

(a) January, February, March and April.

Month	Band limits /(MJ/m²)	Proportion of month	Daily irradiation /(MJ/m²)		Radiation factors		Sunshine duration /(h)	Daily mean long-wave loss /(W/m²)		Dry-bulb temp./°C			Wet-bulb temp./°C			Daily mean wind speed /(m/s)
			Global	Diffuse	k_D	k_d		Roofs	Walls	$t_{max.}$	$t_{min.}$	t_{mean}	$t_{max.}$	$t_{min.}$	t_{mean}	
JAN	4.64 - 4.20	0.026	4.36	2.11	0.84	1.31	5.0	63	15	5.3	1.5	3.0	3.1	0.6	1.8	4.4
	4.20 - 3.75	0.019	3.86	2.13	0.65	1.32	4.5	58	14	4.6	1.6	2.7	2.3	0.5	1.3	3.8
	3.75 - 3.31	0.081	3.55	1.86	0.64	1.16	4.2	55	13	6.1	3.0	4.1	3.9	2.0	2.8	4.4
	3.31 - 2.87	0.081	3.09	2.01	0.41	1.25	3.1	45	11	4.8	1.9	3.0	2.9	1.1	1.8	3.9
$\theta_{max.}$ =	2.87 - 2.42	0.126	2.64	1.69	0.36	1.05	2.6	40	10	5.6	3.1	4.1	3.7	2.1	2.8	4.7
14 GMT	2.42 - 1.98	0.196	2.20	1.60	0.23	0.99	1.8	32	8	5.6	3.3	4.1	3.9	2.4	3.0	4.3
	1.98 - 1.54	0.177	1.74	1.42	0.12	0.88	0.9	23	6	4.9	2.9	3.7	3.5	2.0	2.6	4.1
$\theta_{min.}$ =	1.54 - 1.09	0.126	1.34	1.25	0.03	0.78	0.3	17	5	5.8	3.8	4.7	4.5	3.1	3.8	3.5
07 GMT	1.09 - 0.65	0.126	0.87	0.83	0.02	0.52	0.1	15	4	5.3	3.7	4.5	4.3	3.0	3.7	3.9
	0.65 - 0.21	0.042	0.44	0.42	0.01	0.26	0.01	14	4	3.9	3.3	3.6	3.1	2.6	2.8	5.3
	Average	1.000	2.11	1.48	0.24	0.92	1.7	31	8	5.3	3.1	4.0	3.8	2.3	2.9	4.1
							Possible = 8.1									
FEB	9.59 - 8.68	0.014	9.19	3.16	1.03	1.10	8.1	80	18	7.8	0.2	3.4	4.3	-0.7	1.8	4.6
	8.68 - 7.77	0.018	8.30	3.79	0.77	1.32	5.5	58	14	8.4	2.6	5.4	5.3	1.6	3.7	5.2
	7.77 - 6.86	0.014	7.33	3.68	0.62	1.28	5.8	61	14	6.0	2.1	3.6	3.3	1.1	2.1	4.6
	6.86 - 5.95	0.067	6.45	3.26	0.55	1.13	4.4	50	12	6.7	2.7	4.4	3.9	1.5	2.7	4.7
$\theta_{max.}$ =	5.95 - 5.04	0.088	5.43	3.31	0.36	1.15	3.4	42	10	6.8	3.2	4.8	4.1	2.0	3.1	4.8
14 GMT	5.04 - 4.13	0.159	4.51	2.67	0.32	0.93	3.3	41	10	7.9	4.2	5.6	5.3	3.2	4.1	4.3
	4.13 - 3.22	0.215	3.64	2.71	0.16	0.94	1.9	29	7	6.3	3.5	4.7	4.2	2.4	3.2	4.6
$\theta_{min.}$ =	3.22 - 2.31	0.177	2.78	2.36	0.07	0.82	0.8	20	5	6.7	4.4	5.3	4.9	3.5	4.1	4.3
07 GMT	2.31 - 1.40	0.156	1.90	1.77	0.02	0.62	0.3	16	4	6.7	4.5	5.4	5.3	3.7	4.4	3.7
	1.40 - 0.49	0.092	1.04	1.00	0.01	0.35	0.1	15	4	4.8	3.4	4.0	3.7	2.7	3.1	4.2
	Average	1.000	3.74	2.49	0.21	0.87	2.0	30	8	6.6	3.7	4.9	4.6	2.8	3.6	4.3
							Possible = 9.8									
MAR	18.23 - 16.49	0.013	17.58	4.09	1.24	0.87	10.5	86	19	16.6	4.4	10.3	10.3	3.8	7.1	4.3
	16.49 - 14.75	0.010	15.45	4.90	0.97	1.04	8.7	73	17	16.0	4.9	10.3	9.9	3.8	7.0	3.2
	14.75 - 13.00	0.042	13.60	4.40	0.85	0.93	8.4	71	16	13.6	4.7	8.8	8.3	3.7	6.0	4.2
	13.00 - 11.26	0.090	11.99	5.24	0.62	1.11	7.2	63	15	9.6	3.5	6.4	5.6	2.4	4.1	5.0
$\theta_{max.}$ =	11.26 - 9.52	0.155	10.20	4.74	0.50	1.00	6.0	55	13	9.6	3.4	6.2	5.8	2.4	4.1	4.3
15 GMT	9.52 - 7.77	0.184	8.64	4.86	0.35	1.03	4.3	43	10	10.2	4.7	7.2	6.8	3.7	5.2	4.3
	7.77 - 6.03	0.164	6.90	4.74	0.20	1.00	2.9	34	8	9.3	4.8	6.9	6.5	3.7	5.1	4.5
$\theta_{min.}$ =	6.03 - 4.29	0.181	5.17	4.05	0.10	0.86	1.6	25	6	8.8	5.4	6.9	6.4	4.4	5.4	4.5
06 GMT	4.29 - 2.54	0.100	3.67	3.33	0.03	0.71	0.5	17	5	7.7	5.4	6.4	5.8	4.4	5.0	4.9
	2.54 - 0.80	0.061	1.67	1.65	0.00	0.35	0.01	14	4	6.3	5.0	5.5	4.7	4.0	4.3	4.6
	Average	1.000	7.80	4.37	0.32	0.93	3.8	40	10	9.5	4.6	6.8	6.3	3.6	4.9	4.5
							Possible = 11.6									
APR	22.72 - 20.61	0.010	22.23	7.12	0.87	1.00	12.1	84	19	18.9	6.0	12.6	12.4	5.4	9.3	1.6
	20.61 - 18.51	0.033	19.30	7.53	0.68	1.06	9.8	71	16	16.6	6.5	11.3	11.0	5.4	8.3	3.5
	18.51 - 16.41	0.063	17.19	7.60	0.55	1.07	8.7	64	15	13.5	6.1	9.6	8.8	5.1	7.0	4.0
	16.41 - 14.30	0.117	15.28	7.56	0.45	1.06	7.4	57	13	13.6	6.2	9.8	9.0	5.1	7.2	4.1
$\theta_{max.}$ =	14.30 - 12.20	0.163	13.33	7.62	0.33	1.07	5.5	46	11	12.9	6.7	9.6	8.7	5.6	7.2	4.0
15 GMT	12.20 - 10.09	0.218	11.16	6.84	0.25	0.96	4.3	39	9	12.5	7.0	9.6	8.9	6.1	7.6	4.4
	10.09 - 7.99	0.150	9.07	6.27	0.16	0.88	3.3	33	8	11.6	6.7	9.1	8.5	5.7	7.1	4.5
$\theta_{min.}$ =	7.99 - 5.89	0.130	6.94	5.95	0.06	0.84	1.3	22	6	11.9	7.5	9.4	9.2	6.6	7.8	4.1
05 GMT	5.89 - 3.78	0.063	4.90	4.48	0.02	0.63	0.6	18	5	10.0	7.5	8.5	8.1	6.6	7.1	4.7
	3.78 - 1.68	0.053	2.58	2.51	0.00	0.35	0.1	15	4	6.9	4.9	5.9	5.6	4.0	4.7	5.4
	Average	1.000	11.11	6.57	0.26	0.93	4.4	40	10	12.3	6.7	9.4	8.7	5.7	7.3	4.2
							Possible = 13.6									

$\theta_{max.}$, $\theta_{min.}$ —approximate times of occurrence of $t_{max.}$ and $t_{min.}$.

Table A2.7—*continued*

(b) May, June, July and August.

Month	Band limits /(MJ/m²)	Proportion of month	Daily irradiation /(MJ/m²)		Radiation factors		Sunshine duration /(h)	Daily mean long-wave loss /(W/m²)		Dry-bulb temp./°C			Wet-bulb temp./°C			Daily mean wind speed /(m/s)
			Global	Diffuse	k_D	k_d		Roofs	Walls	$t_{max.}$	$t_{min.}$	t_{mean}	$t_{max.}$	$t_{min.}$	t_{mean}	
MAY	30.62 - 27.76	0.006	29.98	11.80	0.80	1.29	13.8	85	19	17.1	5.9	11.8	10.3	4.9	7.8	4.6
	27.76 - 24.90	0.029	25.44	9.19	0.72	1.00	12.5	78	18	20.2	8.3	14.8	13.5	7.2	10.8	2.9
	24.90 - 22.04	0.093	23.16	8.90	0.63	0.97	11.2	71	16	19.5	9.1	14.6	12.9	8.0	10.8	3.5
	22.04 - 19.18	0.097	20.38	9.02	0.50	0.99	9.8	64	15	17.6	9.2	13.6	12.0	8.1	10.2	4.1
$\theta_{max.}=$	19.18 - 16.32	0.203	17.65	9.20	0.37	1.01	7.6	53	12	16.2	8.8	12.6	11.3	7.7	9.8	3.9
15 GMT	16.32 - 13.45	0.210	14.86	9.28	0.25	1.02	5.7	43	10	15.4	9.1	12.3	11.0	7.9	9.6	4.1
	13.45 - 10.59	0.181	12.20	8.42	0.17	0.92	3.8	34	8	14.1	9.0	11.6	10.6	7.9	9.4	4.2
$\theta_{min.}=$	10.59 - 7.73	0.110	9.36	7.33	0.09	0.80	2.2	25	6	13.4	9.5	11.5	10.6	8.5	9.6	4.2
04 GMT	7.73 - 4.87	0.052	6.47	6.09	0.02	0.67	0.5	16	4	12.1	8.8	10.4	9.7	7.5	8.6	4.7
	4.87 - 2.01	0.019	3.39	3.31	0.00	0.36	0.1	14	4	12.0	9.9	10.8	10.5	8.9	9.6	4.7
	Average	1.000	15.51	8.58	0.31	0.94	6.2	46	11	15.6	9.1	12.5	11.2	8.0	9.8	4.0
							Possible = 15.4									
JUNE	28.53 - 26.00	0.070	27.06	7.48	0.78	0.73	13.4	78	18	20.9	10.2	15.9	14.1	9.0	11.8	3.6
	26.00 - 23.46	0.093	24.71	8.33	0.65	0.82	12.2	73	17	21.7	11.4	16.7	14.7	9.8	12.5	3.5
	23.46 - 20.93	0.107	22.14	9.39	0.50	0.92	10.3	64	15	21.8	12.0	17.1	15.2	10.6	13.2	3.5
	20.93 - 18.40	0.137	19.82	10.09	0.39	0.99	8.3	54	13	20.0	11.6	16.1	14.4	10.4	12.6	3.5
$\theta_{max.}=$	18.40 - 15.87	0.190	17.11	10.00	0.28	0.98	6.4	45	11	19.0	12.3	15.8	14.1	11.0	12.7	3.9
16 GMT	15.87 - 13.33	0.166	14.66	9.70	0.20	0.95	4.9	38	9	18.6	12.5	15.7	14.2	11.2	12.9	3.6
	13.33 - 10.80	0.140	12.22	9.24	0.12	0.90	3.1	29	7	17.6	12.6	15.3	14.2	11.4	13.0	3.8
$\theta_{min.}=$	10.80 - 8.27	0.063	9.76	8.03	0.07	0.79	2.0	24	6	17.3	13.1	15.3	14.5	11.9	13.3	4.2
04 GMT	8.27 - 5.73	0.017	7.39	6.35	0.04	0.62	1.2	20	5	15.2	11.9	13.6	13.1	11.0	12.0	3.9
	5.73 - 3.20	0.017	4.49	4.31	0.01	0.42	0.1	14	4	15.6	13.3	14.2	13.9	12.4	13.0	3.4
	Average	1.000	17.49	9.21	0.33	0.90	6.9	47	11	19.3	12.1	15.9	14.4	10.8	12.8	3.7
							Possible = 16.4									
JUL	27.06 - 24.75	0.036	25.60	7.05	0.76	0.72	13.4	80	18	25.8	13.8	20.1	17.4	12.5	15.4	2.6
	24.75 - 22.44	0.055	23.45	8.56	0.61	0.87	11.9	73	17	22.7	12.2	17.8	15.6	11.1	13.6	2.9
	22.44 - 20.13	0.087	20.98	9.54	0.47	0.97	10.1	64	15	23.5	14.3	19.1	17.1	13.0	15.3	3.1
	20.13 - 17.82	0.116	18.89	9.91	0.37	1.01	8.3	55	13	21.3	13.6	17.6	15.5	12.2	14.0	3.4
$\theta_{max.}=$	17.82 - 15.51	0.200	16.56	10.22	0.26	1.04	6.3	45	11	20.0	13.4	16.8	14.9	12.0	13.6	3.3
15 GMT	15.51 - 13.20	0.203	14.45	10.18	0.18	1.04	4.5	36	9	19.2	13.4	16.4	14.7	12.1	13.6	3.6
	13.20 - 10.89	0.171	12.11	9.24	0.12	0.94	3.1	29	7	18.4	13.7	16.1	14.6	12.5	13.6	3.8
$\theta_{min.}=$	10.89 - 8.58	0.090	9.85	8.23	0.07	0.84	1.8	23	6	18.0	13.4	15.7	14.7	12.3	13.6	3.7
04 GMT	8.58 - 6.27	0.032	7.82	6.88	0.04	0.70	1.2	20	5	17.3	13.8	15.4	14.5	12.8	13.5	3.3
	6.27 - 3.96	0.010	4.69	4.37	0.01	0.45	0.1	14	4	17.4	14.8	16.0	15.8	13.8	14.8	4.9
	Average	1.000	15.67	9.37	0.26	0.96	5.8	43	10	20.0	13.5	16.9	15.1	12.3	13.8	3.4
							Possible = 16.0									
AUG	23.30 - 21.24	0.026	22.08	6.17	0.80	0.76	11.7	78	18	21.7	11.3	16.5	15.0	10.5	13.1	2.6
	21.24 - 19.18	0.068	20.19	6.26	0.70	0.77	11.2	75	17	23.0	13.0	18.0	16.2	11.9	14.3	2.9
	19.18 - 17.12	0.081	17.78	7.94	0.49	0.98	8.8	62	14	21.8	13.8	17.7	16.1	12.7	14.5	3.1
	17.12 - 15.06	0.197	16.11	8.56	0.38	1.05	7.2	53	12	20.7	13.2	16.9	15.3	12.1	14.0	3.2
$\theta_{max.}=$	15.06 - 13.00	0.177	14.02	8.07	0.30	0.99	5.8	46	11	19.9	13.3	16.5	15.0	12.2	13.8	3.4
15 GMT	13.00 - 10.93	0.206	12.07	7.87	0.21	0.97	4.4	38	9	18.8	13.2	15.9	14.8	12.2	13.5	3.6
	10.93 - 8.87	0.113	10.02	7.41	0.13	0.91	3.1	31	8	18.0	13.3	15.6	14.6	12.3	13.5	3.8
$\theta_{min.}=$	8.87 - 6.81	0.087	8.01	6.76	0.06	0.83	1.7	23	6	18.9	14.8	16.7	16.0	13.8	14.8	3.9
05 GMT	6.81 - 4.75	0.026	5.64	5.22	0.02	0.64	0.6	17	5	16.8	13.8	15.1	14.6	12.8	13.6	3.4
	4.75 - 2.69	0.019	3.34	3.29	0.00	0.40	0.01	14	4	16.3	14.5	15.4	15.2	13.8	14.4	4.4
	Average	1.000	13.49	7.56	0.30	0.93	5.6	44	11	19.7	13.4	16.5	15.2	12.3	13.9	3.4
							Possible = 14.5									

$\theta_{max.}$, $\theta_{min.}$ —approximate times of occurrence of $t_{max.}$ and $t_{min.}$

Table A2.7—continued

(c) September, October, November and December.

Month	Band limits /(MJ/m²)	Proportion of month	Daily irradiation /(MJ/m²)		Radiation factors		Sun-shine duration /(h)	Daily mean long-wave loss /(W/m²)		Dry-bulb temp./°C			Wet-bulb temp./°C			Daily mean wind speed /(m/s)
			Global	Diffuse	k_D	k_d		Roofs	Walls	$t_{max.}$	$t_{min.}$	t_{mean}	$t_{max.}$	$t_{min.}$	t_{mean}	
SEPT	19.09 - 17.37	0.010	18.04	5.80	0.88	1.00	9.9	76	17	20.3	13.2	16.4	14.9	12.3	13.5	4.4
	17.37 - 15.65	0.033	16.40	5.84	0.76	1.00	9.0	71	16	20.4	11.0	15.5	14.8	10.1	12.6	2.6
	15.65 - 13.94	0.093	14.70	5.57	0.66	0.96	8.7	69	16	20.0	10.7	15.0	14.4	10.0	12.3	3.1
	13.94 - 12.21	0.137	12.89	5.83	0.51	1.00	7.2	59	14	20.1	11.4	15.5	14.5	10.5	12.7	2.7
$\theta_{max.}$ =	12.21 - 10.50	0.187	11.27	6.03	0.38	1.04	5.6	49	12	18.2	11.5	14.5	13.7	10.5	12.2	3.3
15 GMT	10.50 - 8.78	0.243	9.69	5.80	0.28	1.00	4.5	42	10	17.5	11.9	14.3	13.6	10.9	12.2	3.4
	8.78 - 7.06	0.130	8.07	5.17	0.21	0.89	3.4	35	9	17.2	12.5	14.6	14.1	11.7	12.8	3.2
$\theta_{min.}$ =	7.06 - 5.34	0.107	6.34	5.03	0.09	0.87	1.8	25	6	16.6	12.9	14.5	14.0	12.0	12.9	3.4
05 GMT	5.34 - 3.62	0.037	4.50	4.09	0.03	0.70	0.5	17	5	16.8	13.5	15.0	14.8	12.8	13.8	3.3
	3.62 - 1.90	0.023	2.96	2.88	0.00	0.50	0.1	14	4	15.8	13.2	14.5	14.3	12.4	13.3	3.4
	Average	1.000	10.15	5.47	0.34	0.94	4.9	45	11	18.0	11.9	14.7	13.9	11.0	12.5	3.2
					Possible =	12.6										
OCT	11.83 - 10.75	0.016	11.42	4.06	0.93	1.11	8.3	76	17	19.7	10.7	14.6	14.7	9.8	12.2	3.2
	10.75 - 9.66	0.058	10.11	4.04	0.77	1.11	7.6	71	16	18.5	11.0	14.3	13.6	10.0	11.9	3.6
	9.66 - 8.58	0.048	8.90	4.02	0.62	1.10	6.3	61	14	15.9	8.4	11.6	11.9	7.7	9.8	2.5
	8.58 - 7.50	0.119	7.96	3.79	0.53	1.04	5.7	57	13	15.7	10.3	12.4	12.0	9.4	10.6	3.5
$\theta_{max.}$ =	7.50 - 6.42	0.161	6.97	3.83	0.40	1.05	4.3	46	11	14.4	9.1	11.3	11.3	8.3	9.7	3.4
14 GMT	6.42 - 5.33	0.165	5.83	3.49	0.30	0.96	3.5	40	10	14.4	9.6	11.5	11.6	8.8	10.1	3.1
	5.33 - 4.25	0.155	4.79	3.23	0.20	0.88	2.4	32	8	14.2	10.1	11.9	11.8	9.2	10.4	3.4
$\theta_{min.}$ =	4.25 - 3.16	0.155	3.73	3.03	0.09	0.83	1.3	24	6	13.5	10.4	11.7	11.5	9.5	10.4	3.5
05 GMT	3.16 - 2.08	0.087	2.68	2.40	0.04	0.66	0.4	17	5	12.5	10.0	11.1	10.9	9.2	9.9	3.2
	2.08 - 1.00	0.036	1.71	1.63	0.01	0.45	0.1	15	4	12.4	10.8	11.5	11.0	9.6	10.3	3.5
	Average	1.000	5.80	3.35	0.31	0.92	3.4	39	10	14.5	9.9	11.8	11.6	9.0	10.2	3.3
					Possible =	10.6										
NOV	6.86 - 6.22	0.020	6.47	2.24	1.16	1.10	6.4	72	17	10.3	5.9	7.9	6.9	4.5	5.9	4.9
	6.22 - 5.57	0.017	5.80	2.53	0.90	1.24	6.2	70	16	9.8	5.5	7.1	6.8	4.5	5.5	3.8
	5.57 - 4.93	0.037	5.23	2.72	0.69	1.34	4.2	52	12	10.6	6.3	8.2	8.0	5.5	6.7	3.7
	4.93 - 4.28	0.080	4.55	2.57	0.54	1.26	3.9	50	12	9.5	5.1	7.0	6.8	4.2	5.5	3.9
$\theta_{max.}$ =	4.28 - 3.64	0.103	3.87	2.37	0.41	1.16	3.2	43	10	10.0	6.1	7.8	7.8	5.3	6.5	3.6
14 GMT	3.64 - 2.99	0.150	3.27	2.10	0.32	1.03	2.5	37	9	9.5	6.5	7.5	7.4	5.6	6.2	4.0
	2.99 - 2.35	0.183	2.65	1.91	0.20	0.94	1.7	30	7	8.7	5.8	7.0	7.0	4.9	5.8	4.0
$\theta_{min.}$ =	2.35 - 1.70	0.173	2.03	1.59	0.12	0.78	1.1	24	6	9.4	7.0	7.9	7.7	6.1	6.8	3.6
06 GMT	1.70 - 1.06	0.150	1.38	1.27	0.03	0.62	0.3	17	5	9.0	7.0	7.9	7.8	6.1	6.9	3.6
	1.06 - 0.41	0.087	0.85	0.83	0.01	0.41	0.01	14	4	8.5	7.1	7.7	7.2	6.1	6.7	4.6
	Average	1.000	2.77	1.83	0.26	0.90	1.9	31	8	9.2	6.4	7.5	7.3	5.5	6.3	3.9
					Possible =	8.7										
DEC	4.04 - 3.66	0.013	3.95	1.69	1.11	1.25	5.5	71	16	7.0	3.3	4.7	4.3	2.0	3.1	4.8
	3.66 - 3.28	0.026	3.46	1.55	0.94	1.15	4.8	64	15	5.0	1.3	2.7	2.8	0.4	1.4	3.2
	3.28 - 2.91	0.052	3.11	1.53	0.78	1.13	4.1	57	13	4.8	2.2	3.3	2.5	1.0	1.8	4.4
	2.91 - 2.53	0.048	2.68	1.53	0.57	1.13	3.2	47	11	6.1	3.5	4.6	4.1	2.5	3.4	4.1
$\theta_{max.}$ =	2.53 - 2.16	0.119	2.31	1.36	0.47	1.00	2.7	42	10	5.1	2.7	3.6	3.3	1.8	2.4	3.9
14 GMT	2.16 - 1.78	0.164	1.98	1.29	0.34	0.95	2.0	35	8	5.9	3.6	4.5	4.3	2.7	3.5	4.1
	1.78 - 1.40	0.184	1.60	1.23	0.18	0.91	1.0	24	6	7.1	5.2	5.8	5.6	4.3	4.8	4.1
$\theta_{min.}$ =	1.40 - 1.03	0.174	1.20	1.05	0.08	0.77	0.4	18	5	7.1	5.4	6.0	5.7	4.4	4.9	4.6
07 GMT	1.03 - 0.65	0.126	0.86	0.81	0.02	0.60	0.1	15	4	5.8	3.8	4.8	4.7	3.0	3.9	3.7
	0.65 - 0.27	0.094	0.48	0.46	0.01	0.34	0.01	14	4	5.8	4.8	5.3	4.9	4.0	4.5	4.0
	Average	1.000	1.68	1.13	0.27	0.84	1.5	30	7	6.1	4.2	4.9	4.6	3.3	3.8	4.1
					Possible =	7.6										

$\theta_{max.}$, $\theta_{min.}$ approximate times of occurrence of $t_{max.}$ and $t_{min.}$

Table A2.8 Weather data banded on dry-bulb temperature for Kew. Period 1959-68.

(a) January, February, March and April.

Month	Band limits /°C	Proportion of month	Daily irradiation /(MJ/m²) Global	Diffuse	Radiation factors k_D	k_d	Sunshine duration /(h)	Daily mean long-wave loss /(W/m²) Roofs	Walls	Dry-bulb temp./°C $t_{max.}$	$t_{min.}$	t_{mean}	Wet-bulb temp./°C $t_{max.}$	$t_{min.}$	t_{mean}	Daily mean wind speed /(m/s)
JAN	10.8 - 9.2	0.068	1.80	1.56	0.09	0.97	0.7	21	6	11.0	9.4	10.0	9.4	8.3	8.8	5.2
	9.2 - 7.6	0.116	1.98	1.52	0.17	0.94	1.1	25	6	9.4	7.6	8.3	7.9	6.6	7.1	5.3
	7.6 - 6.0	0.126	2.39	1.62	0.29	1.01	1.9	33	8	8.0	5.8	6.7	6.3	4.8	5.5	5.1
	6.0 - 4.4	0.161	2.12	1.44	0.26	0.90	1.7	31	8	6.6	4.2	5.2	5.0	3.4	4.0	3.7
$\theta_{max.}$ =	4.4 - 2.9	0.142	1.97	1.36	0.23	0.84	1.6	30	7	5.0	2.7	3.6	3.5	1.8	2.5	3.4
14 GMT	2.9 - 1.3	0.155	2.03	1.41	0.23	0.88	1.8	32	8	3.5	1.1	2.0	1.9	0.3	1.0	3.6
	1.3 - -0.3	0.132	1.91	1.33	0.22	0.83	1.9	33	8	1.8	-0.5	0.5	0.3	-1.3	-0.5	3.8
$\theta_{min.}$ =	-0.3 - -1.9	0.055	2.21	1.40	0.30	0.87	2.6	39	10	0.1	-2.0	-1.0	-1.2	-2.8	-1.9	4.4
06 GMT	-1.9 - -3.5	0.032	3.07	1.86	0.46	1.15	3.3	46	11	-1.1	-4.0	-2.7	-2.6	-4.8	-3.7	5.1
	-3.5 - -5.1	0.013	2.40	1.82	0.22	1.13	1.1	25	6	-2.7	-6.6	-4.7	-3.5	-6.9	-5.2	1.3
	Average	1.000	2.11	1.48	0.24	0.92	1.7	31	8	5.3	3.1	4.0	3.8	2.3	2.9	4.1
					Possible =	8.1										
FEB	11.7 - 10.3	0.025	3.34	2.22	0.19	0.77	1.7	28	7	12.6	10.0	11.1	10.7	8.9	9.8	6.3
	10.3 - 8.8	0.109	3.93	2.65	0.22	0.92	2.2	32	8	11.2	8.4	9.4	9.0	7.3	8.0	4.9
	8.8 - 7.4	0.145	3.77	2.49	0.22	0.87	2.3	33	8	9.9	6.9	8.1	7.8	5.8	6.7	4.9
	7.4 - 6.0	0.110	3.29	2.42	0.15	0.84	1.3	24	6	8.4	5.2	6.6	6.1	4.1	5.1	4.1
$\theta_{max.}$ =	6.0 - 4.6	0.106	3.57	2.33	0.21	0.81	2.1	31	8	7.0	4.1	5.3	4.7	3.1	3.9	3.9
14 GMT	4.6 - 3.1	0.180	3.52	2.43	0.19	0.85	1.7	28	7	5.6	2.4	3.8	3.5	1.6	2.5	3.8
	3.1 - 1.7	0.187	3.61	2.40	0.21	0.84	2.0	30	8	4.1	1.3	2.4	2.1	0.4	1.2	4.1
$\theta_{min.}$ =	1.7 - 0.3	0.092	4.02	2.47	0.26	0.86	2.6	35	8	2.7	0.0	1.1	0.7	-1.0	-0.2	4.5
06 GMT	0.3 - -1.2	0.035	4.62	2.94	0.29	1.02	2.8	37	9	0.9	-1.8	-0.6	-1.0	-2.7	-1.8	4.8
	-1.2 - -2.6	0.011	3.36	2.94	0.07	1.03	1.1	23	6	-0.7	-3.2	-2.2	-2.2	-3.9	-3.1	4.5
	Average	1.000	3.74	2.49	0.21	0.87	2.0	30	8	6.6	3.7	4.9	4.6	2.8	3.6	4.3
					Possible =	9.8										
MAR	13.2 - 11.8	0.016	13.59	4.00	0.88	0.85	7.8	67	15	18.4	7.0	12.2	11.9	6.1	9.1	3.0
	11.8 - 10.3	0.042	9.55	4.42	0.47	0.94	4.7	46	11	14.7	8.2	11.2	10.4	7.0	8.7	4.8
	10.3 - 8.9	0.164	7.74	4.47	0.30	0.95	3.6	38	9	12.0	7.4	9.4	9.0	6.5	7.6	4.7
	8.9 - 7.4	0.277	7.71	4.50	0.30	0.95	3.6	38	9	10.8	6.1	8.2	7.7	5.1	6.3	4.4
$\theta_{max.}$ =	7.4 - 6.0	0.194	7.94	4.28	0.34	0.91	4.0	41	10	9.3	4.3	6.6	6.2	3.3	4.8	4.2
15 GMT	6.0 - 4.6	0.103	7.04	4.11	0.27	0.87	3.4	37	9	7.7	3.2	5.3	4.8	2.1	3.5	4.9
	4.6 - 3.1	0.084	6.81	4.23	0.24	0.90	3.1	35	8	6.1	1.8	3.8	3.1	0.7	1.9	4.7
$\theta_{min.}$ =	3.1 - 1.7	0.058	6.66	4.14	0.23	0.88	3.1	35	8	4.5	0.8	2.4	1.7	-0.3	0.6	4.6
06 GMT	1.7 - 0.2	0.052	8.03	4.19	0.35	0.89	4.9	47	11	3.8	-1.3	1.0	1.0	-2.2	-0.7	4.6
	0.2 - -1.2	0.010	6.97	3.68	0.30	0.78	3.9	40	10	1.7	-3.5	-0.6	-0.4	-3.9	-1.8	4.7
	Average	1.000	7.80	4.37	0.32	0.93	3.8	40	10	9.5	4.6	6.8	6.3	3.6	4.9	4.5
					Possible =	11.6										
APR	16.2 - 14.9	0.003	16.38	8.40	0.46	1.18	8.4	63	14	21.0	11.9	16.2	16.3	10.6	13.2	2.5
	14.9 - 13.5	0.020	14.46	7.78	0.38	1.10	5.8	48	10	17.7	10.2	13.9	13.6	9.3	11.5	3.3
	13.5 - 12.2	0.057	14.27	7.16	0.41	1.01	6.0	49	12	16.6	8.9	12.6	12.0	7.9	10.1	3.3
	12.2 - 10.8	0.220	12.18	7.23	0.29	1.02	5.0	43	10	14.7	8.6	11.5	10.8	7.6	9.3	3.7
$\theta_{max.}$ =	10.8 - 9.5	0.230	11.08	6.75	0.25	0.95	4.1	38	9	13.0	7.5	10.1	9.5	6.6	8.1	4.4
15 GMT	9.5 - 8.1	0.190	10.52	6.33	0.24	0.89	4.1	38	9	11.6	6.3	8.8	8.2	5.2	6.7	4.2
	8.1 - 6.8	0.140	10.53	6.23	0.25	0.88	4.3	39	9	10.1	4.9	7.4	6.8	3.8	5.4	4.9
$\theta_{min.}$ =	6.8 - 5.4	0.077	8.69	5.76	0.17	0.81	3.3	33	8	8.7	4.0	6.1	5.6	3.0	4.2	5.1
05 GMT	5.4 - 4.1	0.043	10.45	5.49	0.29	0.77	5.0	43	10	7.5	2.0	4.8	4.1	1.2	2.8	3.6
	4.1 - 2.7	0.020	3.57	2.92	0.37	0.41	0.8	19	5	3.8	3.1	3.4	2.3	1.6	2.1	6.5
	Average	1.000	11.11	6.57	0.26	0.93	4.4	40	10	12.3	6.7	9.4	8.7	5.7	7.3	4.2
					Possible =	13.6										

$\theta_{max.}$, $\theta_{min.}$ —approximate times of occurrence of $t_{max.}$ and $t_{min.}$

Table A2.8—*continued*

(b) May, June, July and August

Month	Band limits /°C	Proportion of month	Daily irradiation /(MJ/m²)		Radiation factors		Sun-shine duration /(h)	Daily mean long-wave loss /(W/m²)		Dry-bulb temp./°C			Wet-bulb temp./°C			Daily mean wind speed /(m/s)
			Global	Diffuse	k_D	k_d		Roofs	Walls	$t_{max.}$	$t_{min.}$	t_{mean}	$t_{max.}$	$t_{min.}$	t_{mean}	
MAY	19.4 - 18.0	0.019	20.75	8.93	0.52	0.98	9.9	65	15	24.2	13.3	18.6	17.1	12.1	14.5	2.8
	18.0 - 16.7	0.039	18.74	8.73	0.44	0.96	8.8	59	14	22.3	11.8	17.1	15.5	10.6	13.3	3.2
	16.7 - 15.3	0.100	19.03	9.05	0.44	0.99	8.5	58	13	20.5	11.1	16.0	14.5	9.9	12.4	3.3
	15.3 - 14.0	0.097	17.27	8.66	0.38	0.95	7.2	51	12	18.5	10.4	14.6	13.1	9.4	11.5	3.4
$\theta_{max.} =$	14.0 - 12.6	0.152	16.49	8.98	0.33	0.98	6.4	47	11	16.5	9.8	13.2	12.2	8.8	10.6	4.2
15 GMT	12.6 - 11.2	0.271	14.93	8.71	0.28	0.95	5.9	44	10	14.6	8.9	11.9	10.6	7.8	9.4	4.8
	11.2 - 9.9	0.203	13.59	8.40	0.23	0.92	4.9	39	9	13.1	7.6	10.5	9.4	6.6	8.2	4.2
$\theta_{min.} =$	9.9 - 8.5	0.090	11.74	7.57	0.18	0.83	4.1	35	8	11.6	6.5	9.2	8.2	5.4	6.9	3.7
04 GMT	8.5 - 7.2	0.023	10.43	6.55	0.17	0.72	3.6	32	8	10.3	5.6	8.0	7.3	4.4	5.9	3.8
	7.2 - 5.8	0.006	15.42	8.19	0.32	0.90	5.8	44	10	9.2	3.4	6.0	5.0	2.5	3.8	4.3
	Average	1.000	15.51	8.58	0.31	0.94	6.2	46	11	15.6	9.1	12.5	11.2	8.0	9.8	4.0
					Possible = 15.4											
JUN	21.2 - 20.0	0.023	21.30	8.96	0.49	0.88	9.4	59	14	25.1	15.4	20.5	18.4	14.1	16.5	3.6
	20.0 - 18.8	0.050	20.25	8.43	0.47	0.82	9.2	58	14	23.7	14.1	19.2	17.0	12.7	15.2	3.0
	18.8 - 17.6	0.113	19.69	9.63	0.40	0.94	8.3	54	13	22.6	13.3	18.1	16.6	12.0	14.6	3.2
	17.6 - 16.4	0.200	18.01	9.42	0.34	0.92	7.1	48	11	20.7	13.0	17.0	15.5	11.8	13.8	3.6
$\theta_{max.} =$	16.4 - 15.2	0.280	17.34	9.14	0.32	0.89	6.8	47	11	18.9	12.3	15.8	14.2	10.9	12.8	4.1
16 GMT	15.2 - 13.9	0.180	16.36	9.20	0.28	0.90	6.3	44	10	17.6	11.0	14.5	13.2	9.9	11.7	3.7
	13.9 - 12.7	0.107	14.93	9.31	0.22	0.91	5.3	40	10	16.0	10.5	13.4	12.0	9.2	10.8	3.5
$\theta_{min.} =$	12.7 - 11.5	0.020	16.61	8.52	0.32	0.83	6.8	47	11	15.2	8.7	11.9	11.1	7.5	9.3	3.7
04 GMT	11.5 - 10.3	0.020	14.23	6.60	0.30	0.64	5.7	42	10	13.6	7.4	10.7	10.0	6.2	8.2	3.7
	10.3 - 9.1	0.007	20.93	8.94	0.48	0.88	11.1	68	16	12.8	4.7	9.3	7.7	3.1	5.8	4.6
	Average	1.000	17.49	9.21	0.33	0.90	6.9	47	11	19.3	12.1	15.9	14.4	10.8	12.8	3.7
					Possible = 16.4											
JUL	23.4 - 22.3	0.016	24.53	7.53	0.70	0.77	12.8	77	18	29.0	16.2	22.7	19.8	14.8	17.9	2.7
	22.3 - 21.1	0.023	22.06	7.73	0.59	0.79	10.9	68	16	26.4	15.9	21.5	18.8	14.3	16.9	3.0
	21.1 - 20.0	0.048	19.03	9.50	0.39	0.97	8.9	58	13	25.0	15.9	20.5	18.7	14.7	16.9	3.0
	20.0 - 18.9	0.084	19.27	9.15	0.42	0.93	9.0	58	14	23.7	15.1	19.4	17.2	13.6	15.5	3.1
$\theta_{max.} =$	18.9 - 17.8	0.129	16.50	9.68	0.28	0.99	6.2	45	11	21.8	14.7	18.2	16.5	13.4	15.0	3.4
15 GMT	17.8 - 16.6	0.197	15.48	9.66	0.24	0.98	5.5	41	10	20.3	13.8	17.1	15.5	12.5	14.2	3.5
	16.6 - 15.5	0.267	14.92	9.63	0.22	0.98	5.2	40	10	18.8	13.0	15.9	14.1	11.7	13.0	3.6
$\theta_{min.} =$	15.5 - 14.4	0.184	13.32	9.13	0.17	0.93	4.1	34	8	17.5	12.2	15.0	13.6	11.1	12.5	3.3
04 GMT	14.4 - 13.2	0.042	13.00	9.11	0.16	0.93	4.0	34	8	15.9	11.4	13.9	12.1	10.0	11.2	4.0
	13.2 - 12.1	0.010	13.20	9.42	0.16	0.96	3.0	29	7	15.1	9.5	12.6	10.8	8.2	9.6	2.9
	Average	1.000	15.67	9.37	0.26	0.96	5.8	43	10	20.0	13.5	16.9	15.1	12.3	13.8	3.4
					Possible = 16.0											
AUG	22.3 - 21.4	0.013	18.26	5.39	0.64	0.66	10.6	72	16	27.4	17.2	21.9	18.9	15.5	17.4	3.3
	21.4 - 20.4	0.026	16.57	7.98	0.43	0.98	7.8	56	13	25.4	16.8	20.6	19.3	15.4	17.3	2.9
	20.4 - 19.5	0.029	17.18	6.85	0.52	0.84	8.7	61	14	25.1	15.6	20.0	18.6	14.2	16.5	2.8
	19.5 - 18.5	0.094	15.22	7.84	0.37	0.96	6.8	51	12	23.0	15.2	18.9	17.7	14.1	16.0	2.9
$\theta_{max.} =$	18.5 - 17.6	0.097	14.55	7.84	0.34	0.96	6.3	48	11	21.8	14.6	18.0	16.9	13.6	15.3	3.1
15 GMT	17.6 - 16.7	0.167	13.49	8.13	0.27	1.00	5.1	42	10	20.2	14.2	17.1	15.8	13.2	14.6	3.5
	16.7 - 15.7	0.238	12.54	7.47	0.25	0.92	5.0	41	10	19.0	13.4	16.1	14.6	12.3	13.6	3.8
$\theta_{min.} =$	15.7 - 14.8	0.171	12.62	7.41	0.26	0.91	5.0	41	10	18.0	12.4	15.2	13.9	11.3	12.8	3.7
05 GMT	14.8 - 13.8	0.113	13.22	7.28	0.30	0.90	5.5	44	10	17.3	11.1	14.3	13.1	10.1	11.8	3.4
	13.8 - 12.9	0.052	12.77	7.44	0.27	0.92	5.3	43	10	16.3	10.0	13.4	12.3	9.2	11.2	2.9
	Average	1.000	13.49	7.56	0.30	0.93	5.6	44	11	19.7	13.4	16.5	15.2	12.3	13.9	3.4
					Possible = 14.5											

$\theta_{max.}, \theta_{min.}$ approximate times of occurrence of $t_{max.}$ and $t_{min.}$

Table A2.8—*continued*

(c) September, October, November and December.

Month	Band limits /°C	Proportion of month	Daily irradiation /(MJ/m²)		Radiation factors		Sunshine duration /(h)	Daily mean long-wave loss /(W/m²)		Dry-bulb temp./°C			Wet-bulb temp./°C			Daily mean wind speed /(m/s)
			Global	Diffuse	k_D	k_d		Roofs	Walls	$t_{max.}$	$t_{min.}$	t_{mean}	$t_{max.}$	$t_{min.}$	t_{mean}	
SEP	19.8 - 18.8	0.023	12.88	6.15	0.49	1.06	7.2	59	14	24.6	14.6	19.1	18.1	13.6	15.8	3.1
	18.8 - 17.9	0.047	12.88	5.54	0.53	0.95	7.2	59	14	22.7	14.6	18.2	16.6	13.6	15.2	3.4
	17.9 - 16.9	0.077	10.86	6.00	0.35	1.03	5.3	47	11	20.6	14.4	17.3	16.1	13.5	14.8	3.4
	16.9 - 15.9	0.133	10.16	5.81	0.31	1.00	4.7	44	10	19.4	13.5	16.2	15.5	12.5	14.0	3.5
$\theta_{max.}$ =	15.9 - 15.0	0.163	9.62	5.68	0.28	0.98	4.1	40	10	18.4	12.9	15.4	14.5	12.0	13.3	3.2
15 GMT	15.0 - 14.0	0.180	9.66	5.27	0.32	0.91	4.7	44	10	17.5	12.0	14.5	14.0	11.2	12.5	3.4
	14.0 - 13.0	0.180	10.23	5.38	0.35	0.93	4.9	45	11	16.7	10.7	13.4	12.8	9.8	11.3	3.0
$\theta_{min.}$ =	13.0 - 12.0	0.140	10.48	5.17	0.38	0.89	5.6	49	12	16.3	9.1	12.5	12.5	8.4	10.5	2.9
05 GMT	12.0 - 11.1	0.047	10.25	5.65	0.33	0.97	4.8	44	10	14.8	8.8	11.6	10.8	7.9	9.4	3.2
	11.1 - 10.1	0.010	9.65	6.29	0.24	1.08	3.6	37	9	13.6	7.9	10.7	9.7	6.9	8.4	3.4
	Average	1.000	10.15	5.47	0.34	0.94	4.9	45	11	18.0	11.9	14.7	13.9	11.0	12.5	3.2
					Possible = 12.6											
OCT	18.0 - 16.8	0.016	9.92	3.93	0.76	1.08	8.1	74	17	22.5	13.8	17.5	16.7	13.0	14.8	3.1
	16.8 - 15.5	0.064	6.28	3.77	0.32	1.03	3.2	38	9	18.9	14.3	16.1	15.6	13.2	14.3	3.9
	15.5 - 14.3	0.081	6.99	4.13	0.36	1.13	3.8	42	10	17.7	13.0	14.9	14.5	12.1	13.2	3.3
	14.3 - 13.1	0.161	6.12	3.71	0.31	1.02	3.4	39	10	16.2	11.9	13.7	13.5	11.1	12.2	3.4
$\theta_{max.}$ =	13.1 - 11.9	0.203	5.66	3.45	0.28	0.94	3.0	36	9	14.9	10.6	12.4	12.2	9.7	10.9	3.4
14 GMT	11.9 - 10.6	0.190	5.63	3.09	0.32	0.85	3.5	40	10	13.8	9.4	11.3	11.1	8.6	9.8	3.6
	10.6 - 9.4	0.094	5.46	3.11	0.30	0.85	3.5	40	10	13.0	8.1	10.0	10.3	7.3	8.6	2.7
$\theta_{min.}$ =	9.4 - 8.2	0.094	4.32	2.82	0.19	0.77	2.4	32	8	11.2	7.0	8.8	8.6	6.1	7.3	3.5
06 GMT	8.2 - 6.9	0.071	5.82	2.95	0.36	0.81	4.2	45	11	10.4	5.3	7.6	7.6	4.5	6.1	3.1
	6.9 - 5.7	0.026	7.00	3.21	0.48	0.88	5.1	52	12	10.1	3.5	6.3	6.9	2.7	4.7	2.7
	Average	1.000	5.80	3.35	0.31	0.92	3.4	39	10	14.5	9.9	11.8	11.6	9.0	10.2	3.3
					Possible = 10.6											
NOV	13.9 - 12.5	0.023	2.71	1.93	0.22	0.94	1.4	27	7	14.4	11.9	12.8	12.3	10.8	11.4	5.0
	12.5 - 11.2	0.070	2.94	2.00	0.26	0.98	1.8	30	8	13.1	10.6	11.6	11.3	9.7	10.3	4.5
	11.2 - 9.8	0.150	2.69	1.80	0.24	0.88	1.8	30	8	11.9	9.7	10.4	10.0	8.7	9.1	4.2
	9.8 - 8.4	0.147	2.61	1.83	0.22	0.90	1.5	28	7	10.7	8.0	9.1	8.8	7.2	7.9	4.0
$\theta_{max.}$ =	8.4 - 7.1	0.166	2.82	1.80	0.28	0.88	2.1	33	8	9.3	6.5	7.7	7.3	5.6	6.4	3.9
14 GMT	7.1 - 5.7	0.200	2.78	1.82	0.26	0.89	1.8	30	8	8.2	5.2	6.4	6.3	4.3	5.2	3.5
	5.7 - 4.3	0.147	3.09	1.91	0.32	0.94	2.6	38	9	7.1	3.7	5.0	5.2	2.8	3.8	3.9
$\theta_{min.}$ =	4.3 - 2.9	0.060	2.56	1.78	0.22	0.87	1.8	30	8	5.5	1.9	3.5	4.0	1.3	2.6	2.7
06 GMT	2.9 - 1.6	0.020	2.57	1.70	0.24	0.84	2.2	34	8	3.9	1.3	2.3	2.2	0.1	1.1	4.1
	1.6 - 0.2	0.017	2.98	1.95	0.28	0.96	2.8	40	10	3.2	–1.2	1.0	1.5	–2.0	–0.2	3.8
	Average	1.000	2.77	1.83	0.26	0.90	1.9	31	8	9.2	6.4	7.5	7.3	5.5	6.3	3.9
					Possible = 8.7											
DEC	12.4 - 10.9	0.032	1.31	1.08	0.11	0.80	0.6	20	5	12.2	11.2	11.5	10.4	10.0	10.2	6.9
	10.9 - 9.4	0.036	1.22	1.01	0.10	0.74	0.6	20	5	11.1	9.0	10.1	9.6	7.7	8.8	5.7
	9.4 - 8.0	0.094	1.55	1.09	0.22	0.81	1.1	25	6	9.7	8.0	8.6	8.0	6.8	7.3	5.4
	8.0 - 6.5	0.180	1.60	1.11	0.24	0.82	1.3	28	7	8.3	6.7	7.2	6.7	5.7	6.0	4.9
$\theta_{max.}$ =	6.5 - 5.0	0.147	1.85	1.23	0.30	0.91	1.6	31	8	7.2	5.0	5.8	5.7	4.1	4.7	3.9
14 GMT	5.0 - 3.5	0.200	1.58	1.07	0.25	0.79	1.3	28	7	5.3	3.6	4.2	3.9	2.7	3.2	3.6
	3.5 - 2.0	0.123	1.61	1.12	0.24	0.83	1.2	26	7	4.0	2.1	2.9	2.7	1.3	1.9	3.0
$\theta_{min.}$ =	2.0 - 0.6	0.068	2.14	1.33	0.40	0.98	2.4	39	9	2.8	0.0	1.2	1.3	–0.7	0.3	2.7
06 GMT	0.6 - –0.9	0.094	2.01	1.21	0.39	0.90	2.3	38	9	1.3	–1.3	–0.1	–0.2	–2.1	–1.1	4.0
	–0.9 - –2.4	0.026	1.79	1.23	0.28	0.91	1.8	33	8	–0.2	–2.7	–1.6	–1.2	–3.2	–2.2	2.2
	Average	1.000	1.68	1.13	0.27	0.84	1.5	30	7	6.1	4.2	4.9	4.6	3.3	3.8	4.1
					Possible = 7.6											

$\theta_{max.}$, $\theta_{min.}$ —approximate times of occurrence of $t_{max.}$ and $t_{min.}$.

The procedure for simulating temperatures assumes separate sinsusoidal interpolations (see Fig. A2.13) between minimum and maximum, and between maximum and minimum temperatures, the times of occurrence of the maximum and minimum being those given in the left-hand column of the banded data tables. Table A2.9 gives factors f_1 and f_2 which help to perform this interpolation where, for a particular combination of θ_{max} and θ_{min} and for a particular time of day, the required temperature ($t_{d(\theta)}$) is given by:

$$t_{d(\theta)} = f_1\, t_{min} + f_2\, t_{max} \quad .. \quad .. \quad .. \quad .. \quad \text{A2.5}$$

where:

t_{min} = daily minimum outside temperature .. °C
t_{max} = daily maximum outside temperature .. °C

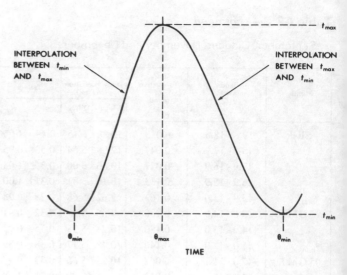

Fig. A2.13 Sinusoidal interpolations of outdoor temperatures.

Table A2.9 Factors for simulating hourly values of dry-bulb and wet-bulb temperatures.

Time (GMT)	(1) 14 GMT / 07 GMT 7h f_1	f_2	(2) 14 GMT / 06 GMT 8h f_1	f_2	(3) 14 GMT / 05 GMT 9h f_1	f_2	(4) 15 GMT / 06 GMT 9h f_1	f_2	(5) 15 GMT / 05 GMT 10h f_1	f_2	(6) 15 GMT / 04 GMT 11h f_1	f_2	(7) 16 GMT / 04 GMT 12h f_1	f_2
00	0.64	0.36	0.69	0.31	0.75	0.25	0.65	0.35	0.72	0.28	0.78	0.22	0.75	0.25
01	0.72	0.28	0.78	0.22	0.83	0.17	0.75	0.25	0.81	0.19	0.87	0.13	0.85	0.15
02	0.80	0.20	0.85	0.15	0.90	0.10	0.83	0.17	0.89	0.11	0.94	0.06	0.93	0.07
03	0.87	0.13	0.92	0.08	0.96	0.04	0.90	0.10	0.95	0.05	0.99	0.01	0.98	0.02
04	0.92	0.08	0.96	0.04	0.99	0.01	0.96	0.04	0.99	0.01	1.00	0	1.00	0
05	0.97	0.03	0.99	0.01	1.00	0	0.99	0.01	1.00	0	0.98	0.02	0.98	0.02
06	0.99	0.01	1.00	0	0.97	0.03	1.00	0	0.98	0.02	0.92	0.08	0.93	0.07
07	1.00	0	0.96	0.04	0.88	0.12	0.97	0.03	0.90	0.10	0.83	0.17	0.85	0.15
08	0.95	0.05	0.85	0.15	0.75	0.25	0.88	0.12	0.79	0.21	0.71	0.29	0.75	0.25
09	0.81	0.19	0.69	0.31	0.59	0.41	0.75	0.25	0.65	0.35	0.57	0.43	0.63	0.37
10	0.61	0.39	0.50	0.50	0.41	0.59	0.59	0.41	0.50	0.50	0.43	0.57	0.50	0.50
11	0.39	0.61	0.31	0.69	0.25	0.75	0.41	0.59	0.35	0.65	0.29	0.71	0.37	0.63
12	0.19	0.81	0.15	0.85	0.12	0.88	0.25	0.75	0.21	0.79	0.17	0.83	0.25	0.75
13	0.05	0.95	0.04	0.96	0.03	0.97	0.12	0.88	0.10	0.90	0.08	0.92	0.15	0.85
14	0	1.00	0	1.00	0	1.00	0.03	0.97	0.02	0.98	0.02	0.98	0.07	0.93
15	0.01	0.99	0.01	0.99	0.01	0.99	0	1.00	0	1.00	0	1.00	0.02	0.98
16	0.03	0.97	0.04	0.96	0.04	0.96	0.01	0.99	0.01	0.99	0.01	0.99	0	1.00
17	0.08	0.92	0.08	0.92	0.10	0.90	0.04	0.96	0.05	0.95	0.06	0.94	0.02	0.98
18	0.13	0.87	0.15	0.85	0.17	0.83	0.10	0.90	0.11	0.89	0.13	0.87	0.07	0.93
19	0.20	0.80	0.22	0.78	0.25	0.75	0.17	0.83	0.19	0.81	0.22	0.78	0.15	0.85
20	0.28	0.72	0.31	0.69	0.35	0.65	0.25	0.75	0.28	0.72	0.32	0.68	0.25	0.75
21	0.36	0.64	0.40	0.60	0.45	0.55	0.35	0.65	0.39	0.61	0.44	0.56	0.37	0.63
22	0.45	0.55	0.50	0.50	0.55	0.45	0.45	0.55	0.50	0.50	0.56	0.44	0.50	0.50
23	0.55	0.45	0.60	0.40	0.65	0.35	0.55	0.45	0.61	0.39	0.68	0.32	0.63	0.37

Banding on: *Global solar radiation*   *Dry-bulb temperature*

Column *(1)* applies to: January, February and December   —
   ,,   *(2)*   ,,   ,,   November   January, February, October, November and December
   ,,   *(3)*   ,,   ,,   March   March
   ,,   *(4)*   ,,   ,,   October   —
   ,,   *(5)*   ,,   ,,   April, August and September   April, August and September
   ,,   *(6)*   ,,   ,,   May and July   May and July
   ,,   *(7)*   ,,   ,,   June   June

Use *'Global solar radiation'* columns for monthly average dry-bulb and wet-bulb temperatures.

Example
Determine the dry-bulb and wet-bulb temperatures corresponding to the sixth band of the global solar radiation analysis at 13 GMT in March. From Table A2.7(*a*), the dry-bulb temperatures for the sixth band in March are:

$$t_{max} : 10.2\,°C \ (\theta_{max} = 15\ GMT)$$
$$t_{min} : 4.7\,°C \ (\theta_{min} = 06\ GMT)$$

For $\theta_{max} = 15$ GMT, $\theta_{min} = 06$ GMT, column (4) of Table A2.9 applies.

At 13 GMT:
$f_1 = 0.12, f_2 = 0.88$

The required dry-bulb temperature is then given by:

$$t_{d(13)} = (0.12 \times 4.7) + (0.88 \times 10.2) = 9.5\,°C$$

Similarly, the wet-bulb temperature at 13 GMT is given by:

$$t_{w(13)} = (0.12 \times 3.7) + (0.88 \times 6.8) = 6.4\,°C$$

Note that the method gives a daily mean temperature of $\frac{1}{2}(t_{max} + t_{min})$. This will only fortuitously agree with the observed mean temperature. For instance, in the worked example above, the 'simulated' mean dry-bulb temperature is $\frac{1}{2}(10.2 + 4.7) = 7.45\,°C$ and the observed value is $7.2\,°C$. On the other hand, the 'simulated' wet-bulb temperature ($\frac{1}{2}(6.8 + 3.7) = 5.25\,°C$) agrees closely with the observed value of $5.2\,°C$.

In practice, it is likely that the above procedure would be included in any associated environmental computer program together, possibly, with sinusoidal functions replacing factors f_1 and f_2 such that hourly values of temperature could be immediately simulated either from a data bank of banded weather held in the computer or by declaring t_{max}, t_{min}, θ_{max} and θ_{min} in the data input for each month and each band being examined.

The simulation procedure has been used to derive the hourly values of dry-bulb temperature which are coincident with the design monthly 'maximum' irradiances (Table A2.28), see *Design Monthly Maximum Irradiances*.

Example Weather Year

When comparing different procedures for calculating plant energy consumptions for heating, ventilating and air conditioning, or when comparing different plant designs using one particular calculation procedure, it is desirable that the weather data being used should have a common basis. These data are required to span twelve months of weather and have led to proposals for a reference year derived either as a synthesis of different aspects of the weather observed over a number of years or as the weather actually occurring in a particular year broadly representative of the average of that occurring over a long-term period. The advantage of a real year over a synthetic year is that the inter-relationships between the climatic elements are preserved. To avoid any discontinuity, the year is regarded as commencing at the start of the heating season on 1 October. This has the added advantage that sequential calculations would start at a time of light load and any initial errors would be minimised.

The CIBSE has used a selection technique[13] in which values of dry-bulb temperature, global and diffuse solar radiation and wind speed for individual years in the period 1956–75 have been compared with average values for the entire period with the object of producing a year of data that does not contain large fluctuations from the most frequently observed values of these parameters. The sole meteorological station to which this technique has been applied so far is Kew, SE England. This led to the years 1957–58, 1964–65 and 1966–67 being selected for further examination. The distribution of dry-bulb temperature was considered to be of prime importance. The 'coarse filter' selection described above was therefore supplemented by an analysis of monthly degree days calculated to different base temperatures. Using this procedure, the year 1964–65 was found to have a dry-bulb temperature distribution which is close to the long-term average. Thus, for Kew, SE England, the year 1 October 1964 to 30 September 1965 has been adopted and is known as the *CIBSE Example Weather Year–Kew*.[14]

A magnetic tape of hourly values of the following coincidentally occurring climatological parameters for the Example Year is obtainable from the Meteorological Office (see *Introduction*):
   Global and diffuse solar radiation
   Direct normal solar radiation
   Sunshine duration
   Dry-bulb and wet-bulb temperatures
   Specific enthalpy
   Atmospheric pressure
   Wind speed and direction
   Rainfall amount and duration
   Dew-point temperature
   Vapour pressure
   Relative humidity
   Radiation balance (net radiation)
   Global and diffuse illuminance

The selection technique described above can be readily applied to any locality for which the relevant climatological data are available.

WIND

Values of daily mean wind speed for one specific locality (Kew, SE England) are given in *Banded Weather Data* (Tables A2.7 and A2.8). More comprehensive data on wind speed and direction for the United Kingdom are published by the Meteorological Office and include tabulated values for about 100 stations[15] and contour maps of hourly mean wind speeds exceeded for percentages of time between 0.1% and 75% of the period 1965-73[16]. Figures A2.14 and A2.15 show such maps for wind speeds exceeded for 10% and 50% of the time, respectively.

Figure A2.15 can be used in conjunction with the multipliers given in Table A2.10[16] to obtain estimates of the hourly mean wind speed exceeded for any selected proportion of the time between 10% and 80% at any location in the UK.

Table A2.10 Multipliers for use with Fig. A2.15 to obtain hourly mean wind speeds exceeded for stated proportion of time.[16]

Proportion of time for which hourly mean wind speed is exceeded /(%)	Multiplier	
	Exposed location (coastal)	Sheltered location (inland)
80	0.56	0.46
75	0.64	0.56
70	0.71	0.65
60	0.86	0.83
50	1.00	1.00
40	1.15	1.18
30	1.33	1.39
25	1.42	1.51
20	1.54	1.66
15	1.70	1.81
10	1.84	2.03

Figure A2.15 has also been used to derive Fig. A2.16, which shows contours of the wind energy available in the UK, this being an updated version of the contours produced by Rayment[17].

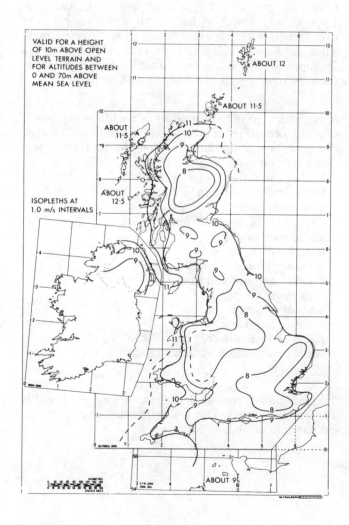

Fig. A2.14 Isopleths of hourly mean wind speeds exceeded for 10% of the time over the UK.

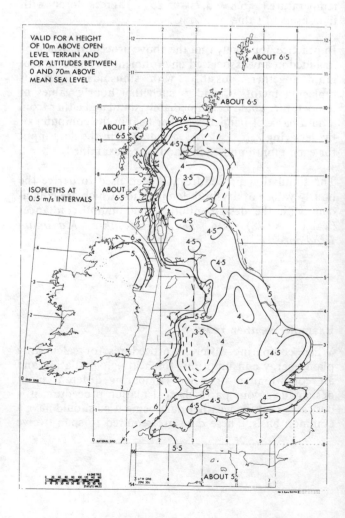

Fig. A2.15 Isopleths of hourly mean wind speeds exceeded for 50% of the time over the UK.

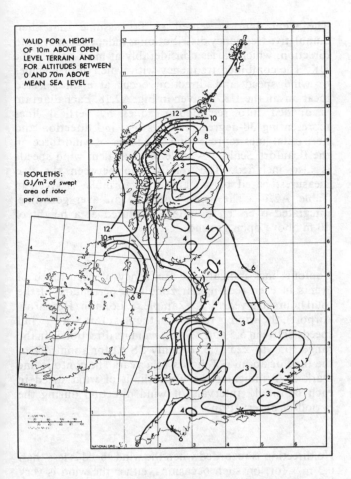

Fig. A2.16 Isopleths of wind energy over the UK.

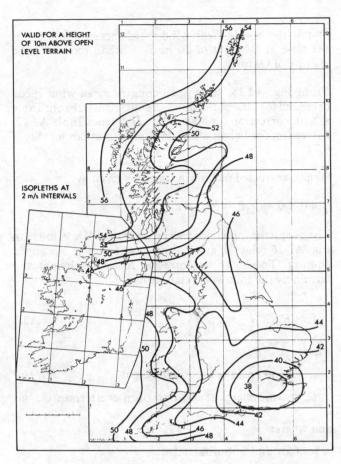

Fig. A2.17 Isopleths of maximum 3-second gust speed over the UK.

A wind contour map, showing the maximum 'surface' 3-second gust speed likely to be exceeded on average only once in 50 years, is given in Fig. A2.17[18]. Such data are used as the basis for wind load calculations. Factors relating to local topography, land surface roughness, gust duration, building dimensions and design life are applied to the gust speeds to obtain the design wind speed.

'Surface' wind data normally refer to a datum height of 10m above ground on a level and unobstructed site. It has been shown[19] that, when the wind is strong, the increase in mean wind speed with height, over given ground conditions, is approximately given by:

$$u = u_m\, K_s\, z^a \qquad \dots \quad \dots \quad \dots \quad \dots \quad \dots \quad \text{A2.6}$$

where:
 u = mean wind speed at required height .. m/s
 u_m = mean wind speed at height of 10m .. m/s
 z = height above ground .. .. .. m

K_s and a are parameters, relating wind speed to terrain and height above ground, which take the values given in Table A2.11.

Equation A2.6 may be used to correct wind speed readings at the specified datum height in open country to the wind speed expected to occur at any given height in the same or another terrain, as described by appropriate values of the parameters K_s and a. The equation has been used to compile Table A2.12 which

lists multipliers to enable the mean wind speed at a height of 10m in open country to be corrected to give the mean wind speed at a given height in each of four types of terrain.

Table A2.11 Values of parameters K_s and a[20].

Terrain	K_s	a
Open flat country	0.68	0.17
Country with scattered windbreaks	0.52	0.20
Urban	0.35	0.25
City	0.21	0.33

Table A2.12 Multipliers relating 10 m open country mean wind speed to terrain and height above ground.

Height/ (m)	Terrain			
	Country		Urban	City
	Open flat	With scattered windbreaks		
5	0.89	0.72	0.52	—
10	1.00	0.82	0.62	0.45
20	1.13	0.95	0.74	0.56
30	1.21	1.03	0.82	0.64
40	1.27	1.09	0.88	0.71
50	1.32	1.14	0.93	0.76

Example

Obtain the hourly mean wind speed exceeded for 80% of the time at a height of 20 m over urban terrain in the vicinity of Oxford.

From Fig. A2.15, 10 m open country mean wind speed exceeded for 50% of the time is about 4.0 m/s. From Table A2.10, correction for 80% is 0.46 and, from Table A2.12, correction for height above ground and urban locality is 0.74.

Hence, corrected mean wind speed is given by:

$$4.0 \times 0.46 \times 0.74 \approx 1.5 \text{ m/s}$$

The isopleths of wind energy over the UK shown in Fig. A2.16 relate to an effective height of 10 m over open country. These can be corrected for actual height and terrain by the following relationship:

$$E = E_m \, K_e \left(\frac{z}{z_r + 10} \right)^b \quad \dots \quad \dots \quad \dots \quad \text{A2.7}$$

where:

E = wind energy at required height   .. GJ/m^2

E_m = wind energy at 10 m over open level terrain GJ/m^2

and where:

for City and Suburban terrains:

$z = z_r$ + height above general roof top level ..   m

z_r = general roof top level ..   ..   m

for Open and Coastal terrains:

z = height above ground ..   ..   m

z_r = zero

and for Hill terrain:

z = height of hill above open level terrain   ..   m

z_r = zero

K_e and b are parameters, relating wind energy to terrain and height, which take the values in Table A2.13. These relationships represent updated versions of those given by Rayment[17].

Table A2.13   Values of parameters K_e and b.

Terrain	K_e	b
City	0.33	1.0
Urban	0.5	0.75
Open	1.0	0.50
Coastal	1.2	0.42
Hill	1.7*	0.50
* Factor strictly depends on hill shape.		

The wind data presented so far assume that their cumulative frequency distribution is independent of wind direction, which varies considerably at most sites in the UK. The combined frequency with which hourly values of wind speed and direction occur at eight selected locations in the UK is given in Fig. A2.18. Each diagram is divided into rectangular zones by vertical lines representing 30-degree intervals of wind direction and horizontal lines representing categories of wind force on the Beaufort Scale.[21] A scale of equivalent wind speeds is also included. The relationship between the two measures, based on an empirical formula, is given in Table A2.14. The wind speed is an average value, integrated over ten minutes, measured at a height of 10 m above open ground.

Contour lines indicate the frequency of occurrence of events in each rectangular zone as a percentage of the total hours in a year. For example, at London (Heathrow Airport), the wind is force 4 on the Beaufort Scale (wind speeds between 5.5 and 7.9 m/s) and its direction is in the range 195° to 225° (ie, roughly SSW) for about 4% of the time or about 350 hours in a year. The contour line marked '0' indicates the upper limit of wind speed in each of the 12 intervals of wind direction during the period of observation.

No direction is recorded when the wind speed is less than 0.3 m/s for, on such occasions, either the wind is very light and its direction is variable, or there is complete calm. The frequency of occurrence of hours of 'calm' (ie wind speed < 0.3 m/s) is given below each diagram. Also given is the aggregate frequency of occurrence of hours of both 'calm' and 'light air' (ie wind speed < 1.6 m/s), a value which would be difficult to estimate from the diagram.

The direction frequencies at the top of each diagram give the percentages of hours for which the wind is in each of the twelve intervals of wind direction. The frequencies do not include 'calm' conditions and so exclude those occasions when the wind speed was less than 0.3 m/s (ie for 7.2% of hours at London (Heathrow Airport), so giving an aggregate direction frequency of 92.8% rather than 100.0%).

The wind blows most frequently from a direction between south and west in open country, but where nearby hills deflect the wind, the pattern may differ from this as, for example, at Glasgow and Manchester. These differences may be important when considering ventilation and atmospheric pollution.

The effect of the wind on human comfort outdoors is discussed by Penwarden[22] and Cohen et al[23].

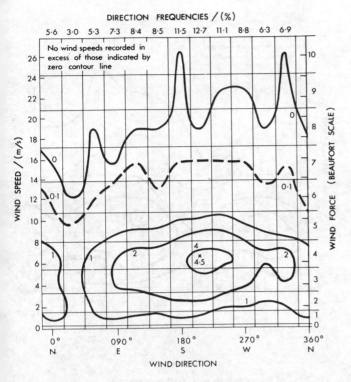

On 4.6% of hours speed was <0.3 m/s (calm)
On 14.0% of hours speed was <1.6 m/s

(a)   Belfast (Aldergrove Airport). Period 1957-66.
      Effective height 10 m.

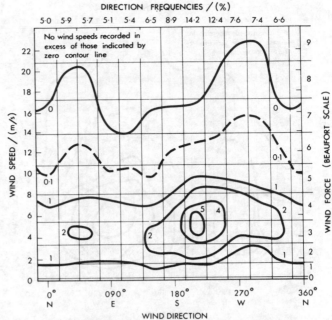

On 6.7% of hours speed was <0.3 m/s (calm)
On 18.3% of hours speed was <1.6 m/s

(b)   Birmingham (Elmdon Airport). Period 1957-66.
      Effective height 10 m.

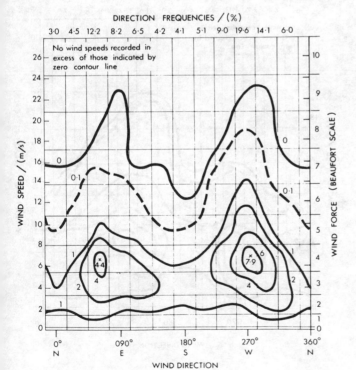

On 3.5% of hours speed was <0.3 m/s (calm)
On 7.6% of hours speed was <1.6m/s

(c)   Cardiff (Rhoose Airport). Period 1961-70.
      Effective height 10 m.

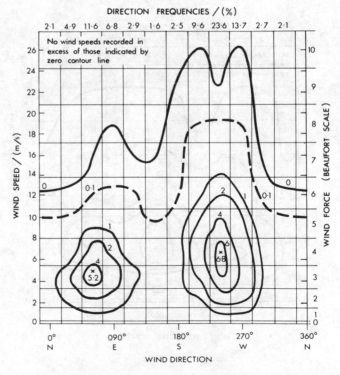

On 15.9% of hours speed was <0.3 m/s (calm)
On 20.7% of hours speed was <1.6 m/s

(d)   Edinburgh (Turnhouse Airport). Period 1957-66.
      Effective height 10 m.

Fig. A2.18   Wind speed and direction frequencies at selected stations, all hours. (Building Research Establishment[8]; Crown copyright).

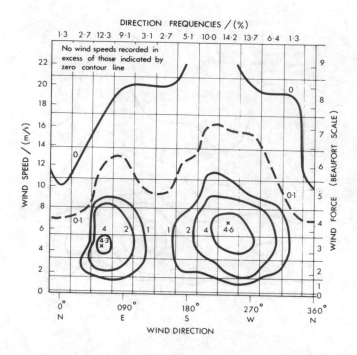

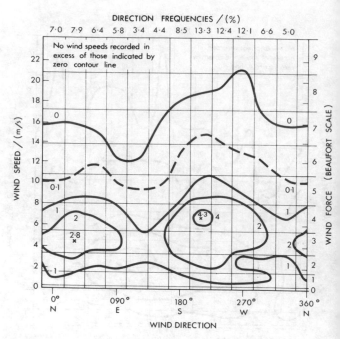

On 18.8% of hours speed was <0.3 m/s (calm)
On 23.1% of hours speed was <1.6 m/s

(e) Glasgow (Renfrew Airport). Period 1956-65.
Effective height 12 m.

On 7.2% of hours speeds was <0.3 m/s (calm)
On 17.6% of hours speed was <1.6 m/s

(f) London (Heathrow Airport). Period 1957-66.
Effective height 10 m.

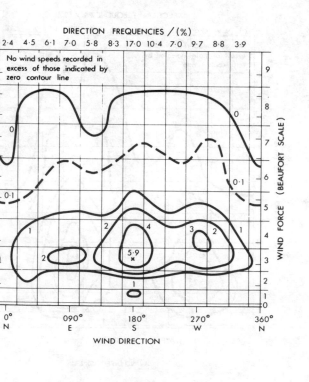

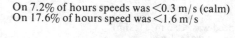

On 9.1% of hours speed was <0.3 m/s (calm)
On 17.2% of hours speed was <1.6 m/s

(g) Manchester (Ringway Airport). Period 1957-66.
Effective height 10 m.

On 4.0% of hours speed was <0.3 m/s (calm)
On 13.3% of hours speed was <1.6 m/s

(h) Plymouth (Mount Batten). Period 1965-73.
Effective height 13 m.

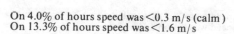

Fig. A2.18—continued

Table A2.14 The Beaufort scale of wind force.[21]

Beaufort Number	Description of Wind	Observation	Wind Speed/ m/s
0	Calm	Smoke rises vertically.	0 to 0.2
1	Light air	Direction of wind shown by smoke drift but not by wind vanes.	0.3 to 1.5
2	Light breeze	Wind felt on face; leaves rustle; ordinary vanes moved by wind.	1.6 to 3.3
3	Gentle breeze	Leaves and small twigs in constant motion; wind extends light flag.	3.4 to 5.4
4	Moderate breeze	Raises dust and loose paper; small branches are moved.	5.5 to 7.9
5	Fresh breeze	Small trees in leaf begin to sway.	8.0 to 10.7
6	Strong breeze	Large branches in motion; whistling heard in telegraph wires.	10.8 to 13.8
7	Near gale	Whole trees in motion; inconvenience felt when walking into wind.	13.9 to 17.1
8	Gale	Twigs broken off trees; generally impedes progress.	17.2 to 20.7
9	Strong gale	Slight structural damage occurs (slates and chimney pots removed from roofs).	20.8 to 24.4
10	Storm	Seldom experienced inland; trees uprooted; considerable structural damage occurs.	24.5 to 28.4
11	Violent storm	Very rarely experienced; accompanied by widespread damage.	28.5 to 32.6
12	Hurricane		32.7 and over

PRECIPITATION

Precipitation is the term used to describe the deposition of all types of water from the atmosphere onto the ground. The main forms are rain, snow, sleet (rain and snow mixed) and hail but dew and hoar frost can also be included. Table A2.15 gives, for a number of typical stations in the United Kingdom, the average annual precipitation totals, including the liquid water equivalent of any snow and hail, together with the average monthly totals for the driest and the wettest months for the period 1941-70. The Meteorological Office can supply detailed data for the whole of the UK.

Rainfall is however a very variable quantity both in space and time and there are many engineering applications for which it is necessary to take into account the high rates of rainfall that only occur rarely at any given point. Such rainfall rates are required to be known, for instance, in the design of drainage systems. In these instances it is not usually economically justifiable, or indeed feasible, to allow for the maximum possible rainfall; a calculated risk has to be taken and the designer then needs to know the (low) probability that the design rate that he has chosen will be exceeded. A useful concept in this respect is that of the "return period". The return period (measured in years) when referred to rainfall is the average length of time in years between occasions when a given rainfall (e.g. average rate in a given time) is exceeded. Thus for instance, a return period of a few years may be considered appropriate for some structures (e.g. storm sewers) but for other structures, where the results of any failure are assessed as being very much more serious, the design figure chosen may be that corresponding to a longer return period.

Table A2.15 Average precipitation at eight stations in the UK. Period 1941-70.

Station	Annual Total/ (mm)	Wettest Month	Total/ (mm)	Driest Month(s)	Total/ (mm)
Belfast	912	December	92	April	57
Birmingham	679	August	71	February	46
Cardiff	947	August	99	March & January	58
Edinburgh	677	August	82	March	39
Glasgow	982	October	103	March, April, May	61
London	617	August	65	February & March	39
Manchester	819	August	91	March	48
Plymouth	990	December	110	April	57

A detailed examination of rainfall data in the UK[24] enables designers to estimate for any point in the UK rates of rainfall in given periods of time corresponding to given return periods. Reference should be made to this report or to the Meteorological Office for detailed guidance but Table A2.16 gives values for two areas of the UK, northern Scotland and south-eastern England, these being chosen because they encompass the range of heavy rainfall conditions in the UK. Values are of rainfall amounts in various periods of time from 1 minute to 48 hours which are likely to occur not more than once in various return periods from 1 to 100 years. It will be seen that, as would be expected, very high rates of rainfall last for only a short time and that as the return period is increased the highest rates of rainfall occurring in that period also increase. Moreover, whereas long duration rainfalls are greatest in northern Scotland, short duration high-intensity rainfalls are greatest in south-eastern England.

Table A2.16 Rainfall duration and frequency for two regions in the UK.

(a) Northern Scotland

Duration	Return Period/(years)					
	1	2	5	10	50	100
	Rainfall/(mm)					
1 min	0.8	0.9	1.2	1.3	1.8	2.0
5 min	2.8	3.4	4.2	4.9	6.8	7.7
15 min	6	7	9	10	14	16
1 hour	12	14	18	21	29	34
3 hours	21	25	30	35	48	55
6 hours	31	35	41	47	64	73
24 hours	60	67	78	88	113	125
48 hours	84	95	107	119	149	163

(b) South Eastern England

Duration	Return Period/(years)					
	1	2	5	10	50	100
	Rainfall/(mm)					
1 min	1.5	1.8	2.3	2.6	3.5	3.9
5 min	4.5	5.5	7.3	8.5	11.7	13.4
15 min	8	9	13	15	21	24
1 hour	13	15	20	24	35	41
3 hours	18	21	27	32	47	55
6 hours	22	26	33	38	55	64
24 hours	33	39	47	54	75	85
48 hours	40	47	55	64	86	98

The data in Table A2.16 refer to rainfall at one particular point, the values being generally applicable to any place in the areas concerned which is not more than about 200 m above sea-level. If however, an area of 1 square kilometre or more is being considered (e.g. the drainage system of a town) then some reduction in the highest rainfall rate corresponding to a given return period can be allowed because the highest rate of rainfall for a given duration does not occur simultaneously over an extended area. Indeed the larger the area the lower is the highest rate of rainfall for a given return period and duration. This leads to the concept of the areal reduction factor which is defined as the factor by which the point rainfall rates corresponding to given durations and return periods should be multiplied to produce the corresponding rainfall rate over the area. Table A2.17 gives some typical values of the areal reduction factor as a function of the size of area and the duration of rainfall. These factors apply to all return periods.

Table A2.17 Areal reduction factor to be applied to point rainfall.

Duration	Reduction Factor for stated area / km²					
	1	5	30	100	1000	10 000
1 min	0.76	0.61	0.40	0.27	—	—
5 min	0.90	0.82	0.65	0.51	—	—
15 min	0.94	0.89	0.77	0.64	0.39	—
1 hour	0.96	0.93	0.86	0.79	0.62	0.44
3 hours	0.97	0.96	0.91	0.87	0.78	0.62
6 hours	0.98	0.97	0.93	0.90	0.83	0.73
24 hours	0.99	0.98	0.96	0.94	0.89	0.83
48 hours	1.00	0.99	0.97	0.96	0.91	0.86

The detailed application of these data and recommended practices are covered by a number of relevant Standards and Codes of Practice such as those issued by the British Standards Institution. Reference should be made to these as appropriate; the Meteorological Office can often help by supplying data or estimates for a particular site. Enquiries should be addressed to the Meteorological Office Rainfall Enquiries Bureau (Met. O. 8c) at Bracknell, Berkshire.

DAYLIGHT AVAILABILITY

To assess the energy consumption of artificial lighting, it is necessary to know the total hours of use of the lights. Where the use of artificial lighting is determined by the available daylight, Tables A2.18 and A2.19[25] may be used to estimate the probable hours of use. Table A2.18 gives the total hours of use corresponding to different levels of sky illuminance for working days having various combinations of start and finish times and Table A2.19 gives similar information on a monthly basis but for a 'standard' working day from 09.00 to 17.30 hours clocktime.

Values are based on sky illuminance measurements made at Kew, SE England, during the ten-year period 1964 to 1973. The times of start and finish of the working day are expressed in clock time, that is GMT or BST (British Summer Time) as appropriate, it being assumed that BST applies between April and October inclusive. The errors in the total hours of use resulting from variations in the actual starting and finishing dates for BST are small and may be neglected.

In using Tables A2.18 and A2.19, a limiting sky illuminance, below which level artificial lighting will be required, has first to be calculated as follows:

$$\text{Limiting sky illuminance (klx)} = \frac{\text{Limiting daylight illuminance (lx)}}{10 \times \text{Daylight factor (\%)}}$$

$$\quad \cdots \quad \cdots \quad \text{A2.8}$$

Note that the limiting daylight illuminance indoors is expressed in lux which yields the limiting sky illuminance in terms of kilolux.

Example

For a particular building, the artificial lighting is controlled by a photo-electric sensing element designed to operate when the daylight illuminance falls below 200 lux, the daylight factor at the sensing element being 2.2%. Determine the likely hours of use of the artificial lighting.

Limiting daylight illuminance = 200 lx

Daylight factor = 2.2%

Therefore:

$$\text{Limiting sky illuminance} = \frac{200}{10 \times 2.2} = 9.1 \text{ klx}$$

For a 'standard' working day, i.e. 09.00 to 17.30 hours clocktime, both Tables A2.18 and A2.19 give 855 hours of use (interpolating between the values given for 9 klx and 10 klx). Table A2.19 shows that this represents about 27% of a 'working year' of 3102 hours. In addition, this table shows how these hours are distributed through the year.

Table A2.18 shows the effect on the likely hours of use resulting from variations in the start and finish times of the working day. It will be seen that the relative benefit of an early or late start depends upon the length of the working day and the level of sky illuminance. For example, in the case of an 8 h working day and a limiting sky illuminance not exceeding 6 klx the hours of use are less for a start time of 08.00 than for 09.00. However, with a limiting illuminance of greater than 6 klx, the later start time is favoured.

The durations given in Tables A2.18 and A2.19 make no allowance for weekends or public holidays. A simple proportional correction factor may be introduced to account for these non-working days. For example, for a 5 day working week and 8 public holidays per year, the correction factor is:

$$\left(\frac{5}{7} - \frac{8}{365}\right) = 0.7$$

In the above example, the corrected hours of use then becomes 600 h.

There is no simple correction factor that can be used to account for lunch breaks and it is assumed that the lights will be in use for all of that part of the working day when the limiting sky illuminance is less than the stated value.

Further information on design for the daylight illumination of buildings is given elsewhere.[26,27]

Table A2.18 Annual availability of daylight for working day of different durations for Kew, SE England. Period 1964-73.

Sky illuminance /(klx)	Hours during the working year when illuminance is below the stated value												
	Start of working day (clock time)												
	07.00				08.00				09.00				
	Finish of working day (clock time)												
	16.00	17.00	18.00	19.00	16.00	17.00	18.00	19.00	16.00	17.00	17.30	18.00	19.00
0.5	109	188	311	476	13	92	215	380	7	86	147	209	374
1	160	250	382	559	42	132	264	441	21	111	176	242	420
2	275	386	532	722	126	236	383	572	69	180	252	326	515
3	383	504	659	860	216	338	493	693	132	253	330	408	609
4	488	617	784	994	306	434	602	812	200	328	412	496	706
5	591	726	903	1123	394	529	706	926	270	404	492	582	801
6	693	834	1021	1251	481	621	809	1039	342	482	575	669	900
7	795	945	1140	1381	570	719	915	1155	416	566	663	761	1002
8	902	1059	1262	1512	661	818	1021	1271	495	652	753	855	1105
9	1008	1174	1385	1644	754	920	1131	1390	575	741	846	952	1211
10	1115	1291	1510	1779	848	1024	1243	1512	654	831	940	1050	1319
15	1623	1842	2102	2420	1303	1523	1783	2100	1049	1269	1398	1529	1846
20	2039	2294	2595	2948	1685	1941	2241	2594	1382	1637	1787	1938	2290
25	2388	2682	3021	3385	2024	2318	2657	3021	1686	1980	2149	2319	2683
30	2682	3008	3366	3731	2317	2643	3002	3366	1960	2286	2465	2645	3009
35	2917	3267	3631	3996	2552	2902	3266	3631	2188	2538	2720	2902	3267
40	3081	3442	3807	4172	2716	3077	3442	3807	2351	2712	2894	3077	3442
45	3186	3550	3915	4280	2821	3185	3550	3915	2456	2820	3002	3185	3550
50	3245	3610	3975	4340	2880	3245	3610	3975	2515	2880	3062	3245	3610
55	3273	3638	4003	4368	2908	3273	3638	4003	2543	2908	3090	3273	3638
60	3281	3646	4011	4376	2916	3281	3646	4011	2551	2916	3098	3281	3646
65	3284	3649	4014	4379	2919	3284	3649	4014	2554	2919	3101	3284	3649
70	3285	3650	4015	4380	2920	3285	3650	4015	2555	2920	3102	3285	3650
Length of working day (hours)	9	10	11	12	8	9	10	11	7	8	8½	9	10

Notes:
1. 09.00 to 17.30 is considered to be the 'standard' working day.
2. British Summer Time (BST) applies from April to October inclusive.
3. Durations of working year (hours) are given by the 70 klx values.
4. Derived from Table A4.2 of Ref. 25.

Table A2.19   Annual and monthly availability of daylight for 'standard' (09.00-17.30) working day at Kew, SE England. Period 1964-73.

Sky illuminance (klx)	Proportion of working year that illuminance is below stated value		Hours during working month with sky illuminance below stated value											
	%	hours	Jan	Feb	Mar	Apr	May	June	July	Aug	Sept	Oct	Nov	Dec
0.5	5	147	43	17	2	0	0	0	0	0	0	1	34	50
1	6	176	49	22	5	0	0	0	0	0	0	1	41	58
2	8	252	69	35	11	0	1	0	0	0	0	4	54	78
3	11	330	89	44	16	1	1	1	0	0	1	10	65	102
4	13	412	110	55	24	2	1	1	0	0	3	16	79	121
5	16	492	127	65	30	3	2	1	0	1	6	26	91	140
6	19	575	144	75	38	6	2	3	1	2	7	33	104	160
7	21	663	159	87	47	10	4	3	3	4	10	43	117	176
8	24	753	175	97	54	15	6	4	3	7	15	54	131	192
9	27	846	192	108	61	18	8	5	5	9	19	68	145	208
10	30	940	205	117	69	23	10	8	6	12	25	81	162	222
15	45	1398	250	175	114	56	27	22	19	33	63	153	227	259
20	58	1787	263	214	166	96	56	49	43	63	115	209	251	262
25	69	2149	263	232	217	146	97	84	78	103	167	244	255	263
30	79	2465	263	238	245	192	143	125	120	151	211	259	255	263
35	88	2720	264	238	259	225	185	167	165	195	240	264	255	263
40	93.3	2894	264	238	262	244	223	203	202	225	251	264	255	263
45	96.8	3002	264	238	263	251	243	228	232	247	254	264	255	263
50	98.7	3062	264	238	263	254	256	242	250	258	255	264	255	263
55	99.6	3090	264	238	263	255	262	249	260	262	255	264	255	263
60	99.88	3098	264	238	263	255	263	253	262	263	255	264	255	263
65	99.97	3101	264	238	263	255	264	254	263	263	255	264	255	263
70	100	3102	264	238	263	255	264	255	263	263	255	264	255	263

Notes:
1. BST applies from April to October inclusive.
2. Derived from Table A2.2 of Ref. 25.

ATMOSPHERIC POLLUTION

The greater part of pollution of the atmosphere arises from the burning of fuels. Pollutants can be divided into three types:

(i) *Grit and dust.*

These names are given to material coarse enough to settle quickly out of the air. The particles mainly fall close to the chimneys from which they are emitted and are generally a local problem.

(ii) *Smoke.*

Smoke is the name given to particles and droplets which remain suspended in the air for long periods and travel with it. The particles of suspended matter are generally carbonaceous, of a size less than $10\,\mu$m and the majority being less than $5\,\mu$m. Particles settle to the ground very slowly, if at all.

(iii) *Gases.*

The principal gaseous pollutant is sulphur dioxide but at low levels in industrial areas carbon monoxide can constitute a local problem. Nitric oxide may be the critical pollutant from installations burning low sulphur fuels such as natural gas.

Measurements of Atmospheric Pollution

The National Survey of Atmospheric Pollution is organised by the Warren Spring Laboratory of the Department of Industry. Observations of smoke and sulphur dioxide concentrations can be obtained from the Laboratory and reports containing summary tables are published periodically by the Department.

Over the country as a whole, smoke pollution is steadily decreasing, improvement in the south being more rapid than in the north. Sulphur dioxide pollution is decreasing less rapidly. Concentrations of these pollutants vary with location within the UK and with the positions of individual measuring sites within a particular locality. An indication of the site-to-site variation is given by Table A2.20 which shows, for particular locations, the ranges of site annual mean concentrations occurring in the period April 1976 to March 1977[28].

Table A2.20   Range of site annual mean concentrations of smoke and sulphur dioxide at selected locations.

Location	Site annual mean concentration		
	Smoke /(μg/m³)	Sulphur Dioxide /(μg/m³)	/(ppm)
Belfast	46 - 141	45 - 107	0.016 - 0.037
Birmingham	18 - 33	58 - 109	0.020 - 0.038
Cardiff	21 - 50	45 - 75	0.016 - 0.026
Edinburgh	26 - 42	31 - 90	0.011 - 0.032
Glasgow	26 - 59	52 - 128	0.018 - 0.045
London	26 - 31	130 - 149	0.046 - 0.052
Manchester	12 - 56	88 - 155	0.031 - 0.054
Plymouth	10 - 26	21 - 36	0.007 - 0.013

Daily concentrations for individual sites show wide variations from the annual mean values; they also show a seasonal trend, being generally less than the annual mean in summer and greater in winter. On rare occasions, average daily concentrations of sulphur dioxide may exceed $500 \mu g/m^3$ at some town sites. Smoke and sulphur dioxide concentrations will normally be lower in rural areas than at town sites.

Although the concentrations of sulphur dioxide are small compared to the threshold limit value of 5 ppm, the time weighted average concentration to which people at their workplaces may be exposed without adverse effects is generally agreed to be a maximum of 0.2 ppm.

Pollution from Motor Vehicle Exhaust

The main pollutants arising from the combustion of petrol and diesel fuels which could create a health hazard are carbon monoxide, oxides of nitrogen and sulphur, lead compounds, organic compounds and smoke.[29, 30]

The most hazardous of these is carbon monoxide which has a threshold limit of 50 ppm (related to continuous exposure at the work place). Measurements of carbon monoxide concentrations taken in busy streets at a height of 2.75 m have shown that levels of 100 ppm are not uncommon. The concentration will generally decrease at greater heights and at increased distances from traffic.

Table A2.21 gives the mean concentrations of carbon monoxide, lead and smoke measured in central London for typical summer and winter conditions.[31] The concentration of pollutants will normally increase considerably during a temperature inversion.

The size of particles emitted by motor vehicle exhausts is typically between 0.3 and $2.0 \mu m$, with most in the range 0.8 to $1.0 \mu m$.

Table A2.21 Mean concentrations of pollutants at street level in central London.

Season	Mean concentration at street level			
	Carbon monoxide		Smoke	Lead
	$/(mg/m^3)$	$/(ppm)$	$/(\mu g/m^3)$	$/(\mu g/m^3)$
Summer	21	17	200	1
Winter	13	11	350	2

WORLD WEATHER DATA

Table A2.22 gives information on meteorological conditions for selected locations around the world. The purpose of this table is to give general guidance on design temperatures and precipitation. Where possible before finally selecting design values, reference should be made to detailed meteorological data and local codes and regulations, for the data quoted may only refer to a relatively small area around the meteorological station cited. The method used to establish summer external design temperatures is the approximate method described in *UK Warm Weather Data* which uses information available in Meteorological Office publications.[12]

The average diurnal range of dry-bulb temperature is given for the month for which the summer design conditions are calculated. This enables an assessment to be made of the overnight minimum temperature associated with the summer design conditions. Such information may be useful when designing for "heavy" buildings so that advantage can be taken of low night temperatures if they occur.

When making use of the table it must be borne in mind that the method used to calculate the summer external design temperatures is an approximate one. In many cases, where comparisons can be made, agreement with design figures which are in common use and known to be satisfactory is good. The following notes may help in a critical appraisal of the values quoted:

(i) If the average relative humidity for early afternoon, say 14 LAT, is available this is used in preference to the average minimum values.

(ii) In some places vapour pressure varies with the time of day more than in others. Where this variation is great, the error in wet-bulb temperature selection by the approximate method may be several degrees but this particular effect will always lead to an error which is upwards (i.e. to a higher wet-bulb temperature selection than is needed).

(iii) For some situations inspection of the published data may reveal an alternative design condition at a time of year of lower dry-bulb temperature but higher vapour pressure, leading to a higher design wet-bulb temperature. Months with moderately high dry-bulb temperatures and high relative humidity must therefore be investigated in addition to the month of highest average monthly maximum temperature. An alternative design condition is given for selected locations in the table where the higher vapour pressure is likely to be significant.

Winter design temperatures are given in the tables for a number of locations. The source of the data is the *ASHRAE* Handbook of Fundamentals.[32] Where *ASHRAE* data are used the temperature given is that value which is equalled or exceeded during the winter period for 97.5% of the time. For all locations except Canada the winter period for the northern hemisphere is December to February inclusive and for the southern hemisphere is June to August inclusive; for Canadian sites the month of January only is used. Reference to local codes and regulations and to detailed meteorological data is recommended when selecting winter design temperatures.

Precipitation quantities are given for the wettest month, the driest month and the annual fall. The information is taken from Meteorological Office publications[12] and is presented to indicate the general conditions obtaining. Average annual sunshine durations are also given where such information is available in these publications.

Table A2.22 World Weather Data

(a) Northern Europe

Location				Design Temperatures					Precipitation/mm			Sunshine
				Summer				Winter	Average monthly			
Station	Lat.	Long.	Height /(m)	Month	Dry-bulb /°C	Average diurnal range /°C	Screen wet-bulb /°C	Dry-bulb /°C	Wettest month	Driest month	Annual	Average annual duration /(h)
AUSTRIA												
Salzburg	47°48′N	13°00′E	435	July	32	11	22	—	195	64	1286	1712
Vienna (Wien)	48°15′N	16°22′E	203	July	31	9	21	−12	84	39	660	1891
BALEARIC ISLES												
Palma de Majorca	39°33′N	02°39′E	10	July	33	9	25	—	77	3	449	2761
BELGIUM												
Brussels (Bruxelles) ..	50°48′N	04°21′E	100	July	31	11	22	−7	95	53	855	1551
BULGARIA												
Plovdiv	42°29′N	24°45′E	160	July	37	15	24	−13	65	28	492	—
CZECHOSLOVAKIA												
Prague (Praha)	50°04′N	14°26′E	262	July	33	10	*	−13	68	18	411	1872
DENMARK												
Copenhagen	55°41′N	12°33′E	9	July	27	8	19	−7	71	32	603	1603
FINLAND												
Helsinki	60°12′N	24°55′E	46	July	28	9	20	−18	73	36	688	1802
FRANCE												
Bordeaux/Merignac ..	44°50′N	00°42′W	46	Aug	33	12	23	—	109	48	900	2008
Brest	48°27′N	04°25′W	98	July	26	7	19	—	150	56	1129	1729
Lyons/Bron	45°43′N	04°57′E	200	Aug	34	12	22	−10	93	46	813	2018
Marseille/Marignane ..	43°27′N	05°13′E	4	July	34	12	22	−2	76	11	546	2654
Paris/Montsouris	48°49′N	02°20′E	75	July	33	10	22	−4	64	35	619	1840
GERMANY												
Berlin	52°27′N	13°18′E	55	July	32	10	22	−11	73	33	603	1738
Cologne (Köln)	50°58′N	06°58′E	45	Aug	32	10	21	—	75	42	699	—
Hamburg	53°38′N	10°00′E	22	July	31	11	21	−9	83	39	715	1640
Leipzig	51°19′N	12°25′E	141	July	32	10	21	—	83	38	595	1726
Munich (München) ..	48°08′N	11°42′E	524	July	31	11	21	−13	139	47	957	1862
HUNGARY												
Budapest	47°26′N	19°11′E	139	July	34	11	22	−10	72	33	614	2060
ICELAND												
Reykjavik	64°08′N	21°56′W	18	July	18	5	13	−8	94	42	779	1258
IRISH REPUBLIC												
Dublin (Airport)	53°26′N	06°15′W	68	June	23	8	17	−3	80	43	769	1503
Shannon (Airport)	52°41′N	08°55′W	2	June	24	9	18	−2	117	53	929	1386
NETHERLANDS												
DeBilt	52°06′N	05°11′E	3	July	30	9	21	—	87	44	766	1568
Eelde	53°08′N	06°35′E	4	July	28	9	20	—	95	44	767	1465

* Inadequate data.

(a) Northern Europe—*continued*

Location					Design Temperatures					Precipitation/mm			Sunshine
					Summer				Winter	Average monthly			
Station	Lat.	Long.	Height /(m)		Month	Dry-bulb /°C	Average diurnal range /°C	Screen wet-bulb /°C	Dry-bulb /°C	Wettest month	Driest month	Annual	Average annual duration /(h)
NORWAY													
Bergen	60°24'N	05°19'E	43		July	26	7	19	−7	235	83	1930	1259
Narvik	68°25'N	17°23'E	40		July	25	7	18	—	97	44	758	—
Oslo	59°56'N	10°44'E	94		July	28	9	20	−16	95	26	730	—
Trondheim	63°26'N	10°25'E	58		July	27	8	19	—	99	47	870	—
POLAND													
Warsaw (Warszawa) ..	52°13'N	21°03'E	110		July	31	10	22	−13	96	27	555	1676
PORTUGAL													
Lisbon (Lisboa)	38°43'N	09°09'W	77		July	36	10	23	4	111	3	708	3022
Pôrto/Serra do Pilar ..	41°08'N	08°36'W	95		July	34	10	23	—	168	20	1151	2667
ROMANIA													
Bucharest/Baneasa ..	44°30'N	26°05'E	92		July	36	14	26	−13	121	26	592	2159
SWEDEN													
Gothenberg (Göteborg) ..	57°42'N	11°58'E	41		July	28	7	19	—	86	29	670	1928
Stockholm	59°21'N	18°04'E	44		July	28	8	19	−13	76	25	554	1973
Umeà	63°50'N	20°17'E	11		July	26	10	18	—	77	27	601	—
SWITZERLAND													
Basle (Basel)	47°33'N	07°35'E	317		July	34	13	23	—	94	40	784	1680
Bern	46°57'N	07°26'E	572		July	30	16	20	—	123	54	986	1756
Geneva (Genève)	46°12'N	06°09'E	405		July	32	11	22	—	99	51	853	2037
UNITED KINGDOM †													
Belfast (Aldergrove) ..	54°39'N	06°13'W	68		July	23	8	17	*	92	57	912	1281
Birmingham (Elmdon) ..	52°27'N	01°44'W	96		July	26	9	19	*	71	46	679	1385
Cardiff (Rhoose)	51°24'N	03°21'W	67		Aug	25	7	18	*	99	58	947	1571
Edinburgh (Turnhouse) ..	55°57'N	03°21'W	35		July	23	9	17	*	82	39	677	1294
Glasgow (Abbotsinch) ..	55°52'N	04°26'W	5		July	24	9	18	*	103	61	982	1266
London (Heathrow) ..	51°29'N	00°27'W	25		July	29	9	20	*	65	39	617	1475
Manchester (Ringway) ..	53°21'N	02°16'W	75		July	26	8	18	*	91	48	819	1334
Plymouth (Mt. Batten) ..	50°21'N	04°07'W	27		July	25	6	19	*	110	57	990	1678
USSR (EUROPEAN)													
Leningrad	59°58'N	30°18'E	4		July	29	9	20	—	78	30	603	1642
Moscow (Moskva)	55°45'N	37°34'E	156		July	29	10	20	—	88	36	624	—
Rostov-na-Donu	47°15'N	39°49'E	77		July	35	12	22	—	87	29	579	2140

* Winter design temperatures are given in the section *UK Cold Weather Data.*

† Summer design temperatures for the UK are calculated using the approximate method described in the section *UK Warm Weather Data* and based on data for the selected locations provided by the Meteorological Office. and refer to periods of 20 to 30 years ending in 1970.

Table A2.22   World Weather Data—*continued*

(b)   Southern Europe

Location				Design Temperatures					Precipitation/mm			Sunshine
				Summer				Winter	Average monthly			
Station	Lat.	Long.	Height /(m)	Month	Dry-bulb /°C	Average diurnal range /°C	Screen wet-bulb /°C	Dry-bulb /°C	Wettest month	Driest month	Annual	Average annual duration /(h)
ALBANIA												
Vlorë	40°28′N	19°29′E	3	Aug	36	11	24	—	192	9	995	2685
CORSICA												
Ajaccio	41°52′N	08°48′E	4	Aug	34	12	25	—	98	10	672	2770
CYPRUS												
Famagusta	35°07′N	33°56′E	25	Aug	38	12	28	—	106	<1	403	2998
Nicosia	35°09′N	33°21′E	175	July	41	16	26	—	76	1	345	3362
GIBRALTAR												
North Front	36°09′N	05°21′W	2	Aug	34	8	25	—	152	1	767	2850
GREECE												
Athens (Athenai)	37°58′N	24°43′E	107	July	39	9	24	2	71	6	402	2756
Salonica (Thessaloniki) ..	40°37′N	22°57′E	25	July	38	12	26	0	57	14	470	2624
Iraklion (Crete)	35°21′N	25°08′E	29	Aug	35	7	25	—	95	1	453	—
ITALY												
Florence (Firenze)	43°46′N	11°15′E	51	July	35	12	23	—	110	35	825	2488
Genoa (Genova)	44°25′N	08°55′E	21	Aug	31	6	23	—	193	40	1270	2288
Milan (Milano)	45°28′N	09°11′E	121	July	34	10	25	-6	125	44	1017	1906
Naples (Napoli)	40°53′N	14°17′E	110	Aug	34	11	24	2	147	19	915	2396
Rome (Roma)	41°54′N	12°29′E	17	July	35	10	23	1	129	15	744	2491
Venice (Venezia)	45°27′N	12°19′E	1	July	32	8	24	—	94	37	770	2104
MALTA												
Valletta	35°54′N	14°31′E	70	July	36	7	25	—	110	0	519	3066
SARDINIA												
Cagliari (Elmas)	39°12′N	09°05′E	7	July	35	10	26	—	72	1	451	2468
SICILY												
Messina	38°12′N	15°33′E	54	Aug	34	7	25	—	149	19	902	2448
Palermo	38°06′N	13°19′E	31	Aug	36	9	25	—	77	2	512	—
SPAIN												
Barcelona	41°24′N	02°09′E	93	Aug	32	7	24	2	86	27	587	2487
La Coruña	43°22′N	08°25′W	58	July	28	7	21	—	135	28	937	2040
Madrid	40°25′N	03°41′W	660	July	36	13	22	-2	53	11	444	2843
Seville (Sevilla)	37°24′N	06°00′W	9	July	43	16	28	—	90	1	564	2909
YUGOSLAVIA												
Belgrade (Beograd) ..	44°48′N	20°28′E	132	Aug	36	12	23	-11	96	46	700	2112

Table A2.22 World Weather Data—*continued*

(c) Australasia

Station	Lat.	Long.	Height /(m)	Summer Month	Summer Dry-bulb /°C	Summer Average diurnal range /°C	Summer Screen wet-bulb /°C	Winter Dry-bulb /°C	Average monthly Wettest month	Average monthly Driest month	Annual	Average annual duration /(h)
AUSTRALIA												
Adelaide, S.A.	34°56′S	138°35′E	43	Jan	42	14	23	4	76	18	536	—
Albany, W.A...	35°02′S	117°50′E	12	Jan	32	8	22	—	152	25	1008	—
Brisbane, Q.	27°28′S	153°02′E	42	Jan	35	10	25	8	163	48	1135	—
Canberra, N.S.W.	35°20′S	149°15′E	559	Jan	36	15	21	—	56	41	584	—
Cloncurry, Q...	20°43′S	140°30′E	193	Jan	42	13	25	—	112	3	457	—
Condon, W.A.	20°00′S	119°20′E	11	Jan	41	11	31	—	76	<3	302	—
Hobart, Tasmania	42°53′S	147°20′E	54	Jan	33	10	20	—	61	38	610	—
Kalgoorlie, W.A.	30°45′S	121°30′E	380	Jan	42	16	23	—	30	10	246	—
Launceston, Tasmania ..	41°27′S	147°10′E	77	Feb	32	13	20	—	81	30	716	—
Melbourne, V.	37°49′S	144°58′E	35	Jan	39	12	23	3	66	46	653	—
Nullagine, W.A.	21°53′S	120°05′E	386	Jan	44	16	26	—	76	<3	335	—
Perth, W.A.	31°57′S	115°51′E	60	Jan	39	10	24	6	180	8	881	—
Port Darwin, N.T... ..	12°28′S	130°51′E	30	Nov	37	9	28	—	386	<3	1491	—
Sydney, N.S.W.	33°52′S	151°12′E	42	Jan	35	7	24	6	135	71	1181	—
Townsville, Q.	19°14′S	146°51′E	15	Feb	34	7	27	—	284	13	1160	—
PAPUA NEW GUINEA												
Port Moresby	09°29′S	147°09′E	38	Dec	34	8	28	21	193	18	1011	—
New Britain (Rabual) ..	04°13′S	152°15′E	12	Oct	35	11	29	—	376	84	2281	—
NEW ZEALAND												
Auckland	36°47′S	174°39′E	26	Jan	26	7	17	6	145	79	1247	—
Christchurch	43°32′S	172°37′E	10	Jan	30	9	20	-1	69	43	638	—
Dunedin	45°52′S	170°32′E	73	Jan	28	9	19	—	89	69	937	—
Wellington	41°16′S	174°46′E	126	Feb	26	7	19	3	137	81	1204	—
PACIFIC OCEAN												
Fiji Island (Suva)	18°08′S	178°26′E	6	Feb	33	7	27	—	368	124	2974	—
Gilbert Island (Tarawa) ..	01°21′S	172°56′E	3	Dec	33	5	28	—	318	58	1996	—
New Caledonia (Noumea)	22°16′S	166°27′E	9	Jan	34	18	27	—	145	51	1105	—

Table A2.22 World Weather Data—*continued*

(d) Africa

Station	Lat.	Long.	Height /(m)	Summer Month	Summer Dry-bulb /°C	Summer Average diurnal range /°C	Summer Screen wet-bulb /°C	Winter Dry-bulb /°C	Average monthly Wettest month	Average monthly Driest month	Annual	Average annual duration /(h)
ALGERIA												
Algiers	36°46′N	03°03′E	59	Aug	37	8	26	7	137	<3	762	—
Aoulef	27°04′N	00°44′E	275	July	48	16	26	—	5	<3	8	—
Coloumb Bechar	31°36′N	02°10′W	770	July	42	14	25	—	5	3	79	—
Oran	35°44′N	00°39′W	11	Aug	35	7	27	—	71	<3	376	—
Touggourt	33°07′N	06°04′E	69	July	47	17	28	—	13	<3	74	

(d) Africa—continued

Location				Design Temperatures					Precipitation/mm			Sunshine
				Summer				Winter	Average monthly			
Station	Lat.	Long.	Height /(m)	Month	Dry-bulb /°C	Average diurnal range /°C	Screen wet-bulb /°C	Dry-bulb /°C	Wettest month	Driest month	Annual	Average annual duration /(h)
ANGOLA												
Cabinda	05°33′S	12°11′E	30	Mar	33	8	28	—	117	<3	666	—
,,				May	31	—	27	—	—	—	—	—
Luanda	08°49′S	13°13′E	59	Mar	32	7	27	—	117	<3	323	—
Mocamedes	15°12′S	12°09′E	3	Apr	33	9	26	—	18	<3	53	—
Vila Luso	11°47′S	19°55′E	1320	Sept	33	13	22	—	231	<3	1138	—
,,				Feb	31	—	24	—	—	—	—	—
BOTSWANA												
Khanzi	21°30′S	21°45′E	1130	Jan	37	—	24	—	—	—	—	—
,,				Nov	38	17	23	—	104	<3	467	—
Maun	19°59′S	23°25′E	941	Oct	39	17	22	—	109	0	462	—
,,				Jan	37	—	25	—	—	—	—	—
CAMEROON REPUBLIC												
Douala	04°03′N	09°41′E	8	May	32	7	28	—	742	46	4026	—
CHAD REPUBLIC												
Faya (Largeau)	18°00′N	19°10′E	255	May	47	20	27	—	18	0	18	—
,, ,,				Aug	44	—	29	—	—	—	—	—
N'Djamena	12°07′N	15°02′E	294	Apr	44	18	23	—	320	0	744	—
,,				Aug	34	11	28	—	—	—	—	—
DJIBOUTI												
Djibouti	11°36′N	43°09′E	7	June	44	7	31	—	25	<3	130	—
EGYPT												
Alexandria	31°12′N	29°53′E	32	May	37	8	25	—	56	<3	178	—
Cairo/Helwan	29°52′N	31°20′E	116	June	41	15	22	8	5	0	28	—
Dakhla Oasis	25°29′N	29°00′E	122	June	45	18	25	—	<3	0	<3	—
Ismailia	30°37′N	32°15′E	12	June	42	16	24	—	8	<3	38	—
Luxor	25°39′N	32°39′E	78	May	47	19	25	—	<3	0	3	—
Port Said	31°16′N	32°19′E	4	Aug	34	8	26	—	18	0	76	—
Quseir	26°08′N	34°18′E	9	July	37	8	28	—	<3	0	<3	—
Suez/Port Tewfik	29°56′N	32°33′E	10	June	42	14	25	—	5	0	20	—
ETHIOPIA												
Addis Ababa	09°20′N	38°45′E	2445	May	28	15	19	5	300	5	1237	—
Asmara	15°17′N	38°55′E	2292	Apr	28	15	19	6	170	<3	467	—
THE GAMBIA												
Banjul/Yundum	13°21′N	16°40′W	27	Mar	39	17	23	—	500	<3	1295	—
,, ,,				Aug	32	8	27	—	—	—	—	—
GHANA												
Accra	05°33′N	40°12′W	27	Apr	33	7	26	21	178	15	724	—
Kumasi	06°40′N	01°37′W	287	Feb	35	12	27	—	201	20	1402	—
Takoradi	04°53′N	01°46′W	9	Jan	33	8	27	—	277	25	1181	—
Tamale	09°24′N	00°50′W	193	Mar	40	13	26	—	226	3	1041	—
,,				July	33	12	27	—	—	—	—	—
GUINEA-BISSAU												
Bolama	11°34′N	15°26′W	19	Apr	37	10	26	—	701	<3	2182	—

(d) Africa—*continued*

| Location | | | | Design Temperatures | | | | | Precipitation/mm | | | Sunshine |
| | | | | Summer | | | | Winter | Average monthly | | | |
Station	Lat.	Long.	Height /(m)	Month	Dry-bulb /°C	Average diurnal range /°C	Screen wet-bulb /°C	Dry-bulb /°C	Wettest month	Driest month	Annual	Average annual duration /(h)
IVORY COAST												
Abidjan	05° 19′N	04° 01′W	20	Mar	33	8	28	—	495	41	1958	—
KENYA												
Kisumu	00° 06′S	34° 45′E	1148	Jan	33	9	22	—	191	48	1140	—
Mombasa	04° 03′S	39° 39′E	16	Mar	33	6	26	—	320	18	1201	—
Nairobi/Kabeto	01° 16′S	36° 48′E	1819	Feb	28	13	19	10	211	15	958	—
Wajir	01° 45′S	40° 04′E	231	Mar	37	12	27	—	53	3	226	—
LIBERIA												
Monrovia	06° 18′N	10° 48′W	23	Apr	32	8	28	21	996	30	5138	—
LIBYA												
Benghazi	32° 06′N	20° 04′E	25	June	38	8	25	9	66	<3	267	—
El Adem	31° 51′N	23° 55′E	160	June	39	12	23	—	28	<3	102	—
Idris	32° 41′N	13° 10′E	80	July	46	18	27	—	76	<3	310	—
Jaghbub	29° 45′N	24° 31′E	15	June	45	17	25	—	3	0	8	—
Tripoli	32° 54′N	13° 11′E	22	June	39	8	27	—	94	<3	384	—
MADAGASCAR												
Diégo Suarez	12° 17′S	49° 17′E	30	Feb	34	8	29	—	269	5	983	—
Tananarive	18° 55′S	47° 33′E	1369	Nov	31	13	21	8	300	7	1356	—
MALI												
Gao	16° 16′N	00° 03′W	275	May	45	14	24	—	137	0	292	—
,,				Aug	38	9	28	—	—	—	—	
Kayes	14° 26′N	11° 26′W	30	Apr	46	16	25	—	241	0	757	—
,,				Sept	37	15	30	—	—	—	—	
MAURITANIA												
Nouadhibou	20° 56′N	17° 03′W	4	Sept	39	13	27	—	13	0	36	—
MALAWI												
Karonga	09° 57′S	33° 56′E	486	Nov	36	12	25	—	274	0	973	—
,,				Mar	32	9	26	—	—	—	—	
Zomba	15° 23′S	35° 19′E	956	Nov	34	11	25	—	307	5	1344	—
MOROCCO												
Casablanca	33° 35′N	07° 39′W	50	Aug	33	8	25	5	71	0	404	—
Ifrane	33° 31′N	05° 07′W	1633	July	35	18	20	—	163	8	1113	—
Ifni	29° 27′N	10° 11′W	45	Sept	33	6	25	—	46	<3	155	—
Tangier	35° 48′N	05° 49′W	73	Aug	33	8	24	—	147	<3	897	—
MOZAMBIQUE												
Beira	19° 50′S	34° 51′E	9	Nov	36	8	27	—	277	20	1521	—
Maputo	25° 58′S	32° 36′E	59	Dec	38	9	27	—	130	13	760	—
Mossuril	14° 57′S	40° 40′E	15	Dec	36	9	29	—	226	10	950	—
NAMIBIA												
Gobabis	22° 28′S	18° 58′E	1441	Dec	36	15	21	—	86	<3	358	—
Keetmanshoop	26° 35′S	18° 08′E	1002	Jan	39	17	20	—	36	<3	132	—
Tsumeb	19° 14′S	17° 43′E	1310	Oct	37	14	20	—	119	<3	521	—
,,				Feb	34	12	23	—	—	—	—	
Walvis Bay	22° 56′S	14° 30′E	7	May	36	12	24	—	8	<3	23	—
Windhoek	22° 34′S	17° 06′E	1728	Feb	33	12	19	—	79	<3	363	—

(d) Africa—*continued*

Location				Design Temperatures					Precipitation/mm			Sunshine
				Summer				Winter	Average monthly			
Station	Lat.	Long.	Height /(m)	Month	Dry-bulb /°C	Average diurnal range /°C	Screen wet-bulb /°C	Dry-bulb /°C	Wettest month	Driest month	Annual	Average annual duration /(h)
NIGERIA												
Calabar	04°58′N	08°19′E	12	Mar	34	9	28	—	455	43	3058	—
Enugu	06°27′N	07°29′E	232	Feb	36	9	25	—	325	13	1816	—
Ibadan	07°26′N	03°54′E	200	Mar	37	11	27	—	170	8	1120	—
Kaduna	10°35′N	07°26′E	643	Mar	38	13	21	—	302	<3	1273	—
,,				Aug	31	—	25	—	—	—	—	—
Kano	12°02′N	08°32′E	467	Apr	42	14	22	—	310	0	869	—
,,				Aug	33	8	26	—	—	—	—	—
Lagos	06°27′N	03°24′E	3	Mar	34	6	27	22	460	25	1836	—
Lokoja	07°48′N	06°44′E	97	Mar	38	11	28	—	236	5	1242	—
Maiduguri	11°51′N	13°05′E	354	Apr	43	18	22	—	221	0	643	—
,,				Aug	34	10	27	—	—	—	—	—
Port Harcourt	04°46′N	07°01′E	15	Feb	34	9	27	—	384	33	2497	—
Sokoto	13°01′N	05°16′E	350	Apr	44	16	24	—	244	0	691	—
,,				Aug	35	10	27	—	—	—	—	—
SENEGAL												
Dakar	14°42′N	17°29′W	40	Mar	37	9	23	17	254	<3	541	—
,,				Aug	34	8	28	—	—	—	—	—
SIERRA LEONE												
Freetown (Falconbridge)	08°30′N	13°14′W	11	Apr	33	6	27	—	927	5	3495	—
SOMALIA												
Bosaso	11°17′N	49°10′E	7	June	42	10	34	—	5	0	10	—
Berbera	10°26′N	45°02′E	14	June	44	12	32	—	13	<3	51	—
Hargeisa	09°29′N	44°05′E	1332	June	33	13	21	—	79	<3	389	—
Mogadishu	02°02′N	45°21′E	12	Apr	33	7	29	21	97	<3	429	—
S. AFRICAN REPUBLIC												
Capetown	33°54′S	18°32′E	17	Feb	34	11	23	6	89	8	508	—
Durban	29°50′S	31°02′E	5	Sept	32	13	22	—	130	28	1008	—
East London	33°02′S	27°50′E	125	Sept	33	9	22	—	97	36	808	—
Johannesburg/Germiston	26°14′S	28°09′E	1168	Jan	31	11	21	1	124	8	709	—
Kimberley	28°48′S	24°46′E	1198	Jan	37	15	22	—	79	5	409	—
Oudtshoorn	33°35′S	22°12′E	334	Jan	41	17	24	—	30	10	226	—
Port Elizabeth	33°59′S	25°36′E	58	Mar	34	9	24	—	61	30	577	—
Pretoria	25°45′S	28°14′E	1368	Dec	32	12	21	2	132	5	785	—
SPANISH SAHARA												
Villa Cisneros	23°42′N	15°52′W	11	Oct	35	8	24	—	36	0	76	—
SUDAN												
El Fasher	13°38′N	25°21′E	729	May	43	19	21	—	135	0	310	—
,,				Aug	39	13	25	—	—	—	—	—
El Obeid	13°11′N	30°14′E	574	Apr	42	17	22	—	122	0	368	—
,,				Aug	36	14	26	—	—	—	—	—
Juba	04°51′N	31°37′E	459	Feb	41	15	25	—	150	5	968	—
Khartoum	15°37′N	32°33′E	390	May	45	15	23	—	71	0	157	—
,,				Aug	41	13	27	—	—	—	—	—
Port Sudan	19°37′N	37°13′E	5	July	46	13	31	—	43	<3	94	—
Wadi Halfa	21°55′N	31°20′E	125	June	46	19	22	—	<3	0	<3	—

(d) Africa—*continued*

Location				Design Temperatures					Precipitation/mm			Sunshine
				Summer				Winter	Average monthly			
Station	Lat.	Long.	Height /(m)	Month	Dry-bulb /°C	Average diurnal range /°C	Screen wet-bulb /°C	Dry-bulb /°C	Wettest month	Driest month	Annual	Average annual duration /(h)
TANZANIA												
Chukwani (Zanzibar) ..	06°15′S	39°13′E	19	Feb	36	8	29	—	320	28	1410	—
Dar Es Salaam	06°50′S	39°18′E	14	Mar	33	7	28	18	290	25	1064	—
Lindi	10°00′S	39°42′E	8	Apr	33	8	28	—	173	5	897	—
Tabora	05°02′S	32°49′E	1264	Sept	33	12	20	—	173	0	889	—
,,				Dec	32	—	23	—	—	—	—	—
TUNISIA												
Gabes	33°53′N	10°07′E	2	Aug	39	11	28	—	30	<3	170	—
Tunis	36°47′N	10°12′E	66	Aug	42	12	27	5	64	3	419	—
UGANDA												
Entebbe	00°04′N	32°29′E	1180	Nov	29	8	23	—	257	66	1506	—
Kampala	00°20′N	32°36′E	1310	Feb	32	9	23	—	175	46	1173	—
Masindi	01°41′N	31°43′E	1144	Feb	35	13	24	—	150	28	1295	—
UPPER VOLTA												
Ouagadougou	12°22′N	01°31′W	302	Apr	44	13	28	—	277	0	894	—
,,				Aug	34	—	29	—	—	—	—	—
ZAIRE												
Albertville	05°54′S	29°12′E	759	Oct	32	11	27	—	213	<3	1153	—
Lubumbashi	11°39′S	27°28′E	1229	Oct	36	18	21	—	269	0	1237	—
,,				Dec	32	11	24	—	—	—	—	—
Kisangani	00°26′N	25°14′E	417	Feb	36	11	27	20	218	53	1704	—
Kinshasa	04°20′S	15°18′E	325	Apr	35	9	28	17	221	3	1354	—
ZAMBIA												
Kabwe	14°24′S	28°24′E	1139	Oct	36	14	21	—	269	0	940	—
Livingstone	17°50′S	25°49′E	962	Oct	38	15	22	—	152	0	673	—
,,				Jan	34	12	25	—	—	—	—	—
Lusaka	15°25′S	28°19′E	1276	Oct	35	13	20	—	231	0	836	—
,,				Jan	29	8	23	—	—	—	—	—
Ndola	12°59′S	28°37′E	1268	Oct	34	17	19	—	351	0	1293	—
,,				Jan	30	10	22	—	—	—	—	—
ZIMBABWE												
Bulawayo	20°09′S	28°37′E	1341	Oct	35	14	20	—	142	<3	594	—
,,				Dec	33	12	22	—	—	—	—	—
Salisbury	17°50′S	31°08′E	1470	Oct	32	11	18	—	180	<3	828	—
,,				Dec	30	—	22	—	—	—	—	—

Table A2.22 World Weather Data—*continued*

(e) Middle East*

Location				Design Temperatures					Precipitation/mm			Sunshine
				Summer				Winter	Average monthly			
Station	Lat.	Long.	Height /(m)	Month	Dry-bulb /°C	Average diurnal range /°C	Screen wet-bulb /°C	Dry-bulb /°C	Wettest month	Driest month	Annual	Average annual duration /(h)
BAHRAIN												
Manama	26°12′N	50°30′E	5	July	42	8	33	—	18	0	81	—
IRAN												
Isfahan	32°34′N	51°44′E	1771	July	39	17	21	—	25	<3	109	—
Meshed	36°17′N	59°36′E	946	July	37	16	21	−10	56	<3	221	—
Tehran	35°41′N	51°25′E	1220	July	40	15	27	−5	46	3	246	—
IRAQ												
Baghdad	33°20′N	44°24′E	34	Aug	47	19	24	2	28	<3	140	—
Basra	30°34′N	47°47′E	2	July	46	13	29	—	36	0	185	—
ISRAEL												
Eilat	29°33′N	34°57′E	2	Aug	44	12	26	—	8	0	28	—
Haifa	32°48′N	34°59′E	10	May	38	10	26	—	185	<3	663	—
,,				Aug	34	8	28	—	2	—	—	—
Jerusalem	31°47′N	35°13′E	757	June	36	14	21	3	132	0	528	—
JORDAN												
Amman	31°57′N	35°57′E	777	Aug	38	12	22	2	74	0	277	—
KUWAIT												
Kuwait City	29°21′N	48°00′E	5	Aug	45	10	31	—	28	0	130	—
LEBANON												
Beirut	33°54′N	35°28′E	34	Aug	33	8	26	7	191	<3	892	—
OMAN												
Masira Island	20°41′N	58°54′E	16	May	41	10	28	—	10	0	15	—
Muscat	23°37′N	58°35′E	5	June	43	6	34	—	28	0	99	—
Salalah	17°03′N	54°06′E	17	June	37	6	29	—	28	<3	81	—
SAUDI ARABIA												
Jidda	21°28′N	39°10′E	6	June	42	12	30	16	30	0	64	—
Riyadh	24°39′N	46°42′E	590	June	44	17	28	4	25	0	81	—
SYRIA												
Esh Sham (Damascus) ..	33°30′N	36°20′E	720	Aug	41	19	23	0	43	0	218	—
TURKEY												
Ankara	39°57′N	32°53′E	861	July	36	15	21	−11	48	10	345	—
Istanbul/Kandilli	41°06′N	29°03′E	114	Aug	34	9	24	−1	119	34	816	2395
Izmir (Smyrna)	38°27′N	27°15′E	28	Aug	38	13	24	−2	122	5	648	—
UNITED ARAB EMIRATES												
Sharjah	25°20′N	55°24′E	5	Aug	44	12	34	—	36	0	107	—
YEMEN P.D.R.												
Aden (Khormaksar) ..	12°50′N	45°01′E	7	June	39	8	29	21	5	<3	23	—
Socoma	12°38′N	53°53′E	43	May	38	8	29	—	81	0	193	

* See CIBSE Design Notes for the Middle East[33]

Table A2.22   World Weather Data—*continued*

(f)   The Americas and the West Indies

Location				Design Temperatures					Precipitation/mm			Sunshine
				Summer				Winter	Average monthly			
Station	Lat.	Long.	Height /(m)	Month	Dry-bulb /°C	Average diurnal range /°C	Screen wet-bulb /°C	Dry-bulb /°C	Wettest month	Driest month	Annual	Average annual duration /(h)
ALASKA												
Anchorage	61°10'N	149°59'W	28	July	25	9	17	−28	65	11	372	—
Barrow Point	71°18'N	156°47'W	7	July	17	7	11	−41	23	3	110	—
Fairbanks	64°19'N	147°52'W	133	July	29	12	19	−44	56	6	286	2233
ARGENTINA												
Bahia Blanca	30°43'S	62°16'W	29	Jan	39	14	24	—	64	23	523	—
Buenos Aires	34°35'S	58°29'W	27	Jan	36	12	26	1	109	56	950	—
Cordoba	31°22'S	64°15'W	422	Jan	40	15	26	0	122	8	716	—
Mendoza	32°53'S	68°49'W	800	Jan	39	17	25	—	31	5	191	—
Santa Cruz	50°01'S	68°32'W	12	Jan	32	12	18	—	18	8	135	—
BAHAMAS												
Nassau	25°05'N	77°21'W	4	Aug	33	7	28	17	175	33	1179	—
BARBADOS												
Bridgetown	13°08'N	59°36'W	55	Sept	32	7	27	—	206	28	1275	—
BELIZE												
Belize City	17°31'N	88°11'W	5	Oct	32	7	29	—	305	38	1890	—
BERMUDA												
Fort George	32°23'N	64°41'W	50	Aug	32	6	27	—	162	97	1423	2585
BOLIVIA												
Conception	16°15'S	62°03'W	490	Nov	36	17	27	—	206	15	1143	—
BRAZIL												
Belem (Para)	01°27'S	48°29'W	13	Nov	34	11	30	22	358	66	2438	—
Manaos	03°08'S	60°01'W	44	Oct	36	9	28	—	262	38	1811	—
Parana	12°26'S	48°06'W	260	Oct	37	20	28	—	310	<3	1582	—
Rio de Janeiro	22°55'S	43°12'W	61	Jan	35	6	26	16	137	41	1082	—
Santos	23°56'S	46°19'W	3	Jan	36	6	27	—	312	104	2238	—
CANADA												
Calgary	51°06'N	114°01'W	1079	July	32	14	20	−31	88	15	444	2156
Coppermine	67°49'N	115°05'W	9	July	25	8	17	—	44	8	234	1536
Edmonton	53°34'N	113°31'W	676	July	31	13	20	−32	82	20	460	2205
Goose	53°19'N	60°23'W	44	July	32	10	20	−31	91	56	836	1565
Hopedale	55°27'N	60°14'W	11	July	27	8	18	—	87	49	741	—
Inoucdjouac	58°27'N	78°08'W	20	July	21	8	14	−18	62	9	395	1333
Montreal	45°30'N	73°35'W	57	July	32	9	22	−23	98	76	1047	1859
Ottawa	45°24'N	75°43'W	79	July	33	12	22	−25	83	58	865	1989
Toronto	43°40'N	79°24'W	116	July	33	10	23	—	74	58	773	2024
Vancouver	49°11'N	123°10'W	5	July	28	10	20	−7	243	39	1529	1835
Winnipeg	49°54'N	97°14'W	240	July	34	13	23	−33	86	20	522	2192
CHILE												
Antofagasta	23°42'S	70°24'W	94	Jan	27	7	22	—	6	0	13	—
Santiago	33°27'S	70°42'W	520	Jan	33	18	21	2	84	3	358	—
Valparaiso	33°01'S	71°38'W	41	Feb	27	9	20	8	150	<3	506	—
COLOMBIA												
Bogota	04°36'N	74°05'W	2645	Mar	23	9	16	8	160	51	1059	—

(f) The Americas and the West Indies—*continued*

| Location | | | | Design Temperatures | | | | | Precipitation/mm | | | Sunshine |
| | | | | Summer | | | | Winter | Average monthly | | | |
Station	Lat.	Long.	Height /(m)	Month	Dry-bulb /°C	Average diurnal range /°C	Screen wet-bulb /°C	Dry-bulb /°C	Wettest month	Driest month	Annual	Average annual duration /(h)
CUBA												
Havana	23°08′N	82°21′W	24	Sept	33	7	27	17	173	46	1224	—
ECUADOR												
Quito	00°13′S	78°32′W	2879	Sept	27	16	17	4	175	20	1115	—
FALKLAND ISLANDS												
Stanley	51°42′S	57°51′W	2	Jan	20	8	14	—	71	38	681	—
GREENLAND												
Angmagssalik	65°37′N	37°38′W	29	July	17	8	12	—	91	39	771	—
Godhavn	69°15′N	53°31′W	8	July	16	6	12	—	60	12	389	—
Torgilsbu	60°32′N	43°11′W	24	Aug	19	5	12	—	239	71	1930	—
GUATEMALA												
Guatemala City	14°37′N	90°31′W	1480	May	31	13	23	11	274	3	1316	—
GUYANA												
Georgetown	06°50′N	58°12′W	2	Sep/Oct	32	6	26	23	302	76	2253	—
HAITI												
Port-au-Prince	18°33′N	72°20′W	37	July	37	11	25	19	231	33	1354	—
HAWAII												
Honolulu	21°20′N	157°55′W	2	Aug	30	6	24	17	97	8	557	—
JAMAICA												
Kingston	17°58′N	76°48′W	34	Aug	34	9	28	—	102	15	800	—
ST. KITTS/NEVIS/ANGUILLA												
La Guerite	17°20′N	62°45′W	48	Sept	31	6	27	—	185	51	1293	—
MEXICO												
Mexico City/Tacubaya ..	19°24′N	99°11′W	2309	Apr	31	18	17	4	160	4	709	2598
Veracruz..	19°12′N	96°08′W	16	Aug	33	7	30	17	430	10	1809	2119
PARAGUAY												
Ascuncion	25°17′S	57°30′W	139	Jan	40	13	29	8	158	38	1316	—
PERU												
Cusco	13°33′S	71°55′W	3225	Nov	26	17	15	—	163	5	813	—
Lima	12°05′S	77°03′W	120	Feb	31	9	25	13	8	<3	41	—
TRINIDAD												
Port of Spain	10°40′N	61°31′W	22	May	34	11	26	19	246	41	1631	—
URUGUAY												
Montevideo	34°52′S	56°12′W	22	Jan	33	12	23	4	99	66	950	—
U.S.A.												
Bismarck	46°46′N	100°45′W	502	July	38	15	25	−28	86	10	384	2760
Chicago	41°47′N	87°45′W	186	July	36	9	24	−20	103	41	843	2565
Dallas	32°51′N	96°51′W	147	Aug	40	11	28	−6	122	48	874	2910
Kansas City	39°17′N	94°43′W	309	July	39	12	27	−14	117	30	869	2839
Los Angeles	33°56′N	118°23′W	30	Sept	33	8	22	4	74	<1	327	3348

(f) The Americas and the West Indies—*continued*

| Location | | | | Design Temperatures | | | | | Precipitation/mm | | | Sunshine |
| Station | Lat. | Long. | Height /(m) | Summer | | | | Winter | Average monthly | | Annual | Average annual duration /(h) |
				Month	Dry-bulb /°C	Average diurnal range /°C	Screen wet-bulb /°C	Dry-bulb /°C	Wettest month	Driest month		
Miami, Florida	25°48′N	80°16′W	2	Aug	34	8	27	8	188	43	1518	2943
New Orleans	29°59′N	90°15′W	1	July	36	10	28	1	170	71	1363	2635
New York	40°42′N	74°01′W	3	July	34	8	24	−9	119	74	1100	2656
St. Louis	38°45′N	90°23′W	163	July	38	12	26	−14	109	51	900	2737
Salt Lake City	40°46′N	111°58′W	1286	July	38	15	22	−13	46	13	353	3073
San Francisco	37°37′N	122°23′W	2	Sept	33	11	22	3	104	<1	477	3037
Santa Fé	35°40′N	105°55′W	2195	July	33	15	20	−12	58	15	350	—
Seattle	47°32′N	122°18′W	4	July	32	11	22	−9	145	17	919	2044
Washington	38°54′N	77°03′W	22	July	36	10	26	−8	120	68	1080	—
VENEZUELA												
Calabozo	08°56′N	67°20′W	106	Apr	36	4	25	—	231	<3	1303	—
Maracaibo	10°39′N	71°36′W	6	Aug	37	9	29	23	150	<3	577	—
Santa Elena	04°36′N	61°07′W	858	Mar	33	13	25	—	252	51	1628	—
WINDWARD ISLANDS												
Roseau	15°18′N	61°23′W	18	Oct	34	9	28	—	274	61	1979	—

Table A2.22　World Weather Data—*continued*

(g)　Asia

| Location | | | | Design Temperatures | | | | | Precipitation/mm | | | Sunshine |
| Station | Lat. | Long. | Height /(m) | Summer | | | | Winter | Average monthly | | Annual | Average annual duration /(h) |
				Month	Dry-bulb /°C	Average diurnal range /°C	Screen wet-bulb /°C	Dry-bulb /°C	Wettest month	Driest month		
AFGHANISTAN												
Kabul	34°30′N	69°13′E	1815	July	37	17	21	−13	102	<3	338	—
BANGLADESH												
Chittagong	22°21′N	91°50′E	27	May	34	9	29	12	597	5	2731	—
Narayanganj	23°37′N	90°30′E	8	Mar	36	10	25	—	338	5	1877	—
,,				June	34	5	29	—	—	—	—	—
BURMA												
Akyab	20°08′N	92°55′E	9	Apr	35	8	29	—	1400	3	5154	—
Mandalay	21°59′N	96°06′E	77	Apr	42	13	27	13	160	3	828	—
,,				Oct	36	8	30					
Mengui	12°26′N	98°36′E	19	Apr	35	9	30		836	20	4122	—
Rangoon	16°46′N	96°11′E	5	Apr	39	12	31	17	582	3	2616	—
CHINA (PEOPLE'S REPUBLIC)												
Canton	23°06′N	113°18′E	9	Aug	36	7	28	—	269	36	1618	—
Hankow	30°35′N	114°17′E	37	July	37	8	29	—	244	28	1257	—
Shanghai	31°12′N	121°26′E	7	July	37	9	28	−3	135	13	693	—
Tientsin	39°10′N	117°10′E	4	July	38	9	28	—	188	3	533	—
Shenyang	41°48′N	123°23′E	43	June	36	13	23	—	183	8	709	—
,,				July	35	10	26	—	—	—	—	—

(g) Asia—*continued*

Location				Design Temperatures					Precipitation/mm			Sunshine
				Summer				Winter	Average monthly			
Station	Lat.	Long.	Height /(m)	Month	Dry-bulb /°C	Average diurnal range /°C	Screen wet-bulb /°C	Dry-bulb /°C	Wettest month	Driest month	Annual	Average annual duration /(h)
HONG KONG												
Hong Kong	22°18'N	114°10'E	33	July	33	5	28	10	394	30	2162	—
INDIA												
Allahabad	25°17'N	81°44'E	98	May	46	11	25	13	320	5	1062	—
„				July	38	7	30	—	—	—	—	—
Bangalore	12°57'N	77°37'E	927	Apr	37	13	23	14	170	5	869	—
Bombay	18°54'N	72°49'E	11	Oct	34	6	28	19	617	<3	1808	—
Calcutta	22°32'N	88°20'E	6	May	39	11	30	12	328	5	1600	—
Madras	13°04'N	80°15'E	16	May	42	11	34	19	356	8	1270	—
New Delhi	28°35'N	77°12'E	218	June	44	11	28	4	180	3	640	—
INDONESIA												
Balikpapan	01°17'S	116°51'E	7	Jan	32	7	27	—	231	132	2228	—
Djakarta	06°11'S	106°50'E	8	Oct	33	7	26	22	300	43	1793	—
Padang	00°56'S	100°22'E	7	Feb	33	7	26	—	518	152	4427	—
JAPAN												
Hiroshima	34°22'N	132°26'E	30	Aug	34	9	26	—	244	46	1527	—
Nagasaki	32°44'N	129°53'E	133	July	33	8	27	—	312	71	1918	—
Osaka	34°39'N	135°26'E	3	Aug	35	9	27	—	188	43	1336	—
Sapporo	43°04'N	141°21'E	17	Aug	32	10	24	-15	127	56	1044	—
Tokyo	35°41'N	139°46'E	6	Aug	33	8	26	-2	234	48	1565	—
KASHMIR												
Srinagar	34°05'N	74°50'E	1586	July	36	13	24	—	94	10	658	—
KOREA												
Seoul (Kyongsong) ..	37°34'N	126°58'E	87	Aug	35	9	26	-13	376	20	1250	—
MALAYSIA												
Kuala Lumpur	03°07'N	101°42'E	39	May	35	9	28	22	292	99	2441	—
Pinang	05°25'N	100°19'E	5	Mar	34	10	28	23	429	79	2736	—
PAKISTAN												
Karachi	24°48'N	66°59'E	4	May	39	8	30	11	81	<3	196	—
Lahore	31°35'N	74°20'E	214	June	46	13	26	3	140	3	503	—
„				Aug	40	11	30	—	—	—	—	—
Quetta	30°10'N	67°01'E	1673	July	38	17	23	—	51	<3	239	—
Hyderabad	25°23'N	68°24'E	29	May	43	16	28	—	76	<3	175	—
PHILIPPINES												
Manila	14°35'N	120°59'E	14	May	36	16	28	23	432	13	2023	—
SINGAPORE												
Singapore	01°18'N	103°50'E	10	May	33	8	28	22	257	170	2413	—
SRI LANKA												
Colombo	06°54'N	79°52'E	7	Feb	33	8	26	21	371	69	2365	—
„				May	32	5	28	—	—	—	—	—
Trincomalee	08°35'N	81°15'E	7	Sept	36	7/8	28	—	363	28	1648	—
THAILAND												
Bangkok	13°45'N	100°28'E	2	Apr	38	10	29	17	305	5	1397	—

(g) Asia—continued)

Location				Design Temperatures					Precipitation/mm			Sunshine
				Summer				Winter	Average monthly			
Station	Lat.	Long.	Height /(m)	Month	Dry-bulb /°C	Average diurnal range /°C	Screen wet-bulb /°C	Dry-bulb /°C	Wettest month	Driest month	Annual	Average annual duration /(h)
USSR												
Krasnoyarsk	56°01′N	92°52′E	152	June	32	6	18	−33	53	3	249	—
Omsk	54°58′N	73°20′E	85	July	32	10	21	—	51	8	318	—
Tashkent	41°20′N	69°18′E	478	July	38	16	24	−13	66	3	373	—
Vladivostok	43°07′N	131°55′E	29	July	29	6	22	−22	119	8	599	—
Moscow	55°45′N	37°34′E	156	July	29	8	20	−21	88	36	624	—
Leningrad	59°58′N	30°18′E	4	July	29	7	20	−21	78	30	603	1642
VIETNAM												
Hanoi	21°02′N	105°52′E	16	June	38	8	30	12	342	18	1682	—
Ho Chi Minh City	10°47′N	106°42′E	9	Apr	37	11	29	19	335	3	1984	—

SOLAR DATA

General

Solar data comprise the following:

(i) sun position—required when determining the overshadowing of buildings and the shading effect of canopies, etc.,

(ii) intensity* of the sun's rays—required when determining the availability of solar energy for utilisation purposes and for the calculation of solar gains in order to determine the temperatures in unconditioned buildings and cooling loads in air conditioned buildings.

Generalised data are given which are applicable to any part of the earth's surface and additional data are given in more detail for the UK. To avoid confusion, all times are quoted as Local Apparent Time (LAT), i.e. sun time, whether they apply world-wide or specifically to the UK. In the latter case, sun time can be approximated to GMT, see *Introduction*.

Sun Position

The angular position of the sun is specified by:

solar altitude *(h)*—measured above the horizon in a vertical plane through the sun

solar azimuth *(φ)*—the compass orientation of this plane, measured clockwise from the north.

These angles are given in Table A2.23 for a range of latitudes.

The direction in which a wall faces, known as the 'wall azimuth', γ, is specified by the compass orientation of a line perpendicular to the wall, measured clockwise from the north.

The horizontal angle between the sun and the wall, known as the 'wall-solar azimuth', γ_s, is specified by the angle between the perpendicular to the wall and a vertical plane through the sun. This angle is positive when measured clockwise from the perpendicular and negative when measured anticlockwise.

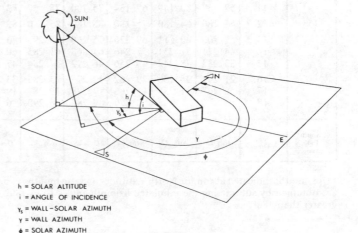

h = SOLAR ALTITUDE
i = ANGLE OF INCIDENCE
γ_s = WALL—SOLAR AZIMUTH
γ = WALL AZIMUTH
ϕ = SOLAR AZIMUTH

Fig. A2.19   Definition of Sun Angles.

---

*The term 'solar intensity' is used in Section A5 of the *Guide*. However, in this Section, the term is more closely defined, as follows.
Solar irradiance (W m⁻²) is used when referring to the rate at which solar energy is received on or transmitted through unit area of a building surface.
Solar irradiation (J m⁻²) is used when referring to the amount of solar energy received during a specified period of time.

Table A2.23 Solar altitude and azimuth angles.

North Latitude	Sun Time	Jan. 21		Feb. 21		Mar. 21		Apr. 22		May 22		June 21		July 23		Aug. 22		Sept. 22		Oct. 22		Nov. 22		Dec. 21		Sun Time
		Alt	Az	Alt	Az	Alt	Az	Alt	Az	Alt	Az	Alt	Az	Alt	Az	Alt	Az	Alt	Az	Alt	Az	Alt	Az	Alt	Az	
	06	0	110	0	101	0	90	0	78	0	70	0	67	0	70	0	78	0	90	0	101	0	110	0	113	06
	07	14	111	15	101	15	90	15	78	14	69	14	66	14	69	15	78	15	90	15	101	14	111	14	114	07
	08	28	113	29	102	30	90	29	76	28	67	27	63	28	67	29	76	30	90	29	102	28	113	27	117	08
	09	42	117	44	105	45	90	44	73	42	62	40	58	42	62	44	73	45	90	44	105	42	117	40	122	09
	10	54	126	58	111	60	90	58	67	54	53	53	49	54	53	58	67	60	90	58	111	54	126	53	131	10
	11	65	145	71	127	75	90	71	51	65	35	62	31	65	35	71	51	75	90	71	127	65	145	62	149	11
0°	12	70	180	79	180	90	0	78	0	70	0	67	0	70	0	78	0	90	0	79	180	70	180	67	180	12
	13	65	215	71	233	75	270	71	309	65	325	62	329	65	325	71	309	75	270	71	233	65	215	62	211	13
	14	54	234	58	249	60	270	58	293	54	307	53	311	54	307	58	293	60	270	58	249	54	234	53	229	14
	15	42	243	44	255	45	270	44	287	42	298	40	302	42	298	44	287	45	270	44	255	42	243	40	238	15
	16	28	247	29	258	30	270	29	284	28	293	27	297	28	293	29	284	30	270	29	258	28	247	27	243	16
	17	14	249	15	259	15	270	15	282	14	291	14	294	14	291	15	282	15	270	15	259	14	249	14	246	17
	18	0	250	0	259	0	270	0	282	0	290	0	293	0	290	0	282	0	270	0	259	0	250	0	247	18
	06					0	90	1	78	2	70	2	67	2	70	1	78	0	90							06
	07	12	112	14	103	15	91	16	79	16	70	16	67	16	70	16	79	15	91	14	103	12	112	12	115	07
	08	26	115	28	105	30	93	30	79	30	69	29	66	30	69	30	79	30	93	28	105	26	115	25	119	08
	09	39	121	42	110	45	95	45	78	44	66	43	62	44	66	45	78	45	95	42	110	39	121	38	125	09
	10	51	131	56	118	60	99	60	75	57	59	56	54	57	59	60	75	60	99	56	118	51	131	49	135	10
	11	61	150	68	137	74	108	74	64	69	42	67	37	69	42	74	64	74	108	68	137	61	150	58	153	11
5°	12	65	180	74	180	85	180	83	0	75	0	72	0	75	0	83	0	85	180	74	180	65	180	62	180	12
	13	61	210	68	223	74	252	74	296	69	318	67	323	69	318	74	296	74	252	68	223	61	210	58	207	13
	14	51	229	56	242	60	261	60	285	57	301	56	306	57	301	60	285	60	261	56	242	51	229	48	225	14
	15	39	239	42	250	45	265	45	282	44	294	43	298	44	294	45	282	45	265	42	250	39	239	38	235	15
	16	26	245	28	255	30	267	30	281	30	291	29	294	30	291	30	281	30	267	28	255	26	245	25	241	16
	17	12	248	14	257	15	269	16	281	16	290	16	293	16	290	16	281	15	269	14	257	12	248	12	245	17
	18					0	270	1	282	2	290	2	293	2	290	1	282	0	270							18
	06					0	90	2	78	3	70	4	67	3	70	2	78	0	90							06
	07	10	113	13	104	15	93	17	80	17	72	18	68	17	72	17	80	15	93	13	104	10	113	9	116	07
	08	24	117	27	108	30	96	31	82	31	72	31	68	31	72	31	82	30	96	27	108	24	117	22	121	08
	09	37	124	41	114	44	100	46	83	46	71	45	67	46	71	46	83	44	100	41	114	37	124	35	128	09
	10	48	136	54	124	59	107	61	83	59	67	58	61	59	67	61	83	59	107	54	124	48	136	45	139	10
	11	57	154	64	144	72	123	75	81	72	52	70	45	72	52	75	81	72	123	64	144	57	154	53	157	11
10°	12	60	180	69	180	80	180	88	0	80	0	77	0	80	0	88	0	80	180	69	180	60	180	57	180	12
	13	57	206	64	216	72	237	75	279	72	308	70	315	72	308	75	279	72	237	64	216	57	206	53	203	13
	14	48	224	54	236	59	253	61	277	59	293	58	299	59	293	61	277	59	253	54	236	48	224	45	221	14
	15	37	236	41	246	44	260	46	277	46	289	45	293	46	289	46	277	44	260	41	246	37	236	35	232	15
	16	24	243	27	252	30	264	31	278	31	288	31	292	31	288	31	278	30	264	27	252	24	243	22	239	16
	17	10	247	13	256	15	267	17	280	17	288	18	292	17	288	17	280	15	267	13	256	10	247	9	244	17
	18					0	270	2	282	3	290	4	293	3	290	2	282	0	270							18
	06					0	90	3	78	5	70	6	67	5	70	3	78	0	90							06
	07	8	113	11	105	15	94	17	82	19	73	19	70	19	73	17	82	15	94	11	105	8	113	7	117	07
	08	21	119	25	110	29	98	32	85	33	75	33	71	33	75	32	85	29	98	25	110	21	119	20	122	08
	09	33	127	38	118	43	104	46	88	47	76	47	71	47	76	46	88	43	104	38	118	33	127	32	130	09
	10	44	139	51	129	57	114	61	92	61	75	60	69	61	75	61	92	57	114	51	129	44	139	42	142	10
	11	52	157	60	149	69	134	75	100	75	67	73	57	75	67	75	100	69	134	60	149	52	157	49	159	11
15°	12	55	180	64	180	75	180	86	180	85	0	82	0	85	0	86	180	75	180	64	180	55	180	52	180	12
	13	52	203	60	211	69	226	75	260	75	293	73	303	75	293	75	260	69	226	60	211	52	203	49	201	13
	14	44	221	51	231	57	246	61	268	61	285	60	291	61	285	61	268	57	246	51	231	44	221	42	218	14
	15	33	233	38	242	43	256	46	272	47	284	47	289	47	284	46	272	43	256	38	242	33	233	32	230	15
	16	21	241	25	250	29	262	32	275	33	285	33	289	33	285	32	275	29	262	25	250	21	241	20	239	16
	17	8	247	11	255	15	266	17	278	19	287	19	290	19	287	17	278	15	266	11	255	8	247	7	243	17
	18					0	270	9	282	5	290	6	293	5	290	3	282	0	270							18
South* Latitude	Sun Time	July 23		Aug. 22		Sept. 22		Oct. 22		Nov. 22		Dec. 21		Jan. 21		Feb. 21		Mar. 21		Apr. 22		May 22		June 21		Sun Time

*Use months indicated at top for North Latitudes and use months at bottom for South Latitudes. Azimuth angles in the southern hemisphere are obtained by subtracting the tabulated azimuth angles from 180° when they are less than or equal to 180° or from 540° when they are greater than 180°.

Table A2.23—*continued*

North Latitude	Sun Time	Jan. 21 Alt	Az	Feb. 21 Alt	Az	Mar. 21 Alt	Az	Apr. 22 Alt	Az	May 22 Alt	Az	June 21 Alt	Az	July 23 Alt	Az	Aug. 22 Alt	Az	Sept. 22 Alt	Az	Oct. 22 Alt	Az	Nov. 22 Alt	Az	Dec. 21 Alt	Az	Sun Time
20°	06					0	90	4	79	7	71	8	68	7	71	4	79	0	90							06
	07	6	114	10	106	14	95	18	83	20	75	21	72	20	75	18	83	14	95	10	106	6	114	5	117	07
	08	19	121	23	112	28	101	32	88	34	78	35	75	34	78	32	88	28	101	23	112	19	121	17	124	08
	09	30	130	36	121	42	109	46	93	48	81	48	77	48	81	46	93	42	109	36	121	30	130	28	133	09
	10	40	142	47	134	54	121	60	101	62	84	62	77	62	84	60	101	54	121	47	134	40	142	38	145	10
	11	47	159	56	153	65	142	74	117	76	86	76	73	76	86	74	117	65	142	56	153	47	159	44	161	11
	12	50	180	59	180	70	180	82	180	90	0	86	0	90	0	82	180	70	180	59	180	50	180	47	180	12
	13	47	201	56	207	65	218	74	243	76	274	76	287	76	274	74	243	65	218	56	207	47	201	44	199	13
	14	40	218	47	226	54	239	60	259	62	276	62	283	62	276	60	259	54	239	47	226	40	218	38	215	14
	15	30	230	36	239	42	251	46	267	48	279	48	283	48	279	46	267	42	251	36	239	30	230	28	227	15
	16	19	239	23	248	28	259	32	272	34	282	35	285	34	282	32	272	28	259	23	248	19	239	17	236	16
	17	6	246	10	254	14	265	18	277	20	285	21	288	20	285	18	277	14	265	10	254	6	246	5	243	17
	18					0	270	4	281	7	289	8	292	7	289	4	281	0	270							18
25°	06					0	90	5	79	8	71	10	68	8	71	5	79	0	90							06
	07	4	114	9	106	14	96	18	85	22	77	22	74	22	77	18	85	14	96	9	106	4	114	3	118	07
	08	16	122	21	114	27	104	32	91	35	82	36	78	35	82	32	91	27	104	21	114	16	122	14	125	08
	09	27	132	33	124	40	113	46	98	48	87	49	82	48	87	46	98	40	113	33	124	27	132	25	134	09
	10	36	144	44	137	52	126	59	109	62	93	63	87	62	93	59	109	52	126	44	137	36	144	34	147	10
	11	43	161	51	156	61	148	71	130	75	105	76	83	75	105	71	130	61	148	51	156	43	161	39	162	11
	12	45	180	54	180	65	180	77	180	85	180	88	180	85	180	77	180	65	180	54	180	45	180	42	180	12
	13	43	199	51	204	61	212	71	230	75	255	76	267	75	255	71	230	61	212	51	204	43	199	39	198	13
	14	36	216	44	223	52	234	59	251	62	267	63	273	62	267	59	251	52	234	44	223	36	216	34	213	14
	15	27	228	33	236	40	247	46	262	48	273	49	278	48	273	46	262	40	247	33	236	27	228	25	226	15
	16	16	238	21	246	27	256	32	269	35	278	36	282	35	278	32	269	27	256	21	246	16	238	14	235	16
	17	4	246	9	254	14	264	18	275	22	283	22	286	22	283	18	275	14	264	9	254	4	246	3	242	17
	18					0	270	5	281	8	289	10	292	8	289	5	281	0	270							18
30°	06					0	90	6	80	10	72	12	69	10	72	6	80	0	90							06
	07	2	115	7	107	13	98	19	87	23	79	24	76	23	79	19	87	13	98	7	107	2	115	0	118	07
	08	14	123	19	116	26	106	32	94	36	85	37	82	36	85	32	94	26	106	19	116	14	123	11	126	08
	09	24	133	30	126	38	117	45	104	48	92	50	88	48	92	45	104	38	117	30	126	24	133	21	136	09
	10	32	146	40	140	49	131	57	116	61	102	62	96	61	102	57	116	49	131	40	140	32	146	29	148	10
	11	38	162	47	158	57	152	67	139	73	122	75	112	73	122	67	139	57	152	47	158	38	162	35	163	11
	12	40	180	49	180	60	180	72	180	80	180	84	180	80	180	72	180	60	180	49	180	40	180	37	180	12
	13	38	198	47	202	57	208	67	221	73	238	75	248	73	238	67	221	57	208	47	202	38	198	35	197	13
	14	32	214	40	220	49	229	57	244	61	258	62	264	61	258	57	244	49	229	40	220	32	214	29	212	14
	15	24	227	30	234	38	243	45	256	48	268	50	272	48	268	45	256	38	243	30	234	24	227	21	224	15
	16	14	237	19	244	26	254	32	266	36	275	37	278	36	275	32	266	26	254	19	244	14	237	11	234	16
	17	2	245	7	253	13	262	19	273	23	281	24	284	23	281	19	273	13	262	7	253	2	245	0	242	17
	18					0	270	6	280	10	288	12	291	10	288	6	280	0	270							18
35°	06					0	90	7	80	12	73	13	70	12	73	7	80	0	90							06
	07	0	115	6	108	12	99	19	88	24	81	25	78	24	81	19	88	12	99	6	108	0	115			07
	08	11	124	17	117	24	108	31	97	36	89	37	86	36	89	31	97	24	108	17	117	11	124	8	127	08
	09	20	135	27	128	35	120	43	108	48	98	49	94	48	98	43	108	35	120	27	128	20	135	18	137	09
	10	28	148	36	143	45	135	54	123	60	111	62	106	60	111	54	123	45	135	36	143	28	148	25	150	10
	11	33	163	42	160	52	155	63	146	70	134	73	128	70	134	63	146	52	155	42	160	33	163	30	164	11
	12	35	180	44	180	55	180	67	180	75	180	78	180	75	180	67	180	55	180	44	180	35	180	32	180	12
	13	33	197	42	200	52	205	63	214	70	226	73	232	70	226	63	214	52	205	42	200	33	197	30	196	13
	14	28	212	36	217	45	225	54	237	60	249	62	254	60	249	54	237	45	225	36	217	28	212	25	210	14
	15	20	225	27	232	35	240	43	252	48	262	49	266	48	262	43	252	35	240	27	232	20	225	18	223	15
	16	11	236	17	243	24	252	31	263	36	271	37	274	36	271	31	263	24	252	17	243	11	236	8	233	16
	17	0	245	6	252	12	261	19	272	24	279	25	282	24	279	19	272	12	261	6	252	0	245			17
	18					0	270	7	280	12	287	13	290	12	287	7	280	0	270							18
South* Latitude	Sun Time	July 23		Aug. 22		Sept. 22		Oct. 22		Nov. 22		Dec. 21		Jan. 21		Feb. 21		Mar. 21		Apr. 22		May 22		June 21		Sun Time

*Use months indicated at top for North Latitudes and use months at bottom for South Latitudes. Azimuth angles in the southern hemisphere are obtained by subtracting the tabulated azimuth angles from 180° when they are less than or equal to 180° or from 540° when they are greater than 180°.

Table A2.23—continued

North Latitude	Sun Time	Jan. 21 Alt	Az	Feb. 21 Alt	Az	Mar. 21 Alt	Az	Apr. 22 Alt	Az	May 22 Alt	Az	June 21 Alt	Az	July 23 Alt	Az	Aug. 22 Alt	Az	Sept. 22 Alt	Az	Oct. 22 Alt	Az	Nov. 22 Alt	Az	Dec. 21 Alt	Az	Sun Time
40°	06					0	90	8	81	13	74	15	72	13	74	8	81	0	90							06
	07			4	108	11	100	19	90	24	83	26	80	24	83	19	90	11	100	4	108					07
	08	8	125	15	118	22	110	31	100	36	92	37	89	36	92	31	100	22	110	15	118	8	125	6	127	08
	09	17	136	24	130	33	123	42	112	47	104	49	100	47	104	42	112	33	123	24	130	17	136	14	138	09
	10	24	149	32	145	42	138	52	128	58	118	60	114	58	118	52	128	42	138	32	145	24	149	21	151	10
	11	28	164	37	161	48	157	59	150	67	142	69	138	67	142	59	150	48	157	37	161	28	164	25	165	11
	12	30	180	39	180	50	180	62	180	70	180	74	180	70	180	62	180	50	180	39	180	30	180	27	180	12
	13	28	196	37	199	48	203	59	210	67	218	69	222	67	218	59	210	48	203	37	199	28	196	25	195	13
	14	24	211	32	215	42	222	52	232	58	242	60	246	58	242	52	232	42	222	32	215	24	211	21	209	14
	15	17	224	24	230	33	237	42	248	47	256	49	260	47	256	42	248	33	237	24	230	17	224	14	222	15
	16	8	235	15	242	22	250	31	260	36	268	37	271	36	268	31	260	22	250	15	242	8	235	6	233	16
	17			4	252	11	260	19	270	24	277	26	280	24	277	19	270	11	260	4	252					17
	18					0	270	8	279	13	286	15	288	13	286	8	279	0	270							18
45°	06					0	90	8	81	14	75	16	73	14	75	8	81	0	90							06
	07			3	108	10	101	19	92	25	85	27	83	25	85	19	92	10	101	3	108					07
	08	5	125	12	120	21	112	30	103	35	96	37	93	35	96	30	103	21	112	12	120	5	125	2	127	08
	09	13	137	21	132	30	125	40	116	46	108	48	105	46	108	40	116	30	125	21	132	13	137	10	139	09
	10	19	150	28	146	38	141	48	133	55	125	58	121	55	125	48	133	38	141	28	146	19	150	16	152	10
	11	24	165	32	162	43	159	55	154	62	148	65	146	62	148	55	154	43	159	32	162	24	165	20	165	11
	12	25	180	34	180	45	180	57	180	65	180	68	180	65	180	57	180	45	180	34	180	25	180	22	180	12
	13	24	195	32	198	43	201	55	206	62	212	65	214	62	212	55	206	43	201	32	198	24	195	20	195	13
	14	19	210	28	214	38	219	48	227	55	235	58	239	55	235	48	227	38	219	28	214	19	210	16	208	14
	15	13	223	21	228	30	235	40	244	46	252	48	255	46	252	40	244	30	235	21	228	13	223	10	221	15
	16	5	235	12	240	21	248	30	257	35	264	37	267	35	264	30	257	21	248	12	240	5	235	2	233	16
	17			3	252	10	259	19	268	25	275	27	277	25	275	19	268	10	259	3	252					17
	18					0	270	8	279	14	285	16	287	14	285	8	279	0	270							18
50°	06					0	90	9	82	16	76	18	74	16	76	9	82	0	90							06
	07			1	108	10	102	19	94	25	88	27	85	25	88	19	94	10	102	1	108					07
	08	2	126	10	120	19	114	28	106	35	99	37	97	35	99	28	106	19	114	10	120	2	126			08
	09	10	138	18	133	27	128	37	120	44	113	46	110	44	113	37	120	27	128	18	133	10	138	6	139	09
	10	15	151	24	148	34	143	45	136	52	130	55	128	52	130	45	136	34	143	24	148	15	151	12	152	10
	11	19	165	28	163	38	161	50	157	58	153	61	151	58	153	50	157	38	161	28	163	19	165	15	166	11
	12	20	180	29	180	40	180	52	180	60	180	64	180	60	180	52	180	40	180	29	180	20	180	17	180	12
	13	19	195	28	197	38	199	50	203	58	207	61	209	58	207	50	203	38	199	28	197	19	195	15	194	13
	14	15	209	24	212	34	217	45	224	52	230	55	232	52	230	45	224	34	217	24	212	15	209	12	208	14
	15	10	222	18	227	27	232	37	240	44	247	46	250	44	247	37	240	27	232	18	227	10	222	6	221	15
	16	2	234	10	240	19	246	28	254	35	261	37	263	35	261	28	254	19	246	10	240	2	234			16
	17			1	252	10	258	19	266	25	272	27	275	25	272	19	266	10	258	1	252					17
	18					0	270	9	278	16	284	18	286	16	284	9	278	0	270							18
55°	06					0	90	10	83	17	78	19	76	17	78	10	83	0	90							06
	07					8	102	18	95	25	90	28	88	25	90	18	95	9	103							07
	08			7	121	17	115	27	108	34	103	36	100	34	103	27	108	18	115	7	121					08
	09	6	138	14	134	24	129	34	123	42	117	44	115	42	117	34	123	24	129	14	134	6	138	3	140	09
	10	11	151	20	149	30	145	41	140	49	135	51	133	49	135	41	140	30	145	20	149	11	151	8	152	10
	11	14	166	23	164	34	162	45	159	54	156	56	154	54	156	45	159	34	162	23	164	14	166	10	166	11
	12	15	180	24	180	35	180	47	180	55	180	58	180	55	180	47	180	35	180	24	180	15	180	12	180	12
	13	14	194	23	196	34	198	45	201	54	204	56	206	54	204	45	201	34	198	23	196	14	194	10	194	13
	14	11	209	20	211	30	215	41	220	49	225	51	227	49	225	41	220	30	215	20	211	11	209	8	208	14
	15	6	222	14	226	24	231	34	237	42	243	44	245	42	243	34	237	24	231	14	226	6	222	3	220	15
	16			7	239	17	245	27	252	34	257	36	260	34	257	27	252	18	245	7	239					16
	17					8	258	18	265	25	270	28	272	25	270	18	265	9	257							17
	18					0	270	10	277	17	282	19	284	17	282	10	277	0	270							18

South* Latitude	Sun Time	July 23		Aug. 22		Sept. 22		Oct. 22		Nov. 22		Dec. 21		Jan. 21		Feb. 21		Mar. 21		Apr. 22		May 22		June 21		Sun Time

*Use months indicated at top for North Latitudes and use months at bottom for South Latitudes. Azimuth angles in the southern hemisphere are obtained by subtracting the tabulated azimuth angles from 180° when they are less than or equal to 180° or from 540° when they are greater than 180°.

The angle of incidence on a building surface, i, is specified by the angle between the sun's direction and the perpendicular to the surface. For a horizontal surface, it is equal to the complement of the solar altitude, that is:

$$i = 90 - h \qquad \qquad \qquad \text{A2.9}$$

where:

i = angle of incidence .. .. degree
h = solar altitude .. .. degree

For a vertical surface, the angle of incidence is given by:

$$\cos i = \cos h \cos \gamma_s \qquad \qquad \text{A2.10}$$

where:

γ_s = wall-solar azimuth .. .. .. degree

For surfaces of intermediate inclination, e.g. sloping roofs, a more complex relationship exists[34].

When finding the shading effect of vertical fins and louvers, the horizontal shadow angle, σ_H, is required and is specified by the wall-solar azimuth. When finding the shading effect of horizontal fins, louvers and canopies, the vertical shadow angle, σ_V, is required. This is specified by the angle between two planes through the line of the shading device, one horizontal and the other through the sun. It is given by:

$$\tan \sigma_V = \tan h \sec \gamma_s \qquad \qquad \text{A2.11}$$

where:

σ_V = vertical shadow angle .. .. .. degree

Sunpath diagram

Fig. A2.20 shows solar altitude and azimuth data presented in an alternative form. The diagram[35,36] represents a plan of the hemispherical sky vault in stereographic projection with the zenith at the centre and the horizon around the circumference. Concentric circles and radial lines form a co-ordinate grid with the circles representing contours of equal solar altitude, the lines representing solar azimuths and with the vertical and horizontal diameters corresponding to the N-S and E-W lines respectively. Fig. A2.20 has been drawn for a latitude of 51.7 °N, but may be used with relatively little error for buildings anywhere in southern England.

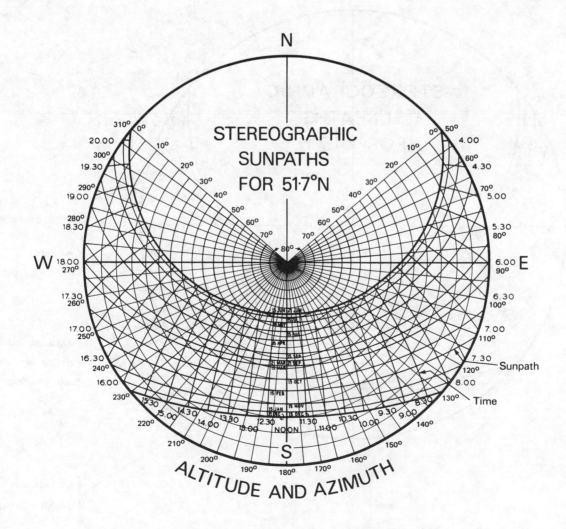

Fig. A2.20 Sunpath diagram for latitude 51.7 °N.

Arcs of circles superimposed on the grid represent the sun's path across the sky for different periods of the year. Corresponding times on the different sunpaths are joined by other arcs of circles. The sun's position at any time of the day and period of the year can be read off in terms of solar altitude and azimuth against the co-ordinates of the grid.

If the outline of a window is superimposed on the sunpath diagram, the angular positions of its edges in relation to an indoor position having been identified on the co-ordinate grid, then the times when it is possible for the sun to reach the indoor position can be read off. For example, in Fig. A2.21 the outline of a rectangular window facing SE has been superimposed and shows that the sun can reach the indoor position between mid-January and mid-April and between the end of August and the end of November, having a maximum possible duration of two hours at the end of February and in mid-October.

Alternatively, the sunpath diagram can be used in conjunction with a series of overlays[35, 36] enabling, by appropriate superimposition, shadow angles, hourly irradiances of direct and diffuse solar radiation, and glass and blind solar performance characteristics to be determined.

INTENSITY OF SOLAR RADIATION

General

Solar radiation perpendicular to the sun's rays at the top of the earth's atmosphere has an annual mean irradiance[37] (the 'solar constant') of approximately 1370 W/m² and is subject to a seasonal variation of about ±3.5 W/m², being highest in early January and lowest in early July. In passing through the atmosphere, part of this extra-terrestrial energy is absorbed by the atmosphere, part is scattered by the atmosphere—some back into space and some to the earth (the latter termed 'diffuse (sky) radiation')—and the remainder (termed 'direct radiation') is transmitted through the atmosphere unchanged.

For cloudless skies, the irradiances of direct and diffuse radiation at the earth's surface depend on the absorption and scattering due to atmospheric constituents such as water vapour, dust, and ozone, and also on the solar altitude and on height above sea level, which determine the depth of the layer of atmosphere in which the absorption and scattering processes take place. For cloudy and overcast skies, a further, and generally overriding, factor determining terrestrial direct and diffuse irradiances is the absorption and scattering produced by cloud cover, these varying with the nature and extent of this cover.

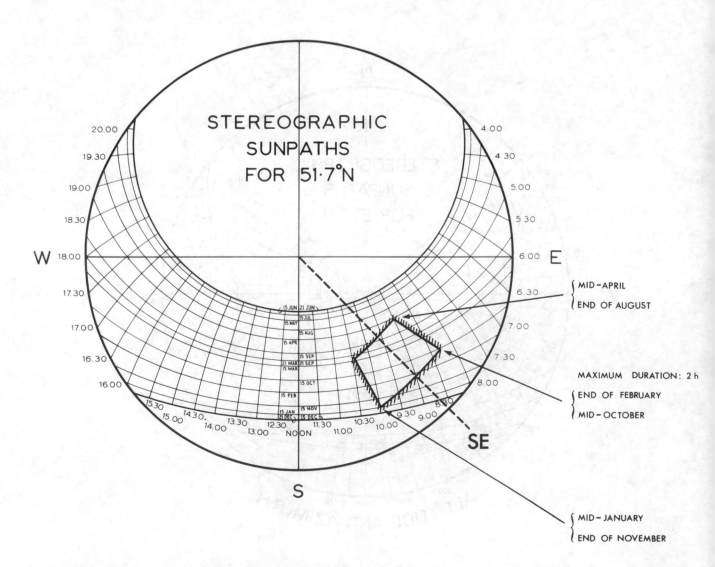

Fig. A2.21 Outline of window superimposed on sunpath diagram.

Basic Radiation Data

To simulate solar irradiances at the earth's surface, basic radiation data are proposed related only to solar altitude and applicable irrespective of latitude or local climate. By applying relationships based on solar geometry, these data can be converted to basic irradiances on specific surfaces at particular latitudes and, by applying radiation correction factors, can be further converted to design irradiances appropriate to the radiation climates at particular localities.

Table A2.24 gives, for specified solar altitudes, basic direct irradiances on surfaces normal to the sun's rays, I_{DN}, and on horizontal surfaces, I_{DH}, calculated from the widely-accepted empirical relationship proposed by Moon.[38] The table also gives basic direct irradiances on vertical surfaces, I_{DV}, for a range of values of wall-solar azimuth.

Basic direct irradiances apply to a particular clear sky condition. It is shown later *(Design Radiation Data)* how design direct irradiances for other types of clear sky, and also for cloudy skies, can be obtained from the basic direct irradiances by applying direct radiation factors, k_D, of appropriate magnitude.

Basic diffuse (sky) irradiances on a horizontal surface, I_{dH}, for various solar altitudes are given in Table A2.25. These values have been derived for both clear and cloudy skies from empirical relationships proposed by Loudon[39].

Basic diffuse (sky) irradiances apply to particular clear and cloudy sky conditions. It is shown later *(Design Radiation Data)* how diffuse irradiances for other types of clear and cloudy sky can be obtained from the basic diffuse irradiances by applying diffuse factors, k_d, of appropriate magnitude.

Table A2.25 Basic diffuse (sky) irradiance on horizontal surface, I_{dH}, for places between 0 and 300 m above sea level.

Solar altitude /(degrees)	Basic diffuse (sky) irradiance/(W/m²)	
	Clear	Cloudy
5	25	25
10	40	50
15	55	75
20	65	100
25	70	125
30	75	150
35	80	175
40	85	200
45	90	225
50	95	250
60	100	300
70	105	355
80	110	405
90	115	455

Note: Guidance on the choice between clear and cloudy sky irradiances is given in *Design Radiation Data*.

For a particular latitude, date and time of day, the solar altitude and the angle of incidence onto a surface of given slope and orientation are uniquely determined. This means that the associated direct and diffuse (sky) irradiances onto this surface can be found.

For any particular latitude, a table may be compiled giving, for specified surfaces, hourly and daily mean direct and diffuse (sky) irradiances. Table A2.26 provides these data for southern England (approximate latitude 51½ °N). Similar data for other latitudes are given in Table A2.35.

Table A2.24 Basic direct solar irradiances on normal, horizontal and vertical surfaces for places between 0 and 300 m above sea level with a clear sky.

Solar altitude (degrees)	Basic direct irradiance/(W/m²)																
	Normal to sun I_{DN}	Horizontal surface I_{DH}	Vertical surface, I_{DV}, for stated wall-solar azimuth													
			0	10	20	30	40	45	50	55	60	65	70	75	80
5	210	20	210	205	195	180	160	150	135	120	105	90	70	55	35
10	390	65	380	375	360	330	295	270	245	220	190	160	130	100	65
15	525	135	505	500	475	440	390	360	325	290	255	215	175	130	90
20	620	215	585	575	550	505	450	415	375	335	290	245	200	150	100
25	690	290	625	615	585	540	480	440	400	360	310	265	215	160	110
30	740	370	640	630	605	555	490	455	410	370	320	270	220	165	110
35	780	450	640	630	600	555	490	455	410	365	320	270	220	165	110
40	815	525	625	615	585	540	480	440	400	360	310	265	215	160	110
45	840	595	595	585	560	515	455	420	380	340	295	250	205	155	105
50	860	660	555	545	520	480	425	390	355	315	275	235	190	145	95
60	895	775	445	440	420	385	340	315	285	255	225	190	155	115	80
70	910	855	310	305	295	270	240	220	200	180	155	130	105	80	55
80	920	905	160	160	150	140	125	115	105	90	80	70	55	40	30
90	930	930	0	0	0	0	0	0	0	0	0	0	0	0	0

Table A2.26 Basic direct solar irradiances (W/m²) on vertical, I_{DV}, and horizontal, I_{DH}, surfaces and basic diffuse (cloudy and clear sky) solar irradiances (W/m²) on horizontal surface, I_{dH}, for southern England.

Date	Orien-tation	Daily mean	___ Sun Time ___																
			04	05	06	07	08	09	10	11	12	13	14	15	16	17	18	19	20
June 21	N	35	40	160	145	45	0	0	0	0	0	0	0	0	0	45	145	160	40
	NE	85	70	350	485	480	380	230	50	0	0	0	0	0	0	0	0	0	0
	E	140	55	330	540	635	630	545	400	210	0	0	0	0	0	0	0	0	0
	SE	135	10	120	280	415	510	540	515	435	300	135	0	0	0	0	0	0	0
	S	105	0	0	0	0	90	220	330	400	425	400	330	220	90	0	0	0	0
	SW	135	0	0	0	0	0	0	0	135	300	435	515	540	510	415	280	120	10
	W	140	0	0	0	0	0	0	0	0	0	210	400	545	630	635	540	330	55
	NW	85	0	0	0	0	0	0	0	0	0	0	50	230	380	480	485	350	70
	H	295	0	60	185	330	475	600	700	770	790	770	700	600	475	330	185	60	0
Diff (cldy)		120	10	50	90	140	185	230	270	300	310	300	270	230	185	140	90	50	10
Diff (clr)		50	5	40	60	75	85	90	100	100	100	100	100	90	85	75	60	40	5
July 23 and May 22	N	20		115	115	15	0	0	0	0	0	0	0	0	0	0	15	115	115	
	NE	75		265	445	455	360	210	30	0	0	0	0	0	0	0	0	0	
	E	135		260	510	625	630	550	405	215	0	0	0	0	0	0	0	0	
	SE	140		100	280	430	530	570	545	460	330	160	0	0	0	0	0	0	
	S	115		0	0	0	120	255	365	440	465	440	365	255	120	0	0	0	
	SW	140		0	0	0	0	0	0	160	330	460	545	570	530	430	280	100	
	W	135		0	0	0	0	0	0	0	0	215	405	550	630	625	510	260	
	NW	75		0	0	0	0	0	0	0	0	0	30	210	360	455	445	265	
	H	270		35	150	290	435	565	670	735	760	735	670	565	435	290	150	35	
Diff (cldy)		110		35	80	125	170	215	255	285	295	285	255	215	170	125	80	35	
Diff (clr)		45		30	55	70	80	90	95	100	100	100	95	90	80	70	55	30	
August 22 and April 22	N	5		5	50	0	0	0	0	0	0	0	0	0	0	0	50	5	
	NE	45		15	290	370	300	155	0	0	0	0	0	0	0	0	0	0	
	E	115		15	360	565	610	545	410	215	0	0	0	0	0	0	0	0	
	SE	150		5	220	430	560	620	605	525	390	220	30	0	0	0	0	0	
	S	150		0	0	40	185	330	445	525	550	525	445	330	185	40	0	0	
	SW	150		0	0	0	0	0	30	220	390	525	605	620	560	430	220	5	
	W	115		0	0	0	0	0	0	0	0	215	410	545	610	565	360	15	
	NW	45		0	0	0	0	0	0	0	0	0	0	155	300	370	290	15	
	H	215		0	60	190	335	470	575	640	665	640	575	470	335	190	60	0	
Diff (cldy)		90		0	45	95	140	185	220	245	255	245	220	185	140	95	45	0	
Diff (clr)		40		0	40	60	75	80	90	95	95	95	90	80	75	60	40	0	
Sept. 22 and March 21	N	0			0	0	0	0	0	0	0	0	0	0	0	0			
	NE	20			0	195	195	75	0	0	0	0	0	0	0	0			
	E	80			0	350	510	495	380	205	0	0	0	0	0	0			
	SE	145			0	300	525	625	635	570	445	280	95	0	0	0			
	S	175			0	75	230	390	520	600	630	600	520	390	230	75	0		
	SW	145			0	0	0	0	95	280	445	570	635	625	525	300	0		
	W	80			0	0	0	0	0	0	0	205	380	495	510	350	0		
	NW	20			0	0	0	0	0	0	0	0	0	75	195	195	0		
	H	140			0	60	180	305	410	475	500	475	410	305	180	60	0		
Diff (cldy)		60			0	45	90	130	165	185	195	185	165	130	90	45	0		
Diff (clr)		30			0	40	60	70	80	85	85	85	80	70	60	40	0		
October 22 and Feb. 21	N	5				0	0	0	0	0	0	0	0	0	0	0			
	NE	5				10	90	15	0	0	0	0	0	0	0	0			
	E	50				25	305	385	320	180	0	0	0	0	0	0			
	SE	120				25	345	535	590	555	450	300	135	0	0	0			
	S	165				10	180	370	515	605	635	605	515	370	180	10			
	SW	120				0	0	0	135	300	450	555	590	535	345	25			
	W	50				0	0	0	0	0	0	180	320	385	305	25			
	NW	5				0	0	0	0	0	0	0	0	15	90	10			
	H	80				0	55	160	250	310	330	310	250	160	55	0			
Diff (cldy)		35				5	45	85	110	130	140	130	110	85	45	5			
Diff (clr)		20				5	35	55	65	70	75	70	65	55	35	5			
Nov. 22 and January 21	N	0					0	0	0	0	0	0	0	0	0				
	NE	0					10	0	0	0	0	0	0	0	0				
	E	25					45	220	230	140	0	0	0	0	0				
	SE	90					55	325	460	470	395	275	135	15	0				
	S	125					30	240	420	525	560	525	420	240	30				
	SW	90					0	15	135	275	395	470	460	325	55				
	W	25					0	0	0	0	0	140	230	220	45				
	NW	0					0	0	0	0	0	0	0	0	10				
	H	35					0	45	115	165	185	165	115	45	0				
Diff (cldy)		20					5	40	70	85	90	85	70	40	5				
Diff (clr)		15					5	35	50	55	60	55	50	35	5				
Dec. 21	N	0						0	0	0	0	0	0	0					
	NE	0						0	0	0	0	0	0	0					
	E	20						140	185	115	0	0	0	0					
	SE	70						215	375	410	355	245	115	15					
	S	100						165	350	465	505	465	350	165					
	SW	70						15	115	245	355	410	375	215					
	W	20						0	0	0	0	115	185	140					
	NW	0						0	0	0	0	0	0	0					
	H	25						20	70	115	135	115	70	20					
Diff (cldy)		15						25	55	70	75	70	55	25					
Diff (clr)		10						20	40	50	50	50	40	20					

Note: Direct radiation factor $(k_D) = 1.0$ Diffuse radiation factor $(k_d) = 1.0$ Height correction factor $(k_a) = 1.0$

Design Radiation Data

For a particular locality, the basic irradiances, whether from Tables A2.24 and A2.25 or, for a given latitude, from Tables A2.26 or A2.35, must be corrected to give design irradiances appropriate to the prevailing radiation climate. This is done by applying a height correction factor and direct and diffuse radiation factors, as follows:

Design direct irradiance is given by;

$$I_{Dd} = k_a k_D I_D \qquad .. \qquad .. \qquad .. \qquad .. \qquad .. \qquad A2.12$$

where:

I_{Dd} = design direct irradiance .. .. .. W/m²
k_a = height correction factor
k_D = direct radiation factor
I_D = basic direct irradiance .. .. .. W/m²
   (Tables A2.24, A2.26 or A2.35)

Design diffuse (sky) irradiance is given by;

$$I_{dd} = k_a k_d I_d \qquad .. \qquad .. \qquad .. \qquad .. \qquad .. \qquad A2.13$$

where:

I_{dd} = design diffuse (sky) irradiance .. .. W/m²
k_d = diffuse radiation factor
I_d = basic diffuse (sky) irradiance .. .. W/m²
   (Tables A2.25, A2.26 or A2.35)

The height correction factor depends on solar altitude and the height of the locality above sea level.[40] Values are given in Fig. A2.22. For heights between 0 and 300 m, a height correction factor of unity may be assumed, irrespective of solar altitude.

Direct and diffuse radiation factors depend on sky clarity and cloud cover at the locality in question, as determined by the weather conditions for which the design irradiances are required. Two methods for their derivation are available, as shown below.

(i) 'Augmented direct/uniform background diffuse' simulation[39]:

For clear skies:

$$k_D = \frac{\text{(Measured total rad.-Basic diffuse (clear sky) rad.)}}{\text{Basic direct radiation}}$$

k_d = 1.0 (applied to basic diffuse (clear sky) radiation)

For cloudy skies:

$$k_D = \frac{\text{(Measured total rad.-Basic diffuse (cloudy sky) rad.)}}{\text{Basic direct radiation}}$$

k_d = 1.0 (applied to basic diffuse (cloudy sky) radiation)

(ii) 'One-to-one' simulation (clear and cloudy skies):

$$k_D = \frac{\text{Measured direct radiation}}{\text{Basic direct radiation}}$$

$$k_d = \frac{\text{Measured diffuse (sky) radiation}}{\text{Basic diffuse (cloudy sky) radiation}}$$

(applied to basic diffuse (cloudy sky) radjation)

In both of these methods, the radiation measure is the daily irradiation or 24-hour mean irradiance on a horizontal surface (i.e. excluding ground-reflected radiation).

For clear skies, simulation *(i)* gives the best agreement with measurements. However, for other types of sky, simulation *(ii)* gives good general agreement and has been used throughout this Section, both for *Design Monthly 'Maximum' Irradiances* and for the irradiances contained in *Banded Weather Data*.

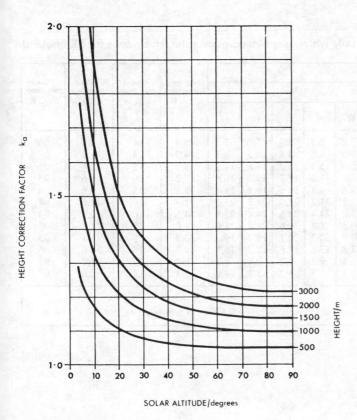

Fig. A2.22. Variation of height correction factor, k_a, with solar altitude and height above sea level.

As an example of the derivation of k_D and k_d, the noon values of the total and diffuse (sky) irradiances on a horizontal surface for a June day of near maximum irradiance in SE England (Table A2.27) are 850 W/m² (H) and 205 W/m² (Diff), respectively. Hence, derived direct irradiance is equal to:

$$(850 - 205) = 645 \text{ W/m}^2$$

The corresponding noon values of the basic direct and diffuse (cloudy sky) irradiances for this surface, date and locality are, from Table A2.26, 790 W/m² and 310 W/m², respectively.

Therefore;

$$k_D = 645/790 = 0.82$$

$$k_d = 205/310 = 0.66$$

The following sections give direct and diffuse radiation factors for various design criteria. The calculation of design total irradiances (direct plus diffuse) is dealt with in *Design Total Irradiances*.

Design Monthly 'Maximum' Irradiances

For some design purposes it is required to know the hourly and daily mean irradiances which, month by month, are the near-maxima that are likely to occur. Such values are given in Table A2.27, the criterion being

that, within each month, the irradiances are likely to be exceeded on 2½% of occasions (e.g. on approximately eight March days in a ten-year period).

The design irradiances in this table are based on horizontal surface radiation measurements at Kew (1959-68), for which locality a height correction factor of unity has been assumed, and can be regarded as being generally applicable to SE England. The values of the direct and diffuse radiation factors (k_D and k_d) used in their derivation from the basic irradiances of Table A2.26 are given in the left-hand column of the table, cloudy sky conditions being assumed for the basic diffuse (sky) irradiances.

For the period 06 GMT to 18 GMT, hourly values of dry-bulb temperature occurring coincidentally month-by-month with the design maximum irradiances are given in Table A2.28. The table also includes data whereby the hourly values can be simulated by the procedure described in *Banded Weather Data*.

For the months March to October, hourly and daily values of the coincident dry-bulb temperature are also given in the second column of Table A2.33.

For vertical surfaces facing N, E, S and W and for a horizontal surface, the diurnal variation of solar irradiance at different times of the year is illustrated in Fig. A2.23.

Table A2.28 Dry-bulb temperatures occurring coincidentally with design 'maximum' solar irradiances for SE England.

Month	Hourly dry-bulb temperature/°C Sun time													Daily max. temperature t_{max}/°C	Time of max. temp. θ_{max}/h	Daily min. temperature t_{min}/°C	Time of min. temp. θ_{min}/h
	06	07	08	09	10	11	12	13	14	15	16	17	18				
January	2.0	2.2	2.6	3.2	4.0	4.7	5.3	5.8	5.9	5.9	5.8	5.6	5.3	5.9	14	2.0	06
February	2.3	2.3	2.6	3.5	4.9	6.4	7.7	8.7	9.0	8.9	8.8	8.5	8.1	9.0	14	2.3	07
March	4.8	5.1	6.0	7.4	9.1	11.0	12.7	14.1	15.0	15.3	15.2	14.8	14.3	15.3	15	4.8	06
April	6.9	7.5	8.5	9.7	11.2	12.7	14.1	15.4	16.4	17.0	17.2	17.1	16.6	17.2	16	6.6	05
May	9.5	10.5	11.9	13.4	15.0	16.5	17.9	18.9	19.6	19.8	19.6	19.1	18.4	19.8	15	8.6	04
June	11.8	12.6	13.8	15.1	16.5	17.9	19.2	20.3	21.2	21.7	21.9	21.7	21.2	21.9	16	11.0	04
July	13.7	14.6	15.8	17.3	18.8	20.3	21.7	22.9	23.8	24.4	24.6	24.4	23.8	24.6	16	12.9	04
August	12.0	12.5	13.4	14.6	16.0	17.4	18.7	19.9	20.8	21.4	21.6	21.4	21.0	21.6	16	11.8	05
September	11.3	12.0	13.0	14.2	15.6	17.0	18.3	19.3	20.0	20.2	20.1	19.7	19.2	20.2	15	11.1	05
October	10.0	10.3	11.1	12.4	13.9	15.4	16.7	17.6	17.8	17.8	17.6	17.2	16.7	17.8	14	10.0	06
November	5.1	5.1	5.3	5.9	6.7	7.7	8.6	9.2	9.4	9.3	9.2	9.0	8.8	9.4	14	5.1	07
December	2.0	2.0	2.2	2.6	3.3	4.0	4.7	5.2	5.3	5.3	5.2	5.1	4.9	5.3	14	2.0	07

Note:

Use data in last four columns, in conjunction with Table A2.9, to simulate hourly values of dry-bulb temperature.

Table A2.27 Design 'maxima' of total solar irradiance (W/m²) on vertical, I_{TVd}, and horizontal, I_{THd}, surfaces and diffuse irradiance (W/m²) on horizontal surfaces, I_{dHd}, for SE England. (Irradiances exceeded on 2½% of occasions in each month).

Date	Orientation	Daily mean	04	05	06	07	08	09	10	11	12	13	14	15	16	17	18	19	20
June 21	N	90	35	155	165	105	100	125	145	160	165	160	145	125	100	105	165	155	35
	NE	135	60	305	445	465	420	320	195	170	175	170	155	130	105	75	50	20	5
	E	185	50	295	495	600	625	585	490	355	185	180	165	140	110	80	50	25	5
	SE	180	10	120	280	420	525	580	585	535	430	290	165	140	110	80	50	25	5
	S	155	5	25	50	80	185	320	435	510	535	510	435	320	185	80	50	25	5
	SW	180	5	25	50	80	110	140	165	290	430	535	585	580	525	420	280	120	10
	W	185	5	25	50	80	100	140	165	180	185	355	490	585	625	600	495	295	50
$k_D = 0.82$	NW	135	5	20	50	75	105	130	155	170	175	170	195	320	420	465	445	305	60
$k_d = 0.66$	H	315	5	80	210	360	505	640	750	825	850	825	750	640	505	360	210	80	5
	Diff	80	5	30	60	90	120	150	180	195	205	195	180	150	120	90	60	30	5
July 23 and May 22	N	85		100	130	90	110	140	165	180	185	180	165	140	110	90	130	100	
	NE	125		210	370	410	380	300	195	195	200	195	175	145	115	80	50	20	
	E	175		210	420	540	580	555	480	360	215	205	185	155	125	90	55	20	
	SE	180		95	255	400	510	570	580	540	450	320	185	155	125	90	55	20	
	S	165		20	55	90	210	340	450	525	550	525	450	340	210	90	55	20	
	SW	180		20	55	90	125	155	185	320	450	540	580	570	510	400	255	95	
	W	175		20	55	90	125	155	185	205	215	360	480	555	580	540	420	210	
$k_D = 0.72$	NW	125		20	50	80	115	145	175	195	200	195	195	300	380	410	370	210	
$k_d = 0.89$	H	295		55	180	325	470	605	715	785	815	785	715	605	470	325	180	55	
	Diff	100		30	70	115	155	195	230	255	265	255	230	195	155	115	70	30	
August 22 and April 22	N	60		5	60	60	90	120	145	160	165	160	145	120	90	60	60	5	
	NE	95		10	240	330	315	240	155	170	180	170	155	125	95	65	30	0	
	E	145		10	295	475	545	535	460	340	190	185	165	135	105	65	30	0	
	SE	175		5	190	380	510	585	600	565	470	340	185	135	105	65	30	0	
	S	175		0	30	95	235	375	490	565	590	565	490	375	235	95	30	0	
	SW	175		0	30	65	105	135	185	340	470	565	600	585	510	380	190	5	
	W	145		0	30	65	105	135	165	185	190	340	460	535	545	475	295	10	
$k_D = 0.73$	NW	95		0	30	65	95	125	155	170	180	170	155	240	315	330	240	10	
$k_d = 0.93$	H	240		0	90	225	375	510	620	690	715	690	620	510	375	225	90	0	
	Diff	80		0	45	90	130	170	205	225	235	225	205	170	130	90	45	0	
Sept 22 and March 21	N	40			0	30	60	90	115	130	135	130	115	90	60	30	0		
	NE	60			0	205	235	165	125	140	145	140	125	100	65	30	0		
	E	120			0	340	515	535	465	330	155	150	130	105	70	35	0		
	SE	175			0	295	525	650	685	665	545	395	215	105	70	35	0		
	S	200			0	95	270	445	585	675	710	675	585	445	270	95	0		
	SW	175			0	35	70	105	215	395	545	665	685	650	525	295	0		
	W	120			0	35	70	105	130	150	155	330	465	535	515	340	0		
$k_D = 0.88$	NW	60			0	30	65	100	125	140	145	140	125	165	235	205	0		
$k_d = 0.97$	H	180			0	95	245	395	515	595	625	595	515	395	245	95	0		
	Diff	60			0	45	90	125	160	180	190	180	160	125	90	45	0		
Oct 22 and Feb 21	N	30				0	30	60	90	105	110	105	90	60	30	0			
	NE	35				10	105	80	95	110	120	110	95	65	30	0			
	E	75				25	290	395	370	265	125	120	100	70	35	0			
	SE	135				20	320	515	590	580	500	370	215	70	35	0			
	S	170				10	185	380	530	620	655	620	530	380	185	10			
	SW	135				0	35	70	215	370	500	580	590	515	320	20			
	W	75				0	35	70	100	120	125	265	370	395	290	25			
$k_D = 0.83$	NW	35				0	30	65	95	110	120	110	95	80	105	10			
$k_d = 1.18$	H	110				5	100	230	340	415	440	415	340	230	100	5			
	Diff	45				5	55	100	135	155	165	155	135	100	55	5			
Nov 22 and Jan 21	N	15					5	30	55	70	75	70	55	30	5				
	NE	20					15	35	60	75	80	75	60	35	5				
	E	40					45	230	265	200	90	80	65	35	5				
	SE	100					55	325	470	495	440	325	180	50	5				
	S	130					35	250	435	545	585	545	435	250	35				
	SW	100					5	50	180	325	440	495	470	325	55				
	W	40					5	35	65	80	90	200	265	230	45				
$k_D = 0.88$	NW	20					5	35	60	75	80	75	60	35	15				
$k_d = 1.29$	H	60					10	95	190	260	285	260	190	95	10				
	Diff	25					10	55	90	110	120	110	90	55	10				
Dec 21	N	10						15	40	50	55	50	40	15					
	NE	10						20	40	55	60	55	40	20					
	E	30						155	225	175	65	60	45	20					
	SE	85						230	410	460	410	300	155	35					
	S	115						180	385	510	555	510	385	180					
	SW	85						35	155	300	410	460	410	230					
	W	30						20	45	60	65	175	225	155					
$k_D = 0.97$	NW	10						20	40	55	60	55	40	20					
$k_d = 1.18$	H	40						50	130	195	220	195	130	50					
	Diff	20						30	60	80	90	80	60	30					

Notes:
1. Height correction factor, $k_a = 1.0$
   Ground reflection factor, $k_r = 0.2$
2. N, NE, E, etc.: Total irradiance on vertical surface, I_{TVd}
   H: Total irradiance on horizontal surface, I_{THd}
   Diff: Diffuse (sky) irradiance on horizontal surface, I_{dHd}
3. Diffuse (sky) irradiance on E, SE, SW and W facing vertical surfaces = 0.5 Diff
   Diffuse (sky) irradiance on NE and NW facing vertical surfaces = 0.45 Diff
   Diffuse (sky) irradiance on N facing vertical surface = 0.4 Diff
4. The table is based on horizontal surface measurements at Kew for the period 1959–68; weather for two consecutive days averaged.

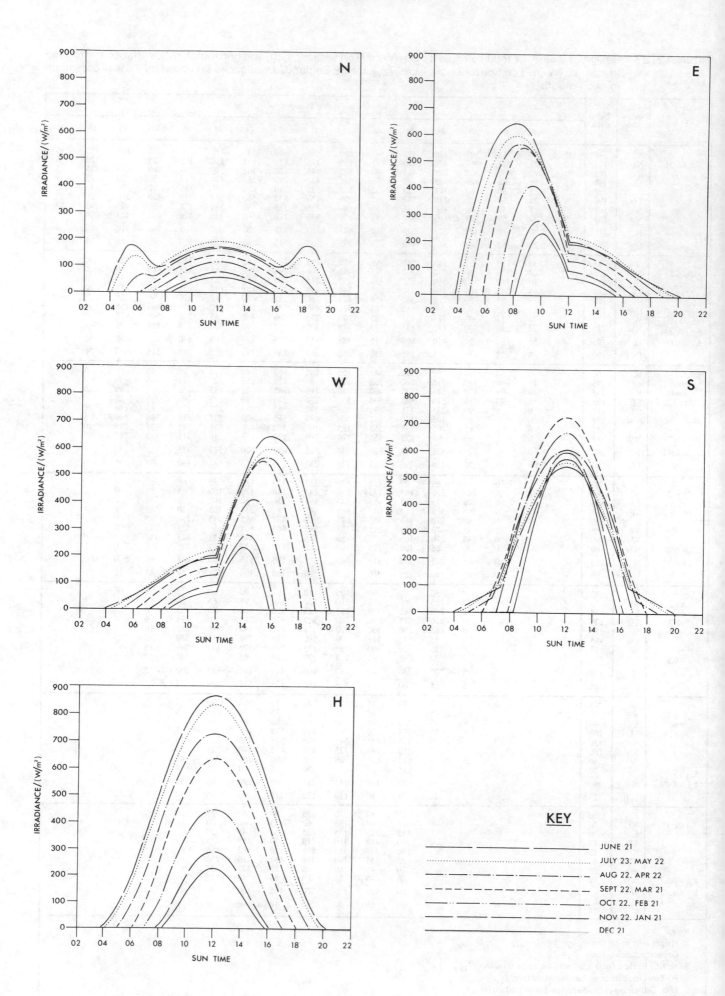

Fig. A2.23. Diurnal variation of solar irradiance on vertical and horizontal surfaces (design 'maximum' irradiances—SE England).

Overheating Design

Temperate localities

For summer overheating design, measures of coincidentally occurring weather parameters are required which lead to indoor temperatures likely to be exceeded for given periods within the year—that is, introducing a small but acceptable risk into the overheating design. The two parameters principally concerned are solar radiation and dry-bulb temperature.

In Table A2.29, these parameters have been selected such that, when applied to peak summer conditions (i.e. July—SW orientation, in the case of rooms with windows in a single external wall in temperate localities), predicted indoor temperatures are likely to be exceeded for the stated number of days in a ten year period.

Table A2.29 Radiation factors and dry-bulb temperatures for summer overheating design—temperate localities.

Design risk (working days per 10 years)	Radiation factor		Daily mean dry-bulb temperature	Peak dry-bulb temperature	Time of peak
	Direct k_D	Diffuse* k_d	/ (°C)	/ (°C)	(GMT)
10	0.58	0.92	21.5	26.5	16
30	0.5	1.00	20.5	25.5	15
50	0.48	0.99	20.0	25.0	15
100	0.42	1.05	19.0	23.5	15

Note:
*apply to basic (cloudy sky) irradiances

Tropical localities

Comprehensive information, comparable with that given in the previous section, for overheating design in tropical localities is generally difficult to obtain.[33] In the absence of such information, radiation factors should be taken from Table A2.30.

Table A2.30 Radiation factors for overheating design—tropical localities.

Situation	Radiation factor	
	Direct k_D	Diffuse k_d
Humid climate	0.5	1.1*
Arid climate	1.1	0.9**

Note:

* apply to basic (cloudy sky) irradiances

**apply to basic (clear sky) irradiances

Simulation of Solar Irradiances

Simulation for Solar Cooling Loads

The solar cooling load tables in the 1979 edition of Section A9, *Estimation of plant capacity*, quotes following climatic constants:

I = overall radiation correction factor
k_c = direct radiation (sky clarity) correction factor (as in the 1970 edition)
k_r = ground reflection factor
C = cloudiness (hours that sun does not shine, expressed as a proportion of possible sunshine hours; 0 for clear sky)

I, k_c and C combine to give solar irradiances as follows:

(i) Clear sky conditions (Tables A9.16 to A9.35), $C = 0$

Design direct irradiance = $I k_c I_D$

where:

I_D = basic direct irradiance—Table A2.24

Design diffuse irradiance = $I I_d$ (clr)

where:

I_d (clr) = basic diffuse (clear sky) irradiance— Table A2.25

Note that in Tables A9.16 to A9.35,

$I = 1.00$
$k_c = 1.00$

That is, solar cooling loads in these tables have been calculated for direct and diffuse (clear sky) irradiances corresponding to the basic values.

(ii) Cloudy sky conditions (Tables A9.14 and A9.15), $0 < C < 1.0$

Design direct irradiance = $I k_c (0.71 - 0.56\ C)\ I_D$
$= k_D I_D$

Therefore,

$k_D = I k_c (0.71 - 0.56 C)$

Design diffuse irradiance = $I I_d$ (cldy)
$= k_d I_d$ (cldy)

where:

I_d (cldy) = basic diffuse (cloudy sky) irradiance— Table A2.25

Therefore,

$k_d = I$

For example, for August, the design 'maximum' irradiances (that is, the irradiances exceeded on 2½% of occasions in that month) are given by:

$$I = 0.93$$
$$k_c = 1.34$$
$$C = 0.23$$

(see Tables A9.14 or A9.15)

Hence,

$$k_D = 0.93 \times 1.34 \times (0.71 - (0.56 \times 0.23))$$

Therefore,

$$k_D = 0.72$$

(Greater precision in the values for I, k_c and C leads to the value $k_D = 0.73$ given in Table A2.27)

Also,

$$k_d = 0.93 \text{ (As given in Table A2.27)}$$

Simulation from Banded Weather Data

The simulation of solar irradiance using banded weather data requires values of k_D and k_d for each band and for each particular month. Such values are given in Tables A2.7 and A2.8. These factors are applied to basic direct and diffuse (sky) irradiances which may be obtained from Table A2.26 or, with the aid of a suitable computer program, from the fundamental formulae.[34]

Example

Obtain the horizontal irradiance at 13 GMT during the month of March for a location in SE England both for average weather and for weather corresponding to the fourth band of the global solar radiation analysis.

From Table A2.7 (a), the radiation factors are;

Monthly average: $k_D = 0.32$ and $k_d = 0.93$

Fourth band
(13.00 to 11.26 MJ/m²): $k_D = 0.62$ and $k_d = 1.11$

The basic direct and diffuse irradiances for a horizontal surface are obtained from Table A2.26;

Direct: $I_{DH} = 475 \text{ W/m}^2$ (i.e. value corresponding to 'H')

Diffuse (cloudy sky):
$I_{dH} = 185 \text{ W/m}^2$ (i.e. value corresponding to 'Diff (cldy)')

Assuming a height correction factor, k_a, of 1.0 the required irradiances are obtained from equations A2.12 and A2.13 as follows:

	Fourth band	Monthly average
Direct irradiance:	1.0 (0.62 × 475) = 295 W/m²	1.0 (0.32 × 475) = 152 W/m²
Diffuse (sky) irradiance:	1.0 (1.11 × 185) = 205 W/m²	1.0 (0.93 × 185) = 172 W/m²
Total irradiance:	295 + 205 = 500 W/m²	152 + 172 = 324 W/m²

The fourth band total irradiance (500 W/m²) is that which would be likely to occur at 13 GMT as the average for a group of March days comprising a proportion of 0.09 of the sample of 310 days—that is, twenty-eight March days in ten years or, approximately, three March days per year. Similarly, total irradiances and their frequencies of occurrence may be derived for the remaining nine bands given in the 'March' segment of Table A2.7(a). This process is then repeated for all the months for which the data are required (e.g. in the estimation of heating or cooling load energy requirements).

The monthly average total irradiance (324 W/m²) is that which would be likely to occur at 13 GMT as the average for all March days.

To determine irradiances on vertical and sloping surfaces, a similar calculation procedure is employed, as described in the following sections.

Design Total Irradiance

Horizontal surfaces

The design total (global) irradiance on a horizontal surface is given by:

$$I_{THd} = I_{DHd} + I_{dHd} \qquad \dots \qquad \dots \qquad \dots \qquad \text{A2.14}$$

where:

I_{THd} = design total (global) irradiance on a horizontal surface $\dots$ $\dots$ $\dots$ W/m²
I_{DHd} = design direct irradiance on a horizontal surface $\dots$ $\dots$ $\dots$ $\dots$ W/m²
I_{dHd} = design diffuse (sky) irradiance on a horizontal surface $\dots$ $\dots$ $\dots$ W/m²

However, I_{DHd} and I_{dHd} may be expressed in terms of basic irradiances using equations A2.12 and A2.13, hence:

$$I_{THd} = k_a (k_D I_{DH} + k_d I_{dH}) = k_a I_{TH} \qquad \dots \qquad \dots \qquad \text{A2.15}$$

where:

$$I_{TH} = k_D I_{DH} + k_d I_{dH} \qquad \dots \qquad \dots \qquad \dots \qquad \text{A2.16}$$

Vertical surfaces

The design total (global) irradiance on a vertical surface is given by:

$$I_{TVd} = I_{DVd} + 0.5 I_{dHd} + 0.5 k_r I_{THd} \qquad \dots \qquad \dots \qquad \text{A2.17}$$

where:

I_{TVd} = design total (global) irradiance on a vertical surface $\dots$ $\dots$ $\dots$ $\dots$ W/m²
I_{DVd} = design direct irradiance on a vertical surface $\dots$ $\dots$ $\dots$ $\dots$ $\dots$ W/m²
k_r = ground reflection factor (Table A2.31)

Therefore:

$$I_{TVd} = k_a (k_D I_{DV} + 0.5 k_d I_{dH} + 0.5 k_r I_{TH}) \qquad \dots \qquad \text{A2.18}$$

Table A2.31   Ground reflection factors.

Situation	Ground reflection factor, k_r
Temperate localities	0.2
Tropical localities (humid)	0.2
Tropical localities (arid)	0.5

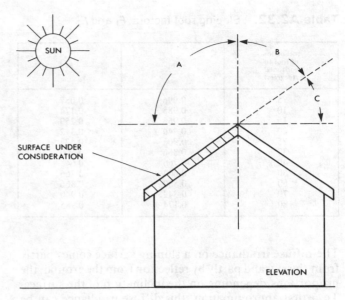

(a) Solar altitude

Equation A2.18 over-estimates irradiances on northerly facing vertical surfaces. For N, NE and NW facing surfaces, a better estimate is given by multiplying the diffuse (sky) irradiance by 0.8, 0.9 and 0.9 respectively.

Therefore, for north facing surface:

$$I_{TVd} = k_a (k_D I_{DV} + 0.4 \, k_d I_{dH} + 0.5 \, k_r I_{TH}) \quad .. \quad \text{A2.19}$$

and for north-east and north-west facing surfaces:

$$I_{TVd} = k_a (k_D I_{DV} + 0.45 \, k_d I_{dH} + 0.5 \, k_r I_{TH}) \quad .. \quad \text{A2.20}$$

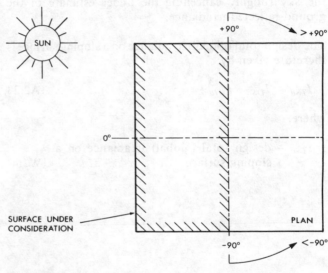

(b) Wall-solar azimuth

Fig. A2.24   Sun position with respect to a sloping surface.

Sloping Surfaces

The design direct irradiance on a sloping surface, such as a pitched roof, depends on the position of the sun relative to the surface under consideration. Fig. A2.24 defines three sectors corresponding to values of wall-solar azimuth.

Sector A: wall-solar azimuth between 0° and +90° or between –90° and 0°.

Sector B: wall-solar azimuth is greater than +90° or less than –90° and sun is above plane of sloping surface.

Sector C: wall-solar azimuth is greater than +90° or less than –90° and sun is below plane of sloping surface.

The design direct irradiance is then given by the following equations:

(i) Sector A

$$I_{DSd} = F_1 I_{DHd} + F_2 I_{DVd} .. \quad .. \quad .. \quad \text{A2.21}$$

where:

I_{DSd} = design direct irradiance on sloping surface   ..   ..   ..   W/m²

I_{DHd} = design direct irradiance on horizontal surface   ..   ..   ..   W/m²

I_{DVd} = design direct irradiance on vertical surface facing same direction as sloping surface   ..   ..   W/m²

F_1, F_2 = sloping roof factors (see Table A2.32)

(ii) Sectors B and C

$$I_{DSd} = F_1 I_{DHd} - F_2 I'_{DVd} .. \quad .. \quad .. \quad \text{A2.22}$$

where:

I'_{DVd} = design direct irradiance on vertical surface facing opposite direction to sloping surface   ..   ..   W/m²

If I_{DSd} is found to be negative, this indicates that the sun is below the plane of the surface, that is, in sector C. Consequently, the total irradiance on the sloping surface is given by the value of the diffuse irradiance alone.

When the sun shines directly along the ridge, i.e. wall-solar azimuth is +90° or –90°, F_2 is zero and there is no vertical component of direct irradiance.

Table A2.32.   Sloping roof factors, F_1 and F_2.

Inclination of roof to horizontal /(degrees)	F_1	F_2
5	0.996	0.087
10	0.985	0.174
15	0.966	0.259
20	0.940	0.342
25	0.906	0.423
30	0.866	0.500
40	0.766	0.643
50	0.643	0.766
60	0.500	0.866
70	0.342	0.940
80	0.174	0.985

The diffuse irradiance on a sloping surface comes partly from the sky and partly by reflection from the ground, the proportions depending on the inclination of the surface. To a first approximation, this diffuse irradiance can be assumed to be equal to the diffuse (sky) irradiance on a horizontal surface, the over-estimate of irradiance from the sky roughly cancelling the under estimate of the ground-reflected irradiance.

The design total (global) irradiance on a sloping surface is therefore given by:

$$I_{TSd} = I_{DSd} + I_{dHd}   \quad .. \quad .. \quad .. \quad .. \quad A2.23$$

where:

I_{TSd} = design total (global) irradiance on a sloping surface .. .. W/m^2

Example

A building at sea level at latitude 51.7°N, has an asymmetrical double pitched roof with a 20° slope (measured to the horizontal) facing 19° west of south and a 60° slope facing 19° east of north, i.e. wall azimuths of 199° and 19° respectively. It is required to find the solar irradiances on the two slopes at 14 GMT in July which are likely to be exceeded on 2½% of July days.

Since the height correction factor, k_a, is unity, the values of total irradiance for horizontal and vertical surfaces and the value of diffuse irradiance on a horizontal surface may be read from Table A2.27.

For 14 GMT on July 23:

I_{THd} = 715 W/m^2
I_{TVd} = 505 W/m^2 (wall azimuth 199° —linear interpolation between 180° and 225°)
I_{dHd} = 230 W/m^2

From equation A2.14,

$I_{DHd} = I_{THd} - I_{dHd}$

Therefore,

$$I_{DHd} = 715 - 230 = 485 \ W/m^2$$

From equation A2.17,

$$I_{DVd} = I_{TVd} - 0.5 \ I_{dHd} - 0.5 \ k_r I_{THd}$$

$$I_{DVd} = 505 - (0.5 \times 230) - (0.5 \times 0.2 \times 715)$$

Therefore,

$$I_{DVd} = 318 \ W/m^2$$

Since I_{DVd} is positive, a vertical surface of wall azimuth 199° is exposed to direct radiation at 14 GMT and therefore its wall-solar azimuth must lie in the range 0° ± 90° (i.e. sector A in Fig. A2.24).

For a slope of 20° to the horizontal, from Table A2.32:

F_1 = 0.940 and F_2 = 0.342

Therefore, using equation A2.21,

$$I_{DSd} = (0.940 \times 485) + (0.342 \times 318)$$

Hence,

$$I_{DSd} = 565 \ W/m^2$$

Total irradiance is given by equation A2.23:

$$I_{TSd} = 565 + 230 = 795 \ W/m^2 \text{ (for the 20° slope)}$$

For a surface facing in the opposite direction, i.e. wall azimuth 19°, the wall-solar azimuth is either greater than +90° or less than –90°. Therefore, at the required time, the sun must be in sector B or C with respect to the 60° slope. In this case, the design direct irradiance on a vertical surface facing in the opposite direction to the sloping surface is required. However, since the two sloping surfaces face in opposite directions,

$$I'_{DVd} = 318 \ W/m^2$$

For a 60° slope, from Table A2.32,

F_1 = 0.500 and F_2 = 0.866

Therefore, using equation A2.22,

$$I_{DSd} = (0.500 \times 485) - (0.866 \times 318)$$

Hence,

$$I_{DSd} = -33 \ W/m^2$$

The negative sign indicates that the sun is below the plane of the 60° slope, therefore the total irradiance results from the diffuse component alone:

$$I_{TSd} = 230 \ W/m^2 \text{ (for the 60° slope)}$$

The method used in the above example involves interpolation between values of I_{DVd} and I'_{DVd} for surfaces orientated at 45° intervals. Care should be taken when interpolating between NW, N and NE facing surfaces since the diffuse (sky) irradiance on these surfaces, used in the derivation of I_{DVd} from tabulated values of I_{TVd}, is not directly given by Table A2.27. Furthermore, a linear interpolation between values of I_{DVd} for adjacent orientations is only valid if the vertical surface receives direct radiation at the specified time for all intermediate orientations.

In the absence of detailed solar irradiance data, such as that of Table A2.27, recourse will need to be made to more fundamental data. In these circumstances the following method should be employed:

(1) Use Table A2.23, interpolating if necessary, to determine the solar altitude and azimuth for a given time, date and latitude.

(2) Determine the wall-solar azimuth and identify in which sector (Fig. A2.24) the sun will be located.

(3) Use solar altitude and wall-solar azimuth in conjunction with Table A2.24 to determine the basic direct irradiances on a horizontal surface and on a vertical surface having the same wall-solar azimuth as the sloping surface under consideration.

(4) Use solar altitude in conjunction with Table A2.25 to determine the basic diffuse (cloudy sky) irradiance.

(5) Apply height correction factor, k_a, and direct and diffuse radiation factors, k_D and k_d, appropriate to the radiation climate at the given locality to obtain design direct and diffuse irradiances.

(6) Use equations A2.21 or A2.22 in conjunction with Table A2.32 to determine the design direct irradiance on the sloping surface.

(7) Add design diffuse (cloudy sky) irradiance on horizontal surface to the design direct irradiance on a sloping surface to obtain the total irradiance on the surface. Note that if the design direct irradiance (step 6) is found to be negative, the sun is below the plane of the sloping surface and the total irradiance is given by the diffuse irradiance alone.

SOL-AIR TEMPERATURE AND LONG-WAVE LOSS

Solar energy absorbed at the outside surface of walls and roofs is partly transmitted to the interior of the building. The absorbed radiation has the same effect as a rise in the outside temperature and the calculation of energy gain is facilitated by the concept of sol-air temperature. This is defined as the outside temperature which, in the absence of solar radiation, would give the same temperature distribution and rate of energy transfer through the wall or roof as exists with the actual outside air temperature and incident solar radiation.

Section A5 of the *Guide* describes the calculation of sol-air temperature and shows that one of the parameters on which this temperature depends is the net long-wave radiation loss, I_l, from a black body at air temperature to the external environment (i.e. sky, ground and nearby buildings). The long-wave loss depends on cloud cover, dry-bulb temperature, orientation of surface and the nature of the external environment.[41] The sol-air temperatures given in this section are obtained using the following simplified relationships:

For horizontal surfaces:
$$I_l = 93 - 79\ C \qquad .. \qquad .. \qquad .. \qquad .. \qquad A2.24$$

For vertical surfaces:
$$I_l = 21 - 17\ C \qquad .. \qquad .. \qquad .. \qquad .. \qquad A2.25$$

where:
I_l = long-wave radiation loss .. .. W/m²
C = cloudiness

For conditions relating to the design 'maximum' irradiances of Table A2.27 (that is, irradiances exceeded on 2½% of occasions in each month) and to the coincidentally occurring dry-bulb temperatures of Table A2.28, the corresponding sol-air temperatures for dark and light surfaces for the months March to October are given in Table A2.33.

When estimating the temperatures reached by outdoor surfaces exposed to the sun, the sol-air temperature concept gives the temperatures of such surfaces when backed by an infinite thermal resistance. The actual surface temperature will generally be less than the sol-air temperature and therefore a safety factor is introduced into the estimate.

The requirement is frequently for the maximum sol-air temperature likely to be reached, generally on a horizontal surface. For this purpose it is suggested that, for the UK, one of the following combinations of solar irradiance and dry-bulb temperature should be used in the determination of sol-air temperature:

(a) Solar irradiance, I_{THd} = 885 W/m²

Dry-bulb temperature, t_{ao} = 23 °C

This combination is based on measurements at Kew for the ten year period from 1959 to 1968 and lends itself to statistical interpretation, i.e. it leads to an hourly mean sol-air temperature likely to be achieved on one occasion in ten years.

(b) Solar irradiance, I_{THd} = 840 W/m²

Dry-bulb temperature, t_{ao} = 27.5 °C

This is based on measurements at Garston during the extreme summer of 1976 (Fig. A2.7) and leads to an hourly mean sol-air temperature in excess of any achieved in the ten year period of (a).

The maximum sol-air temperature, t_{eo}, for a horizontal surface (having solar absorptance, α, of 0.9 and long-wave emissity, ϵ, of 0.9) would be given by the following:

From Section A5 (equation A5.110),

$$t_{eo} = (\alpha I_{THd} - \epsilon I_l) R_{so} + t_{ao}$$

I_l is given be equation A2.24. Thus, for a cloudless sky $(C = 0)$,

$$I_l = 93 \text{ W/m}^2$$

R_{so} is taken from Section A3 of the Guide for a horizontal surface in a 'sheltered' location (Table A3.6),

$$R_{so} = 0.07 \text{ m}^2 \text{ K/W}$$

Therefore, putting these values in equation A5.110, the following values are obtained:
For (a), t_{eo} = 72.9 °C
For (b), t_{eo} = 74.6 °C

Sol-air temperature, and therefore surface temperature, also depend on the magnitude of the external surface resistance, R_{so}, which partly depends on the wind speed across the surface. An extreme of surface temperature is given when R_{so} is high, as under 'calm' conditions, or in a position exposed to the sun but sheltered from the wind. A further influence, which cannot be readily taken into account, is that the radiation and convection coefficients, which determine the magnitude of R_{so}, are themselves temperature dependent. Consequently, at the elevated temperatures of surfaces exposed to the sun, R_{so} deviates from its usual value.

The sol-air temperatures given in Table A2.33 are based on measurements taken at Kew during the ten year period 1959-68, the weather for two consecutive days being averaged. The values of solar absorptance are taken as 0.9 for dark surfaces and 0.5 for light surfaces.

Table A2.33 Sol-air temperatures, t_{eo}, for SE England — 2½% day of highest radiation

(a) March 21

Sun Time	Air Temp, t_{ao}/(°C)	Sol-air temperature, t_{eo}/(°C)															
		Horizontal		North		North-East		East		South-East		South		South-West		West		North-West	
		Dark	Light	Dark	Light	Dark	Light	Dark	Light	Dark	Light	Dark	Light	Dark	Light	Dark	Light	Dark	Light
00	8.5	5.5	5.5	7.5	7.5	7.5	7.5	7.5	7.5	7.5	7.5	7.5	7.5	7.5	7.5	7.5	7.5	7.5	7.5
01	7.5	4.5	4.5	6.5	6.5	6.5	6.5	6.5	6.5	6.5	6.5	6.5	6.5	6.5	6.5	6.5	6.5	6.5	6.5
02	6.5	3.5	3.5	5.5	5.5	5.5	5.5	5.5	5.5	5.5	5.5	5.5	5.5	5.5	5.5	5.5	5.5	5.5	5.5
03	6.0	3.0	3.0	5.0	5.0	5.0	5.0	5.0	5.0	5.0	5.0	5.0	5.0	5.0	5.0	5.0	5.0	5.0	5.0
04	5.0	2.5	2.5	4.5	4.5	4.5	4.5	4.5	4.5	4.5	4.5	4.5	4.5	4.5	4.5	4.5	4.5	4.5	4.5
05	5.0	2.0	2.0	4.0	4.0	4.0	4.0	4.0	4.0	4.0	4.0	4.0	4.0	4.0	4.0	4.0	4.0	4.0	4.0
06	5.0	2.0	2.0	4.0	4.0	4.0	4.0	4.0	4.0	4.0	4.0	4.0	4.0	4.0	4.0	4.0	4.0	4.0	4.0
07	5.0	6.0	4.5	5.5	5.0	14.5	10.0	21.0	13.5	19.0	12.5	9.0	7.0	6.0	5.0	6.0	5.0	6.0	5.0
08	6.0	13.0	8.5	8.0	7.0	17.0	11.5	30.5	19.5	31.0	19.5	18.5	12.5	8.5	7.0	8.5	7.0	8.5	7.0
09	7.5	20.5	13.5	11.0	9.0	14.5	11.0	33.0	21.5	39.0	24.5	28.5	19.0	11.5	9.5	11.5	9.5	11.5	9.5
10	9.0	27.0	18.0	14.0	11.5	14.5	11.5	31.5	21.0	42.5	27.0	37.0	24.5	19.0	14.0	15.0	12.0	14.5	11.5
11	11.0	32.0	21.5	16.5	14.0	17.0	14.0	26.5	19.0	43.0	28.5	43.5	28.5	29.5	21.0	17.5	14.0	17.0	14.0
12	12.5	35.0	23.5	18.5	15.5	19.0	16.0	19.5	16.0	39.0	27.0	47.0	31.5	39.0	27.0	19.5	16.0	19.0	16.0
13	14.0	35.0	24.5	20.0	17.0	20.0	17.0	20.5	17.5	33.0	24.0	46.5	32.0	46.0	31.5	29.5	22.5	20.0	17.0
14	15.0	33.0	23.5	20.0	17.5	20.0	17.5	20.5	17.5	25.0	20.0	43.0	30.0	48.0	33.0	37.0	27.0	20.0	17.5
15	15.5	28.5	21.0	19.0	17.0	19.5	17.0	19.5	17.5	19.5	17.5	36.5	26.5	46.5	32.5	41.0	29.0	22.5	19.0
16	15.0	22.0	18.0	17.5	16.0	17.5	16.0	18.0	16.0	18.0	16.0	27.5	22.0	40.5	29.0	39.5	28.5	26.0	21.0
17	15.0	16.0	14.0	15.5	15.0	15.5	15.0	15.5	15.0	15.5	15.0	19.0	16.5	28.5	22.0	31.0	23.5	24.0	19.5
18	14.5	11.5	11.5	13.5	13.5	13.5	13.5	13.5	13.5	13.5	13.5	13.5	13.5	13.5	13.5	13.5	13.5	13.5	13.5
19	13.5	10.5	10.5	12.5	12.5	12.5	12.5	12.5	12.5	12.5	12.5	12.5	12.5	12.5	12.5	12.5	12.5	12.5	12.5
20	12.5	9.5	9.5	12.0	12.0	12.0	12.0	12.0	12.0	12.0	12.0	12.0	12.0	12.0	12.0	12.0	12.0	12.0	12.0
21	11.5	8.5	8.5	11.0	11.0	11.0	11.0	11.0	11.0	11.0	11.0	11.0	11.0	11.0	11.0	11.0	11.0	11.0	11.0
22	10.5	7.5	7.5	10.0	10.0	10.0	10.0	10.0	10.0	10.0	10.0	10.0	10.0	10.0	10.0	10.0	10.0	10.0	10.0
23	9.5	6.5	6.5	8.5	8.5	8.5	8.5	8.5	8.5	8.5	8.5	8.5	8.5	8.5	8.5	8.5	8.5	8.5	8.5
Mean	10.0	14.5	11.0	11.0	10.5	12.0	11.0	15.0	12.5	18.0	14.0	19.0	15.0	18.0	14.0	15.0	12.5	12.0	11.0

Note: I_l (horizontal surface) = 73 W/m², I_l (vertical surface) = 17 W/m²

Table A2.33 Sol-air temperatures for SE England — 2½% day of highest radiation — *continued*

(b) April 22

Sun Time	Air Temp, t_{ao}/(°C)	Sol-air temperature, t_{eo}/(°C)															
		Horizontal		North		North-East		East		South-East		South		South-West		West		North-West	
		Dark	Light	Dark	Light	Dark	Light	Dark	Light	Dark	Light	Dark	Light	Dark	Light	Dark	Light	Dark	Light
00	10.0	7.0	7.0	9.0	9.0	9.0	9.0	9.0	9.0	9.0	9.0	9.0	9.0	9.0	9.0	9.0	9.0	9.0	9.0
01	9.0	6.0	6.0	8.0	8.0	8.0	8.0	8.0	8.0	8.0	8.0	8.0	8.0	8.0	8.0	8.0	8.0	8.0	8.0
02	8.0	5.0	5.0	7.0	7.0	7.0	7.0	7.0	7.0	7.0	7.0	7.0	7.0	7.0	7.0	7.0	7.0	7.0	7.0
03	7.0	4.5	4.5	6.5	6.5	6.5	6.5	6.5	6.5	6.5	6.5	6.5	6.5	6.5	6.5	6.5	6.5	6.5	6.5
04	7.0	4.0	4.0	6.0	6.0	6.0	6.0	6.0	6.0	6.0	6.0	6.0	6.0	6.0	6.0	6.0	6.0	6.0	6.0
05	6.5	3.5	3.5	6.5	6.5	6.5	6.0	6.5	6.0	6.0	6.0	6.0	6.0	6.0	6.0	6.0	6.0	6.0	6.0
06	7.0	7.5	6.0	8.5	7.5	15.5	11.5	18.0	12.5	14.0	10.5	7.5	6.5	7.5	6.5	7.5	6.5	7.0	6.5
07	7.5	13.5	9.5	9.0	8.0	20.0	14.0	26.0	17.5	22.0	15.0	10.5	9.0	9.5	8.0	9.5	8.0	9.0	8.0
08	8.5	20.5	14.0	11.0	9.5	20.5	14.5	29.5	20.0	28.5	19.0	17.0	13.0	12.0	10.0	12.0	10.0	11.5	10.0
09	9.5	27.5	18.0	13.5	11.5	18.5	14.5	30.5	21.0	32.5	22.0	24.0	17.5	14.5	12.0	14.5	12.0	14.0	12.0
10	11.0	33.5	22.0	16.0	13.5	16.5	14.0	29.0	20.5	34.5	24.0	30.0	21.5	18.0	14.5	17.0	14.0	16.5	14.0
11	12.5	37.5	25.5	18.5	15.5	19.0	15.5	25.5	15.5	34.5	24.5	34.5	24.5	25.5	19.5	19.5	16.0	19.0	15.5
12	14.0	40.0	27.5	20.0	17.0	20.5	17.5	21.0	17.5	32.5	24.0	37.0	26.5	32.5	24.0	21.0	17.5	20.5	17.5
13	15.5	40.5	28.0	21.0	18.0	21.5	18.5	22.0	18.5	28.5	22.0	37.5	27.0	37.5	27.0	28.5	22.0	21.5	18.5
14	16.5	38.5	27.5	21.5	19.0	22.0	19.0	22.0	19.0	23.0	19.5	35.5	26.5	40.0	29.0	34.0	26.0	22.0	19.0
15	17.0	34.5	25.5	21.0	19.0	21.5	19.0	21.5	19.0	21.5	19.0	31.5	24.5	40.0	29.5	38.0	28.0	26.0	21.5
16	17.0	29.5	22.5	20.0	18.5	20.0	18.5	20.5	18.5	20.5	18.5	26.0	21.5	37.0	28.0	38.5	28.5	29.0	23.5
17	17.0	23.5	19.0	18.5	17.5	19.0	17.5	19.0	17.5	19.0	17.5	20.0	18.5	31.5	24.5	35.5	27.0	29.5	23.5
18	16.5	17.0	15.5	18.5	17.0	17.0	16.5	17.0	16.5	17.0	16.5	17.0	16.5	23.5	20.0	27.5	22.5	25.5	21.0
19	16.0	13.0	13.0	15.5	15.0	15.0	15.0	15.0	15.0	15.0	15.0	15.0	15.0	15.5	15.0	15.5	15.5	15.5	15.5
20	15.0	12.0	12.0	14.0	14.0	14.0	14.0	14.0	14.0	14.0	14.0	14.0	14.0	14.0	14.0	14.0	14.0	14.0	14.0
21	14.0	11.0	11.0	13.0	13.0	13.0	13.0	13.0	13.0	13.0	13.0	13.0	13.0	13.0	13.0	13.0	13.0	13.0	13.0
22	12.5	9.5	9.5	11.5	11.5	11.5	11.5	11.5	11.5	11.5	11.5	11.5	11.5	11.5	11.5	11.5	11.5	11.5	11.5
23	11.5	8.5	8.5	10.5	10.5	10.5	10.5	10.5	10.5	10.5	10.5	10.5	10.5	10.5	10.5	10.5	10.5	10.5	10.5
Mean	12.0	18.5	14.5	13.5	12.5	15.0	13.0	17.0	14.5	18.0	15.0	18.0	15.0	18.0	15.0	17.0	14.5	15.0	13.0

Note: I_1 (horizontal surface) = 74 W/m², I_1 (vertical surface) = 17 W/m²

(c) May 22

Sun Time	Air Temp, t_{ao}/(°C)	Sol-air temperature, t_{eo}/(°C)															
		Horizontal		North		North-East		East		South-East		South		South-West		West		North-West	
		Dark	Light	Dark	Light	Dark	Light	Dark	Light	Dark	Light	Dark	Light	Dark	Light	Dark	Light	Dark	Light
00	11.0	8.0	8.0	10.0	10.0	10.0	10.0	10.0	10.0	10.0	10.0	10.0	10.0	10.0	10.0	10.0	10.0	10.0	10.0
01	10.0	7.0	7.0	9.0	9.0	9.0	9.0	9.0	9.0	9.0	9.0	9.0	9.0	9.0	9.0	9.0	9.0	9.0	9.0
02	9.0	6.0	6.0	8.5	8.5	8.5	8.5	8.5	8.5	8.5	8.5	8.5	8.5	8.5	8.5	8.5	8.5	8.5	8.5
03	9.0	5.5	5.5	8.0	8.0	8.0	8.0	8.0	8.0	8.0	8.0	8.0	8.0	8.0	8.0	8.0	8.0	8.0	8.0
04	8.5	5.5	5.5	7.5	7.5	7.5	7.5	7.5	7.5	7.5	7.5	7.5	7.5	7.5	7.5	7.5	7.5	7.5	7.5
05	9.0	8.0	7.0	13.0	11.0	18.5	14.0	18.5	13.5	12.5	10.5	9.0	8.5	9.0	8.5	9.0	8.5	9.0	8.5
06	9.5	13.5	10.5	15.0	12.0	27.0	19.0	29.5	20.0	21.0	15.5	11.0	10.0	11.0	10.0	11.0	10.0	11.0	10.0
07	10.5	20.5	14.5	14.0	12.0	30.0	21.0	36.5	24.5	29.5	20.5	14.0	12.0	14.0	12.0	14.0	12.0	13.5	12.0
08	12.0	28.0	19.5	16.5	14.0	29.5	21.5	39.5	27.0	36.0	25.0	21.5	17.0	17.0	14.5	17.0	14.5	16.5	14.0
09	13.5	34.5	24.0	19.5	16.5	27.5	20.5	40.0	28.0	40.5	28.0	29.5	22.0	20.5	17.0	20.5	17.0	20.0	16.5
10	15.0	40.5	28.0	22.0	18.5	24.0	19.5	38.0	27.5	43.0	30.0	36.5	26.5	23.5	19.5	23.5	19.0	23.0	19.0
11	16.5	45.0	31.0	24.5	20.5	25.0	21.0	33.5	25.5	42.5	30.5	41.5	30.0	31.5	24.5	26.0	21.5	25.0	21.0
12	18.0	47.5	33.0	26.0	22.0	27.0	22.5	27.5	23.0	39.5	29.5	44.0	32.0	39.5	29.5	27.5	23.0	27.0	22.5
13	19.0	47.5	33.5	27.0	23.0	27.5	23.5	28.0	23.5	34.0	27.0	44.0	32.5	45.0	33.0	36.0	28.0	27.5	23.5
14	19.5	45.5	32.5	26.5	23.0	27.5	23.5	28.0	24.0	28.0	24.0	41.0	31.0	47.5	34.5	42.5	32.0	28.5	24.0
15	20.0	41.0	30.0	25.5	22.5	26.0	23.0	26.5	23.0	26.5	23.0	36.0	28.5	47.0	34.5	46.5	34.0	33.5	27.0
16	19.5	35.5	27.0	24.0	21.5	24.5	22.0	25.0	22.0	25.0	22.0	29.0	24.5	44.0	32.5	47.5	34.5	37.5	29.0
17	19.0	29.0	23.5	22.5	20.5	22.5	20.5	22.5	20.5	22.5	20.5	22.5	20.5	38.0	29.0	45.0	33.0	38.5	29.5
18	18.5	22.5	19.0	24.0	21.0	20.0	19.0	20.0	19.0	20.0	19.0	20.0	19.0	30.0	24.5	38.5	29.0	36.0	27.5
19	17.5	16.5	15.5	21.5	19.5	17.5	17.0	17.5	17.0	17.5	17.0	17.5	17.0	21.0	19.0	27.0	22.0	27.0	22.5
20	16.0	13.0	13.0	15.5	15.5	15.5	15.5	15.5	15.5	15.5	15.5	15.5	15.5	15.5	15.5	15.5	15.5	15.5	15.5
21	15.0	11.5	11.5	14.0	14.0	14.0	14.0	14.0	14.0	14.0	14.0	14.0	14.0	14.0	14.0	14.0	14.0	14.0	14.0
22	13.5	10.5	10.5	12.5	12.5	12.5	12.5	12.5	12.5	12.5	12.5	12.5	12.5	12.5	12.5	12.5	12.5	12.5	12.5
23	12.0	9.0	9.0	11.5	11.5	11.5	11.5	11.5	11.5	11.5	11.5	11.5	11.5	11.5	11.5	11.5	11.5	11.5	11.5
Mean	14.0	23.0	17.5	17.5	15.5	19.5	17.0	22.0	18.0	22.5	18.5	21.5	18.0	22.5	18.5	22.0	18.0	19.5	17.0

Note: I_1 (horizontal surface) = 78 W/m², I_1 (vertical surface) = 18 W/m²

Table A2.33　Sol-air temperatures for SE England — 2½% day of highest radiation — *continued*

(d) June 21

Sun Time	Air Temp, t_{ao}/ (°C)	Horizontal		North		North-East		East		South-East		South		South-West		West		North-West	
		Dark	Light	Dark	Light	Dark	Light	Dark	Light	Dark	Light	Dark	Light	Dark	Light	Dark	Light	Dark	Light
00	14.0	10.5	10.5	13.0	13.0	13.0	13.0	13.0	13.0	13.0	13.0	13.0	13.0	13.0	13.0	13.0	13.0	13.0	13.0
01	12.5	9.5	9.5	11.5	11.5	11.5	11.5	11.5	11.5	11.5	11.5	11.5	11.5	11.5	11.5	11.5	11.5	11.5	11.5
02	12.0	8.5	8.5	11.0	11.0	11.0	11.0	11.0	11.0	11.0	11.0	11.0	11.0	11.0	11.0	11.0	11.0	11.0	11.0
03	11.0	8.0	8.0	10.5	10.5	10.5	10.5	10.5	10.5	10.5	10.5	10.5	10.5	10.5	10.5	10.5	10.5	10.5	10.5
04	11.0	8.0	8.0	12.0	11.0	13.0	12.0	12.5	11.5	10.5	10.5	10.5	10.0	10.5	10.0	10.5	10.0	10.5	10.0
05	11.0	11.5	10.0	18.0	14.5	25.5	18.5	25.0	18.5	16.5	13.5	11.5	11.0	11.5	11.0	11.5	11.0	11.5	11.0
06	12.0	17.0	13.5	19.0	15.5	33.0	23.0	35.5	24.0	24.5	18.5	13.5	12.5	13.5	12.5	13.5	12.5	13.0	12.0
07	12.5	24.0	17.5	17.0	14.5	35.0	24.5	41.5	28.0	32.5	23.5	15.5	14.0	15.5	14.0	15.5	14.0	15.5	14.0
08	14.0	31.0	22.0	18.0	15.5	33.5	24.5	44.0	30.0	39.0	27.5	22.0	18.0	18.5	16.0	18.5	16.0	18.5	16.0
09	15.0	38.0	26.5	20.5	17.5	30.0	23.0	43.0	30.5	43.0	30.0	30.0	23.0	21.0	18.0	21.0	18.0	20.5	18.0
10	16.5	43.5	30.0	23.0	19.5	25.5	21.0	40.0	29.0	44.5	31.5	37.0	27.5	23.5	20.0	23.5	20.0	23.5	20.0
11	18.0	48.0	33.0	25.0	21.5	25.5	21.5	34.5	26.5	43.5	31.5	42.0	31.0	31.5	25.0	26.0	22.0	25.5	21.5
12	19.0	50.5	35.0	26.5	23.0	27.0	23.0	27.5	23.5	39.5	30.0	44.5	33.0	39.5	30.0	27.5	23.5	27.0	23.0
13	20.5	50.5	35.5	27.5	24.0	28.0	24.0	28.5	24.5	34.0	27.5	44.5	33.5	46.0	34.0	37.0	29.0	28.0	24.0
14	21.0	48.5	34.5	27.5	24.5	28.0	24.5	28.5	25.0	28.5	25.0	41.5	32.0	49.5	36.5	44.5	34.0	30.0	25.5
15	21.5	44.5	33.0	27.0	24.5	27.5	24.5	28.0	24.0	28.0	24.5	36.5	29.5	49.5	37.0	50.0	37.0	36.5	29.5
16	22.0	39.0	30.0	26.0	24.0	26.5	24.0	26.5	24.0	26.5	24.0	30.0	26.0	47.0	35.5	52.0	38.0	41.5	32.5
17	21.5	33.0	26.5	26.0	24.0	24.5	23.0	25.0	23.0	25.0	23.0	25.0	23.0	41.5	32.5	50.5	37.5	44.0	33.5
18	21.0	26.5	22.5	28.5	25.0	22.5	21.5	23.0	21.5	23.0	21.5	23.0	21.5	34.0	28.0	44.5	34.0	42.5	32.5
19	20.5	20.5	19.0	27.0	23.5	20.5	20.0	20.5	20.0	20.5	20.0	20.5	20.0	25.5	23.0	34.0	27.5	34.5	28.0
20	19.0	16.5	16.0	20.0	19.5	18.5	18.5	18.5	18.5	18.5	18.5	18.5	18.5	19.0	18.5	20.5	19.5	21.5	20.0
21	18.0	14.5	14.5	17.0	17.0	17.0	17.0	17.0	17.0	17.0	17.0	17.0	17.0	17.0	17.0	17.0	17.0	17.0	17.0
22	16.5	13.0	13.0	15.5	15.5	15.5	15.5	15.5	15.5	15.5	15.5	15.5	15.5	15.5	15.5	15.5	15.5	15.5	15.5
23	15.0	12.0	12.0	14.0	14.0	14.0	14.0	14.0	14.0	14.0	14.0	14.0	14.0	14.0	14.0	14.0	14.0	14.0	14.0
Mean	16.5	26.0	20.5	20.0	18.0	22.5	19.5	24.5	20.5	24.5	20.5	23.5	20.0	24.5	20.5	24.5	20.5	22.5	19.5

Note: I_l (horizontal surface) = 80 W/m², I_l (vertical surface) = 18 W/m²

(e) July 23

Sun Time	Air Temp, t_{ao}/ (°C)	Horizontal		North		North-East		East		South-East		South		South-West		West		North-West	
		Dark	Light	Dark	Light	Dark	Light	Dark	Light	Dark	Light	Dark	Light	Dark	Light	Dark	Light	Dark	Light
00	16.0	12.5	12.5	15.0	15.0	15.0	15.0	15.0	15.0	15.0	15.0	15.0	15.0	15.0	15.0	15.0	15.0	15.0	15.0
01	14.5	11.5	11.5	14.0	14.0	14.0	14.0	14.0	14.0	14.0	14.0	14.0	14.0	14.0	14.0	14.0	14.0	14.0	14.0
02	13.5	10.5	10.5	13.0	13.0	13.0	13.0	13.0	13.0	13.0	13.0	13.0	13.0	13.0	13.0	13.0	13.0	13.0	13.0
03	13.0	10.0	10.0	12.0	12.0	12.0	12.0	12.0	12.0	12.0	12.0	12.0	12.0	12.0	12.0	12.0	12.0	12.0	12.0
04	13.0	9.5	9.5	12.0	12.0	12.0	12.0	12.0	12.0	12.0	12.0	12.0	12.0	12.0	12.0	12.0	12.0	12.0	12.0
05	13.0	12.0	11.0	17.5	15.0	22.5	18.0	22.5	18.0	17.0	15.0	13.5	13.0	13.5	13.0	13.5	13.0	13.0	13.0
06	13.5	17.5	14.5	19.5	16.5	31.0	23.0	33.5	24.5	25.5	20.0	15.5	14.5	15.5	14.5	15.5	14.5	15.5	14.0
07	14.5	24.5	18.5	18.0	16.0	34.0	25.0	40.5	28.5	33.5	24.5	18.0	16.0	18.0	16.0	18.0	16.0	18.0	16.0
08	16.0	31.5	23.0	20.5	18.0	33.5	25.5	43.5	31.0	40.0	29.0	25.5	20.5	21.0	18.5	21.0	18.5	20.5	18.0
09	17.5	38.5	27.5	23.0	20.0	31.0	24.5	44.0	31.5	44.5	32.0	33.5	26.0	24.0	20.5	24.0	20.5	23.5	20.5
10	19.0	44.5	31.5	26.0	22.5	27.5	23.5	41.5	31.0	46.5	34.0	40.0	30.5	27.0	23.0	27.0	23.0	26.5	22.5
11	20.5	49.0	34.5	28.5	24.5	29.0	24.5	37.5	29.5	46.0	34.5	45.5	34.0	35.0	28.0	29.5	25.0	29.0	24.5
12	21.5	51.5	36.5	30.0	26.0	30.5	26.5	31.5	26.5	43.0	33.0	48.0	36.0	43.0	33.0	31.5	26.5	30.5	26.5
13	23.0	51.5	37.5	31.0	27.0	31.5	27.5	32.0	27.5	38.0	31.0	48.0	36.5	49.0	37.0	40.0	32.0	31.5	27.5
14	24.0	49.5	36.5	31.0	27.5	31.5	28.0	32.0	28.0	32.0	28.0	45.0	35.5	51.5	39.0	46.5	36.0	32.5	28.5
15	24.5	45.5	35.0	30.5	27.5	31.0	27.5	31.5	28.0	31.5	28.0	40.5	33.0	51.5	39.0	51.0	39.0	38.5	32.0
16	24.5	40.5	32.0	29.0	26.5	29.5	27.0	30.0	27.0	30.0	27.0	34.0	29.5	49.0	37.5	52.5	39.5	42.5	34.0
17	24.5	34.5	28.5	28.0	26.0	27.5	26.0	28.0	26.0	28.0	26.0	28.0	26.0	43.5	34.5	50.5	38.5	45.0	35.0
18	24.0	28.0	24.5	29.5	26.5	25.5	24.5	25.5	24.5	25.5	24.5	25.5	24.5	35.5	30.0	44.0	34.5	41.5	33.0
19	23.0	22.0	21.0	27.0	25.0	23.0	22.5	23.0	22.5	23.0	22.5	23.0	22.5	26.5	24.5	32.5	27.5	32.5	28.0
20	21.5	18.5	18.5	21.0	21.0	21.0	21.0	21.0	21.0	21.0	21.0	21.0	21.0	21.0	21.0	21.0	21.0	21.0	21.0
21	20.5	17.0	17.0	19.5	19.5	19.5	19.5	19.5	19.5	19.5	19.5	19.5	19.5	19.5	19.5	19.5	19.5	19.5	19.5
22	19.0	15.5	15.5	18.0	18.0	18.0	18.0	18.0	18.0	18.0	18.0	18.0	18.0	18.0	18.0	18.0	18.0	18.0	18.0
23	17.5	14.0	14.0	16.5	16.5	16.5	16.5	16.5	16.5	16.5	16.5	16.5	16.5	16.5	16.5	16.5	16.5	16.5	16.5
Mean	19.0	27.5	22.0	22.0	20.0	24.0	21.5	26.5	22.5	27.0	23.0	26.0	22.5	27.0	23.0	26.5	22.5	24.0	21.5

Note: I_l (horizontal surface) = 79 W/m², I_l (vertical surface) = 18 W/m²

Table A2.33 Sol-air temperatures for SE England — 2½% day of highest radiation — *continued*

(f) August 22

Sun Time	Air Temp, t_{ao}/(°C)	Horizontal		North		North-East		East		South-East		South		South-West		West		North-West	
		Dark	Light	Dark	Light	Dark	Light	Dark	Light	Dark	Light	Dark	Light	Dark	Light	Dark	Light	Dark	Light
00	15.0	12.0	12.0	14.0	14.0	14.0	14.0	14.0	14.0	14.0	14.0	14.0	14.0	14.0	14.0	14.0	14.0	14.0	14.0
01	14.0	11.0	11.0	13.0	13.0	13.0	13.0	13.0	13.0	13.0	13.0	13.0	13.0	13.0	13.0	13.0	13.0	13.0	13.0
02	13.0	10.0	10.0	12.0	12.0	12.0	12.0	12.0	12.0	12.0	12.0	12.0	12.0	12.0	12.0	12.0	12.0	12.0	12.0
03	12.5	9.5	9.5	11.5	11.5	11.5	11.5	11.5	11.5	11.5	11.5	11.5	11.5	11.5	11.5	11.5	11.5	11.5	11.5
04	12.0	9.0	9.0	11.0	11.0	11.0	11.0	11.0	11.0	11.0	11.0	11.0	11.0	11.0	11.0	11.0	11.0	11.0	11.0
05	12.0	9.0	8.5	11.0	11.0	11.5	11.0	11.5	11.0	11.0	11.0	11.0	11.0	11.0	11.0	11.0	11.0	11.0	11.0
06	12.0	12.5	11.0	13.5	12.5	21.0	16.5	23.0	17.5	19.0	15.5	12.5	12.0	12.5	12.0	12.5	12.0	12.5	12.0
07	12.5	18.5	14.5	14.0	13.0	25.0	19.0	31.0	22.5	27.0	20.0	15.5	14.0	14.5	13.0	14.5	13.0	14.0	13.0
08	13.5	25.5	19.0	16.0	14.5	25.5	19.5	34.5	25.0	33.0	24.0	22.0	18.0	17.0	15.0	17.0	15.0	16.5	14.5
09	14.5	32.0	23.0	18.5	16.5	23.5	19.0	35.5	26.0	37.5	27.0	29.0	22.0	19.5	17.0	19.5	17.0	19.0	16.5
10	16.0	38.0	27.0	21.0	18.5	21.5	18.5	33.5	25.5	39.5	28.5	35.0	26.0	22.5	19.0	21.5	19.0	21.5	18.5
11	17.5	42.5	30.0	23.0	20.0	23.5	20.5	30.5	24.0	39.5	29.0	39.5	29.0	30.5	24.0	24.0	20.5	23.5	20.5
12	18.5	44.5	32.0	24.5	21.5	25.0	22.0	25.5	22.0	37.0	28.5	41.5	31.0	37.0	28.5	25.5	22.0	25.0	22.0
13	20.0	45.0	32.5	25.5	22.5	26.0	23.0	26.5	23.0	33.0	26.5	42.0	31.5	42.0	31.5	33.0	26.5	26.0	23.0
14	21.0	43.0	31.5	26.0	23.0	26.0	23.5	26.5	23.5	27.5	24.0	39.5	31.0	44.5	33.5	38.5	30.5	26.0	23.5
15	21.5	39.0	30.0	25.5	23.0	25.5	23.5	26.0	23.5	26.0	23.5	35.5	29.0	44.0	33.5	42.0	32.5	30.0	26.0
16	21.5	33.5	27.0	24.5	22.5	24.5	23.0	25.0	23.0	25.0	23.0	30.5	26.0	41.5	32.0	43.0	33.0	33.5	28.0
17	21.5	27.5	23.5	23.0	22.0	23.0	22.0	23.0	22.0	23.0	22.0	24.5	22.5	36.0	29.0	40.0	31.5	34.0	28.0
18	21.0	21.5	20.0	22.5	21.5	21.5	21.0	21.5	21.0	21.5	21.0	21.5	21.0	28.0	24.5	32.0	26.5	30.0	25.5
19	20.5	17.5	17.5	19.5	19.5	19.5	19.5	19.5	19.5	19.5	19.5	19.5	19.5	19.5	19.5	20.0	19.5	20.0	19.5
20	19.5	16.5	16.5	18.5	18.5	18.5	18.5	18.5	18.5	18.5	18.5	18.5	18.5	18.5	18.5	18.5	18.5	18.5	18.5
21	18.5	15.5	15.5	17.5	17.5	17.5	17.5	17.5	17.5	17.5	17.5	17.5	17.5	17.5	17.5	17.5	17.5	17.5	17.5
22	17.0	14.0	14.0	16.5	16.5	16.5	16.5	16.5	16.5	16.5	16.5	16.5	16.5	16.5	16.5	16.5	16.5	16.5	16.5
23	16.0	13.0	13.0	15.0	15.0	15.0	15.0	15.0	15.0	15.0	15.0	15.0	15.0	15.0	15.0	15.0	15.0	15.0	15.0
Mean	16.5	23.5	19.0	18.0	17.0	19.5	18.0	22.0	19.0	23.0	19.5	23.0	19.5	23.0	19.5	22.0	19.0	19.5	18.0

Note: I_l (horizontal surface) = 76 W/m², *I_l* (vertical surface) = 17 W/m²

(g) September 22

Sun Time	Air Temp, t_{ao}/(°C)	Horizontal		North		North-East		East		South-East		South		South-West		West		North-West	
		Dark	Light	Dark	Light	Dark	Light	Dark	Light	Dark	Light	Dark	Light	Dark	Light	Dark	Light	Dark	Light
00	13.5	10.5	10.5	13.0	13.0	13.0	13.0	13.0	13.0	13.0	13.0	13.0	13.0	13.0	13.0	13.0	13.0	13.0	13.0
01	13.0	10.0	10.0	12.0	12.0	12.0	12.0	12.0	12.0	12.0	12.0	12.0	12.0	12.0	12.0	12.0	12.0	12.0	12.0
02	12.0	9.0	9.0	11.0	11.0	11.0	11.0	11.0	11.0	11.0	11.0	11.0	11.0	11.0	11.0	11.0	11.0	11.0	11.0
03	11.5	8.5	8.5	10.5	10.5	10.5	10.5	10.5	10.5	10.5	10.5	10.5	10.5	10.5	10.5	10.5	10.5	10.5	10.5
04	11.0	8.0	8.0	10.5	10.5	10.5	10.5	10.5	10.5	10.5	10.5	10.5	10.5	10.5	10.5	10.5	10.5	10.5	10.5
05	11.0	8.0	8.0	10.0	10.0	10.0	10.0	10.0	10.0	10.0	10.0	10.0	10.0	10.0	10.0	10.0	10.0	10.0	10.0
06	11.5	8.5	8.5	10.5	10.5	10.5	10.5	10.5	10.5	10.5	10.5	10.5	10.5	10.5	10.5	10.5	10.5	10.5	10.5
07	12.0	13.0	11.0	12.5	12.0	21.0	16.5	28.0	20.5	26.0	19.5	16.0	14.0	13.0	12.0	13.0	12.0	12.5	12.0
08	13.0	20.0	15.5	15.0	14.0	24.0	18.5	37.5	26.0	38.0	26.5	25.5	19.5	15.5	14.0	15.5	14.0	15.5	14.0
09	14.0	27.5	20.0	18.0	16.0	21.5	18.0	40.0	28.0	45.5	31.5	35.5	25.5	18.5	16.5	18.5	16.5	18.0	16.0
10	15.5	33.5	24.5	20.5	18.0	21.0	18.0	38.0	27.5	49.0	33.5	43.5	31.0	25.5	21.0	21.5	18.5	21.0	18.0
11	17.0	38.0	27.5	22.5	20.0	23.0	20.0	32.5	25.5	49.0	34.5	49.5	35.0	36.0	27.0	23.5	20.5	23.0	20.0
12	18.5	40.5	29.5	24.5	21.0	25.0	21.5	25.0	22.0	44.5	32.5	52.5	37.0	44.5	32.5	25.0	22.0	25.0	21.5
13	19.5	40.5	30.0	25.0	22.0	25.5	22.5	26.0	22.5	38.0	29.5	52.0	37.0	51.5	37.0	35.0	27.5	25.5	22.5
14	20.0	38.0	28.5	25.0	22.5	25.0	22.5	25.5	22.5	30.0	25.0	48.0	35.0	53.0	38.0	42.0	32.0	25.0	22.5
15	20.0	33.0	26.0	24.0	22.0	24.0	22.0	24.5	22.0	24.5	22.0	41.5	31.5	51.5	37.5	46.0	34.0	27.5	24.0
16	20.0	27.0	22.5	22.0	21.0	22.5	21.0	22.5	21.0	22.5	21.0	32.5	26.5	45.5	33.5	44.5	33.5	31.0	26.0
17	19.5	20.5	19.0	20.5	19.5	20.5	20.0	20.5	20.0	20.5	20.0	23.5	21.5	33.5	27.0	35.5	28.5	29.0	24.5
18	19.0	16.0	16.0	18.5	18.5	18.5	18.5	18.5	18.5	18.5	18.5	18.5	18.5	18.5	18.5	18.5	18.5	18.5	18.5
19	18.5	15.5	15.5	17.5	17.5	17.5	17.5	17.5	17.5	17.5	17.5	17.5	17.5	17.5	17.5	17.5	17.5	17.5	17.5
20	17.5	14.5	14.5	17.0	17.0	17.0	17.0	17.0	17.0	17.0	17.0	17.0	17.0	17.0	17.0	17.0	17.0	17.0	17.0
21	16.5	13.5	13.5	16.0	16.0	16.0	16.0	16.0	16.0	16.0	16.0	16.0	16.0	16.0	16.0	16.0	16.0	16.0	16.0
22	15.5	12.5	12.5	15.0	15.0	15.0	15.0	15.0	15.0	15.0	15.0	15.0	15.0	15.0	15.0	15.0	15.0	15.0	15.0
23	14.5	11.5	11.5	14.0	14.0	14.0	14.0	14.0	14.0	14.0	14.0	14.0	14.0	14.0	14.0	14.0	14.0	14.0	14.0
Mean	15.5	20.0	16.5	17.0	16.0	18.0	16.5	20.5	18.0	23.5	19.5	25.0	20.5	23.5	19.5	20.5	18.0	18.0	16.75

Note: I_l (horizontal surface) = 73 W/m², *I_l* (vertical surface) = 17 W/m²

Table A2.33   Sol-air temperatures for SE England — 2½% day of highest radiation — *continued*

(h) October 22

Sun Time	Air Temp, t_{ao}/(°C)	Horizontal		North		North-East		East		South-East		South		South-West		West		North-West	
		Dark	Light	Dark	Light	Dark	Light	Dark	Light	Dark	Light	Dark	Light	Dark	Light	Dark	Light	Dark	Light
00	12.5	9.5	9.5	11.5	11.5	11.5	11.5	11.5	11.5	11.5	11.5	11.5	11.5	11.5	11.5	11.5	11.5	11.5	11.5
01	11.5	8.5	8.5	11.0	11.0	11.0	11.0	11.0	11.0	11.0	11.0	11.0	11.0	11.0	11.0	11.0	11.0	11.0	11.0
02	11.0	8.0	8.0	10.5	10.5	10.5	10.5	10.5	10.5	10.5	10.5	10.5	10.5	10.5	10.5	10.5	10.5	10.5	10.5
03	10.5	7.5	7.5	10.0	10.0	10.0	10.0	10.0	10.0	10.0	10.0	10.0	10.0	10.0	10.0	10.0	10.0	10.0	10.0
04	10.5	7.5	7.5	9.5	9.5	9.5	9.5	9.5	9.5	9.5	9.5	9.5	9.5	9.5	9.5	9.5	9.5	9.5	9.5
05	10.0	7.0	7.0	9.0	9.0	9.0	9.0	9.0	9.0	9.0	9.0	9.0	9.0	9.0	9.0	9.0	9.0	9.0	9.0
06	10.0	7.0	7.0	9.0	9.0	9.0	9.0	9.0	9.0	9.0	9.0	9.0	9.0	9.0	9.0	9.0	9.0	9.0	9.0
07	10.5	7.5	7.5	9.5	9.5	10.0	10.0	10.5	10.0	10.5	10.0	10.0	9.5	9.5	9.5	9.5	9.5	9.5	9.5
08	11.0	12.0	11.0	12.0	11.0	15.0	13.0	24.5	18.5	26.0	19.0	19.5	15.5	12.0	11.5	12.0	11.5	12.0	11.0
09	12.5	18.5	14.5	14.5	13.5	15.5	13.5	31.0	22.5	37.0	25.5	30.5	22.0	15.0	13.5	15.0	13.5	15.0	13.5
10	14.0	24.5	18.5	17.5	15.5	17.5	15.5	31.5	23.0	42.5	29.5	39.0	27.5	23.5	19.0	18.0	16.0	17.5	15.5
11	15.5	29.0	21.5	19.5	17.5	20.0	17.5	28.0	22.0	43.5	30.5	45.5	31.5	33.0	24.5	20.5	18.0	20.0	17.5
12	16.5	31.5	23.5	21.5	19.0	21.5	19.0	22.0	19.5	40.5	29.5	48.0	34.0	40.5	29.5	22.0	19.5	21.5	19.0
13	17.5	31.5	24.0	22.0	19.5	22.0	20.0	22.5	20.0	35.0	27.0	47.5	34.0	45.5	32.5	23.0	24.0	22.0	20.0
14	18.0	28.5	22.5	21.5	19.5	21.5	19.5	22.0	20.0	27.5	23.0	43.0	31.5	46.5	33.5	35.0	27.0	21.5	19.5
15	18.0	24.0	20.0	20.0	18.5	20.5	19.0	20.5	19.0	20.5	19.0	35.5	27.5	42.5	31.0	36.5	28.0	21.0	19.0
16	17.5	18.5	17.0	18.5	17.5	18.5	17.5	18.5	17.5	18.5	17.5	26.0	22.0	32.5	25.5	31.0	24.5	22.0	19.5
17	17.0	14.5	14.5	16.5	16.5	16.5	16.5	16.5	16.5	16.5	16.5	17.0	16.5	17.5	17.0	17.5	17.0	17.0	16.5
18	16.5	13.5	13.5	16.0	16.0	16.0	16.0	16.0	16.0	16.0	16.0	16.0	16.0	16.0	16.0	16.0	16.0	16.0	16.0
19	16.0	13.0	13.0	15.5	15.5	15.5	15.5	15.5	15.5	15.5	15.5	15.5	15.5	15.5	15.5	15.5	15.5	15.5	15.5
20	15.5	12.5	12.5	14.5	14.5	14.5	14.5	14.5	14.5	14.5	14.5	14.5	14.5	14.5	14.5	14.5	14.5	14.5	14.5
21	14.5	11.5	11.5	14.0	14.0	14.0	14.0	14.0	14.0	14.0	14.0	14.0	14.0	14.0	14.0	14.0	14.0	14.0	14.0
22	14.0	11.0	11.0	13.0	13.0	13.0	13.0	13.0	13.0	13.0	13.0	13.0	13.0	13.0	13.0	13.0	13.0	13.0	13.0
23	13.0	10.0	10.0	12.5	12.5	12.5	12.5	12.5	12.5	12.5	12.5	12.5	12.5	12.5	12.5	12.5	12.5	12.5	12.5
Mean	14.0	15.5	13.5	14.5	14.0	15.0	14.0	17.0	15.0	19.5	16.5	21.5	18.0	19.5	17.0	17.0	15.0	15.0	14.0

Note: I_t (horizontal surface) = 74 W/m², I_t (vertical surface) = 17 W/m²

AVAILABILITY OF SOLAR ENERGY

For the estimation of solar collector performance and for the calculation of available solar gain through windows, information is required on the irradiation of horizontal, vertical and sloping surfaces.

Monthly and annual means of the daily solar irradiation on surfaces of different orientations and slopes are given in Table A2.34. The values are derived from solar radiation measurements at Kew, averaged over the ten year period 1959–68.

For a horizontal surface, the monthly values of diffuse and total (global) solar irradiation are also to be found against 'average' weather in the tables of banded weather data (Tables A2.7 and A2.8). These tables also give the direct and diffuse radiation factors k_D and k_d used in calculating the daily irradiances on sloping and vertical surfaces.

Solar irradiation varies with locality, partly due to changes in latitude and partly to the different sky conditions prevailing. Isopleths of daily totals of global solar irradiation for the United Kingdom are given, month by month, in Fig. A2.25 *(a)* to *(l)* and, for the whole year, in Fig. A2.26.[42] They represent the best attempt to interpolate between available long-term radiation measurements using data on sunshine durations and taking account of significant geographical features. If the maps are used to apply the data of Table A2.34 to localities other than Kew, care should be taken in interpreting the different effects of a latitude shift on the irradiation of horizontal and non-horizontal surfaces.

Maps and tables of the monthly and annual availability of global solar irradiation have also been produced for the whole of Europe,[43] see *Basic Radiation Data — World Values.*

Table A2.34 Monthly and annual means of daily solar irradiation on surfaces of different orientations and slopes, in SE England

(a) South Facing

Month	Direct irradiation incident on surface at stated angle /(MJ/m²)					Diffuse irradiation incident on surface at stated angle /(MJ/m²)					Total irradiation incident on surface at stated angle /(MJ/m²)				
	Horiz	30°	45°	60°	Vert	Horiz	30°	45°	60°	Vert	Horiz	30°	45°	60°	Vert
January	0.6	1.7	2.1	2.4	2.4	1.5	1.4	1.3	1.2	0.9	2.1	3.1	3.4	3.6	3.3
February	1.2	2.5	2.9	3.1	3.0	2.5	2.3	2.2	2.0	1.6	3.7	4.8	5.1	5.1	4.6
March	3.4	5.4	5.9	5.9	4.8	4.4	4.2	3.9	3.7	3.0	7.8	9.6	9.8	9.6	7.8
April	4.5	5.7	5.7	5.3	3.6	6.6	6.2	5.9	5.4	4.4	11.1	11.9	11.6	10.7	8.0
May	6.9	7.5	7.0	6.1	3.3	8.6	8.2	7.7	7.1	5.8	15.5	15.7	14.7	13.2	9.1
June	8.2	8.3	7.5	6.3	3.0	9.3	8.8	8.3	7.8	6.3	17.5	17.1	15.8	14.1	9.3
July	6.3	6.5	6.0	5.1	2.6	9.4	8.9	8.4	7.8	6.2	15.7	15.4	14.4	12.9	8.8
August	5.9	6.9	6.6	6.0	3.7	7.6	7.2	6.8	6.3	5.1	13.5	14.1	13.4	12.3	8.8
September	4.7	6.5	6.9	6.7	5.1	5.6	5.2	4.9	4.6	3.7	10.1	11.7	11.8	11.3	8.8
October	2.4	4.4	5.0	5.2	4.6	3.4	3.2	3.0	2.8	2.3	5.8	7.6	8.0	8.0	6.9
November	0.9	2.3	2.8	3.1	3.0	1.9	1.7	1.6	1.5	1.2	2.8	4.0	4.4	4.6	4.2
December	0.5	1.7	2.1	2.3	2.3	1.2	1.0	1.0	0.9	0.8	1.7	2.7	3.1	3.2	3.1
Year	3.8	4.9	5.0	4.8	3.5	5.2	4.9	4.6	4.3	3.4	9.0	9.8	9.6	9.1	6.9

Note: Diffuse irradiation includes the ground reflected contribution

(b) South-East and South-West Facing

Month	Direct irradiation incident on surface at stated angle /(MJ/m²)					Diffuse irradiation incident on surface at stated angle /(MJ/m²)					Total irradiation incident on surface at stated angle /(MJ/m²)				
	Horiz	30°	45°	60°	Vert	Horiz	30°	45°	60°	Vert	Horiz	30°	45°	60°	Vert
January	0.6	1.4	1.6	1.8	1.7	1.5	1.4	1.3	1.2	0.9	2.1	2.8	2.9	3.0	2.6
February	1.2	2.1	2.3	2.4	2.2	2.5	2.3	2.2	2.0	1.6	3.7	4.4	4.5	4.4	3.8
March	3.4	4.7	5.0	4.9	3.8	4.4	4.2	3.9	3.7	3.0	7.8	8.9	8.9	8.6	6.8
April	4.5	5.3	5.2	4.9	3.4	6.6	6.2	5.9	5.4	4.4	11.1	11.5	11.1	10.3	7.8
May	6.9	7.2	6.8	6.1	3.9	8.6	8.2	7.7	7.1	5.8	15.5	15.4	14.5	13.2	9.7
June	8.2	8.2	7.5	6.6	3.9	9.3	8.8	8.3	7.8	6.3	17.5	17.0	15.8	14.4	10.2
July	6.3	6.3	5.9	5.2	3.2	9.4	8.9	8.4	7.8	6.2	15.7	15.2	14.3	13.0	9.4
August	5.9	6.5	6.3	5.7	3.8	7.6	7.2	6.8	6.3	5.1	13.5	13.7	13.1	12.0	8.9
September	4.7	5.9	6.0	5.8	4.4	5.6	5.2	4.9	4.6	3.7	10.1	11.1	10.9	10.4	8.1
October	2.4	3.8	4.1	4.2	3.4	3.4	3.2	3.0	2.8	2.3	5.8	7.0	7.1	7.0	5.7
November	0.9	1.9	2.2	2.3	2.1	1.9	1.7	1.6	1.5	1.2	2.8	3.6	3.8	3.8	3.3
December	0.5	1.3	1.6	1.7	1.6	1.2	1.0	1.0	0.9	0.8	1.7	2.3	2.6	2.6	2.4
Year	3.8	4.5	4.6	4.3	3.1	5.2	4.9	4.6	4.3	3.4	9.0	9.4	9.2	8.6	6.5

Note: Diffuse irradiation includes the ground reflected contribution

(c) East and West Facing

Month	Direct irradiation incident on surface at stated angle /(MJ/m²)					Diffuse irradiation incident on surface at stated angle /(MJ/m²)					Total irradiation incident on surface at stated angle /(MJ/m²)				
	Horiz	30°	45°	60°	Vert	Horiz	30°	45°	60°	Vert	Horiz	30°	45°	60°	Vert
January	0.6	0.6	0.6	0.6	0.5	1.5	1.4	1.3	1.2	0.9	2.1	2.0	1.9	1.8	1.4
February	1.2	1.2	1.2	1.1	0.8	2.5	2.3	2.2	2.0	1.6	3.7	3.5	3.4	3.1	2.4
March	3.4	3.2	3.0	2.8	2.0	4.4	4.2	3.9	3.7	3.0	7.8	7.4	6.9	6.5	5.0
April	4.5	4.2	3.9	3.5	2.4	6.6	6.2	5.9	5.4	4.4	11.1	10.4	9.8	8.9	6.8
May	6.9	6.3	5.8	5.1	3.5	8.6	8.2	7.7	7.1	5.8	15.5	14.5	13.5	12.2	9.3
June	8.2	7.5	6.8	5.9	4.0	9.3	8.8	8.3	7.8	6.3	17.5	16.3	15.1	13.7	10.3
July	6.3	5.7	5.2	4.5	3.1	9.4	8.9	8.4	7.8	6.2	15.7	14.6	13.6	12.3	9.3
August	5.9	5.4	5.0	4.5	3.1	7.6	7.2	6.8	6.3	5.1	13.5	12.6	11.8	10.8	8.2
September	4.7	4.4	4.1	3.7	2.7	5.6	5.2	4.9	4.6	3.7	10.1	9.6	9.0	8.3	6.4
October	2.4	2.3	2.2	2.1	1.5	3.4	3.2	3.0	2.8	2.3	5.8	5.5	5.2	4.9	3.8
November	0.9	0.9	0.9	0.9	0.7	1.9	1.7	1.6	1.5	1.2	2.8	2.6	2.5	2.4	1.9
December	0.5	0.5	0.5	0.5	0.4	1.2	1.0	1.0	0.9	0.8	1.7	1.5	1.5	1.4	1.2
Year	3.8	3.5	3.3	2.9	2.1	5.2	4.9	4.6	4.3	3.4	9.0	8.4	7.9	7.2	5.5

Note: Diffuse irradiation includes the ground reflected contribution

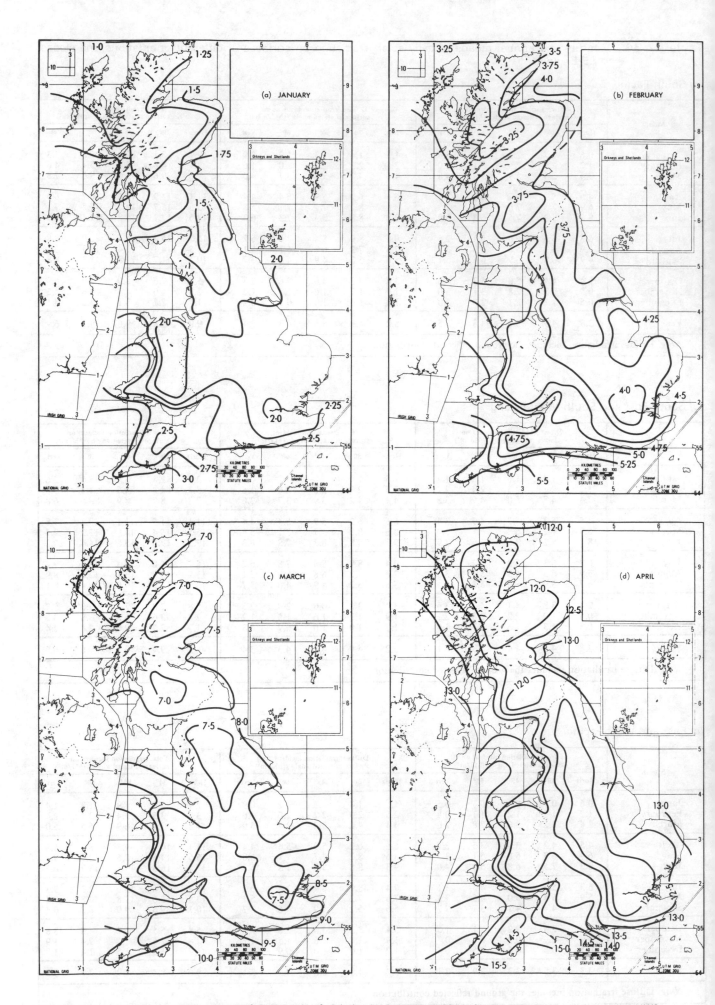

Fig. A2.25 Isopleths of monthly means of daily totals of global solar irradiation (MJ/m²), showing distribution over the UK[42]. (Reproduced by permission of the Controller of H.M. Stationery Office).

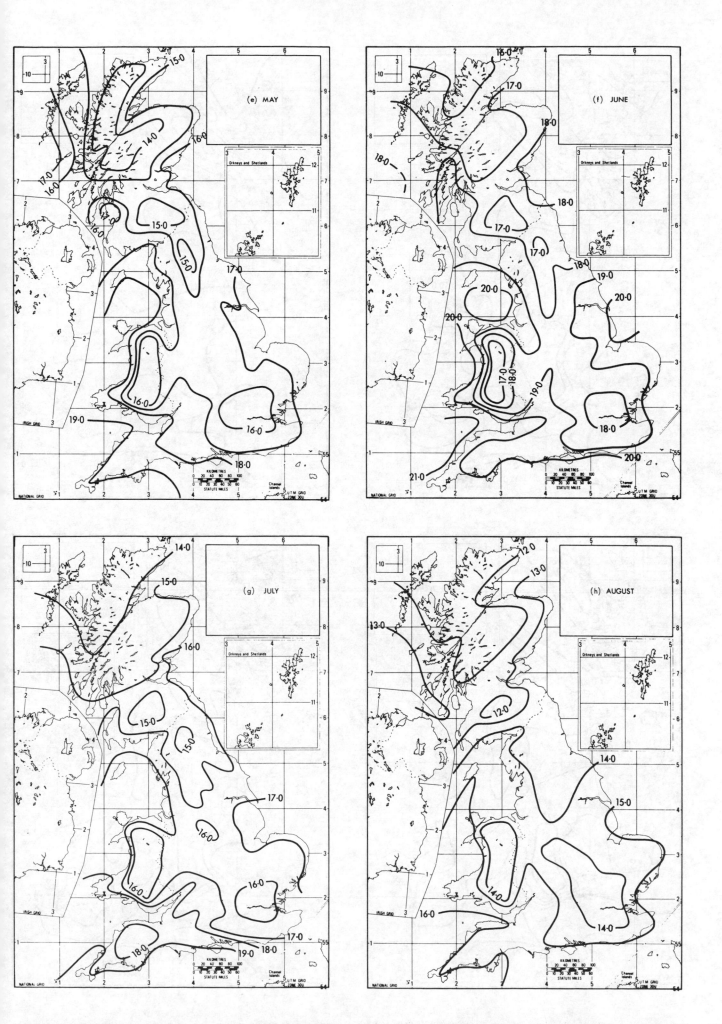

Fig. A2.25 Isopleths of monthly means of daily totals of global solar irradiation (MJ/m²), showing distribution over the UK[42] — *continued*.

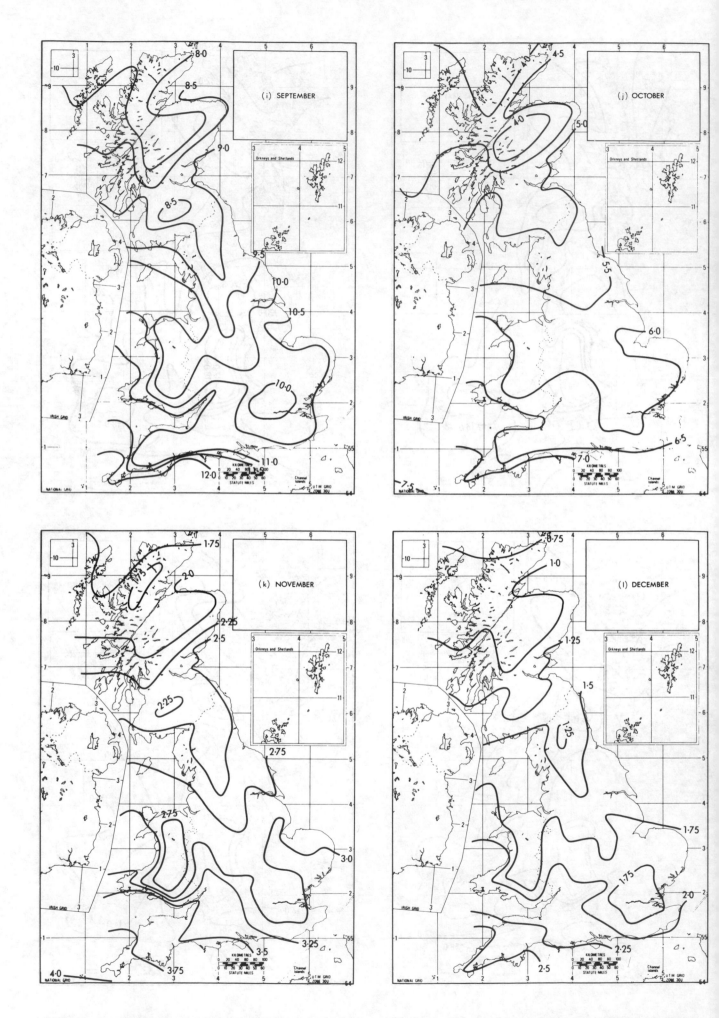

Fig. A2.25 Isopleths of monthly means of daily totals of global solar irradiation (MJ/m²), showing distribution over the UK[42] — *continued*.

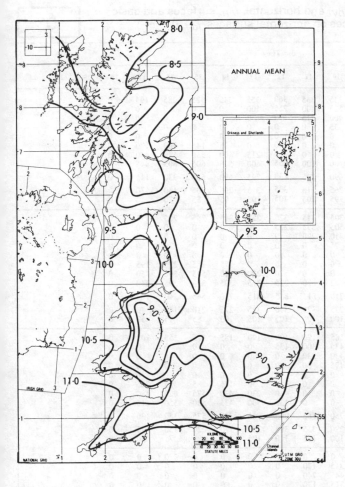

Fig. A.26 Isopleths of annual means of daily totals of global solar irradiation (MJ/m²), showing distribution over the UK[42].

Example

(a) Latitude 5 °N, humid climate, sea level —
At noon, for September 22 and March 21, basic direct and diffuse (cloudy sky) irradiances on a horizontal surface are:

Direct: I_{DH} = 915 W/m²   (Table A2.35 *(b)*)
Diffuse: I_{dH} = 430 W/m²   (Table A2.35 *(b)*)

Radiation factors are as follows:

k_D = 0.5   (Table A2.30)
k_d = 1.1   (Table A2.30)

Therefore, near maximum irradiance is given by:

$$I_{THd} = (0.5 \times 915) + (1.1 \times 430) = 930 \text{ W/m}^2$$

(b) Latitude 30 °N, arid climate, sea level —
At noon, for June 21, basic direct and diffuse (clear sky) irradiances on a horizontal surface are:

Direct: I_{DH} = 915 W/m²   (Table A2.35 *(g)*)
Diffuse: I_{dH} = 110 W/m²   (Table A2.35 *(g)*)

Radiation factors are as follows:

k_D = 1.1   (Table A2.30)
k_d = 0.9   (Table A2.30)

Therefore, near maximum irradiance is given by:

$$I_{THd} = (1.1 \times 915) + (0.9 \times 110) = 1105 \text{ W/m}^2$$

BASIC RADIATION DATA — WORLD VALUES

The concepts of basic direct and diffuse (sky) irradiances have been fully described and hourly and daily mean values for vertical and horizontal surfaces in southern England (that is, approximately 51½ °N) are given in Table A2.26. The present section gives similar data for latitudes between 0 °N (the equator) and 60 °N at intervals of 5 °. Table A2.35 gives basic direct irradiances on vertical surfaces, I_{DV}, and basic direct and diffuse (sky) irradiances on a horizontal surface, I_{DH} and I_{dH} respectively, the latter applying to both clear and cloudy sky conditions.

The derivation of design total (i.e. direct plus diffuse) irradiances from these basic values has been described earlier (see *Design Radiation Data*). The following example shows the use of Table A2.35 in conjunction with the correction factors k_D and k_d.

Comprehensive values of the direct and diffuse radiation factors, k_D and k_d, are generally not available for localities other than SE England. It is expected that these deficiencies will be met as opportunities arise to analyse long-term measurements of solar radiation at other localities.

Monthly and annual totals of both sunshine duration and global solar irradiation obtained at 56 European meteorological stations are given in a European solar radiation atlas.[43] The Atlas also includes isopleths similar to those of Figs. A2.25 and A2.26, but covering the whole of Europe. The isopleths also show the distribution of maximum and minimum irradiation during June and December.

Table A2.35 *(a)* Basic direct solar irradiances on vertical, I_{DV}, and horizontal, I_{DH}, surfaces and basic diffuse (cloudy and clear sky) solar irradiances on horizontal surfaces, I_{dH}, (W/m²).

0°

Date	Orientation	Daily mean	03	04	05	06	07	08	09	10	11	12	13	14	15	16	17	18	19	20	21
June 21	N	140				0	195	285	325	345	355	360	355	345	325	285	195	0			
	NE	120				0	445	605	605	525	400	255	100	0	0	0	0	0			
	E	90				0	430	570	530	400	215	0	0	0	0	0	0	0			
	SE	25				0	170	200	145	35	0	0	0	0	0	0	0	0			
	S	0				0	0	0	0	0	0	0	0	0	0	0	0	0			
	SW	25				0	0	0	0	0	0	0	0	35	145	200	170	0			
	W	90				0	0	0	0	0	0	0	215	400	530	570	430	0			
	NW	120				0	0	0	0	0	100	255	400	525	605	605	445	0			
	H	240				0	115	330	530	690	795	830	795	690	530	330	115	0			
	Diff (Cldy)	95				0	70	140	205	265	315	335	315	265	205	140	70	0			
	Diff (Clr)	40				0	50	70	85	95	105	105	105	95	85	70	50	0			
July 23 and May 22	N	125				0	175	255	285	305	315	320	315	305	285	255	175	0			
	NE	115				0	440	595	590	505	375	225	70	0	0	0	0	0			
	E	90				0	450	590	545	410	220	0	0	0	0	0	0	0			
	SE	30				0	195	235	185	75	0	0	0	0	0	0	0	0			
	S	0				0	0	0	0	0	0	0	0	0	0	0	0	0			
	SW	30				0	0	0	0	0	0	0	0	75	185	235	195	0			
	W	90				0	0	0	0	0	0	0	220	410	545	590	450	0			
	NW	115				0	0	0	0	0	70	225	375	505	590	595	440	0			
	H	245				0	120	340	545	710	815	855	815	710	545	340	120	0			
	Diff (Cldy)	100				0	70	140	210	275	325	350	325	275	210	140	70	0			
	Diff (Clr)	40				0	50	75	85	100	105	105	105	100	85	75	50	0			
August 22 and April 22	N	75				0	105	155	175	185	190	190	190	185	175	155	105	0			
	NE	100				0	415	550	530	435	300	135	0	0	0	0	0	0			
	E	100				0	480	625	575	430	230	0	0	0	0	0	0	0			
	SE	45				0	265	335	285	175	30	0	0	0	0	0	0	0			
	S	0				0	0	0	0	0	0	0	0	0	0	0	0	0			
	SW	45				0	0	0	0	0	0	0	30	175	285	335	265	0			
	W	100				0	0	0	0	0	0	0	230	430	575	625	480	0			
	NW	100				0	0	0	0	0	0	135	300	435	530	550	415	0			
	H	260				0	130	360	575	750	865	905	865	750	575	360	130	0			
	Diff (Cldy)	105				0	75	150	220	290	355	395	355	290	220	150	75	0			
	Diff (Clr)	40				0	50	75	90	100	105	110	105	100	90	75	50	0			
September 22 and March 21	N	0				0	0	0	0	0	0	0	0	0	0	0	0	0			
	NE	70				0	355	455	420	315	170	0	0	0	0	0	0	0			
	E	100				0	500	645	595	445	240	0	0	0	0	0	0	0			
	SE	70				0	355	455	420	315	170	0	0	0	0	0	0	0			
	S	0				0	0	0	0	0	0	0	0	0	0	0	0	0			
	SW	70				0	0	0	0	0	0	0	170	315	420	455	355	0			
	W	100				0	0	0	0	0	0	0	240	445	595	645	500	0			
	NW	70				0	0	0	0	0	0	0	170	315	420	455	355	0			
	H	270				0	135	375	595	770	890	900	890	770	595	375	135	0			
	Diff (Cldy)	115				0	75	150	225	300	380	455	380	300	225	150	75	0			
	Diff (Clr)	40				0	50	75	90	100	110	115	110	100	90	75	50	0			
October 22 and February 21	N	0				0	0	0	0	0	0	0	0	0	0	0	0	0			
	NE	50				0	275	345	300	190	40	0	0	0	0	0	0	0			
	E	100				0	485	630	580	435	235	0	0	0	0	0	0	0			
	SE	95				0	410	545	520	425	285	125	0	0	0	0	0	0			
	S	70				0	95	140	160	165	175	175	175	165	160	140	95	0			
	SW	95				0	0	0	0	0	0	125	285	425	520	545	410	0			
	W	100				0	0	0	0	0	0	0	235	435	580	630	485	0			
	NW	50				0	0	0	0	0	0	0	40	190	300	345	275	0			
	H	265				0	130	365	580	750	870	910	870	750	580	365	130	0			
	Diff (Cldy)	110				0	75	150	220	295	360	400	360	295	220	150	75	0			
	Diff (Clr)	40				0	50	75	90	100	110	110	110	110	90	75	50	0			
November 22 and January 21	N	0				0	0	0	0	0	0	0	0	0	0	0	0	0			
	NE	30				0	200	240	185	80	0	0	0	0	0	0	0	0			
	E	95				0	450	590	550	410	220	0	0	0	0	0	0	0			
	SE	115				0	440	595	585	500	375	220	65	0	0	0	0	0			
	S	125				0	170	250	285	300	310	315	310	300	285	250	170	0			
	SW	115				0	0	0	0	0	65	220	375	500	585	595	440	0			
	W	95				0	0	0	0	0	0	0	220	410	550	590	450	0			
	NW	30				0	0	0	0	0	0	0	0	80	185	240	200	0			
	H	250				0	120	340	550	710	820	860	820	710	550	340	120	0			
	Diff (Cldy)	100				0	70	140	210	275	330	350	330	275	210	140	70	0			
	Diff (Clr)	40				0	50	75	85	100	105	105	105	100	85	75	50	0			
December 21	N	0				0	0	0	0	0	0	0	0	0	0	0	0	0			
	NE	25				0	170	200	145	35	0	0	0	0	0	0	0	0			
	E	90				0	430	570	530	400	215	0	0	0	0	0	0	0			
	SE	120				0	445	605	605	525	400	255	100	0	0	0	0	0			
	S	140				0	195	285	325	345	355	360	355	345	325	285	195	0			
	SW	120				0	0	0	0	0	100	255	400	525	605	605	445	0			
	W	90				0	0	0	0	0	0	0	215	400	530	570	430	0			
	NW	25				0	0	0	0	0	0	0	0	35	145	200	170	0			
	H	240				0	115	330	530	690	795	830	795	690	530	330	115	0			
	Diff (Cldy)	95				0	70	140	205	265	315	335	315	265	205	140	70	0			
	Diff (Clr)	40				0	50	70	85	95	105	105	105	95	85	70	50	0			

THE TABULATED VALUES HAVE THE FOLLOWING BASIS:

Direct radiation factor, $k_D = 1.0$
Diffuse radiation factor, $k_d = 1.0$
Height correction factor, $k_a = 1.0$

For southern latitudes, this table may be used by reading northern values for southern aspects and vice-versa, substituting dates as follows:

NORTH	June	May July	April August	March September	February October	January November	December
SOUTH	December	November January	October February	September March	August April	July May	June

Table A2.35 *(b)* Basic direct solar irradiances on vertical, I_{DV}, and horizontal, I_{DH}, surfaces and basic diffuse (cloudy and clear sky) solar irradiances on horizontal surfaces, I_{dH}, (W/m²).

5°N

Date	Orientation	Daily mean	03	04	05	06	07	08	09	10	11	12	13	14	15	16	17	18	19	20	21
June 21	N	125				35	200	265	280	285	290	290	290	285	280	265	200	35			
	NE	120				85	475	605	580	485	355	205	50	0	0	0	0	0			
	E	95				85	475	590	540	400	215	0	0	0	0	0	0	0			
	SE	30				35	195	230	180	80	0	0	0	0	0	0	0	0			
	S	0				0	0	0	0	0	0	0	0	0	0	0	0	0			
	SW	30				0	0	0	0	0	0	0	0	80	180	230	195	35			
	W	95				0	0	0	0	0	0	0	215	400	540	590	475	85			
	NW	120				0	0	0	0	0	50	205	355	485	580	605	475	85			
	H	255				5	145	365	565	725	830	870	830	725	565	365	145	5			
	Diff (Cldy)	105				10	80	150	215	280	335	360	335	280	215	150	80	10			
	Diff (Clr)	40				10	55	75	90	100	105	110	105	100	90	75	55	10			
July 23 and May 22	N	105				30	175	230	240	245	245	245	245	245	240	230	175	30			
	NE	110				75	465	590	560	465	330	175	15	0	0	0	0	0			
	E	100				75	485	605	555	415	220	0	0	0	0	0	0	0			
	SE	35				35	220	265	220	120	0	0	0	0	0	0	0	0			
	S	0				0	0	0	0	0	0	0	0	0	0	0	0	0			
	SW	35				0	0	0	0	0	0	0	0	120	220	265	220	35			
	W	100				0	0	0	0	0	0	0	220	415	555	605	485	75			
	NW	110				0	0	0	0	0	15	175	330	465	560	590	465	75			
	H	260				0	145	370	575	740	850	890	850	740	575	370	145	0			
	Diff (Cldy)	105				10	80	150	220	285	345	375	345	285	220	150	80	10			
	Diff (Clr)	40				5	55	75	90	100	105	110	105	100	90	75	55	5			
August 22 and April 22	N	55				10	100	125	125	120	115	115	115	120	125	125	100	10			
	NE	90				40	425	535	530	390	245	80	0	0	0	0	0	0			
	E	100				50	505	635	580	435	235	0	0	0	0	0	0	0			
	SE	55				25	285	360	325	225	85	0	0	0	0	0	0	0			
	S	0				0	0	0	0	0	0	0	0	0	0	0	0	0			
	SW	55				0	0	0	0	0	0	0	85	225	325	360	285	25			
	W	100				0	0	0	0	0	0	0	235	435	580	635	505	50			
	NW	90				0	0	0	0	0	0	80	245	390	500	535	425	40			
	H	270				0	145	380	595	765	885	915	885	765	595	380	145	0			
	Diff (Cldy)	110				5	80	155	225	300	370	420	370	300	225	155	80	5			
	Diff (Clr)	40				5	55	75	90	100	100	110	110	100	90	75	55	5			
September 22 and March 21	N	0				0	0	0	0	0	0	0	0	0	0	0	0	0			
	NE	65				0	345	435	385	265	115	0	0	0	0	0	0	0			
	E	100				0	500	645	595	445	240	0	0	0	0	0	0	0			
	SE	80				0	360	480	455	360	225	55	0	0	0	0	0	0			
	S	25				0	10	30	50	65	80	80	80	65	50	30	10	0			
	SW	80				0	0	0	0	0	0	55	225	360	455	480	360	0			
	W	100				0	0	0	0	0	0	0	240	445	595	645	500	0			
	NW	65				0	0	0	0	0	0	0	115	265	385	435	345	0			
	H	265				0	135	370	590	765	885	915	885	765	590	370	135	0			
	Diff (Cldy)	110				0	75	150	225	300	375	430	375	300	225	150	75	0			
	Diff (Clr)	40				0	50	75	90	100	110	115	110	100	90	75	50	0			
October 22 and February 21	N	0					0	0	0	0	0	0	0	0	0	0	0				
	NE	40					255	320	260	140	0	0	0	0	0	0	0				
	E	95					460	620	575	430	230	0	0	0	0	0	0				
	SE	105					400	555	550	470	340	180	10	0	0	0	0				
	S	90					100	170	205	230	245	250	245	230	205	170	100				
	SW	105					0	0	0	0	10	180	340	470	550	555	400				
	W	95					0	0	0	0	0	0	230	430	575	620	460				
	NW	40					0	0	0	0	0	0	0	140	260	320	255				
	H	255					115	345	560	730	845	885	845	730	560	345	115				
	Diff (Cldy)	105					70	140	215	285	345	375	345	285	215	140	70				
	Diff (Clr)	40					50	75	90	100	105	110	105	100	90	75	50				
November 22 and January 21	N	0					0	0	0	0	0	0	0	0	0	0	0				
	NE	25					175	215	150	35	0	0	0	0	0	0	0				
	E	90					410	570	540	405	215	0	0	0	0	0	0				
	SE	125					405	595	610	540	420	270	110	0	0	0	0				
	S	140					165	270	325	355	375	380	375	355	325	270	165				
	SW	125					0	0	0	0	110	270	420	540	610	595	405				
	W	90					0	0	0	0	0	0	215	405	540	570	410				
	NW	25					0	0	0	0	0	0	0	35	150	215	175				
	H	230					95	310	515	675	780	815	780	675	515	310	95				
	Diff (Cldy)	95					60	130	200	260	305	325	305	260	200	130	60				
	Diff (Clr)	35					45	70	85	95	100	105	100	95	85	70	45				
December 21	N	0					0	0	0	0	0	0	0	0	0	0	0				
	NE	20					145	175	110	0	0	0	0	0	0	0	0				
	E	85					385	550	520	390	210	0	0	0	0	0	0				
	SE	130					400	600	625	560	445	300	150	5	0	0	0				
	S	155					180	300	365	400	420	425	420	400	365	300	180				
	SW	130					0	0	0	5	150	300	445	560	625	600	400				
	W	85					0	0	0	0	0	0	210	390	520	550	385				
	NW	20					0	0	0	0	0	0	0	0	110	175	145				
	H	220					90	290	490	645	750	785	750	645	490	290	90				
	Diff (Cldy)	90					60	125	190	250	290	310	290	250	190	125	60				
	Diff (Clr)	35					45	70	85	95	100	105	100	95	85	70	45				

THE TABULATED VALUES HAVE THE FOLLOWING BASIS:

Direct radiation factor, $k_D = 1.0$
Diffuse radiation factor, $k_d = 1.0$
Height correction factor, $k_a = 1.0$

For southern latitudes, this table may be used by reading northern values for southern aspects and vice-versa, substituting dates as follows:

NORTH	June	May July	April August	March September	February October	January November	December
SOUTH	December	November January	October February	September March	August April	July May	June

Table A2.35 *(c)* Basic direct solar irradiances on vertical, I_{DV}, and horizontal, I_{DH}, surfaces and basic diffuse (cloudy and clear sky) solar irradiances on horizontal surfaces, I_{dH}, (W/m²).

10°N

Date	Orientation	Daily mean	03	04	05	06	07	08	09	10	11	12	13	14	15	16	17	18	19	20	21
June 21	N	110				70	200	235	235	225	220	215	220	225	235	235	200	70			
	NE	115				160	500	595	550	445	310	150	0	0	0	0	0	0			
	E	100				160	510	605	545	405	215	0	0	0	0	0	0	0			
	SE	35				65	215	260	220	130	0	0	0	0	0	0	0	0			
	S	0				0	0	0	0	0	0	0	0	0	0	0	0	0			
	SW	35				0	0	0	0	0	0	0	0	130	220	260	215	65			
	W	100				0	0	0	0	0	0	0	215	405	545	605	510	160			
	NW	115				0	0	0	0	0	0	150	310	445	550	595	500	160			
	H	270				10	175	395	595	755	860	900	860	755	595	395	175	10			
	Diff (Cldy)	110				20	90	160	225	295	355	385	355	295	225	160	90	20			
	Diff (Clr)	40				15	60	75	90	100	105	110	105	100	90	75	60	15			
July 23 and May 22	N	85				55	170	200	190	180	170	165	170	180	190	200	170	55			
	NE	105				140	485	575	530	420	280	120	0	0	0	0	0	0			
	E	105				145	515	615	560	415	225	0	0	0	0	0	0	0			
	SE	45				65	245	295	260	165	35	0	0	0	0	0	0	0			
	S	0				0	0	0	0	0	0	0	0	0	0	0	0	0			
	SW	45				0	0	0	0	0	0	0	35	165	260	295	245	65			
	W	105				0	0	0	0	0	0	0	225	415	560	615	515	145			
	NW	105				0	0	0	0	0	0	120	280	420	530	575	485	140			
	H	275				10	170	395	600	765	875	910	875	765	600	395	170	10			
	Diff (Cldy)	115				20	90	160	230	300	365	400	365	300	230	160	90	20			
	Diff (Clr)	40				15	55	75	90	100	110	110	110	100	90	75	55	15			
August 22 and April 22	N	30				20	90	90	70	50	40	30	40	50	70	90	90	20			
	NE	85				80	430	515	465	345	190	25	0	0	0	0	0	0			
	E	105				95	520	640	585	435	235	0	0	0	0	0	0	0			
	SE	65				50	305	390	360	270	140	0	0	0	0	0	0	0			
	S	0				0	0	0	0	0	0	0	0	0	0	0	0	0			
	SW	65				0	0	0	0	0	0	0	140	270	360	390	305	50			
	W	105				0	0	0	0	0	0	0	235	435	585	640	520	95			
	NW	85				0	0	0	0	0	0	25	190	345	465	515	430	80			
	H	275				5	160	390	605	775	890	910	890	775	605	390	160	5			
	Diff (Cldy)	115				10	85	155	230	305	380	445	380	305	230	155	85	10			
	Diff (Clr)	40				10	55	75	90	100	110	115	110	100	90	75	55	10			
September 22 and March 21	N	0				0	0	0	0	0	0	0	0	0	0	0	0	0			
	NE	55				0	335	410	345	220	60	0	0	0	0	0	0	0			
	E	100				0	495	640	590	440	240	0	0	0	0	0	0	0			
	SE	90				0	365	500	490	405	275	115	0	0	0	0	0	0			
	S	45				0	25	65	105	135	155	160	155	135	105	65	25	0			
	SW	90				0	0	0	0	0	0	115	275	405	490	500	365	0			
	W	100				0	0	0	0	0	0	0	240	440	590	640	495	0			
	NW	55				0	0	0	0	0	0	0	60	220	345	410	335	0			
	H	265				0	130	365	580	755	875	910	875	755	580	365	130	0			
	Diff (Cldy)	110				0	75	150	220	295	365	405	365	295	220	150	75	0			
	Diff (Clr)	40				0	50	75	90	100	110	110	110	100	90	75	50	0			
October 22 and February 21	N	0					0	0	0	0	0	0	0	0	0	0	0				
	NE	35					235	290	225	95	0	0	0	0	0	0	0				
	E	95					435	605	570	425	230	0	0	0	0	0	0				
	SE	115					380	565	580	505	385	230	60	0	0	0	0				
	S	110					105	195	250	290	315	325	315	290	250	195	105				
	SW	115					0	0	0	0	60	230	385	505	580	565	380				
	W	95					0	0	0	0	0	0	230	425	570	605	435				
	NW	35					0	0	0	0	0	0	0	95	225	290	235				
	H	240					100	320	535	700	810	850	810	700	535	320	100				
	Diff (Cldy)	100					65	135	205	270	325	350	325	270	205	135	65				
	Diff (Clr)	40					45	70	85	100	105	105	105	100	85	70	45				
November 22 and January 21	N	0					0	0	0	0	0	0	0	0	0	0	0				
	NE	20					150	190	120	0	0	0	0	0	0	0	0				
	E	85					360	550	530	400	215	0	0	0	0	0	0				
	SE	130					360	590	630	570	460	315	155	5	0	0	0				
	S	155					150	285	360	405	435	445	435	405	360	285	150				
	SW	130					0	0	0	5	155	315	460	570	630	590	360				
	W	85					0	0	0	0	0	0	215	400	530	550	360				
	NW	20					0	0	0	0	0	0	0	0	120	190	150				
	H	215					70	270	475	630	735	770	735	630	475	270	70				
	Diff (Cldy)	85					50	120	185	240	285	300	285	240	185	120	50				
	Diff (Clr)	35					40	70	80	95	100	100	100	95	80	40	40				
December 21	N	0					0	0	0	0	0	0	0	0	0	0	0				
	NE	15					120	150	80	0	0	0	0	0	0	0	0				
	E	80					330	520	510	385	205	0	0	0	0	0	0				
	SE	135					345	590	640	590	480	345	190	40	0	0	0				
	S	170					160	310	395	445	475	485	475	445	395	310	160				
	SW	135					0	0	0	40	190	345	480	590	640	590	345				
	W	80					0	0	0	0	0	0	205	385	510	520	330				
	NW	15					0	0	0	0	0	0	0	0	80	150	120				
	H	200					60	250	445	600	700	735	700	600	445	250	60				
	Diff (Cldy)	80					50	115	175	230	270	285	270	230	175	115	50				
	Diff (Clr)	35					40	65	80	90	95	100	95	90	80	65	40				

THE TABULATED VALUES HAVE THE FOLLOWING BASIS:

Direct radiation factor, $k_D = 1.0$
Diffuse radiation factor, $k_d = 1.0$
Height correction factor, $k_a = 1.0$

For southern latitudes, this table may be used by reading northern values for southern aspects and vice-versa, substituting dates as follows:

NORTH	June	May July	April August	March September	February October	January November	December
SOUTH	December	November January	October February	September March	August April	July May	June

Table A2.35 *(d)* Basic direct solar irradiances on vertical, I_{DV}, and horizontal, I_{DH}, surfaces and basic diffuse (cloudy and clear sky) solar irradiances on horizontal surfaces, I_{dH}, (W/m²).

15°N

Date	Orientation	Daily mean	03	04	05	06	07	08	09	10	11	12	13	14	15	16	17	18	19	20	21
June 21	N	90				95	195	205	185	160	145	135	145	160	185	205	195	95			
	NE	110				230	520	580	520	400	255	95	0	0	0	0	0	0			
	E	105				230	540	615	550	410	220	0	0	0	0	0	0	0			
	SE	45				95	240	290	260	175	55	0	0	0	0	0	0	0			
	S	0				0	0	0	0	0	0	0	0	0	0	0	0	0			
	SW	45				0	0	0	0	0	0	0	55	175	260	290	240	95			
	W	105				0	0	0	0	0	0	0	220	410	550	615	540	230			
	NW	110				0	0	0	0	0	0	95	255	400	520	580	520	230			
	H	280				25	200	420	620	775	880	915	880	775	620	420	200	25			
	Diff (Cldy)	120				30	100	165	235	305	370	410	370	305	235	165	100	30			
	Diff (Clr)	45				25	60	80	90	100	110	110	110	100	90	80	60	25			
July 23 and May 22	N	65				75	165	165	140	115	95	85	95	115	140	165	165	75			
	NE	100				200	500	560	495	375	225	60	0	0	0	0	0	0			
	E	110				210	540	625	560	420	225	0	0	0	0	0	0	0			
	SE	55				95	265	325	300	215	90	0	0	0	0	0	0	0			
	S	0				0	0	0	0	0	0	0	0	0	0	0	0	0			
	SW	55				0	0	0	0	0	0	0	90	215	300	325	265	95			
	W	110				0	0	0	0	0	0	0	225	420	560	625	540	210			
	NW	100				0	0	0	0	0	0	60	225	375	495	560	500	200			
	H	280				20	195	420	620	780	890	915	890	780	620	420	195	20			
	Diff (Cldy)	120				25	95	165	235	305	375	425	375	305	235	165	95	25			
	Diff (Clr)	45				20	60	80	90	100	110	110	110	100	90	80	60	20			
August 22 and April 22	N	15				30	75	55	20	0	0	0	0	0	20	55	75	30			
	NE	80				115	435	495	425	295	135	0	0	0	0	0	0	0			
	E	105				135	535	645	585	435	235	0	0	0	0	0	0	0			
	SE	75				75	325	415	400	320	195	35	0	0	0	0	0	0			
	S	5				0	0	0	0	15	40	50	40	15	0	0	0	0			
	SW	75				0	0	0	0	0	0	35	195	320	400	415	325	75			
	W	105				0	0	0	0	0	0	0	235	435	585	645	535	135			
	NW	80				0	0	0	0	0	0	0	135	295	425	495	435	115			
	H	275				5	170	400	610	775	890	915	890	775	610	400	170	5			
	Diff (Cldy)	115				15	90	160	235	305	380	440	380	305	235	160	90	15			
	Diff (Clr)	40				15	55	80	90	100	110	115	110	100	90	80	55	15			
September 22 and March 21	N	0				0	0	0	0	0	0	0	0	0	0	0	0	0			
	NE	50				0	320	385	310	170	5	0	0	0	0	0	0	0			
	E	100				0	490	635	590	440	235	0	0	0	0	0	0	0			
	SE	100				0	370	515	525	450	330	170	0	0	0	0	0	0			
	S	70				0	35	95	150	195	230	240	230	195	150	95	35	0			
	SW	100				0	0	0	0	0	0	170	330	450	525	515	370	0			
	W	100				0	0	0	0	0	0	0	235	440	590	635	490	0			
	NW	50				0	0	0	0	0	0	0	5	170	310	385	320	0			
	H	255				0	125	355	570	735	850	890	850	735	570	355	125	0			
	Diff (Cldy)	105				0	75	145	215	285	345	380	345	285	215	145	75	0			
	Diff (Clr)	40				0	50	75	90	100	105	110	105	100	90	75	50	0			
October 22 and February 21	N	0					0	0	0	0	0	0	0	0	0	0	0				
	NE	30					210	265	190	55	0	0	0	0	0	0	0				
	E	90					405	590	560	420	225	0	0	0	0	0	0				
	SE	120					360	570	605	545	430	280	110	0	0	0	0				
	S	130					105	215	295	345	380	395	380	345	295	215	105				
	SW	120					0	0	0	0	110	280	430	545	605	570	360				
	W	90					0	0	0	0	0	0	225	420	560	590	405				
	NW	30					0	0	0	0	0	0	0	55	190	265	210				
	H	225					85	295	500	665	770	810	770	665	500	295	85				
	Diff (Cldy)	90					55	125	195	255	305	325	305	255	195	125	55				
	Diff (Clr)	35					45	70	85	95	100	105	100	95	85	70	45				
November 22 and January 21	N	0					0	0	0	0	0	0	0	0	0	0	0				
	NE	15					120	165	90	0	0	0	0	0	0	0	0				
	E	80					305	520	515	395	210	0	0	0	0	0	0				
	SE	135					310	575	640	600	495	355	195	45	0	0	0				
	S	170					135	290	390	455	490	500	490	455	390	290	135				
	SW	135					0	0	0	45	195	355	495	600	640	575	310				
	W	80					0	0	0	0	0	0	210	395	515	520	305				
	NW	15					0	0	0	0	0	0	0	0	90	165	120				
	H	195					50	235	430	585	680	715	680	585	430	235	50				
	Diff (Cldy)	80					40	110	170	225	260	275	260	225	170	110	40				
	Diff (Clr)	35					35	65	80	90	95	100	95	90	80	65	35				
December 21	N	0					0	0	0	0	0	0	0	0	0	0	0				
	NE	10					95	125	50	0	0	0	0	0	0	0	0				
	E	75					265	490	495	380	205	0	0	0	0	0	0				
	SE	135					280	565	645	610	515	380	225	75	0	0	0				
	S	180					135	310	420	485	525	535	525	485	420	310	135				
	SW	135					0	0	0	75	225	380	515	610	645	565	280				
	W	75					0	0	0	0	0	0	205	380	495	490	265				
	NW	10					0	0	0	0	0	0	0	0	50	125	95				
	H	180					40	210	400	550	645	675	645	550	400	210	40				
	Diff (Cldy)	75					35	100	160	210	245	260	245	210	160	100	35				
	Diff (Clr)	35					30	65	80	85	95	95	95	85	80	65	30				

THE TABULATED VALUES HAVE THE FOLLOWING BASIS:

Direct radiation factor, $k_D = 1.0$
Diffuse radiation factor, $k_d = 1.0$
Height correction factor, $k_a = 1.0$

For southern latitudes, this table may be used by reading northern values for southern aspects and vice-versa, substituting dates as follows:

NORTH	June	May July	April August	March September	February October	January November	December
SOUTH	December	November January	October February	September March	August April	July May	June

Table A2.35 *(e)* Basic direct solar irradiances on vertical, I_{DV}, and horizontal, I_{DH}, surfaces and basic diffuse (cloudy and clear sky) solar irradiances on horizontal surfaces, I_{dH}, (W/m²).

20°N

Date	Orientation	Daily mean	03	04	05	06	07	08	09	10	11	12	13	14	15	16	17	18	19	20	21
June 21	N	65				120	185	170	130	90	65	55	65	90	130	170	185	120			
	NE	100				290	530	560	480	355	200	40									
	E	110				290	560	620	555	410	220	0	0	0	0	0	0	0			
	SE	55				120	265	320	300	225	110	0	0	0	0	0	0	0			
	S	0				0	0	0	0	0	0	0	0	0	0	0	0	0			
	SW	55				0	0	0	0	0	0	0	110	225	300	320	265	120			
	W	110				0	0	0	0	0	0	0	220	410	555	620	560	290			
	NW	100				0	0	0	0	0	0	40	200	355	480	560	530	290			
	H	290				45	230	445	635	790	895	915	895	790	635	445	230	45			
	Diff (Cldy)	125				40	105	175	245	310	380	435	380	310	245	175	105	40			
	Diff (Clr)	45				30	65	80	95	105	110	115	110	105	95	80	65	30			
July 23 and May 22	N	45				95	150	130	85	45	15	5	15	45	85	130	150	95			
	NE	95				255	505	540	460	330	170	5	0	0	0	0	0	0			
	E	110				265	565	635	565	420	225	0	0	0	0	0	0	0			
	SE	65				125	290	355	340	265	145	0	0	0	0	0	0	0			
	S	0				0	0	0	0	0	0	0	0	0	0	0	0	0			
	SW	65				0	0	0	0	0	0	0	145	265	340	355	290	125			
	W	110				0	0	0	0	0	0	0	225	420	565	635	565	265			
	NW	95				0	0	0	0	0	0	5	170	330	460	540	505	255			
	H	290				35	215	435	630	790	895	905	895	790	630	435	215	35			
	Diff (Cldy)	125				35	100	170	240	310	385	450	385	310	240	170	100	35			
	Diff (Clr)	45				30	65	80	95	105	110	115	110	105	95	80	65	30			
August 22 and April 22	N	10				35	65	20	0	0	0	0	0	0	0	20	65	35			
	NE	75				150	435	475	390	250	80	0	0	0	0	0	0	0			
	E	110				175	550	645	585	435	235	0	0	0	0	0	0	0			
	SE	85				100	345	440	435	365	250	90	0	0	0	0	0	0			
	S	25				0	0	0	35	85	115	130	115	85	35	0	0	0			
	SW	85				0	0	0	0	0	0	90	250	365	435	440	345	100			
	W	110				0	0	0	0	0	0	0	235	435	585	645	550	175			
	NW	75				0	0	0	0	0	0	0	80	250	390	475	435	150			
	H	275				15	180	405	610	770	880	915	880	770	610	405	180	15			
	Diff (Cldy)	115				20	90	160	230	305	370	415	370	305	230	160	90	20			
	Diff (Clr)	45				15	60	80	90	100	110	110	110	100	90	80	60	15			
September 22 and March 21	N	0				0	0	0	0	0	0	0	0	0	0	0	0	0			
	NE	45				0	310	355	270	125	0	0	0	0	0	0	0	0			
	E	100				0	480	630	585	435	235	0	0	0	0	0	0	0			
	SE	110				0	370	535	555	490	375	220	45	0	0	0	0	0			
	S	90				0	45	125	200	260	300	315	300	260	200	125	45	0			
	SW	110				0	0	0	0	0	45	220	375	490	555	535	370	0			
	W	100				0	0	0	0	0	0	0	235	435	585	630	480	0			
	NW	45				0	0	0	0	0	0	0	0	125	270	355	310	0			
	H	250				0	120	340	550	710	820	860	820	710	550	340	120	0			
	Diff (Cldy)	100				0	70	140	210	275	330	355	330	275	210	140	70	0			
	Diff (Clr)	40				0	50	75	85	100	105	105	105	100	85	75	50	0			
October 22 and February 21	N	0					0	0	0	0	0	0	0	0	0	0	0				
	NE	25					185	240	155	15	0	0	0	0	0	0	0				
	E	90					370	570	550	415	225	0	0	0	0	0	0				
	SE	125					330	565	620	575	470	320	155	0	0	0	0				
	S	145					100	230	330	395	440	455	440	395	330	230	100				
	SW	125					0	0	0	0	155	320	470	575	620	565	330				
	W	90					0	0	0	0	0	0	225	415	550	570	370				
	NW	25					0	0	0	0	0	0	0	15	155	240	185				
	H	210					70	265	465	625	725	760	725	625	465	265	70				
	Diff (Cldy)	85					50	120	180	240	280	300	280	240	180	120	50				
	Diff (Clr)	35					40	65	80	95	100	100	100	95	80	65	40				
November 22 and January 21	N	0					0	0	0	0	0	0	0	0	0	0	0				
	NE	10					95	140	60	0	0	0	0	0	0	0	0				
	E	75					245	485	500	385	205	0	0	0	0	0	0				
	SE	135					250	550	645	620	525	390	235	75	0	0	0				
	S	175					110	290	410	490	535	550	535	490	410	290	110				
	SW	135					0	0	0	75	235	390	525	620	645	550	250				
	W	75					0	0	0	0	0	0	205	385	500	485	245				
	NW	10					0	0	0	0	0	0	0	0	60	140	95				
	H	175					30	195	380	530	625	655	625	530	380	195	30				
	Diff (Cldy)	70					30	95	155	205	240	250	240	205	155	95	30				
	Diff (Clr)	30					25	60	75	85	95	95	95	85	75	60	25				
December 21	N	0					0	0	0	0	0	0	0	0	0	0	0				
	NE	10					65	105	25	0	0	0	0	0	0	0	0				
	E	70					190	450	475	370	200	0	0	0	0	0	0				
	SE	140					205	530	640	625	540	410	260	105	0	0	0				
	S	185					100	300	435	520	565	580	565	520	435	300	100				
	SW	140					0	0	0	105	260	410	540	625	640	530	205				
	W	70					0	0	0	0	0	0	200	370	475	450	190				
	NW	10					0	0	0	0	0	0	0	0	25	105	65				
	H	160					20	165	345	490	580	615	580	490	345	165	20				
	Diff (Cldy)	65					25	85	145	190	225	235	225	190	145	85	15				
	Diff (Clr)	30					20	55	75	85	90	90	90	85	75	55	20				

THE TABULATED VALUES HAVE THE FOLLOWING BASIS:

Direct radiation factor, $k_D = 1.0$
Diffuse radiation factor, $k_d = 1.0$
Height correction factor, $k_a = 1.0$

For southern latitudes, this table may be used by reading northern values for southern aspects and vice-versa, substituting dates as follows:

NORTH	June	May July	April August	March September	February October	January November	December
SOUTH	December	November January	October February	September March	August April	July May	June

Table A2.35 *(f)* Basic direct solar irradiances on vertical, I_{DV}, and horizontal, I_{DH}, surfaces and basic diffuse (cloudy and clear sky) solar irradiances on horizontal surfaces, I_{dH}, (W/m²).

25°N

Date	Orientation	Daily mean	03	04	05	06	07	08	09	10	11	12	13	14	15	16	17	18	19	20	21
June 21	N	45				135	170	130	75	20	0	0	0	20	75	130	170	135			
	NE	95				340	535	540	445	305	145	0	0	0	0	0	0	0			
	E	115				345	585	630	555	410	220	0	0	0	0	0	0	0			
	SE	65				150	290	350	340	275	165	15	0	0	0	0	0	0			
	S	0				0	0	0	0	0	15	25	15	0	0	0	0	0			
	SW	65				0	0	0	0	0	0	15	165	275	340	350	290	150			
	W	115				0	0	0	0	0	0	0	220	410	555	630	585	345			
	NW	95				0	0	0	0	0	0	0	145	305	445	540	535	340			
	H	295				65	250	460	645	795	895	910	895	795	645	460	250	65			
	Diff (Cldy)	125				50	115	180	245	315	385	445	385	315	245	180	115	50			
	Diff (Clr)	45				40	65	80	95	105	110	115	110	105	95	80	65	40			
July 23 and May 22	N	30				105	135	95	30	0	0	0	0	0	30	95	135	105			
	NE	90				300	510	515	420	280	115	0	0	0	0	0	0	0			
	E	115				320	580	640	565	420	225	0	0	0	0	0	0	0			
	SE	75				150	315	385	380	315	200	50	0	0	0	0	0	0			
	S	10				0	0	0	0	25	60	75	60	25	0	0	0	0			
	SW	75				0	0	0	0	0	0	50	200	315	380	385	315	150			
	W	115				0	0	0	0	0	0	0	225	420	565	640	580	320			
	NW	90				0	0	0	0	0	0	0	115	280	420	515	510	300			
	H	295				50	235	450	640	790	895	915	895	790	640	450	235	50			
	Diff (Cldy)	125				45	110	175	245	310	380	430	380	310	245	175	110	45			
	Diff (Clr)	45				35	65	80	95	105	110	115	110	105	95	80	65	35			
August 22 and April 22	N	10				40	50	0	0	0	0	0	0	0	0	0	50	40			
	NE	70				180	430	450	350	200	25	0	0	0	0	0	0	0			
	E	110				215	560	645	580	435	230	0	0	0	0	0	0	0			
	SE	95				120	360	470	475	410	300	145	0	0	0	0	0	0			
	S	45				0	0	15	85	150	195	210	195	150	85	15	0	0			
	SW	95				0	0	0	0	0	0	145	300	410	475	470	360	120			
	W	110				0	0	0	0	0	0	0	230	435	580	645	560	215			
	NW	70				0	0	0	0	0	0	0	25	200	350	450	430	180			
	H	275				20	185	405	600	760	865	900	865	760	600	405	185	20			
	Diff (Cldy)	115				25	95	160	230	295	355	390	355	295	230	160	95	25			
	Diff (Clr)	45				20	60	80	90	100	105	110	105	100	90	80	60	20			
September 22 and March 21	N	0				0	0	0	0	0	0	0	0	0	0	0	0	0			
	NE	40				0	295	330	235	80	0	0	0	0	0	0	0	0			
	E	95				0	465	620	575	430	230	0	0	0	0	0	0	0			
	SE	115				0	370	545	580	530	420	270	95	0	0	0	0	0			
	S	110				0	55	150	245	315	365	380	365	315	245	150	55	0			
	SW	115				0	0	0	0	0	95	270	420	530	580	545	370	0			
	W	95				0	0	0	0	0	0	0	230	430	575	620	465	0			
	NW	40				0	0	0	0	0	0	0	0	80	235	330	295	0			
	H	235				0	115	325	525	680	780	820	780	680	525	325	115	0			
	Diff (Cldy)	95				0	70	135	200	260	310	330	310	260	200	135	70	0			
	Diff (Clr)	40				0	50	70	85	95	105	105	105	95	85	70	50	0			
October 22 and February 21	N	0					0	0	0	0	0	0	0	0	0	0	0				
	NE	20					165	215	125	0	0	0	0	0	0	0	0				
	E	85					325	545	540	410	220	0	0	0	0	0	0				
	SE	130					300	555	635	600	505	360	195	25	0	0	0				
	S	155					95	240	360	440	495	510	495	440	360	240	95				
	SW	130					0	0	0	25	195	360	505	600	635	555	300				
	W	85					0	0	0	0	0	0	220	410	540	545	325				
	NW	20					0	0	0	0	0	0	0	0	125	215	165				
	H	195					50	235	425	575	675	705	675	575	425	235	50				
	Diff (Cldy)	80					45	110	170	220	260	275	260	220	170	110	45				
	Diff (Clr)	35					35	65	80	90	95	100	95	90	80	65	35				
November 22 and January 21	N	0					0	0	0	0	0	0	0	0	0	0	0				
	NE	10					65	120	35	0	0	0	0	0	0	0	0				
	E	70					170	445	475	375	200	0	0	0	0	0	0				
	SE	135					175	510	635	630	550	420	265	105	0	0	0				
	S	180					80	280	425	520	575	595	575	520	425	280	80				
	SW	135					0	0	0	105	265	420	550	630	635	510	175				
	W	70					0	0	0	0	0	0	200	375	475	445	170				
	NW	10					0	0	0	0	0	0	0	0	35	120	65				
	H	150					15	155	330	470	560	595	560	470	330	155	15				
	Diff (Cldy)	65					20	80	135	185	215	225	215	185	135	80	20				
	Diff (Clr)	30					20	55	70	80	90	90	90	80	70	55	20				
December 21	N	0					0	0	0	0	0	0	0	0	0	0	0				
	NE	5					35	85	0	0	0	0	0	0	0	0	0				
	E	65					110	400	445	355	195	0	0	0	0	0	0				
	SE	135					115	480	625	635	560	435	285	130	0	0	0				
	S	185					55	280	435	540	600	615	600	540	435	280	55				
	SW	135					0	0	0	130	285	435	560	635	625	480	115				
	W	65					0	0	0	0	0	0	195	355	445	400	110				
	NW	5					0	0	0	0	0	0	0	0	5	85	35				
	H	135					5	125	290	430	515	545	515	430	290	125	5				
	Diff (Cldy)	55					15	70	125	170	200	210	200	170	125	70	15				
	Diff (Clr)	30					10	50	70	80	85	85	85	80	70	50	10				

THE TABULATED VALUES HAVE THE FOLLOWING BASIS:

Direct radiation factor, $k_D = 1.0$
Diffuse radiation factor, $k_d = 1.0$
Height correction factor, $k_a = 1.0$

For southern latitudes, this table may be used by reading northern values for southern aspects and vice-versa, substituting dates as follows:

NORTH	June	May July	April August	March September	February October	January November	December
SOUTH	December	November January	October February	September March	August April	July May	June

Table A2.35 *(g)* Basic direct solar irradiances on vertical, I_{DV}, and horizontal, I_{DH}, surfaces and basic diffuse (cloudy and clear sky) solar irradiances on horizontal surfaces, I_{dH}, (W/m²).

30°N

Date	Orien-tation	Daily mean	03	04	05	06	07	08	09	10	11	12	13	14	15	16	17	18	19	20	21
June 21	N	35				150	155	90	15	0	0	0	0	0	15	90	155	150			
	NE	90				385	530	515	405	255	90	0	0	0	0	0	0	0			
	E	115				395	600	635	555	410	220	0	0	0	0	0	0	0			
	SE	80				175	315	385	380	325	220	75	0	0	0	0	0	0			
	S	15				0	0	0	0	45	90	105	90	45	0	0	0	0			
	SW	80				0	0	0	0	0	0	75	220	325	380	385	315	175			
	W	115				0	0	0	0	0	0	0	220	410	555	635	600	395			
	NW	90				0	0	0	0	0	0	0	90	255	405	515	530	385			
	H	300				85	275	475	650	795	890	915	890	795	650	475	275	85			
Diff (Cldy)		125				60	120	185	250	315	380	420	380	315	250	185	120	60			
Diff (Clr)		45				45	70	85	95	105	110	110	110	105	95	85	70	45			
July 23 and May 22	N	25				115	120	55	0	0	0	0	0	0	0	55	120	115			
	NE	85				340	505	490	380	230	60	0	0	0	0	0	0	0			
	E	115				365	595	640	565	420	225	0	0	0	0	0	0	0			
	SE	85				175	335	415	415	360	255	110	0	0	0	0	0	0			
	S	30				0	0	0	25	90	140	155	140	90	25	0	0	0			
	SW	85				0	0	0	0	0	0	110	255	360	415	415	335	175			
	W	115				0	0	0	0	0	0	0	225	420	565	640	595	365			
	NW	85				0	0	0	0	0	0	0	60	230	380	490	505	340			
	H	295				70	255	460	640	785	880	910	880	785	640	460	255	70			
Diff (Cldy)		120				50	115	180	245	310	370	405	370	310	245	180	115	50			
Diff (Clr)		45				40	65	80	95	105	110	110	110	105	95	80	65	40			
August 22 and April 22	N	5				45	30	0	0	0	0	0	0	0	0	0	30	45			
	NE	65				205	420	420	310	155	0	0	0	0	0	0	0	0			
	E	110				245	565	645	580	430	230	0	0	0	0	0	0	0			
	SE	105				145	375	490	510	455	350	200	25	0	0	0	0	0			
	S	70				0	0	50	140	215	265	285	265	215	140	50	0	0			
	SW	105				0	0	0	0	0	25	200	350	455	510	490	375	145			
	W	110				0	0	0	0	0	0	0	230	430	580	645	565	245			
	NW	65				0	0	0	0	0	0	0	0	155	310	420	420	205			
	H	270				25	195	400	590	735	835	875	835	735	590	400	195	25			
Diff (Cldy)		110				30	95	160	225	285	340	365	340	285	225	160	95	30			
Diff (Clr)		45				25	60	80	90	100	105	110	105	100	90	80	60	25			
September 22 and March 21	N	0				0	0	0	0	0	0	0	0	0	0	0	0	0			
	NE	35				0	275	305	200	40	0	0	0	0	0	0	0	0			
	E	95				0	450	605	570	425	230	0	0	0	0	0	0	0			
	SE	125				0	365	550	605	565	460	315	140	0	0	0	0	0			
	S	130				0	60	175	285	370	425	445	425	370	285	175	60	0			
	SW	125				0	0	0	0	0	140	315	460	565	605	550	365	0			
	W	95				0	0	0	0	0	0	0	230	425	570	605	450	0			
	NW	35				0	0	0	0	0	0	0	0	40	200	305	275	0			
	H	220				0	105	305	490	640	735	770	735	640	490	305	105	0			
Diff (Cldy)		90				0	65	130	190	245	285	300	285	245	190	130	65	0			
Diff (Clr)		35				0	45	70	85	95	100	100	100	95	85	70	45	0			
October 22 and February 21	N	0					0	0	0	0	0	0	0	0	0	0	0				
	NE	20					140	190	95	0	0	0	0	0	0	0	0				
	E	80					280	515	520	400	215	0	0	0	0	0	0				
	SE	135					260	540	640	625	535	395	230	55	0	0	0				
	S	170					85	245	385	480	540	560	540	480	385	245	85				
	SW	135					0	0	0	55	230	395	535	625	640	540	260				
	W	80					0	0	0	0	0	0	215	400	520	515	280				
	NW	20					0	0	0	0	0	0	0	0	95	190	140				
	H	175					35	200	380	525	615	645	615	525	380	200	35				
Diff (Cldy)		70					35	95	155	200	235	245	235	200	155	95	35				
Diff (Clr)		30					30	60	75	85	90	95	90	85	75	60	30				
November 22 and January 21	N	0					0	0	0	0	0	0	0	0	0	0	0				
	NE	5					35	95	15	0	0	0	0	0	0	0	0				
	E	60					95	395	450	360	195	0	0	0	0	0	0				
	SE	135					95	460	620	635	565	440	290	125	0	0	0				
	S	180					45	260	425	540	605	625	605	540	425	260	45				
	SW	135					0	0	0	125	290	440	565	635	620	460	95				
	W	60					0	0	0	0	0	0	195	360	450	395	95				
	NW	5					0	0	0	0	0	0	0	0	15	95	35				
	H	130					5	115	275	410	495	525	495	410	275	115	5				
Diff (Cldy)		55					10	70	120	160	190	200	190	160	120	70	10				
Diff (Clr)		30					10	50	70	80	85	85	85	80	70	50	10				
December 21	N	0					0	0	0	0	0	0	0	0	0	0	0				
	NE	5					5	65	0	0	0	0	0	0	0	0	0				
	E	55					15	340	415	340	185	0	0	0	0	0	0				
	SE	130					15	415	595	625	570	450	305	150	10	0	0				
	S	180					10	245	425	550	615	640	615	550	425	245	10				
	SW	130					0	0	10	150	305	450	570	625	595	415	15				
	W	55					0	0	0	0	0	0	185	340	415	340	15				
	NW	5					0	0	0	0	0	0	0	0	0	65	5				
	H	115					0	85	230	360	445	475	445	360	230	85	0				
Diff (Cldy)		50					0	55	105	150	175	185	175	150	105	55	0				
Diff (Clr)		25					0	45	65	75	80	85	80	75	65	45	0				

THE TABULATED VALUES HAVE THE FOLLOWING BASIS:	For southern latitudes, this table may be used by reading northern values for southern aspects and vice-versa, substituting dates as follows:							
Direct radiation factor, $k_D = 1.0$ Diffuse radiation factor, $k_d = 1.0$ Height correction factor, $k_a = 1.0$	NORTH	June	May July	April August	March September	February October	January November	December
	SOUTH	December	November January	October February	September March	August April	July May	June

Table A2.35 *(h)* Basic direct solar irradiances on vertical, I_{DV}, and horizontal, I_{DH}, surfaces and basic diffuse (cloudy and clear sky) solar irradiances on horizontal surfaces, I_{dH}, (W/m²).

35°N

Date	Orientation	Daily mean	03	04	05	06	07	08	09	10	11	12	13	14	15	16	17	18	19	20	21
June 21	N	30			40	155	130	50	0	0	0	0	0	0	0	50	130	155	40		
	NE	90			85	415	525	485	365	210	35	0	0	0	0	0	0	0	0		
	E	125			80	435	615	635	555	410	220	0	0	0	0	0	0	0	0		
	SE	90				25	200	340	415	420	370	275	130	0	0	0	0	0	0		
	S	35			0	0	0	0	40	115	165	185	165	115	40	0	0	0	0		
	SW	90			0	0	0	0	0	0	0	130	275	370	420	415	340	200	25		
	W	125			0	0	0	0	0	0	0	0	220	410	555	635	615	435	80		
	NW	90			0	0	0	0	0	0	0	0	35	210	365	485	525	415	85		
	H	305			5	110	290	485	650	785	875	905	875	785	650	485	290	110	5		
	Diff (Cldy)	125			10	65	125	185	250	310	365	395	365	310	250	185	125	65	10		
	Diff (Clr)	50			10	50	70	85	95	105	110	110	110	105	95	85	70	50	10		
July 23 and May 22	N	20			0	125	100	15	0	0	0	0	0	0	0	15	100	125	0		
	NE	80			5	375	500	465	340	180	5	0	0	0	0	0	0	0	0		
	E	120			5	405	610	640	565	415	220	0	0	0	0	0	0	0	0		
	SE	100			0	200	360	445	455	405	310	165	0	0	0	0	0	0	0		
	S	50			0	0	0	0	80	160	215	230	215	160	80	0	0	0	0		
	SW	100			0	0	0	0	0	0	0	165	310	405	455	445	360	200	0		
	W	120			0	0	0	0	0	0	0	0	220	415	565	640	610	405	5		
	NW	80			0	0	0	0	0	0	0	0	5	180	340	465	500	375	5		
	H	295			0	85	270	460	630	770	860	895	860	700	630	460	270	85	0		
	Diff (Cldy)	120			0	60	120	180	240	300	355	380	355	300	240	180	120	60	0		
	Diff (Clr)	45			0	45	70	80	95	100	105	110	105	100	95	80	70	45	0		
August 22 and April 22	N	5				50	15	0	0	0	0	0	0	0	0	0	15	50			
	NE	60				230	410	395	275	105	0	0	0	0	0	0	0	0			
	E	115				280	565	640	575	425	225	0	0	0	0	0	0	0			
	SE	120				160	390	515	540	495	395	250	75	0	0	0	0	0			
	S	90				0	0	85	190	275	335	355	335	275	190	85	0	0			
	SW	120				0	0	0	0	0	75	250	395	495	540	515	390	160			
	W	115				0	0	0	0	0	0	0	225	425	575	640	565	280			
	NW	60				0	0	0	0	0	0	0	105	275	395	410	230	0			
	H	260				35	195	395	570	710	800	835	800	710	570	395	195	35			
	Diff (Cldy)	105				35	95	160	220	275	320	340	320	275	220	160	95	35			
	Diff (Clr)	45				30	60	75	90	100	105	105	105	100	90	75	60	30			
September 22 and March 21	N	0					0	0	0	0	0	0	0	0	0	0	0				
	NE	30					260	280	170	0	0	0	0	0	0	0	0				
	E	95					435	590	560	420	225	0	0	0	0	0	0				
	SE	130					355	555	620	590	500	355	180	0	0	0	0				
	S	145					65	195	320	415	480	500	480	415	320	195	65				
	SW	130					0	0	0	0	180	355	500	590	620	555	355				
	W	95					0	0	0	0	0	0	225	420	560	590	435				
	NW	30					0	0	0	0	0	0	0	0	170	280	260				
	H	205					95	280	455	595	685	715	685	595	455	280	95				
	Diff (Cldy)	85					60	120	180	230	265	275	265	230	180	120	60				
	Diff (Clr)	35					45	70	80	90	95	100	95	90	80	70	45				
October 22 and February 21	N	0					0	0	0	0	0	0	0	0	0	0	0				
	NE	15					110	165	70	0	0	0	0	0	0	0	0				
	E	75					230	480	500	390	210	0	0	0	0	0	0				
	SE	140					215	510	635	635	555	425	260	85	0	0	0				
	S	175					75	245	400	510	575	600	575	510	400	245	75				
	SW	140					0	0	0	85	260	425	555	635	635	510	215				
	W	75					0	0	0	0	0	0	210	390	500	480	230				
	NW	15					0	0	0	0	0	0	0	0	70	165	110				
	H	150					25	165	330	465	550	580	550	465	330	165	25				
	Diff (Cldy)	65					30	85	140	180	210	220	210	180	140	85	30				
	Diff (Clr)	30					25	55	75	80	90	90	90	80	75	55	25				
November 22 and January 21	N	0					0	0	0	0	0	0	0	0	0	0	0				
	NE	5					0	75	0	0	0	0	0	0	0	0	0				
	E	55					5	335	415	340	190	0	0	0	0	0	0				
	SE	130					5	395	585	625	570	455	305	145	0	0	0				
	S	175					5	225	410	545	620	645	620	545	410	225	5				
	SW	130					0	0	0	145	305	455	570	625	585	395	5				
	W	55					0	0	0	0	0	0	190	340	415	335	5				
	NW	5					0	0	0	0	0	0	0	0	0	75	0				
	H	105					0	75	215	340	420	450	420	340	215	75	0				
	Diff (Cldy)	45					0	55	100	140	165	175	165	140	100	55	0				
	Diff (Clr)	25					0	45	65	75	80	80	80	75	65	45	0				
December 21	N	0						0	0	0	0	0	0	0	0	0					
	NE	0						50	0	0	0	0	0	0	0	0					
	E	45						270	370	315	175	0	0	0	0	0					
	SE	125						330	545	605	565	460	315	160	20	0					
	S	175						200	400	540	620	645	620	540	400	200					
	SW	125						0	20	160	315	460	565	605	545	330					
	W	45						0	0	0	0	0	175	315	370	270					
	NW	0						0	0	0	0	0	0	0	0	50					
	H	90						50	175	290	370	400	370	290	175	50					
	Diff (Cldy)	40						45	90	125	150	160	150	125	90	45					
	Diff (Clr)	25						35	60	70	75	80	75	70	60	35					

THE TABULATED VALUES HAVE THE FOLLOWING BASIS:

Direct radiation factor, $k_D = 1.0$

Diffuse radiation factor, $k_d = 1.0$

Height correction factor, $k_a = 1.0$

For southern latitudes, this table may be used by reading northern values for southern aspects and vice-versa, substituting dates as follows:

NORTH	June	May July	April August	March September	February October	January November	December
SOUTH	December	November January	October February	September March	August April	July May	June

Table A2.35 *(j)* Basic direct solar irradiances on vertical, I_{DV}, and horizontal, I_{DH}, surfaces and basic diffuse (cloudy and clear sky) solar irradiances on horizontal surfaces, I_{dH}, (W/m²).

40°N

Date	Orien-tation	Daily mean	03	04	05	06	07	08	09	10	11	12	13	14	15	16	17	18	19	20	21
June 21	N	30			85	155	105	10	0	0	0	0	0	0	0	10	105	155	85		
	NE	85			175	445	515	455	325	160	0	0	0	0	0	0	0	0	0		
	E	130			165	470	625	635	555	410	215	0	0	0	0	0	0	0	0		
	SE	105			55	220	365	445	460	420	325	185	20	0	0	0	0	0	0		
	S	55			0	0	0	0	95	185	240	260	240	185	95	0	0	0	0		
	SW	105			0	0	0	0	0	0	20	185	325	420	460	445	365	220	55		
	W	130			0	0	0	0	0	0	0	0	215	410	555	635	625	470	165		
	NW	85			0	0	0	0	0	0	0	0	0	160	325	455	515	445	175		
	H	305			15	130	310	485	645	770	855	880	855	770	645	485	310	130	15		
Diff (Cldy)		125			20	75	130	190	245	300	350	370	350	300	245	190	130	75	20		
Diff (Clr)		50			15	50	70	85	95	100	105	110	105	100	95	85	70	50	15		
July 23 and May 22	N	20			45	125	75	0	0	0	0	0	0	0	0	0	75	125	45		
	NE	75			95	400	490	435	300	135	0	0	0	0	0	0	0	0	0		
	E	125			90	440	615	640	560	415	220	0	0	0	0	0	0	0	0		
	SE	110			35	220	380	475	490	450	355	215	45	0	0	0	0	0	0		
	S	70			0	0	0	25	135	225	285	305	285	225	135	25	0	0	0		
	SW	110			0	0	0	0	0	0	45	215	355	450	490	475	380	220	35		
	W	125			0	0	0	0	0	0	0	0	220	415	560	640	615	440	90		
	NW	75			0	0	0	0	0	0	0	0	0	135	300	435	490	400	95		
	H	290			5	105	280	460	620	745	830	860	830	745	620	460	280	105	5		
Diff (Cldy)		120			10	65	120	180	235	290	335	355	335	290	235	180	120	65	10		
Diff (Clr)		45			10	50	70	80	90	100	105	105	105	100	90	80	70	50	10		
August 22 and April 22	N	5			50	0	0	0	0	0	0	0	0	0	0	0	0	50			
	NE	55			250	400	370	235	65	0	0	0	0	0	0	0	0	0			
	E	115			305	570	635	570	420	225	0	0	0	0	0	0	0	0			
	SE	130			180	405	530	570	535	440	295	120	0	0	0	0	0	0			
	S	105				0	0	115	235	330	395	420	395	330	235	115	0	0			
	SW	130				0	0	0	0	0	120	295	440	535	570	530	405	180			
	W	115				0	0	0	0	0	0	0	225	420	570	635	570	305			
	NW	55				0	0	0	0	0	0	0	0	65	235	370	400	250			
	H	250				40	195	380	545	675	760	790	760	675	545	380	195	40			
Diff (Cldy)		100				40	95	155	210	260	295	315	295	260	210	155	95	40			
Diff (Clr)		40				30	60	75	85	95	100	105	100	95	85	75	60	30			
September 22 and March 21	N	0				0	0	0	0	0	0	0	0	0	0	0	0	0		
	NE	25				0	240	255	140	0	0	0	0	0	0	0	0	0		
	E	90				0	415	570	545	410	220	0	0	0	0	0	0	0		
	SE	140				0	345	550	630	615	530	390	220	35	0	0	0	0		
	S	160				0	70	210	350	460	530	550	530	460	350	210	70	0		
	SW	140				0	0	0	0	35	220	390	530	615	630	550	345	0		
	W	90				0	0	0	0	0	0	0	220	410	545	570	415	0		
	NW	25				0	0	0	0	0	0	0	0	0	140	255	240	0		
	H	190				0	85	250	415	545	630	655	630	545	415	250	85	0		
Diff (Cldy)		75				0	55	115	165	210	240	250	240	210	165	115	55	0		
Diff (Clr)		35				0	45	65	80	85	95	95	95	85	80	65	45	0		
October 22 and February 21	N	0					0	0	0	0	0	0	0	0	0	0	0	0		
	NE	10					85	140	50	0	0	0	0	0	0	0	0	0		
	E	70					175	435	475	375	205	0	0	0	0	0	0	0		
	SE	140					165	475	620	640	570	445	285	110	0	0	0	0		
	S	180					55	235	405	530	605	630	605	530	405	235	55			
	SW	140					0	0	0	110	285	445	570	640	620	475	165			
	W	70					0	0	0	0	0	0	205	375	475	435	175			
	NW	10					0	0	0	0	0	0	0	0	50	140	85			
	H	130					15	130	280	405	485	510	485	405	280	130	15			
Diff (Cldy)		55					20	75	120	160	185	195	185	160	120	75	20			
Diff (Clr)		30					15	50	70	80	85	85	85	80	70	50	15			
November 22 and January 21	N	0						0	0	0	0	0	0	0	0	0	0			
	NE	0						55	0	0	0	0	0	0	0	0	0			
	E	45						265	370	315	175	0	0	0	0	0	0			
	SE	120						315	530	600	560	455	310	150	10	0	0			
	S	170						185	385	530	615	645	615	530	385	185				
	SW	120						0	10	150	310	455	560	600	530	315				
	W	45						0	0	0	0	0	175	315	370	265				
	NW	0						0	0	0	0	0	0	0	0	55				
	H	85						45	160	270	345	370	345	270	160	45				
Diff (Cldy)		40						40	85	120	145	150	145	120	85	40				
Diff (Clr)		25						35	55	70	75	75	75	70	55	35				
December 21	N	0						0	0	0	0	0	0	0	0	0	0			
	NE	0						30	0	0	0	0	0	0	0	0	0			
	E	40						185	320	290	165	0	0	0	0	0	0			
	SE	115						230	480	565	545	450	310	160	25	0				
	S	160						140	355	510	605	635	605	510	355	140				
	SW	115						0	25	160	310	450	545	565	480	230				
	W	40						0	0	0	0	0	165	290	320	185				
	NW	0						0	0	0	0	0	0	0	0	30				
	H	70						20	120	220	295	315	295	220	120	20				
Diff (Cldy)		35						25	70	105	125	135	125	105	70	25				
Diff (Clr)		20						20	50	65	70	70	70	65	50	20				

THE TABULATED VALUES HAVE THE FOLLOWING BASIS:

Direct radiation factor, $k_D = 1.0$
Diffuse radiation factor, $k_d = 1.0$
Height correction factor, $k_a = 1.0$

For southern latitudes, this table may be used by reading northern values for southern aspects and vice-versa, substituting dates as follows:

NORTH	June	May July	April August	March September	February October	January November	December
SOUTH	December	November January	October February	September March	August April	July May	June

Table A2.35 *(k)* Basic direct solar irradiances on vertical, I_{DV}, and horizontal, I_{DH}, surfaces and basic diffuse (cloudy and clear sky) solar irradiances on horizontal surfaces, I_{dH}, (W/m²).

45°N

Sun Time

Date	Orien-tation	Daily mean	03	04	05	06	07	08	09	10	11	12	13	14	15	16	17	18	19	20	21
June 21	N	30			120	155	80	0	0	0	0	0	0	0	0	0	80	155	120		
	NE	85			255	465	505	425	285	110	0	0	0	0	0	0	0	0	0		
	E	130			240	500	630	635	550	405	215	0	0	0	0	0	0	0	0		
	SE	120			85	245	390	475	495	460	370	235	70	0	0	0	0	0	0		
	S	75			0	0	0	35	150	245	310	335	310	245	150	35	0	0	0		
	SW	120			0	0	0	0	0	0	70	235	370	460	495	475	390	245	85		
	W	130			0	0	0	0	0	0	0	0	215	405	550	635	630	500	240		
	NW	85			0	0	0	0	0	0	0	0	0	110	285	425	505	465	255		
	H	300			30	155	320	485	630	745	820	845	820	745	630	485	320	155	30		
	Diff (Cldy)	120			35	80	135	190	240	290	330	345	330	290	240	190	135	80	35		
	Diff (Clr)	50			25	55	70	85	95	100	105	105	105	100	95	85	70	55	25		
July 23 and May 22	N	20			80	125	50	0	0	0	0	0	0	0	0	0	50	125	80		
	NE	75			175	420	475	405	265	90	0	0	0	0	0	0	0	0	0		
	E	130			170	470	620	640	560	410	215	0	0	0	0	0	0	0	0		
	SE	125			65	245	405	500	525	490	405	265	95	0	0	0	0	0	0		
	S	90			0	0	0	65	185	285	350	375	350	285	185	65	0	0	0		
	SW	125			0	0	0	0	0	0	95	265	405	490	525	500	405	245	65		
	W	130			0	0	0	0	0	0	0	0	215	410	560	640	620	470	170		
	NW	75			0	0	0	0	0	0	0	0	0	90	265	405	475	420	175		
	H	285			15	125	290	455	600	720	795	820	795	720	600	455	290	125	15		
	Diff (Cldy)	115			20	70	125	180	230	280	315	330	315	280	230	180	125	70	20		
	Diff (Clr)	45			20	50	70	80	90	100	105	105	105	100	90	80	70	50	20		
August 22 and April 22	N	5				50	0	0	0	0	0	0	0	0	0	0	0	50			
	NE	50				270	385	340	200	20	0	0	0	0	0	0	0	0			
	E	115				330	565	630	565	415	220	0	0	0	0	0	0	0			
	SE	140				200	415	550	595	565	480	340	165	0	0	0	0	0			
	S	125				0	20	145	280	385	455	480	455	385	280	145	20	0			
	SW	140				0	0	0	0	0	165	340	480	565	595	550	415	200			
	W	115				0	0	0	0	0	0	0	220	415	565	630	565	330			
	NW	50				0	0	0	0	0	0	0	0	20	200	340	385	270			
	H	235				50	195	365	520	635	710	740	710	635	520	365	195	50			
	Diff (Cldy)	95				45	95	150	200	245	275	285	275	245	200	150	95	45			
	Diff (Clr)	40				35	60	75	85	95	100	100	100	95	85	75	60	35			
September 22 and March 21	N	0				0	0	0	0	0	0	0	0	0	0	0	0	0			
	NE	25				0	225	230	110	0	0	0	0	0	0	0	0	0			
	E	85				0	390	545	525	400	215	0	0	0	0	0	0	0			
	SE	145				0	325	540	635	630	555	420	250	65	0	0	0	0			
	S	170				0	75	220	375	490	570	595	570	490	375	220	75	0			
	SW	145				0	0	0	0	65	250	420	555	630	635	540	325	0			
	W	85				0	0	0	0	0	0	0	215	400	525	545	390	0			
	NW	25				0	0	0	0	0	0	0	0	110	230	225	0			
	H	170				0	75	220	375	490	570	595	570	490	375	220	75	0			
	Diff (Cldy)	70				0	55	105	150	190	215	225	215	190	150	105	55	0			
	Diff (Clr)	35				0	40	65	75	85	90	90	90	85	75	65	40	0			
October 22 and February 21	N	0					0	0	0	0	0	0	0	0	0	0	0				
	NE	10					55	120	30	0	0	0	0	0	0	0	0				
	E	60					115	385	440	355	195	0	0	0	0	0	0				
	SE	135					110	425	590	630	575	455	300	125	0	0	0				
	S	175					40	215	395	535	615	645	615	535	395	215	40				
	SW	135					0	0	0	125	300	455	575	630	590	425	110				
	W	60					0	0	0	0	0	0	195	355	440	385	115				
	NW	10					0	0	0	0	0	0	0	0	30	120	55				
	H	110					5	95	225	340	410	435	410	340	225	95	5				
	Diff (Cldy)	50					15	60	105	140	165	170	165	140	105	60	15				
	Diff (Clr)	25					10	45	65	75	80	80	80	75	65	45	10				
November 22 and January 21	N	0						0	0	0	0	0	0	0	0	0					
	NE	0						35	0	0	0	0	0	0	0	0					
	E	40						180	315	285	165	0	0	0	0	0					
	SE	110						220	460	555	535	445	305	150	15	0					
	S	155						125	335	495	595	625	595	495	335	125					
	SW	110						0	15	150	305	445	535	555	460	220					
	W	40						0	0	0	0	0	165	285	315	180					
	NW	0						0	0	0	0	0	0	0	0	35					
	H	60						20	105	200	270	290	270	200	105	20					
	Diff (Cldy)	30						25	65	100	120	125	120	100	65	25					
	Diff (Clr)	20						20	50	60	70	70	70	60	50	20					
December 21	N	0						0	0	0	0	0	0	0	0	0					
	NE	0						15	0	0	0	0	0	0	0	0					
	E	30						90	255	250	145	0	0	0	0	0					
	SE	100						110	385	500	500	420	295	150	25	0					
	S	140						70	290	460	565	595	565	460	290	70					
	SW	100						0	25	150	295	420	500	500	385	110					
	W	30						0	0	0	0	0	145	250	255	90					
	NW	0						0	0	0	0	0	0	0	0	15					
	H	45						5	70	155	215	235	215	155	70	5					
	Diff (Cldy)	25						15	50	80	100	110	100	80	50	15					
	Diff (Clr)	15						10	40	55	65	65	65	55	40	10					

THE TABULATED VALUES HAVE THE FOLLOWING BASIS:

Direct radiation factor, $k_D = 1.0$

Diffuse radiation factor, $k_d = 1.0$

Height correction factor, $k_a = 1.0$

For southern latitudes, this table may be used by reading northern values for southern aspects and vice-versa, substituting dates as follows:

NORTH	June	May / July	April / August	March / September	February / October	January / November	December
SOUTH	December	November / January	October / February	September / March	August / April	July / May	June

Table A2.35 *(l)* Basic direct solar irradiances on vertical, I_{DV}, and horizontal, I_{DH}, surfaces and basic diffuse (cloudy and clear sky) solar irradiances on horizontal surfaces, I_{dH}, (W/m²).

50°N

Date	Orien-tation	Daily mean	03	04	05	06	07	08	09	10	11	12	13	14	15	16	17	18	19	20	21
June 21	N	30	15	150	145	55	0	0	0	0	0	0	0	0	0	0	0	55	145	150	15
	NE	85	25	325	480	485	395	245	65	0	0	0	0	0	0	0	0	0	0	0	
	E	135	20	310	530	635	635	550	400	210	0	0	0	0	0	0	0	0	0	0	
	SE	130	5	110	270	410	500	530	500	415	285	115	0	0	0	0	0	0	0	0	
	S	95					0	75	205	310	375	400	375	310	205	75	0				
	SW	130										115	285	415	500	530	500	410	270	110	5
	W	135												210	400	550	635	635	530	310	20
	NW	85		20											65	245	395	485	480	325	25
	H	295		0	55	175	330	480	610	710	780	805	780	710	610	480	330	175	55	0	
	Diff (Cldy)	120		5	45	90	135	185	230	275	305	320	305	275	230	185	135	90	45	5	
	Diff (Clr)	50		0	35	60	70	85	90	100	100	105	100	100	90	85	70	60	35	0	
July 23 and May 22	N	20		110	120	25												25	120	110	
	NE	75		250	435	460	375	225	45												
	E	130		245	495	635	635	555	405	215											
	SE	135		95	265	425	525	560	530	445	310	140									
	S	110						105	235	345	415	440	415	345	235	105					
	SW	135										140	310	445	530	560	525	425	265	95	
	W	130												215	405	555	635	625	495	245	
	NW	75													45	225	375	460	435	250	
	H	275			30	140	295	445	580	685	750	775	750	685	580	445	295	140	30		
	Diff (Cldy)	110			30	80	125	175	220	265	295	305	295	265	220	175	125	80	30		
	Diff (Clr)	45			25	55	70	80	90	95	100	100	100	95	90	80	70	55	25		
August 22 and April 22	N	5				50												50			
	NE	45				285	370	310	165												
	E	115				355	565	615	555	410	215										
	SE	145				215	425	560	615	595	510	375	205	15							
	S	145					35	175	315	430	505	530	505	430	315	175	35				
	SW	145								15	205	375	510	595	615	560	425	215			
	W	115											215	410	555	615	565	355			
	NW	45													165	310	370	285			
	H	225				60	190	345	485	590	660	680	660	590	485	345	190	60			
	Diff (Cldy)	90				45	95	145	185	225	250	260	250	225	185	145	95	45			
	Diff (Clr)	40				40	60	75	85	90	95	95	95	90	85	75	60	40			
September 22 and March 21	N	0																			
	NE	20					205	205	85												
	E	85					360	515	505	390	210										
	SE	145					310	525	630	640	570	440	275	90							
	S	175					75	230	390	515	595	625	595	515	390	230	75				
	SW	145								90	275	440	570	640	630	525	310				
	W	85											210	390	505	515	360				
	NW	20													85	205	205				
	H	150					60	190	325	435	500	525	500	435	325	190	60				
	Diff (Cldy)	60					50	95	135	170	195	200	195	170	135	95	50				
	Diff (Clr)	30					40	60	70	80	85	85	85	80	70	60	40				
October 22 and February 21	N	0																			
	NE	5						20	95	15											
	E	55						50	325	395	330	185									
	SE	125						45	365	545	600	565	455	305	135						
	S	170					15	190	375	520	615	645	615	520	375	190	15				
	SW	125							135	305	455	565	600	545	365	45					
	W	55										185	330	395	325	50					
	NW	5												15	95	20					
	H	85						65	175	270	335	360	335	270	175	65					
	Diff (Cldy)	40					5	50	90	120	140	145	140	120	90	50	5				
	Diff (Clr)	25					5	40	60	70	75	75	75	70	60	40	5				
November 22 and January 21	N	0																			
	NE	0						15													
	E	30						85	245	245	145										
	SE	95						100	365	480	485	410	280	135	15						
	S	135						60	270	440	545	580	545	440	270	60					
	SW	95							15	135	280	410	485	480	365	100					
	W	30											145	245	245	85					
	NW	0														15					
	H	40						5	60	135	190	210	190	135	60	5					
	Diff (Cldy)	25						10	50	75	95	100	95	75	50	10					
	Diff (Clr)	15						10	40	50	60	65	60	50	40	10					
December 21	N	0																			
	NE	0																			
	E	20						175	200	125											
	SE	80						265	410	435	375	260	125	20							
	S	110							205	380	490	530	490	380	205						
	SW	80								20	125	260	375	435	410	265					
	W	20												125	200	175					
	NW	0																			
	H	30							30	90	140	155	140	90	30						
	Diff (Cldy)	20							30	60	80	85	80	60	30						
	Diff (Clr)	15							25	45	55	55	55	45	25						

THE TABULATED VALUES HAVE THE FOLLOWING BASIS:

Direct radiation factor, $k_D = 1.0$
Diffuse radiation factor, $k_d = 1.0$
Height correction factor, $k_a = 1.0$

For southern latitudes, this table may be used by reading northern values for southern aspects and vice-versa, substituting dates as follows:

NORTH	June	May July	April August	March September	February October	January November	December
SOUTH	December	November January	October February	September March	August April	July May	June

Table A2.35 *(m)* Basic direct solar irradiances on vertical, I_{DV}, and horizontal, I_{DH}, surfaces and basic diffuse (cloudy and clear sky) solar irradiances on horizontal surfaces, I_{dH}, (W/m²).

55°N

Date	Orientation	Daily mean	03	04	05	06	07	08	09	10	11	12	13	14	15	16	17	18	19	20	21
June 21	N	35	95	175	135	25	0	0	0	0	0	0	0	0	0	0	0	25	135	175	95
	NE	85	160	385	485	470	365	205	20	0	0	0	0	0	0	0	0	0	0	0	0
	E	145	130	365	550	640	630	545	395	210	0	0	0	0	0	0	0	0	0	0	0
	SE	145	20	135	290	435	530	565	540	455	325	160	0	0	0	0	0	0	0	0	0
	S	115	0	0	0	0	0	115	255	365	435	465	435	365	255	115	0	0	0	0	0
	SW	145	0	0	0	0	0	0	0	0	0	160	325	455	540	565	530	435	290	135	20
	W	145	0	0	0	0	0	0	0	0	0	0	0	210	395	545	630	640	550	365	130
	NW	85	0	0	0	0	0	0	0	0	0	0	0	0	20	205	365	470	485	385	160
	H	290		10	80	195	335	465	585	675	735	755	735	675	585	465	335	195	80	10	
	Diff (Cldy)	115		20	55	95	140	180	225	260	285	295	285	260	225	180	140	95	55	20	
	Diff (Clr)	50		15	45	60	75	80	90	95	100	100	100	95	90	80	75	60	45	15	
July 23 and May 22	N	25	25	135	110	0	0	0	0	0	0	0	0	0	0	0	0	0	110	135	25
	NE	75	45	310	445	445	345	185	0	0	0	0	0	0	0	0	0	0	0	0	0
	E	135	35	305	520	625	630	545	400	210	0	0	0	0	0	0	0	0	0	0	0
	SE	150	5	120	290	445	545	585	565	480	350	185	0	0	0	0	0	0	0	0	0
	S	130	0	0	0	0	0	145	285	395	470	495	470	395	285	145	0	0	0	0	0
	SW	150	0	0	0	0	0	0	0	0	0	185	350	480	565	585	545	445	290	120	5
	W	135	0	0	0	0	0	0	0	0	0	0	0	210	400	545	630	625	520	305	35
	NW	75	0	0	0	0	0	0	0	0	0	0	0	0	0	185	345	445	445	310	45
	H	265		0	50	160	295	430	550	640	700	720	700	640	550	430	295	160	50	0	
	Diff (Cldy)	110		5	40	85	125	170	210	245	270	280	270	245	210	170	125	85	40	5	
	Diff (Clr)	50		5	35	55	70	80	90	95	100	100	100	95	90	80	70	55	35	5	
August 22 and April 22	N	5		20	45	0	0	0	0	0	0	0	0	0	0	0	0	45	20	
	NE	45		60	295	355	285	135	0	0	0	0	0	0	0	0	0	0	0	
	E	115		65	370	555	605	540	400	215	0	0	0	0	0	0	0	0	0	
	SE	155		30	230	430	570	630	620	540	410	240	50	0	0	0	0	0	0	
	S	160		0	0	0	50	200	350	470	550	580	550	470	350	200	50	0	0	
	SW	155		0	0	0	0	0	0	0	50	240	410	540	620	630	570	430	230	30
	W	115		0	0	0	0	0	0	0	0	0	0	215	400	540	605	555	370	65
	NW	45		0	0	0	0	0	0	0	0	0	0	0	0	135	285	355	295	60
	H	205			0	65	185	320	445	540	600	620	600	540	445	320	185	65	0		
	Diff (Cldy)	85			5	50	95	135	175	205	230	235	230	205	175	135	95	50	5		
	Diff (Clr)	40			5	40	60	70	80	85	90	90	90	85	80	70	60	40	5		
September 22 and March 21	N	0				0	0	0	0	0	0	0	0	0	0	0	0			
	NE	20				0	180	180	60	0	0	0	0	0	0	0	0			
	E	80				0	330	480	480	370	200	0	0	0	0	0	0			
	SE	145				0	285	500	615	635	575	455	290	110	0	0	0			
	S	180				0	70	225	390	530	615	645	615	530	390	225	70	0		
	SW	145				0	0	0	0	110	290	455	575	635	615	500	285	0		
	W	80				0	0	0	0	0	0	0	200	370	480	480	330	0		
	NW	20				0	0	0	0	0	0	0	0	0	60	180	180	0		
	H	125				0	50	160	275	370	430	450	430	370	275	160	50	0		
	Diff (Cldy)	55				0	45	85	120	150	170	175	170	150	120	85	45	0		
	Diff (Clr)	30				0	35	55	70	75	80	80	80	75	70	55	35	0		
October 22 and February 21	N	0						0	0	0	0	0	0	0	0	0				
	NE	5						70	5	0	0	0	0	0	0	0				
	E	45						255	345	300	170	0	0	0	0	0				
	SE	115						290	480	555	535	440	295	135	0	0				
	S	155						155	335	490	585	620	585	490	335	155				
	SW	115						0	0	135	295	440	535	555	480	290				
	W	45						0	0	0	0	0	170	300	345	255				
	NW	5						0	0	0	0	0	0	0	5	70				
	H	65						40	120	200	260	280	260	200	120	40				
	Diff (Cldy)	30						35	70	100	115	120	115	100	70	35				
	Diff (Clr)	20						30	50	60	65	70	65	60	50	30				
November 22 and January 21	N	0							0	0	0	0	0	0	0					
	NE	0							0	0	0	0	0	0	0					
	E	20							160	190	120	0	0	0	0					
	SE	75							245	385	410	355	240	115	15					
	S	105							180	350	460	500	460	350	180					
	SW	75							15	115	240	355	410	385	245					
	W	20							0	0	0	0	120	190	160					
	NW	0							0	0	0	0	0	0	0					
	H	25							25	75	120	135	120	75	25					
	Diff (Cldy)	15							30	55	70	75	70	55	30					
	Diff (Clr)	10							25	45	50	50	50	45	25					
December 21	N	0							0	0	0	0	0	0	0					
	NE	0							0	0	0	0	0	0	0					
	E	15							80	140	95	0	0	0	0					
	SE	55							120	290	340	300	205	90	10					
	S	80							90	270	385	420	385	270	90					
	SW	55							10	90	205	300	340	290	120					
	W	15							0	0	0	0	95	140	80					
	NW	0							0	0	0	0	0	0	0					
	H	15							5	40	75	85	75	40	5					
	Diff (Cldy)	10							15	40	55	60	55	40	15					
	Diff (Clr)	10							10	30	40	45	40	30	10					

THE TABULATED VALUES HAVE THE FOLLOWING BASIS:

Direct radiation factor, $k_D = 1.0$

Diffuse radiation factor, $k_d = 1.0$

Height correction factor, $k_a = 1.0$

For southern latitudes, this table may be used by reading northern values for southern aspects and vice-versa, substituting dates as follows:

NORTH	June	May July	April August	March September	February October	January November	December
SOUTH	December	November January	October February	September March	August April	July May	June

Table A2.35 *(n)* Basic direct solar irradiances on vertical, I_{DV}, and horizontal, I_{DH}, surfaces and basic diffuse (cloudy and clear sky) solar irradiances on horizontal surfaces, I_{dH}, (W/m²).

60°N

Date	Orien-tation	Daily mean	03	04	05	06	07	08	09	10	11	12	13	14	15	16	17	18	19	20	21
	N	45	40	165	190	125	0	0	0	0	0	0	0	0	0	0	0	125	190	165	40
	NE	90	55	270	430	490	450	330	165	0	0	0	0	0	0	0	0	0	0	0	5
	E	150	35	220	415	570	640	625	535	390	205	0	0	0	0	0	0	0	0	0	0
	SE	155	0	40	160	315	455	550	590	570	495	365	200	20	0	0	0	0	0	0	0
June 21	S	135	0	0	0	0	5	155	300	415	490	520	490	415	300	155	5	0	0	0	0
	SW	155	0	0	0	0	0	0	0	20	200	365	495	570	590	550	455	315	160	40	0
	W	150	0	0	0	0	0	0	0	0	0	0	205	390	535	625	640	570	415	220	35
	NW	90	5	0	0	0	0	0	0	0	0	0	0	0	165	330	450	490	430	270	55
	H	280	0	30	105	215	335	450	555	630	680	700	680	630	555	450	335	215	105	30	0
Diff (Cldy)		115	5	35	65	100	140	175	210	240	260	270	260	240	210	175	140	100	65	35	5
Diff (Clr)		50	5	25	50	65	75	80	90	95	95	95	95	95	90	80	75	65	50	25	5
	N	30		100	155	100	0	0	0	0	0	0	0	0	0	0	0	100	155	100	
	NE	80		170	365	450	425	315	150	0	0	0	0	0	0	0	0	0	0	0	
	E	145		140	360	535	625	540	395	205	0	0	0	0	0	0	0	0	0	0	
July 23	SE	160		30	145	310	460	565	610	590	515	385	220	35	0	0	0	0	0	0	
and	S	145		0	0	0	25	175	325	445	520	550	520	445	325	175	25	0	0	0	
May 22	SW	160		0	0	0	0	0	0	35	220	385	515	590	610	565	460	310	145	30	
	W	145		0	0	0	0	0	0	0	0	0	205	395	540	625	625	535	360	140	
	NW	80		0	0	0	0	0	0	0	0	0	0	0	150	315	425	450	365	170	
	H	255		10	70	175	295	410	515	595	645	665	645	595	515	410	295	175	70	10	
Diff (Cldy)		105		20	50	90	125	165	200	225	245	255	245	225	200	165	125	90	50	20	
Diff (Clr)		50		15	40	60	70	80	85	90	95	95	95	90	85	80	70	60	40	15	
	N	5			45	40	0	0	0	0	0	0	0	0	0	0	0	0	40	45		
	NE	45			125	305	340	260	105	0	0	0	0	0	0	0	0	0	0	0		
	E	115			130	390	545	585	525	390	210	0	0	0	0	0	0	0	0	0		
August 22	SE	165			60	245	435	570	640	635	560	435	265	80	0	0	0	0	0	0		
and	S	170			0	0	65	220	375	505	585	615	585	505	375	220	65	0	0		
April 22	SW	165			0	0	0	0	0	80	265	435	560	635	640	570	435	245	60		
	W	115			0	0	0	0	0	0	0	0	210	390	525	585	545	390	130		
	NW	45			0	0	0	0	0	0	0	0	0	0	105	260	340	305	125		
	H	185			5	70	175	295	400	485	535	555	535	485	400	295	175	70	5		
Diff (Cldy)		80			15	50	90	125	160	185	205	210	205	185	160	125	90	50	15		
Diff (Clr)		40			15	40	60	70	80	85	85	90	85	85	80	70	60	40	15		
	N	0				0	0	0	0	0	0	0	0	0	0	0	0	0			
	NE	15				0	160	155	40	0	0	0	0	0	0	0	0	0			
	E	70				0	295	440	445	350	190	0	0	0	0	0	0	0			
September 22	SE	140				0	255	465	585	620	570	455	300	125	0	0	0	0			
and	S	180				0	70	220	385	525	615	645	615	525	385	220	70	0			
March 21	SW	140				0	0	0	0	125	300	455	570	620	585	465	255	0			
	W	70				0	0	0	0	0	0	0	190	350	445	440	295	0			
	NW	15				0	0	0	0	0	0	0	0	0	40	155	160	0			
	H	105				0	40	125	220	305	355	375	355	305	220	125	40	0			
Diff (Cldy)		45				0	35	75	105	130	145	150	145	130	105	75	35	0			
Diff (Clr)		25				0	30	50	65	70	75	75	75	70	65	50	30	0			
	N	0						0	0	0	0	0	0	0	0	0				
	NE	0						50	0	0	0	0	0	0	0	0				
	E	35						175	280	255	150	0	0	0	0	0				
October 22	SE	100						200	395	485	480	400	275	125	0	0				
and	S	135						105	280	435	535	570	535	435	280	105				
February 21	SW	100						0	0	125	275	400	480	485	395	200				
	W	35						0	0	0	0	0	150	255	280	175				
	NW	0						0	0	0	0	0	0	0	0	50				
	H	40						15	75	135	180	195	180	135	75	15				
Diff (Cldy)		25						25	55	75	90	95	90	75	55	20				
Diff (Clr)		15						20	40	50	60	60	60	50	40	20				
	N	0							0	0	0	0	0	0	0					
	NE	0							0	0	0	0	0	0	0					
	E	10							60	125	85	0	0	0	0					
November 22	SE	50							95	250	300	270	180	75	5					
and	S	70							70	230	340	380	340	230	70					
January 21	SW	50							5	75	180	270	300	250	95					
	W	10							0	0	0	0	85	125	60					
	NW	0							0	0	0	0	0	0	0					
	H	10							5	30	55	65	55	30	5					
Diff (Cldy)		10							10	30	45	50	45	30	10					
Diff (Clr)		10							10	25	35	40	35	25	10					
	N	0								0	0	0	0	0						
	NE	0								0	0	0	0	0						
	E	5								65	55	0	0	0						
December 21	SE	30								130	205	190	125	40						
	S	40								120	235	270	235	120						
	SW	30								40	125	190	205	130						
	W	5								0	0	0	55	65						
	NW	0								0	0	0	0	0						
	H	5								5	25	30	25	5						
Diff (Cldy)		5								15	30	35	30	15						
Diff (Clr)		5								10	25	25	25	10						

THE TABULATED VALUES HAVE THE FOLLOWING BASIS:	For southern latitudes, this table may be used by reading northern values for southern aspects and vice-versa, substituting dates as follows:							
Direct radiation factor, $k_D = 1.0$								
Diffuse radiation factor, $k_d = 1.0$	NORTH	June	May July	April August	March September	February October	January November	December
Height correction factor, $k_a = 1.0$	SOUTH	December	November January	October February	September March	August April	July May	June

REFERENCES

1 JAMIESON, H. C., Meteorological Data and Design Temperatures, *JIHVE*, 1955, **22**, 465–495.

2 KNIGHT, J. C., Engineering Services in a Laboratory, *JIHVE*, 1955, **23**, 33–69. (See also written contribution by H. C. Jamieson to discussion on this paper *ibid.*, 73–78).

3 HARRISON, R., Air Conditioning at Home and Abroad, *JIHVE*, 1958, **26**, 177–194.

4 Post-War Building Studies No. 33, Basic Design Temperatures for Space-Heating, HMSO, London, 1955.

5 CIBS Building Energy Code, Part 2(a), Calculation of Energy Demands and Targets for the Design of New Buildings and Services (Heated and Naturally Ventilated Buildings), CIBS, London, 1981.

6 COTTIS, J. G. and GROOM, H. J., Low Temperatures related to Surface Wind Speed and Direction at London Airport, December 1948 – February 1958, Meteorological Office Climatological Memorandum No. 21, Meteorological Office, Bracknell, Berks. (out of print).

7 Energy Management – published monthly. Department of Energy, London.

8 LACY, R. E., Climate and Building in Britain, HMSO, London, 1977.

9 CHANDLER, T. J., The Climate of London, Hutchinson, London, 1965.

10 Percentage Frequency of Hourly Values of Dry-Bulb and Wet-Bulb Temperatures, Meteorological Office, Climatological Memoranda:
No. 80, Birmingham Airport, 1960–74;
No. 81, London (Heathrow Airport), 1960–74;
No. 82, Manchester Airport, 1960–74;
No. 91, Glamorgan Airport (Cardiff), 1960–74;
No. 92, Plymouth (Mount Batten), 1960–74;
No. 97, Edinburgh Airport, 1960–74;
No. 99, Renfrew/Abbotsinch, 1960–74;
No. 102, Aldergrove, 1960–74;
Meteorological Office, Bracknell, Berks.

11 Percentage Frequency of Hourly Values of Dry-Bulb and Wet-Bulb Temperatures, Meteorological Office Climatological Memoranda:
No. 83, Dishforth/Leeming, 1960–74;
No. 84, Waddington, 1960–74;
No. 85, Mildenhall/Honington, 1960–74;
No. 86, Boscombe Down, 1960–74;
No. 87, Manston, 1961–74;
No. 88, Thorney Island, 1960–74;
No. 89, Valley, 1960–74;
No. 90, Aberporth, 1960–74;
No. 93, Lerwick, 1960–74;
No. 94, Wick, 1960–74;
No. 95, Stornoway, 1960–74;
No. 96, Kinloss, 1960–74;
No. 98, Tiree, 1960–74;
No. 100, Prestwick, 1960–74;
No. 101, Eskdalemuir, 1960–74;
Meteorological Office, Bracknell, Berks.

12 Tables of Temperature, Relative Humidity and Precipitation for the World:
Part 1 (second edition), North America and Greenland (including Hawaii and Bermuda);
Part 2, Central and South America;
Part 3 (second edition), Europe and the Azores;
Part 4, Africa;
Part 5, Asia;
Part 6, Australasia;
Parts 2 (1967), 4 (1967), 5 (1966) and 6 (1967) are reference Met. 0.617 and Parts 1 (1980) and 3 (1972) (second edition) are reference Met. 0.856.

13 HOLMES, M. J. and HITCHIN, E. R., An Example Year for the Calculation of Energy Demand in Buildings, *BSE*, 1978, **45**, 186–189.

14 LETHERMAN, K. M. and WAI, F. M., Condensed Statistics on the CIBS Example Year – Kew, *BSER & T*, 1980, **1**, 157–159; *BSER & T*, 1981, **2**, 165–173.

15 SHELLARD, H. C., Tables of Surface Wind Speed and Direction over the United Kingdom, Met. 0.792, Meteorological Office, Bracknell, Berks., 1968.

16 CATON, P. G. F., Maps of Hourly Mean Wind Speed over the U.K., 1965–73, Meteorological Office Climatological Memorandum 79, Meteorological Office, Bracknell, Berks., 1976.

17 RAYMENT, R., Wind Energy in the U.K., *BSE*, 1976, **44**, 63–69.

18 British Standard Code of Practice No. 3, Chapter V, Part 2: 1972, Wind Loads, BSI, London, 1972.

19 DAVENPORT, A. G., The Relationship of Wind Structure to Wind Loading, *Proc. Conf. on Wind Effects on Buildings and Structures, N.P.L. 1963*, HMSO, London, 1965.

20 BS 5925, Code of Practice for Design of Buildings: Ventilation Principles and Designing for Natural Ventilation, BSI, London, 1980.

21 Guide to Meteorological Instrument and Observing Practices, World Meteorological Organisation No. 8, TP3., 4th Edition, WMO, Geneva, 1971.

22 PENWARDEN, A. D., Acceptable Wind Speeds in Towns, *Building Science*, 1973, **8**, 259–267.

23 COHEN, H., McLAREN, T. I., MOSS, S. M., PETYK, R. and ZUBE, E. H., Pedestrians and Wind in the Urban Environment, Environment and Behaviour Research Centre, University of Massachusetts & Weather Dynamics Inc., Massachusetts, USA, 1977. (Publication No. UMASS/IME/R-77/13, December 1977.)

24 Flood Studies Report, 1975, National Environment Research Council, London.

25 HUNT, D. R. G., Availability of Daylight, Building Research Establishment, 1979.

26 CIBSE Applications Manual, Window Design, CIBSE, London, to be published.

27 HUNT, D. R. G., Improved Daylight Data for Predicting Energy Savings from Photo-electric Controls, *LR&T*, 1979, **11**, 9–23.

28 The Investigation of Air Pollution: National Survey—Smoke and Sulphur Dioxide, April 1976 – March 1977. Department of Industry, Warren Spring Laboratory, Stevenage, Herts.

29 LAWTHER, P. J., Vehicle Exhausts in Relation to Health, *Proceedings, Royal Society of Health Symposium*, 1966.

30 PURSALL, B. R. and SWANN, C. D., Air Pollution in Vehicular Road Tunnels, *Tunnels and Tunnelling*, July/August 1972.

31 PURSALL, B. R., Some Problems of Air Pollution in Industrial Environments, *Proc. 6th Congress, Int. Council for Building Research Studies and Documentation (CIB)*, Budapest, 1974.

32 ASHRAE Handbook and Product Directory, Fundamentals, ASHRAE, New York, 1977.

33 CIBS Technical Memorandum, TM4, Design Notes for the Middle East, CIBS, London, 1979.

34 Some Fundamental Data Used by Building Services Engineers, IHVE, London, 1973 (out of print).

35 PETHERBRIDGE, P., Sunpath Diagrams and Overlays for Solar Heat Gain Calculations, HMSO, London, 1969 (out of print).

36 MARKUS, T. A. and MORRIS, E. W., Buildings, Climate and Energy, Pitman, London, 1980.

37 FRÖHLICH, C., The Solar Constant: A Critical Review, *Proc. Symp. on Radiation in the Atmosphere*, Science Press, Princeton, N.J., 1977.

38 MOON, P., Proposed Standard Solar-Radiation Curves for Engineering Use, *J. Franklin Inst.*, 1940, **230**, 583–617.

39 LOUDON, A. G., The Interpretation of Solar Radiation Measurements for Building Problems, *BRE Current Paper* R73, 1967.

40 CURTIS, D. M. and LAWRENCE, J., Atmospheric Effects on Solar Radiation for Computer Analysis of Cooling Loads for Buildings at Various Location Heights, *JIHVE*, 1972, **39**, 254–260.

41 COLE, R. J., The Longwave Radiation Incident upon the External Surface of Buildings, *BSE*, 1976, **44**, 195–206.

42 Solar Radiation Data for the United Kingdom 1951–75, Met. 0.912, Meteorological Office, Bracknell, 1980.

43 European Solar Radiation Atlas, Vol. 1 : Global Radiation on Horizontal Surfaces, Commission of the European Communities, W. Grösschen – Verlag, Dortmund, Germany, 1979.

SECTION A3 THERMAL PROPERTIES OF BUILDING STRUCTURES

Introduction	*Page*	A3–3
Notation		A3–3
Building Regulations		A3–4
Steady State Thermal Characteristics		A3–4
Thermal transmittance (*U*-value)		A3–4
Thermal resistance of homogeneous materials		A3–5
Surface resistances		A3–6
Airspace resistance		A3–7
Example 1 : Calculation of *U*-value for simple construction		A3–8
U-values of non-homogeneous and heat-bridged constructions		A3–8
Proportional area method		A3–9
Example 2 : Calculation of *U*-value for wall with bridged inner leaf		A3–10
Combined method		A3–11
Example 3 : Calculation of thermal resistance of slotted block		A3–14
Example 4 : Calculation of thermal resistance of foam-filled block		A3–15

U-values of roofs	*Page*	A3–16
Heat loss through ground floors		A3–17
Example 5 : Calculation of *U*-values for solid and suspended floors		A3–19
Heat loss through glazing		A3–20
Non-steady State Thermal Characteristics		A3–20
Admittance		A3–21
Decrement Factor		A3–21
Surface Factor		A3–21
Internal constructions		A3–21
Overall thermal performance		A3–21
Thermal bridges		A3–21
Appendix 1 : Tables of Thermal Transmittance (*U*) and Admittance (*Y*) Values		A3–22
Appendix 2 : Properties of Materials		A3–31
Appendix 3 : Moisture Content of Masonry Materials		A3–43
Appendix 4 : Thermal Conductivity and Conductance Testing		A3–44
Appendix 5 : Derivation of Admittance, Decrement Factor and Surface Factor		A3–45

This edition of Section A3 first published: 1980

SECTION A3 THERMAL PROPERTIES
OF BUILDING STRUCTURES

INTRODUCTION

Since the publication of the 1970 *Guide*, there has been an increasing need for further authoritative data on the thermal properties of building materials and structures. Recent amendments to the UK Building Regulations have laid down standards of thermal insulation which require the calculation of *U*-values for the structure to ensure compliance. Furthermore, the increasing importance of energy conservation has placed a responsibility upon the designer to ensure that new buildings do not waste energy.

The 1970 *Guide* introduced the concept of thermal admittance and a subsequent paper[1] gave the theory of admittances. Sections A5 and A9 of the *Guide* published in 1979 deal with the use of admittances in great detail

and it has been felt appropriate to include a summary of their method of calculation in this section.

The tables of properties of materials posed a problem. The values had to be selected impartially and, wherever possible, only those with a traditionally accepted value, as given in the 1970 edition of the *Guide*, have been taken. Nevertheless, the Institution recognises that new products will become available and Appendix 4 lays down the test criteria that should be fulfilled before a material is included in the *Guide*.

The problems associated with heat flow through bridged and non-homogeneous materials are covered and examples on the calculation methods are given. Finally the problems of moisture content are discussed.

NOTATION

The notation used in the main body of this document is given below. For Appendix 5, some additional symbols are used and these are defined within the appendix.

$A(x)$	= area of slice (x) etc. of masonry block	m^2
A_1	= area of material 1, etc. in slice of masonry block	m^2
A_f	= area of floor	m^2
B	= dimensionless constant for solid floor	
E	= emissivity factor	
F	= surface factor	
N	= number of room air changes per hour	h^{-1}
P_1	= proportion of total area of element 1, etc. of composite structure	
R_A	= combined thermal resistance of materials in plane of pitched part of roof	$m^2 K/W$
R_B	= combined thermal resistance of materials in plane of ceiling	$m^2 K/W$
R_L	= lower limit of thermal resistance of masonry block	$m^2 K/W$
R_M	= mean thermal resistance of masonry block	$m^2 K/W$
R_R	= thermal resistance of roof void	$m^2 K/W$
R_U	= upper limit of thermal resistance of masonry block	$m^2 K/W$
$R(x)$	= thermal resistance of slice (x) etc. of masonry block	$m^2 K/W$
R_a	= thermal resistance of airspace	$m^2 K/W$
R_b	= thermal resistance of bridged element	$m^2 K/W$
R_c	= equivalent thermal resistance due to convection	$m^2 K/W$
R_e	= thermal resistance of the earth	$m^2 K/W$
R_g	= thermal resistance of floor slab	$m^2 K/W$
R_h	= thermal resistance of homogeneous element	$m^2 K/W$
$R_m(x)$	= thermal resistance of material in slice (x) etc., of masonry block	$m^2 K/W$
R_r	= equivalent thermal resistance due to radiation	$m^2 K/W$
R_s	= surface resistance	$m^2 K/W$
R_{si}	= inside surface resistance	$m^2 K/W$
R_{so}	= outside surface resistance	$m^2 K/W$
R_{t1}	= transform resistance 1, etc.	$m^2 K/W$
R_v	= equivalent thermal resistance due to ventilation	$m^2 K/W$
R_{vo}	= thermal resistance of void	$m^2 K/W$
U	= thermal transmittance of a structural element	$W/m^2 K$
U_g	= thermal transmittance of floor slab	$W/m^2 K$
U_1	= thermal transmittance of element 1, etc. of composite structure	$W/m^2 K$
V	= room volume	m^3
V_f	= ventilation rate under a suspended floor	m^3/s
Y	= thermal admittance of a structural element	$W/m^2 K$
b	= breadth (lesser dimension) of floor	m
c_v	= specific heat capacity	$J/m^2 K$
f	= decrement factor	
f_r	= response factor of a building	
h_c	= convective heat transfer coefficient	$W/m^2 K$
h_r	= radiative heat transfer coefficient	$W/m^2 K$
l	= thickness of a structural element	m

l_f	= length (greater dimension) of floor		m
l_1	= thickness of element 1, etc. of a composite structure		m
r	= thermal resistivity of a material..		m K/W
t_{ao}	= outside air temperature ..		°C
t_{ei}	= inside environmental temperature		°C
v	= wind velocity		m/s
w	= thickness of wall surrounding floor slab		m
Σ	= sum of		
Θ	= form (shape) factor		
a	= free area of floor per metre length of floor		m²/m
β	= angle of pitch of roof		degree

ϵ_1	= emissivity of surface 1, etc. (see section C3 of the *Guide*)		
λ	= thermal conductivity of a material*		W/m K
λ_e	= thermal conductivity of the earth*		W/m K
λ_1	= thermal conductivity of material 1, etc.*		W/m K
ϕ	= time lag for decrement factor ..		h
ψ	= time lag for surface factor ..		h
ω	= time lead for admittance ..		h

* The symbol λ has been adopted for thermal conductivity, in place of k, in accordance with current international practice. This is embodied in ISO Standard 31, Part 4: 1978, which has been adopted by the British Standards Institution as BS 5775 : Part 4 : 1979.

BUILDING REGULATIONS

The Building Regulations (for thermal insulation) in the United Kingdom were introduced initially to minimise the risk of condensation in dwellings. With the increasing cost and scarcity of energy, the regulations have been extended in scope to conserve energy in the majority of building types. These regulations[2] set minimum standards only but higher standards of insulation can often be justified on the grounds of economic energy conservation. (Detailed guidance may be found in Part 1 of the CIBSE Building Energy Code.)

It is, of course, essential that designers are fully conversant with current statutory requirements and are aware of any amendment proposals that may be relevant to work in hand, particularly since members may be called upon to certify compliance with such regulations.

Apart from complying with the Building Regulations, cross checks should be made with regard to the prediction of condensation given in Section A10 of the *Guide*.

The *U*-value gives a good indication of the mean rate of loss of heat from a structure. However, to establish an accurate picture of the thermal performance of a building throughout the year, the dynamic response of the structure should also be considered. This is discussed in detail in Sections A5 and A9 of the *Guide*.

STEADY STATE THERMAL CHARACTERISTICS

Thermal Transmittance (*U*-value)

The thermal transmittance of a building element is obtained by combining the thermal resistances of its component parts and the adjacent air layers. Thermal transmittances of walls and roofs composed of parallel slabs are obtained simply by adding thermal resistances and taking the reciprocal, thus:

$$U = \frac{1}{R_{si}+R_1+R_2+\ldots.+R_a+R_{so}} \qquad \text{.. A3.1}$$

where:

U	= thermal transmittance		W/m² K
R_{si}	= inside surface resistance ..		m² K/W
R_1, R_2	= thermal resistances of structural components		m² K/W
R_a	= airspace resistance		m² K/W
R_{so}	= outside surface resistance ..		m² K/W

Other types of construction, such as elements bridged or partly bridged by other materials, require a different approach. In all cases the first step is to determine the appropriate thermal resistances and the following information is necessary.

Thermal resistance of materials

This depends on the nature, thickness and disposition of the materials. For insulating materials, thermal conductivity test data and the degree of protection from moisture are required. For masonry materials, either the bulk dry density of the material or thermal conductivity test data and the degree of protection from moisture are needed.

Surface resistances

The disposition and whether the surface is of a wall, floor or roof are needed. The direction of heat flow, horizontal, upward or downward and whether the surfaces are of normal building materials with high emissivity or polished metal with low emissivity are also relevant.

Thermal resistance of airspaces

This depends on the thickness and, if <25 mm, other dimensions of airspaces. Other factors are whether the airspace is lined with normal high emissivity surfaces or reflective, low emissivity surfaces and whether it is ventilated or unventilated.

Thermal resistance of heat bridges

The important factor is whether the building element is bridged through its entire thickness or only the inner or outer leaf of the element is bridged.

Thermal resistance of pitched roofs

When combined with a flat ceiling the thermal resistance depends on the angle of slope, loft and (if appropriate) airspace resistances.

Thermal resistance of ground floors

These are a special case where considerable modification of the basic heat flow equation is required, The size and shape of the floor and position of insulation all affect the performance.

Thermal Resistance of Homogeneous Materials

The thermal resistance of unit area of a slab of homogeneous material is calculated by dividing its thickness by its thermal conductivity:

$$R = \frac{l}{\lambda} \qquad .. \qquad .. \qquad .. \qquad .. \qquad A3.2$$

where:

R = thermal resistance .. .. .. m^2 K/W

l = thickness of slab .. .. .. m

λ = thermal conductivity .. .. W/m K

It has been common practice for many years to adopt thermal conductivity values based on historical data for broad classifications of materials. For the majority of masonry materials an empirical relationship between density and thermal conductivity has been used. Table A3.1 gives appropriate values.

More recently, manufacturers have produced materials the thermal conductivities of which are claimed to depart radically from the traditional values. The thermal conductivities and other properties of materials contained in this section are drawn mainly from historical data.

Table A3.1. Thermal conductivities of homogeneous masonry.

Material and standard moisture content (% by volume)	Bulk dry density (kg/m³)	Thermal conductivity (W/m K)	
		Protected	Exposed
	400	0·15	0·16
	500	0·16	0·18
	600	0·19	0·20
	700	0·21	0·23
	800	0·23	0·26
	900	0·27	0·30
	1000	0·30	0·33
	1100	0·34	0·38
	1200	0·38	0·42
Concrete work	1300	0·44	0·49
Aerated concrete and dense concrete at standard moisture content:	1400	0·51	0·57
protected 3%	1500	0·59	0·65
exposed 5%	1600	0·66	0·73
	1700	0·76	0·84
	1800	0·87	0·96
	1900	0·99	1·09
	2000	1·13	1·24
	2100	1·28	1·40
	2200	1·45	1·60
	2300	1·63	1·80
	2400	1·83	2·00
	1000	0·23	0·25
	1100	0·26	0·28
	1200	0·29	0·32
	1300	0·33	0·37
	1400	0·38	0·43
Concrete work	1500	0·44	0·49
Foamed slag aggregate concrete at standard moisture content:	1600	0·50	0·55
protected 3%	1700	0·57	0·63
exposed 5%	1800	0·65	0·72
	1900	0·74	0·82
	2000	0·85	0·93
	2100	0·96	1·05
	1200	0·31	0·42
	1300	0·36	0·49
	1400	0·42	0·57
	1500	0·48	0·65
Brickwork	1600	0·54	0·73
At standard moisture content:	1700	0·62	0·84
protected 1%	1800	0·71	0·96
exposed 5%	1900	0·81	1·09
	2000	0·92	1·24

Notes:
1. 'Protected' refers to internal partitions; inner leaves separated from outer leaves by a continuous airspace; masonry protected by tile hanging; sheet cladding, or other such protection, separated by a continuous airspace.
2. 'Exposed' refers to masonry directly exposed to rain, unrendered or rendered.
3. The standard thermal conductivities apply to the standard moisture contents in the first column and represent typical values. They are given for a range of densities and it is not implied that the materials are available at all the densities indicated.
4. These values assume mortar joints of similar thermal conductivity and density as those of the bulk material.

It is suggested that these values continue to be used until new values are verified by approved test methods and quality control procedures. Appendix 4 discusses appropriate methods.

It should be noted that a number of manufacturers, particularly of insulants, are beginning to define the thermal properties of their products by means of thermal resistance (R-value) rather than thermal conductivity.

This may be more convenient in certain circumstances but, in general, the thickness of the material is still required to ensure that it will fit within the proposed structure. Equation A3.2 may be used in these cases to calculate the thermal conductivity.

The thermal conductivity of a porous building material is determined by its nature and density and, if moist, by the percentage of moisture in the pores.

Insulating materials are normally used where they are roughly in thermal equilibrium with the ambient air and standard methods are used to determine the thermal conductivity. It is less easy, however, to measure the thermal conductivity for masonry materials (brickwork and concrete). The chief difficulty is that many such materials contain appreciable amounts of moisture, either because they are hygroscopic and absorb moisture from the surrounding air or because they are exposed to rain. Corrections for the moisture content of masonry materials are given in Appendix 3.

For masonry materials, the standard values of moisture content are given in Table A3.2. For other materials, it is usual to assume that the material is conditioned to constant weight at 20°C and 65% rh, as specified in BS 874 : 1973, 'Methods of determining thermal insulating properties, with definitions of thermal insulating terms'.

Table A3.2. Standard moisture contents for protected and exposed masonry.

Material	Moisture content by volume / (%)	
	Protected	Exposed
Brickwork	1·0	5·0
Concrete work	3·0	5·0

Note:
Protected covers internal partitions, inner leaves separated from outer leaves by a continuous airspace, masonry protected by tile hanging, sheet cladding or other such protection, separated by a continuous airspace.

Exposed covers masonry directly exposed to rain, unrendered or rendered.

Surface Resistances
Heat transfer by radiation and convection at the surfaces of building elements can be treated as flow through thermal resistances which may be combined to give a surface resistance as follows:

$$R_s = \frac{1}{Eh_r + h_c} \qquad \qquad \qquad A3.3$$

where:

R_s = surface resistance .. .. .. m² K/W
E = emissivity factor
h_r = radiative heat transfer coefficient .. W/m² K
h_c = convective heat transfer coefficient W/m² K

The radiative heat transfer coefficient depends upon the temperature of the radiating surface and values between −10°C and 20°C are given in Table A3.3.

Table A3.3. Radiative heat transfer coefficient, h_r.

Temperature of surface / °C	h_r / (W/m² K)
−10	4·1
0	4·6
10	5·1
20	5·7

Radiative heat transfer also depends upon the shape of the radiating surface, its emissivity and the shape and emissivity of the surface to which it radiates and these are combined into a single emissivity factor, E, as follows:

$$E = \Theta\, \epsilon_1\, \epsilon_2 \quad .. \qquad .. \qquad .. \qquad .. \qquad A3.4$$

where:

Θ = form (or shape) factor
ϵ_1, ϵ_2 = emissivities of surfaces involved

Section C3 of the *Guide* gives form factors for various configurations and values of emissivity for a range of materials, although a different symbol is used for form factor.

In general, the common building materials have high emissivities ($\epsilon \simeq 0·9$) but polished metal finishes, e.g. aluminium foil, have low emissivities ($\epsilon \simeq 0·05$).

The convective heat transfer coefficient depends upon the direction of the heat flow, i.e. upward, downward, or horizontal, the wind speed across the surface and whether the building element is a wall, floor or ceiling.

For still air conditions (i.e. air speed not greater than 0·1 m/s) values of convective heat transfer coefficient are given in Table A3.4 and these have been used in the calculation of the inside surface resistances contained in the following paragraphs.

Table A3.4. Convective heat transfer coefficient, h_c.

Heat flow direction	h_c / (W/m² K)
Horizontal	3·0
Upward	4·3
Downward	1·5
Average	3·0

Note: Air speed at the surface is assumed to be not greater than 0·1 m/s.

In cases where significant air movement takes place, heat transfer by convection becomes more complex and this is dealt with in detail in Section C3 of the *Guide*.

Inside Surface Resistance

The theory of environmental temperature[4], see also Section A5 of the *Guide*, considers that the internal heat transfer is made between the surface and the environmental point and consequently, the shape factor is multiplied by 6/5. Depending on the assumptions made in the equations, the values of R_{si} will vary but standard values of the inside surface resistance are given in Table A3.5.

Table A3.5. Inside surface resistance, R_{si}.

Building element	Heat flow	Surface resistance / (m² K/W)	
		High emissivity factor ($\frac{6}{5}E = 0.97$)	Low emissivity factor ($\frac{6}{5}E = 0.05$)
Walls	Horizontal	0·12	0·30
Ceilings or roofs, flat or pitched, floors	Upward	0·10	0·22
Ceilings and floors	Downward	0·14	0·55

Notes:
1. High emissivity factor assumes $\epsilon_1 = \epsilon_2 = 0.9$
   Low emissivity factor assumes $\epsilon_1 = 0.9, \epsilon_2 = 0.05$
2. Surface temperature is assumed to be 20°C
3. Air speed at the surface is assumed to be not greater than 0·1 m/s.

Outside Surface Resistance

The outside surface resistance for 'standard' *U*-values is based on a wind speed at roof surfaces of 3 m/s. This corresponds to the values of outside surface resistance for 'normal' exposure given in Table A3.6.

Table A3.6. Outside surface resistance (R_{so}) for stated exposure.

Building element	Emissivity of surface	Surface resistance for stated exposure / (m² K/W)		
		Sheltered	Normal	Severe
Wall	High	0·08	0·06	0·03
	Low	0·11	0·07	0·03
Roof	High	0·07	0·04	0·02
	Low	0·09	0·05	0·02

Note: Form (shape) factor for radiative heat transfer is taken to be unity.

These values were obtained by assuming turbulent air flow for which the convective heat transfer coefficients are more complex than those given in Table A3.4. They represent the commonly accepted values for R_{so}.

The effect of differing exposures is small for well insulated structures and has been ignored for opaque structures. However, for glazing, the exposure must be taken into account and, for this reason, Table A3.6 also gives outside surface resistances under sheltered and severely exposed conditions. These conditions are defined thus:

Sheltered: up to third floor of buildings in city centres.

Normal: most suburban and rural buildings; fourth to eighth floors of buildings in city centres.

Severe: buildings on coastal or hill sites; floors above the fifth in suburban or rural districts; floors above the ninth in city centres.

The effect of sunshine is dealt with in detail in Section A5 of the *Guide*, but it is assumed that in winter heating design weather the walls receive little sunshine and the outside surface resistance is unaffected by orientation.

Airspace Resistance

Airspaces can be treated as media with thermal resistance because the radiation and convection heat transfer across them is approximately proportional to the difference between the temperatures of the boundary surfaces. The thermal resistance of an airspace depends on the following factors.

Surface Emissivity

Most building materials have a high emissivity, 0·9 to 0·95, and radiation accounts for about two-thirds of the heat transfer. Airspaces lined with low emissivity material such as aluminium foil have a much higher resistance because radiation is largely prevented. However, high emissivity should be assumed unless the airspace is known to be lined with such a material.

Dimensions

The thermal resistance of a tall vertical airspace increases with its thickness up to about 25 mm. At greater thicknesses the thermal resistance is virtually constant. Furthermore, if the airspace is not continuous in the horizontal direction but divided into vertical strips or slots, see Fig. A3.1., the thermal resistance of the airspace also depends upon the width of the strip.

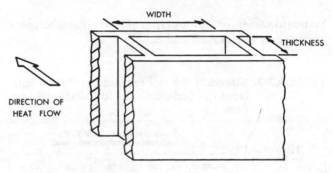

Fig. A3.1. Divided vertical airspace

Direction of Heat Flow

A horizontal airspace presents a higher resistance to downward heat flow than to upward because downward convection is small.

Many heat loss problems are concerned with upward heat flow but it is worth noting that the thermal resistance of an airspace incorporating multiple aluminium foil insulation may be as high as 2·0 for downward heat flow and may therefore be an important factor in reducing summer heat gains through roofs.

A small inclination of an airspace has only a minor effect on the convection transfer and therefore little effect on the airspace resistance. This also applies in the case of pitched roofs above flat ceilings.

Temperature Difference

The temperature difference across the airspace also has a minor effect on convection and the mean temperature has a minor effect on radiation transfer. In general, no allowance need be made for these factors unless the airspace resistance forms a major proportion of the total resistance.

Effect of Airspace Ventilation

Airspace ventilation provides an additional heat flow path which decreases the effective airspace resistance. Its influence can be estimated from heat transfer theory if the rate and distribution of air movement in the airspace is known. However, this varies according to conditions and cannot easily be determined so that estimates of thermal resistance of ventilated airspaces are necessarily approximate.

Airspaces may be ventilated either deliberately, e.g. ventilated loft spaces, or fortuitously, e.g. sheeted constructions with gaps between sheets.

It should be noted that ventilation occurs through gaps between tiles or cladding sheets unless precautions are taken to seal the joints and in these cases the thermal resistance of the tiles should be ignored.

Effect of Corrugations

If the surface of the airspace is corrugated, as in some sheeted constructions, the area for convection transfer is about 20% greater but this has a negligible effect on the airspace resistance. If flat and corrugated sheets are in contact, leaving only narrow air gaps between troughs and crests of the corrugations, the resistance is reduced and the values in Table A3.8 should be used.

Standard values for various types of unventilated airspace are given in Tables A3.7 and A3.8.

Table A3.7. Standard thermal resistances for unventilated divided airspaces for horizontal heat flow.

Thickness of air space/mm	Thermal resistance / (m² K/W) for air space of stated width / (mm)				
	200 or greater	100	50	20	10 or less
5	0·10	0·10	0·11	0·11	0·11
6	0·11	0·12	0·12	0·12	0·13
7	0·12	0·12	0·13	0·13	0·14
8	0·13	0·13	0·13	0·14	0·15
10	0·14	0·14	0·15	0·16	0·17
12	0·15	0·16	0·16	0·18	0·19
15	0·16	0·17	0·18	0·19	0·21
20	0·17	0·18	0·19	0·22	0·24
25 or more	0·18	0·20	0·21	0·24	0·27

Notes:
1. Applies to heat flow in horizontal direction only for airspaces of dimensions as shown in Fig. A3.1.
2. Values are based on recent work by the Building Research Establishment[5].

Example 1: Calculation of *U*-value for Simple Construction

An external wall consisting of 105 mm brickwork, 50 mm unventilated cavity containing 13 mm of expanded polystyrene insulation, 100 mm lightweight concrete block inner leaf finished with 13 mm of lightweight plaster.

Taking thermal conductivities from Appendix 2, the thermal resistance of each element is obtained from equation A3.2 as follows:

Element	Thickness/m	Thermal conductivity/ (W/m K)	Thermal resistance/ (m² K/W)
Brickwork	0·105	0·84	0·13
Expanded polystyrene	0·013	0·035	0·37
Lightweight concrete block	0·100	0·19	0·53
Lightweight plaster	0·013	0·16	0·08

The airspace and surface resistances are:

Outside surface resistance, $R_{so} = 0.06$ m² K/W
(Table A3.6)

Inside surface resistance, $R_{si} = 0.12$ m² K/W
(Table A3.5)

Cavity resistance, $R_a = 0.18$ m² K/W
(Table A3.8)

Substituting these values into equation A3.1:

$$U = \frac{1}{0.12 + (0.13+0.37+0.53+0.08) + 0.18 + 0.06}$$

Therefore:

$$U = 0.68 \text{ W/m}^2 \text{ K}$$

U-values of Non Homogeneous and Heat Bridged Constructions

As with straightforward homogeneous materials the basic calculation of *U*-values involves the combination of the thermal resistances of the separate elements. The surface resistances and air gap resistances are the same as before but the computation of the resistance of the materials is far more complex.

The method of calculating *U*-values, described above, assumes that the direction of heat flow is perpendicular to the plane of the structure and that edge effects are ignored. Where discontinuities due to the presence of dissimilar materials occur, this uni-directional heat flow is disturbed and thermal bridges are formed. The evaluation of these bridged areas is complex and a correct

Table A3.8. Standard thermal resistances for unventilated airspaces.

Type of air space		Thermal resistance / (m² K/W) for heat flow in stated direction		
Thickness	Surface emissivity	Horizontal	Upward	Downward
5 mm	High	0·10	0·10	0·10
	Low	0·18	0·18	0·18
25 mm	High	0·18	0·17	0·22
or more	Low	0·35	0·35	1·06
High emissivity plane and corrugated sheets in contact		0·09	0·09	0·11
Low emissivity multiple foil insulation with airspace on one side.		0·62	0·62	1·76

analysis can only be made if three dimensional heat flow is considered. However, in many instances simpler solutions can be employed.

Thermal bridges can be classified into three distinct types: discrete bridges, multi-webbed bridges and finned element bridges.

Discrete bridges are contained wholly within the main structure where the size of the bridged area in relation to the rest of the structure is small, e.g. solid lintels and concrete beams. The proportional area method of calculation can be used in these cases.

Multi-webbed bridges occur in components such as slotted blocks and perforated bricks. Because the bridges cover a large area of the structure, the disturbance to the perpendicular heat flow is great. In these cases either a three dimensional analysis or the combined method of calculation should be used.

Finned element bridges are formed at the junction of walls and floors and other non-planar elements where the heat flow paths are complex. These can only be assessed satisfactorily by means of three-dimensional techniques involving, for example, finite element computer programs.

A more pragmatic approach is to use thermal breaks to minimise the disturbance as far as possible. An approximation of the effect of a finned element is to treat the area of the fin as being the total exposed area of the finned element as shown in Fig. A3.2.

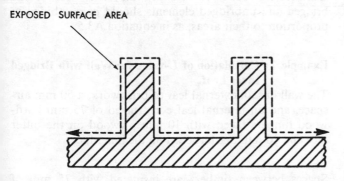

Fig. A3.2. Finned element.

Effects of Mortar Joints

The effect of mortar joints, which can account for 5 to 20% of the area, should be considered in all cases. Where the solid building material has similar thermal properties to the mortar, the effect of bridging is negligible and this has been assumed to be the case in the tables of U-values contained in Appendix 1. However, where the mortar is used with materials of substantially different thermal properties, the effect of heat bridging should be taken into account using the proportional area method (see below). Typically, mortar has a density of 1750 kg/m³, thermal conductivity of 0·8 (inner leaf) and 0·9 (outer leaf) W/m K and a thickness of 10 mm.

Corners and Other Junctions

The above assumes that a building consists of large plane or nearly plane elements and ignores the effects of corners and other junctions between the external envelope and the internal structural elements on the rate of loss of heat from the building.

In such cases, particularly where the insulating layer of the external element is disrupted, the rate of loss of heat can be increased and problems due to surface condensation or pattern staining may arise. A pragmatic solution in buildings where there is a risk of condensation is either to continue the insulation across the junction or to line the interior faces of the internal structure with a layer of insulant for some distance back from the junction. These methods are indicated in Fig. A3.3.

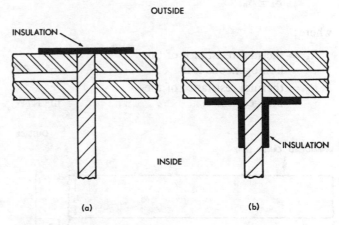

Fig. A3.3. Insulation at junctions.

Other Thermal Effects

The average U-values of non-homogeneous structures can be estimated with a reasonable degree of accuracy. However, the presence of thermal bridges of any form may have repercussions in the form of condensation (both surface and interstitial) and pattern staining, see Section A10 of the *Guide*.

Proportional Area Method (applicable to Discrete Bridges)

The proportional area method assumes that heat flow is in one direction, perpendicular to the surfaces of the construction. Consequently the thermal transmittance of each heat flow path can be calculated separately and then added together in direct proportion to their areas.

Single Leaf Walls

For a single leaf wall, see Fig. A3.4, the overall U-value is given by:

$$U = P_1U_1 + P_2U_2 + \quad .. \quad .. \quad .. \quad \text{A3.5}$$

where:

P_1 = unbridged proportion of the total area

P_2 = bridged proportion of the total area

OUTSIDE

UNBRIDGED PROPORTION P_1 OF TOTAL AREA

BRIDGED PROPORTION P_2 OF TOTAL AREA

INSIDE

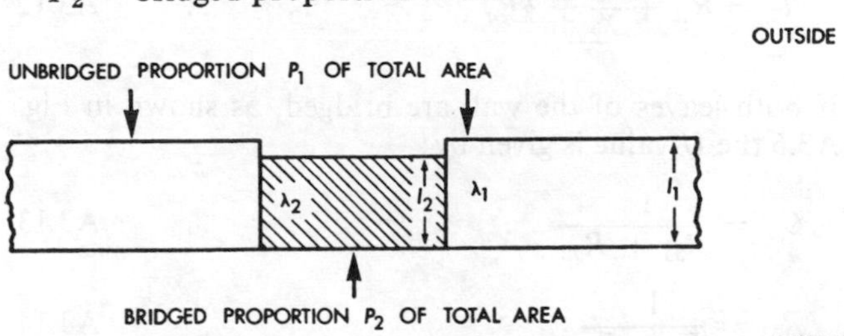

Fig. A3.4. Bridged single leaf wall.

The U-value of each component is calculated, as for a homogeneous structure, from equation A3.1, so in this case:

$$U_1 = \frac{1}{R_{si} + \frac{l_1}{\lambda_1} + R_{so}} \qquad \ldots \qquad \ldots \qquad \ldots \qquad \text{A3.6}$$

$$U_2 = \frac{1}{R_{si} + \frac{l_2}{\lambda_2} + R_{so}} \qquad \ldots \qquad \ldots \qquad \ldots \qquad \text{A3.7}$$

Twin Leaf Walls

For the twin leaf wall shown in Fig. A3.5, where only one leaf is bridged, the overall U-value is given by:

$$U = \frac{1}{R_b + R_h} \qquad \ldots \qquad \ldots \qquad \ldots \qquad \ldots \qquad \text{A3.8}$$

where:

R_h = thermal resistance of the
       homogeneous leaf   ..   ..   ..   m² K/W

R_b = thermal resistance of the
       bridged leaf ..   ..   m² K/W

Fig. A3.5. Twin leaf wall – inner leaf bridged.

The boundary between the two leaves is taken as mid-way across the air gap so that half the air gap resistance is added to each leaf. Thus the resistances are:

$$R_h = \tfrac{1}{2}R_a + \frac{l_3}{\lambda_3} + R_{so} \qquad \ldots \qquad \ldots \qquad \ldots \qquad \text{A3.9}$$

$$R_b = \frac{1}{\frac{P_1}{R_1} + \frac{P_2}{R_2}} \qquad \ldots \qquad \ldots \qquad \ldots \qquad \text{A3.10}$$

and in this case:

$$R_1 = R_{si} + \frac{l_1}{\lambda_1} + \tfrac{1}{2}R_a \qquad \ldots \qquad \ldots \qquad \ldots \qquad \text{A3.11}$$

$$R_2 = R_{si} + \frac{l_2}{\lambda_2} + \tfrac{1}{2}R_a \qquad \ldots \qquad \ldots \qquad \ldots \qquad \text{A3.12}$$

If both leaves of the wall are bridged, as shown in Fig. A3.6 the U-value is given by:

$$U = \frac{1}{R_{b1} + R_{b2}} \qquad \ldots \qquad \ldots \qquad \ldots \qquad \text{A3.13}$$

$$R_{b1} = \frac{1}{\frac{P_1}{R_1} + \frac{P_2}{R_2}} \qquad \ldots \qquad \ldots \qquad \ldots \qquad \text{A3.14}$$

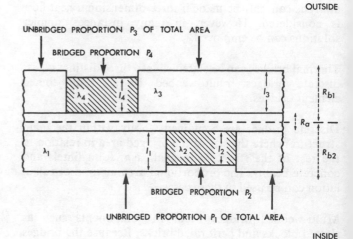

Fig. A3.6. Twin leaf wall – both leaves bridged.

$$R_{b2} = \frac{1}{\frac{P_3}{R_3} + \frac{P_4}{R_4}} \qquad \ldots \qquad \ldots \qquad \ldots \qquad \text{A3.15}$$

$$R_1 = R_{si} + \frac{l_1}{\lambda_1} + \tfrac{1}{2}R_a \qquad \ldots \qquad \ldots \qquad \ldots \qquad \text{A3.16}$$

$$R_2 = R_{si} + \frac{l_2}{\lambda_2} + \tfrac{1}{2}R_a \qquad \ldots \qquad \ldots \qquad \ldots \qquad \text{A3.17}$$

$$R_3 = \tfrac{1}{2}R_a + \frac{l_3}{\lambda_3} + R_{so} \qquad \ldots \qquad \ldots \qquad \ldots \qquad \text{A3.18}$$

$$R_4 = \tfrac{1}{2}R_a + \frac{l_4}{\lambda_4} + R_{so} \qquad \ldots \qquad \ldots \qquad \ldots \qquad \text{A3.19}$$

If both leaves and the cavity are bridged by a single element (e.g. concrete column), the resistances of the bridged and unbridged elements should be combined in proportion to their areas, as in equation A3.5.

Example 2: Calculation of U-value for Wall with Bridged Inner Leaf

The wall has an external leaf of brickwork, a 50 mm airspace, and an internal leaf constructed of 75 mm hardwood timbers faced with 10 mm plywood on the outer face and 10 mm plasterboard on the inner face.

Spaces between timbers are insulated with 75 mm of mineral wool fibre of thermal conductivity of 0·04 W/m K. The wall is 4·275 m long by 3·075 m high, and is constructed of light vertical hardwood timbers at 600 mm centres and horizontal timbers at 1·5 m centres at the top, centre and base of the wall.

Taking thermal conductivities from Appendix 2, the thermal resistance of the elements are obtained from equation A3.2, giving:

Element	Thickness (m)	Thermal conductivity (W/m K)	Thermal resistance (m² K/W)
Brickwork	0·105	0·84	0·13
Mineral Wool Fibre	0·075	0·04	1·88
Plywood	0·010	0·14	0·07
Gypsum Plasterboard	0·010	0·16	0·06
Structural Timbers	0·075	0·15	0·50

The airspace and surface resistances are:

Inside surface resistance, $R_{si} = 0.12$ m² K/W
Outside surface resistance, $R_{so} = 0.06$ m² K/W
Airspace resistance, $R_a = 0.18$ m² K/W

Substituting these values in equation A3.9:

$$R_h = R_{so} + R \text{ (brickwork)} + \tfrac{1}{2}R_a$$
$$= 0.06 + 0.13 + 0.09$$
$$= 0.28 \text{ m}^2 \text{ K/W}$$

The fractions of the wall area occupied by insulation and by structural timbers, P_1 and P_2 are found as follows:

Total wall area: $4.275 \times 3.075 = 13.15$ m²
Area of 14 insulated sections: $14 \times 0.525 \times 1.425$
$= 10.47$ m²
Fraction occupied by insulation, $P_1 = 10.47/13.15$
$= 0.80$
Fraction occupied by timbers, $P_2 = 0.20$

The thermal resistances R_1 and R_2 of the areas incorporating insulation and structural timbers are found as follows:

$$R_1 = \tfrac{1}{2}R_a + R \text{ (plywood)} + R \text{ (mineral wool)} + R \text{ (plaster-board)} + R_{si}$$
$$= 0.09 + 0.07 + 1.88 + 0.06 + 0.12$$
$$= 2.22 \text{ m}^2 \text{ K/W}$$

$$R_2 = \tfrac{1}{2}R_a + R \text{ (plywood)} + R \text{ (timber)} + R \text{ (plaster-board)} + R_{si}$$
$$= 0.09 + 0.07 + 0.50 + 0.06 + 0.12$$
$$= 0.84 \text{ m}^2 \text{ K/W}$$

Hence from equation A3.10:

$$R_b = \cfrac{1}{\dfrac{0.8}{2.22} + \dfrac{0.2}{0.84}}$$
$$= 1.67 \text{ m}^2 \text{ K/W}$$

From equation A3.8:

$$U = \frac{1}{0.28 + 1.67}$$
$$= 0.51 \text{ W/m}^2 \text{ K}$$

Combined Method

The combined method is applicable to masonry or concrete blocks with a pattern of filled or unfilled rectangular voids. The method is also applicable to blocks containing circular or elliptical (oval) voids provided the following assumptions are made:

(a) If the voids are circular, the calculation should be carried out by assuming the voids to be square, of the same area and centred on the same point as the circular voids with two faces parallel to the surface of the block.

(b) If the voids are elliptical, the calculation should be carried out by assuming the voids to be rectangular and of the same area as the elliptical voids, the lengths of the sides of the rectangle being in the ratio of the maximum and minimum dimensions of the ellipse. Again, the rectangular voids are to be centred on the same point as the elliptical voids, the faces being parallel to the surface of the block.

It should be noted that actual dimensions of slots differ from nominal dimensions and mean dimensions should be obtained by measurement. For ease of production,

slots are generally tapered and measurements have to be made at different depths using an internal micrometer screw gauge or similar instrument. Measurements should be made on several blocks and the average cross-section and depth should be used in calculating the conductance of the block.

The thermal conductance can be obtained either by measurement on a specimen prepared from material sliced from the face of the block, or by calculation from the density of the material. The density can be assessed if the mean slot dimensions have been obtained by dividing the mass of the block by its net volume. The net volume is found by subtracting the volume of the slots from the total volume of the block.

The thermal resistance of an unfilled void is a function of many complex factors. Until such time as more reliable data are available, the values of thermal resistance given in Table A3.7 may be used.

The pattern of heat flow in a block with voids is complicated by the effects of lateral heat flow around the voids, see Fig. A3.7 (a), and the effects of adjacent materials and

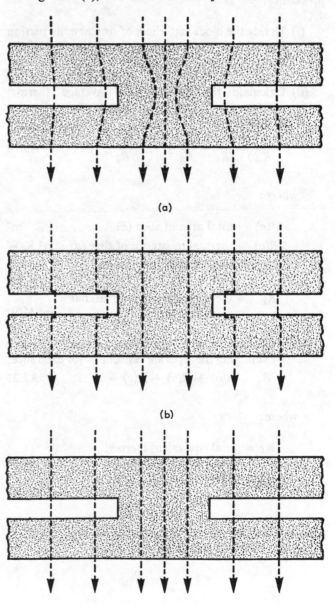

(a)

(b)

(c)

Fig. A3.7. Heat flow around voids (Concentration of lines indicates rate of flow of heat.)

these can only be assessed correctly by means of a multi-dimensional calculation procedure. However, the following manual method is considered to be a reasonable compromise which gives a unique value for a particular block. The method involves the setting of upper and lower limits to the degree of lateral heat flow and the calculation of a mean thermal resistance[14].

Lower Limit

The lower limit of thermal resistance is set by assuming that at each plane of discontinuity of heat flow formed by the edge of a void parallel to the main face of the block, the temperature is uniform and that there is, in effect, no resistance to lateral heat flow, Fig. A3.7 (b).

The equivalent resistance is calculated by the following procedure:

(i) Divide the block into slices of similar construction across their thickness, parallel to the face of the block.

(ii) Calculate the area-weighted average thermal resistance of each slice from the following equation:

$$\frac{A(a)}{R(a)} = \frac{A_1}{R_1} + \frac{A_2}{R_2} + \dots \frac{A_n}{R_n} \qquad \text{A3.20}$$

where:

$A(a)$ = total area of slice (a) .. .. m²

$R(a)$ = thermal resistance of slice (a) m² K/W

A_1 = area of each material in slice 1, etc. .. .. m²

R_1 = thermal resistance of material in slice 1, etc. .. .. m² K/W

(iii) Calculate the total equivalent thermal resistance by summing the separate resistances for each slice:

$$R_L = R(a) + R(b) + R(c) + \qquad .. \qquad \text{A3.21}$$

where:

R_L = total equivalent thermal resistance (lower limit) .. m² K/W

$R(a)$= thermal resistance of slice (a), etc. .. .. .. m² K/W

This method, applied to a specific block type, is shown diagrammatically in Fig. A3.8.

SCHEMATIC DIAGRAM OF SLOTTED BLOCK

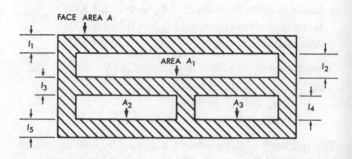

SLICE (a)

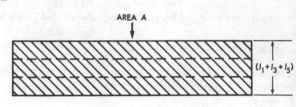

THERMAL RESISTANCE OF MATERIAL; $R_m(a) = \frac{l_1 + l_3 + l_5}{\lambda}$

RESISTANCE OF SLICE (a); $R(a) = R_m(a)$

SLICE (b)

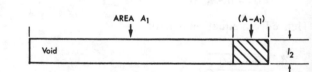

THERMAL RESISTANCE OF MATERIAL; $R_m(b) = \frac{l_2}{\lambda}$

THERMAL RESISTANCE OF VOID; R_{vo}

RESISTANCE OF SLICE (b) IS GIVEN BY; $\frac{A}{R(b)} = \frac{A_1}{R_{vo}} + \frac{(A - A_1)}{R_m(b)}$

SLICE (c)

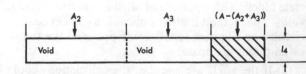

THERMAL RESISTANCE OF MATERIAL; $R_m(c) = \frac{l_4}{\lambda}$

THERMAL RESISTANCE OF VOIDS; R_{vo}

RESISTANCE OF SLICE (c) IS GIVEN BY; $\frac{A}{R(c)} = \frac{(A_2 + A_3)}{R_{vo}} + \frac{(A - (A_2 + A_3))}{R_m(c)}$

Fig. A3.8. Equivalent thermal resistance – lower limit.

Upper Limit

The upper limit of thermal resistance is set by assuming that the outer and inner faces of the block are at uniform temperatures and there is no lateral heat flow, see Fig. A3.7 (c).

The equivalent resistance is calculated as follows:

(i) Divide the block into sections of similar construction at right angles to the face of the block.

(ii) Calculate the thermal resistance of each section by summing the resistances of the separate components in the section, i.e.

$$R(a) = R_1 + R_2 + R_3 + \ldots R_n \ldots \quad \text{A3.22}$$

where:

$R(a)$ = thermal resistance of section (a)

R_1, etc. = thermal resistance of component   ..   .. m² K/W

(iii) Calculate the equivalent resistance of the whole block by combining the resistances of the sections in inverse proportion to their areas, i.e.

$$\frac{A}{R_U} = \frac{A(a)}{R(a)} + \frac{A(b)}{R(b)} + \ldots \frac{A(n)}{R(n)} \quad \text{..} \quad \text{A3.23}$$

where:

A = total area of block

R_U = total equivalent thermal resistance (upper limit)   .. m² K/W

$A(a)$ = area of section (a) ..   ..   m²

$R(a)$ = thermal resistance of section (a) ..   ..   .. m² K/W

Fig. A3.9 shows a diagrammatic representation of this method.

The mean equivalent resistance of the block is derived from the mean of the upper and lower limiting values.

$$R_M = \frac{R_U + R_L}{2} \quad \text{..} \quad \text{..} \quad \text{..} \quad \text{..} \quad \text{A3.24}$$

where:

R_M = mean thermal resistance   ..   .. m² K/W

This equivalent resistance is then used in the normal manner to obtain the overall U-value for the composite construction that contains the block.

SCHEMATIC DIAGRAM OF SLOTTED BLOCK

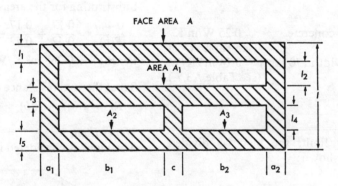

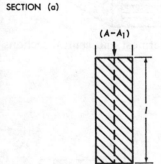

SECTION (a)

THERMAL RESISTANCE OF:

MATERIAL, $R_m(a) = \dfrac{l}{\lambda}$

VOIDS,   none

SECTION (a), $R(a) = R_m(a)$

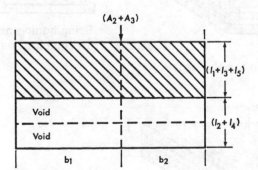

SECTION (b)

THERMAL RESISTANCE OF:

MATERIAL, $R_m(b) = \dfrac{l_1 + l_3 + l_5}{\lambda}$

VOIDS, $2 R_{vo}$

SECTION (b), $R(b) = R_m(b) + 2R_{vo}$

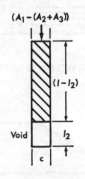

SECTION (c)

THERMAL RESISTANCE OF:

MATERIAL, $R_m(c) = \dfrac{l - l_2}{\lambda}$

VOIDS, R_{vo}

SECTION (c), $R(c) = R_m(c) + R_{vo}$

Fig. A3.9. Equivalent thermal resistance – upper limit.

Example 3: Calculation of Thermal Resistance of Slotted Block

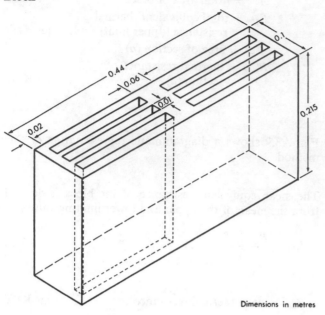

Dimensions in metres

Concrete block, material density 850 kg/m², having three rows of parallel slots, each 10 mm thick, divided into two groups as shown below. The voids are continuous through the block.

Thermal conductivity of concrete   = 0·25 W/m K
                                     (see Table A3.1)
Resistance of airspace (width 170 mm) = 0·14 m² K/W
                                     (see Table A3.7.)

Lower Limit

For calculation of lower limit, the block is divided horizontally into slices, as shown:

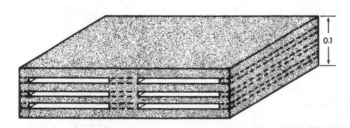

These seven slices may be grouped together as follows:

SLICE (a)

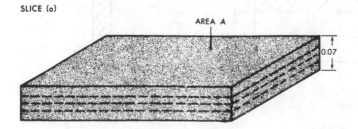

AREA A

Thermal resistance of material in slice (a):

$$R_m(a) = \frac{0 \cdot 07}{0 \cdot 25} = 0 \cdot 28 \text{ m}^2 \text{ K/W}$$

Therefore total thermal resistance of slice (a):

$$R(a) = R_m(a) = 0 \cdot 28 \text{ m}^2 \text{ K/W}$$

SLICE (b)

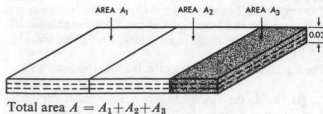

AREA A_1 AREA A_2 AREA A_3

Total area $A = A_1 + A_2 + A_3$

Thermal resistance of material in slice (b):

$$R_m(b) = \frac{0 \cdot 03}{0 \cdot 25} = 0 \cdot 12 \text{ m}^2 \text{ K/W}$$

Total thermal resistance of slice (b):

$$\frac{A}{R(b)} = \frac{A_1}{R_{vo} + R_{vo} + R_{vo}} + \frac{A_2}{R_{vo} + R_{vo} + R_{vo}} + \frac{A_3}{R_m(b)}$$

In this case the resistances of the slots are equal since they are of equal size and unfilled and $R_{vo} = 0 \cdot 14$ m² K/W.

$$\frac{A}{R(b)} = \frac{A_1}{3 \times 0 \cdot 14} + \frac{A_2}{3 \times 0 \cdot 14} + \frac{A_3}{0 \cdot 12}$$

$$A_1 = 0 \cdot 170 \times 0 \cdot 215 \text{ m}^2$$
$$A_2 = 0 \cdot 170 \times 0 \cdot 215 \text{ m}^2$$
$$A_3 = 0 \cdot 100 \times 0 \cdot 215 \text{ m}^2$$
$$A \ = 0 \cdot 440 \times 0 \cdot 215 \text{ m}^2$$

Substituting for the areas and dividing through by 0·215:

$$\frac{0 \cdot 440}{R(b)} = \frac{0 \cdot 17}{0 \cdot 42} + \frac{0 \cdot 17}{0 \cdot 42} + \frac{0 \cdot 10}{0 \cdot 12}$$

i.e. $R(b) = 0 \cdot 268$ m² K/W

Total thermal resistance of block (lower limit):

$$R_L = R(a) + R(b) = 0 \cdot 548 \text{ m}^2 \text{ K/W}$$

Upper Limit

The block is considered in sections as follows:

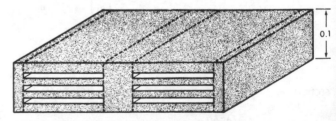

Being homogeneous, the outermost and central sections are combined as follows:

SECTION (a)

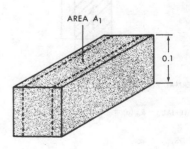

AREA A_1

Thermal resistance of section (a) is:

$$R(a) = \frac{0 \cdot 1}{0 \cdot 25} = 0 \cdot 4 \text{ m}^2 \text{ K/W}$$

SECTIONS (b) AND (c)

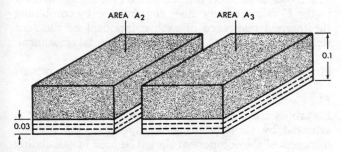

Thermal resistance of section (b) is:

$$R(b) = R_{vo} + R_{vo} + R_{vo} + R_m(b)$$

i.e.

$$R(b) = (3 \times 0.14) + \frac{0.07}{0.25} = 0.7 \text{ m}^2 \text{ K/W}$$

Thermal resistance of section (c) is identical to section (b), hence:

Total thermal resistance of block (upper limit) is given by:

$$\frac{A}{R_U} = \frac{A_1}{R(a)} + \frac{A_2}{R(b)} + \frac{A_3}{R(c)}$$

Area:

$$A_1 = 0.10 \times 0.215 \text{ m}^2$$
$$A_2 = 0.17 \times 0.215 \text{ m}^2$$
$$A_3 = 0.17 \times 0.215 \text{ m}^2$$
$$A = A_1 + A_2 + A_3 = 0.44 \times 0.215 \text{ m}^2$$

Substituting for the areas and dividing throughout by 0.215:

$$\frac{0.44}{R_U} = \frac{0.10}{0.4} + \frac{0.17}{0.7} + \frac{0.17}{0.7}$$

i.e. $R_U = 0.598 \text{ m}^2 \text{ K/W}$

Finally, mean equivalent resistance of block,

$$R_M = \frac{R_U + R_L}{2}$$

Hence:

$$R_M = 0.57 \text{ m}^2 \text{ K/W}$$

Example 4: Calculation of Thermal Resistance of Foam-filled Block

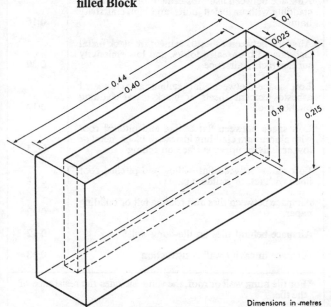

Dimensions in metres

Concrete block, density 1400 kg/m³, with single slot 25 mm thick, closed at one end and filled with expanded polystyrene.

Thermal conductivity of concrete	$= 0.51 \text{ W/m K}$ (see Table A3.15)
Thermal conductivity of expanded polystyrene	$= 0.035 \text{ W/m K}$ (see Table A3.15)

Lower Limit

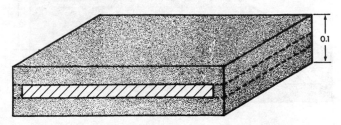

The outermost slices are grouped together as follows:

SLICE (a)

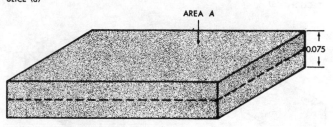

Thermal resistance of material in slice (a):

$$R_m(a) = \frac{0.075}{0.51} = 0.147 \text{ m}^2 \text{ K/W}$$

Total thermal resistance of slice (a)

$$R(a) = R_m(a) = 0.147 \text{ m}^2 \text{ K/W}$$

SLICE (b)

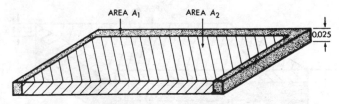

Thermal resistance of material (1), i.e. concrete, in slice (b):

$$R_{m1}(b) = \frac{0.025}{0.51} = 0.049 \text{ m}^2 \text{ K/W}$$

Thermal resistance of material (2), i.e. EPS foam, in slice (b):

$$R_{m2}(b) = \frac{0.025}{0.035} = 0.714 \text{ m}^2 \text{ K/W}$$

Total thermal resistance of slice (b):

$$\frac{A}{R(b)} = \frac{A_1}{R_{m1}(b)} + \frac{A_2}{R_{m2}(b)}$$

Area:

$$A = 0.44 \times 0.215 = 0.0946 \text{ m}^2$$
$$A_2 = 0.40 \times 0.19 = 0.076 \text{ m}^2$$
$$A_1 = (A - A_2) = 0.0186 \text{ m}^2$$

$$\frac{0.0946}{R(b)} = \frac{0.0186}{0.049} + \frac{0.076}{0.714}$$

i.e. $R(b) = 0.195$ m² K/W

Thus, total resistance of block (lower limit)

$$R_L = R(a) + R(b) = 0.342 \text{ m}^2 \text{ K/W}$$

Upper Limit

The block is divided into two sections, as shown:

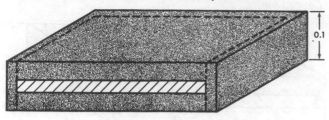

Taking the '*U*-shaped' homogeneous section:

SECTION (a)

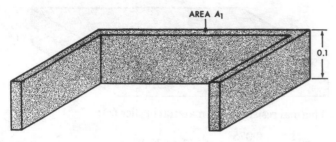

AREA A_1

Thermal resistance of section (*a*)

$$R(a) = \frac{0.10}{0.51} = 0.196 \text{ m}^2 \text{ K/W}$$

SECTION (b)

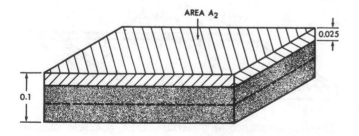

AREA A_2

Thermal resistance of section (*b*):

$$R(b) = \frac{0.025}{0.035} + \frac{0.075}{0.51} = 0.861 \text{ m}^2 \text{ K/W}$$

Total thermal resistance of block (upper limit) is given by:

$$\frac{A}{R_U} = \frac{A_1}{R(a)} + \frac{A_2}{R(b)}$$

$$\frac{0.0946}{R_U} = \frac{0.0186}{0.196} + \frac{0.076}{0.861}$$

$$R_U = 0.517 \text{ m}^2 \text{ K/W}$$

Finally, mean equivalent thermal resistance of block:

$$R_M = \frac{R_L + R_U}{2}$$

i.e.

$$R_M = 0.43 \text{ m}^2 \text{ K/W}$$

U-values of Roofs

The *U*-values of roofs are calculated in a similar fashion to the *U*-values of any other construction by combining the thermal resistance of each component of the roof structure and taking the reciprocal of the total resistance.

However, the following types merit special consideration:

Flat Roofs

Flat roofs are normally laid to falls. Where this effect is achieved by the tapering of components, the average thickness of the component should be used in calculating the overall performance of the roof.

However, if the tapered component is the main insulant, the variation of the *U*-value over the roof structure should be allowed for in designing the heating system.

Pitched Roofs

For simple pitched roofs the *U*-value is calculated normal to the plane of the roof. However when the pitched roof contains a horizontal ceiling, the *U*-value is measured with respect to the plane of the ceiling and has to be corrected for the roof pitch as follows:

$$U = \frac{1}{R_A \cos \beta + R_R + R_B} \quad \cdots \quad \cdots \quad \cdots \quad \text{A3.25}$$

where:

R_A = combined resistance of materials in the plane of pitched part of the roof, including outside surface resistance   m² K/W

β = angle of pitch of the roof.

R_R = resistance of the roof void (Table A3.9) ..   ..   m² K/W

R_B = combined resistance of materials in the plane of the ceiling, including inside surface resistance   ..   ..   m² K/W

Table A3.9. Standard thermal resistance of ventilated airspaces.

Type of airspace (thickness 25 mm minimum)	Thermal resistances (m² K/W)
Airspace between asbestos cement or black metal cladding with unsealed joints, and high emissivity lining	0·16
Airspace between asbestos cement or black metal cladding with unsealed joints, and low emissivity surface facing airspace	0·30
Loft space between flat ceiling and unsealed asbestos cement sheets or black metal cladding pitched roof	0·14
Loft space between flat ceiling and pitched roof with aluminium cladding instead of black metal or low emissivity upper surface on ceiling	0·25
Loft space between flat ceiling and pitched roof lined with felt or building paper.	0·18
Airspace between tiles and roofing felt or building paper.	0·12
Airspace behind tiles on tile-hung wall*	0·12
Airspace in cavity wall construction	0·18

*For tile hung wall or roof, the value includes the resistance of the tile.

Heat Loss Through Ground Floors

Solid Ground Floors

Table A3.10 gives U-values for calculating the heat flow through solid ground floors in contact with the earth. The values given are applicable to dense concrete floors with or without a bed of hard core[6, 7].

The thermal conductivity of the earth, λ_e, depends upon the moisture content and can vary from 0·7 to 2·1 W/m K. An average value of 1·4 W/m K was used in calculating the U-values and, since this is about the same as the thermal conductivity of the floor slabs, Table A3.10 may be used for slabs of any thickness. The U-value will not be affected by a hard dense floor finish such as granolithic concrete or terrazzo tiling nor by a thin finish of little insulation value such as thermoplastic tiles. The values given in Table A3.10 should be used with the temperature difference $(t_{et} - t_{ao})$.

For floors with four exposed edges, Table A3.11 is based on the equation:

$$U = \frac{2\lambda_e B}{\frac{1}{2}b \pi} \text{ artanh } \left(\frac{\frac{1}{2}b}{\frac{1}{2}b + \frac{1}{2}w}\right) \quad \text{..} \quad \text{..} \quad \text{A3.26}$$

where:

$b =$ breadth (lesser dimension) of floor ..   m

$w =$ thickness of surrounding wall (taken to be 0·3 m) ..   ..   m

The constant B depends on the ratio of the floor dimensions, i.e.:

$$B = \exp \left(\frac{\frac{1}{2}b}{l_f}\right) \quad \text{..} \quad \text{..} \quad \text{..} \quad \text{..} \quad \text{A3.27}$$

where:

$l_f =$ length (greater dimension) of floor ..   m

The U-values given in Table A3.10 were evaluated using values of B from Table A3.11

Table A3.11. Values of B in equation A3.26.

l_f/b	B
1	1·6
2	1·3
3	1·2
4	1·13
6	1·1
∞	1·0

Table A3.10. U-values for solid and suspended floors.

Length (m)	Breadth (m)	U-value / (W/m² K)		
		4 edges exposed	2 perpendicular edges exposed	Suspended floor‡
Very long	100	0·06*	0·03†	0·07
Very long	60	0·09*	0·05†	0·11
Very long	40	0·12*	0·07†	0·15
Very long	20	0·22*	0·12†	0·26
Very long	10	0·38*	0·22†	0·43
Very long	6	0·55*	0·33†	0·60
Very long	4	0·74*	0·45†	0·76
Very long	2	1·19*	0·74†	1·04
100	100	0·10	0·05	0·11
100	60	0·12	0·07	0·14
100	40	0·15	0·09	0·18
100	20	0·24	0·14	0·28
60	60	0·15	0·08	0·16
60	40	0·17	0·10	0·20
60	20	0·26	0·15	0·30
60	10	0·41	0·24	0·46
40	40	0·21	0·12	0·22
40	20	0·28	0·16	0·31
40	10	0·43	0·25	0·47
40	6	0·59	0·35	0·63
20	20	0·36	0·21	0·37
20	10	0·48	0·28	0·51
20	6	0·64	0·38	0·65
20	4	0·82	0·49	0·79
10	10	0·62	0·36	0·59
10	6	0·74	0·44	0·71
10	4	0·90	0·54	0·83
10	2	1·31	0·82	1·08
6	6	0·91	0·54	0·79
6	4	1·03	0·62	0·89
6	2	1·40	0·87	1·11
4	4	1·22	0·73	0·96
4	2	1·52	0·95	1·15
2	2	1·96	1·22	1·27

*These values can be used for a floor with two parallel edges exposed taking the breadth as the distance between the exposed edges.
†These values can be used for a floor with one exposed edge taking the breadth as the distance between the exposed edge and the edge opposite it.
‡These values have been computed for $R_g = 0.2$ m² K/W.
For other values of R_g, a corrected U-value can be obtained from:
$$U' = (\frac{1}{U} - 0.2 + R_g)^{-1}$$

For floors with two parallel edges exposed, equation A3.26 is used for a floor the appropriate breadth but of infinite length.

For floors with two edges at right angles exposed, the U-value is the same as for floors of twice the length and twice the breadth with four edges exposed.

For floors with a single exposed edge, the U-value is the same as for floors with two parallel edges exposed but of twice the breadth.

Insulation of Solid Floors

If a floor finish or screed with thermal insulating properties is used, the U-value of the floor can be calculated sufficiently accurately by adding the thermal resistance of the layer to the thermal resistance of the floor and taking the reciprocal.

It has been shown[6] that the heat flow through a ground floor consists of two components:

(*i*) an edge loss which is proportional to the perimeter length and the inside/outside temperature difference;

(*ii*) a ground loss which depends on the inside/earth temperature difference and the floor area.

The edge loss is the most significant part and the cost of insulating the slab overall is seldom justifiable. An alternative procedure that will give good results is to treat only the edges of the slab as shown in Fig. A3.10.

A vertical layer of insulating material, see Fig. A3.10(*a*) can be used as shown. Alternatively, a horizontal strip about 1 m wide can be laid in conjunction with a vertical strip through the full thickness of the floor around all the exposed edges, see Fig. A3.10(*b*). The insulating material used for these applications should be of a type that is unaffected by, or protected from, moisture.

Corrections to Table A3.10 to allow for the effects of the edge insulation on solid floors in Fig. A3.10(*a*) are given in Table A3.12. The edge insulation of Fig. A3.10(*b*) will be at least as good.

Table A3.12. Corrections to U-values of solid floors with edge insulation.

Floor dimensions/m	Percent reduction in U-value for insulation extending to indicated depth/m		
	0·25	0·5	1·0
Very long × 100 m	2	6	10
Very long × 60 m	2	6	11
Very long × 40 m	3	7	11
Very long × 20 m	3	8	11
Very long × 10 m	4	9	14
Very long × 6 m	4	9	15
Very long × 4 m	5	12	20
Very long × 2 m	6	15	25
100 m × 100 m	3	11	16
60 m × 60 m	4	11	17
40 m × 40 m	4	12	18
20 m × 20 m	5	13	19
10 m × 10 m	6	14	22
6 m × 6 m	6	15	25
4 m × 4 m	7	18	28
2 m × 2 m	10	20	35

Note:
These corrections are based on thermal insulation having a minimum thermal resistance of 0·25 m² K/W.

Suspended Ground Floors

A suspended ground floor above an enclosed airspace is exposed to air on both sides but the air temperature below the floor is higher than the outside air temperature because the underfloor ventilation rate is usually low. Table A3.10 gives the basic thermal transmittances for suspended ground floors.

Fig. A3.11(*a*) shows the thermal resistance network for the flow of heat through a suspended floor to outside. The heat transfer from the lower surface of the floor follows two parallel paths.

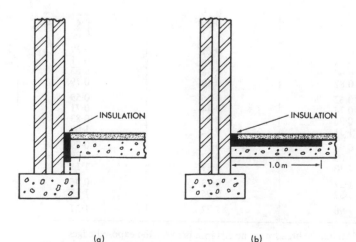

(a) Vertical insulation.

(b) Vertical and horizontal insulation.

Fig. A3.10. Edge insulation of solid floors.

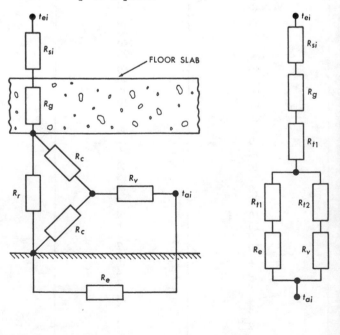

(a) Delta arrangement.

(b) Equivalent star arrangement.

Fig. A3.11. Thermal resistance network through suspended floors.

Heat is radiated directly to the earth from the surface of the floor, or is convected to the airspace. Some of this heat then flows directly to the outside, due to the ventilation of the space, but there is also a further convective exchange with the earth.

The values of the various resistances in the network are obtained as follows. The inside surface resistance is obtained from Table A3.5. The resistance of the floor slab itself is calculated from equation A3.2 in the normal way. The resistance of the earth can be found by using Table A3.10 for solid floors with 4 exposed edges to obtain the U-value for the ground floor and then deducting the inside surface resistance from its reciprocal:

$$R_e = \frac{1}{U_g} - R_{si} \qquad .. \qquad .. \qquad .. \qquad \text{A3.28}$$

The assumption used earlier that the earth has the same conductivity as a floor slab (1·4 W/m K) is used here. The convective and radiative resistances are the reciprocals of the respective heat transfer coefficients.
The ventilation resistance, R_v, is derived as follows:
The ventilation rate V_f, in m³/s, under a suspended floor is given by[8]:

$$V_f = 0{\cdot}66\, a\, v\, l_f \qquad .. \qquad .. \qquad .. \qquad \text{A3.29}$$

where:

a = free area of floor (per metre length, l_f)   m²/m

v = wind velocity ..   ..   m/s

This yields a thermal resistance per unit area of floor, given by:

$$R_v = \frac{A_f}{V_f c_v} \qquad .. \qquad .. \qquad .. \qquad .. \qquad \text{A3.30}$$

where:

A_f = floor area ..   ..   m²

c_v = volumetric specific heat capacity of air ..   ..   J/m³ K

Hence:

$$R_v = \frac{1{\cdot}5\, b}{c_v a\, v} \qquad .. \qquad .. \qquad .. \qquad \text{A3.31}$$

where:

b = breadth (lesser dimension) of floor ..   m

Taking c_v as 1200 J/m³ K, a as 0·002 m²/m and a wind velocity of 1 m/s, equation A3.31 becomes:

$$R_v = 0{\cdot}63\, b\,.. \qquad .. \qquad .. \qquad .. \qquad \text{A3.32}$$

Finally, the convective resistance, R_c, is simply the reciprocal of the convective heat transfer coefficient, h_c, given in Table A3.4.

$$R_c = \frac{1}{h_c} \qquad .. \qquad .. \qquad .. \qquad .. \qquad \text{A3.33}$$

The calculation of the combined thermal resistance is simplified by transforming[9] the 'delta' configuration of Fig. A3.11(a) into the 'star' arrangement shown in Fig. A3.11(b). This is achieved using the transform resistances R_{t1} and R_{t2} which are defined as follows:

$$R_{t1} = \frac{R_r R_c}{R_r + 2R_c} \qquad .. \qquad .. \qquad .. \qquad \text{A3.34}$$

$$R_{t2} = \frac{R^2_c}{R_r + 2R_c} \qquad .. \qquad .. \qquad .. \qquad \text{A3.35}$$

The thermal transmittance of the suspended floor is then obtained by taking the reciprocal of the combined thermal resistance of the network.

Insulation of a Suspended Ground Floor
Additional insulation of a suspended wooden ground floor is commonly provided either in the form of a continuous layer of semi-rigid or flexible material laid over the joists. The thermal resistance of boards or slabs laid over joists and of any resulting airspaces, or the thermal resistance of the overall insulation above the structural floor must be added to the basic resistance and the resistance of the floor structure to calculate the new U-value. Blankets and quilts are effective between joists as the resistance of the joists compensates for the absence of insulation.

Example 5: Calculation of U-values for Solid and Suspended Floors

For a floor 60 m × 20 m calculate:

the U-value if it is a solid floor,

the U-value if it is a suspended floor.

Solid ground floor with four exposed edges
From Table A3.11, $B = 1{\cdot}2$

Thermal conductivity of earth = 1·4 W/m K

Wall thickness = 0·3 m

Hence, from equation A3.26:

$$U = \frac{2 \times 1{\cdot}4 \times 1{\cdot}2}{10\pi} \text{ artanh}\left(\frac{10}{10{\cdot}15}\right)$$

$$= 0{\cdot}107 \text{ artanh } (0{\cdot}985)$$

$$= 0{\cdot}26 \text{ W/m}^2 \text{ K}$$

Suspended floor
From Table A3.5, $R_{si} = 0{\cdot}14$ m² K/W

Resistance of floor slab,

$$R_g = 0{\cdot}2 \text{ m}^2 \text{ K/W}$$

Radiative resistance,

$$R_r = (Eh_r)^{-1}$$

$$= (0{\cdot}9 \times 5{\cdot}7)^{-1}$$

$$= 0{\cdot}2 \text{ m}^2 \text{ K/W}$$

Convective resistance,

$$R_c = (h_c)^{-1}$$

$$= 1{\cdot}5^{-1}$$

$$= 0{\cdot}67 \text{ m}^2 \text{ K/W}$$

The transform resistances are calculated from R_c and R_r:

$$R_{t1} = \frac{R_r R_c}{R_r + 2R_c}$$

$$= 0{\cdot}09 \text{ m}^2 \text{ K/W}$$

$$R_{t2} = \frac{R^2_c}{R_r + 2R_c}$$

$$= 0{\cdot}29 \text{ m}^2 \text{ K/W}$$

Resistance of earth,

$$R_e = \frac{1}{0{\cdot}26} - 0{\cdot}14$$

$$= 3{\cdot}7 \text{ m}^2 \text{ K/W}$$

From equation A3.32,

$$R_v = 0.63 \times 20$$
$$= 12.6 \text{ m}^2 \text{ K/W}$$

hence:

$$R = 0.14 + 0.2 + 0.09$$
$$+ \left(\frac{1}{0.09 + 3.7} + \frac{1}{0.29 + 12.6} \right)^{-1}$$
$$= 3.36 \text{ m}^2 \text{ K/W}$$

therefore:

$$U = 0.30 \text{ W/m}^2 \text{ K}$$

Heat Loss Through Glazing

In Tables A3.13 and 14, thermal resistances are given for glazing under three conditions of exposure–normal, sheltered and severe. These are defined on page A3.7.

Table A3.13. U-values for glazing (without frames).

Construction	U-value for stated exposure (W/m² K)		
	Sheltered	Normal (Standard)	Severe
Single window glazing ..	5.0	5.6	6.7
Double window glazing with airspace			
25 mm or more ..	2.8	2.9	3.2
12 mm	2.8	3.0	3.3
6 mm	3.2	3.4	3.8
3 mm	3.6	4.0	4.4
Triple window glazing with airspace			
25 mm or more ..	1.9	2.0	2.1
12 mm	2.0	2.1	2.2
6 mm	2.3	2.5	2.6
3 mm	2.8	3.0	3.3
Roof glazing skylight ..	5.7	6.6	7.9
Horizontal laylight with skylight or lantern light over			
Ventilated	3.5	3.8	4.2
Unventilated	2.8	3.0	3.3

Note: In calculating these values, the thermal resistance of the glass has been ignored (typically $\lambda = 1.05$ W/m K, hence $R = 0.0057 \text{ m}^2 \text{ K/W}$).

The U-values for single glazing given in Table A3.13 have been obtained by adding the appropriate inside and outside thermal resistances and taking the reciprocal of the sum. For double and triple glazing the resistances of the airspaces have been added. Where the glazing is bridged by metal members, the U-value should be calculated by the proportional area method described earlier.

The effect of frame profile on the total heat loss, and the occurrence of condensation on the inside of the frame is related to the overall area of frame surface exposed externally and to the ratio of this area to the area of the frame surface exposed internally. Furthermore, the effectiveness of a thermal break is similarly dependent on the ratio of exposed areas. The values given in Table A3.14 are based on typical window constructions encountered in practice. If a frame is of a particularly unusual design, the U-value should be calculated using the methods described for non-homogeneous or heat-bridged constructions.

Low emissivity metallic films applied to the inside surface of glazing can be effective in increasing the inside surface resistance. However, durability of the film can be a serious problem when exposed to room conditions.

Double and triple glazing is normally filled with dry air. It has been shown[10] that by using a gas having improved thermal properties (i.e. lower thermal conductivity) a reduction in the heat loss can be achieved.

However, this is strictly true for small separations only since convection effects reduce the improvement as the glass separation is increased.

Table A3.14. U-values for typical windows.

Window type	Fraction of area occupied by frame	U-value for stated exposure (W/m² K)		
		Sheltered	Normal	Severe
SINGLE GLAZING Wood frame	10%	4.7	5.3	6.3
	20%	4.5	5.0	5.9
	30%	4.2	4.7	5.5
Aluminium frame (no thermal break)	10%	5.3	6.0	7.1
	20%	5.6	6.4	7.5
	30%	5.9	6.7	7.9
Aluminium frame (with thermal break)	10%	5.1	5.7	6.7
	20%	5.2	5.8	6.8
	30%	5.2	5.8	6.8
DOUBLE GLAZING Wood frame	10%	2.8	3.0	3.2
	20%	2.7	2.9	3.2
	30%	2.7	2.9	3.1
Aluminium frame (no thermal break)	10%	3.3	3.6	4.1
	20%	3.9	4.3	4.8
	30%	4.4	4.9	5.6
Aluminium frame (with thermal break)	10%	3.1	3.3	3.7
	20%	3.4	3.7	4.0
	30%	3.7	4.0	4.4

Note: Where the proportion of the frame differs appreciably from the above values, particularly with wood or plastic, the U-value should be calculated (metal members have a U-value similar to that of glass).

NON-STEADY STATE THERMAL CHARACTERISTICS

There are several methods available for assessing the non-steady state or dynamic performance of a structure, but one of the simplest is the admittance procedure, which is discussed in Section A5. This procedure requires the calculation of three factors additional to the U-value in assessing the thermal performance of a building. These are the admittance, surface factor and decrement factor[1].

These factors are functions of the thickness, thermal conductivity, density and specific heat capacity of each of the materials used in the construction. The position of materials within the construction and the frequency of the energy inputs (a 24 h cycle is usually assumed) are also required. The factors are complex in form and are normally expressed as an amplitude and time lag, see Appendix 5.

Admittance (Y-value)

The admittance is the rate of heat flow between the internal surface of the construction and the space temperature, for each degree of swing in space temperature about its mean value. It can be considered as the cyclic U-value for heat flow between the space and the construction.

For thin structures the admittance is equal to the U-value and tends to a limiting value for thicknesses greater than 100 mm.

With multi-layer constructions, the admittance is determined primarily by the characteristics of the materials in the layers next to the internal surface, e.g. lining a heavy concrete slab with insulation will decrease the admittance to near the value for the insulation alone, whereas placing the insulation within the construction or on the external surface will have little or no effect on the admittance of the construction.

Decrement Factor (f)

The decrement factor is the ratio of the rate of heat flow through the structure to the internal space temperature for each degree of swing in external temperature about its mean value, to the steady state rate of heat flow or U-value. For thin structures of low thermal capacity the decrement factor is unity and decreases in value with increasing thickness and/or thermal capacity.

Surface Factor (F)

The surface factor is the ratio of the variation of heat flow about its mean value readmitted to a space from the surface, to the variation of heat flow about its mean value absorbed in the surface. The surface factor decreases and its time lag increases with increasing thermal capacity and they are virtually constant with thickness.

Internal Constructions

For internal constructions, floors, partitions, etc. which are not symmetrical about their mid-plane the dynamic responses will be different for each face and therefore two sets of admittances and surface factors are required for the construction. The decrement factor is the same, however, in both directions. For the special cases of partitions, etc., separating spaces of identical thermal conditions, the energy transfers can be simplified by combining the admittance and surface factor respectively with the decrement factor to give modified values of admittance and surface factor.

Overall Thermal Performance

Of the three factors, the admittance has by far the greatest effect on the buildings dynamic thermal performance. A convenient method of expressing the overall performance of a building is by the ratio known as response factor, given by:

$$f_r = \frac{\Sigma(AY) + \frac{1}{3}NV}{\Sigma(AU) + \frac{1}{3}NV} \qquad .. \qquad .. \qquad .. \qquad A3.36$$

A thermally lightweight building will have a response factor of about 2·5 and a heavyweight building a response factor of about 6. With the increasing use of insulation in buildings response factors of 10 are possible, i.e. buildings with thermal characteristics approaching those of medieval churches and particular care should be taken in designing the heating systems for such buildings.

Thermal Bridges (Dynamic Conditions)

The presence of thermal bridges within a structure will alter its overall dynamic performance. However, since the value of admittance is controlled mainly by the properties of the materials immediately adjacent to the interior spaces of a building, e.g. plaster, etc., the presence of a bridge has little effect on the overall performance of the structure in the majority of cases. Where it is considered necessary to allow for the effect of bridges, an area-weighted mean approach, similar to the proportional area method for steady state conditions, should be used.

APPENDIX 1. Tables of Thermal Transmittance (U) and Admittance (Y) Values

In this appendix, values of thermal transmittance and admittance have been calculated for composite constructions using building materials having the values of density, thermal conductivity and specific heat capacity stated in Table A3.15. Furthermore, to ensure consistency with current building regulations in the UK[2], it is assumed in the Tables that mortar joints have densities and thermal properties similar to those of the bulk material used in the construction. For constructions which deviate in these respects, values of thermal transmittance and admittance should be calculated by the methods described earlier in this Section.

The Tables of U and Y values for composite constructions are presented as follows:

Table A3.16 Exterior Walls – Single Leaf Construction

Table A3.17 Exterior Walls – Cavity Construction

Table A3.18 Roofs – Pitched

Table A3.19 Roofs – Flat

Table A3.20 Internal Walls/Partitions

Table A3.21 Internal Floors/Ceilings

Some of the values given in these Tables differ from those contained in the first impression of this Section. This is mainly due to the correction of some inconsistencies in rounding to two significant figures.

In the case of Table A3.21, the corrections are the result of recalculation using the values of surface resistance given in the footnote to Table A3.15. The format of this Table has also been modified to remove any ambiguity regarding the surface under consideration.

Additionally, the opportunity has been taken to include U-values for internal structural elements.

Table A3.15. Values used in calculating U- and Y-values.

Material	Density (kg/m³)	Thermal Conductivity (W/m K)	Specific Heat Capacity (J/kg K)
WALLS (External and Internal)			
Asbestos cement sheet	700	0·36	1050
Asbestos cement decking	1500	0·36	1050
Brickwork (outer leaf)	1700	0·84	800
Brickwork (inner leaf)	1700	0·62	800
Cast concrete (dense)	2100	1·40	840
Cast concrete (lightweight)	1200	0·38	1000
Concrete block (heavyweight)	2300	1·63	1000
Concrete block (mediumweight)	1400	0·51	1000
Concrete block (lightweight)	600	0·19	1000
Fibreboard	300	0·06	1000
Plasterboard	950	0·16	840
Tile hanging	1900	0·84	800
SURFACE FINISHES			
External rendering	1300	0·50	1000
Plaster (dense)	1300	0·50	1000
Plaster (lightweight)	600	0·16	1000
ROOFS			
Aerated concrete slab	500	0·16	840
Asphalt	1700	0·50	1000
Felt/Bitumen layers	1700	0·50	1000
Screed	1200	0·41	840
Stone chippings	1800	0·96	1000
Tile	1900	0·84	800
Wood wool slab	500	0·10	1000
FLOORS			
Cast concrete	2000	1·13	1000
Metal tray	7800	50·00	480
Screed	1200	0·41	840
Timber flooring	650	0·14	1200
Wood blocks	650	0·14	1200
INSULATION			
Expanded polystyrene (EPS) slab	25	0·035	1400
Glass fibre quilt	12	0·040	840
Glass fibre slab	25	0·035	1000
Mineral fibre slab	30	0·035	1000
Phenolic foam	30	0·040	1400
Polyurethane Board	30	0·025	1400
Urea formaldehyde (UF) foam	10	0·040	1400

Note:
Surface resistances have been assumed as follows:

External walls
$R_{so} = 0.06 \text{ m}^2\text{K/W}$
$R_{si} = 0.12 \text{ m}^2\text{K/W}$
$R_a = 0.18 \text{ m}^2\text{K/W}$

Roofs
$R_{so} = 0.04 \text{ m}^2\text{K/W}$
$R_{si} = 0.10 \text{ m}^2\text{K/W}$
$R_a = 0.18 \text{ m}^2\text{K/W}$ (pitched)
$R_a = 0.16 \text{ m}^2\text{K/W}$ (flat)

Internal walls
$R_{so} = R_{si} = 0.12 \text{ m}^2\text{K/W}$
$R_a = 0.18 \text{ m}^2\text{K/W}$

Internal floors
$R_{so} = R_{si} = 0.12 \text{ m}^2\text{K/W}$
$R_a = 0.20 \text{ m}^2\text{K/W}$

Table A3.16. External walls – Single leaf construction.

No.	Construction (outside to inside)	U-value (W/m² K)	Admittance		Decrement factor		Surface factor	
			Y-value (W/m² K)	ω/h	f	φ/h	F	ψ/h
Brickwork								
1. (a)	105 mm brickwork, unplastered	3·3	4·2	1	0·88	3	0·54	1
(b)	220 mm brickwork, unplastered	2·3	4·6	1	0·54	6	0·52	2
(c)	335 mm brickwork, unplastered	1·7	4·7	1	0·29	9	0·51	2
2. (a)	105 mm brickwork, 13 mm dense plaster	3·0	4·1	1	0·83	3	0·56	1
(b)	220 mm brickwork, 13 mm dense plaster	2·1	4·4	1	0·49	7	0·53	1
(c)	335 mm brickwork, 13 mm dense plaster	1·7	4·4	1	0·26	10	0·53	1
3. (a)	105 mm brickwork, 13 mm light plaster	2·6	3·3	1	0·82	3	0·63	1
(b)	220 mm brickwork, 13 mm light plaster	1·9	3·6	1	0·46	7	0·61	1
(c)	335 mm brickwork, 13 mm light plaster	1·5	3·6	1	0·24	10	0·60	1
4. (a)	105 mm brickwork, 10 mm plasterboard	2·7	3·5	1	0·83	3	0·61	1
(b)	220 mm brickwork, 10 mm plasterboard	2·0	3·8	1	0·47	7	0·59	1
(c)	335 mm brickwork, 10 mm plasterboard	1·6	3·8	1	0·25	10	0·58	1
5.	220 mm brickwork, 25 mm airgap 10 mm plasterboard (on dabs)*	1·5	2·5	1	0·40	7	0·72	0
6.	220 mm brickwork 25 mm airgap, 10 mm foil-backed plasterboard (on dabs)	1·2	1·8	1	0·37	7	0·78	0
7. (a)	220 mm brickwork, 20 mm glass fibre quilt, 10 mm plasterboard	1·0	1·4	1	0·34	7	0·84	0
(b)	As 7(a) but with 20 mm EPS slab	0·93	1·3	2	0·33	7	0·85	0
(c)	As 7(a) but with 25 mm EPS slab	0·82	1·2	2	0·32	8	0·87	0
(d)	As 7(a) but with 25 mm polyurethane slab ...	0·66	0·98	2	0·31	8	0·90	0
8. (a)	220 mm brickwork, 25 mm airgap, 25 mm EPS slab, 10 mm plasterboard	0·71	1·0	2	0·31	8	0·89	0
(b)	As 8(a) but with 25 mm polyurethane slab	0·59	0·91	2	0·30	8	0·91	0
9. (a)	19 mm render, 25 mm mineral fibre slab, 220 mm brickwork, 13 mm lightweight plaster	0·73	3·4	1	0·17	10	0·62	1
(b)	As 9(a) but with 40 mm EPS slab	0·56	3·4	1	0·15	10	0·62	1
Concrete Blockwork								
10.	200 mm heavyweight concrete block, 25 mm airgap 10 mm plasterboard (on dabs)	1·8	2·5	1	0·35	7	0·64	0
11.	200 mm heavyweight concrete block, 25 mm cavity, 10 mm foil-backed plasterboard (on dabs)	1·5	1·9	1	0·33	7	0·76	0
12. (a)	200 mm heavyweight concrete block, 20 mm glass fibre quilt, 10 mm plasterboard	1·2	1·5	1	0·34	7	0·83	0
(b)	As 12(a) but with 20 mm EPS slab	1·1	1·4	1	0·33	7	0·84	0
(c)	As 12(a) but with 25 mm EPS slab	0·93	1·2	2	0·32	7	0·87	0
(d)	As 12(a) but with 25 mm polyurethane slab	0·73	1·0	2	0·31	7	0·90	0
13. (a)	200 mm heavyweight concrete block, 25 mm airgap, 25 mm EPS slab, 10 mm plasterboard	0·79	1·1	2	0·29	7	0·89	0
(b)	As 13(a) but with 25 mm polyurethane slab	0·65	0·91	2	0·29	7	0·91	0
14. (a)	19 mm render, 25 mm mineral fibre slab, 200 mm heavyweight concrete block, 13 mm lightweight plaster ...	0·88	4·2	1	0·15	8	0·51	1
(b)	As 14(a) but with 40 mm EPS slab	0·64	4·2	1	0·14	8	0·51	1
15.	200 mm lightweight concrete block, 25 mm airgap 10 mm plasterboard (on dabs)	0·68	1·8	2	0·47	7	0·82	1
16.	200 mm lightweight concrete block, 25 mm airgap, 10 mm foil-backed plasterboard (on dabs)	0·62	1·6	2	0·44	8	0·84	0
17. (a)	200 mm lightweight concrete block, 20 mm glass fibre quilt, 10 mm plasterboard	0·56	1·3	2	0·40	8	0·87	0
(b)	As 17(a) but with 20 mm EPS slab	0·54	1·2	2	0·39	8	0·88	0
(c)	As 17(a) but with 25 mm EPS slab	0·50	1·1	2	0·37	8	0·89	0
(d)	As 17(a) but with 25 mm polyurethane slab ...	0·44	1·0	3	0·34	8	0·91	0
18. (a)	200 mm lightweight concrete block, 25 mm airgap, 25 mm EPS slab, 10 mm plasterboard	0·46	1·0	3	0·35	8	0·90	0
(b)	As 18(a) but with 25 mm polyurethane slab	0·40	0·89	3	0·33	8	0·92	0
19. (a)	19 mm render, 25 mm mineral fibre slab, 200 mm lightweight concrete block, 13 mm lightweight plaster ...	0·48	2·2	2	0·30	9	0·78	1
(b)	As 19(a) but with 40 mm EPS slab	0·40	2·2	2	0·26	10	0·78	1

*'dabs' may be taken to include timber studding.

Table A3.16—*continued*

No.	Construction (outside to inside)	U-value (W/m² K)	Admittance Y-value (W/m² K)	Admittance ω/h	Decrement factor f	Decrement factor φ/h	Surface factor F	Surface factor ψ/h
Cast Concrete and Pre-cast Panels								
20. (a)	150 mm cast concrete, unplastered	3·5	5·2	1	0·71	4	0·44	2
(b)	200 mm cast concrete, unplastered	3·1	5·4	1	0·57	5	0·42	2
21. (a)	150 mm cast concrete, 50 mm wood wool slab, 13 mm dense plaster	1·2	2·3	3	0·50	7	0·80	1
(b)	200 mm cast concrete, 50 mm wood wool slab, 13 mm dense plaster	1·2	2·3	3	0·36	8	0·79	1
22. (a)	150 mm cast concrete, 50 mm wood wool slab, 13 mm lightweight plaster...	1·2	1·7	2	0·49	6	0·82	0
(b)	200 mm cast concrete, 50 mm wood wool slab, 13 mm lightweight plaster...	1·1	1·7	2	0·35	8	0·82	0
23.	75 mm pre-cast concrete panels (consisting of three 25 mm sheets)	4·3	4·9	1	0·92	2	0·43	1
24.	75 mm pre-cast concrete panels (incorporating 5 mm asbestos cement sheet), 25 mm airgap 25 mm EPS slab, 10 mm plasterboard	0·83	1·0	2	0·82	3	0·90	0
25.	250 mm pre-cast sandwich (consisting of 75 mm cast concrete, 25 mm EPS slab, 150 mm lightweight concrete)	0·74	3·8	2	0·28	10	0·62	1
Tile Hanging								
26. (a)	10 mm tile on battens (combined resistance = 0.12 m² K/W), breather paper, 25 mm airgap, 50 mm glass fibre quilt, 10 mm plasterboard	0·56	0·78	3	0·99	1	0·93	0
(b)	As 26(a) but with 50 mm EPS slab	0·51	0·77	3	0·99	1	0·94	0
(c)	As 26(a) but with 75 mm glass fibre quilt	0·41	0·70	3	0·99	1	0·95	0
(d)	As 26(a) but with 75 mm EPS slab	0·37	0·72	4	0·99	1	0·95	0
(e)	As 26(a) but with 100 mm glass fibre quilt	0·33	0·66	4	0·99	1	0·96	0
(f)	As 26(a) but with 100 mm EPS slab	0·29	0·71	4	0·99	1	0·96	0

Table A3.17. External walls – Cavity construction.

No.	Construction (outside to inside)	U-value (W/m² K)	Admittance		Decrement factor		Surface factor	
			Y-value (W/m² K)	ω/h	f	ϕ/h	F	ψ/h
Brick: Cavity: Brick								
1. (a)	105 mm brickwork, 25 mm airgap, 105 mm brickwork, 13 mm dense plaster	1·5	4·4	2	0·44	8	0·58	2
(b)	As 1(a) but with 13 mm lightweight plaster	1·4	3·5	1	0·40	8	0·63	1
(c)	220 mm brickwork, 25 mm airgap, 220 mm brickwork, 13 mm dense plaster	1·0	4·3	2	0·09	15	0·56	1
(d)	As 1(c) but with 13 mm lightweight plaster	0·95	3·4	1	0·08	15	0·63	1
2. (a)	105 mm brickwork, 25 mm airgap, 25 mm phenolic foam, 105 mm brickwork, 13 mm lightweight plaster	0·73	3·6	2	0·31	9	0·61	1
(b)	As 2(a) but with 25 mm mineral fibre, glass fibre or expanded polystyrene (EPS) slab	0·69	3·6	2	0·30	9	0·61	1
(c)	As 2(a) but with 40 mm phenolic foam	0·58	3·6	2	0·28	9	0·61	1
(d)	As 2(a) but with 40 mm EPS slab	0·53	3·6	2	0·28	9	0·61	1
(e)	As 2(a) but with 50 mm mineral fibre, glass fibre or EPS slab	0·46	3·7	2	0·27	9	0·61	1
3. (a)	105 mm brickwork, 50 mm urea formaldehyde (UF) foam, 105 mm brickwork, 13 mm lightweight plaster	0·55	3·6	2	0·28	9	0·61	1
(b)	As 3(a) but with 50 mm mineral fibre, glass fibre or EPS slab	0·50	3·7	2	0·28	9	0·61	1
(c)	As 3(a) but with 75 mm UF foam	0·41	3·7	2	0·27	9	0·61	1
(d)	As 3(a) but with 75 mm mineral fibre, glass fibre or EPS slab	0·37	3·7	2	0·26	10	0·61	1
Brick: Cavity: Block								
4.	105 mm brickwork, 25 mm airgap, 100 mm heavyweight concrete block, 13 mm lightweight plaster	1·6	4·3	1	0·31	8	0·52	1
5. (a)	105 mm brickwork, 25 mm airgap, 25 mm phenolic foam, 100 mm heavyweight concrete block, 13 mm lightweight plaster	0·80	4·3	1	0·23	9	0·51	1
(b)	As 5(a) but with 25 mm mineral fibre, glass fibre or EPS slab	0·75	4·3	1	0·22	9	0·51	1
(c)	As 5(a) but with 40 mm phenolic foam	0·61	4·3	1	0·21	9	0·51	1
(d)	As 5(a) but with 40 mm EPS slab	0·56	4·3	1	0·21	9	0·51	1
(e)	As 5(a) but with 50 mm mineral fibre, glass fibre or EPS slab	0·49	4·3	1	0·20	9	0·51	1
6. (a)	105 mm brickwork, 50 mm UF foam, 100 mm heavyweight concrete block, 13 mm lightweight plaster	0·59	4·3	1	0·21	9	0·51	1
(b)	As 6(a) but with 50 mm mineral fibre, glass fibre or EPS slab	0·53	4·3	1	0·20	9	0·51	1
(c)	As 6(a) but with 75 mm UF foam	0·43	4·3	1	0·20	9	0·51	1
(d)	As 6(a) but with 75 mm mineral fibre, glass fibre or EPS slab	0·39	4·3	1	0·19	10	0·51	1
7.	105 mm brickwork, 25 mm airgap, 100 mm medium concrete block, 13 mm lightweight plaster	1·3	3·4	1	0·40	8	0·64	1
8. (a)	105 mm brickwork, 25 mm airgap, 25 mm phenolic foam, 100 mm medium concrete block, 13 mm lightweight plaster	0·72	3·5	2	0·30	9	0·63	1
(b)	As 8(a) but with 25 mm mineral fibre, glass fibre or EPS slab	0·68	3·5	2	0·30	9	0·62	1
(c)	As 8(a) but with 40 mm phenolic foam	0·57	3·5	2	0·28	9	0·62	1
(d)	As 8(a) but with 40 mm EPS slab	0·52	3·5	2	0·28	9	0·62	1
(e)	As 8(a) but with 50 mm mineral fibre, glass fibre or EPS slab	0·46	3·6	2	0·27	9	0·62	1
9. (a)	105 mm brickwork, 50 mm UF foam, 100 mm medium concrete block, 13 mm lightweight plaster	0·55	3·5	2	0·28	9	0·62	1
(b)	As 9(a) but with 50 mm mineral fibre, glass fibre or EPS slab	0·50	3·5	2	0·27	9	0·62	1
(c)	As 9(a) but with 75 mm UF foam	0·41	3·6	2	0·26	9	0·62	1
(d)	As 9(a) but with 75 mm mineral fibre, glass fibre or EPS slab	0·37	3·6	2	0·26	10	0·62	1
10.	105 mm brickwork, 25 mm airgap, 100 mm lightweight concrete block, 13 mm lightweight plaster	0·92	2·2	2	0·55	7	0·80	1
11. (a)	105 mm brickwork, 25 mm airgap, 25 mm phenolic foam, 100 mm light concrete block, 13 mm lightweight plaster	0·58	2·3	2	0·46	8	0·79	1
(b)	As 11(a) but with 25 mm mineral fibre, glass fibre or EPS slab	0·55	2·3	2	0·45	8	0·79	1
(c)	As 11(a) but with 40 mm phenolic foam	0·48	2·3	2	0·43	8	0·79	1
(d)	As 11(a) but with 40 mm EPS slab	0·45	2·4	2	0·42	9	0·79	1
(e)	As 11(a) but with 50 mm mineral fibre, glass fibre or EPS slab	0·40	2·4	2	0·41	9	0·79	1

Table A3.17—continued

No.	Construction (outside to inside)	U-value (W/m² K)	Admittance Y-value (W/m² K)	ω/h	Decrement factor f	φ/h	Surface factor F	ψ/h
	Brick: Cavity: Block (*cont'd.*)							
12.	(a) 105 mm brickwork, 50 mm UF foam, 100 mm light concrete block, 13 mm lightweight plaster	0·46	2·4	2	0·43	8	0·79	1
	(b) As 12(a) but with 50 mm mineral fibre, glass fibre or EPS slab	0·43	2·4	2	0·42	9	0·79	1
	(c) As 12(a) but with 75 mm UF foam	0·36	2·4	2	0·39	9	0·79	1
	(d) As 12(a) but with 75 mm mineral fibre, glass fibre or EPS slab	0·33	2·4	2	0·39	9	0·78	1
	Block: Cavity: Brick							
13.	100 mm heavyweight concrete block, 25 mm airgap, 105 mm brickwork, 13 mm lightweight plaster	1·5	3·4	1	0·37	8	0·63	1
14.	(a) 100 mm heavyweight concrete block, 25 mm airgap, 25 mm phenolic foam, 105 mm brickwork, 13 mm lightweight plaster	0·77	3·6	2	0·28	9	0·61	1
	(b) As 14(a) but with 25 mm mineral fibre, glass fibre or EPS slab	0·72	3·6	2	0·27	9	0·61	1
	(c) As 14(a) but with 40 mm phenolic foam	0·60	3·6	2	0·26	9	0·61	1
	(d) As 14(a) but with 40 mm EPS slab	0·55	3·6	2	0·25	9	0·61	1
	(e) As 14(a) but with 50 mm mineral fibre, glass fibre or EPS slab	0·48	3·7	2	0·25	10	0·61	1
15.	(a) 100 mm heavyweight concrete block, 50 mm UF foam, 105 mm brick, 13 mm lightweight plaster	0·57	3·6	2	0·26	9	0·61	1
	(b) As 15(a) but with 50 mm mineral fibre, glass fibre or EPS slab	0·52	3·7	2	0·25	10	0·61	1
	(c) As 15(a) but with 75 mm UF foam	0·42	3·7	2	0·24	10	0·61	1
	(d) As 15(a) but with 75 mm mineral fibre, glass fibre or EPS slab	0·38	3·7	2	0·24	10	0·61	1
16.	100 mm lightweight concrete block, 25 mm airgap, 105 mm brickwork, 13 mm lightweight plaster	0·88	3·6	1	0·36	8	0·62	1
17.	(a) 100 mm lightweight concrete block, 25 mm airgap, 25 mm phenolic foam, 105 mm brickwork, 13 mm lightweight plaster	0·57	3·6	2	0·31	9	0·61	1
	(b) As 17(a) but with 25 mm mineral fibre, glass fibre or EPS slab	0·54	3·6	2	0·30	9	0·61	1
	(c) As 17(a) but with 40 mm phenolic foam	0·47	3·7	2	0·29	9	0·61	1
	(d) As 17(a) but with 40 mm EPS slab	0·44	3·7	2	0·28	9	0·61	1
	(e) As 17(a) but with 50 mm mineral fibre, glass fibre or EPS slab	0·39	3·7	2	0·28	9	0·61	1
18.	(a) 100 mm lightweight concrete block, 50 mm UF foam, 105 mm brick, 13 mm lightweight plaster	0·45	3·7	2	0·29	9	0·61	1
	(b) As 18(a) but with 50 mm mineral fibre, glass fibre or EPS slab	0·42	3·7	2	0·28	9	0·61	1
	(c) As 18(a) but with 75 mm UF foam	0·35	3·7	2	0·27	10	0·61	1
	(d) As 18(a) but with 75 mm mineral fibre, glass fibre or EPS slab	0·32	3·7	2	0·26	10	0·61	1
	Block: Cavity: Block							
19.	100 mm heavyweight concrete block, 25 mm airgap, 100 mm heavyweight concrete block, 13 mm lightweight plaster	1·8	4·2	1	0·29	8	0·53	1
20.	(a) 100 mm heavyweight concrete block, 25 mm airgap, 25 mm phenolic foam, 100 mm heavyweight concrete block, 13 mm lightweight plaster...	0·84	4·3	1	0·20	9	0·51	1
	(b) As 20(a) but with 25 mm mineral fibre, glass fibre or EPS slab	0·78	4·3	1	0·20	9	0·51	1
	(c) As 20(a) but with 40 mm phenolic foam	0·64	4·3	1	0·19	10	0·51	1
	(d) As 20(a) but with 40 mm EPS slab	0·59	4·3	1	0·19	10	0·51	1
	(e) As 20(a) but with 50 mm mineral fibre, glass fibre or EPS slab	0·50	4·3	1	0·18	10	0·51	1
21.	(a) 100 mm heavyweight concrete block, 50 mm UF foam, 100 mm heavyweight concrete block, 13 mm lightweight plaster	0·61	4·3	1	0·19	9	0·51	1
	(b) As 21(a) but with 50 mm mineral fibre, glass fibre or EPS slab	0·55	4·3	1	0·19	10	0·51	1
	(c) As 21(a) but with 75 mm UF foam	0·44	4·3	1	0·18	10	0·51	1
	(d) As 21(a) but with 75 mm mineral fibre, glass fibre or EPS slab	0·40	4·3	1	0·18	10	0·51	1
22.	100 mm heavyweight concrete block, 25 mm airgap, 100 mm medium concrete block, 13 mm lightweight plaster	1·4	3·4	1	0·37	8	0·65	1

Table A3.17—*continued*

No.	Construction (outside to inside)	U-value (W/m² K)	Admittance Y-value (W/m² K)	Admittance ω/h	Decrement factor f	Decrement factor φ/h	Surface factor F	Surface factor ψ/h
	Block: Cavity: Block (*cont'd.*)							
23. (a)	100 mm heavyweight concrete block, 25 mm airgap, 25 mm phenolic foam, 100 mm medium concrete block, 13 mm lightweight plaster	0·76	3·5	2	0·28	9	0·63	1
(b)	As 23(a) but with 25 mm mineral fibre, glass fibre or EPS slab	0·71	3·5	2	0·27	9	0·63	1
(c)	As 23(a) but with 40 mm phenolic foam	0·59	3·5	2	0·26	10	0·62	1
(d)	As 23(a) but with 40 mm EPS slab	0·54	3·5	2	0·25	10	0·62	1
(e)	As 23(a) but with 50 mm mineral fibre, glass fibre or EPS slab	0·47	3·6	2	0·24	10	0·62	1
24. (a)	100 mm heavyweight concrete block, 50 mm UF foam, 100 mm medium weight concrete block, 13 mm lightweight plaster	0·57	3·5	2	0·25	10	0·62	1
(b)	As 24(a) but with 50 mm mineral fibre, glass fibre or EPS slab	0·51	3·5	2	0·25	10	0·62	1
(c)	As 24(a) but with 75 mm UF foam	0·42	3·6	2	0·24	10	0·62	1
(d)	As 24(a) but with 75 mm mineral fibre, glass fibre or EPS slab	0·38	3·6	2	0·23	10	0·62	1
25.	100 mm heavyweight concrete block, 25 mm airgap, 100 mm lightweight concrete block, 13 mm lightweight plaster	0·97	2·1	2	0·49	7	0·80	1
26. (a)	100 mm heavyweight concrete block, 25 mm airgap, 25 mm phenolic foam, 100 mm lightweight concrete block, 13 mm lightweight plaster	0·60	2·3	3	0·42	8	0·79	1
(b)	As 26(a) but with 25 mm mineral fibre, glass fibre or EPS slab	0·57	2·3	3	0·41	8	0·79	1
(c)	As 26(a) but with 40 mm phenolic foam	0·49	2·3	3	0·39	9	0·79	1
(d)	As 26(a) but with 40 mm EPS slab	0·46	2·4	3	0·38	9	0·79	1
(e)	As 26(a) but with 50 mm mineral fibre, glass fibre, or EPS slab	0·41	2·4	3	0·37	9	0·79	1
27. (a)	100 mm heavyweight concrete block, 50 mm UF foam, 100 mm lightweight concrete block, 13 mm lightweight plaster	0·48	2·4	3	0·39	9	0·79	1
(b)	As 27(a) but with 50 mm mineral fibre, glass fibre or EPS slab	0·44	2·4	3	0·38	9	0·79	1
(c)	As 27(a) but with 75 mm UF foam	0·37	2·4	3	0·36	9	0·79	1
(d)	As 27(a) but with 75 mm mineral fibre, glass fibre or EPS slab	0·33	2·4	3	0·35	9	0·78	1
28.	100 mm lightweight concrete block, 25 mm airgap, 100 mm heavyweight concrete block, 13 mm lightweight plaster	0·97	4·3	1	0·28	8	0·52	1
29. (a)	100 mm lightweight concrete block, 25 mm airgap, 25 mm phenolic foam, 100 mm heavyweight concrete block, 13 mm lightweight plaster...	0·60	4·3	1	0·23	9	0·51	1
(b)	As 29(a) but with 25 mm mineral fibre, glass fibre or EPS slab	0·57	4·3	1	0·23	9	0·51	1
(c)	As 29(a) but with 40 mm phenolic foam	0·49	4·3	1	0·22	9	0·51	1
(d)	As 29(a) but with 40 mm EPS slab	0·46	4·3	1	0·21	9	0·51	1
(e)	As 29(a) but with 50 mm mineral fibre, glass fibre or EPS slab	0·41	4·3	1	0·21	9	0·51	1
30. (a)	100 mm lightweight concrete block, 50 mm UF foam, 100 mm heavyweight concrete block, 13 mm lightweight plaster	0·48	4·3	1	0·21	9	0·51	1
(b)	As 30(a) but with 50 mm mineral fibre, glass fibre or EPS slab	0·44	4·3	1	0·21	9	0·51	1
(c)	As 30(a) but with 75 mm UF foam	0·37	4·3	1	0·20	10	0·51	1
(d)	As 30(a) but with 75 mm mineral fibre, glass fibre or EPS slab	0·33	4·3	1	0·20	10	0·51	1
31.	100 mm lightweight concrete block, 25 mm airgap, 100 mm medium concrete block, 13 mm lightweight plaster	0·86	3·5	1	0·36	8	0·63	1
32. (a)	100 mm lightweight concrete block, 25 mm airgap, 25 mm phenolic foam, 100 mm medium concrete block, 13 mm lightweight plaster	0·56	3·5	2	0·30	9	0·62	1
(b)	As 32(a) but with 25 mm mineral fibre, glass fibre or EPS slab	0·53	3·5	2	0·30	9	0·62	1
(c)	As 32(a) but with 40 mm phenolic foam	0·46	3·5	2	0·29	9	0·62	1
(d)	As 32(a) but with 40 mm EPS slab	0·43	3·6	2	0·28	9	0·62	1
(e)	As 32(a) but with 50 mm mineral fibre, glass fibre or EPS slab	0·39	3·6	2	0·27	10	0·62	1

Table A3.17—*continued*

No.	Construction (outside to inside)	U-value (W/m² K)	Admittance		Decrement factor		Surface factor	
			Y-value (W/m² K)	ω/h	f	φ/h	F	ψ/h
33. (a)	100 mm lightweight concrete block, 50 mm UF foam, 100 mm medium concrete block, 13 mm lightweight plaster	0·45	3·5	2	0·28	9	0·62	1
(b)	As 33(a) but with 50 mm mineral fibre, glass fibre or EPS slab	0·41	3·6	2	0·28	10	0·62	1
(c)	As 33(a) but with 75 mm UF foam	0·35	3·6	2	0·27	10	0·62	1
(d)	As 33(a) but with 75 mm mineral fibre, glass fibre, or EPS slab	0·32	3·6	2	0·26	10	0·62	1
34.	100 mm lightweight concrete block, 25 mm airgap, 100 mm lightweight concrete block, 13 mm lightweight plaster	0·67	2·3	2	0·51	8	0·79	1
35. (a)	100 mm lightweight concrete block, 25 mm airgap, 25 mm phenolic foam, 100 mm lightweight concrete block, 13 mm lightweight plaster	0·47	2·3	2	0·45	8	0·79	1
(b)	As 35(a) but with 25 mm mineral fibre, glass fibre or EPS slab	0·45	2·3	2	0·45	8	0·79	1
(c)	As 35(a) but with 40 mm phenolic foam	0·40	2·4	2	0·43	9	0·79	1
(d)	As 35(a) but with 40 mm EPS slab	0·38	2·4	2	0·42	9	0·79	1
(e)	As 35(a) but with 50 mm mineral fibre, glass fibre or EPS slab	0·34	2·4	3	0·41	9	0·78	1
36. (a)	100 mm lightweight concrete block, 50 mm UF foam, 100 mm lightweight concrete block, 13 mm lightweight plaster	0·39	2·4	3	0·43	9	0·79	1
(b)	As 36(a) but with 50 mm mineral fibre, glass fibre or EPS slab	0·36	2·4	3	0·42	9	0·79	1
(c)	As 36(a) but with 75 mm UF foam	0·31	2·4	3	0·40	9	0·78	1
(d)	As 36(a) but with 75 mm mineral fibre, glass fibre or EPS slab	0·29	2·4	3	0·39	9	0·78	1

Table A3.18. Roofs – pitched.

No.	Construction (outside to inside)	U-value (W/m² K)	Admittance		Decrement factor		Surface factor	
			Y-value (W/m² K)	ω/h	f	φ/h	F	ψ/h
1.	5 mm asbestos cement sheet	6·5	6·5	0	1·0	0	0·35	0
2.	5 mm asbestos cement sheet, loft space, 10 mm plasterboard ceiling	2·6	2·6	0	1·0	0	0·74	0
3. (a)	5 mm asbestos cement sheet, loft space, 25 mm glass fibre quilt, 10 mm plasterboard ceiling	0·99	1·1	2	1·0	0	0·90	0
(b)	As 3(a) but with 50 mm glass fibre quilt	0·61	0·82	2	1·0	1	0·94	0
(c)	As 3(a) but with 75 mm glass fibre quilt	0·44	0·71	3	1·0	1	0·95	0
(d)	As 3(a) but with 100 mm glass fibre quilt	0·35	0·67	4	1·0	0	0·96	0
4.	10 mm tile, loft space, 10 mm plasterboard ceiling ...	2·6	2·6	0	1·0	0	0·74	0
5. (a)	10 mm tile, loft space, 25 mm glass fibre quilt, 10 mm plasterboard ceiling	0·99	1·1	2	1·0	1	0·90	0
(b)	As 5(a) but with 50 mm glass fibre quilt	0·61	0·82	2	1·0	1	0·94	0
(c)	As 5(a) but with 75 mm glass fibre quilt	0·44	0·71	3	1·0	1	0·95	0
(d)	As 5(a) but with 100 mm glass fibre quilt	0·35	0·67	4	1·0	1	0·96	0

Note: A pitch of 35° has been assumed.

Table A3.19. Roofs – flat.

No.	Construction (outside to inside)	U-value (W/m² K)	Admittance		Decrement factor		Surface factor	
			Y-value (W/m² K)	ω/h	f	φ/h	F	ψ/h
1.	19 mm asphalt, 75 mm screed, 150 mm cast concrete (dense), 13 mm dense plaster	1·9	5·7	1	0·34	8	0·50	1·
2.	19 mm asphalt, 150 mm aerated concrete slab, 13 mm dense plaster	0·88	2·5	3	0·80	5	0·85	1
3.	25 mm stone chippings, 19 mm asphalt, 40 mm screed, 150 mm heavyweight concrete block	2·5	7·0	1	0·40	7	0·41	2
4.	25 mm stone chippings, 19 mm asphalt, 40 mm screed, 150 mm lightweight concrete block	0·92	2·3	2	0·58	7	0·83	1
5.	19 mm asphalt, 13 mm fibreboard, 10 mm asbestos cement decking, 25 mm airgap, 10 mm asbestos cement decking	1·6	2·1	2	0·96	2	0·82	1
6.	19 mm asphalt, 13 mm fibreboard, 25 mm airgap, 10 mm foil-backed plasterboard (cavity resistance assumed to be 0·30 m² K/W)	1·3	1·4	1	0·99	1	0·87	0
7. (a)	19 mm asphalt, 13 mm fibreboard, 25 mm airgap, 25 mm glass fibre quilt, 10 mm plasterboard	0·81	0·97	2	0·99	1	0·92	0
(b)	As 7(a) but with 50 mm glass fibre quilt	0·54	0·77	3	0·99	1	0·94	0
(c)	As 7(a) but with 75 mm glass fibre quilt	0·40	0·70	3	0·99	1	0·96	0
8. (a)	19 mm asphalt, 13 mm fibreboard, 25 mm EPS slab, 25 mm airgap, 10 mm plasterboard	0·75	0·93	2	0·99	1	0·92	0
(b)	As 8(a) but with 50 mm EPS slab	0·49	0·76	3	0·99	1	0·95	0
9.	19 mm asphalt, 13 mm screed, 50 mm wood wool slab, 25 mm airgap, 10 mm plasterboard	1·1	1·4	2	0·94	2	0·88	0
10.	19 mm felt/bitumen layers, 25 mm EPS slab on metal decking	1·1	1·2	1	0·99	1	0·89	0

Table A3.20. Internal walls/Partitions.

No.	Construction	U-value (W/m² K)	Admittance		Decrement factor		Surface factor	
			Y-value (W/m² K)	ω/h	f	φ/h	F	ψ/h
1. (a)	105 mm brickwork	2·4	4·1	4	—	—	0·81	2
(b)	As 1(a) but with 13 mm lightweight plaster each side ...	1·8	3·6	3	—	—	0·72	2
2. (a)	105 mm brickwork, 25 mm airgap, 105 mm brickwork...	1·3	4·9	2	—	—	0·57	2
(b)	As 2(a) but with 13 mm lightweight plaster each side ...	1·1	3·8	2	—	—	0·61	1
3. (a)	100 mm heavyweight concrete block	3·3	5·7	3	—	—	0·68	3
(b)	As 3(a) but with 13 mm lightweight plaster each side ...	2·2	4·3	2	—	—	0·61	2
4. (a)	100 mm heavyweight concrete block, 25 mm airgap, 100 mm heavyweight concrete block	1·8	6·5	2	—	—	0·42	3
(b)	As 4(a) but with 13 mm lightweight plaster each side ...	1·4	4·4	1	—	—	0·51	1
5. (a)	100 mm mediumweight concrete block	2·3	4·0	4	—	—	0·80	2
(b)	As 5(a) but with 13 mm lightweight plaster each side ...	1·7	3·5	3	—	—	0·72	1
6. (a)	100 mm mediumweight concrete block, 25 mm airgap, 100 mm mediumweight concrete block	1·2	4·7	·2	—	—	0·58	2
(b)	As 6(a) but with 13 mm lightweight plaster each side ...	1·0	3·6	2	—	—	0·62	1
7. (a)	100 mm lightweight concrete block	1·3	2·0	4	—	—	0·93	1
(b)	As 7(a) but with 13 mm lightweight plaster each side ...	1·1	2·3	4	—	—	0·88	1
8. (a)	100 mm lightweight concrete block, 25 mm airgap, 100 mm lightweight concrete block	0·68	2·6	3	—	—	0·79	1
(b)	As 8(a) but with 13 mm lightweight plaster each side ...	0·61	2·5	3	—	—	0·78	1
9. (a)	65 mm lightweight cast concrete	2·4	2·6	4	—	—	0·92	1
(b)	As 9(a) but with 13 mm lightweight plaster each side ...	1·7	2·8	4	—	—	0·85	1
10.	25 mm plasterboard, 25 mm airgap, 25 mm plaster board	1·4	1·4	5	—	—	0·97	1
11.	12 mm fibreboard, 25 mm airgap, 12 mm fibreboard ...	1·2	0·26	6	—	—	1·00	0

Table A3.21. Internal floors/Ceilings.

No.	Construction	U-value (W/m² K)	Surface	Admittance		Decrement factor		Surface factor	
				Y-value (W/m² K)	ω/h	f	φ/h	F	ψ/h
1. (a)	50 mm screed, 150 mm cast concrete	2·0	Floor	4·3	2	—	—	0·59	2
			Ceiling	6·0	2	—	—	0·46	3
(b)	As 1(a) but with 25 mm wood block floor	1·5	Floor	2·9	2	—	—	0·70	1
			Ceiling	6·0	1	—	—	0·42	3
2. (a)	65 mm cast concrete > 25 mm airgap, 16 mm plasterboard ceiling	1·7	Floor	5·2	3	—	—	0·72	3
			Ceiling	2·2	3	—	—	0·86	1
(b)	As 2(a) but with 25 mm wood block floor	1·3	Floor	3·2	2	—	—	0·70	1
			Ceiling	2·4	2	—	—	0·78	1
3.	25 mm wood block, 65 mm cast concrete, 25 mm airgap, 25 mm glass fibre quilt, 16 mm plasterboard ceiling	0·71	Floor	3·3	2	—	—	0·67	1
			Ceiling	1·4	3	—	—	0·89	1
4.	25 mm wood block, 65 mm cast concrete, 25 mm airgap, 25 mm glass fibre quilt, 2 mm metal tray	0·77	Floor	3·2	2	—	—	0·67	1
			Ceiling	1·3	3	—	—	0·89	0
5.	10 mm timber floor, > 25 mm airgap, 16 mm plasterboard ceiling	1·6	Floor	0·68	6	—	—	0·99	0
			Ceiling	0·81	6	—	—	0·99	0
6.	10 mm timber floor, > 25 mm airgap, 25 mm glass fibre quilt, 16 mm plasterboard ceiling	0·81	Floor	0·63	6	—	—	1·00	0
			Ceiling	0·88	6	—	—	0·99	0
7.	10 mm timber floor > 25 mm airgap, 25 mm glass fibre quilt, 2 mm metal tray	0·88	Floor	0·55	6	—	—	1·00	0
			Ceiling	0·57	6	—	—	1·00	0

Note: The U-values quoted are averages. In steady-state conditions, the actual values may differ by up to ± 10% depending on whether the heat flow is upwards or downwards, respectively.

APPENDIX 2. Properties of materials

Table A3.22.—Thermal conductivities and resistivities of miscellaneous materials.

Material			Thermal Properties			
Detail	Condition (where known)	Bulk Density (kg/m³)	λ $\left(\dfrac{W}{m\,K}\right)$	r $\left(\dfrac{m\,K}{W}\right)$	For face temperatures (°C)	
					Hot	Cold
ALUMINA						
Activated gel	dry	700	0·13	7·7	100	10
Insulating brick	dry	720	0·29	3·5	500	40
			0·31	3·2	750	40
			0·34	2·9	1000	40
Solid, electrical insulator at 100°C	dry	3600	17	0·06		
at 600°C			9	0·11		
ASBESTOS CEMENT SHEET		1360	0·25	4·0		
	conditioned*	1520	0·37	2·7		
		1600†	0·40	2·5		
		2000	0·55	1·8		
ASBESTOS CLOTH	dry	450	0·11	9·1		
	dry	560	0·17	5·9		
ASBESTOS FELT	dry	144	0·078	13		
ASBESTOS HARD SETTING COMPOSITION	dry	1200	0·25	4·0	70	25
ASBESTOS INSULATING BOARD	conditioned	720	0·11	9·1		
	conditioned	750	0·12	8·3		
	conditioned	800	0·14	7·1		
	conditioned	900	0·16	6·2		
	wet	845	0·21	4·8		
ASBESTOS, 85% MAGNESIA	dry	190	0·060	16·7	100	25
			0·065	15·4	200	25
			0·072	13·9	300	25
			0·080	12·5	400	25
		235	0·065	15·4	150	25
	dry		0·067	14·9	200	25
	dry	235	0·074	13·5	300	25
			0·083	12·0	400	25
			0·090	11·1	500	25
ASBESTOS MILLBOARD		720	0·11	9·1		
		1050	0·19	5·3		
ASBESTOS PAPER						
Plain sheet	dry	950	0·15	6·7		
Corrugated and plain bonded	dry	190	0·087	11·5		
Corrugated and aluminium foil bonded	dry	145	0·065	15·4		
ASBESTOS PLASTIC INSULATING COMPO-SITION	dry	275	0·075	13·3	100	40
			0·080	12·5	200	40
			0·085	11·8	300	40
			0·095	10·5	400	40
			0·105	9·5	500	40
		400	0·120	8·3	100	40
	dry		0·125	8·0	200	40
			0·130	7·7	300	40
			0·135	7·4	400	40
ASBESTOS/RESIN BONDED BOARD	dry	1280	0·30	3·3		
ASBESTOS ROPE						
25 mm diameter, one layer	dry		0·15	6·67	270	120
ASBESTOS SLABS						
High amosite asbestos content	dry	145	0·055	18·2	100	40
			0·060	16·7	200	40
			0·068	14·7	300	40
			0·075	13·3	400	40
			0·083	12·0	500	40
	dry	320	0·080	12·5	100	40
			0·085	11·8	200	40
			0·090	11·1	300	40
			0·097	10·3	400	40
			0·110	9·09	500	40
Same specimen	dry	135	0·050	20·0		
	wet		0·150	6·67		
	soaked		0·200	5·00		
Lightweight slab		70	0·050	20·0		
		95	0·053	18·9		

Table A3.22—continued

Material			Thermal Properties			
Detail	Condition (where known)	Bulk Density (kg/m³)	λ $\left(\dfrac{W}{m\,K}\right)$	r $\left(\dfrac{m\,K}{W}\right)$	For face temperatures (°C)	
					Hot	Cold
ASBESTOS, SPRAYED		80	0·043	23·3		
		130	0·046	21·7		
		160	0·061	16·4		
		240	0·075	13·3		
ASBESTOS/VERMICULITE SLABS		260	0·080	12·5		
		320	0·095	10·5		
		400	0·115	8·7		
	dry	400	0·130	7·7	80	25
ASBESTOS WALLBOARD	conditioned	900	0·16	6·3		
		1200	0·25	4·0		
ASH Pulverized fuel powder		720	0·10	10·0		
ASPHALT (bitumen containing mineral matter)	dry	2250	1·20	0·83		
roofing	dry	1600	0·43	2·33		
		1700	0·50	2·00		
		1925	0·58	1·72		
mastic asphalt roofing, heavy, 20% grit	dry	2325	1·15	0·87		
BALSA WOOD Fluffy wood fibres		40	0·040	25·0		
BEESWAX	dry	1000	0·26	3·85		
BITUMEN Pure	dry	1055	0·16	6·25		
Sand or slate filled	dry	1300	0·26	3·85		
	dry	1450	0·35	2·86		
	dry	1600	0·50	2·00		
Composition for floors	dry	2400	0·85	1·18		
BLANKET Wool, closely woven		65	0·043	23·3		
BOILER LAGGING Light	dry	255	0·063	15·9	100	25
		400	0·115	8·7	100	25
Heavy	dry	720	0·170	5·9	70	25
		880	0·190	5·3	100	25
CALCIUM SILICATE INSULATING COMPOSITION	dry	200	0·068	14·7	300	25
			0·075	13·3	400	25
			0·082	12·2	500	25
			0·090	11·1	600	25
			0·100	10·0	700	25
Low temperature	dry	160	0·046	21·7	10	—10
			0·034	29·4	—10	—190
High-density slab		430	0·095	10·5		
CARDBOARD Plain sheet			0·22	4·6		
Plain sheet, waxed		710	0·12	8·3		
Corrugated and plain sheets, bonded		105	0·047	21·3		
CARPETING Wilton type			0·058	17·2		
Simulated sheepswool			0·055	18·2		
Wool felt underlay		160	0·045	22·2		
Cellular rubber underlay		270	0·065	15·4		
		400	0·10	10·0		
CELLULAR CONCRETE PIPE INSULATION	dry	400	0·095	10·5	40	10
			0·100	10·0	100	10
CELLULOSE WADDING		30	0·038	26·3		
CEMENT Acid resisting, phenolic binder		1700	0·80	1·25		
Heat conducting, graphite filled at 100°C	dry	1600	17	0·059		
at 300°C			15	0·067		

Table A3.22—*continued*

Material			Thermal Properties			
Detail	Condition (where known)	Bulk Density (kg/m³)	λ $\left(\dfrac{W}{m\,K}\right)$	r $\left(\dfrac{m\,K}{W}\right)$	For face temperatures (°C)	
					Hot	Cold
CHALK						
Crushed Brighton chalk	dry		0·25	4·00		
	10% d.w.		0·50	2·00		
	20% d.w.		0·80	1·25		
CHARCOAL						
Loose	dry	190	0·055	18·2		
COAL						
Pulverized, powder	conditioned	575	0·065	15·4		
COIR FIBRE MATS		80	0·047	21·3		
		210	0·050	20·0		
CORK						
Loose baked granules	damp	100	0·039	25·6		
	dry	100	0·045	22·2	80	25
Loose raw granules	damp	115	0·046	21·7		
	dry	115	0·052	19·2	80	25
CORKBOARD						
(Variation with density)		110	0·039	25·6		
		130	0·040	25·0		
		145	**0·042**	**23·8**		
		160	0·045	22·2		
(Variation with temperature)		130	0·033	30·3	15	—70
			0·038	26·3	15	—20
			0·039	25·6	15	0
	dry		0·043	23·3	65	15
	dry		0·046	21·7	90	15
Cork slab, baked	dry	130	0·040	25·0		
soaked in water and drained	wet	195	0·054	18·5		
soaked in water	saturated	325	0·085	11·8		
ice-logged	saturated	325	0·080	12·5	—5	—70
baked, high density		200	0·046	21·7		
		265	0·050	20·0		
raw	damp	160	0·050	20·0		
raw, heavy density	damp	465	0·080	12·5		
Cork with cement binder		280	0·073	13·7		
		400	0·100	10·0		
Cork with bitumen or asphalt binder		240	0·055	18·2		
		640	0·145	6·90		
		1040	0·290	3·45		
Cork with rubber latex binder		320	0·062	16·1		
		480	0·080	12·5		
Cork with resin binder	conditioned (40% r.h.)	250	0·050	20·0		
Cork floor tiles	conditioned (40% r.h.)	**540**	**0·085**	**11·8**		
DIATOMACEOUS EARTH						
Kieselguhr or infusorial earth (9% moisture content)		480	0·090	11·1		
DIATOMACEOUS INSULATING POWDER	dry	220	0·067	14·9	300	40
			0·080	12·50	500	40
			0·095	10·5	700	40
	dry	360	0·090	11·1	300	40
			0·105	9·52	500	40
			0·115	8·70	700	40
Crushed diatomaceous brick		510	0·150	6·67		
EEL GRASS						
Insulating blanket		80	0·039	25·6		
		145	0·043	23·3		
		215	0·049	20·4		
EBONITE						
Solid sheet at 20°C	dry	1200	0·155	6·45		
at 30°C	dry		0·160	6·25		
Cellular insulation board	dry	64	0·026	38·5	15	—70
	dry		0·030	33·3	20	0
	dry		0·033	30·3	40	20

Table A3.22—*continued*

Material			Thermal Properties			
Detail	Condition (where known)	Bulk Density (kg/m³)	λ $\left(\dfrac{W}{m\,K}\right)$	r $\left(\dfrac{m\,K}{W}\right)$	For face temperatures (°C)	
					Hot	Cold
FELT						
Hair felt		80	0·039	25·6		
Car body lining felt		30	0·039	25·6		
Undercarpet felt		**120**	**0·045**	**22·2**		
Wool felt		150	0·039	25·6		
Asbestos felt		144	0·078	12·8		
Roofing felt		960	0·19	5·4		
		1120	0·20	5·0		
Sacking felt, bitumen		**1100**	**0·20**	**5·0**		
FIBRE BUILDING BOARDS						
Bitumen impregnated board	conditioned	270–340	0·051	19·6		
Fibre insulating board						
(Variation with density)	conditioned	240	0·053	18·9		
	conditioned	280	0·056	17·9		
	conditioned	**300**	**0·057**	**17·5**		
	conditioned	320	0·059	17·0		
	conditioned	360	0·062	16·1		
	conditioned	400	0·065	15·4		
(Variation with temperature)		290	0·049	20·4	10	—40
			0·052	19·2	10	—10
	dry		0·056	17·9	30	10
	dry		0·059	17·0	45	20
(Variation with dryness)	dry	265	0·052	19·2		
	conditioned	290	0·056	17·9		
	damp	320	0·065	15·4		
	wet	345	0·080	12·5		
FIBRE SHEET						
Hard vulcanized sheet		1200	0·300	3·3		
FLAX SHIVE						
Loose shive	conditioned	240	0·044	22·7		
Resin-bonded insulating board		300	0·070	14·3		
Resin-bonded board		670	0·110	9·1		
FLOORING						
Bitumen with inert mineral matter	dry	1700	0·75	1·3		
Mastic asphalt with limestone	dry	2250	1·22	0·8		
Asphalt with foamed slag	dry	1200	0·22	4·6		
Bitumen emulsion, cement and aggregate	dry	1600	0·55	1·8		
		2000	0·60	1·7		
Composition flooring	conditioned	1600	0·44	2·3		
	wet	1730	0·58	1·7		
	soaked	1890	0·85	1·2		
Composition, hard	dry	2100	0·65	1·5		
	wet	2200	0·80	1·2		
Pitch with inert mastic mineral matter	dry	1850	0·68	1·5		
Pitch mastic flooring	dry	2250	1·10	0·9		
Wood fibre and cement blocks	conditioned	1550	0·32	3·1		
FLOOR COVERING						
See under Carpeting						
Linoleum						
Plastics						
Rubber						
Tiles						
FOAMED SLAG						
Loose granules		480	0·10	10·0		
		640	0·13	7·7		
GASES						
Air		1·17	0·026	38·5		
Carbon dioxide		1·84	0·017	58·8		
Hydrogen		0·082	0·18	5·6		
GASKET MATERIALS						
Cork		480	0·06	16·7		
Graphited		1750	0·40	2·5		
Metallic		1900	0·40	2·5		
GATCH						
Aerated and baked		650	0·22	4·6		

Table A3.22—*continued*

Material			Thermal Properties			
Detail	Condition (where known)	Bulk Density (kg/m³)	λ $\left(\dfrac{W}{mK}\right)$	r $\left(\dfrac{mK}{W}\right)$	For face temperatures (°C)	
					Hot	Cold
GLASS						
Cellular slab		175	0·063	15·9		
Cloth, woven		480	0·06	16·7		
		800	0·09	11·1		
Sheet, window		**2500**	**1·05**	**0·95**		
heat-resisting		2250	1·10	0·91		
flint glass		3500	0·70	1·4		
Hollow glass block wall			0·68	1·5		
GLASS FIBRE						
Lightweight mats, quilts	dry	**12**	**0·040**	**25·0**	**10** Average	
	dry		0·042	23·8	40	10
	dry	50	0·033	30·3	15	0
	dry		0·036	27·8	40	10
	conditioned (40% r.h.)	65	0·032	31·3		
Loose, mats, quilts	dry	80	0·035	28·6	40	10
	dry		0·039	25·6	90	40
	dry	130	0·045	22·2	90	40
	dry		0·053	18·9	200	40
	dry		0·062	16·1	300	40
	dry		0·075	13·3	400	40
Loose wool blanket	dry	145	0·042	23·8	40	25
	dry		0·046	21·7	100	25
	dry		0·053	18·9	200	25
	dry		0·062	16·1	300	25
Rigid pipe sections	dry	160	0·042	23·8	100	25
	dry		0·046	21·7	150	25
	dry		0·052	19·2	200	25
	dry		0·058	17·2	250	25
GRANOLITHIC		2085	0·865	1·16		
GRAPHITE						
Achreson, solid at 50°C	dry	1600	140	0·007		
at 25°C			115	0·009		
Reactor grade at 50°C	dry		70	0·01		
at 250°C			65	0·02		
GRAVEL						
Ham River, loose, grading 10 to 19 mm	dry	1250	0·30	3·3		
GREASE, LUBRICATING		950	0·14	7·1		
GROUND NUT SHELL BOARD						
Resin-bonded	conditioned	650	0·12	8·3		
GYPSUM						
Powder		320	0·065	15·4		
Foamed plaster		880	0·25	4·0		
Plasterboard		**950**	**0·16**	**6·3**		
Plastering		1100	0·38	2·6		
		1300	0·46	2·2		
HARDBOARD						
Medium		560	0·079	12·7		
		600	**0·08**	**12·5**		
Standard		750	0·094	10·6		
		880	0·123	8·1		
		900	**0·13**	**7·7**		
		1010	0·144	6·9		
HONEYCOMB PAPER BOARD						
Empty cores, 19 mm across			0·18	5·6		
Granulated cork-filled			0·08	12·5		
Vermiculite filled			0·10	10·0		
HUSKS						
Bonded with cement	(conditioned 6% m.c.)	560	0·11	9·1		
		720	0·15	6·7		
Rice husks bonded with cement	dry	720	0·15	6·7		
	conditioned	800	0·29	3·5		
ICE at −45°C		925	2·74	0·4		
at −20°C		920	2·45	0·4		
at −1°C		920	2·24	0·4		

Table A3.22—*continued*

Material			Thermal Properties			
Detail	Condition (where known)	Bulk Density (kg/m³)	λ $\left(\dfrac{W}{m\,K}\right)$	r $\left(\dfrac{m\,K}{W}\right)$	For face temperatures (°C)	
					Hot	Cold
INSULATING BOARD						
See under Asbestos						
Ebonite						
Fibreboard						
Flax shive						
Ground nut shell						
Jute						
Papyrus grass						
Strawslabs						
JUTE						
Bonded fibre mat		50	0·036	27·8		
Resin-bonded board		430	0·065	15·4		
KAPOK						
Insulating quilt		20	0·035	28·6		
		30	0·030	33·3	10	—10
	dry		0·039	25·6	80	25
LINOLEUM						
Cork		510	0·07	14·3		
Inlaid		1150	0·22	4·6		
Plastic		1750	0·35	2·9		
P.V.C.		1600	0·22	4·6		
Rubber		1600	0·31	3·2		
LIQUIDS						
Cylinder oil		890	0·15	6·67		
Glycerol		1200	0·29	3·45		
Paraffin		810	0·12	8·34		
Quenching oil		895	0·13	7·69		
Transformer oil		880	0·12	8·34		
Water at 20°C		1000	0·60	1·67		
at 40°C		990	0·63	1·59		
at 80°C		970	0·67	1·49		
Sea water at 20°C		1025	0·58	1·72		
MAGNESIA ASBESTOS 85%						
See under Asbestos 85% Magnesia						
METALS						
Aluminium alloy, typical		2800	160	0·006		
Brass		8400	130	0·008		
Copper, commercial		8900	200	0·005		
Iron, cast		7000	40	0·025		
Steel, carbon		7800	50	0·020		
Steel, high alloy		8000	15	0.067		
MICA						
Mica flakes bonded with shellac			0·31	3·2		
Muscorite sheet		2900	0·69	1·5		
Phlogonite sheet		2900	0·62	1·6		
MINERAL WOOL						
Felted		16	0·040	25·0		
		50	0·036	27·8	20	0
	dry	50	0·039	25·6	40	10
		80	0·035	28·6	20	0
	dry	80	0·038	26·3	40	10
	dry		0·045	22·2	100	40
Semi-rigid felted mat	dry	130	0·036	27·8	40	10
	dry		0·044	22·7	100	40
	dry		0·056	17·9	200	40
	dry		0·070	14·3	300	40
Loose, felted slab or mat	dry	180	0·042	23·8	40	10
	dry		0·048	20·8	100	40
	dry		0·059	17·0	200	40
	dry		0·071	14·1	300	40
	dry		0·084	11·9	400	40
Rigid slab	dry	155	0·050	20·0	150	40
	dry		0·060	16·7	300	40
	dry		0·071	14·1	400	40
	dry		0·082	12·2	500	40
	dry		0·095	10·5	600	40
High-density slab, at low temperature		290	0·025	40·0	10	—150
			0·030	33·3	10	—70
			0·035	28·6	10	—20

Table A3.22—*continued*

Material			Thermal Properties			
Detail	Condition (where known)	Bulk Density (kg/m³)	λ $\left(\dfrac{W}{m\,K}\right)$	r $\left(\dfrac{m\,K}{W}\right)$	For face temperatures (°C)	
					Hot	Cold
MUD						
	5% d.w.	1840	0·43	2·3		
	10% d.w.	1920	0·72	1·4		
	20% d.w.	2115	1·44	0·69		
	40% d.w.	1920	1·15	0·87		
	80% d.w.	1570	0·94	1·1		
	150% d.w.	1315	0·79	1·3		
MUTTY		1350	0·33	3·0		
PAINTS						
Aluminium			0·46	2·2		
Anti-condensation		800	0·16	6·3		
Thermo-setting varnish		1075	0·19	5·3		
Varnish			0·32	3·1		
Zinc-filled paint		4645	2·16	0·46		
PAPER		1090	0·14	7·1		
Kraft building paper			0·06	16·7		
PAPYRUS GRASS						
Insulating board		255	0·055	18·2		
Building board		480	0·085	11·8		
PEAT SLAB		160	0·043	23·3		
	conditioned (10%)	240	0·058	17·2		
		400	0·094	10·6		
		481	0·101	9·9		
PERLITE						
Loose, expanded granules		65	0·042	23·8		
	dry	65	0·046	21·7	100	40
	dry		0·06	16·7	200	40
	dry		0·07	14·3	300	40
	dry		0·085	11·8	400	40
Perlite cement, sprayed	dry	350	0·08	12·5		
	wet	420	0·11	9·1		
Perlite plaster		400	0·08	12·5		
	conditioned	600	0·19	5·3		
Perlite plasterboard	conditioned (2% m.c.)	800	0·18	5·6		
PITCH	dry	1000	0·14	6·9		
PLASTER						
Foamed		400	0·10	9·9		
		640	0·16	6·3		
		880	0·25	4·1		
PLASTERBOARD						
Gypsum		950	0·16	6·25		
Perlite		800	0·18	5·56		
PLASTERING						
Gypsum		1120	0·38	2·7		
		1280	0·46	2·2		
Perlite		400	0·079	12·7		
		610	0·19	5·4		
Vermiculite		480	0·14	6·9		
		640	0·20	5·0		
		800	0·26	3·9		
		960	0·30	3·3		
Sand, cement	conditioned	1570	0·53	1·9		
Sand, cement and lime	conditioned	1440	0·48	2·1		
Sand, gypsum, 3 : 1	conditioned	1555	0·65	1·5		
PLASTICINE		1760	0·65	1·5		
PLASTICS, CELLULAR						
Phenolic foam board	dry	30	0·038	26·3		
	dry	50	0·036	27·8		
Polyether, flexible sheet	dry	30	0·039	25·6	20	0
	dry		0·045	22·2	45	20
	dry		0·050	20·0	80	20
Polystyrene, expanded board	dry	15	0·037	27·0		
	dry	15	0·033	30·3	10	−10
	dry		0·035	28·6	20	0
	dry		0·039	25·6	45	20

Table A3.22—*continued*

Material			Thermal Properties			
Detail	Condition (where known)	Bulk Density (kg/m³)	λ $\left(\dfrac{W}{m\,K}\right)$	r $\left(\dfrac{m\,K}{W}\right)$	For face temperatures (°C)	
					Hot	Cold
Polystyrene, expanded board	dry	25	0·034	29·4		
	dry	25	0·031	32·3	10	—10
	dry		0·033	30·3	20	0
	dry		0·037	27·0	45	20
	dry	30	0·030	33·3	20	0
Polyurethane, gas-filled rigid board (As received)	dry	30	0·020	50·0	10	—10
	dry		0·021	47·6	20	0
	dry		0·024	41·7	45	20
(After 1½ years, aged)	dry	30	0·023	43·5	10	—10
	dry		0·025	40·0	20	0
	dry		0·027	37	45	20
Polyurethane foam (aged)	dry	30	0·026	38·5		
Polyvinyl chloride, rigid foam (small pores)	dry	25	0·035	28·6	20	0
	dry		0·041	24·4	45	20
	dry	50	0·034	29·4	20	0
	dry		0·040	25·0	45	20
	dry	80	0·035	28·6	20	0
Urea formaldehyde foam	dry	8-12	0·031	32·3		
	dry	15	0·032	31·3		
	dry	30	0·032	31·3		
P.V.C. floor covering	dry		0·40	2·5		
PLASTICS, SOLID SHEET						
Acrylic resin	dry	1440	0·20	5·0		
Epoxy casting	dry	1200	0·20	5·0		
Epoxy glass cloth laminate	dry	1750	0·38	2·6		
Epoxy glass fibre	dry	1500	0·23	4·4		
Epoxy silica flour (33% Wht.)	dry	1400	0·34	2·9		
Melamine glass cloth	dry	2000	0·55	1·8		
Nylon	dry	1100	0·30	3·3		
Phenolic, asbestos cloth	dry	1300	0·30	3·3		
		1700	0·50	2·0		
Phenolic, asbestos flock	dry	1600	0·38	2·6		
Phenolic, cotton fabric	dry	1350	0·34	2·9		
Phenolic, paper	dry	1370	0·27	3·7		
Polycarbonate	dry	1150	0·23	4·4		
Polyethylene, low density	dry	920	0·35	2·9		
Polyethylene, high density	dry	960	0·50	2·0		
Polyester, glass mat	dry	1450	0·23	4·4		
Polypropylene	dry	915	0·24	4·2		
Polystyrene	dry	1050	0·17	5·9		
P.T.F.E.	dry	2200	0·24	4·2		
P.T.F.E. glass cloth	dry	2250	0·30	3·3		
P.V.C., rigid	dry	1350	0·16	6·2		
Silicone, asbestos mat	dry	1600	0·34	2·9		
Silicone, glass fabric	dry	1800	0·34	2·9		
PORCELAIN						
Electrical grade	dry	2400	1·44	0·68		
POWDERS						
Alumina						
Aluminium			0·20	5·0		
Carborundum		1350	0·19	5·3		
Copper		5100	0·45	2·2		
Diatomaceous		210	0·06	16·7		
Graphite		320	0·10	10·0		
		460	0·21	4·8		
Gypsum		320	0·065	15·4		
Phosphate rock fertilizer	dry	1600	0·23	4·4		
	damp (90% r.h.)	1760	0·40	2·5		
Sand, fine silver	dry	1600	0·30	3·3		
Silica aerogel	dry	130	0·024	41·7		
PUMICE						
Loose granules		350	0·07	14·3		
Loose 19 mm granules		480	0·09	11·1		
PYROPHYLITE						
Fired high-temperature refractory		2500	1·90	0·53		
REFRACTORY BRICK						
Alumina insulating grade	dry	720	0·29	3·5	500	40
	dry		0·31	3·2	750	40
	dry		0·34	2·9	1000	40

Table A3.22—*continued*

Material			Thermal Properties			
Detail	Condition (where known)	Bulk Density (kg/m³)	λ $\left(\dfrac{W}{mK}\right)$	r $\left(\dfrac{mK}{W}\right)$	For face temperatures (°C)	
					Hot	Cold
Diatomaceous brick	dry	480	0·125	8·0	500	40
	dry		0·13	7·7	750	40
	dry		0·135	7·4	900	40
	dry	560	0·14	7·1	500	40
	dry		0·145	6·9	750	40
	dry		0·15	6·7	900	40
	dry	720	0·18	5·6	500	40
	dry		0·20	5·0	750	40
	dry		0·21	4·8	900	40
Firebrick at 500°C	dry	2000	1·00	1·00		
at 1000°C	dry		1·30	0·77		
Silica brick 95% $S_1 O_2$ at 500°C	dry	1900	1·30	0·77		
at 1000°C	dry		1·40	0·71		
Vermiculite insulating brick	dry	700	0·26	3·8	500	40
	dry		0·28	3·6	750	40
	dry		0·29	3·4	1000	40
REFRACTORY INSULATING CONCRETE						
Diatomaceous aggregate, cement	dry	1050	0·25	4·00	300	40
	dry		0·26	3·8	500	40
	dry		0·27	3·7	800	40
Refractory aggregate, aluminious cement, 4 : 1 volume	dry	1350	0·45	2·2	400	40
	dry		0·47	2·1	600	40
	dry		0·49	2·0	800	40
ROOFING						
Asphalt (bitumen with inert mineral matter)	dry	1600	0·43	2·3		
		1925	0·58	1·7		
Mastic asphalt, heavy, 20% grit	dry	2325	1·15	0·87		
ROOFING FELT	dry	960	0·19	5·4		
	dry	1120	0·20	5·0		
RUBBER						
Cellular slabs		80	0·040	25·00		
		160	0·043	23·3		
		240	0·055	18·2		
		400	0·085	11·8		
Sheet:						
Natural rubber	dry	930	0·16	6·2		
40% vulcanized rubber, mineral-filled		1500	0·29	3·4		
50% vulcanized rubber, mineral-filled		1380	0·20	5·0		
Synthetic rubber		960	0·16	6·2		
Synthetic rubber, filled		1500	0·27	3·7		
Silicone rubber at 20°C		1200	0·25	4·0		
at 100°C			0·23	4·3		
Rubber floor covering			0·40	2·5		
SALT						
Loose grains		1450	0·24	4·2		
SAND						
Building	dry	1500	0·30	3·3		
Sand 3 to 6 mm pebbles	dry	1540	0·42	2·4		
Sand 20 to 100 mesh	dry	1750	0·42	2·4		
Mixture of 30% of 20 to 100 mesh, and 70% of 3 to 6 mm	dry	2000	0·80	1·2		
Fine silver sand at 20°C	dry	1600	0·32	3·1		
at 150°C	dry		0·35	2·9		
at 250°C	dry		0·37	2·7		
SAND/EPOXY RESIN BLOCKS	dry	2000	1·10	0·9		
SARKING FELT, BITUMEN		1100	0·20	5·06		
SAWDUST						
Loose	conditioned	145	0·08	12·5		
Slabs, lightly bonded	conditioned	160	0·05	20·0		
Slabs, bonded with glue	conditioned	550	0·10	10·0		
SEALING COMPOUND						
Flexible, for windows and joints		1350	0·40	2·5		

Table A3.22—*continued*

Material			Thermal Properties			
Detail	Condition (where known)	Bulk Density (kg/m³)	λ $\left(\dfrac{W}{m\,K}\right)$	r $\left(\dfrac{m\,K}{W}\right)$	For face temperatures (°C)	
					Hot	Cold
SEED						
Flax	conditioned	650	0·11	9·1		
Wheat	conditioned	880	0·16	6·2		
SILICA						
Aerogel insulating powder at −20°C	dry	90	0·020	50·00		
at 0°C	dry		0·021	47·6		
at 10°C	dry		0·022	45·4		
at 20°C	dry	130	0·024	41·7		
Fibre insulating blanket	dry	50	0·11	9·1	650	40
	dry		0·20	5·00	950	40
	dry	95	0·085	11·8	650	40
	dry		0·14	7·1	950	40
Solid fused quartz at 40°C	dry	2190	1·40	0·7		
at 250°C	dry		1·50	0·7		
Woven cloth at 40°C	dry	1000	0·08	12·5		
at 500°C	dry		0·10	10·0		
SILT						
Very hard	5% d.w.	1840	0·43	2·3		
Hard	10% d.w.	1920	0·72	1·4		
Stiff	20% d.w.	2115	1·44	0·7		
Firm	40% d.w.	1920	1·15	0·9		
Soft	80% d.w.	1570	0·94	1		
Very soft	150% d.w.	1315	0·79	1·3		
SLATE		2700	1·9	0·5		
			2·0	**0·5**		
SNOW						
Freshly fallen		190	0·17	5·9		
Compacted		400	0·43	2·3		
SOIL						
Clay soil						
From depth of 1·5 m	11% d.w. (typical)		1·10	0·91		
3 m	11% d.w. (typical)		1·10	0·91		
6 m	11% d.w. (typical)		1·15	0·87		
8 m	11% d.w. (typical)		1·25	0·80		
Clay soil			**1·50**	**0·67**		
Loosely packed	14% d.w. (typical)	1200	0·38	2·6		
Loaded 5 kPa	14% d.w. (typical)	1280	0·70	1·4		
Loaded 100 kPa	14% d.w. (typical)	1550	1·20	0·83		
Liverpool clay	17% d.w. very damp	2100	1·70	0·59		
London clay	25% d.w. wet	1900	1·40	0·71		
Crushed Brighton chalk	dry		0·25	4·00		
	10% d.w.		0·50	2·00		
	20% d.w.		0·80	1·25		
Loam over sand and gravel 1 m deep (seasonal change due to moisture content)			1·27	0·79		
Sandy loam, seasonal variation	5% d.w.		0·55	1·82		
	10% d.w.		0·85	1·18		
	15% d.w.		1·20	0·83		
Loam	wet		**1·20**	**0·83**		
SPONGE CLIPPINGS		30	0·043	23·3		
		80	0·035	28·6		
STONE						
Artificial		1750	1·3	0·77		
Granite			**2·5**	**0·40**		
		2650	2·9	0·34		
(Variation with temperature) at 25°C		2600	2·3	0·43		
at −100°C			2·4	0·42		
Limestone	dry	**2180**	**1·5**	**0·67**		
Marble	dry	2500	2·0	0·50		
		2700	2·5	0·40		
Sandstone		**2000**	**1·3**	**0·77**		
Slate		2700	1·9	0·53		
			2·0	**0·50**		
STONEWARE	conditioned	2150	1·40	0·71		
STRAWSLAB, COMPRESSED	conditioned	260	0·085	11·8		
		330	0·098	10·2		
		350	**0·11**	**9·1**		

Table A3.22—*continued*

Material			Thermal Properties			
Detail	Condition (where known)	Bulk Density (kg/m³)	λ $\left(\dfrac{W}{m\,K}\right)$	r $\left(\dfrac{m\,K}{W}\right)$	For face temperatures (°C)	
					Hot	Cold
SUGAR						
Yellow, demarara		770	0·19	5·3		
White, granulated		900	0·21	4·8		
TERRAZZO	conditioned	2435	1·59	0·63		
THATCH						
Reed		**270**	**0·09**	**11·1**		
Straw		**240**	**0·07**	**14·3**		
TILES						
Asphalt and asbestos	conditioned	1900	0·55	1·82		
Burnt clay	conditioned	**1900**	**0·85**	**1·18**		
Concrete	conditioned	2100	1·10	0·91		
Cork	conditioned	530	0·085	11·8		
Plastic		1050	0·50	2·00		
P.V.C. asbestos		2000	0·85	1·18		
Rubber		1600	0·30	3·3		
		1800	0·50	2·0		
Sand, epoxy resin	conditioned	2000	1·10	0·91		
TIMBER						
Across grain:						
Softwood	conditioned		**0·13**	**7·7**		
Hardwood			**0·15**	**6·7**		
Balsa	conditioned	100	0·048	20·8		
		150	0·055	18·2		
		200	0·060	16·7		
		250	0·065	15·4		
Beech	conditioned	700	0·165	6·06		
Deal	conditioned	610	0·125	8·00		
Mahogany	conditioned	700	0·155	6·45		
Oak	conditioned	770	0·160	6·25		
Pitch pine	conditioned	660	0·140	7·14		
Plywood	conditioned	**530**	**0·140**	**7·14**		
Plywood, fireproofed	conditioned	560	0·150	6·67		
Spruce	conditioned	415	0·105	9·52		
Teak	conditioned	700	0·170	5·88		
Walnut	conditioned	660	0·140	7·14		
Along grain:						
Deal	conditioned	610	0·215	4·65		
Oak	conditioned	770	0·290	3·45		
VERMICULITE						
Loose granules		**100**	**0·065**	**15·4**		
Granules 5 to 10 mm diameter	dry	100	0·075	13·3		
	dry		0·090	11·1	100	20
	dry		0·135	7·4	250	20
Plastering		480	0·144	6·9	500	20
		640	0·20	5·0		
		800	0·260	3·9		
		960	0·303	3·3		
WALL AND CEILING BOARDS						
Diatomaceous board	conditioned	1200	0·23	4·4		
	conditioned 40%	830	0·14	7·1		
	wet	1355	0·32	3·1		
Plasterboard:						
Gypsum		**950**	**0·16**	**6·3**		
Perlite	conditioned	**800**	**0·18**	**5·6**		
Pulpboard, paper		600	0·07	14·3		
WATER						
at 20°C		1000	0·60	1·67		
at 40°C		990	0·63	1·59		
at 80°C		970	0·67	1·49		
Seawater at 20°C		1025	0·58	1·72		
WOOD CHIP BOARD						
Bonded with synthetic resin	conditioned	350	0·070	14·29		
	conditioned	500	0·100	10·00		
	conditioned	600	0·120	8·33		
	conditioned	**800**	**0·150**	**6·67**		
	conditioned	950	0·180	5·56		
Wood chips and rubber		1350	0·21	4·76		

Table A3.22—*continued*

Material			Thermal Properties			
Detail	Condition (where known)	Bulk Density (kg/m³)	λ $\left(\dfrac{W}{m\,K}\right)$	r $\left(\dfrac{m\,K}{W}\right)$	For face temperatures (°C)	
					Hot	Cold
WOOD WASTE BOARD Bonded with bitumen and cement		500	0·090	11·11		
WOOD WOOL BUILDING SLABS	conditioned	400	0·080	12·50		
	conditioned	**500**	**0·100**	**10·00**		
	conditioned	600	0·110	9·09		
	conditioned	700	0·120	8·33		
	conditioned	750	0·130	7·69		
		800	0·130	7·69		
	wet	480	0·130	7·69		
	wet	860	0·200	5·00		
WOOL Aluminium wool at 40°C	dry	30	0·09	11·11		
	dry	40	0·17	5·88	200	25
Sheep's wool		50	0·045	22·22		
Steel wool	dry	100	0·11	9·09	200	25
Wood wool, fluffy		40	0·040	25·00		

Notes:

* Conditioned to a constant weight at 20°C and 65% rh.

† Data printed in heavy type indicate representative values to be used in the absence of precise information.

Appendix 3: Moisture Content of Masonry Materials

While insulating materials in buildings are generally 'air-dry', i.e. in equilibrium with the internal environment, this is not true for masonry materials in external walls. Research has shown that typical moisture contents of inner leaves as well as outer leaves[3] of external twin-leaf masonry walls are above air-dry values, and thermal conductivities used for calculating U-values take account of the presence of moisture.

There are wide variations in practical moisture contents in occupied buildings depending on climate, type of masonry, workmanship, whether or not the wall is rendered, local exposure to rain which varies across the building, temperature gradient across the masonry which depends on internal temperature, disposition of insulation, wall thickness etc.

However, it is not feasible to take account of those factors, whose effects have not been delineated, and it is convenient in calculating U-values to adopt standard moisture contents typical of walls in heated buildings. Calculations are thus carried out on the same basis for any defined wall construction. Investigations have shown that a typical average moisture content of masonry exposed to the external climate – i.e. solid masonry or outer leaves of cavity walls without protective cladding – is 5 % by volume. This value is adopted as standard in the UK for all types of masonry, rendered or unrendered.

With masonry protected from rain, i.e. inner leaf masonry, or solid walls or outer leaves protected by cladding such as tile hanging or weather boarding, it has been found that the average moisture content of concrete blockwork is higher than that of brickwork, and standard moisture contents are taken as 3 % by volume for protected blockwork and 1 % by volume for protected brickwork. Standard moisture contents are set out in Table A3.2.

It is also convenient to adopt a standard factor to correct measured thermal conductivities to the standard moisture content. It has been found that the relationship between thermal conductivity and moisture content (as a percentage by volume) is similar for all materials and the relationship in Table A3.23 was proposed by Jakob[11] in 1949.

Table A3.23 gives factors to correct the thermal conductivity for dry materials to values appropriate to the moisture content.

Table A3.23. Correction factor for moisture content

Moisture content (%)	Correction factor
0·5	1·15
1·0	1·30
1·5	1·40
2·0	1·48
2·5	1·55
3·0	1·60
4·0	1·67
5·0	1·75
6·0	1·82
8·0	1·96
10·0	2·10
15·0	2·35
20·0	2·55
25·0	2·75

Jespersen[12] showed from a series of careful measurements on moist masonry materials that this relationship is broadly correct at moisture contents above 1% by volume, but at lower moisture contents there are considerable deviations between one material and another. Provided measurements are made with care, avoiding distillation of moisture etc., it seems desirable to use measurements made in the moisture content range 1–5 % by volume and to correct these to the standard moisture content. Measurement on dry materials could in some cases lead to errors in the correction factor.

The correction to standard moisture content is performed as follows:

(i) Divide the measured thermal conductivity by the factor appropriate to the moisture content of the specimen.

(ii) Multiply the result by the factor appropriate to the standard moisture content.

The values in Table A3.1 are derived from thermal conductivity measurements in this moisture range derived from research papers and sources judged to be reliable; they apply to the mean or best-fit curve through the measured values, and they are corrected to the standard moisture contents.

Results of other thermal conductivity measurements corrected to the appropriate standard moisture content are also acceptable provided the measurements are carried out in conformity with the recommendations in Appendix 4.

Appendix 4: Thermal Conductivity and Conductance Testing

With the increasing demand for thermal insulation and the subsequent development of new forms of insulants, guidance is required on appropriate methods of determining the thermal performance of these materials. In the UK, the recommended method of determining the thermal conductivity of materials is the use of either the guarded or unguarded hot plate apparatus as laid down in BS 874. This method, which is carried out on a comparatively small sample of the material, is considered suitable for the majority of available materials. However, the method requires considerable skill and expertise for the tests to be performed correctly, particularly in the preparation of the samples. The British Calibration Service (BCS) is now offering a monitoring service for laboratories which will ensure an independent check on the laboratories' capability to carry out tests to BS 874. It is, therefore, recommended that values of thermal conductivity, apart from the standardised values listed in this section, should only be accepted when based on tests carried out by a laboratory accredited by the BCS.

Thermal conductivity tests are only of use when the tests are carried out on samples of the material which are representative of the actual product. This is a problem of quality assurance which should be the subject of discussions between the supplier and the user. The use of appropriate BSI Kite-marked materials or similar schemes is recommended wherever possible. If there is no appropriate scheme available, the use of a mean value based on at least three test certificates, at least one of which should be for tests undertaken in the previous 12 months, is suggested. Where the material has a large density range, which is common with some masonry or concrete materials, the test certificates should normally be for samples within $100 kg/m^3$ of the maximum density offered and within the manufacturers' stated density range, for example, a material of maximum density of $1250 kg/m^3$ should have certified values lying in the range 1150 to $1250 kg/m^3$.

Other forms of thermal conductivity testing, using probes etc., are available. These are only suitable, because of their quickness etc., for routine quality control and are not considered suitable at the moment for precise determinations.

Thermal conductance testing, which is an attempt to determine the thermal performance of a complete or almost complete construction is also becoming more common. Unfortunately, there are no precise standards available in the UK for such methods, therefore great care should be taken before accepting values based on such tests. Multiple tests are, of course, necessary and checks on the repeatability of the apparatus should be made from time to time.

Conductance test data cannot be corrected to standard moisture content by the Jakob procedure. Conductance tests should therefore be performed at a minimum of three values of moisture content* spanning the standard moisture content, and the thermal conductance at this value may then be obtained by interpolation.

---

*The moisture content should be measured relative to the volume of the solid material within the block.

APPENDIX 5: Derivation of Admittance, Decrement Factor and Surface Factor

The temperature distribution in a homogeneous slab subject to one dimensional heat flow is given by the diffusion equation:

$$\frac{\partial^2 t}{\partial x^2} = \frac{\rho c}{\lambda} \frac{\partial t}{\partial \theta} \quad \dots \quad \dots \quad \dots \quad \text{A3.37}$$

where:

t = temperature   ..   ..   ..   °C

x = x-direction (perpendicular to surface of slab) ..   ..   m

ρ = density ..   ..   kg/m³

c = specific heat capacity   ..   ..   J/kg K

λ = thermal conductivity ..   ..   W/m K

θ = time   ..   ..   s

For finite slabs and for sinusoidal temperature variations the temperature and energy cycles can be linked by the use of matrix algebra[13]:

$$\begin{bmatrix} t_1 \\ q_1 \end{bmatrix} = \begin{bmatrix} m_1 & m_2 \\ m_3 & m_1 \end{bmatrix} \begin{bmatrix} t_2 \\ q_2 \end{bmatrix} \quad \dots \quad \dots \quad \text{A3.38}$$

where:

q = heat flow   ..   ..   W

For a slab of homogeneous material, the coefficients of the matrix are given by:

$$m_1 = \cosh(p + ip) \quad \dots \quad \dots \quad \text{A3.39}$$

$$m_2 = \frac{l \sinh(p + ip)}{\lambda(p + ip)} \quad \dots \quad \dots \quad \text{A3.40}$$

$$m_3 = \frac{\lambda(p + ip)\sinh(p + ip)}{l} \quad \dots \quad \text{A3.41}$$

and for a 24 hour cycle:

$$p = \left(\frac{\pi l^2 \rho c}{86400\lambda}\right)^{0.5} \quad \dots \quad \dots \quad \text{A3.42}$$

For an air gap, or a surface resistance between a layer and the air, where the diffusivity ($= \lambda/\rho c$) is high, the coefficients of the matrix are given by:

$$m_1 = 1 \quad .. \quad .. \quad .. \quad .. \quad \text{A3.43}$$

$$m_2 = R_a \text{ or } R_s \quad .. \quad .. \quad .. \quad \text{A3.44}$$

$$m_3 = 0 \quad .. \quad .. \quad .. \quad .. \quad \text{A3.45}$$

Clearly, for a composite wall, the matrices of each of the layers can be multiplied together to give the relation between inside and outside as:

$$\begin{bmatrix} t_i \\ q_i \end{bmatrix} = \begin{bmatrix} 1 & R_{si} \\ 0 & 1 \end{bmatrix} \begin{bmatrix} m_1 & m_2 \\ m_3 & m_1 \end{bmatrix} \begin{bmatrix} n_1 & n_2 \\ n_3 & n_1 \end{bmatrix} \cdots \begin{bmatrix} 1 & R_{so} \\ 0 & 1 \end{bmatrix} \begin{bmatrix} t_o \\ q_o \end{bmatrix}$$
$$\dots \quad \dots \quad \dots \quad \text{A3.46}$$

which can be written:

$$\begin{bmatrix} t_i \\ q_i \end{bmatrix} = \begin{bmatrix} M_1 & M_2 \\ M_3 & M_4 \end{bmatrix} \begin{bmatrix} t_o \\ q_o \end{bmatrix} \quad \dots \quad \dots \quad \text{A3.47}$$

Note that the components of this matrix will be complex numbers.

The non-steady state parameters are now derived as follows:

Admittance

$$Y_c = \frac{M_4}{M_2} \quad .. \quad .. \quad .. \quad .. \quad \text{A3.48}$$

$$Y = |Y_c| \quad .. \quad .. \quad .. \quad .. \quad \text{A3.49}$$

$$\omega = \frac{12}{\pi} \arctan\left(\frac{\text{Im}(Y_c)}{\text{Re}(Y_c)}\right) \quad .. \quad .. \quad \text{A3.50}$$

The arctangent should be evaluated in the range 0 to π radians thus ω is a time lead.

Decrement Factor

$$f_c = \frac{1}{UM_2} \quad .. \quad .. \quad .. \quad .. \quad \text{A3.51}$$

$$f = |f_c| \quad .. \quad .. \quad .. \quad .. \quad \text{A3.52}$$

$$\phi = \frac{12}{\pi} \arctan\left(\frac{\text{Im}(f_c)}{\text{Re}(f_c)}\right) \quad .. \quad .. \quad \text{A3.53}$$

The arctangent should be evaluated in the range $-\pi$ to 0 radians. Thus ϕ is a time lag.

Surface Factor

$$F_c = 1 - R_{si} Y_c \quad .. \quad .. \quad .. \quad \text{A3.54}$$

$$F = |F_c| \quad .. \quad .. \quad .. \quad .. \quad \text{A3.55}$$

$$\psi = \frac{12}{\pi} \arctan\left(\frac{\text{Im}(F_c)}{\text{Re}(F_c)}\right) \quad .. \quad .. \quad \text{A3.56}$$

As with the decrement factor, the arctangent should be evaluated in the range $-\pi$ to 0 radians, thus ψ is a time lag.

Internal Partitions

For internal partitions, the decrement factor is combined with the admittance and surface factor.

$$Y_{ci} = Y_c - Uf_c \quad .. \quad .. \quad .. \quad \text{A3.57}$$

$$= \frac{M_4 - 1}{M_2} \quad .. \quad .. \quad .. \quad \text{A3.58}$$

$$F_{ci} = 1 - R_{si} Y_{ci} \quad .. \quad .. \quad .. \quad \text{A3.59}$$

Equations A3.49, A3.50, A3.55, and A3.56 can then be used as before.

Example

Calculate the non-steady state properties of a 220 mm external brick wall.

The properties of brick are:

$\rho = 1700$ kg/m³;

$\lambda = 0.84$ W/m K;

$c = 800$ J/kg K.

The U-value is:

$$U = \frac{1}{0.12 + \frac{0.22}{0.84} + 0.06}$$

$$= 2.3 \text{ W/m}^2 \text{ K}.$$

From equation A3.42

$p = 1.688.$

For manual calculations, it is convenient to express cosh $(p + ip)$ and sinh $(p + ip)$ in terms of the functions $\sin p$, $\cos p$ and e^p which are available on most slide rules, pocket calculators and books of tables.

$$\cosh (p + ip) = \tfrac{1}{2}[(e^p + e^{-p}) \cos p + i(e^p - e^{-p}) \sin p] \qquad \qquad \qquad \qquad \qquad \text{A3.60}$$

$$\sinh (p + ip) = \tfrac{1}{2}[(e^p - e^{-p}) \cos p + i(e^p + e^{-p}) \sin p] \qquad \qquad \qquad \qquad \qquad \text{A3.61}$$

In the matrix, the coefficient m_1, is given by equation A3.60 while m_2 and m_3 are given by:

$$m_2 = \frac{l[(e^p - e^{-p}) \cos p + (e^p + e^{-p}) \sin p - i(e^p - e^{-p}) \cos p + i(e^p + e^{-p}) \sin p]}{4\lambda p} \qquad \qquad \qquad \text{A3.62}$$

$$m_3 = \frac{\lambda p[(e^p - e^{-p}) \cos p - (e^p + e^{-p}) \sin p + i(e^p - e^{-p}) \cos p + i(e^p + e^{-p}) \sin p]}{2l} \qquad \qquad \qquad \text{A3.63}$$

Which gives the matrix as:

$$\begin{bmatrix} -0\cdot33 + i2\cdot59 & 0\cdot19 + i0\cdot24 \\ -19\cdot9 + i15\cdot9 & -0\cdot33 + i2\cdot59 \end{bmatrix}$$

Performing the matrix multiplication from left to right (which corresponds to inside to outside):

$$\begin{bmatrix} 1 & 0\cdot12 \\ 0 & 1 \end{bmatrix} \times \begin{bmatrix} -0\cdot33 + i2\cdot59 & 0\cdot19 + i0\cdot24 \\ -19\cdot9 + i15\cdot9 & -0\cdot33 + i2\cdot59 \end{bmatrix} = \begin{bmatrix} -2\cdot72 + i4\cdot50 & 0\cdot150 + i0\cdot551 \\ -19\cdot9 + i15\cdot9 & -0\cdot33 + i2\cdot59 \end{bmatrix}$$

The second stage only requires the evaluation of the right-hand column of the product matrix as only M_2 and M_4 are required.

$$\begin{bmatrix} -2\cdot72 + i4\cdot50 & 0\cdot150 + i0\cdot551 \\ -19\cdot9 + i15\cdot9 & -0\cdot33 + i2\cdot59 \end{bmatrix} \begin{bmatrix} 1 & 0\cdot06 \\ 0 & 1 \end{bmatrix} = \begin{bmatrix} * & -0\cdot013 + i0\cdot821 \\ * & -1\cdot52 + i3\cdot54 \end{bmatrix}$$

From equation A3.48

$$Y_c = \frac{-1\cdot52 + i3\cdot54}{-0\cdot013 + i0\cdot821} = \frac{(-1\cdot52 + i3\cdot54)(-0\cdot013 - i0\cdot821)}{0\cdot013^2 + 0\cdot821^2} = 4\cdot35 + i1\cdot78$$

$$Y = 4\cdot70$$

$$\omega = 1\cdot48 \text{ h.}$$

From equation A3.51

$$f_c = \frac{1}{2\cdot3(-0\cdot013 + i0\cdot821)} = \frac{-(0\cdot013 + i0\cdot821)}{2\cdot3(0\cdot013^2 + 0\cdot821^2)} = -0\cdot0084 - i0\cdot530$$

$$f = 0\cdot53$$

$$\phi = -6\cdot0 \text{ h.}$$

From equation A3.54

$$F_c = 1 - 0\cdot12(4\cdot35 + i1\cdot78) = 0\cdot478 - i0\cdot214$$

$$F = 0\cdot52$$

$$\psi = -1\cdot6 \text{ h.}$$

REFERENCES

[1] MILBANK, N. O. and HARRINGTON-LYNN, J., 'Thermal Response and the Admittance Procedure', *BSE*, May 1974, **42**, 38–51.

[2] The Building Regulations 1985; HMSO.

[3] ARNOLD, P. J., 'Thermal Conductivity of Masonry Materials', BRE Current Paper CP 1/70, 1970, Building Research Establishment.

[4] IHVE Symposium, 'Environmental Temperature and the Calculation of Heat Losses and Gains', June 1973.

[5] ANDERSON, B. R., 'The Thermal Resistance of Airspaces in Building Constructions', *Building and Environment,* 1981, **16**, 35-39.

[6] BILLINGTON, N. S., 'Heat Loss through Solid Ground Floors', *JIHVE*, Nov. 1951, **19**, 351–372.

[7] MACEY, H. H., 'Heat Loss through a Solid Floor', *J. Inst. F.*, 1949, **22**, 369.

[8] DICK, J. B., 'The Fundamentals of Natural Ventilation of Houses', *JIHVE*, June 1950, **18**, 123–134.

[9] LOUDON, A. G., private communication.

[10] OWENS, P. G. T. and BARNETT, M., 'Reducing Glazing U-Values with Low Emissivity Coatings and Low Conductivity Gases', *BSE*, Feb. 1974, **41**, 250-252.

[11] JAKOB, M., 'Heat Transfer, Part 1', London, Chapman and Hall, 1949.

[12] JESPERSEN, H. B., 'Thermal Conductivity of Moist Materials and its Measurement', *JIHVE*, August 1953, **21**, 157–174.

[13] PIPES, L. A., 'Matrix Analysis of Heat Transfer Problems', *J. Franklin Inst.*, 1957, **623**, 195–206.

[14] GARRETT, K. W., 'An Assessment of the Calculation Methods to Determine the Thermal Performance of Slotted Building Blocks,' *B.S.E.R. & T.*, 1980, **1**, 24–30.

SECTION A4 AIR INFILTRATION AND NATURAL VENTILATION

Introduction .... *Page* A4—3

Notation .... A4—3

Calculation of Infiltration and Natural Ventilation .... A4—4

    Flow Through Openings .... A4—4

    Meteorological Data .... A4—5

    Pressures Acting on a Building .... A4—5

Prediction of Natural Ventilation and Infiltration Rates .... A4—6

    Natural Ventilation Rates .... A4—6

    Infiltration Rates for Design Purposes .... A4—8

    Example .... A4—12

Empirical Values for Air Infiltration .... A4—13

    Exposure .... A4—13

References .... A4—15

This edition of Section A4 first published: 1986

SECTION A4 AIR INFILTRATION AND NATURAL VENTILATION

INTRODUCTION

Infiltration is the fortuitous leakage of air through a building due to imperfections in the structure—mainly as cracks round doors, windows or infill panels or between cladding sheets and such other joints or perforations as may exist in the structure. It is closely dependent on the construction, materials, workmanship and condition of a building, factors normally outside the control of the building services engineer.

Natural ventilation is the air flow resulting from the designed provision of specified apertures such as openable windows, ventilators, shafts, etc. and can usually be controlled to some extent by the occupant. Infiltration, on the other hand, cannot be so controlled.

Both infiltration and natural ventilation are at the mercy of natural forces, and cannot be relied upon to provide a constant rate of air interchange under all conditions. In particular, infiltration may sometimes be far in excess of fresh air requirements whilst in other circumstances it may be grossly inadequate. Therefore, the designer must always check to determine whether infiltration alone will provide sufficient fresh air or if additional means of supply, either natural or mechanical, will be required.

In the interests of economy of design of the heating installation and of fuel conservation, the building designer should endeavour to reduce infiltration by making the structure as airtight as possible when all doors and windows are closed. Where air change rates are suggested in this Section, these apply to the average case and the designer's judgement will determine whether deviation from the given value is warranted.

The rate of air flow through a building depends upon the areas and resistances of the various apertures (both intentionally provided and fortuitous) and the pressure difference across the building. The pressure differential may be caused either by wind, in which case air will enter through cracks and openings in the leeward side, or by differences in density of the air due to the indoor/outdoor temperature differences (commonly referred to as the 'stack effect'). In the latter case, air will move from low level inlets to high level outlets in a heated building or in the opposite direction if the air in the building is cooler than outside. Other factors which may influence the pressure distribution are the presence of atria, stairwells, lift shafts, flue shafts, ventilators and mechanical ventilation and exhaust systems.

NOTATION

$\dot{A}$	= area of opening		m^2
A_B	= equivalent area for ventilation by stack effect only		m^2
A_W	= equivalent area for ventilation by wind only		m^2
A_{rep}	= representative area		m^2
C_d	= discharge coefficient		
C_i	= window infiltration coefficient		litre/s m
C_p	= pressure coefficient		
F	= factor relating flow rate to applied pressure difference		
$J(\phi)$	= function of angle of window opening		
K_s	= parameter relating wind speed to nature of terrain		
L	= length of opening window joint (crack length)		m
L_r	= crack length per unit area of glazed facade		m/m^2
N	= air change rate		h^{-1}
Q	= flow rate through opening		m^3/s
Q_B	= volume flow rate due to stack effect only		m^3/s
Q_T	= total volume flow rate		m^3/s
Q_W	= volume flow rate due to wind only		m^3/s
Q_r	= room infiltration rate		litre/s
Q_t	= total infiltration rate		litre/s
Q_v	= volume flow rate		litre/s
Q'_b	= basic infiltration rate per unit length of window opening joint		litre/s m
Q'_u	= uncorrected infiltration rate per unit length of window opening joint		litre/s m
a	= exponent relating wind speed to height above ground		
a, b	= plan dimensions of building (glazed facades)		m

c	=	specific heat capacity of air	..	J/kg K	t_1, t_2	=	temperature of air column 1, 2 etc.	°C
f_1	=	correction factor for geographical location			t_i	=	mean inside air temperature ..	°C
f_2	=	correction factor for internal resistance			t_o	=	outside ambient temperature ..	°C
					$\bar{t}$	=	mean of temperature t_i and t_o ..	°C
g	=	gravitational constant (= 9.81)..		m/s²	u	=	mean wind speed	m/s
h	=	height of building		m	u_m	=	mean wind speed at 10m height in open country	m/s
h_a	=	height of air column		m				
h_o	=	height of opening		m	u_r	=	mean wind speed at height equal to the building height ..	m/s
h_r	=	height of room above ground level		m	x	=	increase in infiltration rate above average	%
n	=	exponent relating volume flow rate to applied pressure difference			z	=	height above ground	m
					ΔC_p	=	difference in pressure coefficient	
p	=	mean pressure at any point on the surface of a building ..		Pa	Δp	=	applied pressure difference ..	Pa
					Δt	=	difference between t_i and t_o ..	°C
p_o	=	static pressure in undisturbed wind		Pa	ε	=	ratio of areas of openings	
					ρ	=	density of air	kg/m³
q_v	=	ventilation allowance per unit volume of room		W/K m³	ϕ	=	angle of window opening ..	degree

CALCULATION OF INFILTRATION AND NATURAL VENTILATION

Flow through Openings

The magnitude of the flow through an opening due to an applied pressure difference depends upon the dimensions and shape of the opening and on the Reynolds Number for the flow. In general terms this relationship may be written[1] as:

$$Q = A F \left(\frac{2\Delta p}{\rho}\right)^{0.5} \quad .. \quad .. \quad .. \quad .. \quad \text{A4.1}$$

where:

Q	=	flow rate through opening..	..	m³/s
A	=	area of opening	..	m²
Δp	=	applied pressure difference	..	Pa
ρ	=	density of air..	..	kg/m³
F	=	factor relating flow rate to applied pressure difference		

The factor, F, depends upon the size, shape and nature of the opening and the value of the Reynolds number appropriate to the flow through the opening.

For openings with a typical cross-sectional dimension greater than about 10mm (i.e. most purpose built ventilators including air-bricks, open windows and doors etc.) F may be regarded as constant for the range of pressure differences which are normally expected, and is conventionally termed the discharge coefficient, C_d. For such openings, equation A4.1 may be written in the form:

$$Q = A C_d \left(\frac{2\Delta p}{\rho}\right)^{0.5} \quad .. \quad .. \quad .. \quad .. \quad \text{A4.2}$$

where:

C_d	=	discharge coefficient

The theoretical value of C_d for a sharp-edged opening is 0.61 and it is common practice to refer other openings, for which the airflow is governed by the square root of the pressure difference, to this value. Measurements of flow rate and applied pressure difference are used to calculate an equivalent area assuming a discharge coefficient of 0.61. This approach is particularly useful where the nature of the opening makes the determination of its geometrical area difficult.

For small openings, such as the cracks around openable windows, the form of the factor F is much more complex[2]. However, for most practical applications equation A4.1 may be replaced by a simple power law expression of the following form:

$$Q_v = L C_i (\Delta p)^n \quad .. \quad .. \quad .. \quad .. \quad \text{A4.3}$$

where:

Q_v	=	volume flow rate through small opening		litre/s
L	=	length of opening (crack length)		m
C_i	=	infiltration coefficient		litre/s m
n	=	exponent relating volume flow rate to applied pressure difference		

The infiltration coefficient is defined as the volume flow rate of air per unit length of opening at an applied pressure difference of 1 Pa. The value of the exponent generally lies in the range 0.6 to 0.7.

Meteorological Data

As noted earlier, the prime agencies for infiltration and natural ventilation are the wind and the differences between internal and external air temperatures. The way in which these act will be discussed but it is useful to note certain characteristics relevant to the choice of design value. Section A2 of the *Guide* gives detailed information on external air temperatures and wind speeds and directions for the UK.

Wind speed varies with height. Section A2 gives the following expression which relates this variation to the nature of the terrain across which the wind is passing:

$$u = u_m K_s z^a \quad \ldots \quad \ldots \quad \ldots \quad \text{A4.4}$$

where:

u = mean wind speed at height z ..   m/s

u_m = mean wind speed at 10m height in open country ..   ..   m/s

z = height above ground ..   ..   m

K_s = parameter relating wind speed to nature of terrain

a = exponent relating wind speed to height above ground

Values of K_s and a for four types of terrain are given in Table A4.1.

Table A4.1 Values[3] of parameters K_s and a.

Terrain	K_s	a
Open flat country	0.68	0.17
Country with scattered windbreaks	0.52	0.20
Urban	0.35	0.25
City	0.21	0.33

Wind speed also varies with time and for any location recorded meteorological data may be analysed to give the frequency of occurrence for which particular wind speeds are exceeded. These data are valuable for design purposes such as the calculation of design heat load where a wind speed exceeded for a small proportion of the time, say 10%, may be relevant. Alternatively, for summertime cooling calculations, it may be helpful to know the wind speed likely to prevail for a high proportion, say 80%, of the summer months. Section A2 contains suitable data to enable the calculation of the frequency of occurrence of particular wind speeds in the UK.

Pressures Acting on a Building

Wind

Provided that a building has relatively sharp corners the pattern of air flow around the building due to wind from a particular direction is independent of wind speed. Therefore, the pressure generated at any point on the surface is dependent only upon the dynamic pressure of the upstream wind, defined by the expression ($\frac{1}{2} \rho u_r^2$). This represents the wind speed at a height equal to that of the building, for the appropriate terrain as defined by equation A4.4. Thus the mean pressure, p, at any point on the surface of a building may be defined in the terms of a dimensionless pressure coefficient, C_p, given by:

$$C_p = \frac{(p - p_o)}{\frac{1}{2} \rho u_r^2} \quad \ldots \quad \ldots \quad \ldots \quad \ldots \quad \text{A4.5}$$

where:

C_p = pressure coefficient

p = mean pressure at any point on surface of building ..   ..   ..   Pa

p_o = static pressure in undisturbed wind   Pa

u_r = mean wind speed at height equal to building height ..   ..   ..   m/s

Few data exist on pressure coefficients for buildings of differing form and degrees of shelter. This is gradually being remedied, primarily by wind tunnel tests. For buildings of simple form which stand alone, or are much higher than surrounding buildings and obstructions, BS5925[3] gives average surface pressure coefficients. Typically, the difference in pressure coefficient, ΔC_p, between windward and leeward faces is about 1.0. However, for buildings in sheltered locations the difference may be as low as 0.1[4].

The above deals with mean pressures. In practice, surface pressures fluctuate considerably about the mean due to turbulence. However, this is only important in cases where the mean pressure across an opening (or building) is small. In such cases, the flow direction may alternate, giving rise to a higher rate of exchange of air than expected. At present, only limited information is available on this effect but in the absence of better data this may be taken into account by using a minimum value for C_p of 0.2[1].

Stack Effect

Air density varies approximately as the inverse of absolute temperature. The weight of two vertical columns of air at different temperatures separated by a vertical surface will differ and a pressure difference will be created across the intervening surface. When openings exist in the surface the pressure difference will cause a flow of air to occur. The maximum pressure difference, Δp, which may be created by two columns of height h_a, is given by:

$$\Delta p = 3462 \, h_a \left[\frac{1}{(t_1 + 273)} - \frac{1}{(t_2 + 273)} \right] \quad .. \quad \text{A4.6}$$

where:

Δp = pressure difference .. .. .. Pa

h_a = height of air column .. .. m

t_1, t_2 = temperature of air column 1, 2 etc. °C

For the range of temperatures found in practice, equation A4.6 approximates to:

$$\Delta p = 0.043\, h_a\, (t_2 - t_1) \quad .. \quad .. \quad .. \quad \text{A4.7}$$

The values in Table A4.2 have been calculated from this expression for a range of temperature differences and variations in height.

Table A4.2 Pressure differences due to stack effect.

$(t_2 - t_1)$ /(°C)	Pressure difference (P_a) for the stated vertical difference in height (m)				
	5	10	20	50	100
−10	−2·2	−4·3	−8·6	−22	−43
0	0	0	0	0	0
10	2·2	4·3	8·6	22	43
20	4·3	8·6	17·0	43	86

PREDICTION OF NATURAL VENTILATION AND INFILTRATION RATES

General

In principle, the airflow through a building and the ventilation rates of individual spaces within a building can be determined for a given set of weather conditions (i.e. wind speed, wind direction and external air temperature) if the following are known:

(a) the position and characteristics of all openings through which flow can occur,

(b) the detailed distribution of surface mean pressure coefficients for the wind direction under consideration,

(c) the internal air temperatures.

In practice, because equation A4.1 and its simplified forms are non-linear and because of the number of flow paths likely to be present in any but the simplest building, solutions can only be obtained by computer methods. A number of programs, varying in degree of sophistication, for predicting natural ventilation and infiltration are available and some preliminary trials to validate these against measured data from full-scale buildings have been undertaken[5]. However, the predictions of such programs are only as accurate as the input data, as set out above and these are rarely known for existing buildings, far less for those at the design stage.

However, the magnitude and characteristics of natural ventilation and infiltration can be demonstrated by examining simplified situations. This is dealt with in the following sections.

Natural Ventilation Rates

Figure A4.1 represents a section through a simple two-dimensional building in which internal divisions are ignored and the openings are as shown. The openings are considered to be large, hence the flow through them is governed by equation A4.2. The equivalent areas are indicated and these may be taken as the minimum cross-sectional area perpendicular to the flow for large openings such as windows and doors. Table A4.3[1] gives experimentally determined values for a number of common types of smaller, purpose-built openings. Table A4.4[1,3] shows schematically the expected air flow patterns for different conditions and gives the formulae from which the natural ventilation rate can be calculated.

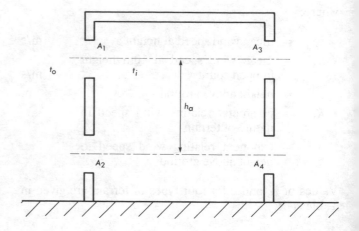

Fig. A4.1 Section through simple building – internal divisions ignored; see Table A4.4.

Table A4.3 Equivalent areas of ventilation openings.

Type	Overall size /mm	Equivalent area /mm
Air brick, terra cotta, square holes	225 × 75	1 400
Air brick, terra cotta, square holes	225 × 150	4 300
Air brick, terra cotta, square holes	225 × 225	6 400
Air brick, terra cotta, louvres	225 × 150	2 000
Air brick, terra cotta, louvres	225 × 225	4 300
Air brick, cast iron, square holes	225 × 75	7 200
Air brick, cast iron, square holes	225 × 150	12 700
Air brick, cast iron, square holes	225 × 225	19 600
Air brick, cast iron, louvres	225 × 75	3 100
Air brick, cast iron, louvres	225 × 150	11 300
Air brick, cast iron, louvres	225 × 225	19 200
Typical internal louvres grille	225 × 75	2 400
Typical internal louvres grille	225 × 150	7 200
Typical internal louvres grille	225 × 225	10 700

Table A.4.4 Cross ventilation of simple building.

Conditions	Schematic	Formula
(a) Wind only		$$Q_W = C_d A_W u_r (\Delta C_p)^{0.5}$$ $$\frac{1}{A_W^2} = \frac{1}{(A_1 + A_2)^2} + \frac{1}{(A_3 + A_4)^2}$$
(b) Temperature difference only		$$Q_B = C_d A_B \left(\frac{2\,\Delta t\, h_a\, g}{(\bar{t} + 273)}\right)^{0.5}$$ $$\frac{1}{A_B^2} = \frac{1}{(A_1 + A_3)^2} + \frac{1}{(A_2 + A_4)^2}$$
(c) Wind and temperature difference together		$Q_T = Q_B$ for: $$\frac{u}{\sqrt{\Delta t}} < 0.26\left(\frac{A_B}{A_W}\right)\left(\frac{h_a}{\Delta C_p}\right)^{0.5}$$ $Q_T = Q_W$ for: $$\frac{u}{\sqrt{\Delta t}} > 0.26\left(\frac{A_B}{A_W}\right)\left(\frac{h_a}{\Delta C_p}\right)^{0.5}$$

The formulae given in Tables A4.4 and A4.5 illustrate a number of general characteristics of natural ventilation, as follows:

(a) The effective area of a number of openings combined in parallel, across which the same pressure difference is applied, can be obtained by simple addition.

(b) The effective area of a number of openings combined in series, across which the same pressure difference is applied, can be obtained by adding the inverse squares and taking the inverse of the square root of the total.

(c) When wind is the dominating mechanism the ventilation rate is proportional to wind speed and to the square root of the difference in pressure coefficient. Thus, although ΔC_p may cover a range of 10:1, this implies a range of only about 3:1 in the resulting ventilation rates.

(d) When stack effect is the dominating mechanism the ventilation rate is proportional to the square root of both temperature difference and height between upper and lower openings.

When wind and stack effects are of the same order of magnitude their interaction is complicated. However, to a first approximation, for the simple case illustrated, the actual rate may be considered equal to the larger of the rates for the two alternative approaches, taken separately. This is shown in Table A4.4 (c).

Whereas Table A4.4 deals with a situation in which cross ventilation is uninhibited by internal partitions, Table A4.5 deals with the opposite case, in which there is no cross ventilation and all air exchange must take place across openings in one wall. This is typical of the summertime situation for offices or classrooms adjoining a central corridor, the doors to which are kept closed.

Measurements[6] have shown that the magnitude of the resulting 'single-sided' ventilation, while smaller than cross ventilation with similar areas of opening under comparable conditions, can be large enough to contribute to natural cooling with normally sized windows. Table A4.5 gives formulae which enable ventilation rates to be calculated for wind and stack effect. It is suggested that calculations are carried out using both formulae and the larger value taken. The formula for wind represents a minimum which will be enhanced up to threefold for certain wind directions.

Table A.4.5 Internal spaces with openings on one wall only.

Conditions	Schematic	Formula
(a) Due to wind		$Q = 0.025\,A\,u_r$
(b) Due to temperature difference — two openings	t_o A_1 t_i h_a A_2	$Q = C_d(A_1 + A_2)\left(\dfrac{\sqrt{2}\,.\,\varepsilon}{(1+\varepsilon)\,(1+\varepsilon^2)^{0.5}}\right)\left(\dfrac{\Delta t\,h_a\,g}{(\bar{t}+273)}\right)^{0.5}$ $\varepsilon = \dfrac{A_1}{A_2}$
(c) Due to temperature difference — one opening	t_o t_i A h_o	$Q = C_d\dfrac{A}{3}\left(\dfrac{\Delta t\,h_o\,g}{(\bar{t}+273)}\right)^{0.5}$ If opening light is present: $Q = C_d\dfrac{A}{3}\mathrm{J}(\phi)\left(\dfrac{\Delta t\,h_o\,g}{(\bar{t}+273)}\right)^{0.5}$ Where $\mathrm{J}(\phi)$ is given by Fig. A4.2.

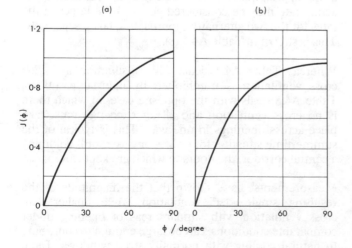

Fig. A4.2 Variation of $\mathrm{J}(\phi)$ with angle of opening for: (a) side-mounted casement windows, (b) centre-pivoted windows.

Infiltration Rates for Design Purposes

Introduction

For design purposes the following procedure[7] may be used where the building layout and window leakage characteristics are known. If these data are not available empirical values may be used, such as those tabulated later in this Section.

Infiltration Chart

The likely infiltration rate in a rectangular building may be determined by using the infiltration chart, Figure A4.3, which provides the basis of a simple technique for estimating infiltration from a knowledge of wind speed, building height, location and window characteristics.

The chart has been constructed on the basis of the following assumptions:

(i) The difference in pressure coefficient across the building is 1.1.

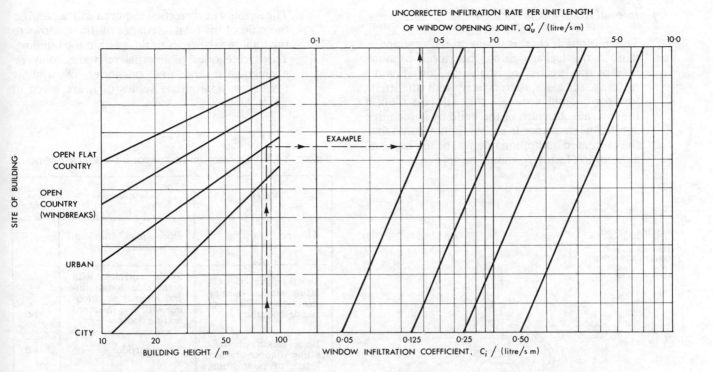

Fig. A4.3   Infiltration chart.

(*ii*)   The wind speed is that exceeded for 10% of the time.

(*iii*)   Flow through window cracks is of the form given in equation A4.3.

(*iv*)   The exponent, n, for flow through window cracks is 0.63.

(*v*)   The geographical location is assumed to give a 50% wind speed of 4 m/s.

(*vi*)   The window leakage characteristics are assumed to be identical on both sides of the building.

The sequence for using the chart is as follows:

(*a*)   Enter the building height on the left-hand horizontal axis.

(*b*)   Plot a line vertically until it intersects with the sloping line appropriate to the general terrain in which the building is situated.

(*c*)   Plot a line horizontally until it intersects with the sloping line on the right-hand section of the chart which is appropriate to the type of window installed.

(*d*)   Plot a line vertically until it intersects with the horizontal axis and read off the infiltration rate per unit length of opening window joint.

The range of window infiltration coefficients given in the chart should cover the wide range found in practice and enable interpolation where specific values are known. Table A4.6 lists upper limit values for different types of metal framed windows. In general a pessimistic estimate of window infiltration coefficient should be made to allow for infiltration through other small gaps in the building fabric.

Table A4.6   Air infiltration through windows.

Window type	Window infiltration coefficient for pressure difference of 1Pa, C_i / (litre/s m)
Horizontally or vertically pivoted—weather stripped	0·05
Horizontally or vertically pivoted—non-weather stripped	0·25
Horizontally or vertically sliding—weather stripped	0·125
Horizontally or vertically sliding—non-weather stripped	0·25

Where appropriate, other more specific criteria may be used in place of Table A4.6 such as those defined in BS6375[8].

Correction Factors

To determine an infiltration rate appropriate to a particular building it may be necessary to apply the following corrections to the rate obtained from Fig. A4.3.

(*a*)   *Geographical Location*

In Figure A4.3 the geographical location is assumed to give a 50% wind speed of 4 m/s. The 50% wind speed for any chosen location may be found from Fig. A4.4, and where this differs from 4 m/s a correction factor, f_1, may be determined from Table A4.7.

(b) *Internal Resistance to Air Flow*

The infiltration chart is based on the assumption that, in the leakage paths, the closed windows present the greatest resistance to flow. For the majority of cases, particularly with the trend towards open-plan design, this will be so, but if the internal structure of the building is such that substantial resistance to air flow is introduced then the estimated infiltration rate will be too high and a correction factor, f_2, should be applied.

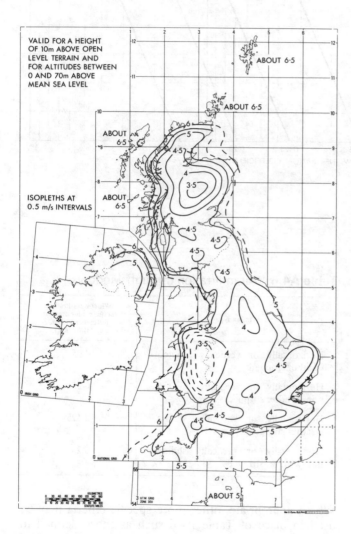

VALID FOR A HEIGHT OF 10m ABOVE OPEN LEVEL TERRAIN AND FOR ALTITUDES BETWEEN 0 AND 70m ABOVE MEAN SEA LEVEL

ISOPLETHS AT 0.5 m/s INTERVALS

Fig. A4.4 Isopleths of hourly mean wind speed exceeded for 50% of the time in the UK.

Table A4.7 Correction factor for geographical location.

Wind speed exceeded for 50% of time /(m/s)	Correction factor, f_1	
	Sheltered location (inland)	Exposed location (coastal)
3.5	0.85	0.79
4.0	1.0	0.94
4.5	1.16	1.09
5.0	1.32	1.25
5.5	1.49	1.40
6.0	1.67	1.57
6.5	1.84	1.73

The amount of correction required will depend on the ratio of the total resistance of the windows to the total resistance to air flow within the building. Three categories of internal resistance may be distinguished and five categories of window resistance; appropriate values of f_2 are given in Table A4.8.

Table A4.8 Correction factor for internal resistance.

Window type	Internal structure	Correction factor (f_2)
All types	Open plan (no full partitioning)	1·0
Short length of well-fitting window opening joint (say, 20% of facade openable)	Single corridor with many side doors: liberal internal partitioning with few interconnecting doors	1·0
Long length of well-fitting window or short length of poor fitting window joint (say, 20 to 40% of facade openable)	Single corridor	1·0
	Liberal partitioning	0·8
Long length of poor-fitting window joint (say, 40 to 50% of facade openable)	Single corridor	0·8
	Liberal partitioning	0·65
Very long length of poor-fitting window joint (say, >50% of facade openable)	Single corridor	0·65
	Liberal partitioning	0·4

Basic Infiltration Rates

The basic infiltration rate is the maximum likely to occur at a given wind speed, whatever its direction and is determined from the following:

$$Q'_b = Q'_u f_1 f_2 \qquad \qquad \qquad \qquad \text{A4.8}$$

where:

Q'_b = basic infiltration rate per unit length of window opening joint .. litre/s m

Q'_u = uncorrected infiltration rate per unit length of window opening joint .. .. litre/s m

f_1 = correction factor for geographical location

f_2 = correction factor for internal resistance

Buoyancy forces (stack effect) have little effect on the total infiltration into a multi-storey building under design wind conditions, except in the unlikely event that there are vertical shafts or stairwells with unrestricted access to every floor. The rates are average values taken over the whole height of the building. Therefore, it is necessary to consider how the basic infiltration rate is to be utilized in order to determine:

(i) the room infiltration, hence the size of the room appliance,

(ii) the total infiltration, hence the size of the central boiler plant.

Room Infiltration

The infiltration into an individual room with windows on one external wall only is calculated by multiplying the basic infiltration rate by the crack length for the room, thus:

$$Q_r = Q'_b L \quad .. \quad .. \quad .. \quad .. \quad \text{A4.9}$$

where:

Q_r = room infiltration rate .. .. litre/s

L = crack length .. .. m

In the case of corner rooms, with openable windows on two adjacent walls, the infiltration rate will be increased to 1.5 times that calculated for a room with windows on one face only.

Adjustments should be made to allow for stack effect and this depends on the height of the room above ground level. Although buoyance forces do not normally affect the total flow through the building, they may affect the air distribution between floors (except where each floor is sealed off from the others). Thus in winter, the infiltration rate for the lower floors will be greater than the average value and less than the average for the topmost floors.

In summer this situation may be reversed. The maximum deviations from the average values are given in Table A4.9 for buildings of five, ten or twenty storeys, with corridor doors separating each floor level from the stairwell.

Table A4.9 Deviation from average infiltration rates due to wind and stack effect.

Condition	Building storeys	Percentage increase in infiltration above average (x)	Level of maximum ventilation
Wind acting alone	5 10 20	3 6 8	Topmost floor
9 m/s wind plus stack effect (20°C heating season)	5 10 20	3 10 20	Lowest floor

Thus in a building of twenty floors, the basic infiltration rate in winter should be increased by 20% for the ground floor, the percentage allowance, x, decreasing linearly to zero at mid-height. In order to ensure that maximum infiltration rates are determined for design purposes, no reduction in infiltration rate due to stack effect should be allowed in the top half of the building. Thus:

(a) For $h_r < \frac{1}{2}h$:

$$Q_r = Q'_b L \left[1 + \frac{x}{100} \left(1 - \frac{2\,h_r}{h} \right) \right] \quad .. \quad \text{A4.10}$$

where:

x = increase in infiltration rate above average value .. %

h_r = height of room above ground level .. .. m

h = overall height of building .. m

(b) For $h_r \geq \frac{1}{2}h$:

$$Q_r = Q'_b L \quad .. \quad .. \quad .. \quad .. \quad \text{A4.11}$$

It will be noted that the calculated rates (adjusted as necessary) are the probable maxima and therefore represent the air-change due to infiltration with which the room heating appliance must cope.

The procedure outlined applies to any tall building. In the case of blocks of flats with internal staircase and lifts, the internal resistance to air flow between room and corridor will usually be high so that the correction factor f_2 (see Table A4.8) will have values between 0.4 and 0.65. The lower value applies to flats having large or ill-fitting windows and the higher value to flats having windows of normal size or better quality.

Where the access to each flat is open to the outside air (e.g. via balconies or open lift halls) no allowances should be made for stack effect and values of x (see Table A4.9) should be chosen to take account of wind only.

Total Infiltration

At any one time, outside air enters the windward rooms only, and imposes a heating or cooling load upon them. The corresponding volume of air which must leave the building by passing through the leeward rooms will already be at room temperature and will add nothing to the total heat load of the building (assuming that all rooms are heated or cooled to the same temperature).

Thus, the total load at a given moment, heating or cooling, will not equal the sum of the maximum infiltration loads expected in each room. Usually this sum will be between two and three times the maximum total infiltration load, and it is this latter quantity which is relevant to the sizing of the central boiler plant.

The total infiltration may be determined as follows:

$$Q_t = Q'_b L_r A_{rep} \quad .. \quad .. \quad .. \quad .. \quad \text{A4.12}$$

where:

Q_t = total infiltration rate .. .. litre/s

Q'_b = basic infiltration rate .. .. litre/s m

L_r = crack length per unit area of glazed facade.. .. .. m/m^2

A_{rep} = representative area .. .. .. m^2

The crack length per unit area of glazing is given by:

$$L_r = \frac{\Sigma L}{2(a + b)\,h} \quad .. \quad .. \quad .. \quad .. \quad \text{A4.13}$$

where:

ΣL = total crack length for building ..   m

a, b = plan dimensions of building (glazed facades) .. ..   m

h = height of building .. .. ..   m

The representative area is given by:

$$A_{rep} = (a^2 + b^2)^{0.5}\,h \quad .. \quad .. \quad .. \quad .. \quad \text{A4.14}$$

The representative area may be thought of as the area through which the air passes from one side of the building to the other, and this depends on the number of walls in which openable windows are located, see Fig. A4.5.

For a building with sealed end walls (usually a long rectangular building) the representative area is the area of one of the glazed faces. In the case of a building with openable glazing on all four sides, the representative area is that of the vertical diagonal plane; this makes allowances for the increased overall infiltration with wind approaching at an angle other than perpendicular to one of the building faces.

The total rate of infiltration so derived will be the maximum expected at the design outdoor conditions and this value may be used in the calculation of heating load imposed on the central boiler.

For convenience, Table A4.10 gives values of the representative area for various building configurations.

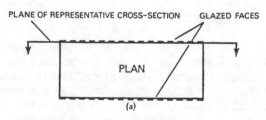

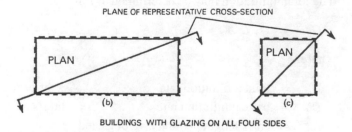

Fig. A4.5 Representative cross-sections.

Table A4.10 Representative areas.

$\dfrac{a}{b}$	$\dfrac{(a^2 + b^2)^{0.5}}{2(a + b)}$	A_{rep}	See figure
Any value if end walls are unglazed	0·5	ah	A4.5a
With glazing on all facades:			
10	0·45	$10bh$	
4	0·41	$4·1bh$	A4.5b
2	0·37	$2·2bh$	
1	0·35	$1·4bh$	A4.5c

Example

Find the total rate of infiltration and the infiltration in individual rooms for the purposes of sizing the central boiler plant and the room appliances in a twenty-storey rectangular plan building of 50m × 20m × 85m high, located in an urban area in central England. The building incorporates 5m × 5m × 3m high offices around its periphery and a central open-plan area at each floor level. Metal, horizontally-pivoted windows are fitted on all four sides of the building such that the length of opening joint (weather stripped) per unit area of glazing is 1.5m/m².

From the infiltration chart (Fig. A4.3) the mean pressure difference is determined for the building height of 85m (indicated by broken line on chart). The horizontal line is then traced until it crosses the line for the appropriate window infiltration coefficient, in this case, 0.05 litre/s m (see Table A4.6). A vertical line is projected from the point of intersection to the right-hand scale giving an uncorrected infiltration rate per metre of window-opening joint of 0.39 litre/s m.

This value is multiplied by 0.8 to correct for internal resistance, assuming that each office has a single door leading to the central area (see Table A4.8). Thus the basic average infiltration rate per unit length of opening window joint becomes:

$$Q'_b = 0.39 \times 1.0 \times 0.8 \qquad = 0.31 \text{ litre/s m}$$

(a) *Individual Rooms*

Multiplying Q'_b by the length of window-opening joint in the external wall of each office gives the average rate of infiltration for that office.

Thus infiltration rate for each room is:

$$Q_r = 0.31 \times 1.5\,(5 \times 3) \qquad = 7.0 \text{ litre/s}$$

The infiltration rate should be adjusted for height of the room above ground level using Table A4.9. This shows that at the lowest floor the ventilation is 20% above average, the adjustment decreasing linearly to mid-height and zero thereafter.

For convenience, several floors may be grouped together, taking the adjustment in each group as equal to that for the lowest floor of the group, as shown in Table A4.11.

Table A4.11   Adjustments for example building.

Floor level	Addition	Infiltration rate (litre/s)	
		Normal office	Corner office (+50%)
Ground to 3rd ..	+20%	8·4	12·6
4th to 7th ..	+12%	7·8	11·7
8th to 9th ..	+ 4%	7·3	11·0
10th to 19th ..	+ 0%	7·0	10·5

(b)   *Total Infiltration*

This is given by equation A4.12, in which the representative area is the diagonal vertical cross-sectional area.

Thus:

$$Q_t = Q'_b L_r A_{rep}$$
$$= 0.31 \times 1.5 \times 85 \times (50^2 + 20^2)^{0.5}$$
$$= 2130 \text{ litre/s}$$

This total infiltration rate would be used in the determination of the overall capacity of the central heating plant, whereas the infiltration rates calculated for the individual offices would be used for sizing the heat appliances in each room.

In this case, summation of the infiltration rates in each office gives a total of $(24 \times 20 \times 7) = 3360$ litre/s, which is nearly twice the total to be used for boiler capacity allowance. However, the natural infiltration into each office, 7.0 litre/s, is more than adequate to meet the fresh air requirements for a single occupant (5 to 6 litre/s). This rate would be increased considerably by opening doors and/or windows or if doors are in frequent use.

EMPIRICAL VALUES FOR AIR INFILTRATION

Tables A4.12 and 13 give empirical values of the infiltration which may be expected in buildings of typical construction in normal use in winter. They are not necessarily coincident with the fresh air requirement (see Section A1). The infiltration is expressed in two ways; as an air infiltration rate and as a ventilation allowance. The former is for use when it is desired to compare the natural infiltration with the required ventilation and the latter can be used directly in heat loss calculations.

The ventilation allowance has been obtained thus:

$$q_v = \frac{c \rho N}{3600} \quad .. \quad .. \quad .. \quad .. \quad .. \quad \text{A4.15}$$

where:

q_v	=	ventilation allowance per unit volume of room	W/K m³
c	=	specific heat capacity of air ..	J/kg K
N	=	air change rate	h⁻¹
ρ	=	density of air..	kg/m³

At room temperatures; $c \rho /3600 \approx \frac{1}{3}$.

Hence, for practical purposes; $q_v = \frac{1}{3} N$.

During periods when the building is unoccupied, the infiltration rate and ventilation allowance can be taken as half that obtaining in normal use.

The values in Table A4.12 are rates applicable to single rooms or spaces, and are appropriate to the estimation of room heat loads. As before, the load on the central plant will be about half the total of those for the individual rooms, except in some special cases, where all the rooms have at least two opposite external walls with windows and doors.

Exposure

The air infiltration rates and the ventilation allowances given in Table A4.12 are considered adequate to meet the average case. However, in view of the many variables, they may need to be adjusted according to local conditions of exposure. In this context*, the following definitions may be used:

Sheltered:	Up to third floor of buildings in city centres.
Normal:	Most suburban and country premises: fourth to eighth floors of buildings in city centres.
Severely exposed:	Buildings on the coasts or exposed on hill sites: floors above the fifth of buildings in suburban or country districts: floors above the ninth of buildings in city centres.

The tabulated infiltration rates are based on normal exposure and on an average ratio (25%) of openable areas (windows and doors) to external wall area. If the ratio much exceeds 25% in one external wall only, the infiltration rate should be increased by one-quarter; if in two or more walls, an increase of one half should be allowed. On severely exposed sites a 50% increase should be allowed, and on sheltered sites the infiltration may be reduced by 33%.

---

*The empirical definitions quoted here should not be confused with the more precise data included in Fig. A4.3.

The air change rate in rooms in tall buildings may be increased above the values given by the direct action of the wind and by stack effect. The design of tall buildings should include barriers against vertical air movement through stairwells and shafts to minimize stack effect. If this is not done, the balance of internal temperatures can be seriously upset.

Where warm air is supplied mechanically for ventilation, rates of infiltration applicable to a closed building (i.e. half the tabulated values) should be used for calculating the room heat requirements, so that room temperatures can be maintained, if required, when the mechanical ventilation system is not operating. However, the warm air requirement must be included in the total load on the central plant.

Table A4.12 Empirical values for air infiltration and ventilation allowance for buildings on normal sites in winter, (These values should be adjusted for local conditions of exposure.)

Type of building	Air infiltration rate (h^{-1})	Ventilation allowance ($W/m^3 K$)
Art galleries and museums	1	0·33
Assembly halls, lecture halls	½	0·17
Banking halls:		
Large (height > 4m)	1	0·33
Small (height < 4m)	1½	0·50
Bars	1	0·33
Canteens and dining rooms	1	0·33
Churches and chapels:		
Up to 7000 m³	½	0·17
> 7000 m³	¼	0·08
Vestries	1	0·33
Dining and banqueting halls	½	0·17
Exhibition halls:		
Large (height > 4m)	¼	0·08
Small (height < 4m)	½	0·17
Factories:		
Sedentary work	(see table A4.13)	
Light work		
Heavy work		
Fire stations; ambulance stations:		
Appliance rooms	½	0·17
Watch rooms	½	0·17
Recreation rooms	1	0·33
Flats, residences, and hostels:		
Living rooms	1	0·33
Bedrooms	½	0·17
Bed-sitting rooms	1	0·33
Bathrooms	2	0·67
Lavatories and cloakrooms	1½	0·50
Service rooms	½	0·17
Staircase and corridors	1½	0·50
Entrance halls and foyers	1½	0·50
Public rooms	1	0·33
Gymnasia	¾	0·25
Hospitals:		
Corridors	1	0·33
Offices	1	0·33
Operating theatre suite	½	0·17
Stores	½	0·17
Wards and patient areas	2	0·67
Waiting rooms	1	0·33
(*See also DHSS Building Notes*)		

Type of building	Air infiltration rate (h^{-1})	Ventilation allowance ($W/m^3 K$)
Hotels:		
Bedrooms (standard)	1	0·33
Bedrooms (luxury)	1	0·33
Public Rooms	1	0·33
Corridors	1½	0·50
Foyers	1½	0·50
Laboratories	1	0·33
Law Courts	1	0·33
Libraries:		
Reading rooms (height > 4m)	½	0·17
(height < 4m)	¾	0·25
Stack rooms	½	0·17
Store rooms	¼	0·08
Offices:		
General	1	0·33
Private	1	0·33
Stores	½	0·17
Police stations:		
Cells	5	1·65
Restaurants and tea shops	1	0·33
Schools and colleges:		
Classrooms	2	0·67
Lecture rooms	1	0·33
Studios	1	0·33
(*See also DES Bulletins*)		
Shops and showrooms:		
Small	1	0·33
Large	½	0·17
Department store	¼	0·08
Fitting rooms	1½	0·50
Store rooms	½	0·17
Sports pavilions:		
Dressing rooms	1	0·33
Swimming baths:		
Changing rooms	½	0·17
Bath hall	½	0·17
Warehouses:		
Working and packing spaces	½	0·17
Storage space	¼	0·08

The Table is not to be used for the design of mechanical ventilation, air conditioning or warm air heating systems for which see Sections B2 and B3.

Table A4.13 Rates of air infiltration on which heat loss calculations for factories should be based where number of occupants is unknown.

Construction	Air infiltration rate (h^{-1})	Ventilation allowance ($W/m^3 K$)
Multi-storey, brick or concrete construction:		
Lower and intermediate floors	1	0·33
Top floor with flat roof	1	0·33
Top floor with sheeted roof, lined	$1\frac{1}{4}$	0·42
Top floor with sheeted roof, unlined	$1\frac{1}{2}$	0·50
Single-storey unpartitioned spaces:		
Brick or concrete construction:		
Up to 300 m³	$1\frac{1}{2}$	0·50
300 to 3000 m³	$\frac{3}{4}$	0·25
3000 to 10 000 m³	$\frac{1}{2}$	0·17
Over 10 000 m³	$\frac{1}{4}$	0·08
Curtain wall or sheet construction, lined:		
Up to 300 m³	$1\frac{3}{4}$	0·58
300 to 3000 m³	1	0·33
3000 to 10 000 m³	$\frac{3}{4}$	0·25
Over 10 000 m³	$\frac{1}{2}$	0·17
Sheet construction, unlined:		
Up to 300 m³	$2\frac{1}{2}$	0·75
300 to 3000 m³	$1\frac{1}{2}$	0·50
3000 to 10 000 m³	1	0·33
Over 10 000 m³	$\frac{3}{4}$	0·25

Note: The rates of air infiltration given in this Table are those to be allowed for heat loss calculation but additional allowances must also be made for exceptional conditions such as are produced by large doorways and ventilators, and also where the processes carried on require additional ventilation for the extraction of dust, fumes or other impurities.

REFERENCES

[1] Building Research Establishment Digest 210, Principles of Natural Ventilation, BRE, Garston, 1982.

[2] ETHERIDGE, D. W., Crack Flow Equations and Scale Effect, *Building and Environment,* **12**, 3, 1977.

[3] BS 5925: 1980. Code of practice for design of buildings; ventilation principles and designing for natural ventilation, BSI, London, 1980.

[4] EATON, K. J. and MAYNE, J. R., The Measurement of Wind Pressure on Two Storey Houses at Aylesbury, *BRE Current Paper CP 70/74,* Garston, 1974.

[5] LIDDAMENT, M. and ALLEN, C., The Validation and Comparison of Mathematical Models of Air Infiltration, *Technical Note TN-11-83,* Air Infiltration Centre, Bracknell, 1983.

[6] WARREN, P. R., Ventilation through Openings on One Wall Only, Proceedings of the ICHMT Conference — Energy Conservation in Heating, Cooling and Ventilating Buildings, ICHMT, 1977.

[7] JACKMAN, P. J., A Study of the Natural Ventilation of Tall Office Buildings, *Laboratory Report No. 53,* HVRA, Bracknell, 1969.

[8] BS 6375: Part 1: 1983, Classification for weather-tightness (including guidance on selection and specification), BSI, London, 1983.

SECTION A5 THERMAL RESPONSE OF BUILDINGS

Introduction..*Page* A5–2

Notation A5–2

Temperatures A5–4

    Inside Air Temperature.................................. A5–4

    Mean Surface Temperature............................ A5–4

    Mean Radiant Temperature............................ A5–4

    Inside Environmental Temperature.................... A5–4

    Dry Resultant Temperature at the Centre of a Room.. A5–4

    Outside Air Temperature................................ A5–4

    Sol-Air Temperature...................................... A5–4

Steady State Energy Balances............................ A5–4

    Temperatures A5–4

    Energy Balance Triangle................................ A5–5

Cyclic Conditions.. A5–6

    Fabric Transfers due to External Fluctuations A5–6

    Fabric Transfers due to Fluctuations of Inside Temperature.. A5–6

    Cyclic Ventilation Transfers............................ A5–6

    Cyclic Energy Balance with respect to Dry Resultant Temperature.................................. A5–7

    Cyclic Energy Balance with respect to Air Temperature.. A5–7

Energy Inputs.. A5–7

    Radiant Energy from which Occupants are Screened.. A5–7

    Radiant Energy which falls on Room Occupants.. A5–8

Back Losses...*Page* A5–8

    Solar Gains through Windows.......................... A5–8

Application to Heating.. A5–9

    Continuous Operation to Maintain Dry Resultant Temperature.. A5–9

    Intermittent Operation to Maintain Dry Resultant Temperature.. A5–9

Air Conditioning Plant Sizing—Sensible Heat Load.. A5–9

    Continuous Operation to Maintain Dry Resultant Temperature.. A5–9

    Continuous Operation at Constant Air Temperature.. A5–10

    Fluctuations in Control Temperature.............. A5–10

    Intermittent Operation.................................. A5–10

Summertime Temperatures.................................. A5–10

Calculating Annual Energy Consumption............. A5–11

Appendices.. A5–11

    1. Derivation of Environmental Temperature A5–11

    2. Derivation of Sol-Air Increment and Sol-Air Temperature.. A5–12

    3. Derivation of Hypothetical Conductances A5–12

    4. Steady State Energy Balance...................... A5–13

    5. Solar Gains through Glass/Blind Combinations A5–14

    6. Derivation of F_1 and F_2 .... A5–16

    7. Intermittent Operation.............................. A5–17

References.. A5–18

This edition of Section A5 first published: 1979

SECTION A5 THERMAL RESPONSE OF BUILDINGS

Note:

In the equations appearing in this section $\Sigma(A)$ = the total area of *all surfaces* bounding the enclosure

INTRODUCTION

With the publication of the 1970 *Guide* and the subsequent presentation of a number of papers on the admittance procedure, a calculation method has become generally available which gives great improvements in accuracy over previous design methods for the sizing of heating and cooling plant.

This section of the *Guide* sets out these theories. The section should prove of most use to those who wish to develop advanced methods for temperature prediction, heating and cooling requirements and energy calculations. It is not intended for use in manual calculations which, for heating and cooling loads, are dealt with in Section A9.

Earlier methods of calculation relied on the application of empirical correction factors which have produced successful installations in the majority of cases since they provided an adequate safety margin but this, and a conservative design approach, have often led to excessive central plant capacity.

Achievement of comfort conditions demands that both radiant and air temperature be considered in calculations. The procedures set out in this section not only provide this facility but also take account of the modifying effect which the room enclosing surfaces have due to their ability to absorb and release heat, a characteristic expressed by the admittance of the materials.

The calculation method described in this section involves consideration of several inside temperatures such as air, mean surface and dry resultant. Energy flow is related to these temperatures and an analysis of the energy flow paths results in energy balance equations for both steady state and cyclic conditions. These energy balance equations may then be used to determine:

(*a*) the required plant input to provide given inside temperatures;

(*b*) the various inside temperatures arising from known values of energy input.

Applications of the method to heating plant sizing and air conditioning plant sizing and also to summer time temperatures round off the section.

As with all design procedures, it is necessary to strike a balance between accuracy and simplicity. The balance point taken in this section is most suitable for calculations where the temperature swings and/or the energy inputs in the course of the day are changing steadily. It is

less suitable for step shape inputs, especially if transient temperature calculations are needed at the time of change. In this situation it might be necessary to use a much more complex model such as the response factor methods developed by the Division of Building Research of the National Research Council of Canada, but such complex methods are usually more relevant to research than design.

NOTATION

Many of the quantities in this section occur in three forms. The quantity itself, symbolised by X (which may also be considered as the instantaneous value of X); the 24 hour mean or steady state value, $\bar{X}$ and the instantaneous variation about the mean, $\tilde{X}$. Where time lags occur, the variation symbol may be given a subscript to indicate at what time it occurs, e.g. $\tilde{X}_\theta$ is the value of $\tilde{X}$ at time θ.

In the list below, only the basic symbol is given unless the quantity involved only occurs in the mean or cyclic form in which case the appropriate sign is included.

A	= area	m^2
A_g	= area of glazing	m^2
A_h	= area of heater	m^2
A_s	= area of a surface	m^2
B	= boost factor	
C	= specific heat of air	J/kg K
E	= proportion of energy transfer which is at the environmental point	
F_{au}	= dimensionless room factor w.r.t. air point	
F_{ay}	= dimensionless room factor w.r.t. air point	
F_b	= back loss factor	
F_r	= radiant energy factor	
F_s	= surface factor	
F_u	= dimensionless room factor w.r.t. dry resultant point	
F_v	= dimensionless room factor w.r.t. dry resultant point	
F_y	= dimensionless room factor w.r.t. dry resultant point	
F_1	= temperature ratio	
F_2	= temperature ratio	

I_l = net long wave radiation exchange between a black body at outside air temperature and the outside environment .. .. .. W/m²

I_t = total intensity of solar radiation .. W/m²

K = proportion of energy transfer which is at the air point

Q = energy transfer .. .. .. W

Q_a = energy transfer at air point .. W

Q_{ac} = energy transfer between air and dry resultant points .. .. W

Q_{am} = miscellaneous energy gains at air point .. .. W

$\bar{Q}_b$ = 24 hour mean of continuous plant load during OFF hours .. .. W

Q_{bl} = back loss .. .. .. W

Q_e = energy transfer at environmental point .. .. W

Q_{ec} = energy transfer between environmental and dry resultant points W

$\tilde{Q}_f$ = cyclic energy transfer at environmental point due to fluctuations of outside conditions .. .. W

Q_g = energy gain through glazing .. W

Q_i = room energy input .. .. W

Q_{in} = room energy input during intermittent operation.. .. .. W

Q_l = unaccounted energy gain .. W

Q_o = energy transfer at outside air point .. .. W

Q_p = plant energy output .. .. W

Q_{pb} = plant output under boosted intermittent operation.. .. .. W

Q_{pn} = plant energy output during intermittent operation.. .. .. W

Q_{rs} = radiant energy from which room occupants are screened .. .. W/m²

Q_s = incident solar radiation .. .. W/m²

Q_u = energy transfer through fabric .. W

Q_v = ventilation energy transfer .. W

$\tilde{Q}_{vt}$ = cyclic ventilation transfer due to fluctuation of t_{ai} .. .. .. W

$\tilde{Q}_{vo}$ = cyclic ventilation transfer due to fluctuation of t_{ao} .. .. .. W

$\tilde{Q}_y$ = cyclic energy transfer due to fluctuation of t_{ei} .. .. .. W

R_s = resistance between environmental point and any plane in a building m²K/W

R_{si} = inside surface resistance .. .. m² K/W

R_{so} = outside surface resistance .. m² K/W

S_a = solar gain factor w.r.t. air point

S_c = shading coefficient

S_e = solar gain factor w.r.t. environmental point

U = thermal transmittance .. .. W/m² K

U' = modified thermal transmittance.. W/m² K

Y = thermal admittance .. .. W/m² K

f = decrement factor

h_a = heat transfer coefficient between air and environmental points .. W/m² K

h_{ac} = heat transfer coefficient between air and dry resultant points .. W/m² K

h_c = average convective heat transfer coefficient .. .. W/m² K

h_{ec} = heat transfer coefficient between environmental and dry resultant points .. .. W/m² K

h_r = radiant heat transfer coefficient .. W/m² K

h_l = calculation surface heat transfer coefficient .. .. .. W/m² K

n = hours of plant operation .. h

n_b = hours of plant ON operation at boost .. .. h

n_n = hours of plant operation at normal load .. .. h

r = intermittent operation ratio

t = temperature .. .. .. °C

t_{ai} = inside air temperature .. .. °C

t_{ao} = outside air temperature .. .. °C

t_c = dry resultant temperature at centre of room .. .. .. °C

t_d = design temperature .. .. °C

t_{ei} = inside environmental temperature °C

t_{eo} = sol-air temperature .. .. °C

t_h = temperature of heater .. .. °C

t_l = mean temperature of all room surfaces bar one .. .. .. °C

t_m = mean surface temperature .. °C

t_r = mean radiant temperature .. °C

t_s = temperature of a surface .. °C

t_x = calculation temperature .. .. °C

v = natural ventilation rate .. .. m³/s

v_m = mechanical ventilation rate .. m³/s

Δ = change, increase or decrease in

Δt_{eo} = sol-air excess temperature difference .. .. °C

ΔQ = change in energy transfer .. W

ΔQ_p = change in plant output .. .. W

ε = emissivity factor

Σ = sum of

α = absorption coefficient

β = proportion of indirect radiation

γ = proportion of direct radiation

δ = proportion of convection

ϵ = emissivity

θ = time .. .. .. h

λ = amplitude

ρ = density of air .. .. .. kg/m³

ϕ = time lag (decrement factor) .. h

ψ = time lag (surface factor) .. h

ω = time lead (admittance) .. .. h

TEMPERATURES

Inside Air Temperature (t_{ai})

Inside air temperature is the average of the bulk air temperature of the enclosed space. For practical purposes it is the reading of a dry thermometer, shielded from radiation, suspended at the centre of the space.

Mean Surface Temperature (t_m)

The mean surface temperature is determined by totalling the products of the areas and temperatures of the surrounding surfaces and dividing this total by the sum of the areas, i.e.:

$$t_m = \frac{\Sigma(At_s)}{\Sigma(A)} \quad .. \quad .. \quad .. \quad .. \quad .. \quad \text{A5.1}$$

At any instant of time there is only one value of mean surface temperature for a room.

Mean Radiant Temperature

The mean radiant temperature sensed at any point within the enclosure is a function of the respective areas, shapes and surface temperatures of the enclosing elements as viewed from that point. In contrast to the mean surface temperature, the mean radiant temperature usually changes with position in the room. Determination of precise values is complex due to the effect of the shape factor. However, the mean radiant temperature is the same as the mean surface temperature at the centre point of a cubical room where all surfaces have the same emissivity. It is a good approximation at the room centre for other shapes.

Inside Environmental Temperature (t_{ei})

Environmental temperature is used to calculate the heat exchange between a surface and an enclosed space. Its precise value depends on room configuration and the convective and radiant heat transfer coefficients.

Typical values for these coefficients, applicable in the UK and in hot climates give:

$$t_{ei} = \tfrac{1}{3} t_{ai} + \tfrac{2}{3} t_m \quad .. \quad .. \quad .. \quad .. \quad \text{A5.2}$$

Appendix 1 gives the detailed derivation of environmental temperature. In winter, in cold continental climates, the inside convective heat transfer coefficient increases for single glazed windows, hence $t_{ei} \rightarrow \tfrac{1}{2} t_{ai} + \tfrac{1}{2} t_m$.

Dry Resultant Temperature at the Centre of a Room (t_c).

Thermal comfort is discussed at length in Section A1 of the CIBSE *Guide*. It concludes that in most practical situations where air movement is low, an acceptable index temperature for comfort is the average of air and mean radiant temperature, usually referred to as dry resultant temperature.

In the rest of this section, dry resultant temperature at the centre of the space is defined as:

$$t_c = \tfrac{1}{2} t_{ai} + \tfrac{1}{2} t_m \quad .. \quad .. \quad .. \quad .. \quad .. \quad \text{A5.3}$$

where t_m approximates to t_r at the room centre and t_{ai} is the air temperature at the same point.

Outside Air Temperature (t_{ao})

Outside air temperature is the bulk temperature of the air surrounding the building.

Sol-air Temperature (t_{eo}) and Sol-air Excess Temperature Difference (Δt_{eo})

Sol-air temperature is that temperature which, in the absence of solar radiation, would give the same rate of heat transfer through the wall or roof as exists with the actual outdoor temperature and the incident solar radiation. In effect it is the outside environmental temperature and is calculated from the expression:

$$t_{eo} = t_{ao} + R_{so}(aI_t - \epsilon I_l) \quad .. \quad .. \quad .. \quad \text{A5.4}$$

Appendix 2 gives the derivation of this equation.

Where overcast sky conditions can be assumed, the outside sol-air temperature is approximately equal to the outside air temperature but where clear skies lead to radiation loss and/or solar gains by day the external sol-air temperature can be used to calculate conduction transfers through opaque surfaces such as walls and roofs.

Sol-air excess temperature difference is given by:

$$\Delta t_{eo} = R_{so}(aI_t - \epsilon I_l) \quad .. \quad .. \quad .. \quad .. \quad \text{A5.5}$$

It is that quantity which must be added to or subtracted from the outside air temperature in order to calculate the heat transfer through opaque external surfaces resulting from the radiation exchange between those surfaces and the sun and the sky.

STEADY STATE ENERGY BALANCES

Temperatures

Under steady state conditions the relationships between air, dry resultant and environmental temperatures are dependent on the proportions of the convective and radiant energies entering the room, the room dimensions and the relative proportions of fabric and ventilation exchanges with the outside. The conductance $h_a\Sigma(A)$ which links the inside air temperature and the inside environmental temperature as shown in Fig. A5.1 is derived in Appendix 3 and is shown to be:

$$h_a\Sigma(A) = 1.5 h_c \Sigma(A) \quad .. \quad .. \quad .. \quad .. \quad \text{A5.6}$$

For any specific temperature lying between the air and environmental temperatures the conductance $h_a\Sigma(A)$ can be divided into two separate conductances joining the specified temperature to the inside air and environmental temperatures respectively as shown in Fig. A5.2. Appendix 3 shows that when the specified temperature is the dry resultant temperature as defined in equation A5.3, these conductances are given by:

$$h_{ac}\Sigma(A) = \frac{4}{3} h_a \Sigma(A) \quad .. \quad .. \quad .. \quad .. \quad \text{A5.7}$$

$$h_{ec}\Sigma(A) = 4h_a\Sigma(A) \quad .. \quad .. \quad .. \quad .. \quad \text{A5.8}$$

Energy Balance Triangle

The steady state energy balance triangle is shown in Fig. A5.3 where the fabric transfer is given by:

$$\bar{Q}_u = \Sigma(AU)(\bar{t}_{ei} - \bar{t}_{ao}) \quad .. \quad .. \quad ... \quad \text{A5.9}$$

and the ventilation transfer is given by:

$$\bar{Q}_v = C\rho v(\bar{t}_{ai} - \bar{t}_{ao}) \quad .. \quad .. \quad .. \quad \text{A5.10}$$

If the ventilation rate varies during the day, the mean value over 24 hours is given by:

$$\bar{Q}_v = \frac{\int Q_{v\theta}\,d\theta}{\int d\theta} \quad .. \quad .. \quad ... \quad \text{A5.11}$$

$$= \frac{C\rho \int v_\theta (t_{ai} - t_{ao})_\theta\,d\theta}{\int d\theta} \quad .. \quad .. \quad \text{A5.12}$$

Since the net energy balance at each of the temperature points C, E and A must be zero, the following equations hold:

$$\bar{Q}_{ac} = \bar{Q}_{ec} \quad .. \quad .. \quad .. \quad .. \quad \text{A5.13}$$

$$\bar{Q}_a = \bar{Q}_v - \bar{Q}_{ac} \quad .. \quad .. \quad .. \quad \text{A5.14}$$

$$\bar{Q}_e = \bar{Q}_{ec} + \bar{Q}_u \quad .. \quad .. \quad .. \quad \text{A5.15}$$

Equations A5.13 to A5.15 enable a set of energy balance equations to be derived with respect to air, dry resultant or environmental temperature.

Adjacent Rooms at Different Temperatures

The energy balance triangle in Fig. A5.2 shows that all fabric losses are to outside air and assumes that adjacent rooms are at the same temperature as the design room. When the temperature of adjacent rooms differs from the design temperature, then further heat exchanges occur through the internal surfaces. In this situation use can be made of a modified U-value for the dividing wall U' where:

$$U' = \frac{U(\bar{t}_{ei} - \bar{t}'_{ei})}{(\bar{t}_{ei} - \bar{t}_{ao})} \quad .. \quad .. \quad .. \quad \text{A5.16}$$

and $\bar{t}'_{ei}$ is the mean temperature of the adjacent space. $\Sigma(AU)$ is then calculated in the conventional way.

Energy Balance with respect to Dry Resultant Temperature

Appendix 4 shows how the energy balance may be expressed in terms of the energy inputs at the air and environmental points, the difference between the dry resultant and outside air temperature and the conductances in the network. The relationship is:

$$\left(\frac{h_{ac}\Sigma(A)}{h_{ac}\Sigma(A)+C\rho v}\right)\bar{Q}_a + \left(\frac{h_{ec}\Sigma(A)}{h_{ec}\Sigma(A)+\Sigma(AU)}\right)\bar{Q}_e = \left\{\left(\frac{h_{ac}\Sigma(A)}{h_{ac}\Sigma(A)+C\rho v}\right)C\rho v + \left(\frac{h_{ec}\Sigma(A)}{h_{ec}\Sigma(A)+\Sigma(AU)}\right)\Sigma(AU)\right\}(\bar{t}_c - \bar{t}_{ao}) \quad \text{A5.17}$$

For convenience two dimensionless room characteristics can be defined:

$$F_v = \frac{h_{ac}\ \Sigma(A)}{h_{ac}\Sigma(A)+C\rho v} \quad .. \quad .. \quad \text{A5.18}$$

$$F_u = \frac{h_{ec}\Sigma(A)}{h_{ec}\Sigma(A)+\Sigma(AU)} \quad .. \quad .. \quad \text{A5.19}$$

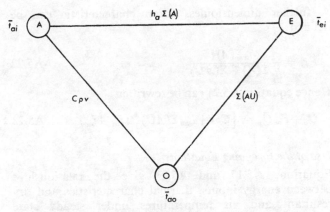

Fig. A5.1. Basic conductance network.

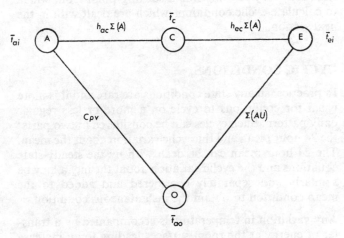

Fig. A5.2. Modified conductance network.

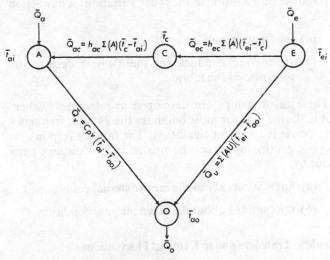

Fig. A5.3. Steady state energy flow.

Hence, equation A5.17 can be written.

$$F_v\bar{Q}_a + F_u\bar{Q}_e = \left(F_vC\rho v + F_u\Sigma(AU)\right)(\bar{t}_c - \bar{t}_{ao}) \quad \text{A5.20}$$

Energy Balance with respect to Air Temperature

Appendix 4 also shows how energy inputs can be expressed in terms of the inside air temperature, viz:

$$\bar{Q}_a + \left(\frac{h_a\Sigma(A)}{h_a\Sigma(A)+\Sigma(AU)}\right)\bar{Q}_e = \left\{C\rho v + \left(\frac{h_a\Sigma(A)}{h_a\Sigma(A)+\Sigma(AU)}\right)\Sigma(AU)\right\}(\bar{t}_{ai} - \bar{t}_{ao}) \quad .. \quad .. \quad .. \quad .. \quad \text{A5.21}$$

A further dimensionless room characteristic can be defined:

$$F_{au} = \frac{h_a \Sigma(A)}{h_a \Sigma(A) + \Sigma(AU)} \qquad .. \qquad .. \qquad .. \qquad \text{A5.22}$$

Hence equation A5.21 can be rewritten:

$$\bar{Q}_a + F_{au}\bar{Q}_e = \left\{ C\rho v + F_{au}\Sigma(AU) \right\}(\bar{t}_{ai} - \bar{t}_{ao}) \quad .. \quad \text{A5.23}$$

Use of the foregoing Equations

Equations A5.17 and A5.21 give the relationships between energy inputs, thermal characteristics and dry resultant and air temperatures under steady state conditions. As well as dealing with the steady state situation, they also provide a starting point from which to calculate cyclic conditions which are dealt with in the next section.

CYCLIC CONDITIONS

In practice, steady state conditions are rare and it is more usual for conditions to cycle on a more or less regular daily pattern. Such cycles can be considered in two parts: the 24 hour mean and the cyclic variation about the mean. The 24 hour mean can be dealt with by the steady-state equations and the cyclic variation about the mean may be similarly and separately considered and added to the mean condition to obtain the instantaneous condition.

Any variation in temperature is accompanied by a transfer of energy at the room surfaces leading to an increase or decrease of energy stored in the structure. The thermal response of the fabric to the cyclic variations is a function of:

(*a*) the frequency of the cycle;

(*b*) the thermal conductivity, specific heat, density and thickness of the fabric.

These relationships are developed in reference 1 where it is shown that for most buildings the 24 hour frequency response is the most significant. The fabric's response to cyclic energy inputs can be treated in two distinct parts due to:

(*a*) fluctuations about the mean external condition;

(*b*) fluctuations about the mean internal condition.

Fabric Transfers due to External Fluctuations

The transmission of fluctuations in external conditions can be calculated by using the decrement factor *f* which is the attenuation of a thermal wave travelling through an element of building structure. Thus, if a cyclic wave of amplitude λ enters at one side of an element, after a period of φ hours a wave of reduced amplitude *f*λ will emerge at the other side. Both the decrement factor and its time lag are characteristics of the material and thickness of the element. Values for typical constructions are listed in Section A3. The resultant cyclic energy input to the room due to the fluctuations of the external conditions about their mean value can be expressed in terms of the sol-air temperature as follows:

$$\tilde{Q}_{f\theta} = \Sigma(fAU)(t_{eo} - \bar{t}_{eo})_{\theta-\phi} \quad .. \qquad .. \qquad \text{A5.24}$$

$$= \Sigma(fAU)(\tilde{t}_{eo})_{\theta-\phi} \quad .. \qquad .. \qquad \text{A5.25}$$

This energy transfer through the fabric flows from the internal surfaces to the room and is therefore an energy gain to the environmental point. For this reason it can be considered as part of the energy transfer at the environmental point and so does not appear independently in the cyclic energy network, see Fig. A5.4.

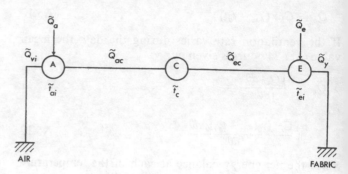

Fig. A.5.4. Cyclic energy flow.

Fabric Transfers due to Fluctuations of Inside Temperature

The cyclic energy flow $\tilde{Q}_y$ is the variation of stored energy in the structure due to fluctuations in the internal environmental temperature. It can be expressed as:

$$\tilde{Q}_{y\theta} = \Sigma(AY)(t_{ei} - \bar{t}_{ei})_{\theta+\omega} \quad .. \qquad .. \qquad \text{A5.26}$$

$$= \Sigma(AY)(\tilde{t}_{ei})_{\theta+\omega} \quad .. \qquad .. \qquad \text{A5.27}$$

The admittance *Y* determines the storage of energy in room surfaces. Admittance is a measure of the construction's response to temperature variations and is related to the diffusivity and thickness of the materials. Admittances for internal and external surfaces are listed in Section A3. Calculation procedures for *f* and *Y* are given in reference 1. It should be noted that the admittances of all room surfaces are included in the calculation of $\Sigma(AY)$.

Cyclic Ventilation Transfers

As with cyclic fabric transfers, the cyclic ventilation transfer has two components, one ($\tilde{Q}_{vo\theta}$) related to fluctuations about the mean outside temperature and the other ($\tilde{Q}_{vi\theta}$) related to fluctuations about the mean inside temperature.

Since external conditions are usually specified it is convenient to treat $\tilde{Q}_{vo\theta}$ as an energy input at the air point, and include it as part of $\tilde{Q}_a$. It does not appear independently in the cyclic energy network.

For constant ventilation rates:

$$\tilde{Q}_{vi\theta} = C\rho \, v\tilde{t}_{ai\theta} \qquad .. \qquad .. \qquad .. \qquad \text{A5.28}$$

and:

$$\tilde{Q}_{vo\theta} = C\rho \, v\tilde{t}_{ao\theta} \qquad .. \qquad .. \qquad .. \qquad \text{A5.29}$$

For variable ventilation rates:

$$\tilde{Q}_{vi\theta} = C\rho v_\theta \tilde{t}_{ai\theta} + C\rho v_\theta \tilde{t}_{ai} - \frac{C\rho \int v_\theta \tilde{t}_{ai\theta} \, d\theta}{\int d\theta} \quad .. \quad \text{A5.30}$$

and:

$$\tilde{Q}_{vo\theta} = C\rho v_\theta \tilde{t}_{ao\theta} + C\rho v_\theta \tilde{t}_{ao} - \frac{C\rho \int v_\theta \tilde{t}_{ao\theta} \, d\theta}{\int d\theta} \quad .. \quad \text{A5.31}$$

Cyclic Energy Balance with respect to Dry Resultant Temperature

The cyclic energy transfer network of Fig. A5.4 gives the following equations representing the energy balance at each node. (For convenience a constant ventilation rate is assumed.)

Node C

$$\tilde{Q}_{ac\theta} = \tilde{Q}_{ec\theta} \quad \cdots \quad \cdots \quad \cdots \quad \cdots \quad \cdots \quad \text{A5.32}$$

Node A

$$\tilde{Q}_{a\theta} = \tilde{Q}_{vi\theta} - \tilde{Q}_{ac\theta} \quad \cdots \quad \cdots \quad \cdots \quad \cdots \quad \text{A5.33}$$

Node E

$$\tilde{Q}_{e\theta} = \tilde{Q}_{ec\theta} + \tilde{Q}_{y\theta} \quad \cdots \quad \cdots \quad \cdots \quad \cdots \quad \text{A5.34}$$

The solution of these equations parallels the solution of equations A5.13 to A5.15, see Appendix 4, with cyclic temperature fluctuations in place of the mean temperature differences and admittances in place of U values.

Hence:

$$\frac{h_{ac}\Sigma(A)}{h_{ac}\Sigma(A)+C\rho v}\tilde{Q}_{a\theta}+\frac{h_{ec}\Sigma(A)}{h_{ec}\Sigma(A)+\Sigma(AY)}\tilde{Q}_{e\theta} = \left\{\frac{h_{ac}\Sigma(A)}{h_{ac}\Sigma(A)+C\rho v}C\rho v+\frac{h_{ec}\Sigma(A)}{h_{ec}\Sigma(A)+\Sigma(AY)}\Sigma(AY)\right\}\tilde{t}_{c\theta} \quad \cdots \quad \text{A5.35}$$

Defining:

$$F_y = \frac{h_{ec}\Sigma(A)}{h_{ec}\Sigma(A)+\Sigma(AY)} \quad \cdots \quad \cdots \quad \cdots \quad \cdots \quad \cdots \quad \text{A5.36}$$

means that equation A5.35 can be rewritten:

$$F_v\tilde{Q}_{a\theta}+F_y\tilde{Q}_{e\theta} = (F_vC\rho v+F_y\Sigma(AY))\tilde{t}_{c\theta} \quad \cdots \quad \cdots \quad \cdots \quad \text{A5.37}$$

Cyclic Energy Balance with respect to Air Temperature

Similarly, the energy network of Fig. A5.4 gives:

$$\tilde{Q}_{a\theta}+\frac{h_a\Sigma(A)}{h_a\Sigma(A)+\Sigma(AY)}\tilde{Q}_{e\theta}= \left\{C\rho v+\frac{h_a\Sigma(A)}{h_a\Sigma(A)+\Sigma(AY)}\Sigma(AY)\right\}\tilde{t}_{ai\theta} \quad \cdots \quad \text{A5.38}$$

Introducing:

$$F_{ay} = \frac{h_a\Sigma(A)}{h_a\Sigma(A)+\Sigma(AY)} \quad \cdots \quad \cdots \quad \cdots \quad \cdots \quad \text{A5.39}$$

gives:

$$\tilde{Q}_{a\theta}+F_{ay}\tilde{Q}_{e\theta} = \left\{C\rho v+F_{ay}\Sigma(AY)\right\}\tilde{t}_{ai\theta} \quad \cdots \quad \cdots \quad \cdots \quad \text{A5.40}$$

ENERGY INPUTS

So far the method has dealt with steady state and cyclic energy inputs at the air and environmental points, without showing how the inputs at these points are derived. In practice three types of energy transfer must be considered, namely radiant energy from which occupants are screened, radiant energy which falls directly on them and convective energy. For convenience these are assumed to be in the fractions $\beta:\gamma:\delta$ respectively, of the total room input Q_i.

This section deals with the transfer of these energies to the air and environmental points in the model.

Radiant Energy from which Occupants are Screened

Radiation will often be introduced, or in the case of solar radiation restricted, so that it does not fall directly on to the occupants and so does not contribute directly to the mean radiant temperature until it has been absorbed by a room surface.

In this case a surface factor must be used to calculate the resultant input at the environmental point.

Steady State Conditions

Under steady state conditions there is no storage within the fabric and only the retransmission and the conduction through the fabric need be considered. For room boundaries subjected to a temperature difference, the steady state surface factor $\bar{F}_s$ allows for the absorption of short wave radiant energy at a room surface and its retransmission to the environmental point:

$$\bar{F}_s = \frac{\dfrac{1}{\bar{U}} - R_{si}}{\dfrac{1}{\bar{U}}} \quad \cdots \quad \cdots \quad \cdots \quad \text{A5.41}$$

$$= 1 - UR_{si} \quad \cdots \quad \cdots \quad \cdots \quad \cdots \quad \text{A5.42}$$

For an internal element, backed by a space at the same thermal conditions, there is no net transmission through the fabric and therefore the factor is unity.

When such radiation is distributed uniformly across all surfaces, the mean radiant energy factor $\bar{F}_r$ for the whole room is the area weighting of the individual factors for each surface, viz:

$$\bar{F}_r = \frac{\Sigma(A\bar{F}_s)}{\Sigma(A)} \quad \cdots \quad \cdots \quad \cdots \quad \text{A5.43}$$

$$= \frac{\Sigma(A) - \Sigma(AUR_{si})}{\Sigma(A)} \quad \cdots \quad \cdots \quad \text{A5.44}$$

The effective steady-state radiation input at the environmental point is the product of $\bar{F}_r$ and the actual steady-state input, i.e.:

$$\bar{Q}_{rs} = \bar{F}_r \times (\beta \times \bar{Q}_i) \quad \cdots \quad \cdots \quad \cdots \quad \text{A5.45}$$

Cyclic Conditions

In a similar manner, cyclic energy inputs are determined by the cyclic radiant energy factor $\tilde{F}_r$. The cyclic surface factor $\tilde{F}_s$ for individual elements, is a function of the density, specific heat and thermal conductivity of the element and has a time lag associated with it in a similar fashion to the admittance and values are given in Section A3 of the CIBSE *Guide*.

Again for a uniform distribution of screened radiant energy the cyclic equivalent energy factor is defined as:

$$\tilde{F}_r = \frac{\Sigma(A\tilde{F}_s)}{\Sigma(A)} \quad .. \quad .. \quad .. \quad .. \quad A5.46$$

The combined time lag associated with the cyclic radiant energy factor can be derived by averaging the time lags of the individual elements. Approximate values of 1, 2 and 3 hours can be assumed for light, medium and heavy structures respectively.

The effective cyclic radiant input at the environmental point is the product of $\tilde{F}_r$ and the actual cyclic radiant input, i.e.:

$$\tilde{Q}_{rs} = \tilde{F}_r \times (\beta \times \tilde{Q}_i) \quad .. \quad .. \quad .. \quad A5.47$$

Radiant Energy which Falls on Room Occupants

When the radiation is generally dispersed within the room so that the occupants are in direct receipt of its energy, it contributes to the mean radiant temperature of the space. Because of this contribution towards the mean radiant temperature, the radiant energy can be regarded as entering directly at the environmental point.

However, the nature of an environmental heat input is that it has radiant and convective components in the proportion 2:1. Therefore the total heat input to the environmental point is equal to $1\frac{1}{2}$ times the radiation component, viz. $1.5\gamma Q_i$ (i.e. γQ_i by radiation plus $0.5\gamma Q_i$ by convection).

Total Energy Input at the Environmental Point (Q_e)

If E is the proportion of Q_i, which is realised at the environmental point then:

$$Q_e = EQ_i \quad .. \quad .. \quad .. \quad .. \quad .. \quad A5.48$$

and:

$$E = 1.5\gamma + F_r\beta \quad .. \quad .. \quad .. \quad .. \quad .. \quad A5.49$$

This formula is applicable to both the steady state and cyclic conditions.

Energy Input at the Air Point (Q_a)

The energy input at the air point, Q_a, is the remaining convective input which has not been included at the environmental point, i.e.:

$$Q_a = (\delta - 0.5\gamma) Q_i \quad .. \quad .. \quad .. \quad A5.50$$

If K is the proportion of Q_i realised at the air point then:

$$Q_a = KQ_i \quad .. \quad .. \quad .. \quad .. \quad .. \quad A5.51$$

and:

$$K = \delta - 0.5\gamma \quad .. \quad .. \quad .. \quad .. \quad A5.52$$

Back Losses

The treatment of plant and casual gains assumes that the energy sources are free standing within the space and that their total energy output enters the space. For energy sources embedded in or fixed to the surfaces surrounding the space a correction is needed for the additional heat loss which arises since that part of the surface is exposed to the temperature of the emitter rather than the environmental temperature of the room. This is commonly referred to as the back loss.

For wall mounted radiators the correction is simply the product of the projected radiator area, the U-value of the exposed wall and the mean temperature difference between the radiator and the room, i.e.:

$$Q_{bl} = A_h U (t_h - t_{ei}) \quad .. \quad .. \quad .. \quad A5.53$$

Air ducts can be dealt with in a similar manner.

The plant capacity is given by:

$$Q_p = Q_i + Q_{bl} \quad .. \quad .. \quad .. \quad .. \quad A5.54$$

For embedded heating systems (e.g. underfloor heating and ceiling heating) the steady state back loss factor can be derived and is given by:

$$\bar{F}_b = 1 - UR_s \quad .. \quad .. \quad .. \quad .. \quad A5.55$$

Consequently:

$$\bar{Q}_p = \frac{\bar{Q}_i}{\bar{F}_b} \quad .. \quad .. \quad .. \quad .. \quad .. \quad A5.56$$

Cyclic back losses can be derived by using admittances in place of U-values.

Solar Gains Through Windows

Solar gains through windows arise due to:

(a) the part of the solar radiation absorbed in the window as a whole which is transmitted to the environmental point;

(b) the transmitted solar radiation which is absorbed at the internal surfaces of the room and subsequently appears also at the environmental point.

Where internal shading devices are used there is an additional convective load which is realised at the air point.

Each part is related to the instantaneous solar intensity and the type of glass and shade. Transmitted radiation is also modified by the thermal characteristics of the room construction. Each component has a daily mean value and an instantaneous cyclic variation about that mean. The effective solar cooling load can be calculated using solar gain factors which deal with the steady and cyclic components respectively. The derivation of these factors is given in Appendix 5 and they are used as follows.

Mean solar gain through window at the air point

$$\bar{Q}_{ga} = A_g \bar{S}_a \bar{I}_t \quad .. \quad .. \quad .. \quad .. \quad A5.57$$

Mean solar gain through window at the environmental point

$$\bar{Q}_{ge} = A_g \bar{S}_e \bar{I}_t \quad .. \quad .. \quad .. \quad .. \quad A5.58$$

Cyclic solar gain through window at the air point

$$\tilde{Q}_{ga\theta} = A_g \tilde{S}_a \tilde{I}_{t(\theta-\psi)} \quad .. \quad .. \quad A5.59$$

Cyclic solar gain through window at the environmental point

$$\bar{Q}_{ge\theta} = A_g \, \tilde{S}_e \, \tilde{I}_{t(\theta-\psi)} \quad \cdots \quad \cdots \quad \cdots \quad \text{A5.60}$$

APPLICATION TO HEATING

The energy balance equations (A5.17 and A5.35) are directly applicable to the winter time situations if full account of all the energy gains (solar, casual etc.) is taken. However, it is more usual to size heating plant for constant conditions and ignore, or only partially correct for, solar, lighting and other casual gains.

Continuous Operation to Maintain Dry Resultant Temperature

The sizing of heating plant for continuous operation (constant internal temperature for 24 hours per day, 7 days per week) is a straight application of the mean energy balance equations for a constant dry resultant temperature:

$$F_v \, \bar{Q}_a + F_u \, \bar{Q}_e = [F_v C \rho v + F_u \, \Sigma(AU)] \, (\bar{t}_c - \bar{t}_{ao}) \quad \text{A5.61}$$

where $\bar{Q}_a$ and $\bar{Q}_e$ are the total inputs at the air and environmental points; i.e. they include plant inputs, casual gains, solar gains and occupancy etc. The designer needs to calculate the total room energy input $\bar{Q}_i$, to be provided by the plant. It has already been noted that $\bar{Q}_i$ has environmental and convective proportions E and K. If other energy inputs are ignored then:

$$\bar{Q}_a = K \bar{Q}_i \quad \cdots \quad \cdots \quad \cdots \quad \cdots \quad \text{A5.62}$$

$$\bar{Q}_e = E \bar{Q}_i \quad \cdots \quad \cdots \quad \cdots \quad \cdots \quad \text{A5.63}$$

And equation A5.61 becomes:

$$\bar{Q}_i(F_v K + F_u E) = (F_v C \rho v + F_u \Sigma(AU))(\bar{t}_c - \bar{t}_{ao}) \quad \text{A5.64}$$

For conventional steady state calculations it is simpler to have an equation in the form:

$$\bar{Q}_i = (F_1 \Sigma(AU) + F_2 C \rho v)(\bar{t}_c - \bar{t}_{ao}) \quad \cdots \quad \cdots \quad \text{A5.65}$$

and to define F_1 and F_2 as follows so that the calculation of room temperatures is easier:

$$F_1 = \frac{\bar{t}_{ei} - \bar{t}_{ao}}{\bar{t}_c - \bar{t}_{ao}} \quad \cdots \quad \cdots \quad \cdots \quad \text{A5.66}$$

$$F_2 = \frac{\bar{t}_{ai} - \bar{t}_{ao}}{\bar{t}_c - \bar{t}_{ao}} \quad \cdots \quad \cdots \quad \cdots \quad \text{A5.67}$$

Pairs of values of F_1 and F_2 can be calculated for given room configurations and stated types of heating system. For the simple case of 100% convective or 100% environmental heating the solution to F_1 and F_2 is straightforward and can be arrived at by simple analysis of the conductance paths. The more general solutions for F_1 and F_2 for a 'mixed' system are given in Appendix 6 which shows:

$$F_1 = \frac{E(F_v C \rho v + F_u \Sigma(AU))}{(\Sigma(AU) + h_{ec}\Sigma(A))(F_v K + F_u E)} + F_u \quad \text{A5.68}$$

$$F_2 = \frac{K(F_v C \rho v + F_u \Sigma(AU))}{(C \rho v + h_{ac}\Sigma(A))(F_v K + F_u E)} + F_v \quad \text{A5.69}$$

In practice the plant capacity $\bar{Q}_p$ may be slightly higher than $\bar{Q}_i$ because of back losses. Where these are important the appropriate correction can be calculated from equations A5.53 and A5.55.

Intermittent Operation to Maintain Dry Resultant Temperature

Appendix 7 gives the theoretical method for deriving intermittent heat requirements and the correction factor F_3, which is tabulated in Section A9. It is used in the equation:

$$Q_{pb} = F_3 Q_p = B r Q_p \cdots \quad \cdots \quad \cdots \quad \cdots \quad \cdots \quad \cdots \quad \cdots \quad \cdots \quad \cdots \quad \cdots \quad \text{A5.70}$$

where Q_{pb} is the plant output under boosted intermittent conditions and Q_p is the plant output to control the temperature with 24 hour operation and where values for B are given in Table A5.6 and r is given by:

$$r = \frac{24(F_v C \rho v + F_y \Sigma(AY))(KF_v + EF_u)}{n(F_v C \rho v + F_y \Sigma(AY))(KF_v + EF_u) + (24-n)(KF_v + EF_y)(F_v C \rho v + F_u \Sigma(AU))} \quad \cdots \quad \cdots \quad \cdots \quad \cdots \quad \cdots \quad \text{A5.71}$$

AIR CONDITIONING PLANT SIZING—SENSIBLE HEAT LOAD

The sizing of air conditioning plant requires the direct application of the energy balance equations developed in the preceding sections.

In determining plant capacity the main points to be considered are:

(a) the choice of control temperature (air, dry resultant etc.);

(b) is the control temperature assumed to vary?

In contrast to heating plant calculations, full account must be taken of *all* heat gains to the conditioned space. In the following treatment it is assumed that all cooling is effected at the air point since it is normal practice to achieve cooling via the air circulation system.

Continuous Operation to maintain Constant Dry Resultant Temperature

Air conditioning loads must allow for the varying energy inputs, from whatever source. For this reason plant capacity is derived by combining the steady state and the cyclic energy equations, viz:

$$F_v \bar{Q}_a + F_u \bar{Q}_e = (F_v C \rho v + F_u \Sigma(AU))(\bar{t}_c - \bar{t}_{ao}) \quad \cdots \quad \text{A5.72}$$

and:

$$F_v \tilde{Q}_a + F_y \tilde{Q}_e = (F_v C \rho v + F_y \Sigma(AY))(\tilde{t}_{c\theta}) \quad \cdots \quad \text{A5.73}$$

Since, under controlled conditions, $\tilde{t}_{c\theta} = 0$ equation A5.73 can be simplified to:

$$F_v \tilde{Q}_a + F_y \tilde{Q}_e = 0 \quad \cdots \quad \cdots \quad \cdots \quad \cdots \quad \text{A5.74}$$

Equations A5.72 and A5.74 can then be combined to give:

$$F_v(\bar{Q}_a+\tilde{Q}_a)+F_u\bar{Q}_e+F_y\tilde{Q}_e = (F_vC\rho v+F_u\Sigma(AU))(\bar{t}_c-\bar{t}_{ao}) \quad \cdots \quad \cdots \quad \cdots \quad \cdots \quad \cdots \quad \cdots \quad \text{A5.75}$$

$\bar{Q}_a$ and $\tilde{Q}_a$ include the plant load, cyclic ventilation gains and other gains, Q_{am}, at the air point. $\bar{Q}_e$ and $\tilde{Q}_e$ represent all the gains at the environmental point, dominated usually by solar gains through window and fabric.

If Q_i is the instantaneous room input from the plant at the air point, equation A5.75 can be rewritten:

$$F_v(Q_i+C\rho v\tilde{t}_{ao}+Q_{am})+F_u\bar{Q}_e+F_y\tilde{Q}_e = (F_vC\rho v+F_u\Sigma(AU))(\bar{t}_c-\bar{t}_{ao}) \quad \cdots \quad \cdots \quad \cdots \quad \cdots \quad \text{A5.76}$$

Hence:

$$Q_i = (C\rho v+\frac{F_u}{F_v}\Sigma(AU))(\bar{t}_c-\bar{t}_{ao})-\frac{F_u}{F_v}\bar{Q}_e-\frac{F_y}{F_v}\tilde{Q}_e-C\rho v\tilde{t}_{ao}-Q_{am} \quad \cdots \quad \cdots \quad \cdots \quad \cdots \quad \cdots \quad \text{A5.77}$$

For air conditioning systems with a central air handling plant, the ventilation rate to calculate F_v in the above equations should be the infiltration rate and *not* the mechanical ventilation rate. In practice, for a well sealed building, F_v equals unity.

Continuous Operation at Constant Air Temperature

It is common to control air conditioning plant to provide a constant air temperature. The solution to the energy equations is similar to that in the preceding section, giving:

$$Q_i = (C\rho v+F_{au}\Sigma(AU))(\bar{t}_{ai}-\bar{t}_{ao})-F_{au}\bar{Q}_e \\ -F_{ay}\tilde{Q}_e-C\rho v\tilde{t}_{ao}-Q_{am} \quad \cdots \quad \cdots \quad \text{A5.78}$$

Fluctuations in Control Temperature

If the control temperature is allowed to rise at the time of peak load then the room sensible load can be reduced. For short periods of swing, when the effect on the 24 hour mean temperature can be ignored, equation A5.74 shows that for a rise in t_c the reduction in cooling load is:

$$\Delta Q_i = \left(C\rho v_m+\frac{F_y}{F_v}\Sigma(AY)\right)\tilde{t}_c \cdots \quad \cdots \quad \cdots \quad \text{A5.79}$$

Similarly for control at the air point, a rise in t_{ai} gives a reduction in load:

$$\Delta Q_i = (C\rho v_m+F_{ay}\Sigma(AY))\tilde{t}_{ai} \quad \cdots \quad \cdots \quad \text{A5.80}$$

where v_m is the sum of mechanical ventilation and infiltration rates.

Intermittent Operation

For the more usual case when the air conditioning plant is operated intermittently for part of the day, the plant size can be calculated directly[2]. If the infiltration ventilation rate is constant or is small, the change in plant load ΔQ_p in going from continuous to intermittent operation can be calculated from:

$$\Delta Q_p = \frac{24\ (F_y\ \Sigma(AY)-F_u\ \Sigma(AU))\ \bar{Q}_b}{(24-n)\ F_u\ \Sigma(AU)+n\ F_y\ \Sigma(AY)+24\ C\rho v\ F_v}$$

A5.81

where $\bar{Q}_b$ is the 24 hour mean of the continuous operation load which would otherwise have occurred during the OFF period.

Alternatively, when the load in the OFF period is small:

$$\Delta Q_p = \bar{Q}_b \quad \cdots \quad \cdots \quad \cdots \quad \cdots \quad \cdots \quad \text{A5.82}$$

SUMMERTIME TEMPERATURES

The prediction of summertime temperature is similar to the calculation of air conditioning loads, coming from the steady state and cyclic energy equations. For a fixed ventilation rate, the steady state equation (A5.20) can be rearranged to give:

$$(\bar{t}_c-\bar{t}_{ao}) = \frac{F_v\ \bar{Q}_a+F_u\ \bar{Q}_e}{F_v\ C\rho v+F_u\ \Sigma(AU)} \quad \cdots \quad \cdots \quad \text{A5.83}$$

where $\bar{Q}_a$ and $\bar{Q}_e$ are the 24 hour means of casual and solar gains at the air and environmental points respectively.

Similarly the cyclic equation (A5.37) can be rearranged to yield:

$$\tilde{t}_{c\theta} = \frac{F_v\ \tilde{Q}_{a\theta}+F_y\ \tilde{Q}_{e\theta}}{F_v\ C\rho v+F_y\ \Sigma(AY)} \quad \cdots \quad \cdots \quad \cdots \quad \text{A5.84}$$

Thus the inside dry resultant temperature at any time is given by summing the mean and fluctuating temperatures.

When the ventilation rate varies during the course of the day the solution is more complicated. It is dealt with relative to environmental temperature in reference 3 and the same method can be used to give the following solutions relative to dry resultant temperature:

$$(\bar{t}_c-\bar{t}_{ao}) = \frac{\sum_1^{24}(F_u\bar{Q}_e+F_{v\theta}Q_{a\theta}+F_{v\theta}C\rho v_\theta\tilde{t}_{ao\theta}) - \sum_1^{24}\left(\frac{F_{v\theta}C\rho v_\theta(F_u\bar{Q}_e+F_{v\theta}Q_{a\theta}+F_{v\theta}C\rho v_\theta\tilde{t}_{ao\theta})}{(F_{v\theta}C\rho v_\theta+F_y\Sigma(AY))}\right)}{\sum_1^{24}(F_u\Sigma(AU))+\sum_1^{24}(F_{v\theta}C\rho v_\theta)-\sum_1^{24}\left(F_{v\theta}C\rho v_\theta\left(\frac{F_u\Sigma(AU)+F_{v\theta}C\rho v_\theta}{F_{v\theta}C\rho v_\theta+F_y\Sigma(AY)}\right)\right)} \quad \cdots \quad \cdots \quad \cdots \quad \text{A5.85}$$

$$\tilde{t}_{c\theta} = \frac{F_u\bar{Q}_e+F_{v\theta}Q_{a\theta}+F_y\tilde{Q}_{e\theta}+F_{v\theta}C\rho v_\theta\tilde{t}_{ao\theta} - (F_u\Sigma(AU)+F_{v\theta}C\rho v_\theta)\ (\bar{t}_c-\bar{t}_{ao})}{F_{v\theta}C\rho v_\theta+F_y\Sigma(AY)} \quad \cdots \quad \cdots \quad \cdots \quad \text{A5.86}$$

CALCULATING ANNUAL ENERGY CONSUMPTION

Although the foregoing procedures were developed originally for use in predicting design or peak conditions, the method used is equally applicable to non-design conditions including estimates of annual energy consumption. Since the admittances and other related factors are calculated from periodic steady-cycle conditions i.e. a series of days of repeatable weather patterns and building usage, the meteorological data used for energy calculations should be processed to match this requirement.

The 'banded' weather data given in Section A2 have been specially prepared for this purpose. Care should also be taken to ensure that items of plant and their associated controls and the actual usage of the buildings by its occupants are adequately represented in the analysis.

(The manual method for calculating energy targets used in the CIBSE Energy Codes has been developed from these procedures.)

APPENDICES

Appendix 1—Derivation of Environmental Temperature

The equation for the heat transfer between a single surface of area A_s and its enclosing space is:

$$Q = A_s[\varepsilon h_r(t_l - t_s) + h_c(t_{ai} - t_s)] \quad \cdots \quad \text{A5.87}$$

Since:

$$t_m \Sigma(A) = A_s t_s + (\Sigma(A) - A_s) t_l \quad \cdots \quad \cdots \quad \text{A5.88}$$

$$\therefore t_l = \frac{t_m \Sigma(A) - A_s t_s}{\Sigma(A) - A_s} \quad \cdots \quad \cdots \quad \text{A5.89}$$

and:

$$t_l - t_s = \frac{(t_m - t_s) \Sigma(A)}{\Sigma(A) - A_s} \quad \cdots \quad \cdots \quad \cdots \quad \text{A5.90}$$

Hence:

$$Q = A_s\left[\varepsilon h_r\left(\frac{(t_m - t_s)\Sigma(A)}{\Sigma(A) - A_s}\right) + h_c(t_{ai} - t_s)\right] \quad \text{A5.91}$$

or:

$$\frac{Q}{A_s} = h_l(t_m - t_s) + h_c(t_{ai} - t_s) \quad \cdots \quad \cdots \quad \text{A5.92}$$

where:

$$h_l = \frac{\varepsilon h_r \Sigma(A)}{\Sigma(A) - A_s} \quad \cdots \quad \cdots \quad \cdots \quad \cdots \quad \text{A5.93}$$

For a cubical room:

$$\frac{\Sigma(A)}{\Sigma(A) - A_s} = \frac{6}{5} \quad \cdots \quad \cdots \quad \cdots \quad \cdots \quad \text{A5.94}$$

and this is a reasonable approximation for other room configurations, see Table A5.1.

Hence:

$$h_l = \frac{6}{5} \varepsilon h_r \quad \cdots \quad \cdots \quad \cdots \quad \cdots \quad \text{A5.95}$$

Equation A5.92 may be simplified by introducing a calculation temperature such that:

Table A5.1. Values of $\dfrac{\Sigma(A)}{\Sigma(A) - A_s}$ for single surface

Ratio of room dimensions			$\Sigma(A) = 2(ab+bc+ca)$	$\Sigma(A)/(\Sigma(A)-A_s)$ for A_s		
a	b	c		ab	bc	ca
1	1	1	6	1.20	1.20	1.20
1	1	2	10	1.11	1.25	1.25
1	1	3	14	1.08	1.27	1.27
1	1	4	18	1.06	1.29	1.29
1	2	2	16	1.14	1.33	1.14
1	2	3	22	1.10	1.38	1.16
1	2	4	28	1.08	1.40	1.17
1	3	3	30	1.11	1.43	1.11
1	3	4	38	1.09	1.46	1.12
1	4	4	48	1.09	1.50	1.09

$$\frac{Q}{A_s} = (h_l + h_c)(t_x - t_s) \quad \cdots \quad \cdots \quad \text{A5.96}$$

Putting the right hand sides of equations A5.92 and A5.96 equal gives:

$$h_l(t_m - t_s) + h_c(t_{ai} - t_s) = (h_l + h_c)(t_x - t_s) \quad \cdots \quad \text{A5.97}$$

$$\therefore t_x = \frac{h_l t_m + h_c t_{ai}}{h_l + h_c} \quad \cdots \quad \cdots \quad \cdots \quad \cdots \quad \text{A5.98}$$

$$= \frac{\frac{6}{5}\varepsilon h_r t_m + h_c t_{ai}}{h_c + \frac{6}{5}\varepsilon h_r} \quad \cdots \quad \cdots \quad \cdots \quad \text{A5.99}$$

In the UK, typical values of the coefficients are:

$\varepsilon = 0.9$ (see Section A3)
$h_r = 5.7$ W/m² K
$h_c = 1.5$ W/m² K (downward flow)
$\quad = 3.0$ W/m² K (horizontal flow)
$\quad = 4.3$ W/m² K (upward flow)
$\quad = 3.0$ W/m² K (average value)

$$\therefore t_x = \frac{3.0\, t_{ai} + (\frac{6}{5} \times 0.9 \times 5.7\, t_m)}{3.0 + (\frac{6}{5} \times 0.9 \times 5.7)} \quad \cdots \quad \text{A5.100}$$

$$= \frac{1}{3} t_{ai} + \frac{2}{3} t_m \quad \cdots \quad \cdots \quad \cdots \quad \text{A5.101}$$

This calculation temperature is called the internal environmental temperature, t_{ei}.

Appendix 2—Derivation of Sol-Air Increment and Sol-Air Temperature

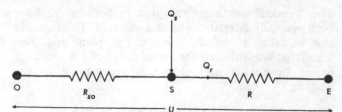

Fig. A5.5. Solar energy flow network.

The incident solar radiation is absorbed by a building element at its surface (point S). The net amount of energy input at the surface is:

$$Q_s = \alpha I_t - \epsilon I_l \qquad \qquad \qquad \text{A5.102}$$

The overall U-value of the wall can be divided into the outside surface resistance and the remaining resistance, i.e.:

$$\frac{1}{U} = R_{so} + R \qquad \qquad \qquad \qquad \text{A5.103}$$

By superposition, for a given value of t_{ei}, Q_r is that part of Q_s which is realised at the environmental point. Since the resistances R_{so} and R are seen in parallel from the building surface, see Fig. A5.5, Q_r is given by:

$$Q_r = Q_s \left(\frac{R_{so}}{R + R_{so}} \right) \qquad \qquad \qquad \text{A5.104}$$

$$= Q_s U R_{so} \qquad \qquad \qquad \qquad \text{A5.105}$$

By definition this is the energy flow given by the sol-air temperature difference between the outside and inside, i.e.:

$$Q_r = U \Delta t_{eo} \qquad \qquad \qquad \qquad \text{A5.106}$$

Hence:

$$U \Delta t_{eo} = Q_s U R_{so} \qquad \qquad \qquad \text{A5.107}$$

$$\therefore \Delta t_{eo} = R_{so} (\alpha I_t - \epsilon I_l) \qquad \qquad \text{A5.108}$$

Thus, by definition, sol-air temperature is:

$$t_{eo} = t_{ao} + \Delta t_{eo} \qquad \qquad \qquad \text{A5.109}$$

$$= t_{ao} + R_{so} (\alpha I_t - \epsilon I_l) \qquad \qquad \text{A5.110}$$

Appendix 3—Derivation of Hypothetical Conductances

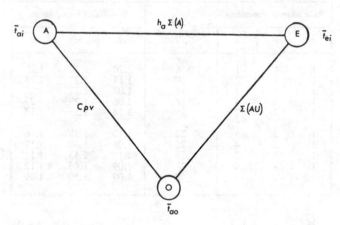

Fig. A5.6. Basic conductance network.

The heat transfer between a surface and the air is:

$$Q = A_s h_c (t_s - t_{ai}) \qquad \qquad \qquad \text{A5.111}$$

Hence in a room, the exchange between all the surfaces and the air is:

$$Q = h_c \Sigma(A) (t_m - t_{ai}) \qquad \qquad \text{A5.112}$$

but:

$$t_{ei} = \tfrac{1}{3} t_{ai} + \tfrac{2}{3} t_m \qquad \qquad \qquad \text{A5.113}$$

$$\therefore Q = h_c \Sigma(A) (\tfrac{3}{2} t_{ei} - \tfrac{3}{2} t_{ai}) \qquad \qquad \text{A5.114}$$

$$= \tfrac{3}{2} h_c \Sigma(A) (t_{ei} - t_{ai}) \qquad \qquad \text{A5.115}$$

$$= h_a \Sigma(A) (t_{ei} - t_{ai}) \qquad \qquad \text{A5.116}$$

where:

$$h_a = \tfrac{3}{2} h_c \qquad \qquad \qquad \qquad \text{A5.117}$$

$$= 4.5 \, \text{W/m}^2 \, \text{K} \qquad \qquad \qquad \text{A5.118}$$

By introducing the dry resultant point, h_a is divided into h_{ac} and h_{ec}, see Fig. A5.7.

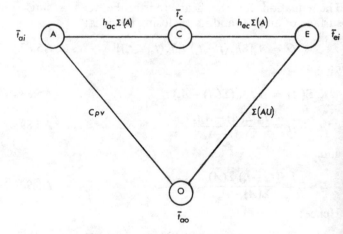

Fig. A5.7. Modified conductance network.

From Fig. A5.7.

$$h_{ec} \Sigma(A) (t_{ei} - t_c) = h_{ac} \Sigma(A) (t_c - t_{ai})$$

$$= h_a \Sigma(A) (t_{ei} - t_{ai}) \qquad \text{A5.119}$$

$$t_c = \tfrac{1}{2} t_{ai} + \tfrac{1}{2} t_m \qquad \qquad \qquad \text{A5.120}$$

$$= \tfrac{1}{2} t_{ai} + \tfrac{1}{2} (\tfrac{3}{2} t_{ei} - \tfrac{1}{2} t_{ai}) \qquad \qquad \text{A5.121}$$

$$= \tfrac{3}{4} t_{ei} + \tfrac{1}{4} t_{ai} \qquad \qquad \qquad \text{A5.122}$$

Hence:

$$h_{ec} \Sigma(A) (\tfrac{1}{4} t_{ei} - \tfrac{1}{4} t_{ai}) = h_a \Sigma(A) (t_{ei} - t_{ai}) \qquad \text{A5.123}$$

$$\therefore h_{ec} = 4 h_a \qquad \qquad \qquad \text{A5.124}$$

$$= 18 \, \text{W/m}^2 \, \text{K} \qquad \qquad \text{A5.125}$$

$$h_{ac} \Sigma(A) (\tfrac{3}{4} t_{ei} - \tfrac{3}{4} t_{ai}) = h_a \Sigma(A) (t_{ei} - t_{ai}) \qquad \text{A5.126}$$

$$\therefore h_{ac} = \tfrac{4}{3} h_a \qquad \qquad \qquad \text{A5.127}$$

$$= 6 \, \text{W/m}^2 \, \text{K} \qquad \qquad \text{A5.128}$$

Appendix 4—Steady State Energy Balance

Energy flows are given by:

$$\bar{Q}_u = \Sigma(AU)(\bar{t}_{ei} - \bar{t}_{ao}) \qquad \qquad \text{A5.129}$$

$$\bar{Q}_v = C\rho v(\bar{t}_{ai} - \bar{t}_{ao}) \qquad \qquad \text{A5.130}$$

$$\bar{Q}_{ac} = h_{ac}\Sigma(A)(\bar{t}_c - \bar{t}_{ai}) \qquad \qquad \text{A5.131}$$

$$\bar{Q}_{ec} = h_{ec}\Sigma(A)(\bar{t}_{ei} - \bar{t}_c) \qquad \qquad \text{A5.132}$$

Energy balances at nodes are given by:

$$\bar{Q}_{ac} = \bar{Q}_{ec} \qquad \qquad \text{A5.133}$$

$$\bar{Q}_a = \bar{Q}_v - \bar{Q}_{ac} \qquad \qquad \text{A5.134}$$

$$\bar{Q}_e = \bar{Q}_u + \bar{Q}_{ec} \qquad \qquad \text{A5.135}$$

$$\bar{Q}_o = \bar{Q}_u + \bar{Q}_v \qquad \qquad \text{A5.136}$$

$$\bar{Q}_a + \bar{Q}_e = \bar{Q}_u + \bar{Q}_v \qquad \qquad \text{A5.137}$$

From equations A5.131, A5.132 and A5.133:

$$h_{ac}\Sigma(A)(\bar{t}_c - \bar{t}_{ai}) = h_{ec}\Sigma(A)(\bar{t}_{ei} - \bar{t}_c) \qquad \text{A5.138}$$

From equations A5.130, A5.131 and A5.134:

$$\bar{Q}_a = C\rho v(\bar{t}_{ai} - \bar{t}_{ao}) - h_{ac}\Sigma(A)(\bar{t}_c - \bar{t}_{ai}) \qquad \text{A5.139}$$

$$= (C\rho v + h_{ac}\Sigma(A))\bar{t}_{ai} - h_{ac}\Sigma(A)\bar{t}_c - C\rho v\bar{t}_{ao} \qquad \text{A5.140}$$

$$\therefore \bar{t}_{ai} = \frac{\bar{Q}_a + h_{ac}\Sigma(A)\bar{t}_c + C\rho v\bar{t}_{ao}}{C\rho v + h_{ac}\Sigma(A)} \qquad \qquad \text{A5.141}$$

From equations A5.129, A5.132 and A5.135:

$$\bar{Q}_e = \Sigma(AU)(\bar{t}_{ei} - \bar{t}_{ao}) + h_{ec}\Sigma(A)(\bar{t}_{ei} - \bar{t}_c) \qquad \text{A5.142}$$

$$= (\Sigma(AU) + h_{ec}\Sigma(A))\bar{t}_{ei} - \Sigma(AU)\bar{t}_{ao} - h_{ec}\Sigma(A)\bar{t}_c$$
$$\text{A5.143}$$

$$\therefore \bar{t}_{ei} = \frac{\bar{Q}_e + \Sigma(AU)\bar{t}_{ao} + h_{ec}\Sigma(A)\bar{t}_c}{\Sigma(AU) + h_{ec}\Sigma(A)} \qquad \qquad \text{A5.144}$$

Substituting equations A5.141 and A5.144 into equation A5.138 gives:

$$h_{ac}\Sigma(A)\left[\frac{(C\rho v + h_{ac}\Sigma(A))\bar{t}_c - (\bar{Q}_a + h_{ac}\Sigma(A)\bar{t}_c + C\rho v\bar{t}_{ao})}{C\rho V + h_{ac}\Sigma(A)}\right] = h_{ec}\Sigma(A)\left[\frac{(\bar{Q}_e + \Sigma(AU)\bar{t}_{ao} + h_{ec}\Sigma(A)\bar{t}_c) - (\Sigma(AU) + h_{ec}\Sigma(A))\bar{t}_c}{\Sigma(AU) + h_{ec}\Sigma(A)}\right]$$
$$\text{A5.145}$$

Hence:

$$\frac{h_{ac}\Sigma(A)}{C\rho v + h_{ac}\Sigma(A)}\bar{Q}_a + \frac{h_{ec}\Sigma(A)}{\Sigma(AU) + h_{ec}\Sigma(A)}\bar{Q}_e = \left[\frac{h_{ac}\Sigma(A)}{C\rho v + h_{ac}\Sigma(A)}C\rho v + \frac{h_{ec}\Sigma(A)}{\Sigma(AU) + h_{ec}\Sigma(A)}\Sigma(AU)\right](\bar{t}_c - \bar{t}_{ao}) \qquad \text{A5.146}$$

For convenience this may be written:

$$F_v\bar{Q}_a + F_u\bar{Q}_e = [F_v C\rho v + F_u\Sigma(AU)](\bar{t}_c - \bar{t}_{ao}) \qquad \text{A5.147}$$

where:

$$F_v = \frac{h_{ac}\Sigma(A)}{C\rho v + h_{ac}\Sigma(A)} \qquad \qquad \text{A5.148}$$

$$F_u = \frac{h_{ec}\Sigma(A)}{\Sigma(AU) + h_{ec}\Sigma(A)} \qquad \qquad \text{A5.149}$$

In terms of air temperature the network is simpler, see Fig. A5.9:

$$\bar{Q}_a = \bar{Q}_v - \bar{Q}_{ae} \qquad \qquad \text{A5.150}$$

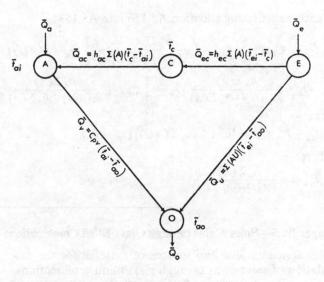

Fig. A5.8. Steady state energy flow.

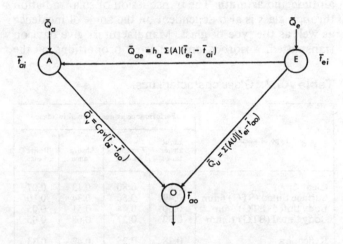

Fig. A5.9. Steady state energy flow (air point control).

$$\bar{Q}_{ae} = h_a\Sigma(A)(\bar{t}_{ei} - \bar{t}_{ai}) \qquad \qquad \text{A5.151}$$

$$\bar{Q}_e = \bar{Q}_u + \bar{Q}_{ae} \qquad \qquad \text{A5.152}$$

Hence:

$$\bar{Q}_a = C\rho v(\bar{t}_{ai} - \bar{t}_{ao}) - h_a\Sigma(A)(\bar{t}_{ei} - \bar{t}_{ai}) \qquad \text{A5.153}$$

and:

$$\bar{Q}_e = \Sigma(AU)(\bar{t}_{ei} - \bar{t}_{ao}) + h_a\Sigma(A)(\bar{t}_{ei} - \bar{t}_{ai}) \qquad \text{A5.154}$$

$$= [\Sigma(AU) + h_a\Sigma(A)]\bar{t}_{ei} - \Sigma(AU)\bar{t}_{ao} - h_a\Sigma(A)\bar{t}_{ai}$$
$$\text{A5.155}$$

$$\therefore \bar{t}_{ei} = \frac{\bar{Q}_e + \Sigma(AU)\bar{t}_{ao} + h_a\Sigma(A)\bar{t}_{ai}}{\Sigma(AU) + h_a\Sigma(A)} \qquad \text{A5.156}$$

Hence, substituting equation A5.156 into A5.153:

$$\bar{Q}_a = C\rho v(\bar{t}_{ai} - \bar{t}_{ao}) - \left(\frac{h_a\,\Sigma(A)}{\Sigma(AU) + h_a\,\Sigma(A)}\right)\left[\bar{Q}_e - \Sigma(AU)(\bar{t}_{ai} - \bar{t}_{ao})\right] \quad\quad\quad\quad\quad\quad\quad \text{A5.157}$$

$$\therefore\ \bar{Q}_a + \frac{h_a\,\Sigma(A)}{\Sigma(AU) + h_a\,\Sigma(A)}\ \bar{Q}_e = \left[C\rho v + \frac{h_a\,\Sigma(A)}{\Sigma(AU) + h_a\,\Sigma(A)}\ \Sigma(AU)\right](\bar{t}_{ai} - \bar{t}_{ao}) \quad\quad\quad\quad \text{A5.158}$$

or:

$$\bar{Q}_a + F_{au}\,\bar{Q}_e = [C\rho v + F_{au}\,\Sigma(AU)]\,(\bar{t}_{ai} - \bar{t}_{ao}) \quad\quad\quad\quad\quad\quad\quad\quad\quad \text{A5.159}$$

where:

$$F_{au} = \frac{h_a\,\Sigma(A)}{\Sigma(AU) + h_a\,\Sigma(A)} \quad\quad\quad\quad\quad\quad\quad\quad\quad\quad\quad\quad\quad \text{A5.160}$$

Appendix 5—Solar Gains through Glass/Blind Combinations

This appendix identifies sources of material for the calculation of solar gains through glass/blind combinations. It also gives definitions of the more common terms used to describe solar transmission characteristics.

The solar intensity on a building façade changes continuously because of time dependent variations in solar altitude and azimuth. The transmission of solar radiation through glass is also dependent on the angle of incidence as well as the type of glass. Manufacturers give data on transmitted, absorbed and reflected proportions of the incident energy. Table A5.2 gives data for a representative range of glasses.

The characteristics of vertical and horizontal slatted opaque blinds are given in a BRE paper[4] from which the critical information is shown to be the absorptivity of the blind surface, the width : spacing ratio of the slats and the angle of the slats to the glass.

The above variables can be compounded to give the instantaneous solar gain through any glass/blind combination at any time or place. (Because of the complexity, computers will usually be used for this calculation.) Where internal blinds are used, the gains are realised partly at the environmental point and partly at the air point. Where internal blinds are not fitted, all the gains appear at the environmental point.

Calculations can be simplified, with a slight loss of accuracy, by using solar gain factors and alternating gain factors. These were developed specifically for the calculation of temperatures in naturally ventilated buildings but they may also be used for calculating solar gains through glass/blinds in air conditioned buildings. They are particularly well suited to admittance procedure calculations where the mean and cyclic responses are analysed separately.

Table A5.2. Glass characteristics.

Type of glass	Performance at near normal incidence			
	Light transmittance	Transmittance	Absorptance	Reflectance
Clear 6mm	0.87	0.80	0.13	0.07
Surface tinted (STG) 6mm	0.49	0.56	0.34	0.10
Body tinted (BTG) 6mm	0.50	0.44	0.51	0.05
Body tinted (BTG) 10mm	0.32	0.27	0.68	0.05
Reflecting	0.38	0.25	0.42	0.33
Strongly reflecting	0.20	0.07	0.36	0.57
Sealed double unit (reflecting+clear 6mm)	0.47	0.25	0.51	0.24
Sealed double unit (strongly reflecting+clear 6mm)	0.20	0.10	0.47	0.43
Clear 6mm with reflecting film (metallic)	0.30	0.25	0.42	0.33
Clear 6mm with strongly reflecting film (metallic)	0.16	0.13	0.41	0.46
Clear 6mm with reflecting film (tinted)	0.15	0.15	0.66	0.19

Solar Gain Factors $\bar{S}$ and Alternating Solar Gain Factors $\tilde{S}$

These factors are used to calculate the mean gain to the conditioned space in the course of 24 hours.

Values are derived from rigorous calculations of conditions in July for south-west façades at latitude 51.7°N and usually the 1500 hours value is taken as standard. The factors are defined as:

$$\bar{S}_a = \frac{\text{Mean solar gain at air point/m}^2\text{ of glazing}}{\text{Mean solar intensity on the façade}}$$

$$\bar{S}_e = \frac{\text{Mean solar gain at environmental point/m}^2\text{ of glazing}}{\text{Mean solar intensity on the façade}}$$

$$\tilde{S}_a = \frac{\text{Instantaneous cyclic solar gain at air point/m}^2\text{ of glazing}}{\text{Instantaneous cyclic solar intensity on the façade}}$$

$$\tilde{S}_e = \frac{\text{Instantaneous cyclic solar gain at environmental point/m}^2\text{ of glazing}}{\text{Instantaneous cyclic solar intensity on the façade}}$$

Values of $\tilde{S}_a$, $\tilde{S}_e$, $\tilde{S}_a$ and $\tilde{S}_e$ for a range of glass/blinds are given in Tables A5.3 and A5.4

Time Delays

The alternating gain usually lags the solar intensity by between 0 and 2 hours, the duration of the lag depending on the surface factors of the internal surfaces. High surface factors (0.8) give rise to delays of about one hour, low surface factors (0.5) give rise to delays of about two hours.

Shading Coefficients S_c

These are a measure of the instantaneous heat gain at normal incidence and are calculated as a fraction of the gain through a reference glass, usually 3 or 4 mm clear glass. Shading coefficients are often used by glass manu-facturers in their technical literature. Shading coefficients do not lend themselves to direct application in admit-tance calculations.

They are defined as:

$$S_c = \frac{\text{Solar gain through selected glass blind at direct normal incidence}}{\text{Solar gain through reference glass at direct normal incidence}}$$

Table A5.3. Solar gain factors with no internal shading.

Description	S_c	S_e light	S_e heavy	Description	S_c	S_e light	S_e heavy
Single glazing				Clear 6mm+miniature louvres (1)	0.16	0.10	0.09
Clear 6mm	0.76	0.64	0.47	Clear 6mm+miniature louvres (2)	0.12	0.09	0.09
Surface tinted (STG) 6mm	0.60	0.53	0.41	BTG 6mm +light horizontal slats	0.13	0.09	0.08
Body tinted (BTG) 6mm	0.52	0.47	0.38	BTG 6mm +light vertical slats	0.14	0.12	0.09
Body tinted (BTG) 10mm	0.42	0.39	0.34				
				Double glazing + external shade			
Clear with reflecting film (metallic)	0.32	0.29	0.23	Clear 6mm+clear 6mm+ light horizontal slats	0.13	0.09	0.07
Clear with strongly reflecting film (metallic)	0.21	0.19	0.16	Clear 6mm+clear 6mm+light vertical slats	0.15	0.10	0.08
Clear with reflecting film (tinted)	0.28	0.26	0.23	Clear 6mm+clear 6mm+light roller blind	0.10	0.09	0.07
Reflecting	0.36	0.33	0.27	Clear 6mm+clear 6mm+miniature louvres (1)	0.12	0.07	0.06
Strongly reflecting	0.18	0.17	0.15				
Double glazing (outer pane first)				Clear 6mm+clear 6mm+miniature louvres (2)	0.09	0.06	0.06
Clear 6mm +clear 6mm	0.64	0.56	0.42	Clear 6mm+clear 6mm+dark horizontal slats	0.10	0.06	0.06
STG +clear 6mm	0.48	0.43	0.34				
BTG 6mm +clear 6mm	0.40	0.37	0.30	*Other*			
BTG 10mm +clear 6mm	0.30	0.28	0.24	Triple glazing clear 6mm+clear 6mm+clear 6mm	0.55	0.50	0.39
Reflecting +clear 6mm	0.28	0.25	0.21	Clear 6mm+clear 6mm+mid pane light slats	0.28	0.26	0.24
Strongly reflecting+clear 6mm	0.13	0.12	0.10				
Lightly reflecting sealed double unit	0.32	0.29	0.21				
Strongly reflecting sealed double unit	0.15	0.14	0.11				
Single glazing with external shade							
Clear 6mm +light horizontal slats	0.16	0.11	0.09				
Clear 6mm +light vertical slats	0.18	0.13	0.10				
Clear 6mm+dark horizontal slats	0.13	0.09	0.08				
Clear 6mm+holland blind	0.13	0.10	0.08				

TYPE OF SHADE			
Light slatted blind (vertical or horizontal)		blade angle (downward tilt)	20°
width/spacing ratio	1.2	blade absorptance	0.96
blade angle (downward tilt for horizontal)	45°	*Miniature fixed louvres* (2)	
blade absorptance	0.4	number of slats per inch	23
Dark slatted blind (vertical or horizontal)		width/spacing ratio	1.15
width/spacing ratio	1.2	blade angle (downward tilt)	20°
blade angle (downward tilt for horizontal)	45°	blade absorptance	0.98
blade absorptance	0.8	*Linen roller blind*	
Miniature fixed louvres (1)		transmittance	0.13
number of slats per inch	17	absorptance	0.20
width/spacing ratio	0.85	reflectance	0.67

Table A5.4 Solar gain factors with internal shading.

Description	S_e	S_a	Lightweight S_e	Lightweight S_a	Heavyweight S_e	Heavyweight S_a
Single glazing + internal shade						
Clear 6mm +light horizontal slats	0.31	0.16	0.28	0.17	0.24	0.17
Clear 6mm +light vertical slats	0.32	0.16	0.30	0.18	0.24	0.18
Clear 6mm +dark horizontal slats	0.35	0.23	0.36	0.26	0.34	0.26
Clear 6mm +linen blinds	0.20	0.11	0.18	0.11	0.14	0.11
BTG 6mm +light slatted blinds	0.19	0.20	0.18	0.22	0.17	0.22
BTG 10mm +light slatted blinds	0.14	0.21	0.14	0.22	0.13	0.22
Reflecting +light slatted blinds	0.14	0.15	0.14	0.16	0.12	0.16
Strongly reflecting+light slatted blinds	0.06	0.10	0.06	0.10	0.06	0.10
Double glazing + internal shades						
Clear 6mm+clear 6mm+light slatted blinds	0.26	0.19	0.25	0.21	0.21	0.21
Clear 6mm+clear 6mm+dark slatted blinds	0.30	0.26	0.31	0.29	0.30	0.29
BTG 6mm+clear 6mm+light slatted blinds	0.15	0.15	0.14	0.16	0.13	0.16
BTG 10mm+clear 6mm+light slatted blinds	0.10	0.13	0.10	0.14	0.09	0.14
Reflecting+clear 6mm+light slatted blinds	0.11	0.10	0.10	0.11	0.09	0.11
Strongly reflecting+clear 6mm+light slatted blinds	0.04	0.06	0.04	0.06	0.04	0.06

Appendix 6—Derivation of F_1 and F_2

$$F_1 = \frac{\bar{t}_{ei} - \bar{t}_{ao}}{\bar{t}_c - \bar{t}_{ao}} \quad \dots \quad \dots \quad \dots \quad \dots \quad \dots \quad \dots \quad \dots \quad \dots \quad \dots \quad \dots \quad \text{A5.161}$$

From Appendix 4, equation A5.147:

$$\bar{t}_c - \bar{t}_{ao} = \frac{F_v \bar{Q}_a + F_u \bar{Q}_e}{F_v C\rho v + F_u \Sigma(AU)} \quad \dots \quad \dots \quad \dots \quad \dots \quad \dots \quad \dots \quad \dots \quad \dots \quad \text{A5.162}$$

From Appendix 4, equation A5.142:

$$\bar{Q}_e = h_{ec} \Sigma(A) (\bar{t}_{ei} - \bar{t}_{ao}) - h_{ec} \Sigma(A) (\bar{t}_c - \bar{t}_{ao}) + \Sigma(AU) (\bar{t}_{ei} - \bar{t}_{ao}) \quad \dots \quad \dots \quad \dots \quad \dots \quad \text{A5.163}$$

$$= [h_{ec} \Sigma(A) + \Sigma(AU)](\bar{t}_{ei} - \bar{t}_{ao}) - h_{ec} \Sigma(A)(\bar{t}_c - \bar{t}_{ao}) \quad \dots \quad \dots \quad \dots \quad \text{A5.164}$$

Thus:

$$\frac{\bar{Q}_e}{\bar{t}_c - \bar{t}_{ao}} + h_{ec} \Sigma(A) = (h_{ec} \Sigma(A) + \Sigma(AU)) \left[\frac{\bar{t}_{ei} - \bar{t}_{ao}}{\bar{t}_c - \bar{t}_{ao}} \right] \quad \dots \quad \dots \quad \dots \quad \text{A5.165}$$

$$\therefore \quad F_1 = \frac{\bar{Q}_e}{[h_{ec} \Sigma(A) + \Sigma(AU)](\bar{t}_c - \bar{t}_{ao})} + \frac{h_{ec} \Sigma(A)}{h_{ec} \Sigma(A) + \Sigma(AU)} \quad \dots \quad \dots \quad \dots \quad \text{A5.166}$$

Thus, combining equations A5.147, A5.148, A5.149 and A5.166

$$F_1 = \frac{\bar{Q}_e (F_v C\rho v + F_u \Sigma(AU))}{[h_{ec} \Sigma(A) + \Sigma(AU)] (F_v \bar{Q}_a + F_u \bar{Q}_e)} + F_u \quad \dots \quad \dots \quad \dots \quad \dots \quad \text{A5.167}$$

And combining with equations A5.48 and A5.51

$$F_1 = \frac{E(F_v C\rho v + F_u \Sigma(AU))}{[h_{ec} \Sigma(A) + \Sigma(AU)] (KF_v + EF_u)} + F_u \quad \dots \quad \dots \quad \dots \quad \dots \quad \dots \quad \text{A5.168}$$

$$F_2 = \frac{\bar{t}_{ai} - \bar{t}_{ao}}{\bar{t}_c - \bar{t}_{ao}} \quad \dots \quad \dots \quad \dots \quad \dots \quad \dots \quad \dots \quad \dots \quad \dots \quad \dots \quad \text{A5.169}$$

$$\bar{Q}_a = C\rho v(\bar{t}_{ai} - \bar{t}_{ao}) - h_{ac} \Sigma(A) (\bar{t}_c - \bar{t}_{ao}) + h_{ac} \Sigma(A) (\bar{t}_{ai} - \bar{t}_{ao}) \dots \quad \dots \quad \dots \quad \text{A5.170}$$

From Appendix 4, equation A5.139:

$$\therefore \frac{\bar{Q}_a}{\bar{t}_c - \bar{t}_{ao}} + h_{ac} \Sigma(A) = (C\rho v + h_{ac} \Sigma(A)) \left(\frac{\bar{t}_{ai} - \bar{t}_{ao}}{\bar{t}_c - \bar{t}_{ao}} \right) \quad \dots \quad \dots \quad \dots \quad \dots \quad \text{A5.171}$$

Hence:

$$F_2 = \frac{\bar{Q}_a}{[C\rho v + h_{ac} \Sigma(A)] (\bar{t}_c - \bar{t}_{ao})} + \frac{h_{ac} \Sigma(A)}{C\rho v + h_{ac} \Sigma(A)} \quad \dots \quad \dots \quad \dots \quad \dots \quad \text{A5.172}$$

Thus, combining equations A5.147, A5.148, A5.149 and A5.172

$$F_2 = \frac{\bar{Q}_a[F_v C\rho v + F_u \Sigma(AU)]}{[C\rho v + h_{ac} \Sigma(A)] (F_v \bar{Q}_a + F_u \bar{Q}_e)} + F_v \quad \dots \quad \dots \quad \dots \quad \dots \quad \text{A5.173}$$

And combining with equations A5.48 and A5.51

$$F_2 = \frac{K[F_v C\rho v + F_u \Sigma(AU)]}{[C\rho v + h_{ac} \Sigma(A)] (KF_v + EF_u)} + F_v \quad \dots \quad \dots \quad \dots \quad \dots \quad \dots \quad \dots \quad \text{A5.174}$$

Appendix 7—Intermittent Operation

Single Step Inputs

Considering continuous (steady state) operation and ignoring all casual gains then the room energy requirement, Q_t, is given as follows:

$$Q_t(KF_v+EF_u)=[F_vC\rho v+F_u\Sigma(AU)](t_d-t_{ao}) \qquad \text{A5.175}$$

This can be solved to find Q_t for a given t_d.

For intermittent operation, the average condition is:

$$\bar{Q}_{in}(KF_v+EF_u)=[F_vC\rho v+F_u\Sigma(AU)](\bar{t}_c-t_{ao}) \qquad \text{A5.176}$$

And the cyclic component in the ON period is:

$$\tilde{Q}_{in}(KF_v+EF_y)=[F_vC\rho v+F_y\Sigma(AY)]\tilde{t}_c \qquad .. \quad \text{A5.177}$$

However:

$$t_d=\bar{t}_c+\tilde{t}_c \quad .. \qquad .. \qquad .. \qquad .. \qquad .. \quad \text{A5.178}$$

So:

$$t_d-t_{ao}=\bar{t}_c-t_{ao}+\tilde{t}_c \quad .. \qquad .. \qquad .. \qquad .. \quad \text{A5.179}$$

Hence, combining equations A5.176, A5.177 and A5.179 gives:

$$t_d-\bar{t}_{ao}=\frac{\bar{Q}_{in}(KF_v+EF_u)}{F_vC\rho v+F_u\Sigma(AU)}+\frac{\tilde{Q}_{in}(KF_v+EF_y)}{F_vC\rho v+F_y\Sigma(AY)} \qquad \text{A5.180}$$

However:

$$24\bar{Q}_{in}=nQ_{in} \quad .. \qquad .. \qquad .. \qquad .. \qquad .. \quad \text{A5.181}$$

$$=n(\bar{Q}_{in}+\tilde{Q}_{in}) \quad .. \qquad .. \qquad .. \qquad .. \quad \text{A5.182}$$

$$\tilde{Q}_{in}=\left(\frac{24}{n}-1\right)\bar{Q}_{in} \quad .. \qquad .. \qquad .. \qquad .. \quad \text{A5.183}$$

$$=\left(1-\frac{n}{24}\right)Q_{in} \quad .. \qquad .. \qquad .. \qquad .. \quad \text{A5.184}$$

Hence, combining equations A5.180, A5.181 and A5.184 gives:

$$t_d-t_{ao}=Q_{in}\left[\frac{\frac{1}{24}n(KF_v+EF_u)}{F_vC\rho v+F_u\Sigma(AU)}+\frac{(1-\frac{1}{24}n)(KF_v+EF_y)}{F_vC\rho v+F_y\Sigma(AY)}\right] \qquad \text{A5.185}$$

But the intermittent plant operation ratio is given by:

$$r=\frac{Q_{pn}}{Q_p} \quad .. \qquad .. \qquad .. \qquad .. \qquad .. \quad \text{A5.186}$$

$$=\frac{Q_{in}}{F_b}\div\frac{Q_t}{F_b} \quad .. \qquad .. \qquad .. \qquad .. \quad \text{A5.187}$$

$$=\frac{Q_{in}}{Q_t} \quad .. \qquad .. \qquad .. \qquad .. \qquad .. \quad \text{A5.188}$$

Thus:

$$r=\frac{\left[\dfrac{KF_v+EF_u}{F_vC\rho v+F_u\Sigma(AU)}\right]}{\left[\dfrac{\frac{1}{24}n(KF_v+EF_u)}{F_vC\rho v+F_u\Sigma(AU)}+\dfrac{(1-\frac{1}{24}n)(KF_v+EF_y)}{F_vC\rho v+F_y\Sigma(AY)}\right]} \quad .. \qquad .. \qquad .. \qquad .. \qquad .. \quad \text{A5.189}$$

or:

$$r=\frac{24[F_vC\rho v+F_y\Sigma(AY)](KF_v+EF_u)}{n[F_vC\rho v+F_y\Sigma(AY)](KF_v+EF_u)+(24-n)[F_vC\rho v+F_u\Sigma(AU)](KF_v+EF_y)} \quad .. \qquad .. \qquad .. \qquad .. \quad \text{A5.190}$$

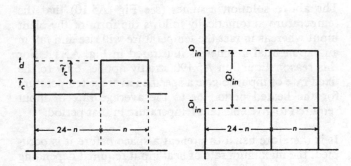

Fig. A5.10. Step inputs.

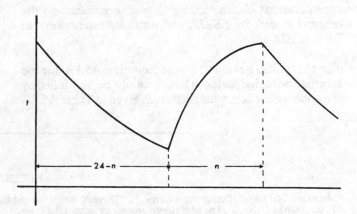

Fig. A5.11. Temperature response.

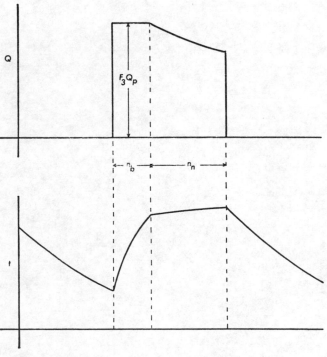

Fig. A5.12 Energy input and Temperature response.

The above solution assumes (see Fig. A5.10) that the temperature automatically follows the form of the plant input whereas in fact the temperature will rise and fall in an exponential manner as illustrated in Fig. A5.11. For this reason Equation A5.190 strictly applies only to the fixed rate of input to give a specified average temperature for the heated period or to the average rate of input required to give constant temperature in that period.

It is therefore usual to preheat a space before it is occupied, the maximum rate of heat input required depending on the length of preheat period adopted. An idealised illustration of the appropriate input cycle is given in Fig. A5.12. The approximate theoretical basis outlined above is insufficient to evaluate these more detailed considerations but the following guidance, based on the original studies by BSRIA and on more recent work at BRE, is offered.

The plant ratio r evaluated from Equation A5.190 for the specified occupied period, n hours, should be multiplied by the appropriate correction factor, B, given in Table A5.6.

The preheat plant capacity is therefore given as follows:

$$Q_{pb} = B\,Q_{pn} \quad .. \quad .. \quad .. \quad .. \quad \text{A5.191}$$

$$= B \times (r \times Q_p) \quad .. \quad .. \quad .. \quad \text{A5.192}$$

which for convenience can be written:

$$Q_{pb} = F_3\,Q_p \quad .. \quad .. \quad .. \quad .. \quad \text{A5.193}$$

where:

$$F_3 = B \times r \quad .. \quad .. \quad .. \quad .. \quad \text{A5.194}$$

Table A5.6. Correction factors for preheating, B.

Preheat period/h	Correction factor
0	1.9
1	1.4
2	1.2
4	1.0
6	0.8
8	0.7

REFERENCES

[1] MILBANK, N. O. and HARRINGTON-LYNN, J., "Thermal Response and the Admittance Procedure" *BSE*, May 1974, **42**, 38–51.
[2] HARRINGTON-LYNN, J., The admittance proceduce: intermittent plant operation, *BSE*, December 1974, **42**, 219–221.
[3] HARRINGTON-LYNN, J., The admittance procedure: variable ventilation, *BSE*, November 1974, **42**, 199–200.
[4] NICOL, J. F. "Radiation Transmission Characteristics of Blind Systems" *Building Science*, 1966, 1.

SECTION A7   INTERNAL HEAT GAINS

General ....*Page*   A7–3

Human and Animal Bodies A7–3

Lighting A7–4

Electric Motors A7–6

Computer and Office Equipment..   A7–6

Miscellaneous Electric Appliances A7–7

Gas Heated Appliances A7–8

This edition of Section A7 first published: 1986

SECTION A7   INTERNAL HEAT GAINS

GENERAL

Internal heat gain is the sensible and latent heat emitted within an internal space by the occupants, lighting, electric motors, electronic equipment, etc. The radiant proportion of sensible heat emitted from internal sources is partially absorbed in the building structure and furnishings, hence reducing the instantaneous heat gain.

HUMAN AND ANIMAL BODIES

Human Bodies

The emission of heat from a human body in relation to the surrounding indoor climate is discussed in Section A1 and the sensible and latent heat emissions of adult males for various activities are listed in Table A7.1. Correction factors for typical occupancies are given in Table A7.2, but specific assessments should be applied where data are available.

The latent heat gain from the human body results in an instantaneous addition to the cooling load, whereas the sensible heat gain is not all directly converted to cooling load. The radiant proportion of the sensible heat loss from the human body is about 70%. Reference should be made to Sections A5 and A9 to determine the effects of radiant energy stored within the building structure.

Table A7.2. Typical proportions for occupancy, men, women and children in buildings overall.

Space	Typical proportions† (%)			Correction to data in table A7.1 (%)*
	Men	Women	Children	
Cinema, matinée	20	70	10	88
evening	45	50	5	92
Dance hall	60	40	—	94
Department store.. ..	25	65	10	88
Factory, light work ..	25	75	—	89
medium work ..	66	33	—	94
heavy work ..	100	—	—	100
Office, commercial ..	50	50	—	93
bank headquarters	40	60	—	91
bank branch ..	33	66	—	89
Restaurant, maximum ..	100	—	—	100
normal ..	40	50	10	90
Theatre, matinée	20	70	10	88
evening	45	50	5	92

* Based on proportions quoted and emissions for women and children of 85% and 75% of rate for adult male.
† Proportions will vary area to area, i.e. a typing pool is likely to be all female.

Table A7.1. Heat emission from the human body. (Adult male, body surface area 2 m^2).

Application			Sensible (s) and latent (l) heat emissions, W, at the stated dry-bulb temperatures, °C.									
			15		20		22		24		26	
Degree of activity	Typical	Total	(s)	(l)	’s)	(l)	(s)	(l)	(s)	(l)	(s)	(l)
Seated at rest	Theatre, hotel lounge	115	100	15	90	25	80	35	75	40	65	50
Light work	Office, restaurant*	140	110	30	100	40	90	50	80	60	70	70
Walking slowly	Store, bank	160	120	40	110	50	100	60	85	75	75	85
Light bench work	Factory	235	150	85	130	105	115	120	100	135	80	155
Medium work	Factory, dance hall	265	160	105	140	125	125	140	105	160	90	175
Heavy work	Factory	440	220	220	190	250	165	275	135	305	105	335

* For restaurants serving hot meals, add 10 W sensible and 10 W latent for food.

Animal Bodies

In the absence of experimental results, an approximation to the basal metabolic rate (bmr) from an animal may be established using the expression:

$$h = 3.2m^{0.75} \qquad .. \qquad .. \qquad .. \qquad .. \qquad A7.1$$

where:

h = basal metabolic rate ..   ..   W

m = mass of animal..   ..   ..   kg

It is further necessary to estimate the effect of the activity since the bmr will be slightly higher if the normal body temperature exceeds 39°C.

The sensible and latent heat emissions from the bodies of a variety of animals of average mass are listed in Table A7.3.

Table A7.3. Sensible (s) and latent (l) heat emissions, etc., from animal bodies at normal body temperature.

Creature	Average body weight (kg)	Rectal temperature (°C)	b.m.r. (W)	Typical occupancy per 10m² floor area	Estimated heat emission (W)*	
					(s)	(l)
Mouse ..	0·02	36·5	0·175	2000	0·5	0·3
Hampster	0·12	36·9	0·483	1350	1·6	0·4
Rat ..	0·30	37·3	1·32	485	3·7	1·2
Guinea Pig	0·41	39·1	1·7	400	4·6	2·2
Rabbit ..	2·6	39·4	5·6	32	8·5	2·5
Cat ..	3·0	38·6	7·35	16	11	3·8
Monkey ..	4·2	38·8	10	16	24	14
Dog ..	16	38·9	26	5	40	13
Goat ..	36	39·2	41	5	62	21
Sheep ..	45	38·8	56	5	81	29
Pig ..	250	39·3	210	1·5	317	106
Pigeon ..	0·27	43·3	1·35	400	2·2	0·5
Chicken ..	2·0	41·4	5·6	195	9·2	1·8

* Based on a 24-hour average. During periods of high activity the heat production may be double that of the estimated 24-hour rate.

LIGHTING

General

All electrical energy used by a lamp is ultimately released as heat. The energy is emitted by means of conduction, convection or radiation. When the lighting is switched on the luminaire itself absorbs some of the heat emitted by the lamp. Some of this heat may then be transmitted to the building structure, depending on the mounting of the luminaire. The radiant energy (both visible and invisible) emitted from a lamp will only result in a heat gain to the space after it has been absorbed by the room surfaces. This storage effect results in a time lag before the electrical energy used at the lamp appears as a part of the cooling load.

Energy Distribution

The total electrical power input to the lighting installation has to be known. For lamps which have associated control gear, it is important to add the power dissipated by the control gear to that dissipated by the lamp. Where a conventional ballast is used, an addition of about 20% of the nominal lamp rating should be allowed. Where an electronic ballast is used the addition should be about 10%.

The performance of individual types of lamp varies from one manufacturer to another. The percentage power absorbed by the ballast also varies with the lamp rating, generally falling as lamp rating increases.

Table A7.4 provides an indication of the relative proportions of heat output from tungsten and fluorescent luminaires, including control gear.

Table A7.4. Energy dissipation in lamps.

Heat output	Energy dissipated in following types of lamp* (%)		
	Fluorescent	Tungsten	High pressure discharge
Conducted or convected	55	15	38
Radiant	45	85	62

*An approximation of the control gear losses is included where appropriate.

Where luminaires are recessed into the ventilated ceiling, or are of the air handling type, the heat transmitted to the room will be reduced below the normal rating of the lamp. Recessed luminaires give about 50% of the heat they produce directly to the room, the other 50% going into the plenum above the suspended ceiling. Air handling luminaires give about 20% of the heat they produce directly to the room, the other 80% being taken away through the extract duct. Heat which is taken away from a luminaire via a ceiling plenum or directly from the luminaire itself will not form part of the room sensible heat gain, but will still constitute part of the total refrigeration load.

Where detailed design is being carried out an accurate assessment of the distribution of energy from particular types of luminaire should be obtained from the manufacturer. In the absence of manufacturers' data, Table A7.5 gives the appropriate energy distribution for typical fittings.

Radiation

As shown earlier, a large proportion of the energy is dissipated by the lamps as radiant energy; this of course includes the proportion which is light. Radiant heat has the same properties as light. It can be reflected, refracted or diffused.

With the increasing levels of lighting the amount of radiant heat generated by an installation will also increase. This heat, which is difficult to control, even by the use of air conditioning, can lead to complaints by the occupants. Radiant heat is mainly detected by the occupant on the forehead or the back of the hand as these parts are more sensitive to radiant heat than other parts of the body.

Reference should be made to Sections A5 and A9 to determine the effects of radiant energy stored within the building structure.

Preliminary Load Assessment

In instances where a preliminary assessment of the heat gain due to lighting load is required prior to the establishment of the detailed design arrangement, the figures quoted in Table A7.6 may be used.

Table A7.5   Measured energy distribution for fluorescent fittings having four 70 W lamps.

Type of fitting		Energy distribution %	
Mounting	Detail	Up	Down
Recessed	Open	38	62
	Louvre	45	55
	Prismatic or opal diffuser	53	47
Surface	Open	12	88
	Enclosed prismatic or opal	22	78
	Enclosed prismatic on metal spine	6	94

Table A7.6.   Typical installed power per unit floor area for different types of lighting installation classified by light source, luminaire type and illuminance provided.

Illuminance/ lux	Installed power per unit floor area/(W/m^2)					
	Incandescent opal sphere	Tubular fluorescent			High pressure mercury discharge, high bay reflector	High pressure sodium discharge, high bay reflector
		Industrial trough	Enclosed surface mounted luminaire	Enclosed recessed luminaire		
300	50–60	5–12	8–19	8–20	7–14	4–8
500		8–20	14–30	15–35	13–25	7–14
750		12–30	20–40	20–50	18–35	10–20

Note: The above figures assume design to good current practice and exisiting installations may exceed the ranges given.

ELECTRIC MOTORS

The heat gain to a building space from electric motors falls into three categories:

(a) Motor, driven equipment and useful output all situated within the space concerned (e.g. machinery in a workshop).

$$q_g = \frac{q_a}{\eta_t} \quad .. \quad .. \quad .. \quad .. \quad .. \quad A7.2$$

(b) Motor situated within the space concerned with driven equipment elsewhere.

$$q_g = q_a \left(\frac{1}{\eta_t} - 1\right) .. \quad .. \quad .. \quad .. \quad A7.3$$

(c) Driven equipment situated within, or related to (e.g. fans), the space concerned with motor elsewhere.

$$q_g = q_a \quad .. \quad .. \quad .. \quad .. \quad .. \quad A7.4$$

where (see Fig. A7.1):

q_g = heat gain to space .. .. .. W

q_a = power at equipment shaft .. W

η_t = overall efficiency of transmission.

The overall efficiency of transmission is the product of the motor efficiency (η_m) and the drive efficiency (η_d).

For precise details of efficiencies, which will vary with motor type, speed, performance and the character of the drive, reference should be made to manufacturers' data. For preliminary system design, reference may be made to Table A7.7.

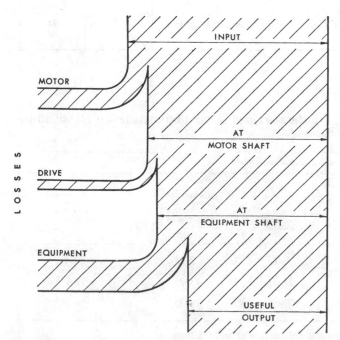

Fig. A7.1. Energy input and output and dissipation by losses.

Table A7.7. Average efficiencies for electric motors and drives.

| Motor output rating | | Average values for motor efficiency (η_m) | | | |
h.p.	kW	d.c.	a.c. Single phase	a.c. Two phase	a.c. Three phase
1	0·75	0·76	0·65	0·73	0·74
5	3·75	0·83	0·78	0·84	0·85
10	7·50	0·86	0·81	0·87	0·88
20	15	0·88	0·83	0·88	0·90
50	38	0·90	0·85	0·91	0·91
75	56	0·92	0·86	0·92	0·92

Drive efficiencies (η_d) are approximately as follows:

Plain bearings 95 to 98%.   Vee-belts 96 to 98%.
Roller bearings 98%.   Spur gears 93%.
Ball bearings 99%.   Bevel gears 92%.

COMPUTER AND OFFICE EQUIPMENT

The heat dissipated by similar types of electronic equipment varies considerably from one manufacturer to another. Therefore it is important to obtain specific data, for both running and standby modes, at the earliest opportunity.

Table A7.8 gives an indication of the typical heat dissipation rates per m² of floor area for rooms containing different types of electronic data-processing equipment. These figures may be used for assessing loads during the preliminary design stage.

Table A7.9 gives an indication of the heat dissipation from typical computer and office equipment. These figures should only be used in the absence of manufacturers' data and their application should be limited to the preliminary design stage.

Table A7.8. Heat dissipated per m² of floor area for rooms containing computer equipment.

Room type	Sensible heat dissipated from equipment/(W/m²)	Typical equipment in room
Hi-tech office	50–70	One VDU per person and one central printer
Computer support room	500–750	Distributive processors. VDU. Printer
Computer equipment room: average high density	450 900	Central processing unit. Tape deck. Disk drive

Table A7.9. Heat dissipated from typical electronic data-processing equipment.

Description	Performance/Status	Base dimensions/ mm x mm	Heat emission/W
VDU terminal	—	470 × 590	200
	Intelligent	470 × 650	500
Printer	300 lpm	760 × 620	450
	430 lpm	930 × 810	1000
	750 lpm	930 × 810	1150
	1000 lpm	930 × 810	1150
Card reader	300 cpm	490 × 360	450
Disk drive	80 mb	480 × 860	980
	300 mb	580 × 910	1300
Magnetic tape deck	9 track	475 × 525	800
CPU	4 mips	640 × 830	3800
Photocopier	Running	Small	1500
	Standby	Small	750
	Running	Large	3500
	Standby	Large	1500
Typewriter:			
electric	Running		50
electronic	Running		100

Notes: lpm = lines per minute; cpm = cards per minute; mb = megabytes; mips = million instructions per second; cpu = central processing unit; vdu = visual display unit.

A feature of the developments in the electronics industry over the past two decades has been the reduction in physical size and power input to components which continue to provide the same processing power. This trend is likely to continue, making published data liable to be outdated very quickly. Businesses making use of computers tend to expand their systems as the demand on their existing facility grows. However, since the equipment available becomes increasingly efficient, the actual heat dissipation attributed to processing equipment is likely to remain roughly constant as processing power increases.

MISCELLANEOUS ELECTRIC APPLIANCES

Tables A7.10 and A7.11 list the probable heat gain from miscellaneous electric appliances under normal use, and are for equipment operating without overhead extract hoods. Where properly designed hoods are used, the sensible and latent heat gains may be reduced by 50%. See Section B3 for recommended hood face velocities.

Table A7.10. Sensible heat and latent heat emissions from miscellaneous electric cooking appliances operating under normal conditions of use.

Appliance	Overall dimensions Less legs and handles (mm) (height quoted last)	Type of control	Miscellaneous data (Dimensions in mm, ratings in W)	Mfgr. rating	Maintaining rate	In average use Sensible (s)	In average use Latent (l)
Coffee brewer—2·5 litre		Man.		0·7	0·1	0·3	0·1
„ warmer—2·5 litre		„		0·1	0·1	0·1	0·1
„ brewing unit with 20 litre tank	500 × 760 × 660	Auto.	Water heater—2000 W Brewers— 3000 W	5·0		1·5	0·4
Coffee urn—14 litre	380 diam. × 870	Auto.	Black finish	3·5	0·1	0·8	0·5
„ „ 23 litre	460 diam. × 940	„	Nickel plated	5·0	1·0	1·0	0·7
„ „ 14 litre	300 × 580 oval × 530	„	„ „	4·5	0·1	0·7	0·5
Food warmer with plate warmer, per m² top surface		Auto.	Insulated, separate heating unit for each pot. Plate warmer in base	4·0	1·5	1·0	1·0
Food warmer without plate warmer, per m² top surface		Auto.	Ditto, without plate warmer	3·0	1·2	0·6	1·1
Fry kettle— 5 kg fat	300 diam. × 360	Auto.		2·6	0·3	0·5	0·7
„ „ 13 kg fat	400 × 460 × 300	„	Frying area 300 × 350	7·0	0·6	1·1	1·7
Grill, meat	360 × 360 × 250	Auto.	Cooking area 250 × 300	3·0	0·6	1·2	0·6
„ sandwich	330 × 360 × 250	„	Grill area 300 × 300	1·7	0·6	0·8	0·2
Toaster, continuous	380 × 380 × 700	Auto.	Two slices wide	2·2	1·5	1·5	0·4
„ „	500 × 380 × 700	„	Four slices wide	3·0	1·8	1·8	0·8
„ pop-up	150 × 280 × 230	„	Two slices	1·2	0·3	0·7	0·2
Waffle iron	300 × 330 × 250	Auto.	One waffle 20 mm diam.	0·8	0·2	0·4	0·2

Table A7.11. Sensible heat and latent heat emissions from miscellaneous electric appliances operating under normal conditions of use.

Appliance	Type of control	Miscellaneous data (Dimensions in mm (height quoted last), ratings in W)	Mfgr. rating	Heat output (kW)	
				In average use	
				Sensible (s)	Latent (l)
Hair dryer, blower type	Man.	Fan 165 W (low 915 W, high 1580 W)	1·7	0·7	0·1
Hair dryer, helmet type	Man.	Fan 80 W (low 300 W, high 710 W)	0·7	0·6	0·1
Permanent wave machine	Man.	60 heaters at 25 W each, 36 in normal use	1·5	0·3	0·1
Pressurized instrument washer and sterilizer		270 × 270 × 540		3·5	7·0
Solution and/or blanket warmer		450 × 750 × 1800		0·4	0·9
		450 × 600 × 1800		0·3	0·7
Sterilizer, dressing	Auto.	400 × 600		2·8	2·6
	,,	500 × 900		7·0	7·0
Sterilizer, rectangular bulk	Auto.	600 × 600 × 900		10·0	6·5
	,,	600 × 600 × 1200		12·5	7·5
	,,	600 × 900 × 1200		16·5	10·5
	,,	600 × 900 × 1500		20·0	13·0
	,,	900 × 1050 × 2150		47·5	28·3
	,,	1050 × 1200 × 2450		54·0	41·0
	,,	1200 × 1350 × 2450		61·5	53·0
Sterilizer, water	Auto.	45 litre		1·2	4·8
	,,	70 litre		1·8	7·2
Sterilizer, instrument	Auto.	150 × 100 × 450		0·8	0·7
	,,	250 × 250 × 500		1·5	1·1
	,,	250 × 300 × 550		2·4	1·7
	,,	250 × 300 × 900		3·0	2·7
	,,	250 × 400 × 600		2·7	2·5
Sterilizer, utensil	Auto.	400 × 400 × 600		3·1	6·0
	,,	500 × 500 × 600		3·5	7·5
Water still		7 mlitre/s		0·5	0·8
X-ray machines, for producing plates		Doctor's and dentist's office		Negligible	
X-ray machines, for therapy		Heat gain may be appreciable		Refer to manufacturer's data	

GAS HEATED APPLIANCES

For practical purposes, the total heat gains from manufactured and natural gas may be taken as 20 MJ/m³ and 40 MJ/m³ respectively, the sensible and latent heat components in each case being in the ratio of nine to one.

The total heat gain from flued gas appliances will be the heat transmitted by radiation and convection from the equipment plus some latent heat if vapour is being generated. For flueless appliances the total heat content of the fuel, sensible plus latent, will pass into the space but the proportions between these components will vary, depending upon the vapour generated by the equipment, if any.

Table A7.12 lists the probable heat gain from miscellaneous gas appliances without overhead extract hoods. Where properly designed hoods are used the sensible and latent heat gains may be reduced by 50%. See Section B3 for recommended hood face velocities.

Table A7.12. Sensible heat and latent heat emissions from miscellaneous gas appliances operating under normal conditions of use.

Appliance	Overall dimensions less legs and handles (mm) (height quoted last)	Type of control	Miscellaneous data (dimensions in mm, ratings in W)	Heat output (kW)			
				Mfgr. rating	Maintaining rate	In average use	
						Sensible (s)	Latent (l)
Coffee brewer 2·5 litre		Man.	Combination brewer	1·0		0·4	0·1
„ warmer 2·5 litre		„	and warmer	0·2	0·2	0·1	0·1
„ brewer unit with tank	480 × 760 × 660		Four brewers and 20-litre tank			2·1	0·5
Coffee urn—14 litre	380 diam. × 870	Auto.	Black finish	1·0	1·2	0·9	0·9
„ „ —14 litre	300 × 580 oval × 530	„	Nickel plated		1·0	0·8	0·8
„ „ —23 litre	460 diam. × 940	„	„ „		1·4	1·2	1·2
Food warmer, per m² top surface		Man.	Water bath type	6·4	3·2	2·7	1·6
Fry kettle— 7 kg fat	300 × 500 × 460	Auto.	Frying area 250 × 250	4·2	0·9	1·2	0·9
„ „ 13 kg fat	380 × 890 × 280	„	„ „ 280 × 410	7·0	1·3	2·1	1·4
Grill-top burner	560 × 360 × 430	Man.	Insulated 6500 W	11·0		4·4	1·1
„ bottom burner	(0·13 m² grill surface)		4500 W				
Stoves, short order—open top, values per m² top surface		Man.	Ring type burners 3500 to 6500 W per burner	44·0		13·5	13·5
Stoves, short order—closed top, values per m² top surface		Man.	Ring type burners 3000 to 3500 W per burner	35·0		11·0	11·0
Toaster, continuous	380 × 380 × 710	Auto.	Two slices wide	3·5	3·0	2·2	1·0
Burners, laboratory: Small bunsen	10 mm diam. barrel	Man.	Town gas	0·5		0·3	0·1
	10 mm diam. barrel	„	Natural gas	0·9		0·5	0·1
Fishtail burner	10 mm diam. barrel	„	„ „	1·0		0·6	0·2
„ „	10 mm diam. barrel	„	„ „	1·6		0·9	0·3
Large bunsen	40 mm diam. mouth	„	„ „	1·8		1·0	0·3

SECTION A8 SUMMERTIME TEMPERATURES IN BUILDINGS

Introduction ....*Page* A8–3

Notation A8–3

Calculation Sequence.. A8–5

Data Required.. A8–5

Mean Heat Gains... A8–5

Mean Internal Environmental Temperature A8–10

Swing, Mean-to-peak, in Heat Gains.. A8–10

Swing, Mean-to-peak, in Internal Environmental Temperature A8–12

Peak Internal Environmental Temperature A8–13

Example Calculations A8–13

References A8–15

This edition of Section A8 first published: 1986

SECTION A8   SUMMERTIME TEMPERATURES IN BUILDINGS

Introduction

During warm sunny periods, buildings with windows facing in a southerly direction—any aspect from East to West through South—are subjected to daily cyclic heat gains from solar radiation: in addition, further gains arise from artificial lighting, occupants and other sources. In designing a building it is important to ensure that it will not become uncomfortably hot during sunny periods, i.e. that the maximum peak temperature should not frequently exceed, say, 27°C. This Section describes a technique[1] which enables the peak environmental temperature to be assessed for any proposed building design.

It should be noted that the data given do not include any allowance for the effect of sunshine falling directly on occupants whose discomfort would be further increased in such circumstances.

As presented here, the method of calculation assumes that neighbouring rooms respond in a similar way to the room under consideration. If this is not the case, suitable adjustments should be made to equations A8.4, A8.7 and A8.9.

If the calculated peak environmental temperature is shown to be excessive and steps cannot be taken to overcome the problem by modification of the building design, the need for mechanical ventilation or, more probably, air conditioning is self evident.

Notation

A	=	surface area of element.. ..	m²
A_f	=	area of opaque exposed fabric..	m²
A_g	=	area of glazing	m²
C_v	=	ventilation loss	W/K
I'_T	=	peak total solar irradiance ..	W/m²
$\bar{I}_T$	=	mean total solar irradiance ..	W/m²
N	=	number of air changes	h⁻¹
$\tilde{Q}_a$	=	swing in effective heat input due to swing in outside air temperature	W
Q'_c	=	total casual gain at peak hour	W
$\bar{Q}_c$	=	mean casual gain	W
$\tilde{Q}_c$	=	swing in effective heat input due to casual heat gain	W
$\tilde{Q}_f$	=	swing in effective heat input due to structural gain	W
$\bar{Q}_s$	=	mean solar gain	W
$\tilde{Q}_s$	=	swing in effective heat input due to solar radiation	W
$\bar{Q}_t$	=	total mean heat gain	W
$\tilde{Q}_t$	=	swing in total heat gain ..	W
$\bar{S}_e$	=	mean solar gain factor	
$\tilde{S}_e$	=	alternating solar gain factor	
U	=	thermal transmittance of element	W/m² K

U_f	=	thermal transmittance of exposed opaque fabric	W/m² K
U_g	=	thermal transmittance of glazing	W/m² K
Y	=	thermal admittance of element	W/m² K
f	=	decrement factor	
f_r	=	response factor	
h_1	=	duration of casual gain from source 1, etc.	h
q_{c1}	=	instantaneous casual gain from source 1, etc.	W
v	=	room volume	m³
$\bar{t}_{ao}$	=	mean outside air temperature	°C
$\tilde{t}_{ao}$	=	swing in outside air temperature	°C
t'_{ei}	=	peak internal environmental temperature	°C
$\bar{t}_{ei}$	=	mean internal environmental temperature	°C
$\tilde{t}_{ei}$	=	swing in internal environmental temperature	°C
t_{eo}	=	sol-air temperature at time $(\theta - \phi)$	°C
t'_{eo}	=	peak sol-air temperature ..	°C
$\bar{t}_{eo}$	=	mean sol-air temperature ..	°C
$\tilde{t}_{eo}$	=	swing in sol-air temperature ..	°C
θ	=	time of day	h
ϕ	=	time lag	h

Table A8.1 Total solar irradiance (W/m²) on vertical and horizontal surfaces for SE England. (Approximately correct for UK.)

51·7°N

Date	Orientation	Daily mean	04	05	06	07	08	09	10	11	12	13	14	15	16	17	18	19	20
June 21	N	90	35	155	165	105	100	125	145	160	165	160	145	125	100	105	165	155	35
	NE	135	60	305	445	465	420	320	195	170	175	170	155	130	105	75	50	20	5
	E	185	50	295	495	600	625	585	490	355	185	180	165	140	110	80	50	25	5
	SE	180	10	120	280	420	525	580	585	535	430	290	165	140	110	80	50	25	5
	S	155	5	25	50	80	185	320	435	510	535	510	435	320	185	80	50	25	5
	SW	180	5	25	50	80	110	140	165	290	430	535	585	580	525	420	280	120	10
	W	185	5	25	50	80	100	140	165	180	185	355	490	585	625	600	495	295	50
	NW	135	5	20	50	75	105	130	155	170	175	170	195	320	420	465	445	305	60
	H	315	5	80	210	360	505	640	750	825	850	825	750	640	505	360	210	80	5
July 23 and May 22	N	85		100	130	90	110	140	165	180	185	180	165	140	110	90	130	100	
	NE	125		210	370	410	380	300	195	195	200	195	175	145	115	80	50	20	
	E	175		210	420	540	580	555	480	360	215	205	185	155	125	90	55	20	
	SE	180		95	255	400	510	570	580	540	450	320	185	155	125	90	55	20	
	S	165		20	55	90	210	340	450	525	550	525	450	340	210	90	55	20	
	SW	180		20	55	90	125	155	185	320	450	540	580	570	510	400	255	95	
	W	175		20	55	90	125	155	185	205	215	360	480	555	580	540	420	210	
	NW	125		20	50	80	115	145	175	195	200	195	195	300	380	410	370	210	
	H	295		55	180	325	470	605	715	785	815	785	715	605	470	325	180	55	
August 22 and April 22	N	60		5	60	60	90	120	145	160	165	160	145	120	90	60	60	5	
	NE	95		10	240	330	315	240	155	170	180	170	155	125	95	65	30	0	
	E	145		10	295	475	545	535	460	340	190	185	165	135	105	65	30	0	
	SE	175		5	190	380	510	585	600	565	470	340	185	135	105	65	30	0	
	S	175		0	30	95	235	375	490	565	590	565	490	375	235	95	30	0	
	SW	175		0	30	65	105	135	185	340	470	565	600	585	510	380	190	5	
	W	145		0	30	65	105	135	165	185	190	340	460	535	545	475	295	10	
	NW	95		0	30	65	95	125	155	170	180	170	155	240	315	330	240	10	
	H	240		0	90	225	375	510	620	690	715	690	620	510	375	225	90	0	
Sept 22 and March 21	N	40			0	30	60	90	115	130	135	130	115	90	60	30	0		
	NE	60			0	205	235	165	125	140	145	140	125	100	65	30	0		
	E	120			0	340	515	535	465	330	155	150	130	105	70	35	0		
	SE	175			0	295	525	650	685	665	545	395	215	105	70	35	0		
	S	200			0	95	270	445	585	675	710	675	585	445	270	95	0		
	SW	175			0	35	70	105	215	395	545	665	685	650	525	295	0		
	W	120			0	35	70	105	130	150	155	330	465	535	515	340	0		
	NW	60			0	30	65	100	125	140	145	140	125	165	235	205	0		
	H	180			0	95	245	395	515	595	625	595	515	395	245	95	0		
Oct 22 and Feb 21	N	30				0	30	60	90	105	110	105	90	60	30	0			
	NE	35				10	105	80	95	110	120	110	95	65	30	0			
	E	75				25	290	395	370	265	125	120	100	70	35	0			
	SE	135				20	320	515	590	580	500	370	215	70	35	0			
	S	170				10	185	380	530	620	655	620	530	380	185	10			
	SW	135				0	35	70	215	370	500	580	590	515	320	20			
	W	75				0	35	70	100	120	125	265	370	395	290	25			
	NW	35				0	30	65	95	110	120	110	95	80	105	10			
	H	110				5	100	230	340	415	440	415	340	230	100	5			
Nov 22 and Jan 21	N	15					5	30	55	70	75	70	55	30	5				
	NE	20					15	35	60	75	80	75	60	35	5				
	E	40					45	230	265	200	90	80	65	35	5				
	SE	100					55	325	470	495	440	325	180	50	5				
	S	130					35	250	435	545	585	545	435	250	35				
	SW	100					5	50	180	325	440	495	470	325	55				
	W	40					5	35	65	80	90	200	265	230	45				
	NW	20					5	35	60	75	80	75	60	35	15				
	H	60					10	95	190	260	285	260	190	95	10				
Dec 21	N	10						15	40	50	55	50	40	15					
	NE	10						20	40	55	60	55	40	20					
	E	30						155	225	175	65	60	45	20					
	SE	85						230	410	460	410	300	155	35					
	S	115						180	385	510	555	510	385	180					
	SW	85						35	155	300	410	460	410	230					
	W	30						20	45	60	65	175	225	155					
	NW	10						20	40	55	60	55	40	20					
	H	40						50	130	195	220	195	130	50					

Notes:

1. N, NE, E etc: total irradiance on vertical surfaces.
   H: total irradiance on horizontal surface.

2. This table is based on horizontal surface measurements at Kew for the period 1959-1968: weather for two consecutive days averaged. See Section A2, Table A2.27.

3. For other latitudes see Section A2, *Basic Radiation Data – World Values.*

Calculation Sequence

Application of the technique requires that the following be calculated in turn:

(a) Mean heat gains from all sources.

(b) Mean internal environmental temperature.

(c) Swing (deviation), from mean-to-peak, in heat gains from all sources.

(d) Swing (deviation), from mean-to-peak, in internal environmental temperature.

(e) Hence, from (b) and (d), the peak internal environmental temperature.

Data Required

In order that these steps may be followed, the following information is needed about the rooms concerned:

Area, aspect and details of construction of internal and external structural elements. From these particulars, thermal transmittances (U-values) and admittances (Y-values) may be determined from the tables given in Section A3. (See also Section A5.)

Area and aspect of all windows and details of blinds and/or shading. From these particulars, mean and alternating solar gains may be determined using Tables A8.1, A8.2 and A8.5 for the UK. (See Section A2 for solar irradiances at latitudes other than 51.7°N.)

Any casual heat gains, constant or intermittent, from electric lighting, occupants or other sources. (See Section A7.)

Details of the ventilation rate. In view of the difficulty of determining the rate for naturally ventilated build-ings, the empirical values given in Table A8.4 may be used. (See also Section A4.)

Peak and mean outdoor temperatures. For the UK it is proposed that, in the present context, the values given in Table A8.3 should be used. These are typical of sunny days (i.e. $2\frac{1}{2}\%$ days of highest solar radiation. (See also Section A2.)

Mean Heat Gains

Mean Solar Heat Gains

The mean solar heat gain into a room is a function of the mean solar irradiance as read from Table A8.1 for the UK (or from the similar tables contained in Section A2 for other latitudes), the mean solar gain factor appropriate to the type of glass and solar protection from Table A8.2 and the area of glazing. Thus:

$$\bar{Q}_s = \bar{S}_e \bar{I}_T A_g \qquad .. \qquad .. \qquad .. \qquad \text{A8.1}$$

where:

$\bar{Q}_s$	= mean solar gain	W
$\bar{I}_T$	= mean total solar irradiance ..	W/m^2
$\bar{S}_e$	= mean solar gain factor	
A_g	= area of glazing	m^2

For instances where the solar protection may vary throughout the 24 hours, by manipulation of blinds (either automatically or manually) some allowance should be made by suitable modification of the mean solar gain factor. However, any such modification cannot be other than very approximate.

Table A8.2 Mean solar gain factors, $\bar{S}_e$, for various types of glazing and shading (strictly accurate for UK only, approximately correct world wide).

		Mean solar gain factors*, $\bar{S}_e$, for stated window type	
Shading	Type of sun protection	Single	Double
None	None ..	0·76	0·64
	Lightly heat absorbing glass	0·51	0·38
	Densely heat absorbing glass	0·39	0·25
	Lacquer coated glass, grey	0·56	—
	Heat reflecting glass, gold (sealed unit when double)	0·26	0·25
Internal	Dark green open weave plastic blind	0·62	0·56
	White venetian blind	0·46	0·46
	White cotton curtain	0·41	0·40
	Cream holland linen blind ..	0·30	0·33
Mid-pane	White venetian blind	—	0·28
External	Dark green open weave plastic blind	0·22	0·17
	Canvas roller blind ..	0·14	0·11
	White louvred sunbreaker, blades at 45° ..	0·14	0·11
	Dark green miniature louvred blind	0·13	0·10

Notes: *All glazing clear except where stated otherwise. Factors are typical values only and variations will occur due to density of blind weave, reflectivity and cleanliness of protection.

Table A8.3   Sol-air and outside air temperatures for SE England – 2½% day of highest radiation. (Approximately correct for UK. See Section A2, *Sol-air Temperature and Long-wave Loss*.)

(a) March 21

Sun Time	Air Temp, t_{ao} /(°C)	Sol-air temperature, t_{eo} /(°C)																
		Horizontal		North		North-East		East		South-East		South		South-West		West		North-West	
		Dark	Light	Dark	Light	Dark	Light	Dark	Light	Dark	Light	Dark	Light	Dark	Light	Dark	Light	Dark	Light
00	8.5	5.5	5.5	7.5	7.5	7.5	7.5	7.5	7.5	7.5	7.5	7.5	7.5	7.5	7.5	7.5	7.5	7.5	7.5
01	7.5	4.5	4.5	6.5	6.5	6.5	6.5	6.5	6.5	6.5	6.5	6.5	6.5	6.5	6.5	6.5	6.5	6.5	6.5
02	6.5	3.5	3.5	5.5	5.5	5.5	5.5	5.5	5.5	5.5	5.5	5.5	5.5	5.5	5.5	5.5	5.5	5.5	5.5
03	6.0	3.0	3.0	5.0	5.0	5.0	5.0	5.0	5.0	5.0	5.0	5.0	5.0	5.0	5.0	5.0	5.0	5.0	5.0
04	5.0	2.5	2.5	4.5	4.5	4.5	4.5	4.5	4.5	4.5	4.5	4.5	4.5	4.5	4.5	4.5	4.5	4.5	4.5
05	5.0	2.0	2.0	4.0	4.0	4.0	4.0	4.0	4.0	4.0	4.0	4.0	4.0	4.0	4.0	4.0	4.0	4.0	4.0
06	5.0	2.0	2.0	4.0	4.0	4.0	4.0	4.0	4.0	4.0	4.0	4.0	4.0	4.0	4.0	4.0	4.0	4.0	4.0
07	5.0	6.0	4.5	5.5	5.0	14.5	10.0	21.0	13.5	19.0	12.5	9.0	7.0	6.0	5.0	6.0	5.0	6.0	5.0
08	6.0	13.0	8.5	8.0	7.0	17.0	11.5	30.5	19.5	31.0	19.5	18.5	12.5	8.5	7.0	8.5	7.0	8.5	7.0
09	7.5	20.5	13.5	11.0	9.0	14.5	11.0	33.0	21.5	39.0	24.5	28.5	19.0	11.5	9.5	11.5	9.5	11.5	9.5
10	9.0	27.0	18.0	14.0	11.5	14.5	11.5	31.5	21.0	42.5	27.0	37.0	24.5	19.0	14.0	15.0	12.0	14.5	11.5
11	11.0	32.0	21.5	16.5	14.0	17.0	14.0	26.5	19.0	43.0	28.5	43.5	28.5	29.5	21.0	17.5	14.0	17.0	14.0
12	12.5	35.0	23.5	18.5	15.5	19.0	16.0	19.5	16.0	39.0	27.0	47.0	31.5	39.0	27.0	19.5	16.0	19.0	16.0
13	14.0	35.0	24.5	20.0	17.0	20.0	17.0	20.5	17.5	33.0	24.0	46.5	32.0	46.0	31.5	29.5	22.5	20.0	17.0
14	15.0	33.0	23.5	20.0	17.5	20.0	17.5	20.5	17.5	25.0	20.0	43.0	30.0	48.0	33.0	37.0	27.0	20.0	17.5
15	15.5	28.5	21.0	19.0	17.0	19.5	17.0	19.5	17.5	19.5	17.5	36.5	26.5	46.5	32.5	41.0	29.0	22.5	19.0
16	15.0	22.0	18.0	17.5	16.0	17.5	16.0	18.0	16.0	18.0	16.0	27.5	22.0	40.5	29.0	39.5	28.5	26.0	21.0
17	15.0	16.0	14.0	15.5	15.0	15.5	15.0	15.5	15.0	15.5	15.0	19.0	16.5	28.5	22.0	31.0	23.5	24.0	19.5
18	14.5	11.5	11.5	13.5	13.5	13.5	13.5	13.5	13.5	13.5	13.5	13.5	13.5	13.5	13.5	13.5	13.5	13.5	13.5
19	13.5	10.5	10.5	12.5	12.5	12.5	12.5	12.5	12.5	12.5	12.5	12.5	12.5	12.5	12.5	12.5	12.5	12.5	12.5
20	12.5	9.5	9.5	12.0	12.0	12.0	12.0	12.0	12.0	12.0	12.0	12.0	12.0	12.0	12.0	12.0	12.0	12.0	12.0
21	11.5	8.5	8.5	11.0	11.0	11.0	11.0	11.0	11.0	11.0	11.0	11.0	11.0	11.0	11.0	11.0	11.0	11.0	11.0
22	10.5	7.5	7.5	10.0	10.0	10.0	10.0	10.0	10.0	10.0	10.0	10.0	10.0	10.0	10.0	10.0	10.0	10.0	10.0
23	9.5	6.5	6.5	8.5	8.5	8.5	8.5	8.5	8.5	8.5	8.5	8.5	8.5	8.5	8.5	8.5	8.5	8.5	8.5
Mean	10.0	14.5	11.0	11.0	10.5	12.0	11.0	15.0	12.5	18.0	14.0	19.0	15.0	18.0	14.0	15.0	12.5	12.0	11.0

Note: I_l (horizontal surface) = 73 W/m², I_l (vertical surface) = 17 W/m²

(b) April 22

Sun Time	Air Temp, t_{ao} /(°C)	Sol-air temperature, t_{eo} /(°C)																
		Horizontal		North		North-East		East		South-East		South		South-West		West		North-West	
		Dark	Light	Dark	Light	Dark	Light	Dark	Light	Dark	Light	Dark	Light	Dark	Light	Dark	Light	Dark	Light
00	10.0	7.0	7.0	9.0	9.0	9.0	9.0	9.0	9.0	9.0	9.0	9.0	9.0	9.0	9.0	9.0	9.0	9.0	9.0
01	9.0	6.0	6.0	8.0	8.0	8.0	8.0	8.0	8.0	8.0	8.0	8.0	8.0	8.0	8.0	8.0	8.0	8.0	8.0
02	8.0	5.0	5.0	7.0	7.0	7.0	7.0	7.0	7.0	7.0	7.0	7.0	7.0	7.0	7.0	7.0	7.0	7.0	7.0
03	7.0	4.5	4.5	6.5	6.5	6.5	6.5	6.5	6.5	6.5	6.5	6.5	6.5	6.5	6.5	6.5	6.5	6.5	6.5
04	7.0	4.0	4.0	6.0	6.0	6.0	6.0	6.0	6.0	6.0	6.0	6.0	6.0	6.0	6.0	6.0	6.0	6.0	6.0
05	6.5	3.5	3.5	6.5	6.0	6.5	6.0	6.5	6.0	6.0	6.0	6.0	6.0	6.0	6.0	6.0	6.0	6.0	6.0
06	7.0	7.5	6.0	8.5	7.5	15.5	11.5	18.0	12.5	14.0	10.5	7.5	6.5	7.5	6.5	7.5	6.5	7.0	6.5
07	7.5	13.5	9.5	9.0	8.0	20.0	14.0	26.0	17.5	22.0	15.0	10.5	9.0	9.5	8.0	9.5	8.0	9.0	8.0
08	8.5	20.5	14.0	11.0	9.5	20.5	14.5	29.5	20.0	28.5	19.0	17.0	13.0	12.0	10.0	12.0	10.0	11.5	10.0
09	9.5	27.5	18.0	13.5	11.5	18.5	14.5	30.5	21.0	32.5	22.0	24.0	17.5	14.5	12.0	14.5	12.0	14.0	12.0
10	11.0	33.5	22.0	16.0	13.5	16.5	14.0	29.0	20.5	34.5	24.0	30.0	21.5	18.0	14.5	17.0	14.0	16.5	14.0
11	12.5	37.5	25.5	18.5	15.5	19.0	15.5	25.5	15.5	34.5	24.5	34.5	24.5	25.5	19.5	19.5	16.0	19.0	15.5
12	14.0	40.0	27.5	20.0	17.0	20.5	17.5	21.0	17.5	32.5	24.0	37.0	26.5	32.5	24.0	21.0	17.5	20.5	17.5
13	15.5	40.5	28.0	21.0	18.0	21.5	18.5	22.0	18.5	28.5	22.0	37.5	27.0	37.5	27.0	28.5	22.0	21.5	18.5
14	16.5	38.5	27.5	21.5	19.0	22.0	19.0	22.0	19.0	23.0	19.5	35.5	26.5	40.0	29.0	34.0	26.0	22.0	19.0
15	17.0	34.5	25.5	21.0	19.0	21.5	19.0	21.5	19.0	21.5	19.0	31.5	24.5	40.0	29.5	38.0	28.0	26.0	21.5
16	17.0	29.5	22.5	20.0	18.5	20.0	18.5	20.5	18.5	20.5	18.5	26.0	21.5	37.0	28.0	38.5	28.5	29.0	23.5
17	17.0	23.5	19.0	18.5	17.5	19.0	17.5	19.0	17.5	19.0	17.5	20.0	18.5	31.5	24.5	35.5	27.0	29.5	23.5
18	16.5	17.0	15.5	18.5	17.0	17.0	16.5	17.0	16.5	17.0	16.5	17.0	16.5	23.5	20.0	27.5	22.5	25.5	21.0
19	16.0	13.0	13.0	15.5	15.0	15.0	15.0	15.0	15.0	15.0	15.0	15.0	15.0	15.5	15.0	15.5	15.5	15.5	15.5
20	15.0	12.0	12.0	14.0	14.0	14.0	14.0	14.0	14.0	14.0	14.0	14.0	14.0	14.0	14.0	14.0	14.0	14.0	14.0
21	14.0	11.0	11.0	13.0	13.0	13.0	13.0	13.0	13.0	13.0	13.0	13.0	13.0	13.0	13.0	13.0	13.0	13.0	13.0
22	12.5	9.5	9.5	11.5	11.5	11.5	11.5	11.5	11.5	11.5	11.5	11.5	11.5	11.5	11.5	11.5	11.5	11.5	11.5
23	11.5	8.5	8.5	10.5	10.5	10.5	10.5	10.5	10.5	10.5	10.5	10.5	10.5	10.5	10.5	10.5	10.5	10.5	10.5
Mean	12.0	18.5	14.5	13.5	12.5	15.0	13.0	17.0	14.5	18.0	15.0	18.0	15.0	18.0	15.0	17.0	14.5	15.0	13.0

Note: I_l (horizontal surface) = 74 W/m², I_l (vertical surface) = 17 W/m²

Table A8.3—*continued.*

(c) May 22

Sun Time	Air Temp, $t_{ao}/$ (°C)	Horizontal		North		North-East		East		South-East		South		South-West		West		North-West	
		Dark	Light	Dark	Light	Dark	Light	Dark	Light	Dark	Light	Dark	Light	Dark	Light	Dark	Light	Dark	Light
00	11.0	8.0	8.0	10.0	10.0	10.0	10.0	10.0	10.0	10.0	10.0	10.0	10.0	10.0	10.0	10.0	10.0	10.0	10.0
01	10.0	7.0	7.0	9.0	9.0	9.0	9.0	9.0	9.0	9.0	9.0	9.0	9.0	9.0	9.0	9.0	9.0	9.0	9.0
02	9.0	6.0	6.0	8.5	8.5	8.5	8.5	8.5	8.5	8.5	8.5	8.5	8.5	8.5	8.5	8.5	8.5	8.5	8.5
03	9.0	5.5	5.5	8.0	8.0	8.0	8.0	8.0	8.0	8.0	8.0	8.0	8.0	8.0	8.0	8.0	8.0	8.0	8.0
04	8.5	5.5	5.5	7.5	7.5	7.5	7.5	7.5	7.5	7.5	7.5	7.5	7.5	7.5	7.5	7.5	7.5	7.5	7.5
05	9.0	8.0	7.0	13.0	11.0	18.5	14.0	18.5	13.5	12.5	10.5	9.0	8.5	9.0	8.5	9.0	8.5	9.0	8.5
06	9.5	13.5	10.5	15.0	12.0	27.0	19.0	29.5	20.0	21.0	15.5	11.0	10.0	11.0	10.0	11.0	10.0	11.0	10.0
07	10.5	20.5	14.5	14.0	12.0	30.0	21.0	36.5	24.5	29.5	20.5	14.0	12.0	14.0	12.0	14.0	12.0	13.5	12.0
08	12.0	28.0	19.5	16.5	14.0	29.5	21.5	39.5	27.0	36.0	25.0	21.5	17.0	17.0	14.5	17.0	14.5	16.5	14.0
09	13.5	34.5	24.0	19.5	16.5	27.5	20.5	40.0	28.0	40.5	28.0	29.5	22.0	20.5	17.0	20.5	17.0	20.0	16.5
10	15.0	40.5	28.0	22.0	18.5	24.0	19.5	38.0	27.5	43.0	30.0	36.5	26.5	23.5	19.5	23.5	19.0	23.0	19.0
11	16.5	45.0	31.0	24.5	20.5	25.0	21.0	33.5	25.5	42.5	30.5	41.5	30.0	31.5	24.5	26.0	21.5	25.0	21.0
12	18.0	47.5	33.0	26.0	22.0	27.0	22.5	27.5	23.0	39.5	29.5	44.0	32.0	39.5	29.5	27.5	23.0	27.0	22.5
13	19.0	47.5	33.5	27.0	23.0	27.5	23.5	28.0	23.5	34.0	27.0	44.0	32.5	45.0	33.0	36.0	28.0	27.5	23.5
14	19.5	45.5	32.5	26.5	23.0	27.5	23.5	28.0	24.0	28.0	24.0	41.0	31.0	47.5	34.5	42.5	32.0	28.5	24.0
15	20.0	41.0	30.0	25.5	22.5	26.0	23.0	26.5	23.0	26.5	23.0	36.0	28.5	47.0	34.5	46.5	34.0	33.5	27.0
16	19.5	35.5	27.0	24.0	21.5	24.5	22.0	25.0	22.0	25.0	22.0	29.0	24.5	44.0	32.5	47.5	34.5	37.5	29.0
17	19.0	29.0	23.5	22.5	20.5	22.5	20.5	22.5	20.5	22.5	20.5	22.5	20.5	38.0	29.0	45.0	33.0	38.5	29.5
18	18.5	22.5	19.0	24.0	21.0	20.0	19.0	20.0	19.0	20.0	19.0	20.0	19.0	30.0	24.5	38.5	29.0	36.0	27.5
19	17.5	16.5	15.5	21.5	19.5	17.5	17.0	17.5	17.0	17.5	17.0	17.5	17.0	21.0	19.0	27.0	22.0	27.0	22.5
20	16.0	13.0	13.0	15.5	15.5	15.5	15.5	15.5	15.5	15.5	15.5	15.5	15.5	15.5	15.5	15.5	15.5	15.5	15.5
21	15.0	11.5	11.5	14.0	14.0	14.0	14.0	14.0	14.0	14.0	14.0	14.0	14.0	14.0	14.0	14.0	14.0	14.0	14.0
22	13.5	10.5	10.5	12.5	12.5	12.5	12.5	12.5	12.5	12.5	12.5	12.5	12.5	12.5	12.5	12.5	12.5	12.5	12.5
23	12.0	9.0	9.0	11.5	11.5	11.5	11.5	11.5	11.5	11.5	11.5	11.5	11.5	11.5	11.5	11.5	11.5	11.5	11.5
Mean	14.0	23.0	17.5	17.5	15.5	19.5	17.0	22.0	18.0	22.5	18.5	21.5	18.0	22.5	18.5	22.0	18.0	19.5	17.0

Note: I_l (horizontal surface) = 78 W/m², I_l (vertical surface) = 18 W/m²

(d) June 21

Sun Time	Air Temp, $t_{ao}/$ (°C)	Horizontal		North		North-East		East		South-East		South		South-West		West		North-West	
		Dark	Light	Dark	Light	Dark	Light	Dark	Light	Dark	Light	Dark	Light	Dark	Light	Dark	Light	Dark	Light
00	14.0	10.5	10.5	13.0	13.0	13.0	13.0	13.0	13.0	13.0	13.0	13.0	13.0	13.0	13.0	13.0	13.0	13.0	13.0
01	12.5	9.5	9.5	11.5	11.5	11.5	11.5	11.5	11.5	11.5	11.5	11.5	11.5	11.5	11.5	11.5	11.5	11.5	11.5
02	12.0	8.5	8.5	11.0	11.0	11.0	11.0	11.0	11.0	11.0	11.0	11.0	11.0	11.0	11.0	11.0	11.0	11.0	11.0
03	11.0	8.0	8.0	10.5	10.5	10.5	10.5	10.5	10.5	10.5	10.5	10.5	10.5	10.5	10.5	10.5	10.5	10.5	10.5
04	11.0	8.0	8.0	12.0	11.0	13.0	12.0	12.5	11.5	10.5	10.5	10.5	10.0	10.5	10.0	10.5	10.0	10.5	10.0
05	11.0	11.5	10.0	18.0	14.5	25.5	18.5	25.0	18.5	16.5	13.5	11.5	11.0	11.5	11.0	11.5	11.0	11.5	11.0
06	12.0	17.0	13.5	19.0	15.5	33.0	23.0	35.5	24.0	24.5	18.5	13.5	12.5	13.5	12.5	13.5	12.5	13.0	12.0
07	12.5	24.0	17.5	17.0	14.5	35.0	24.5	41.5	28.0	32.5	23.5	15.5	14.0	15.5	14.0	15.5	14.0	15.5	14.0
08	14.0	31.0	22.0	18.0	15.5	33.5	24.5	44.0	30.0	39.0	27.5	22.0	18.0	18.5	16.0	18.5	16.0	18.0	16.0
09	15.0	38.0	26.5	20.5	17.5	30.0	23.0	43.0	30.5	43.0	30.0	30.0	23.0	21.0	18.0	21.0	18.0	20.5	18.0
10	16.5	43.5	30.0	23.0	19.5	25.5	21.0	40.0	29.0	44.5	31.5	37.0	27.5	23.5	20.0	23.5	20.0	23.5	20.0
11	18.0	48.0	33.0	25.0	21.5	25.5	21.5	34.5	26.5	43.5	31.5	42.0	31.0	31.5	25.0	26.0	22.0	25.5	21.5
12	19.0	50.5	35.0	26.5	23.0	27.0	23.0	27.5	23.5	39.5	30.0	44.5	33.0	39.5	30.0	27.5	23.5	27.0	23.0
13	20.5	50.5	35.5	27.5	24.0	28.0	24.0	28.5	24.5	34.0	27.5	44.5	33.5	46.0	34.0	37.0	29.0	28.0	24.0
14	21.0	48.5	34.5	27.5	24.5	28.0	24.5	28.5	25.0	28.5	25.0	41.5	32.0	49.5	36.5	44.5	34.0	30.0	25.5
15	21.5	44.5	33.0	27.0	24.5	27.5	24.5	28.0	24.5	28.0	24.5	36.5	29.5	49.5	37.0	50.0	37.0	36.5	29.5
16	22.0	39.0	30.0	26.0	24.0	26.5	24.0	26.5	24.0	26.5	24.0	30.0	26.0	47.0	35.5	52.0	38.0	41.5	32.5
17	21.5	33.0	26.5	26.0	24.0	24.5	23.0	25.0	23.0	25.0	23.0	25.0	23.0	41.5	32.5	50.5	37.5	44.0	33.5
18	21.0	26.5	22.5	28.5	25.0	22.5	21.5	23.0	21.5	23.0	21.5	23.0	21.5	34.0	28.0	44.5	34.0	42.5	32.5
19	20.5	20.5	19.0	27.0	23.5	20.5	20.0	20.5	20.0	20.5	20.0	20.5	20.0	25.5	23.0	34.0	27.5	34.5	28.0
20	19.0	16.5	16.0	20.0	19.5	18.5	18.5	18.5	18.5	18.5	18.5	18.5	18.5	19.0	18.5	20.5	19.5	21.5	20.0
21	18.0	14.5	14.5	17.0	17.0	17.0	17.0	17.0	17.0	17.0	17.0	17.0	17.0	17.0	17.0	17.0	17.0	17.0	17.0
22	16.5	13.0	13.0	15.5	15.5	15.5	15.5	15.5	15.5	15.5	15.5	15.5	15.5	15.5	15.5	15.5	15.5	15.5	15.5
23	15.0	12.0	12.0	14.0	14.0	14.0	14.0	14.0	14.0	14.0	14.0	14.0	14.0	14.0	14.0	14.0	14.0	14.0	14.0
Mean	16.5	26.0	20.5	20.0	18.0	22.5	19.5	24.5	20.5	24.5	20.5	23.5	20.0	24.5	20.5	24.5	20.5	22.5	19.5

Note: I_l (horizontal surface) = 80 W/m², I_l (vertical surface) = 18 W/m²

Table A8.3—*continued.*

(e) July 23

Sun Time	Air Temp, t_{ao}/(°C)	Horizontal Dark	Horizontal Light	North Dark	North Light	North-East Dark	North-East Light	East Dark	East Light	South-East Dark	South-East Light	South Dark	South Light	South-West Dark	South-West Light	West Dark	West Light	North-West Dark	North-West Light
00	16.0	12.5	12.5	15.0	15.0	15.0	15.0	15.0	15.0	15.0	15.0	15.0	15.0	15.0	15.0	15.0	15.0	15.0	15.0
01	14.5	11.5	11.5	14.0	14.0	14.0	14.0	14.0	14.0	14.0	14.0	14.0	14.0	14.0	14.0	14.0	14.0	14.0	14.0
02	13.5	10.5	10.5	13.0	13.0	13.0	13.0	13.0	13.0	13.0	13.0	13.0	13.0	13.0	13.0	13.0	13.0	13.0	13.0
03	13.0	10.0	10.0	12.0	12.0	12.0	12.0	12.0	12.0	12.0	12.0	12.0	12.0	12.0	12.0	12.0	12.0	12.0	12.0
04	13.0	9.5	9.5	12.0	12.0	12.0	12.0	12.0	12.0	12.0	12.0	12.0	12.0	12.0	12.0	12.0	12.0	12.0	12.0
05	13.0	12.0	11.0	17.5	15.0	22.5	18.0	22.5	18.0	17.0	15.0	13.5	13.0	13.5	13.0	13.5	13.0	13.0	13.0
06	13.5	17.5	14.5	19.5	16.5	31.0	23.0	33.5	24.5	25.5	20.0	15.5	14.5	15.5	14.5	15.5	14.5	15.5	14.0
07	14.5	24.5	18.5	18.0	16.0	34.0	25.0	40.5	28.5	33.5	24.5	18.0	16.0	18.0	16.0	18.0	16.0	18.0	16.0
08	16.0	31.5	23.0	20.5	18.0	33.5	25.5	43.5	31.0	40.0	29.0	25.5	20.5	21.0	18.5	21.0	18.5	20.5	18.0
09	17.5	38.5	27.5	23.0	20.0	31.0	24.5	44.0	31.5	44.5	32.0	33.5	26.0	24.0	20.5	24.0	20.5	23.5	20.5
10	19.0	44.5	31.5	26.0	22.5	27.5	23.5	41.5	31.0	46.5	34.0	40.0	30.5	27.0	23.0	27.0	23.0	26.5	22.5
11	20.5	49.0	34.5	28.5	24.5	29.0	24.5	37.5	29.5	46.0	34.5	45.5	34.0	35.0	28.0	29.5	25.0	29.0	24.5
12	21.5	51.5	36.5	30.0	26.0	30.5	26.5	31.5	26.5	43.0	33.0	48.0	36.0	43.0	33.0	31.5	26.5	30.5	26.5
13	23.0	51.5	37.5	31.0	27.0	31.5	27.5	32.0	27.5	38.0	31.0	48.0	36.5	49.0	37.0	40.0	32.0	31.5	27.5
14	24.0	49.5	36.5	31.0	27.5	31.5	28.0	32.0	28.0	32.0	28.0	45.0	35.5	51.5	39.0	46.5	36.0	32.5	28.5
15	24.5	45.5	35.0	30.5	27.5	31.0	27.5	31.5	28.0	31.5	28.0	40.5	33.0	51.5	39.0	51.0	39.0	38.5	32.0
16	24.5	40.5	32.0	29.0	26.5	29.5	27.0	30.0	27.0	30.0	27.0	34.0	29.5	49.0	37.5	52.5	39.5	42.5	34.0
17	24.5	34.5	28.5	28.0	26.0	27.5	26.0	28.0	26.0	28.0	26.0	28.0	26.0	43.5	34.5	50.5	38.5	45.0	35.0
18	24.0	28.0	24.5	29.5	26.5	25.5	24.5	25.5	24.5	25.5	24.5	25.5	24.5	35.5	30.0	44.0	34.5	41.5	33.0
19	23.0	22.0	21.0	27.0	25.0	23.0	22.5	23.0	22.5	23.0	22.5	23.0	22.5	26.5	24.5	32.5	27.5	32.5	28.0
20	21.5	18.5	18.5	21.0	21.0	21.0	21.0	21.0	21.0	21.0	21.0	21.0	21.0	21.0	21.0	21.0	21.0	21.0	21.0
21	20.5	17.0	17.0	19.5	19.5	19.5	19.5	19.5	19.5	19.5	19.5	19.5	19.5	19.5	19.5	19.5	19.5	19.5	19.5
22	19.0	15.5	15.5	18.0	18.0	18.0	18.0	18.0	18.0	18.0	18.0	18.0	18.0	18.0	18.0	18.0	18.0	18.0	18.0
23	17.5	14.0	14.0	16.5	16.5	16.5	16.5	16.5	16.5	16.5	16.5	16.5	16.5	16.5	16.5	16.5	16.5	16.5	16.5
Mean	19.0	27.5	22.0	22.0	20.0	24.0	21.5	26.5	22.5	27.0	23.0	26.0	22.5	27.0	23.0	26.5	22.5	24.0	21.5

Note: I_l (horizontal surface) = 79 W/m², I_l (vertical surface) = 18 W/m²

(f) August 22

Sun Time	Air Temp, t_{ao}/(°C)	Horizontal Dark	Horizontal Light	North Dark	North Light	North-East Dark	North-East Light	East Dark	East Light	South-East Dark	South-East Light	South Dark	South Light	South-West Dark	South-West Light	West Dark	West Light	North-West Dark	North-West Light
00	15.0	12.0	12.0	14.0	14.0	14.0	14.0	14.0	14.0	14.0	14.0	14.0	14.0	14.0	14.0	14.0	14.0	14.0	14.0
01	14.0	11.0	11.0	13.0	13.0	13.0	13.0	13.0	13.0	13.0	13.0	13.0	13.0	13.0	13.0	13.0	13.0	13.0	13.0
02	13.0	10.0	10.0	12.0	12.0	12.0	12.0	12.0	12.0	12.0	12.0	12.0	12.0	12.0	12.0	12.0	12.0	12.0	12.0
03	12.5	9.5	9.5	11.5	11.5	11.5	11.5	11.5	11.5	11.5	11.5	11.5	11.5	11.5	11.5	11.5	11.5	11.5	11.5
04	12.0	9.0	9.0	11.0	11.0	11.0	11.0	11.0	11.0	11.0	11.0	11.0	11.0	11.0	11.0	11.0	11.0	11.0	11.0
05	12.0	9.0	9.0	11.0	11.0	11.5	11.0	11.5	11.0	11.0	11.0	11.0	11.0	11.0	11.0	11.0	11.0	11.0	11.0
06	12.0	12.5	11.0	13.5	12.5	21.0	16.5	23.0	17.5	19.0	15.5	12.5	12.0	12.5	12.0	12.5	12.0	12.5	12.0
07	12.5	18.5	14.5	14.0	13.0	25.0	19.0	31.0	22.5	27.0	20.0	15.5	14.0	14.5	13.0	14.5	13.0	14.0	13.0
08	13.5	25.5	19.0	16.0	14.5	25.5	19.5	34.5	25.0	33.0	24.0	22.0	18.0	17.0	15.0	17.0	15.0	16.5	14.5
09	14.5	32.0	23.0	18.5	16.5	23.5	19.0	35.5	26.0	37.5	27.0	29.0	22.0	19.5	17.0	19.5	17.0	19.0	16.5
10	16.0	38.0	27.0	21.0	18.5	21.5	18.5	33.5	25.5	39.5	28.5	35.0	26.0	22.5	19.0	21.5	19.0	21.5	18.5
11	17.5	42.5	30.0	23.0	20.0	23.5	20.5	30.5	24.0	39.5	29.0	39.5	29.0	30.5	24.0	24.0	20.5	23.5	20.5
12	18.5	44.5	32.0	24.5	21.5	25.0	22.0	25.5	22.0	37.0	28.5	41.5	31.0	37.0	28.5	25.5	22.0	25.0	22.0
13	20.0	45.0	32.5	25.5	22.5	26.0	23.0	26.5	23.0	33.0	26.5	42.0	31.5	42.0	31.5	33.0	26.5	26.0	23.0
14	21.0	43.0	31.5	26.0	23.0	26.0	23.5	26.5	23.5	27.5	24.0	39.5	31.0	44.5	33.5	38.5	30.5	26.0	23.5
15	21.5	39.0	30.0	25.5	23.0	25.5	23.5	26.0	23.5	26.0	23.5	35.5	29.0	44.0	33.5	42.0	32.5	30.0	26.0
16	21.5	33.5	27.0	24.5	22.5	24.5	23.0	25.0	23.0	25.0	23.0	30.5	26.0	41.5	32.0	43.0	33.0	33.5	28.0
17	21.5	27.5	23.5	23.0	22.0	23.0	22.0	23.0	22.0	23.0	22.0	24.5	22.5	36.0	29.0	40.0	31.5	34.0	28.0
18	21.0	21.5	20.0	22.5	21.5	21.5	21.0	21.5	21.0	21.5	21.0	21.5	21.0	28.0	24.5	32.0	26.5	30.0	25.5
19	20.5	17.5	17.5	19.5	19.5	19.5	19.5	19.5	19.5	19.5	19.5	19.5	19.5	19.5	19.5	20.0	19.5	20.0	19.5
20	19.5	16.5	16.5	18.5	18.5	18.5	18.5	18.5	18.5	18.5	18.5	18.5	18.5	18.5	18.5	18.5	18.5	18.5	18.5
21	18.5	15.5	15.5	17.5	17.5	17.5	17.5	17.5	17.5	17.5	17.5	17.5	17.5	17.5	17.5	17.5	17.5	17.5	17.5
22	17.0	14.0	14.0	16.5	16.5	16.5	16.5	16.5	16.5	16.5	16.5	16.5	16.5	16.5	16.5	16.5	16.5	16.5	16.5
23	16.0	13.0	13.0	15.0	15.0	15.0	15.0	15.0	15.0	15.0	15.0	15.0	15.0	15.0	15.0	15.0	15.0	15.0	15.0
Mean	16.5	23.5	19.0	18.0	17.0	19.5	18.0	22.0	19.0	23.0	19.5	23.0	19.5	23.0	19.5	22.0	19.0	19.5	18.0

Note: I_l (horizontal surface) = 76 W/m², I_l (vertical surface) = 17 W/m²

Table A8.3—*continued.*

(g) September 22

Sun Time	Air Temp, $t_{ao}/$(°C)	Horizontal		North		North-East		East		South-East		South		South-West		West		North-West	
		Dark	Light	Dark	Light	Dark	Light	Dark	Light	Dark	Light	Dark	Light	Dark	Light	Dark	Light	Dark	Light
00	13.5	10.5	10.5	13.0	13.0	13.0	13.0	13.0	13.0	13.0	13.0	13.0	13.0	13.0	13.0	13.0	13.0	13.0	13.0
01	13.0	10.0	10.0	12.0	12.0	12.0	12.0	12.0	12.0	12.0	12.0	12.0	12.0	12.0	12.0	12.0	12.0	12.0	12.0
02	12.0	9.0	9.0	11.0	11.0	11.0	11.0	11.0	11.0	11.0	11.0	11.0	11.0	11.0	11.0	11.0	11.0	11.0	11.0
03	11.5	8.5	8.5	10.5	10.5	10.5	10.5	10.5	10.5	10.5	10.5	10.5	10.5	10.5	10.5	10.5	10.5	10.5	10.5
04	11.0	8.0	8.0	10.5	10.5	10.5	10.5	10.5	10.5	10.5	10.5	10.5	10.5	10.5	10.5	10.5	10.5	10.5	10.5
05	11.0	8.0	8.0	10.0	10.0	10.0	10.0	10.0	10.0	10.0	10.0	10.0	10.0	10.0	10.0	10.0	10.0	10.0	10.0
06	11.5	8.5	8.5	10.5	10.5	10.5	10.5	10.5	10.5	10.5	10.5	10.5	10.5	10.5	10.5	10.5	10.5	10.5	10.5
07	12.0	13.0	11.0	12.5	12.0	21.0	16.5	28.0	20.5	26.0	19.5	16.0	14.0	13.0	12.0	13.0	12.0	12.5	12.0
08	13.0	20.0	15.5	15.0	14.0	24.0	18.5	37.5	26.0	38.0	26.5	25.5	19.5	15.5	14.0	15.5	14.0	15.5	14.0
09	14.0	27.5	20.0	18.0	16.0	21.5	18.0	40.0	28.0	45.5	31.5	35.5	25.5	18.5	16.5	18.5	16.5	18.0	16.0
10	15.5	33.5	24.5	20.5	18.0	21.0	18.0	38.0	27.5	49.0	33.5	43.5	31.0	25.5	21.0	21.5	18.5	21.0	18.0
11	17.0	38.0	27.5	22.5	20.0	23.0	20.0	32.5	25.5	49.0	34.5	49.5	35.0	36.0	27.0	23.5	20.5	23.0	20.0
12	18.5	40.5	29.5	24.5	21.0	25.0	21.5	25.0	22.0	44.5	32.5	52.5	37.0	44.5	32.5	25.0	22.0	25.0	21.5
13	19.5	40.5	30.0	25.0	22.0	25.5	22.5	26.0	22.5	38.0	29.5	52.0	37.0	51.5	37.0	35.0	27.5	25.5	22.5
14	20.0	38.0	28.5	25.0	22.5	25.0	22.5	25.5	22.5	30.0	25.0	48.0	35.0	53.0	38.0	42.0	32.0	25.0	22.5
15	20.0	33.0	26.0	24.0	22.0	24.0	22.0	24.5	22.0	24.5	22.0	41.5	31.5	51.5	37.5	46.0	34.0	27.5	24.0
16	20.0	27.0	22.5	22.0	21.0	22.5	21.0	22.5	21.0	22.5	21.0	32.5	26.5	45.5	33.5	44.5	33.5	31.0	26.0
17	19.5	20.5	19.0	20.5	19.5	20.5	20.0	20.5	20.0	20.5	20.0	23.5	21.5	33.5	27.0	35.5	28.5	29.0	24.5
18	19.0	16.0	16.0	18.5	18.5	18.5	18.5	18.5	18.5	18.5	18.5	18.5	18.5	18.5	18.5	18.5	18.5	18.5	18.5
19	18.5	15.5	15.5	17.5	17.5	17.5	17.5	17.5	17.5	17.5	17.5	17.5	17.5	17.5	17.5	17.5	17.5	17.5	17.5
20	17.5	14.5	14.5	17.0	17.0	17.0	17.0	17.0	17.0	17.0	17.0	17.0	17.0	17.0	17.0	17.0	17.0	17.0	17.0
21	16.5	13.5	13.5	16.0	16.0	16.0	16.0	16.0	16.0	16.0	16.0	16.0	16.0	16.0	16.0	16.0	16.0	16.0	16.0
22	15.5	12.5	12.5	15.0	15.0	15.0	15.0	15.0	15.0	15.0	15.0	15.0	15.0	15.0	15.0	15.0	15.0	15.0	15.0
23	14.5	11.5	11.5	14.0	14.0	14.0	14.0	14.0	14.0	14.0	14.0	14.0	14.0	14.0	14.0	14.0	14.0	14.0	14.0
Mean	15.5	20.0	16.5	17.0	16.0	18.0	16.5	20.5	18.0	23.5	19.5	25.0	20.5	23.5	19.5	20.5	18.0	18.0	16.5

Note: I_l (horizontal surface) = 73 W/m², I_l (vertical surface) = 17 W/m²

(h) October 22

Sun Time	Air Temp, $t_{ao}/$(°C)	Horizontal		North		North-East		East		South-East		South		South-West		West		North-West	
		Dark	Light	Dark	Light	Dark	Light	Dark	Light	Dark	Light	Dark	Light	Dark	Light	Dark	Light	Dark	Light
00	12.5	9.5	9.5	11.5	11.5	11.5	11.5	11.5	11.5	11.5	11.5	11.5	11.5	11.5	11.5	11.5	11.5	11.5	11.5
01	11.5	8.5	8.5	11.0	11.0	11.0	11.0	11.0	11.0	11.0	11.0	11.0	11.0	11.0	11.0	11.0	11.0	11.0	11.0
02	11.0	8.0	8.0	10.5	10.5	10.5	10.5	10.5	10.5	10.5	10.5	10.5	10.5	10.5	10.5	10.5	10.5	10.5	10.5
03	10.5	7.5	7.5	10.0	10.0	10.0	10.0	10.0	10.0	10.0	10.0	10.0	10.0	10.0	10.0	10.0	10.0	10.0	10.0
04	10.5	7.5	7.5	9.5	9.5	9.5	9.5	9.5	9.5	9.5	9.5	9.5	9.5	9.5	9.5	9.5	9.5	9.5	9.5
05	10.0	7.0	7.0	9.0	9.0	9.0	9.0	9.0	9.0	9.0	9.0	9.0	9.0	9.0	9.0	9.0	9.0	9.0	9.0
06	10.0	7.0	7.0	9.0	9.0	9.0	9.0	9.0	9.0	9.0	9.0	9.0	9.0	9.0	9.0	9.0	9.0	9.0	9.0
07	10.5	7.5	7.5	9.5	9.5	10.0	10.0	10.5	10.0	10.5	10.0	10.0	9.5	9.5	9.5	9.5	9.5	9.5	9.5
08	11.0	12.0	10.5	12.0	11.0	15.5	13.0	24.5	18.5	26.0	19.0	19.5	15.5	12.0	11.5	12.0	11.5	12.0	11.0
09	12.5	18.5	14.5	14.5	13.5	15.5	13.5	31.0	22.5	37.0	25.5	30.5	22.0	15.0	13.5	15.0	13.5	15.0	13.5
10	14.0	24.5	18.5	17.5	15.5	17.5	15.5	31.5	23.0	42.5	29.5	39.0	27.5	23.5	19.0	18.0	16.0	17.5	15.5
11	15.5	29.0	21.5	19.5	17.5	20.0	17.5	28.0	22.0	43.5	30.5	45.5	31.5	33.0	24.5	20.5	18.0	20.0	17.5
12	16.5	31.5	23.5	21.5	19.0	21.5	19.0	22.0	19.5	40.5	29.5	48.0	34.0	40.5	29.5	22.0	19.5	21.5	19.0
13	17.5	31.5	24.0	22.0	19.5	22.0	20.0	22.5	20.0	35.0	27.0	47.5	34.0	45.5	32.5	23.0	24.0	22.0	20.0
14	18.0	28.5	22.5	21.5	19.5	21.5	19.5	22.0	20.0	27.5	23.0	43.0	31.5	46.5	33.5	35.0	27.0	21.5	19.5
15	18.0	24.0	20.0	20.0	18.5	20.5	19.0	20.5	19.0	20.5	19.0	35.5	27.5	42.5	31.0	36.5	28.0	21.0	19.0
16	17.5	18.5	17.0	18.5	17.5	18.5	17.5	18.5	17.5	18.5	17.5	26.0	22.0	32.5	25.5	31.0	24.5	22.0	19.0
17	17.0	14.5	14.5	16.5	16.5	16.5	16.5	16.5	16.5	16.5	16.5	17.0	16.5	17.5	17.0	17.5	17.0	17.0	16.5
18	16.5	13.5	13.5	16.0	16.0	16.0	16.0	16.0	16.0	16.0	16.0	16.0	16.0	16.0	16.0	16.0	16.0	16.0	16.0
19	16.0	13.0	13.0	15.5	15.5	15.5	15.5	15.5	15.5	15.5	15.5	15.5	15.5	15.5	15.5	15.5	15.5	15.5	15.5
20	15.5	12.5	12.5	14.5	14.5	14.5	14.5	14.5	14.5	14.5	14.5	14.5	14.5	14.5	14.5	14.5	14.5	14.5	14.5
21	14.5	11.5	11.5	14.0	14.0	14.0	14.0	14.0	14.0	14.0	14.0	14.0	14.0	14.0	14.0	14.0	14.0	14.0	14.0
22	14.0	11.0	11.0	13.0	13.0	13.0	13.0	13.0	13.0	13.0	13.0	13.0	13.0	13.0	13.0	13.0	13.0	13.0	13.0
23	13.0	10.0	10.0	12.5	12.5	12.5	12.5	12.5	12.5	12.5	12.5	12.5	12.5	12.5	12.5	12.5	12.5	12.5	12.5
Mean	14.0	15.5	13.5	14.5	14.0	15.0	14.0	17.0	15.0	19.5	16.5	21.5	18.0	19.5	17.0	17.0	15.0	15.0	14.0

Note: I_l (horizontal surface) = 74 W/m², I_l (vertical surface) = 17 W/m²

Mean Casual Heat Gain

The mean heat gain from casual sources, artificial lighting, occupants etc. is found by multiplying the individual items by their duration and averaging over the 24 hours whence:

$$\bar{Q}_c = \frac{(q_{c_1} \times h_1) + (q_{c_2} \times h_2)\ etc}{24} \quad .. \quad .. \quad \text{A8.2}$$

where:

$\bar{Q}_c$ = mean casual gain .. .. W

q_{c_1} and q_{c_2} = instantaneous casual gains .. W

h_1 and h_2 = duration of individual casual gains .. .. h

Total Mean Gain

The total mean heat gain is the sum of the mean solar and mean casual gains determined by equations A8.1 and A8.2 as:

$$\bar{Q}_t = \bar{Q}_s + \bar{Q}_c \quad .. \quad .. \quad .. \quad .. \quad \text{A8.3}$$

Mean Internal Environmental Temperature

Having obtained a value for $\bar{Q}_t$, the mean internal environmental temperature may be determined from the equation:

$$\bar{Q}_t = (\Sigma A_g U_g + C_v)(\bar{t}_{ei} - \bar{t}_{ao}) + \Sigma A_f U_f(\bar{t}_{ei} - \bar{t}_{eo}) \quad \text{A8.4}$$

where:

A_g = area of glazed exposed surface .. m²

U_g = thermal transmittance of glazing .. W/m² K

A_f = area of exposed opaque fabric .. m²

U_f = thermal transmittance of exposed opaque fabric .. .. .. W/m² K

C_v = ventilation loss .. .. .. W/K

$\bar{t}_{ei}$ = mean internal environmental temperature .. .. °C

$\bar{t}_{eo}$ = mean sol-air temperature (Table A8.3 for the UK) .. .. .. °C

$\bar{t}_{ao}$ = mean outdoor temperature (Table A8.3 for the UK) .. .. .. °C

For low rates of ventilation, equivalent to a ventilation loss of say 0·6 W/m³ K (2 air changes per hour) or less,

$$C_v \approx \frac{1}{3} Nv \ .. \quad .. \quad .. \quad .. \quad .. \quad \text{A8.5}$$

where:

N = Rate of air interchange .. .. h⁻¹

v = room volume .. .. .. m³

The above assumes that the air and environmental temperatures are the same. For higher rates of ventilation a more accurate assessment of C_v is necessary, that is:

$$\frac{1}{C_v} = \frac{1}{0·33\ Nv} + \frac{1}{4·8\Sigma A} \ .. \quad .. \quad .. \quad .. \quad \text{A8.6}$$

where:

ΣA = total area of surfaces bounding the enclosure .. .. m²

The empirical values for ventilation rates listed in Table A8.4 may be used for naturally ventilated buildings in the United Kingdom.

Table A8.4 Ventilation rates for naturally ventilated buildings on sunny days.

Position of opening windows	Usage of windows		Effective mean ventilation rate	
	Day	Night	Air changes (h⁻¹)	Ventilation allowance (W/m³ K)
One side only	Closed	Closed	1	0·3
	Open	Closed	3	1·0
	Open	Open	10	3·3
More than one side	Closed	Closed	2	0·6
	Open	Closed	10	3·3
	Open	Open	30	10·0

Swing (deviation), Mean-to-peak, in Heat Gains

The variations in heat input due to solar radiation, outside air temperature and casual gains must be determined separately and added together to give the total swing in heat input. Solar heat gains usually predominate, unless there are large casual heat gains within the room, and an examination of the solar irradiances in Table A8.1 (for the UK), together with the outside air temperatures, will usually indicate when the peak indoor temperature will occur. For rooms with South or West facing external walls, the peak temperatures will occur during early or late afternoon when high solar irradiance coincides with high outside air temperatures.

In north-facing rooms with little solar radiation (which seldom suffer from overheating) the peak indoor temperature can be expected in the afternoon due to the warmth of the ventilating air. In east-facing rooms, the peak indoor temperatures can occur in the morning or afternoon, depending on the size of window, amount of natural ventilation and the presence of casual gains.

In order to determine the swing (mean-to-peak) it is necessary to decide on the time of day when the peak indoor temperature is likely to occur, and compute the mean-to-peak effective heat inputs for this 'peak hour'. If there is a doubt about the choice of the peak hour, the same procedure must be followed for several times of day to ensure that the peak indoor temperature is found.

Response Factor

The response factor of a room may be determined from the following equation:

$$f_r = \frac{\Sigma(AY) + \frac{1}{3} Nv}{\Sigma(AU) + \frac{1}{3} Nv} \quad .. \quad .. \quad .. \quad .. \quad \text{A8.7}$$

where:

f_r = reponse factor of room

$\Sigma(AY)$ = sum of products of areas of all room surfaces and their appropriate admittances .. .. W/K

$\Sigma(AU)$ = sum of products of areas of all exposed surfaces and their appropriate transmittances .. W/K

Structures with a high response factor are often referred to as 'heavyweight' structures and those with a low response factor as 'lightweight'. These terms give only a general guide to the thermal behaviour of buildings. Equation A8.7 shows that the response factor depends both upon the materials of construction and the rate of ventilation. A nominally 'heavyweight' building may have a low response factor if the rate of ventilation is high. Table A8.5 gives some guidance in this respect. Further details may be found in Sections A5 and A9.

Table A8.5 Nominal building classifications and response factors.

Nominal building classification	Construction	Response factor f_r
Heavyweight	Masonry external and internal partitions, bare solid floors and ceilings.	≥ 6
Lightweight	Lightweight external cladding, demountable partitions, suspended ceilings, solid floors with carpet or wood block finish or suspended floors.	≤ 4

Swing in Effective Solar Heat Input

From the solar irradiances listed in Table A8.1 (or the similar tables given in Section A2 for other latitudes), the difference between the irradiance at the peak hour and the mean irradiance may be found, in order to give the effective heat input due to solar radiation. A time lag of 1 hour should be assumed in heavyweight rooms to allow for the response of the room surfaces to the solar radiation, i.e. for a room of heavyweight construction, the radiation intensity incident on the surfaces at 1 hour earlier than the peak hour should be used. For lightweight constructions, no allowance for time lag is necessary. This mean-to-peak difference must be multiplied by the appropriate alternating solar gain factor, as read from Table A8.6, and by the area of the glazing, thus:

Table A8.6 Alternating solar gain factors, $\tilde{S}_e$, for various types of glazing and shading, lightweight and heavyweight structures (strictly accurate for UK only – SW façade).

Position of shading and type of sun protection		Alternating solar gain factors*, $\tilde{S}_e$, for the following building and window types			
		Heavyweight building		Lightweight building	
Shading	Type of sun protection	Single	Double	Single	Double
None	None	0·42	0·39	0·65	0·56
	Lightly heat absorbing glass	0·36	0·27	0·47	0·35
	Densely heat absorbing glass	0·32	0·21	0·37	0·24
	Lacquer coated glass, grey	0·37	—	0·50	—
	Heat reflecting glass, gold (sealed unit when double)	0·21	0·14	0·25	0·20
Internal	Dark green open weave plastic blind	0·55	0·53	0·61	0·57
	White venetian blind	0·42	0·44	0·45	0·46
	White cotton curtain	0·27	0·31	0·35	0·37
	Cream holland linen blind	0·24	0·30	0·27	0·32
Mid-pane	White venetian blind	—	0·24	—	0·27
External	Dark green open weave plastic blind	0·16	0·13	0·22	0·17
	Canvas roller blind	0·10	0·08	0·13	0·10
	White louvred sunbreaker, blades at 45°	0·08	0·06	0·11	0·08
	Dark green miniature louvred blind	0·08	0·06	0·10	0·07

Notes: *All glazing clear except where stated otherwise. Factors are typical values only and variations will occur due to density of blind weave, reflectivity and cleanliness of protection.

$$\tilde{Q}_s = \tilde{S}_e A_g (I'_T - \bar{I}_T) \quad .. \quad .. \quad .. \quad \text{A8.8}$$

where:

$\tilde{Q}_s$ = swing in effective heat input due to solar radiation .. .. .. W

$\tilde{S}_e$ = alternating solar gain factor

I'_T = peak total solar irradiance .. .. W/m²

$\bar{I}_T$ = mean total solar irradiance .. W/m²

It should be noted that the magnitude of the alternating solar gain factor depends on the response factor, see Table A8.5

The values of alternating solar gain factor given in Table A8.6 apply to a South-West facing room in the UK and it is assumed that the peak temperature occurs at 1500 h for lightweight structures and 1600 h for heavyweight structures. These values are approximately correct for other orientations but may lead to overestimation of peak temperature in these cases.

The values given are approximately correct for other locations in the Northern hemisphere and for North-West facing rooms in the Southern hemisphere.

Swing in Structural Heat Gain

The time of occurrence of the peak temperature will normally be determined by the time of occurrence of the maximum solar irradiance (assuming this to be the largest contributing input). However, there will be an additional contribution to this peak load due to the outside sol-air temperature. The swing in sol-air temperature is modified in amplitude and suffers a time delay and these effects are described in terms of the decrement factor, f, and an associated time lag, ϕ. Values of decrement factor and the associated time lag are tabulated in Section A3.

The swing in sol-air temperature is calculated as follows, taking into account the time lag associated with decrement factor:

$$\tilde{t}_{eo} = (t_{eo} - \bar{t}_{eo}) \quad .. \quad .. \quad .. \quad .. \quad .. \quad \text{A8.9}$$

where:

$\tilde{t}_{eo}$ = swing in sol-air temperature at time θ .. .. °C

t_{eo} = sol-air temperature at time $(\theta - \phi)$ °C

$\bar{t}_{eo}$ = mean sol-air temperature .. .. °C

θ = time of day .. .. h

ϕ = time lag .. .. h

The resulting swing in effective heat input due to structural heat gain is given by:

$$\tilde{Q}_f = f A U \tilde{t}_{eo} \quad .. \quad .. \quad .. \quad .. \quad .. \quad \text{A8.10}$$

where:

$\tilde{Q}_f$ = swing in effective heat input due to structural gain .. .. .. W

f = decrement factor (see Section A3)

Swing in Casual Heat Gain

From the examination of casual heat gains made to determine the mean, the value at the peak hour will have been revealed. The mean-to-peak swing may thence be determined from:

$$\tilde{Q}_c = Q'_c - \bar{Q}_c \quad .. \quad .. \quad .. \quad .. \quad \text{A8.11}$$

where:

$$Q'_c = q_{c_1} + q_{c_2} + \text{etc} \quad .. \quad .. \quad .. \quad \text{W}$$

Swing in Heat Gain Air-to-air

The difference between the outdoor air temperature at the peak hour and the mean outdoor air temperature must be found in order to give the variation in heat input due to the outside temperature swing. This temperature difference must be multiplied by the product of the area and U-value of the exposed glass and by the appropriate ventilation heat loss value, thus:

$$\tilde{Q}_a = (\Sigma A_g U_g + C_v) \tilde{t}_{ao} .. \quad .. \quad .. \quad .. \quad \text{A8.12}$$

where:

$\tilde{Q}_a$ = swing in effective heat input due to swing in outside temperature W

$\Sigma A_g U_g$ = sum of products of areas of exposed glazing and the appropriate U-values .. .. .. W/K

$\tilde{t}_{ao}$ = swing in outside air temperature °C (see Table A8.3 for the UK)

Total Swing in Heat Gain

From the components listed, the total swing in effective heat input may be determined as:

$$\tilde{Q}_t = \tilde{Q}_s + \tilde{Q}_f + \tilde{Q}_c + \tilde{Q}_a \quad .. \quad .. \quad .. \quad \text{A8.13}$$

Swing, Mean-to-peak, in Internal Environmental Temperature

The magnitude of the mean-to-peak swing in internal environmental temperature may be determined by the following equation. Values for thermal admittance for various constructions are tabulated in Section A3. Thus:

$$\tilde{Q}_t = (\Sigma A Y + C_v) \tilde{t}_{ei} \quad .. \quad .. \quad .. \quad .. \quad \text{A8.14}$$

where:

$\Sigma A Y$ = sum of products of all room surface areas, internal and external and their appropriate admittance values W/K

$\tilde{t}_{ei}$ = swing in internal environmental temperature .. .. °C

Peak Internal Environmental Temperature

The peak internal environmental temperature is determined by adding the mean-to-peak swing to the mean, thus:

$$t'_{ei} = \bar{t}_{ei} + \tilde{t}_{ei} \quad .. \quad .. \quad .. \quad .. \quad .. \quad \text{A8.15}$$

where:

t'_{ei} = peak internal environmental temperature .. .. °C

Example Calculations

Example 1

An indication is required of the peak internal environmental temperature likely to occur during a sunny period in August for the South-facing office module shown in Fig. A8.1.

The office module under consideration is on an intermediate floor and faces onto a busy traffic route. Table A8.7 gives relevant characteristics of the module and its construction and Table A8.8 gives appropriate values of thermal transmittance, admittance, decrement factor and time lag, taken from Section A3.

Table A8.7 Characteristics of office for Examples 1 and 2.

Item	Detail
Outside wall	105 mm brickwork (dark finish), 50 mm mineral fibre, 105 mm brickwork, 13 mm lightweight plaster
Partitions	105 mm brickwork, lightweight plaster each side
Floor	150 mm cast concrete, 50 mm screed, linoleum tiles
Ceiling	Bare concrete
Lighting	20 W per square metre of floor area; 0700 to 0900 hours, 1700 to 1900 hours
Occupancy	4 persons for 8 h per day (sensible heat output 80 W each)
Window	Single glazing, aluminium frame with thermal break occupying 10% of glazed area

Table A8.8 Values of thermal transmittance, admittance and decrement factor for Examples 1 and 2.

Item	Area / m^2	U-value /(W/m^2 K)	Y-value /(W/m^2 K)	Decrement factor, f	Time lag, ϕ / h
Outside wall	5	0.5	3.7	0.28	9
Partitions	42	1.8	3.6	–	–
Floor	20	2.0	4.3	–	–
Ceiling	20	2.0	6.0	–	–
Window	7	5.7	5.7	–	–

Step (a) – Mean heat gains:

Mean solar gain (equation A8.1, Tables A8.1 and A8.2):

$$\bar{Q}_s = 0.76 \times 175 \times (3.5 \times 2 \times 0.9) \qquad = \quad 838 \quad \text{W}$$

Mean casual gain (equation A8.2):

$$\bar{Q}_c = \frac{(4 \times 80 \times 8) + (4 \times 5 \times 20 \times 4)}{24} \quad = \quad 173 \quad \text{W}$$

Thus:

$$\bar{Q}_t = 838 + 173 \qquad = \quad 1011 \quad \text{W}$$

Step (b) – Mean internal environmental temperature:

It is assumed that the internal environmental temperature of the adjacent rooms is equal to that of the room under consideration. Hence, heat flow is through outside window-wall only. Therefore:

$$\Sigma(AU) = (5 \times 0.5) + (7 \times 5.7) \qquad = \quad 42.4 \quad \text{W/K}$$

$$\Sigma(AY) = (5 \times 3.7) + (42 \times 3.6) + (20 \times 4.3) + (20 \times 6.0) + (7 \times 5.7) \quad = \quad 415.6 \quad \text{W/K}$$

Assuming window closed day and night; number of air changes (Table A8.4):

$$C_v = \frac{(5 \times 4 \times 3)}{3} \qquad = \quad 20 \quad \text{W/K}$$

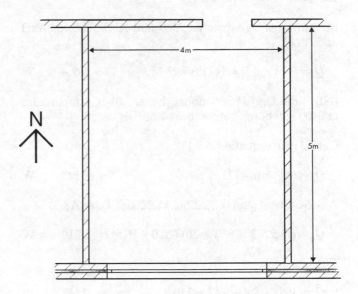

Floor to ceiling height = 3 m

Window dimensions = (3.5 m × 2.0) m

Glazed area = (3.5 × 2.0 × 0.9) m^2

(ie window frame and glazing bars account for 10% of total window area.)

Fig. A8.1 Office module for Examples 1 and 2.

Response factor of room (equation A8.7):

$$f_r = \frac{415.6 + 20}{42.4 + 20} \qquad = \qquad 7$$

Hence, structure is 'heavyweight'.

Assuming thermal conductance of frame material is equal to that of glass; fabric loss through window (Fig. A8.1 and Table A8.8):

$$\Sigma U_g A_g = 5.7\,(3.5 \times 2) \qquad = \qquad 39.9 \quad \text{W/K}$$

Fabric loss through outside wall (Fig. A8.1 and Table A8.8):

$$\Sigma U_f A_f = 0.5\,((4 \times 3) - (3.5 \times 2)) \qquad = \qquad 2.5 \quad \text{W/K}$$

Thus (equation A8.4 and Table A8.3):

$$1011 = (39.9 + 20)(\bar{t}_{ei} - 16.5) + 2.5(\bar{t}_{ei} - 23.0)$$

Hence:

$$\bar{t}_{ei} = 33.0\,°C$$

Step (c) – Swing (mean-to-peak) in heat gain:

Solar gain (equation A8.8, Tables A8.1 and A8.6):

$$\tilde{Q}_s = 0.42\,(3.5 \times 2 \times 0.9)\,(590 - 175) \qquad = \qquad 1098 \quad \text{W}$$

(NB: maximum irradiance occurs at 1200 h. However, for heavyweight building, time lag (ϕ) is 1 hour. Hence, the 'peak-hour' is 1300 h.)

Structural gain (equations A8.9 and A8.10, Tables A8.3 and A8.8):

$$\tilde{Q}_f = 0.28 \times 0.5 \times 5\,(11.0 - 23.0) \qquad = \qquad -8.4 \quad \text{W}$$

(NB: time lag (ϕ) is 9 hours, hence sol-air temperature at 0400 h, 9 hours before 'peak-hour', is used.)

Casual gain (equation A8.11):

$$\tilde{Q}_c = (4 \times 80) - 173 \qquad = \qquad 147 \quad \text{W}$$

Air-to-air heat gain (equation A8.12 and Table A8.3):

$$\tilde{Q}_a = ((3.5 \times 2 \times 5.7) + 20)\,(20.0 - 16.5) = \qquad 210 \quad \text{W}$$

Thus:

$$\tilde{Q}_t = 1098 - 8.4 + 147 + 210 \qquad = \qquad 1447 \quad \text{W}$$

Step (d) – swing (mean-to-peak) in internal environmental temperature:

From equation A8.14:

$$1447 = (415.6 + 20)\,\tilde{t}_{ei}$$

Hence,

$$\tilde{t}_{ei} = 3.3\,°C$$

Step (e) – Peak internal environmental temperature.

From equation A8.15:

$$t'_{ei} = 33.0 + 3.3 \qquad = \qquad 36.3\,°C$$

Example 2

The same module is considered but it is assumed that the windows will be open day and night (10 air changes per hour).

Step (a):

As for Example 1:

$$\bar{Q}_t = 1011 \quad \text{W}$$

Step (b):

The higher rate of ventilation means that a more accurate assessment of the ventilation loss is required.

From equation A8.6:

$$\frac{1}{C_v} = \frac{1}{198} + \frac{1}{(4.8 \times 94)} \qquad = 0.0073 \ \text{K/W}$$

Thus:

$$C_v = 138 \quad \text{W/K}$$

Therefore response factor is:

$$f_r = \frac{415.6 + 138}{42.4 + 138} \qquad = \qquad 3$$

Thus, because of the increased ventilation loss, the structure now behaves as 'lightweight'.

Fabric loss through window, as for Example 1:

$$\Sigma U_g A_g = 39.9 \quad \text{W/K}$$

Fabric loss through outside wall, as for Example 1:

$$\Sigma U_f A_f = 2.5 \quad \text{W/K}$$

Thus (equation A8.4):

$$1011 = (39.9 + 138)\,(\bar{t}_{ei} - 16.5) + 2.5\,(\bar{t}_{ei} - 23.0)$$

Hence:

$$\bar{t}_{ei} = 22.2\,°C$$

Step (c):

Solar heat input (equation A8.8, Tables A8.1 and A8.6):

$$\tilde{Q}_s = 0.65\,(3.5 \times 2 \times 0.9)\,(590 - 175) \qquad = \qquad 1699 \quad \text{W}$$

(NB: lightweight structure, therefore time lag (ϕ) is zero and 'peak-hour' is time of maximum irradiance, 1200 h.)

Structural gain (equations A8.9 and A8.10, Tables A8.3 and A8.9):

$$\tilde{Q}_f = 0.28 \times 0.5 \times 5 \, (11.5 - 23.0) \qquad = \quad -8.0 \qquad W$$

(NB: time lag on decrement (ϕ) is 9 hours, therefore sol-air temperature at 0300 h, 9 hours before 'peak-hour', is appropriate.)

Air-to-air heat gain (equation A8.12 and Table A8.3):

$$\tilde{Q}_a = (3.5 \times 2 \times 5.7) + 138 \, (18.5 - 16.5) = \quad 356 \qquad W$$

Thus:

$$\tilde{Q}_t = 1699 - 8.0 + 147 + 356 \qquad = \quad 2194 \qquad W$$

Step (d):

From equation A8.14:

$$2194 = (415.6 + 138) \, \tilde{t}_{ei}$$

Hence:

$$\tilde{t}_{ei} = 4.0 \, °C$$

Step (e):

From equation A8.15:

$$t'_{ei} = 22.2 + 4.0 \qquad = \quad 26.2 \, °C$$

REFERENCE

[1] LOUDON, A. G., 'Summertime temperatures in buildings', *I.H.V.E./B.R.S. Symposium,* Feb. 1968, *B.R.S. Current Paper 47/68,* Building Research Establishment, Watford, 1968.

SECTION A9   ESTIMATION OF PLANT CAPACITY

Introduction ....*Page* A9–2

Notation A9–2

Temperatures A9–3

   Inside Air Temperature.................................... A9–3

   Mean Surface Temperature.............................. A9–3

   Mean Radiant Temperature.............................. A9–3

   Inside Environmental Temperature.................... A9–3

   Dry Resultant Temperature at the Centre of a
      Room.. A9–3

   Outside Air Temperature.................................. A9–3

   Sol-Air Temperature and Sol-Air Excess
      Temperature Difference............................... A9–3

Heating

   Steady State Heat Requirements...................... A9–4

   Inside Temperatures...................................... A9–6

   Intermittent Heating.. A9–8

   Highly Intermittent Systems............................ A9–9

Radiant Heating ....*Page* A9–9

Storage Systems... A9–9

Central Plant Size... A9–10

Selective Systems.. A9–10

Multiple Boiler Installations............................... A9–10

Air Conditioning... A9–11

   Design Conditions.. A9–12

   Sensible Cooling Loads................................... A9–12

   Intermittent Operation A9–13

   Central Plant Size.. A9–13

Assessment of Reliability................................... A9–13

References... A9–15

Tables—Cooling Load due to Solar Gain through
   Vertical Glazing.. A9–20–41

Appendices A9–16

   1. Heating Example.. A9–16

   2. Air Conditioning Example............................ A9–17

Supplement A9/1 .... A9–43

This edition of Section A9 first published: 1979
Supplement A9/1 first published: 1983

SECTION A9   ESTIMATION OF PLANT CAPACITY

Note:

In the equations appearing in this section $\Sigma(A)$ = the total area of *all surfaces* bounding the enclosure

INTRODUCTION

This section presents design information for the manual calculation of sensible heating and cooling loads and plant capacity. The sensible heating or cooling requirement is determined by:

(*a*) the chosen design temperature conditions inside and outside;

(*b*) the thermal characteristics of the construction;

(*c*) the ventilation rate;

(*d*) the type of system;

(*e*) the hours of plant operation.

This section of the *Guide* gives the calculation procedure for sizing systems when these conditions are known. The section starts with a summary of the temperature indices used and then treats heating and air conditioning in turn. The section ends with a discussion on plant reliability.

Further information, showing the development of the design method, is given in Section A5 which may also be used to derive more detailed design information for calculations with digital computers.

Guidance on the selection of design conditions, the thermal properties of the building and the performance of systems is given elsewhere in the *Guide* and reference to the following sections is advisable:

Comfort conditions	Section A1
Selection of outdoor design conditions	Section A2
Thermal transmittances (*U*-values) and admittances (*Y*-values)	Section A3
Calculation of ventilation rates	Section A4
Calculation of sensible heat loads	Section A5
Estimation of casual and miscellaneous heat gains both sensible and latent	Section A7
Heating equipment	Section B1
Air conditioning equipment and latent heat loads	Sections B2 and B3

NOTATION

Many of the quantities in this section occur in three forms. The quantity itself, symbolised by X (which may also be considered as the instantaneous value of, X); the 24 hour mean or steady state value, $\bar{X}$ and the instantaneous variation about the mean, $\tilde{X}$. Where time lags occur, the variation symbol may be given a subscript to indicate at what time it occurs, e.g. $\tilde{X}_\theta$ is the value of $\tilde{X}$ at time θ.

In the list below, only the basic symbol is given unless the quantity involved only occurs in the mean or cyclic form in which case the appropriate sign is included.

A	=	area	m²
A_s	=	area of surface	m²
C	=	cloudiness (see Section A2 (1982))	
F_{au}	=	dimensionless room factor with respect to the air point	
F_{av}	=	dimensionless room factor with respect to the air point	
F_{ay}	=	dimensionless room factor with respect to the air point	
F_u	=	dimensionless room factor with respect to the environmental point	
F_v	=	dimensionless room factor with respect to the environmental point	

F_1	=	temperature ratio	
F_2	=	temperature ratio	
F_3	=	intermittent operation factor	
F_4	=	highly intermittent operation factor	
I	=	intensity factor	
I_l	=	net long wave radiation exchange between a black body at outside air temperature and the outside enviroment	W/m²
I_t	=	total intensity of solar radiation ..	W/m²
k_c	=	sky clarity (see Section A2 (1982))	
k_r	=	ground reflectance (see Section A2 (1982))	
N	=	number of room air changes per hour	h⁻¹
N_{inf}	=	number of room air changes per hour due to infiltration	h⁻¹
P	=	probability of failure free operation	
Q_i	=	room energy input	W
Q_p	=	plant energy output	W
Q_{pb}	=	plant output under boosted intermittent operation	W
Q_u	=	energy transfer through fabric ..	W
Q_v	=	ventilation energy cansfer	W
R_{si}	=	inside surface resistance ..	m² K/W
U	=	thermal transmittance ..	W/m² K

U' = modified thermal transmittance   W/m² K

V = room volume .. .. m³

Y = thermal admittance .. .. W/m² K

c = specific heat of air .. .. J/kg K

f = decrement factor

k = an index

m = an index

t_a = air temperature .. .. .. °C

t_{ai} = inside air temperature .. .. °C

t_{ao} = outside air temperature .. .. °C

t_c = dry resultant temperature at the centre
of the room .. .. °C

t_{ei} = inside environmental temperature .. °C

t_{eo} = outside environmental temperature .. °C

t_m = mean surface temperature .. .. °C

ΔQ_i = change in room energy input .. .. **W**

Γ = failure rate

Λ = reliability

Σ = sum of

ρ = density of air .. .. kg/m³

θ = time .. .. h

θ_r = recharge time .. .. h

TEMPERATURES *(See Supplement A9/1)*

Inside Air Temperature (t_{ai})

Inside air temperature is the average of the bulk air temperature of the enclosed space. For practical purposes it is the reading of a dry thermometer shielded from radiation suspended at the centre of the space.

Mean Surface Temperature (t_m)

The mean surface temperature is determined by totalling the products of the areas and temperatures of the surrounding surfaces and dividing this total by the sum of the areas, i.e.

$$t_m = \frac{\Sigma(A_s\, t_s)}{\Sigma(A_s)} \quad .. \quad .. \quad .. \quad .. \quad A9.1$$

At any instant of time there is only one value of mean surface temperature for a room.

Mean Radiant Temperature (t_r)

The mean radiant temperature sensed at any point within the enclosure is a function of the respective areas, shapes and surface temperatures of the enclosing elements as viewed from that point. In contrast to the mean surface temperature, the mean radiant temperature usually changes with position in the room. Determination of precise values is complex due to the effect of the shape factor, however, the mean radiant temperature is the same as the mean surface temperature at the centre point of a cubical room where all surfaces have the same emissivity. It is a good approximation at the room centre for other shapes.

Inside Environmental Temperature (t_{ei})

Environmental temperature is used to calculate the heat exchange between a surface and an enclosed space. Its precise value depends on room configuration and the convective and radiant heat transfer coefficients.

Typical values for these coefficients, applicable in the UK and in hot climates give:

$$t_{ei} = \tfrac{1}{3} t_{ai} + \tfrac{2}{3} t_m \quad .. \quad .. \quad .. \quad .. \quad A9.2$$

Dry Resultant Temperature at the Centre of a Room (t_c)

Thermal comfort is discussed at length in Section A1 of the CIBSE *Guide*. It concludes that in most practical situations where air movement is low, an acceptable index temperature for comfort is the average of air and mean radiant temperature, usually referred to as dry resultant temperature.

In the rest of this section, dry resultant temperature at the centre of the space is defined as:

$$t_c = \tfrac{1}{2} t_{ai} + \tfrac{1}{2} t_m \quad .. \quad .. \quad .. \quad .. \quad A9.3$$

where t_m approximates to t_r at the room centre and t_{ai} is the air temperature at the same point.

Outside Air Temperature (t_{ao})

Outside air temperature is the bulk temperature of the air surrounding the building.

Sol-Air Temperature (t_{eo}) and Sol-Air Excess Temperature Difference (Δt_{eo})

Sol-air temperature is that temperature which, in the absence of solar radiation, would give the same rate of heat transfer through the wall or roof as exists with the actual outdoor temperature and the incident solar radiation. In effect it is the outside environmental temperature and is calculated from the expression:

$$t_{eo} = t_{ao} + R_{so}\,(\alpha I_t - \epsilon I_l) \quad .. \quad .. \quad .. \quad A9.4$$

Where overcast sky conditions can be assumed, the outside sol-air temperature is approximately equal to the outside air temperature but where clear skies lead to radiation loss and/or solar gains by day the external sol-air temperature can be used to calculate conduction transfers through opaque surfaces such as walls and roofs.

Sol-air excess temperature difference is given by:

$$\Delta t_{eo} = R_{so}\,(\alpha I_t - \epsilon I_l) \quad .. \quad .. \quad .. \quad A9.5$$

It is that quantity which must be added to or subtracted from the outside air temperature in order to calculate the heat transfer through opaque external surfaces resulting from the radiation exchange between those surfaces and the sun and the sky.

HEATING (See Supplement A9/1)

Steady State Heat Requirements

Buildings lose heat by conduction through their exposed surfaces and by ventilation. These losses are calculated in the following way.

Heat Transfers through the Fabric

These are determined by the thermal transmittance (U-value) and the expected temperature conditions. For any surface:

$$Q_u = \Sigma(AU)(t_{ei} - t_{ao}) \quad\quad\quad\quad\quad \text{A9.6}$$

When adjacent rooms are at different temperatures, heat flows through party walls, floors or ceilings are estimated by using the temperature differential between the two rooms and the ensuing heat flow is added to that through the external wall.

Heat Requirements for Ventilation

Ventilation heat requirements are determined by the rate of ventilation and the difference between supply and exhaust air temperatures. In determining ventilation rates, account must be taken of infiltration, natural ventilation due to open windows and, when appropriate, mechanical ventilation. Guidance on design allowances for ventilation is given in Sections A1 and A4. For outdoor air supplies:

$$Q_v = \frac{c\rho NV}{3600}(t_{ai} - t_{ao}) \quad\quad\quad \text{A9.7}$$

For practical purposes, $c\rho/3600 = \frac{1}{3}$.

Total Steady State Heat Requirements

The total heat requirement is the sum of the fabric and ventilation losses, thus, adding equations A9.6 and A9.7 gives:

$$Q_p = \Sigma(AU)(t_{ei} - t_{ao}) + \tfrac{1}{3}NV(t_{ai} - t_{ao}) \quad \text{A9.8}$$

For winter heating design conditions it is conventional to assume that the sol-air temperature equals the outside air temperature. It is also convenient to introduce the temperature ratios:

$$F_1 = \frac{t_{ei} - t_{ao}}{t_c - t_{ao}} \quad\quad\quad\quad\quad \text{A9.9}$$

and:

$$F_2 = \frac{t_{ai} - t_{ao}}{t_c - t_{ao}} \quad\quad\quad\quad\quad \text{A9.10}$$

When these are substituted into equation A9.8 it can be rewritten:

$$Q_p = (F_1\Sigma(AU) + \tfrac{1}{3}F_2NV)(t_c - t_{ao}) \quad\quad \text{A9.11}$$

The temperature ratios F_1 and F_2 are given in Tables A9.1 to A9.7 for a representative range of heat emitters although for any system not covered, interpolation is permissible. In each table the form of room construction is defined by two measures: $\Sigma(AU)/\Sigma(A)$ and $\frac{1}{3}NV/\Sigma(A)$. For the most precise work, it may be necessary to modify $\Sigma(A)$ to take account of furniture, fittings etc.

The factors F_1 and F_2 automatically compensate for the relationships between inside air and mean surface temperatures and ensure similar comfort conditions at the centre of the room whatever heating system is used.

Tables A9.1 to A9.7 are based on $\Sigma(AU)$ for external walls. Where account is taken of temperature difference across internal partitions a modified U-value should be used where:

$$U' = \frac{U(t_{ei} - t'_{ei})}{(t_{ei} - t_{ao})} \quad\quad\quad\quad \text{A9.12}$$

For a given building design (i.e. known values of $\Sigma(AU)$, $\Sigma(A)$ and NV) the inside temperature relationships will depend on the type of heating system. For warm air systems the highest inside temperature will be air temperature, with resultant, environmental, mean surface and outside temperatures each progressively lower. At

Table A9.1. Values of F_1 and F_2 for 100% convective, 0% radiant (forced warm air heaters).

$\frac{NV}{3\Sigma(A)}$	\multicolumn{20}{c}{$\Sigma(AU)/\Sigma(A)$}
	0.1		0.2		0.4		0.6		0.8		1.0		1.5		2.0		3.0		4.0	
	F_1	F_2	F_1	F_2	F_1	F_2	F_1	F_2	F_1	F_2	F_1	F_2	F_1	F_2	F_1	F_2	F_1	F_2	F_1	F_2
0.1	0.99	1.02	0.99	1.03	0.98	1.07	0.97	1.10	0.96	1.13	0.95	1.16	0.92	1.23	0.90	1.30	0.86	1.43	0.82	1.55
0.2	0.99	1.02	0.99	1.03	0.98	1.07	0.97	1.10	0.96	1.13	0.95	1.16	0.92	1.23	0.90	1.30	0.86	1.43	0.82	1.55
0.4	0.99	1.02	0.99	1.03	0.98	1.07	0.97	1.10	0.96	1.13	0.95	1.16	0.92	1.23	0.90	1.30	0.86	1.43	0.82	1.55
0.6	0.99	1.02	0.99	1.03	0.98	1.07	0.97	1.10	0.96	1.13	0.95	1.16	0.92	1.23	0.90	1.30	0.86	1.43	0.82	1.55
0.8	0.99	1.02	0.99	1.03	0.98	1.07	0.97	1.10	0.96	1.13	0.95	1.16	0.92	1.23	0.90	1.30	0.86	1.43	0.82	1.55
1.0	0.99	1.02	0.99	1.03	0.98	1.07	0.97	1.10	0.96	1.13	0.95	1.16	0.92	1.23	0.90	1.30	0.86	1.43	0.82	1.55
1.5	0.99	1.02	0.99	1.03	0.98	1.07	0.97	1.10	0.96	1.13	0.95	1.16	0.92	1.23	0.90	1.30	0.86	1.43	0.82	1.55
2.0	0.99	1.02	0.99	1.03	0.98	1.07	0.97	1.10	0.96	1.13	0.95	1.16	0.92	1.23	0.90	1.30	0.86	1.43	0.82	1.55
3.0	0.99	1.02	0.99	1.03	0.98	1.07	0.97	1.10	0.96	1.13	0.95	1.16	0.92	1.23	0.90	1.30	0.86	1.43	0.82	1.55
4.0	0.99	1.02	0.99	1.03	0.98	1.07	0.97	1.10	0.96	1.13	0.95	1.16	0.92	1.23	0.90	1.30	0.86	1.43	0.82	1.55

Table A9.2. Values of F_1 and F_2 for 90% convective, 10% radiant (natural convectors and convector radiators).

$\frac{NV}{3\Sigma(A)}$	\multicolumn{20}{c}{$\Sigma(AU)/\Sigma(A)$}
	0.1		0.2		0.4		0.6		0.8		1.0		1.5		2.0		3.0		4.0	
	F_1	F_2	F_1	F_2	F_1	F_2	F_1	F_2	F_1	F_2	F_1	F_2	F_1	F_2	F_1	F_2	F_1	F_2	F_1	F_2
0.1	1.00	1.01	0.99	1.03	0.98	1.05	0.97	1.08	0.96	1.11	0.96	1.13	0.93	1.20	0.91	1.26	0.88	1.37	0.84	1.47
0.2	1.00	1.01	0.99	1.02	0.98	1.05	0.97	1.08	0.97	1.10	0.96	1.13	0.94	1.19	0.92	1.25	0.88	1.37	0.84	1.47
0.4	1.00	1.00	0.99	1.02	0.98	1.05	0.98	1.07	0.97	1.10	0.96	1.12	0.94	1.19	0.92	1.25	0.88	1.36	0.85	1.46
0.6	1.00	1.00	1.00	1.01	0.99	1.04	0.98	1.07	0.97	1.09	0.96	1.12	0.94	1.18	0.92	1.24	0.88	1.35	0.85	1.46
0.8	1.00	0.99	1.00	1.01	0.99	1.04	0.98	1.06	0.97	1.09	0.96	1.11	0.94	1.18	0.92	1.24	0.88	1.35	0.85	1.45
1.0	1.00	0.99	1.00	1.00	0.99	1.03	0.98	1.06	0.97	1.08	0.96	1.11	0.94	1.17	0.92	1.23	0.89	1.34	0.85	1.45
1.5	1.01	0.98	1.00	0.99	0.99	1.02	0.99	1.04	0.98	1.07	0.97	1.10	0.95	1.16	0.93	1.22	0.89	1.33	0.86	1.43
2.0	1.01	0.97	1.01	0.98	1.00	1.01	0.99	1.03	0.98	1.06	0.97	1.08	0.95	1.14	0.93	1.20	0.90	1.31	0.86	1.42
3.0	1.02	0.94	1.01	0.96	1.01	0.98	1.00	1.01	0.99	1.03	0.98	1.06	0.96	1.12	0.94	1.18	0.90	1.29	0.87	1.39
4.0	1.03	0.92	1.02	0.94	1.01	0.96	1.00	0.99	1.00	1.01	0.99	1.04	0.97	1.10	0.95	1.15	0.91	1.26	0.88	1.36

Table A9.3. Values of F_1 and F_2 for 80% convective, 20% radiant (multicolumn radiators).

$\frac{NV}{3\Sigma(A)}$	$\Sigma(AU)/\Sigma(A)$																			
	0.1		0.2		0.4		0.6		0.8		1.0		1.5		2.0		3.0		4.0	
	F_1	F_2	F_1	F_2	F_1	F_2	F_1	F_2	F_1	F_2	F_1	F_2	F_1	F_2	F_1	F_2	F_1	F_2	F_1	F_2
0.1	1.00	1.01	0.99	1.02	0.99	1.04	0.98	1.06	0.97	1.09	0.96	1.11	0.95	1.16	0.93	1.21	0.90	1.31	0.87	1.40
0.2	1.00	1.00	1.00	1.01	0.99	1.04	0.98	1.06	0.97	1.08	0.97	1.10	0.95	1.15	0.93	1.21	0.90	1.30	0.87	1.39
0.4	1.00	0.99	1.00	1.00	0.99	1.03	0.98	1.05	0.98	1.07	0.97	1.09	0.95	1.14	0.94	1.19	0.90	1.29	0.87	1.38
0.6	1.01	0.98	1.00	0.99	0.99	1.02	0.99	1.04	0.98	1.06	0.97	1.08	0.96	1.13	0.94	1.18	0.91	1.28	0.88	1.37
0.8	1.01	0.97	1.01	0.98	1.00	1.01	0.99	1.03	0.98	1.05	0.98	1.07	0.96	1.12	0.94	1.17	0.91	1.27	0.88	1.36
1.0	1.01	0.96	1.01	0.97	1.00	1.00	0.99	1.02	0.99	1.04	0.98	1.06	0.96	1.11	0.95	1.16	0.91	1.26	0.88	1.35
1.5	1.02	0.94	1.02	0.95	1.01	0.97	1.00	1.00	0.99	1.02	0.99	1.04	0.97	1.09	0.95	1.14	0.92	1.23	0.89	1.32
2.0	1.03	0.92	1.02	0.93	1.02	0.95	1.01	0.97	1.00	0.99	1.00	1.01	0.98	1.06	0.96	1.11	0.93	1.21	0.90	1.29
3.0	1.04	0.88	1.04	0.89	1.03	0.91	1.02	0.93	1.02	0.95	1.01	0.97	0.99	1.02	0.98	1.07	0.95	1.16	0.92	1.24
4.0	1.05	0.84	1.05	0.85	1.04	0.87	1.04	0.89	1.03	0.91	1.02	0.93	1.01	0.98	0.99	1.03	0.96	1.11	0.93	1.20

Table A9.4. Values of F_1 and F_2 for 70% convective, 30% radiant (double and treble panel radiators and double column radiators).

$\frac{NV}{3\Sigma(A)}$	$\Sigma(AU)/\Sigma(A)$																			
	0.1		0.2		0.4		0.6		0.8		1.0		1.5		2.0		3.0		4.0	
	F_1	F_2	F_1	F_2	F_1	F_2	F_1	F_2	F_1	F_2	F_1	F_2	F_1	F_2	F_1	F_2	F_1	F_2	F_1	F_2
0.1	1.00	1.00	1.00	1.01	0.99	1.03	0.98	1.05	0.98	1.06	0.97	1.08	0.96	1.12	0.95	1.16	0.92	1.24	0.89	1.32
0.2	1.00	0.99	1.00	1.00	0.99	1.02	0.99	1.04	0.98	1.06	0.98	1.07	0.96	1.12	0.95	1.16	0.92	1.23	0.90	1.31
0.4	1.01	0.98	1.00	0.99	1.00	1.01	0.99	1.02	0.99	1.04	0.98	1.06	0.97	1.10	0.95	1.14	0.93	1.22	0.90	1.29
0.6	1.01	0.97	1.01	0.97	1.00	0.99	1.00	1.01	0.99	1.03	0.99	1.04	0.97	1.08	0.96	1.13	0.93	1.20	0.91	1.28
0.8	1.02	0.95	1.01	0.96	1.01	0.98	1.00	1.00	1.00	1.01	0.99	1.03	0.98	1.07	0.96	1.11	0.94	1.19	0.91	1.26
1.0	1.02	0.94	1.02	0.95	1.01	0.96	1.01	0.98	1.00	1.00	0.99	1.02	0.98	1.06	0.97	1.10	0.94	1.17	0.92	1.24
1.5	1.03	0.91	1.03	0.92	1.02	0.93	1.02	0.95	1.01	0.97	1.01	0.98	0.99	1.02	0.98	1.06	0.96	1.13	0.93	1.21
2.0	1.04	0.88	1.04	0.89	1.03	0.90	1.03	0.92	1.02	0.93	1.02	0.95	1.00	0.99	0.99	1.03	0.97	1.10	0.94	1.17
3.0	1.06	0.82	1.06	0.83	1.05	0.85	1.05	0.86	1.04	0.88	1.04	0.89	1.02	0.93	1.01	0.97	0.99	1.04	0.96	1.11
4.0	1.07	0.78	1.07	0.78	1.07	0.80	1.06	0.81	1.06	0.83	1.05	0.84	1.04	0.88	1.03	0.91	1.01	0.98	0.98	1.05

Table A9.5. Values of F_1 and F_2 for 50% convective, 50% radiant (single column radiators, floor warming systems, block storage heaters).

$\frac{NV}{3\Sigma(A)}$	$\Sigma(AU)/\Sigma(A)$																			
	0.1		0.2		0.4		0.6		0.8		1.0		1.5		2.0		3.0		4.0	
	F_1	F_2	F_1	F_2	F_1	F_2	F_1	F_2	F_1	F_2	F_1	F_2	F_1	F_2	F_1	F_2	F_1	F_2	F_1	F_2
0.1	1.00	0.99	1.00	1.00	1.00	1.00	1.00	1.01	0.99	1.02	0.99	1.03	0.98	1.05	0.98	1.07	0.96	1.11	0.95	1.14
0.2	1.01	0.98	1.01	0.98	1.00	0.99	1.00	1.00	1.00	1.01	0.99	1.02	0.99	1.04	0.98	1.06	0.97	1.09	0.96	1.13
0.4	1.01	0.96	1.01	0.96	1.01	0.97	1.01	0.98	1.01	0.98	1.00	0.99	1.00	1.01	0.99	1.03	0.98	1.07	0.96	1.11
0.6	1.02	0.93	1.02	0.94	1.02	0.95	1.02	0.95	1.01	0.96	1.01	0.97	1.00	0.99	1.00	1.01	0.99	1.04	0.97	1.08
0.8	1.03	0.91	1.03	0.92	1.03	0.92	1.02	0.93	1.02	0.94	1.02	0.95	1.01	0.97	1.00	0.99	0.99	1.02	0.98	1.06
1.0	1.04	0.89	1.03	0.90	1.03	0.90	1.03	0.91	1.03	0.92	1.02	0.93	1.02	0.95	1.01	0.96	1.00	1.00	0.99	1.04
1.5	1.05	0.85	1.05	0.85	1.05	0.86	1.05	0.86	1.04	0.87	1.04	0.88	1.03	0.90	1.03	0.91	1.02	0.95	1.01	0.98
2.0	1.07	0.80	1.06	0.81	1.06	0.81	1.06	0.82	1.06	0.83	1.05	0.84	1.05	0.85	1.04	0.87	1.03	0.90	1.02	0.94
3.0	1.09	0.73	1.09	0.73	1.09	0.74	1.08	0.75	1.08	0.75	1.08	0.76	1.07	0.78	1.07	0.79	1.06	0.82	1.05	0.85
4.0	1.11	0.67	1.11	0.67	1.11	0.68	1.10	0.69	1.10	0.69	1.10	0.70	1.10	0.71	1.09	0.73	1.08	0.76	1.07	0.79

Table A9.6. Values of F_1 and F_2 for $33\frac{1}{3}$% convective, $66\frac{2}{3}$% radiant (vertical and ceiling panel heaters).

$\frac{NV}{3\Sigma(A)}$	$\Sigma(AU)/\Sigma(A)$																			
	0.1		0.2		0.4		0.6		0.8		1.0		1.5		2.0		3.0		4.0	
	F_1	F_2	F_1	F_2	F_1	F_2	F_1	F_2	F_1	F_2	F_1	F_2	F_1	F_2	F_1	F_2	F_1	F_2	F_1	F_2
0.1	1.01	0.98	1.01	0.98	1.01	0.98	1.01	0.98	1.01	0.98	1.01	0.98	1.01	0.98	1.01	0.98	1.01	0.98	1.01	0.98
0.2	1.01	0.97	1.01	0.97	1.01	0.97	1.01	0.97	1.01	0.97	1.01	0.97	1.01	0.97	1.01	0.97	1.01	0.97	1.01	0.97
0.4	1.02	0.94	1.02	0.94	1.02	0.94	1.02	0.94	1.02	0.94	1.02	0.94	1.02	0.94	1.02	0.94	1.02	0.94	1.02	0.94
0.6	1.03	0.91	1.03	0.91	1.03	0.91	1.03	0.91	1.03	0.91	1.03	0.91	1.03	0.91	1.03	0.91	1.03	0.91	1.03	0.91
0.8	1.04	0.88	1.04	0.88	1.04	0.88	1.04	0.88	1.04	0.88	1.04	0.88	1.04	0.88	1.04	0.88	1.04	0.88	1.04	0.88
1.0	1.05	0.86	1.05	0.86	1.05	0.86	1.05	0.86	1.05	0.86	1.05	0.86	1.05	0.86	1.05	0.86	1.05	0.86	1.05	0.86
1.5	1.07	0.80	1.07	0.80	1.07	0.80	1.07	0.80	1.07	0.80	1.07	0.80	1.07	0.80	1.07	0.80	1.07	0.80	1.07	0.80
2.0	1.08	0.75	1.08	0.75	1.08	0.75	1.08	0.75	1.08	0.75	1.08	0.75	1.08	0.75	1.08	0.75	1.08	0.75	1.08	0.75
3.0	1.11	0.67	1.11	0.67	1.11	0.67	1.11	0.67	1.11	0.67	1.11	0.67	1.11	0.67	1.11	0.67	1.11	0.67	1.11	0.67
4.0	1.13	0.60	1.13	0.60	1.13	0.60	1.13	0.60	1.13	0.60	1.13	0.60	1.13	0.60	1.13	0.60	1.13	0.60	1.13	0.60

Table A9.7. Values of F_1 and F_2 for 10% convective, 90% radiant (high temperature radiant systems).

$\frac{NV}{3\Sigma(A)}$	$\Sigma(AU)/\Sigma(A)$																			
	0.1		0.2		0.4		0.6		0.8		1.0		1.5		2.0		3.0		4.0	
	F_1	F_2	F_1	F_2	F_1	F_2	F_1	F_2	F_1	F_2	F_1	F_2	F_1	F_2	F_1	F_2	F_1	F_2	F_1	F_2
0.1	1.01	0.97	1.01	0.97	1.02	0.95	1.02	0.94	1.02	0.93	1.03	0.92	1.04	0.89	1.05	0.86	1.07	0.80	1.09	0.73
0.2	1.02	0.95	1.02	0.95	1.02	0.93	1.03	0.92	1.03	0.91	1.03	0.90	1.04	0.87	1.05	0.84	1.07	0.78	1.10	0.71
0.4	1.03	0.91	1.03	0.91	1.03	0.90	1.04	0.88	1.04	0.87	1.05	0.86	1.06	0.83	1.07	0.80	1.09	0.74	1.11	0.68
0.6	1.04	0.88	1.04	0.87	1.05	0.86	1.05	0.85	1.05	0.84	1.06	0.83	1.07	0.80	1.08	0.77	1.10	0.71	1.12	0.65
0.8	1.05	0.84	1.05	0.84	1.06	0.83	1.06	0.82	1.06	0.81	1.07	0.79	1.08	0.77	1.09	0.74	1.11	0.68	1.12	0.63
1.0	1.06	0.81	1.06	0.81	1.07	0.80	1.07	0.79	1.07	0.78	1.08	0.76	1.09	0.74	1.10	0.71	1.11	0.66	1.13	0.60
1.5	1.09	0.74	1.09	0.74	1.09	0.73	1.09	0.72	1.10	0.71	1.10	0.70	1.11	0.68	1.12	0.65	1.13	0.60	1.15	0.55
2.0	1.10	0.69	1.11	0.68	1.11	0.67	1.11	0.66	1.12	0.65	1.12	0.64	1.13	0.62	1.13	0.60	1.15	0.55	1.17	0.50
3.0	1.14	0.59	1.14	0.59	1.14	0.58	1.14	0.57	1.14	0.57	1.15	0.56	1.15	0.54	1.16	0.52	1.18	0.47	1.19	0.43
4.0	1.16	0.52	1.16	0.52	1.16	0.51	1.17	0.50	1.17	0.50	1.17	0.49	1.18	0.47	1.18	0.45	1.19	0.42	1.21	0.38

the other extreme, heating with high temperature radiant panels gives inside temperatures in reverse order, i.e. mean surface temperature is highest, with environmental, resultant, inside air and outside temperatures each progressively lower.

Most heating systems have characteristics between these two extremes and in many cases the differences between inside air, dry resultant, environmental and mean surface temperatures are not important. In contrast, air conditioning systems provide heating or cooling at the air point. Thus when heating, they provide the same temperature regimes as warm air systems while when cooling, the mean surface temperature is highest with environmental temperature, dry resultant and inside air temperatures each progressively lower.

Allowances for Height of Space

In heat loss calculations a uniform temperature throughout the height of the heated space is assumed. Certain modes of heating cause vertical temperature gradients which lead to enhanced heat losses, particularly through the roof. Additions to the calculated heat loss to allow for this are given in Table A9.8. These percentages should *not* be added to replacement heat to balance that in air mechanically exhausted from process plant.

Allowances for Incidental Heat Gains and Back Losses

Some reduction from the calculated steady state heat requirement can be made where there is continuous 24 hour heating and there are permanent heat sources such as lighting and occupants. The lighting load and metabolic heat from people together with other heat gains from equipment in continuous use can be deducted from the calculated heat loss (see section A7 for detailed information on casual gains). The calculation of back losses is detailed in Section A5.

Inside Temperatures

For unit sizing, condensation studies and comfort assessment it will be necessary to know temperatures other than the dry resultant temperature at the centre of the space. The relevant temperatures under design conditions can be estimated as follows.

Table A9.8. Allowances for height of heated space.

Method of heating and type or disposition of heaters	Percent addition for following heights of heated space (m)		
	5	5 to 10	>10
MAINLY RADIANT			
Warm floor	Nil	Nil	Nil
Warm ceiling	Nil	0 to 5	*
Medium and high temperature downward radiation from high level	Nil	Nil	0 to 5
MAINLY CONVECTIVE			
Natural warm air convection	Nil	0 to 5	*
Forced warm air			
Cross flow at low level	0 to 5	5 to 15	15 to 30
Downward from high level	0 to 5	5 to 10	10 to 20
Medium and high temperature cross radiation from intermediate level	Nil	0 to 5	5 to 10

* Not appropriate to this application.

Mean Inside Air Temperature

From equation A9.10 the inside air temperature at the centre of the room is given by:

$$t_{ai} = F_2(t_c - t_{ao}) + t_{ao} \quad .. \quad .. \quad .. \quad .. \quad A9.13$$

Inside Environmental Temperature

From equation A9.9 the inside environmental temperature is given by:

$$t_{ei} = F_1(t_c - t_{ao}) + t_{ao} \quad .. \quad .. \quad .. \quad .. \quad A9.14$$

Inside Surface Temperature of Exposed Surfaces

Consideration of the heat flow from a room surface shows that:

$$\frac{t_s - t_{ao}}{t_{ei} - t_{ao}} = U\left(\frac{1}{U} - R_{si}\right) \quad .. \quad .. \quad .. \quad A9.15$$

therefore:

$$t_s = (1 - UR_{si})(t_{ei} - t_{ao}) + t_{ao} .. \quad .. \quad .. \quad A9.16$$

$$= (1 - UR_{si}) F_1(t_c - t_{ao}) + t_{ao} \quad .. \quad .. \quad A9.17$$

Dry Resultant Temperature at Other Points

The foregoing calculation procedure gives conditions at the centre of the room concerned. However, there will be an independent variation of air and radiant temperatures in the heated space, changing with the location, size and U-value of the exposed perimeter and with the type and position of the heating unit. The comfort at any point in the room will depend on the dry resultant temperature which is the mean of the air and radiant temperatures at that point.

Mean Radiant Temperature

The mean radiant temperature at any point in a room is calculable and depends on the surface temperature of the surrounding surfaces 'seen' from that point.

Normally the main variation in radiant temperature is in the horizontal plane. Fig. A9.1 shows typical examples of the horizontal distribution of radiant temperature. The variation in radiant temperature is reduced by placing heat sources adjacent to cold surfaces and by improving the U-value of the external walls and glazing.

Air Temperature

The variation in air temperature in a heated space is not, at present, calculable. It varies mainly in the vertical plane except adjacent to cold surfaces such as windows, unless heating units are placed below them to counteract down draught. Fig A9.2 gives an indication of the vertical temperature gradient found with different types of heating systems[10]. It should be noted that the position of the heating unit or warm air inlet is important and affects the temperature gradient. If a radiator is placed at the back of a heated space away from the window, it will induce a circulation of air with a draught of cool air falling down the window, the cool air being drawn across the floor with a warm air stream across the ceiling. This will increase the temperature gradient, and the increased air movement at floor level will accentuate the discomfort of the legs and feet of the occupant.

The position of warm air inlets is also important, a high level inlet giving a much greater temperature gradient than a low level inlet.

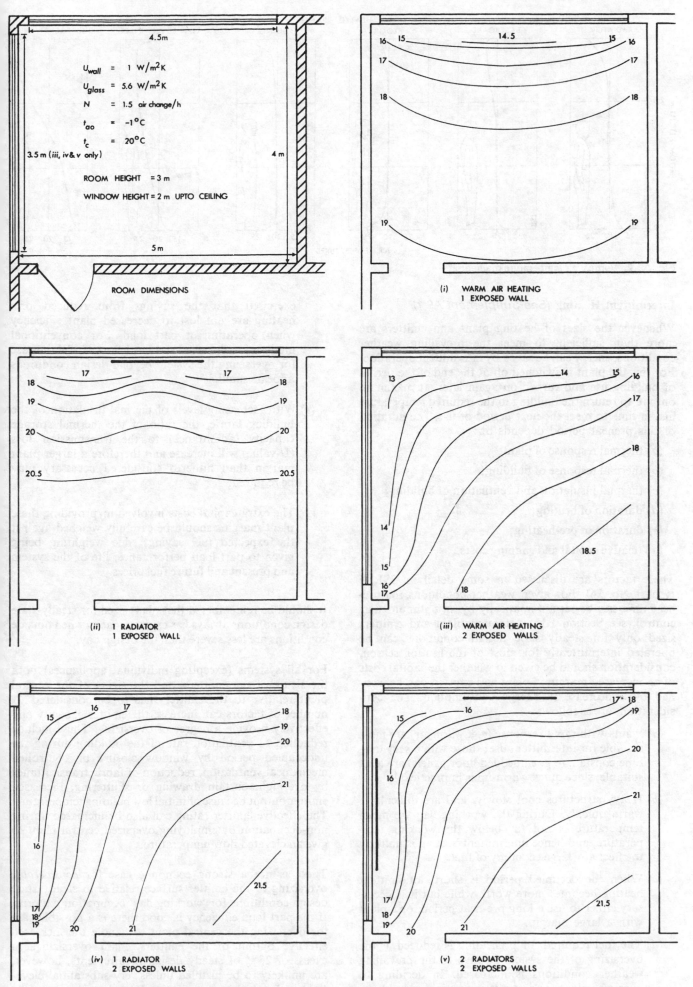

Fig. A9.1. Mean radiant temperature isotherms.

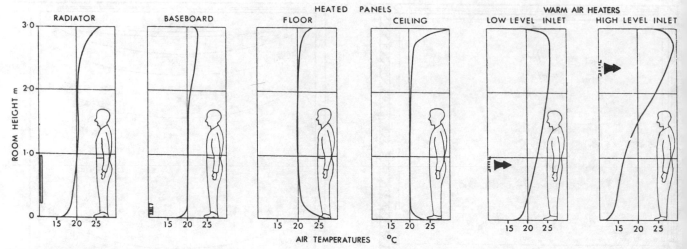

Fig. A9.2. Vertical air temperature gradients[10].

Intermittent Heating *(See Supplement A9/1)*

Whenever the sizes of heating plant and emitters are more than sufficient to meet the prevailing weather conditions, energy can be saved by intermittent operation. For this the plant is switched off at the end of the period of building use and turned on again later, at maximum output, to return the building to the required temperature just in time to meet the next period of use. The duration of this preheat period depends on:

(a) thermal response of plant;

(b) thermal response of building;

(c) thermal insulation and ventilation of building;

(d) duration of heating;

(e) duration of pre-heating;

(f) relative capital and running costs.

These factors are discussed in some detail in BSRIA Report No. 26[1]. For given weather conditions the pre-heat time can be set automatically by an optimum start control, see Section B11. Although plant and emitters sized only for steady state design conditions can be operated intermittently for most of the heating season, consideration should be given to whether the capital costs of an increased margin in plant and emitters can be justified by a decrease in energy consumption. The considerations are as follows:

(a) Plants with rapid response (e.g. warm air) are most suitable for intermittent use; those with a very long time constant (e.g. embedded floor panels) are least suitable, since quick warm-up is impracticable.

(b) Heavy structures cool slowly, and are difficult to warm quickly. During the working day the mean temperature is not far below the working temperature, and hence intermittent heating is unlikely to effect any large economy of fuel.

(c) When the occupied period is short, intermittent heating becomes more worth while but it is necessary either to use a long pre-heat period, or a plant with a large margin.

(d) The fuel required for preheating is reduced as the oversizing of the system relative to the prevailing weather conditions is increased. In deciding to oversize plant and emitter caution should be

exercised that the savings from reduced pre-heating are not lost to decreased plant efficiency when operating at part load. For conventional modern fossil-fuelled systems below 40 kW the case for oversizing the system beyond design conditions appears small.[2,3]

(e) With increasing levels of thermal insulation of the building fabric, the ratio of the thermal storage capacity (admittance) to the transmission loss (U-value) will increase and therefore a larger plant margin than hitherto considered necessary may be required.

(f) The extra capital costs involved in providing these plant margins should be carefully weighed against the expected fuel savings, due weighting being given to part load performance, life of the system and present and future fuel prices.

It should be remembered that plant sized for steady-state design conditions always has excess capacity when outside conditions are less severe than the design day.

For all systems (excepting individual appliances) both the sizing of the emitters, and the sizing of the central plant relative to the emitters has to be considered. A number of factors can increase the emitter capacity and effectively provide a degree of oversizing. These include reduction of ventilation rate of the building during the unoccupied period by window closure or controlled mechanical ventilation, reduction of fabric transmittance by overnight curtain drawing or shuttering, increased emitter output because of initial low building temperature. The effective emitter rating can also be increased during non-occupation by employing oversized central plant to give an elevated flow temperature.

There is not a strong economic case for *considerable* oversizing of the emitter surface relative to steady state design conditions for 'working day' occupation patterns. If the part load efficiency is good there is a possible case for oversizing the central plant to handle the increased effective output of the emitters. Plant oversizings in excess of 25% of steady design requirements, however, are unlikely to be justified unless very substantial elevations in flow temperature can be effected.

Table A9.9. Allowances for intermittent heating, F_3.

Plant ratio	Lightweight construction		Heavyweight construction	
	Preheat time at design/h	Seasonal heat requirement/%	Preheat time at design/h	Seasonal heat requirement/%
1.0	Continuous	59	Continuous	84
1.2	6	52	Very long	86
1.5	3	48	7	74
2.0	1	46	4	70
2.5	0	45	2	68
3.0	0	45	1	67

Notes:
1. The Table is based on an indoor dry resultant temperature of 20°C and an occupied period of 8 h, for a 7 day week.
2. Plant size ratio $= \dfrac{\text{Design maximum heat requirement}}{\text{Steady state design load}}$
3. The preheat times are for short plant response such as warm air and low volume water systems. They should be increased when the plant response time is significant.
4. Seasonal heat requirement is expressed as a percentage of heat needed for continuous operation. If casual gains (e.g. sun, lighting, occupants) are significant the plant input may be further reduced.
5. Lightweight buildings are those with a response factor < 4 while heavyweight buildings have a response factor > 6, where
$$\text{response factor} = \frac{\Sigma(AY) + \frac{1}{3}NV}{\Sigma(AU) + \frac{1}{3}NV}$$

The preheating times of systems for various plant ratios (F_3) are given in Table A9.9 for UK design conditions. The preheating times are based on plant with a short response time (e.g. warm air and low volume water systems). They should be increased if the response time of the heating system is significant.

The intermittent or peak heating load, Q_{pb} is given by the equation:

$$Q_{pb} = F_3 Q_p \quad .. \quad\quad .. \quad\quad .. \quad\quad .. \quad\quad .. \quad\quad \text{A9.18}$$

Table A9.9 also includes estimates of the seasonal heat requirements during intermittent operation compared with continuous operation. These values are based on 8 hours per day, 7 day week operation for a heating season of 260 days. (i.e. when outside temperatures are below 16°C). They assume that the building temperature is 20°C during the occupied period and make no allowances for incidental energy gains from the Sun, from lighting, occupants etc. In using these data to calculate seasonal energy requirements it is necessary to use an appropriate seasonable boiler efficiency, see Section B.18. Estimates of the internal temperature cycles under intermittent operation can be made using Section A5 (Appendix 7).

Methods of control for intermittent operation are dealt with in Section B11.

Highly Intermittent Systems

Where a building is used for very short periods, as for example, a church, the steady-state heat loss calculation is inappropriate. Instead use should be made of the 'admittance' concept which evalutes the heat flow *into* rather than *through* the structure, see Section A5.

The heat output required from the room appliance will be:

$$Q_p = (F_1 \Sigma (AY) + \tfrac{1}{3}F_2 NV)(t_c - t_{ao}) \quad .. \quad\quad .. \quad \text{A9.19}$$

As given, the equation is valid for a 24-hour cycle (i.e. 12 h heating, 12 h off) For other durations of heating values of Y should be multiplied by a correction factor:

$$F_4 = \left(\frac{24}{2\theta}\right)^{0.5} \quad .. \quad\quad .. \quad\quad .. \quad\quad .. \quad\quad .. \quad \text{A9.20}$$

This immediately gives higher input ratings to achieve a given comfort level in and for short periods. Values for F_1 and F_2 are obtained from Tables A9.1 to A9.7 but using $\Sigma(AY)$ instead of $\Sigma(AU)$.

Radiant Heating

High temperature radiant systems are normally chosen for local heating or for highly intermittent use and for neither case are the ordinary heat loss calculations appropriate for the selection of either unit or total output. The limiting factors are discussed in Section A1. Design should be based on consideration of local radiant intensity at the work place, using the polar diagrams of the radiation from the heating unit if these are known.

The sizing of medium and low temperature radiant systems is carried out via the usual heat loss calculations. The total area of panel required is found by dividing the net heat requirement by the emission from the panel.

Once the total area has been found in this way, the distribution of the hot surfaces needs to be considered. BSRIA Laboratory Reports 36[4] and 40[5] suggest a method of doing this, to secure substantial uniformity over the working plane in a factory. Generally, medium-temperature panels should not be equidistant, but closer towards the exposed walls of the space. A single panel in the centre of the ceiling should not normally be used, as this tends to produce a peak of temperature in the middle of the working zone. Low-temperature panels, too, are preferably located adjacent to the exposed perimeter of the room. In every case, the panel area and operating temperature should be checked in relation to the mounting height, to ensure that the comfort criteria are satisfied.

Storage Systems

The previous discussion has been based on the assumption that heat is supplied to the building only during the occupied period and the preheating time. In some circumstances, it may be financially advantageous to supply heat outside normal hours and to store it in water storage vessels, in specially designed storage appliances, or in the fabric of the building. At the present time, such systems are used only when off-peak electric power is cheaply available but they could be used with any fuel for which a different tariff might be introduced to reduce demand variations.

It is necessary to consider two variants—one in which heat is dissipated continuously throughout 24 h (e.g. uncontrolled floor or block-heating) and one in which the heat dissipation takes place only during the hours of use (controlled block-heating or electrically heated water with thermal storage). In each case, energy is supplied to the system during restricted periods, usually at night.

In both cases, the individual room units should be sized according to the method given above, to ensure an adequate rate of emission. With floor-heating, it is necessary to check that the required emission can be obtained without exceeding the maximum permissible floor surface temperature.

With uncontrolled systems, heating is continuous, and no intermittent heating factors should be used. With controlled systems, heating can be intermittent and the usual factors may be applied according to the response time, the hours of use, etc.

The storage and charge must be equal to the total 24 h demand under design conditions. In the case of the uncontrolled 'continuous' systems, this is $24 \times 3600 \times$ the mean heat requirement, but for the others it is less than this, on account of the lower mean daily temperature. The input rating must, in either case, be:

$$Q_p = \frac{\bar{Q}_p}{3600 \, \theta_r} \qquad .. \qquad .. \qquad .. \qquad .. \quad \text{A9.21}$$

With uncontrolled storage systems, the highest room temperature is likely to be at the end of the re-charging period—the minimum at the end of the usage period, just prior to re-charging. For acceptability, this temperature fall during daytime (swing) must be limited to 3°C or less. It depends on the thermal properties of the building as well as those of the appliance.

Temperature Swings

With intermittent operation it is often useful to calculate the temperature swing when the plant is not operating. The calculation may be particularly useful to indicate the extent of overnight cooling and hence the risks of condensation on room surfaces. The appropriate formula is:

$$\tilde{t}_c = \frac{\tilde{Q}_p}{F_1 \Sigma (A Y) + \frac{1}{3} F_2 N V} \qquad .. \qquad .. \qquad .. \quad \text{A9.22}$$

Central Plant Size

In estimating the required duty of a central plant for a building, it should be remembered that the total net infiltration of outdoor air is about half the sum of the rates for the separate rooms. This is because at any one time, infiltration of outdoor air takes place only on the windward part of the building, the flow in the remainder being *outwards*.

When intermittent heating is to be practised, the pre-heating periods for all rooms in a building will generally be coincident. The central plant rating is then the sum of the individual room heat demands, modified to take account of the *net* infiltration.

If heating is to be continuous, some diversity between the several room heating loads can be expected. The values listed in Table A9.10 are suggested. When mechanical ventilation is combined with heating, the heating plant and the ventilation plant may have different hours of

Table A9.10. Diversity factors for central plant (continuous heating).

Space or buildings served by plant	Diversity factor
Single space	1.0
Single building or zone, central control	0.9
Single building, individual room control	0.8
Group of buildings, similar type and use	0.8
Group of buildings, dissimilar uses*..	0.7

* This applies to group and district heating schemes, where there is substantial storage of heat in the distribution mains, whether heating is continuous or intermittent.

use and the peak loads on the two sections of the plant will often occur at different times.

The central plant may also be required to provide a domestic hot water supply, and/or heat for process purposes. These loads may have to be added to the net heating load to arrive at the necessary plant duty, but careful design may avoid the occurrence of simultaneous peaks; and in large installations, the construction of boiler curves may indicate whether savings in boiler rating can be made[6]. In many cases, little or no extra capacity may be needed for the hot water supply, its demands being met by 'robbing' the heating circuits for short periods.

Selective Systems

In some cases the various rooms of a building do not all require heating at the same time of day and in such cases a so-called selective system may be used. The supply of heat is restricted to different parts of the building at different times of the day; the whole building cannot be heated at one time. A typical application is in dwellings where the demands for heat in living spaces and bedrooms do not normally coincide.

In a selective system, the individual room appliances must be sized as indicated above, to provide the appropriate output according to heat loss, gains and intermittency. The central plant need only be capable of meeting the greatest simultaneous demands of those room units which are in use at the same time. This will generally lead to a large power being available to meet the demands of those units which form the lesser part of the load. These units may then be operated with a high degree of intermittency.

Multiple Boiler Installations

Load variation throughout the season is clearly large and consideration should be given to the number of boilers required in the system. Operation at low loads leads to corrosion and loss in efficiency and should be avoided. On the other hand a number of smaller boilers gives an increase in capital costs.

It has been shown[7] that, when boilers are chosen which have a fairly constant and good efficiency over a working range of 30–100%, then the effects on overall costs (running+capital) of varying the number and relative sizes of boilers in the system is less than 5%. The optimum number depends on the frequency of occurrence of low loads.

Under these circumstances the engineer is free to choose the number of boilers in his system based on practical rather than economic considerations.

The following procedure is recommended:

(a) Choose a type of boiler with a fairly constant and high efficiency over its full turndown range. Obtain its efficiency curve.

(b) On the basis of avoiding acid corrosion and obtaining required standby, choose the number of boilers required and their relative sizes.

Equally sized boilers should be used except where the provision of domestic hot water in summer requires one smaller boiler.

Table A9.11 gives suggested relative sizes based on turndown to 30%.

(c) The boilers should be controlled in sequence, the switching points for bringing boilers on line occurring whenever an additional boiler makes the system more efficient (for evaluation of this see Fig. A9.3). Full boiler load is not usually the most economic switching point, but switching points too close to full turndown should also be avoided. At any given system load the boilers on line should share the load between them in proportion (a) then refer to reference 7 for further guidance.

(d) If boilers must be chosen contrary to recommendation (a) then refer to reference 7 for further guidance.

AIR CONDITIONING *(See Supplement A9/1)*

This manual calculation procedure for air conditioning loads assumes that all heat is removed at the air point since this is the practical effect of all current air conditioning methods whether all air systems or a combination of air and water. The procedure permits the calculation of loads to hold either the air or dry resultant temperature at the chosen design value. Loads due to solar gains through glass with and without shading are tabulated for latitudes between 0° and 60°. Corrections are given to deal with intermittent plant operation and to cover fluctuations in the controlled temperature if they are permissible. Finally, guidance is given on the sizing of central plant capacity to take account of diversity in use.

Ultimately, the selection of air conditioning equipment is determined by the interaction of sensible and latent cooling loads. The interplay between sensible and latent loads and the use of psychrometric charts and data are dealt with in Section B3.

The calculation procedure follows the theory set out in Section A5 of the CIBSE *Guide*. This procedure is intended for manual calculations and anyone wishing to write a computer program based on this method is referred to Section A5 which contains all the relevant equations.

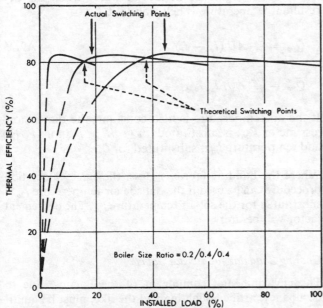

Fig. A9.3. Evaluation of optimum boiler control.

Table A9.11. Appropriate boiler size ratios assuming turn-down to 30% of full load.

Number of boilers	Installed plant ratio*	Heating only			Heating plus domestic hot water			Remarks
		Installed boiler size ratios	Lowest load/%	Load if largest fails/%	Installed boiler size ratios	Lowest load/%	Load if largest fails/%	
1	1.0	1·0	30	0	—	—	—	Use only if load is seldom < 30%. No standby.
2	1.0	0.5/0.5	15	50	—	—	—	Impossible to gain reasonable standby and meet low loads.
	1.0	0.33/0.67	10	33	0.30/0.70	9	30	
	1.25	0.3/0.7	11.3	37	0.25/0.75	9.4	31	
	1.5	0.25/0.75	11.3	37	—	—	—	
3	1.0	0.33/0.33/0.33	10	67	0.2/0.4/0.4	6	60	
	1.25	0.2/0.4/0.4	7.5	75	0.2/0.4/0.4	7.5	75	
	1.50	0.2/0.4/0.4	9	90	0.2/0.4/0.4	9	90	
	1.67	0.2/0.4/0.4	10	100	0.2/0.4/0.4	10	100	
4	1.0	0.25/0.25/0.25/0.25	7.5	75	0.25/0.25/0.25/0.25	7.5	75	
	1.25	0.25/0.25/0.25/0.25	9.4	94	0.1/0.3/0.3/0.3	3.7	87	
	1.50	0.1/0.3/0.3/0.3	4.3	105	0.1/0.3/0.3/0.3	4.5	105	
	1.33	0.25/0.25/0.25/0.25	10	100	0.1/0.3/0.3/0.3	4	93	
5	1.0	0.2/0.2/0.2/0.2/0.2	6	80	0.2/0.2/0.2/0.2/0.2	6	80	
	1.25	0.2/0.2/0.2/0.2/0.2	7.5	100	0.2/0.2/0.2/0.2/0.2	7.5	100	
	1.50	0.2/0.2/0.2/0.2/0.2	9.0	120	0.2/0.2/0.2/0.2/0.2	9	120	

$$\text{* Installed plant ratio} = \frac{\text{Total installed boiler capacity}}{\text{Design maximum heat requirement}}$$

Design Conditions

Internal

Guidance on the choice of internal design conditions is given in Section A1 of the CIBSE *Guide*.

External

The choice of external design conditions must allow for daily variations in climatic conditions since steady state flow is only of minor significance in summer, while variations in sunshine are of major importance. Data on temperature, humidity and solar radiation are given in Section A2 of the CIBSE *Guide*.

Sensible Cooling Loads

The calculation routine falls into the following four parts:

(a) cooling load due to solar gain through windows and blinds;

(b) cooling load due to conduction through the surfaces of the space;

(c) cooling load due to internal gains;

(d) infiltration load.

Cooling Loads through Windows and Blinds

Tables of solar cooling loads have been prepared for direct use. These refer to a building having single 6mm clear glass with and without internal white venetian blinds. The tables are based on:

(a) constant internal temperature held by plant operating 10 hours per day (0800 to 1800 sun time);

(b) four to five days sunny spell;

(c) for the UK (51.7°N), the climatological data in Section A2 have been used. For other latitudes the values taken are; direct radiation factor = 1.0, diffuse radiation factor = 1.0, ground reflectance factor = 0.2, cloudiness = 0.0.

The data in the tables are given for lightweight buildings. These may be considered as having demountable partitioning and suspended ceilings. Floors are either solid with carpet or wood-block finish or of the suspended type (i.e. an average surface factor ≥0.8). Correction factors are given for buildings of heavyweight construction, namely those buildings with solid internal walls and partitions and with solid floors and solid ceilings (i.e. an average surface factor ≤0.5). Surface factors are given in Section A3 of the CIBSE *Guide*. It will be noted that to hold the air temperature constant, the cooling load is generally less than that required to hold the dry resultant temperature constant. The data listed should be applied to the problem as follows.

In order to maintain constant dry resultant temperature, for the UK read the values from Tables A9.14 and A9.15 as appropriate. For world-wide use, read values from Tables A9.16 to A9.35 as appropriate. For glasses other than 6mm clear glass and for buildings of heavyweight construction, the factors at the foot of each table should be used. Where factors are not quoted for the particular design situation, interpolation is permitted.

In order to maintain constant internal air temperature, the procedure follows that for constant dry resultant temperature but the additional factor, related to building weight is used.

Cooling Load due to Conduction

The average rate of heat conduction through an opaque wall or roof is given by:

$$\bar{Q}_u = AU(\bar{t}_{eo} - \bar{t}_{ei}) \quad .. \quad .. \quad .. \quad \text{A9.23}$$

and the cyclic variation about the mean is:

$$\tilde{Q}_u = AUf\,\tilde{t}_{eo\,(\theta-\phi)} \quad .. \quad .. \quad .. \quad \text{A9.24}$$

These are gains at the environmental point and give rise to the following loads at the air point when the dry resultant temperature is held constant.

$$\bar{Q}_{ua} = \frac{F_u}{F_v} AU(\bar{t}_{eo} - \bar{t}_c) \quad .. \quad .. \quad \text{A9.25}$$

$$\tilde{Q}_{ua} = \frac{F_y}{F_v} AUf\,\tilde{t}_{eo\,(\theta-\phi)} \quad .. \quad .. \quad \text{A9.26}$$

If the air temperature is held constant, the dimensionless factor F_{au}, is substituted for (F_u/F_v), F_{ay} for (F_y/F_v) and temperature $\bar{t}_{ai}$ is substituted for $\bar{t}_c$.

Where the building fabric is glass, the same calculation procedure can be used if the outside air temperature t_{ao} is substituted for the sol-air temperature t_{eo}. The decrement factor will be unity.

Cooling Load due to Internal Gains

The environmental component of these gains, due to occupancy, artificial lighting and the like, must be multiplied by the correction factor (F_u/F_v) in order to give the load at the air point when the dry resultant temperature is held constant. When the air temperature is held constant, the multiplying factor is F_{au}. In contrast, the components of the load realised at the air point need no correction factor.

Cooling Load due to Air Infiltration

The heat gain due to air infiltration is given by:

$$Q_v = \tfrac{1}{3}NV(t_{ao} - t_{ai}) \quad .. \quad .. \quad \text{A9.27}$$

When the air temperature is held constant, this equation gives the load at the air point. For those systems in which dry resultant temperature is used for control purposes, the load is given by:

$$Q_v = \tfrac{1}{3}NVF_2(t_{ao} - t_c) \quad .. \quad .. \quad \text{A9.28}$$

Cooling Load due to Outdoor Air Supply

In the majority of air conditioning systems outdoor air is treated in the central air handling plant and is also used as the medium for controlling both temperature and humidity in the room space. For this reason, account must be taken of latent and sensible loads and this is dealt with in Section B3.

Intermittent Operation

The calculation of loads during intermittent plant operation requires the evaluation of loads for all 24 hours of the day. Equations A5.82 and A5.83 can then be used to estimate the actual load. Such a procedure is likely to be too lengthy for manual calculations. However, the tabulated solar gains through windows do allow for intermittent operation and in temperate climates at least, the effect of ignoring intermittency for fabric, internal and infiltration loads is not usually significant. This is because their overnight values are only a small fraction of the peak load.

Fluctuations in Control Temperature

If the controlled temperature is allowed to rise for short periods then the peak room sensible load can be reduced. If the control system is based on dry resultant temperature, the following applies:

$$\Delta Q_p = (\tfrac{1}{3} N_{inf} V + \frac{F_y}{F_v} \Sigma(AY)) \Delta t_c \quad \cdots \qquad \cdots \quad \text{A9.29}$$

For controls based on the air temperature, the relevant equation is:

$$\Delta Q_p = (\tfrac{1}{3} N_{inf} V + F_{ay} \Sigma(AY)) \Delta t_{al} \quad \cdots \qquad \cdots \quad \text{A9.30}$$

Central Plant Size

The sum of the calculated loads (allowance being made where appropriate for non-coincidence) is the cooling load for the space. To estimate the rating of the central plant, it is essential to take account of the times of occurrence of peak loads for the different façades and for this purpose it may be helpful to plot plant demand curves hour by hour.

As with heating, some additional capacity may be needed in the room unit and/or central plant if accurate automatic control is required. In groups of buildings served by one plant, a diversity factor (less than 1) may be used.

The calculations assume that a constant dry resultant temperature is to be maintained for 10 hours, but sometimes it may be possible, in the interest of capital saving, to permit swings to occur as described above, particularly in hot weather. As mentioned above, latent loads need to be taken into account as indicated in Section B3.

ASSESSMENT OF RELIABILITY

Reliability, simply expressed, is the ratio of successful operation of a device or system to all attempted operations.[8]

Reliability theory is complex but a few basic formulae can help the designer in making reliability-related decisions. Some of these formulae are presented here and are a useful means for assessing the overall risk of central plant down time.

The pattern of failure during the lifetime of a system or a piece of equipment is shown in Fig. A9.4. During the normal useful life period, reliability Λ, can be expressed as an exponential function of failure rate, Γ and time, θ.

$$\Lambda = \exp(-\Gamma\theta) \quad \cdots \qquad \cdots \qquad \cdots \qquad \cdots \quad \text{A9.31}$$

Reliability can also be determined independently of time in certain situations by using conventional probability methods. It is a convenient circumstance that analyses of the probability of failure-free operation of various equipment arrangements can be accomplished using these techniques.

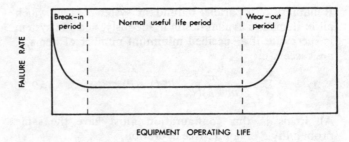

Fig. A9.4. Failure pattern.

Letting P be the probability of failure-free operation, the following formulae can be applied to determine the reliability of a system Λ_s.

Serial System

Fig. A9.5. Serial system.

Reliability of a serial system, Λ_s, in which all items must be successful for system success.

$$\Lambda_s = P_1 P_2 P_3 \ldots \ldots P_n \quad \cdots \qquad \cdots \qquad \cdots \quad \text{A9.33}$$

Parallel System

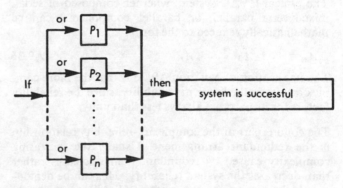

Fig. A9.6. Parallel system.

Reliability of parallel system Λ_s, in which one of the items must be successful before the system is successful:

$$\Lambda_s = 1 - (1 - P_1)(1 - P_2) \ldots \ldots (1 - P_n) \quad \cdots \quad \text{A9.34}$$

Parallel Redundant System

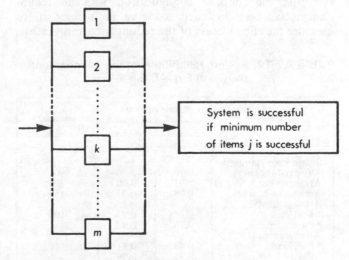

Fig. A9.7. Parallel redundant system.

Reliability of a parallel redundant system, Λ_s, in which all m items are available simultaneously, and the system is successful if a specified minimum number of items, j, are successful:

$$\Lambda_s = \sum_{k=j}^{m} \frac{m!}{(m-k)! \, k!} \, P^k (1-P)^{m-k} \qquad .. \quad \text{A9.35}$$

All items in this configuration must have the same probability P of failure-free operation.

Standby Redundant System

A standby item is turned on only if an on-line item fails. The standby (off-line) items are assumed immune to failure until activated, and switching is always reliable.

Because the standby equipment either cannot fail or will have a lower failure rate than the on-line equipment, a high reliability is inherent in the standby redundant system. However, if standby duty is divided equally among the various items, it can be assumed that the failure rate for each item will be the same when considered over the normal useful life. In this event, the standby redundant system is equivalent to the parallel redundant system for our purposes, and equation A9.35 is applicable. From the foregoing formulae it is possible to examine the relationships between reliability and complexity of various equipment arrangements. The typical HVAC system, whether composed of serial, mixed serial-parallel, or parallel components, can be mathematically reduced to the form:

$$\Lambda_s = \Lambda_1 \Lambda_2 \Lambda_3 \ldots \ldots \Lambda_m \qquad .. \qquad .. \qquad .. \quad \text{A9.36}$$

The implication of equation A9.36 is that the more complex a system, the lower its reliability, since the reliability factors for its parts are always less than unity.

The counterpart of the complexity-reliability relationship is the redundant arrangement. Usually the increasing complexity caused by redundant items increases rather than decreases the system reliability. This can be demonstrated by comparing the system reliabilities of several parallel arrangements commonly used in HVAC systems. Using equation A9.35, system reliability formulae have been derived for each arrangement shown in Fig. A9.8. All items are assumed to have the same probability of failure-free operation, P. Table A9.12 gives the system reliability calculated for each arrangement with values of P at 0.70 and 0.90. A single item of equipment, representing the simplest configuration with no redundancy, has been included to serve as a standard to measure the effectiveness of the redundant arrangements.

Table A9.12. System reliabilities of the arrangements shown in Fig. A9.8.

Arrangement	System reliability		Installed equipment capacity, per cent of full load
	$P = 0.70$	$P = 0.90$	
Single-item standard (no redundancy)	0.70	0.90	100
Arrangement A	0.91	0.99	200
Arrangement B	0.78	0.97	150
Arrangement C			
* Full load	0.34	0.73	100
* Partial load	0.78	0.97	—
Arrangement D			
* Full load	0.49	0.81	150
* Partial load	0.91	0.99	—

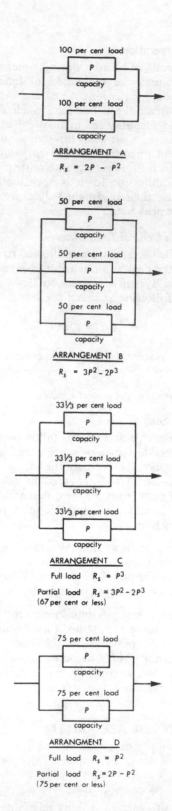

Fig. A9.8. System reliability of various arrangements.

Table A9.12 suggests:

(a) The beneficial effects of 100 per cent redundancy are indicated by Arrangement A, which has the highest reliability.

(b) Arrangements A, B and the single-item standard show the direct relationship between redundant equipment capacity and system reliability: the greater the redundancy, the higher the reliability.

(c) Arrangements C and D have sharply lower system reliabilities at full load conditions because all items in these two arrangements must be successful under full load conditions. Under partial conditions, the system reliabilities increase substantially as redundant capacity emerges. Because of these characteristics, the load profile assumes great importance when applying these two arrangements.

Arrangement pairs B and D as well as C and the single-item standard have equal installed equipment capacities but unequal system reliabilities. The designer must weigh the risks of low reliability at full load while gaining high reliability at partial loads against the benefits of a constant, but lower, reliability under all loads.

The formulae discussed here represent only a very small part of the reliability methodology that can be used in systems design. The fully-fledged application of this evolving discipline, necessitates the availability of reliability data on HVAC equipment, for which some information[9] is tentatively offered in Table A9.13.

Table A9.13 Reliability of HVAC equipment.

Item	Life*	Availability during 10 000 hours operation
Fans	100 000 hrs	97%
Motors	,,	95%
Bearings	,,	97%
Air handlers	,,	95%
DX compressors	,,	83%
Reciprocating chillers	,,	85%
Centrifugal chillers	,,	86%
Cooling towers and pumping	,,	90%
Evaporative condenser	,,	95%
Aircooled condenser	,,	97%

* *Note.* Expected life of all these items under normal operating conditions is between 15 and 20 years. Furthermore, ten years of high reliability can be expected under continuous operation or frequent cycling.

REFERENCES

[1] *BSRIA Laboratory Report* No. 26. "Intermittent Heating" 1964

[2] M. B. GREEN, "Heat Services for Future Housing—Part II— The Design of Gas Systems for Insulated Housing" *B.S.E.* **45**, 155, December 1977.

[3] D. P. BLOOMFIELD and D. J. FISK, "Seasonal Domestic Boiler Efficiencies and Intermittent Heating" *Heating and Ventilating Engineer* **51**, 6, September 1977.

[4] *BSRIA Laboratory Report* No. 36. "Space Heating by Medium Temperature Radiant Panels" 1966.

[5] *BSRIA Laboratory Report* No. 40. "Siting of Medium Temperature Radiant Heating Strip Panels in Long Rooms" 1967.

[6] H. C. JAMIESON, "The Mechanical Services at Shell Centre" *J.I.H.V.E.* **31**, 1, 1963.

[7] P. ROBERTSON, E. McKENZIE, R. RAVENSCROFT, "A New Approach to the Economic Sizing and Operation of Space Heating Boiler Plant", *B.S.E.* **41**, 1, April 1973.

[8] N. G. WARREN, "Reliability Formulas for System Design", *Heating/Piping/Air Conditioning*, June 1975.

[9] *BSRIA Laboratory Report* No. 56, "Reliability of Heating, Ventilating and Air Conditioning Equipment—Introduction and Literature Survey" 1969.

[10] OSCAR FABER and J. R. KELL, "Heating and Air Conditioning of Buildings" Revised by J. R. Kell and P. L. Martin Architectural Press.

APPENDICES

Appendix 1—Heating Example

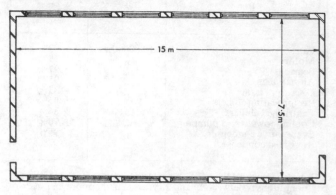

HEIGHT = 5m   OUTSIDE WALL U = 0.5 W/m² °C
DOORS U = 2·9 W/m² °C   WINDOW U = 5·7 W/m² °C
EACH WINDOW = 4m²   DOORS = 6m²

Fig. A9.9. Heating example building.

A small factory (see Fig. A9.9) is to be heated to a dry resultant temperature of 19°C. The ventilation allowance is assumed to be 0.5 W/m³ and the external design temperature is −1.0°C. Calculate the total heat loss, environmental, air and mean radiant temperatures under steady-state design conditions if the factory is to be heated:

    (a) by forced circulation warm air heaters,

    (b) by high temperature radiant strip.

Solution (a)—Warm Air

Establish first the numerical values of $\Sigma(AU)/\Sigma(A)$ and $\frac{1}{3}N\Sigma(V)/\Sigma(A)$ from the data given.

For $\Sigma(AU)/\Sigma(A)$ refer to the dimensions and thermal transmittances given in Fig. A9.9 and calculate total surface area and fabric heat loss for 1°C temperature difference:

Floor	= 113 m²	×	0.5 W/m²K	=	57	W/K
Roof	= 113 m²	×	0.3 W/m²K	=	34	W/K
Walls	= 171 m²	×	0.5 W/m²K	=	86	W/K
Glass	= 48 m²	×	5.7 W/m²K	=	274	W/K
Doors	= 6 m²	×	2.9 W/m²K	=	17	W/K
$\Sigma(A)$	= 451 m²		$\Sigma(AU)$	=	468	W/K

Hence: $\Sigma(AU)/\Sigma(A) = \dfrac{468}{451}$ $= 1.04\,\text{W/m}^2\text{K}$

For $\frac{1}{3}N\Sigma(V)/\Sigma(A)$, the value of $\Sigma(V)$ is the volume of the factory and $\frac{1}{3}N$ the ventilation allowance as given (where $N \approx 1\frac{1}{2}$ air changes).

Hence: $\dfrac{\frac{1}{3}N\,\Sigma(V)}{\Sigma(A)} = \dfrac{563 \times 0.5}{451} = 0.62 \text{ W/m}^2\text{ K}$

From the solutions above and the co-ordinates given in Table A9.1 for forced warm air heaters, select factors F_1 and F_2 for applying to the fabric and ventilation losses respectively. By interpolation, $F_1 = 0.95$ and $F_2 = 1.17$ thus, for the fabric, the loss is:

$$Q_u = \Sigma(AU) \times (19°C + 1°C) \times F_1$$
$$= 468 \times 20 \times 0.95$$
$$= 8.89 \text{ kW}$$

And for the ventilation, the loss is:

$$Q_v = \tfrac{1}{3}N\Sigma(V) \times (19°C + 1°C) \times F_2$$
$$= 563 \times 0.5 \times 20 \times 1.17$$
$$= 6.59 \text{ kW}$$

Hence, total heat loss is:

$$Q_p = Q_u + Q_v$$
$$= 15.5 \text{ kW}$$

The various temperature relationships can now be established as follows.

From equation A9.14:

$$t_{ei} = F_1(t_c - t_{ao}) + t_{ao}$$
$$= (0.95 \times 20) - 1.0$$
$$= 18.0°C$$

From equation A9.13:

$$t_{ai} = F_2(t_c - t_{ao}) + t_{ao}$$
$$= (1.17 \times 20) - 1.0$$
$$= 22.4°C$$

From equation A9.2:

$$t_m = \frac{3t_{ei} - t_{ai}}{2}$$
$$= \frac{(3 \times 18.0) - 22.4}{2}$$
$$= 15.8°C$$

Solution (b)—Radiant strip

The same calculations for the determination of $\Sigma(AU)/\Sigma(A)$ and $\frac{1}{3}N\Sigma(V)/\Sigma(A)$ given in solution (a) apply equally in this example. It is necessary, however, to proceed from here by referring to Table A9.7 for the values of F_1 and F_2 in order to take account of the differing output nature of the radiant heating strips. As before the alternative values for F_1 and F_2 are used for applying to the fabric and ventilation losses respectively. By interpolation, $F_1 = 1.06$ and $F_2 = 0.83$ thus for the fabric, the loss is:

$$Q_u = \Sigma(AU) \times (19°C + 1°C) \times F_1$$
$$= 468 \times 20 \times 1.06$$
$$= 9.92 \text{ kW}$$

And for the ventilation, the loss is:

$$Q_v = \tfrac{1}{3}N\Sigma(V) \times (19°C + 1°C) \times F_2$$
$$= 563 \times 0.5 \times 20 \times 0.83$$
$$= 4.67 \text{ kW}$$

Hence, total heat loss is:

$$Q_p = Q_u + Q_v$$
$$= 9.92 + 4.67$$
$$= 14.6 \text{ kW}$$

The alternative temperature relationships for radiant strip are thus:

$$t_{ei} = F_1(t_c - t_{ao}) + t_{ao}$$
$$= (1.06 \times 20) - 1.0$$
$$= 20.2°C$$

$$t_{ai} = F_2(t_c - t_{ao}) + t_{ao}$$
$$= (0.83 \times 20) - 1.0$$
$$= 15.6°C$$

$$t_m = \frac{3\,t_{et}-t_{at}}{2}$$

$$= \frac{(3\times20.2)-15.6}{2}$$

$$= 22.5°C$$

Note

The two examples, based on heating the same factory, but using different forms of heating, are offered primarily to convey the techniques for carrying out manual calculations. As may be seen, however, the method also permits the direct comparison of one form of heating against another and the likely success each might have in meeting mean comfort conditions in design weather. In the two cases illustrated, neither installation would

prove to be entirely satisfactory under full-load operation even though each would meet the mean comfort (resultant) temperature of 19°C specified. The radiant strip installations would be improved by increasing the proportion of convected heat such as by introducing some, or all, of the ventilating air in forced convection form. In this event a further set of calculations would be needed and reference again made to Tables A9.1 to A9.7 to re-assess the values of F_1 and F_2 according to the radiant/convective proportions of the alternative system.

These calculations have been carried out under design conditions, however, and no account has been taken of other sources of gain i.e. solar energy, gains from processes etc. and therefore the temperature predictions only apply to the unoccupied building.

Appendix 2—Air Conditioning Example
(See Supplement A9/1)

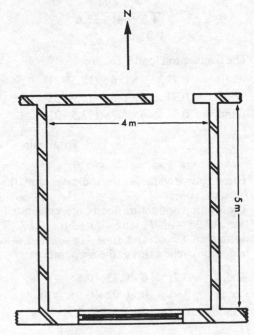

HEIGHT = 3 m

WINDOW = 4 m² ; U = 5.7 W/m² K

ROOF = 200 mm (INSULATED) ; 500 kg/m³ ; U = 0.6 W/m² K

EXT. WALL = 300 mm (BARE) ; 1000 kg/m³ ; U = 0.6 W/m² K

Fig. A9.10. Air Conditioning Example.

The room in Fig.A9.10 is situated on the top floor of an office building in London. It has one occupant and is to be air conditioned during 10 hours of plant operation. The building is of heavyweight construction, having light coloured external walls and a dark roof. The window is of 6 mm single clear glass equipped with a light, close-slatted blind facing south. The infiltration ventilation rate is expected to be one air change per hour. The surrounding rooms are assumed to be at the same temperature.

Solution (a) – Dry Resultant Temperature Control
Assess the sensible cooling load to be extracted at the air point at mid-day (sun time) in late September if the room

is being air conditioned to a dry resultant temperature of 21°C.

The solar gain through the window is found from Table A9.15, allowing a one hour lag for a heavyweight building (i.e. taking the value at 1100 hours). The correction factor for the blind must also be incorporated, hence:

$$\text{Solar gain} = 312\ \text{W/m}^2\times0.77\times4\ \text{m}^2$$

$$= 961\ \text{W}$$

The 24 hour mean conduction loads at the air point through the window, wall and roof are calculated using equation A9.25, which first requires the evaluation of F_u and F_v. From equation A5.19:

$$F_u = \frac{h_{ec}\Sigma(A)}{h_{ec}\Sigma(A)+\Sigma(AU)}$$

where:

$$h_{ec} = 18\ \text{W/m}^2\,\text{K}$$
$$\Sigma(A) = 94\ \text{m}^2$$
$$\Sigma(AU) = (20\times0.6)+(8\times0.6)+(4\times5.7)$$
$$= 39.6\ \text{W/K}$$

Hence:

$$F_u = \frac{18\times94}{(18\times94)+39.6}$$
$$= 0.98$$

From equation A5.18:

$$F_v = \frac{h_{ac}\Sigma(A)}{h_{ac}\Sigma(A)+\frac{1}{3}NV}$$

where:

$$h_{ac} = 6\ \text{W/m}^2\,\text{K}$$
$$\tfrac{1}{3}NV = \tfrac{1}{3}\times1\times60$$
$$= 20\ \text{W/K}$$

Hence:

$$F_v = \frac{6\times94}{(6\times94)+20}$$
$$= 0.96$$

Hence:

$$\frac{F_u}{F_v} = \frac{0.98}{0.96} = 1.02$$

From Table A6.21:

t_{eo} (wall) =   18.5°C
t_{eo} (roof) =   15.9°C
t_{ao} =   13.5°C

Hence, the mean conduction gains at the air point are:

Wall: $1.02 \times 8 \times 0.6 \times (18.5-21)$ =   −12W
Roof: $1.02 \times 20 \times 0.6 \times (15.9-21)$ =   −62W
Window: $1.02 \times 4 \times 5.7 \times (13.5-21)$ =   −174W
                                          _____
          Total gain =   −248W

The negative value indicates that the heat is lost from the room.

The cyclic conduction loads at the air point are calculated from equation A9.26. This requires the decrement factor and time lag of each element of the room to be known.

From Fig. A6.14 and A6.15 the time lags and decrement factors are:

ϕ (wall)   = 11 h f (wall)   = 0.23
ϕ (roof)   = 7 h f (roof)   = 0.22
ϕ (window) = 0 h f (window) = 1.00

From Table A6.21:

$\tilde{t}_{eo}$ (wall) =   8.7°C–18.5°C (at 0100) = − 9.8°C
$\tilde{t}_{eo}$ (roof) =   5.1°C–15.9°C (at 0500) = −10.8°C
$\tilde{t}_{ao}$ =   17.4°C–13.5°C (at 1200) = 3.9°C

Hence, the cyclic gains at the air point are:

Wall: $1.02 \times 8 \times 0.23 \times 0.6 \times -9.8$ = − 11W
Roof: $1.02 \times 20 \times 0.22 \times 0.6 \times -10.8$ = − 29W
Window: $1.02 \times 4 \times 1 \times 5.7 \times 3.9$ = 91W
                                         _____
            Total =   51W

The cooling load due to internal gains is found from the figures in section A7. In this example it is assumed that the only load is from a person engaged in light work from whom the sensible gain is 90W. This is taken as being entirely at the air point and therefore unmodified. When internal gains have an environmental component, this should be corrected by the factor F_u/F_v in the same way as the conduction gains.

The cooling load due to infiltration is found using equation A9.28:

Q_v = $\frac{1}{3} \times 1 \times 60 \times (17.4-21)$
     = −72W

The total sensible cooling load at the air point to hold the dry resultant temperature constant is the sum of the individual components:

$961 - 248 + 51 + 90 - 72 = 782W$

Solution (b) – Air Temperature Control

The calculation of sensible cooling load is now performed to keep the air temperature at 21°C.

The solar gain through the window now has the additional air point correction:

Solar gain   = $312 \times 0.77 \times 4 \times 0.83$
            =   798W

The 24 hour mean conduction loads at the air point, for air point control, require the evaluation of F_{au}. From equation A5.22:

$$F_{au} = \frac{h_a \Sigma(A)}{h_a \Sigma(A) + \Sigma(AU)}$$

where:

h_a =   4.5 W/m² K
$\Sigma(A)$ =   94 m²
$\Sigma(AU)$ =   39.6 W/K

Hence:

$$F_{au} = \frac{4.5 \times 94}{(4.5 \times 94) + 39.6}$$
$$= 0.91$$

The conduction loads are now:

Wall: $0.91 \times 8 \times 0.6 \times (18.5-21)$ = − 11W
Roof: $0.91 \times 20 \times 0.6 \times (15.9-21)$ = − 56W
Window: $0.91 \times 4 \times 5.7 \times (13.5-21)$ = −156W
                                          _____
          Total gain =   −223W

The negative value again indicates that the heat is lost from the room.

The cyclic conduction loads are calculated using equation A9.26 with F_{au} substituted for F_u/F_v. The values of decrement factor and time lag are the same as before, hence the cyclic gains at the air point are:

Wall: $0.91 \times 8 \times 0.23 \times 0.6 \times -9.8$ = − 10W
Roof: $0.91 \times 20 \times 0.22 \times 0.6 \times -10.8$ = − 26W
Window: $0.91 \times 4 \times 1 \times 5.7 \times 3.9$ = 81W
                                         _____
            Total gain =   45W

The cooling load due to internal gains is the same as before, i.e. 90W at the air point. Any input at the environmental point would this time be corrected by F_{au}.

The cooling load due to infiltration is found using equation A9.27:

Q_v = $\frac{1}{3} \times 1 \times 60 (17.4-21)$
     = −72W

The total sensible cooling load at the air point to hold the air temperature constant is:

$798 - 223 + 45 + 90 - 72 = 638W$

COOLING LOAD TABLES

Table A9.14 Cooling load due to solar gain through vertical glazing. (10 h plant operation)—W/m²

FOR CONSTANT DRY RESULTANT TEMPERATURE

LIGHTWEIGHT BUILDING UNPROTECTED 6mm CLEAR GLASS 51.7°N

Date	Climatic constants	Orientation	0800	0900	1000	1100	1200	1300	1400	1500	1600	1700	1800	Orientation
June 21	$I=0.66$ $k_c=1.96$ $k_r=0.20$ $C=0.14$	N	89	104	122	137	147	150	146	135	119	103	92	N
		NE	358	307	220	159	165	169	164	153	138	120	102	NE
		E	465	477	438	355	241	179	175	164	149	131	112	E
		SE	322	392	425	419	372	286	188	149	134	116	98	SE
		S	89	127	208	289	342	359	337	280	196	116	83	S
		SW	102	121	138	158	202	300	381	423	424	386	313	SW
		W	116	135	152	167	177	189	257	366	444	477	460	W
		NW	104	123	140	155	165	169	166	166	232	313	357	NW
July 23 and May 22	$I=0.89$ $k_c=1.33$ $k_r=0.20$ $C=0.18$	N	85	107	128	145	157	161	156	143	125	104	86	N
		NE	314	276	205	162	173	177	172	159	141	120	98	NE
		E	419	440	412	343	244	188	183	170	152	131	109	E
		SE	309	381	418	419	380	304	209	162	144	123	101	SE
		S	97	146	231	309	361	377	356	301	219	134	89	S
		SW	106	128	149	171	224	317	388	421	416	375	300	SW
		W	114	136	156	174	186	197	258	353	417	439	413	W
		NW	102	124	144	162	173	177	173	168	214	281	312	NW
August 24 and April 20	$I=0.93$ $k_c=1.34$ $k_r=0.20$ $C=0.23$	N	59	82	102	119	131	134	129	117	100	79	58	N
		NE	243	214	150	130	142	145	140	128	111	90	67	NE
		E	364	403	385	317	216	158	153	141	123	102	80	E
		SE	296	383	430	435	399	323	219	144	126	105	82	SE
		S	90	167	264	346	398	415	394	338	253	154	80	S
		SW	88	110	131	156	235	335	406	437	427	376	285	SW
		W	86	108	129	146	157	168	233	329	390	402	355	W
		NW	72	95	115	132	143	147	142	135	160	220	240	NW
September 22 and March 22	$I=0.97$ $k_c=1.61$ $k_r=0.20$ $C=0.27$	N	32	55	76	93	104	107	102	90	73	51	29	N
		NE	143	142	91	96	107	110	106	94	76	54	32	NE
		E	263	371	375	306	191	122	118	106	88	67	44	E
		SE	245	396	474	494	459	376	254	136	101	79	56	SE
		S	97	208	329	428	490	510	485	418	315	192	84	S
		SW	62	85	109	153	272	388	466	495	469	383	225	SW
		W	50	73	94	111	122	134	209	318	377	364	243	W
		NW	36	59	80	97	108	111	107	98	97	146	133	NW
October 23 and February 20	$I=1.18$ $k_c=1.31$ $k_r=0.20$ $C=0.31$	N	10	32	53	70	81	85	80	68	50	28	8	N
		NE	19	61	54	71	82	85	81	69	51	29	9	NE
		E	43	215	272	237	149	94	89	77	59	37	17	E
		SE	57	254	379	424	409	345	242	128	71	50	30	SE
		S	51	162	289	390	452	472	447	380	275	145	42	S
		SW	32	54	81	143	255	353	412	420	367	233	43	SW
		W	19	40	62	79	90	101	161	243	268	198	31	W
		NW	10	32	54	71	82	86	81	69	55	58	14	NW
November 21 and January 21	$I=1.29$ $k_c=1.34$ $k_r=0.20$ $C=0.35$	N	4	9	28	44	55	58	54	42	25	7	4	N
		NE	5	11	28	44	55	58	54	42	25	7	4	NE
		E	10	47	160	168	106	63	58	47	30	11	9	E
		SE	23	68	246	338	349	301	212	108	43	24	21	SE
		S	31	60	201	322	396	419	390	310	184	49	29	S
		SW	21	26	51	121	224	308	349	329	228	54	21	SW
		W	9	13	32	49	59	69	115	169	149	36	9	W
		NW	4	9	28	44	55	58	54	42	25	9	4	NW
December 22	$I=1.18$ $k_c=1.70$ $k_r=0.20$ $C=0.40$	N	3	4	16	31	40	43	39	29	14	3	3	N
		NE	3	4	16	31	46	43	39	29	14	3	3	NE
		E	6	13	111	138	87	47	43	32	18	6	6	E
		SE	18	27	180	297	324	283	196	94	71	18	18	SE
		S	25	33	152	287	372	398	365	273	136	25	25	S
		SW	18	20	39	107	207	289	322	286	162	18	18	SW
		W	6	7	20	34	44	52	95	137	100	6	9	W
		NW	3	4	16	31	40	43	39	29	14	3	3	NW

Correction factors for tabulated values

Type of glass	Single glazing		Double glazing with clear 6 mm glass inside		Single glazing and external light slatted blinds used intermittently	
	Lightweight	Heavyweight	Lightweight	Heavyweight	Lightweight	Heavyweight
Clear 6 mm	1.00	0.85	0.85	0.70	0.19	0.19
Body Tinted Glass (BTG) 6 mm	0.70	0.60	0.53	0.45	0.16	0.16
BTG 10 mm	0.58	0.49	0.40	0.34	0.14	0.14
Reflecting	0.49	0.42	0.37	0.31	0.13	0.13
Strongly reflecting	0.25	0.21	0.16	0.14	0.09	0.10
Additional factor for air point control	0.76	0.73	0.76	0.73	0.76	0.73

Table A9.15 Cooling load due to solar gain through vertical glazing. (10 h plant operation)—W/m²

FOR CONSTANT DRY RESULTANT TEMPERATURE

LIGHTWEIGHT BUILDING
INTERMITTENT BLINDS **51.7°N**

Date	Climatic constants	Orientation	0800	0900	1000	1100	1200	1300	1400	1500	1600	1700	1800	Orientation
June 21	$I = 0.66$ $k_c = 1.96$ $k_r = 0.20$ $C = 0.14$	N	81	96	114	128	138	142	137	126	111	95	122	N
		NE	223	169	81	144	151	154	150	139	124	106	87	NE
		E	328	306	254	184	88	156	151	140	125	107	89	E
		SE	252	280	282	257	207	143	69	125	110	93	74	SE
		S	102	124	179	220	238	230	197	145	89	39	61	S
		SW	69	87	105	184	183	239	273	281	261	217	152	SW
		W	78	97	114	129	139	230	227	284	314	313	274	W
		NW	79	98	115	130	140	143	141	217	204	240	243	NW
July 23 and May 22	$I = 0.89$ $k_c = 1.33$ $k_r = 0.20$ $C = 0.18$	N	85	107	128	145	157	161	156	143	125	104	86	N
		NE	205	161	80	155	167	170	165	152	135	114	92	NE
		E	306	292	250	189	90	172	167	154	136	115	93	E
		SE	247	277	283	264	219	159	73	140	122	101	79	SE
		S	75	209	194	234	252	244	212	161	59	112	68	S
		SW	74	96	117	211	196	247	275	278	256	210	144	SW
		W	80	102	123	140	152	248	222	270	293	285	239	W
		NW	81	103	123	141	152	156	152	219	186	213	207	NW
August 24 and April 22	$I = 0.93$ $k_c = 1.34$ $k_r = 0.20$ $C = 0.23$	N	59	82	102	119	131	134	129	117	100	79	58	N
		NE	159	118	57	126	137	141	136	124	106	85	63	NE
		E	277	270	229	166	71	143	138	126	108	87	65	E
		SE	246	283	292	274	228	163	64	121	103	82	59	SE
		S	118	153	212	254	272	264	231	177	111	36	52	S
		SW	56	78	99	205	204	257	285	286	259	203	120	SW
		W	59	81	102	119	130	222	207	254	273	253	177	W
		NW	59	81	102	119	130	134	129	177	148	169	141	NW
September 22 and March 21	$I = 0.97$ $k_c = 1.61$ $k_r = 0.20$ $C = 0.27$	N	32	55	76	93	104	107	102	90	73	51	29	N
		NE	205	39	89	94	105	109	104	92	74	53	30	NE
		E	427	260	220	147	52	109	104	92	75	53	31	E
		SE	402	310	330	313	262	184	59	110	74	53	30	SE
		S	137	189	262	312	333	324	285	219	137	36	48	S
		SW	31	53	78	224	237	298	328	322	274	175	37	SW
		W	31	54	75	92	103	192	201	252	258	192	43	W
		NW	32	54	75	92	103	107	102	93	156	106	28	NW
October 23 and February 21	$I = 1.18$ $k_c = 1.31$ $k_r = 0.20$ $C = 0.31$	N	10	32	53	70	81	85	80	68	50	28	8	N
		NE	19	61	54	71	82	85	81	69	51	29	9	NE
		E	136	183	170	115	37	84	80	67	49	28	7	E
		SE	148	242	283	280	241	175	50	106	50	28	8	SE
		S	78	164	241	291	313	303	264	197	108	23	10	S
		SW	10	32	58	225	221	271	289	265	183	41	21	SW
		W	9	31	52	70	81	155	159	188	158	35	21	W
		NW	10	32	54	71	82	86	81	69	55	58	14	NW
November 21 and January 21	$I = 1.29$ $k_c = 1.34$ $k_r = 0.20$ $C = 0.35$	N	4	9	28	44	55	58	54	42	25	7	4	N
		NE	5	11	28	44	55	58	54	42	25	7	4	NE
		E	7	121	120	38	103	59	55	43	26	8	5	E
		SE	7	165	226	242	216	158	42	92	27	8	5	SE
		S	6	122	198	259	284	273	226	143	30	25	5	S
		SW	5	10	36	203	198	237	236	176	43	39	5	SW
		W	5	9	29	45	56	65	192	117	28	33	5	W
		NW	4	9	28	44	55	58	54	42	25	9	4	NW
December 21	$I = 1.18$ $k_c = 1.70$ $k_r = 0.20$ $C = 0.40$	N	3	4	16	31	40	43	39	29	14	3	3	N
		NE	3	4	16	31	40	43	39	29	14	3	3	NE
		E	5	12	177	32	85	45	41	31	16	5	5	E
		SE	6	15	314	225	206	150	39	82	19	6	6	SE
		S	5	13	267	245	273	261	206	109	26	5	5	S
		SW	4	5	25	186	187	222	211	129	34	4	4	SW
		W	3	4	17	31	41	50	160	81	20	3	3	W
		NW	3	4	16	31	40	43	39	29	14	3	3	NW

Correction factors for tabulated values

Type of glass (outside pane for double glazing)	Building weight	Single glazing			Double glazing, internal shade			Double glazing, mid-pane shade		
		Light slatted blind		Linen roller blind	Light slatted blind		Linen roller blind	Light slatted blind		Linen roller blind
		Open	Closed		Open	Closed		Open	Closed	
Clear 6mm	Light	1.00	0.77	0.66	0.95	0.74	0.65	0.58	0.39	0.42
	Heavy	0.97	0.77	0.63	0.94	0.76	0.64	0.56	0.40	0.40
BTG 6mm	Light	0.86	0.77	0.72	0.66	0.55	0.51	0.45	0.36	0.38
	Heavy	0.85	0.77	0.71	0.66	0.57	0.51	0.44	0.37	0.37
BTG 10mm	Light	0.78	0.73	0.70	0.54	0.47	0.45	0.38	0.34	0.36
	Heavy	0.77	0.73	0.70	0.53	0.48	0.45	0.37	0.34	0.34
Reflecting	Light	0.64	0.57	0.54	0.48	0.41	0.38	0.33	0.27	0.29
	Heavy	0.62	0.57	0.53	0.47	0.41	0.38	0.32	0.27	0.28
Strongly reflecting	Light	0.36	0.34	0.32	0.23	0.21	0.21	0.17	0.16	0.16
	Heavy	0.35	0.34	0.32	0.23	0.21	0.21	0.17	0.16	0.16
Additional factor for air point control	Light	0.91	0.91	0.91	0.91	0.91	0.91	0.80	0.80	0.80
	Heavy	0.83	0.83	0.83	0.90	0.90	0.90	0.78	0.78	0.78

Table A9.16 Cooling load due to solar gain through vertical glazing. (10 h plant operation)—W/m²

FOR CONSTANT DRY RESULTANT TEMPERATURE

LIGHTWEIGHT BUILDING — UNPROTECTED 6mm CLEAR GLASS — 0°N

Date	Climatic constants	Orientation	0800	0900	1000	1100	1200	1300	1400	1500	1600	1700	1800	Orientation
June 21	I = 1.00, k_c = 1.00, k_r = 0.20, C = 0.00	N	184	253	293	318	333	337	331	315	287	244	167	N
		NE	381	498	508	457	364	246	148	120	106	88	65	NE
		E	365	464	443	345	204	126	122	113	99	81	59	E
		SE	135	156	126	98	104	106	103	94	79	61	39	SE
		S	38	59	77	90	99	101	98	89	75	56	34	S
		SW	42	64	81	95	103	106	104	102	132	155	122	SW
		W	61	83	100	114	122	135	221	357	445	455	336	W
		NW	68	89	107	125	161	260	374	462	506	486	350	NW
July 23 and May 22	I = 1.00, k_c = 1.00, k_r = 0.20, C = 0.00	N	160	220	256	280	293	297	292	277	251	212	144	N
		NE	376	489	495	440	341	222	137	120	106	87	65	NE
		E	379	480	457	357	210	129	125	116	101	83	60	E
		SE	160	188	155	110	108	110	107	97	83	64	42	SE
		S	39	61	78	92	101	104	100	91	76	58	35	S
		SW	45	67	84	98	107	110	109	116	160	185	144	SW
		W	63	85	103	116	125	139	229	369	459	470	349	W
		NW	67	89	107	124	148	237	353	445	494	477	346	NW
August 24 and April 22	I = 1.00, k_c = 1.00, k_r = 0.20, C = 0.00	N	95	134	160	179	189	193	188	176	156	128	84	N
		NE	355	454	449	384	276	167	130	120	104	85	62	NE
		E	406	509	484	380	224	135	131	121	106	87	63	E
		SE	223	270	238	166	117	119	115	106	90	71	48	SE
		S	40	63	82	96	105	108	104	96	79	60	37	S
		SW	51	73	92	107	116	119	124	177	243	265	202	SW
		W	66	89	107	122	131	145	243	392	487	499	374	W
		NW	65	87	106	121	136	181	289	391	449	444	326	NW
September 22 and March 21	I = 1.00, k_c = 1.00, k_r = 0.20, C = 0.00	N	41	64	83	98	108	111	107	97	81	61	37	N
		NE	301	376	356	280	177	130	125	115	99	80	56	NE
		E	420	526	499	392	231	139	134	124	109	89	65	E
		SE	301	376	356	280	177	130	125	115	99	80	56	SE
		S	41	64	83	98	108	111	107	97	81	61	37	S
		SW	59	82	101	116	125	137	191	289	358	368	275	SW
		W	68	91	110	125	134	150	251	404	502	515	388	W
		NW	59	82	101	116	125	137	191	289	358	368	275	NW
October 23 and February 21	I = 1.00, k_c = 1.00, k_r = 0.20, C = 0.00	N	40	63	82	97	106	109	105	95	80	60	37	N
		NE	232	282	251	177	120	121	117	107	91	72	49	NE
		E	409	512	487	382	225	136	132	122	107	87	64	E
		SE	351	447	441	374	266	160	129	120	104	85	61	SE
		S	86	122	147	165	175	179	174	163	143	116	75	S
		SW	64	87	106	120	135	173	279	382	441	437	322	SW
		W	66	89	108	123	132	146	244	394	490	502	377	W
		NW	52	74	93	108	117	121	128	188	256	277	210	NW
November 21 and January 21	I = 1.00, k_c = 1.00, k_r = 0.20, C = 0.00	N	39	61	79	93	101	104	100	91	76	58	35	N
		NE	162	190	157	111	108	110	107	97	83	64	42	NE
		E	380	481	458	358	211	129	125	116	101	83	60	E
		SE	376	488	494	438	340	220	137	120	106	87	65	SE
		S	158	218	253	277	290	294	289	274	248	210	142	S
		SW	67	89	107	123	147	235	351	444	493	477	346	SW
		W	63	85	103	117	125	139	229	370	460	471	350	W
		NW	45	67	85	99	107	110	110	118	163	188	146	NW
December 21	I = 1.00, k_c = 1.00, k_r = 0.20, C = 0.00	N	38	59	77	90	99	101	98	89	75	56	34	N
		NE	135	196	126	98	104	106	103	94	79	61	39	NE
		E	365	464	443	345	204	126	122	113	99	81	59	E
		SE	381	498	508	457	364	246	148	120	106	88	65	SE
		S	184	253	293	318	333	337	331	315	287	244	167	S
		SW	68	89	107	125	161	260	374	462	506	486	350	SW
		W	61	83	100	114	122	135	221	357	445	455	336	W
		NW	42	64	81	95	103	106	104	102	132	155	122	NW

Correction factors for tabulated values

Type of glass	Single glazing		Double glazing with clear 6 mm glass inside		Single glazing and external light slatted blinds used intermittently	
	Lightweight	Heavyweight	Lightweight	Heavyweight	Lightweight	Heavyweight
Clear 6 mm	1.00	0.85	0.85	0.70	0.19	0.19
BTG 6 mm	0.70	0.60	0.53	0.45	0.16	0.16
BTG 10 mm	0.58	0.49	0.40	0.34	0.14	0.14
Reflecting	0.49	0.42	0.37	0.31	0.13	0.13
Strongly reflecting	0.25	0.21	0.16	0.14	0.09	0.10
Additional factor for air point control	0.76	0.73	0.76	0.73	0.76	0.73

Table A9.17 Cooling load due to solar gain through vertical glazing. (10 h plant operation)—W/m²

FOR CONSTANT DRY RESULTANT TEMPERATURE

LIGHTWEIGHT BUILDING

INTERMITTENT BLINDS   **0°N**

Date	Climatic constants	Orientation	Sun Time											Orientation
			0800	0900	1000	1100	1200	1300	1400	1500	1600	1700	1800	
June 21	I = 1.00 k_c = 1.00 k_r = 0.20 C = 0.00	N	251	175	196	209	215	215	206	190	164	119	28	N
		NE	584	337	307	250	176	111	55	92	77	59	37	NE
		E	562	301	243	155	61	105	102	92	78	60	38	E
		SE	195	93	45	93	99	102	98	89	75	57	35	SE
		S	37	59	76	90	99	101	98	88	74	56	34	S
		SW	36	58	75	89	98	100	98	143	114	100	26	SW
		W	37	59	76	90	98	185	222	290	313	258	55	W
		NW	37	58	76	135	154	229	293	332	334	265	55	NW
July 23 and May 22	I = 1.00 k_c = 1.00 k_r = 0.20 C = 0.00	N	216	153	173	186	192	192	184	169	145	104	25	N
		NE	577	329	297	237	163	67	111	94	80	61	39	NE
		E	582	311	251	160	63	107	104	94	80	61	39	E
		SE	233	112	51	104	102	105	101	92	77	59	36	SE
		S	38	60	78	92	101	103	100	90	76	57	35	S
		SW	38	59	77	91	100	103	102	169	134	117	29	SW
		W	38	60	78	92	101	190	229	299	323	268	57	W
		NW	38	60	78	94	197	217	283	324	329	263	55	NW
August 24 and April 22	I = 1.00 k_c = 1.00 k_r = 0.20 C = 0.00	N	126	98	115	127	133	132	126	113	94	66	18	N
		NE	541	300	262	197	127	61	107	97	82	62	39	NE
		E	621	329	266	170	66	112	108	99	83	64	41	E
		SE	331	166	126	57	108	109	105	96	80	61	38	SE
		S	40	63	81	96	105	108	104	94	79	60	36	S
		SW	39	61	80	95	104	107	173	164	186	159	37	SW
		W	40	63	81	96	105	201	243	316	342	286	60	W
		NW	39	62	80	95	162	179	248	295	305	249	52	NW
September 22 and March 21	I = 1.00 k_c = 1.00 k_r = 0.20 C = 0.00	N	41	64	83	98	107	111	106	96	80	61	37	N
		NE	454	241	197	136	62	113	109	99	83	63	39	NE
		E	643	339	275	175	68	116	111	101	85	66	42	E
		SE	454	241	197	136	62	113	109	99	83	63	39	SE
		S	41	64	83	98	107	111	106	96	80	61	37	S
		SW	40	63	82	97	106	179	186	236	254	212	46	SW
		W	41	64	83	98	107	207	251	326	353	296	63	W
		NW	40	63	82	97	106	179	186	236	254	212	46	NW
October 23 and February 21	I = 1.00 k_c = 1.00 k_r = 0.20 C = 0.00	N	40	63	82	96	105	108	104	94	79	60	36	N
		NE	345	174	133	59	110	110	106	96	81	62	38	NE
		E	626	331	268	171	67	113	109	99	84	64	41	E
		SE	534	295	256	191	123	61	107	97	82	63	39	SE
		S	115	92	108	120	126	126	120	107	89	35	63	S
		SW	39	62	80	95	159	173	242	289	300	246	52	SW
		W	40	63	82	96	105	202	245	318	344	288	61	W
		NW	39	62	81	95	104	109	181	172	193	165	38	NW
November 21 and January 21	I = 1.00 k_c = 1.00 k_r = 0.20 C = 0.00	N	38	60	78	92	101	103	100	90	76	57	35	N
		NE	236	114	51	105	102	105	101	92	77	59	36	NE
		E	583	311	251	160	63	108	104	95	80	61	39	E
		SE	576	329	296	236	162	66	111	94	80	61	39	SE
		S	214	152	171	184	190	190	182	167	143	103	25	S
		SW	38	60	78	94	196	216	282	324	328	263	55	SW
		W	38	60	78	92	101	191	230	299	324	268	57	W
		NW	38	60	77	91	100	103	102	171	135	118	29	NW
December 21	I = 1.00 k_c = 1.00 k_r = 0.20 C = 0.00	N	37	59	76	90	99	101	98	88	74	56	34	N
		NE	195	93	45	93	99	102	98	89	75	57	35	NE
		E	562	301	243	155	61	105	102	92	78	60	38	E
		SE	584	337	307	250	176	110	55	92	77	59	37	SE
		S	251	175	195	209	215	215	206	190	164	119	28	S
		SW	37	58	76	135	154	229	293	332	334	265	55	SW
		W	37	59	76	90	98	185	222	290	313	258	55	W
		NW	36	58	75	89	98	100	98	143	114	100	26	NW

Correction factors for tabulated values											
Type of glass (outside pane for double glazing)	Building weight	Single glazing			Double glazing, internal shade			Double glazing, mid-pane shade			
		Light slatted blind		Linen roller blind	Light slatted blind		Linen roller blind	Light slatted blind		Linen roller blind
		Open	Closed		Open	Closed		Open	Closed	
Clear 6mm	Light	1.00	0.77	0.66	0.95	0.74	0.65	0.58	0.39	0.42
	Heavy	0.97	0.77	0.63	0.94	0.76	0.64	0.56	0.40	0.40
BTG 6mm	Light	0.86	0.77	0.72	0.66	0.55	0.51	0.45	0.36	0.38
	Heavy	0.85	0.77	0.71	0.66	0.57	0.51	0.44	0.37	0.37
BTG 10mm	Light	0.78	0.73	0.70	0.54	0.47	0.45	0.38	0.34	0.36
	Heavy	0.77	0.73	0.70	0.53	0.48	0.45	0.37	0.34	0.34
Reflecting	Light	0.64	0.57	0.54	0.48	0.41	0.38	0.33	0.27	0.29
	Heavy	0.62	0.57	0.53	0.47	0.41	0.38	0.32	0.27	0.28
Strongly reflecting	Light	0.36	0.34	0.32	0.23	0.21	0.21	0.17	0.16	0.16
	Heavy	0.35	0.34	0.32	0.23	0.21	0.21	0.17	0.16	0.16
Additional factor for air point control	Light	0.91	0.91	0.91	0.91	0.91	0.91	0.80	0.80	0.80
	Heavy	0.83	0.83	0.83	0.90	0.90	0.90	0.78	0.78	0.78

Table A9.18 Cooling load due to solar gain through vertical glazing. (10 h plant operation)—W/m²

FOR CONSTANT DRY RESULTANT TEMPERATURE

LIGHTWEIGHT BUILDING
UNPROTECTED 6mm CLEAR GLASS **10°N**

Date	Climatic constants	Orientation	Sun Time											Orientation
			0800	0900	1000	1100	1200	1300	1400	1500	1600	1700	1800	
June 21	$I = 1.00$ $k_c = 1.00$ $k_r = 0.20$ $C = 0.00$	N	180	208	217	220	221	221	221	220	215	204	168	N
		NE	427	495	475	401	292	183	138	129	115	97	76	NE
		E	430	499	466	364	219	140	136	127	113	95	74	E
		SE	180	210	188	138	115	118	114	105	91	73	52	SE
		S	46	67	84	98	106	109	105	96	82	64	43	S
		SW	55	75	93	106	115	117	120	147	192	207	166	SW
		W	76	97	114	128	136	149	237	376	469	491	405	W
		NW	78	99	116	129	145	197	305	409	476	487	402	NW
July 23 and May 22	$I = 1.00$ $k_c = 1.00$ $k_r = 0.20$ $C = 0.00$	N	148	171	178	181	182	182	182	181	177	168	137	N
		NE	412	479	456	378	266	165	137	127	113	95	73	NE
		E	435	509	477	373	223	141	137	128	113	95	74	E
		SE	204	243	222	164	120	121	117	108	93	75	54	SE
		S	46	67	85	99	107	110	106	97	82	64	43	S
		SW	56	78	95	109	118	122	127	174	226	239	189	SW
		W	76	97	115	129	137	151	242	385	480	502	410	W
		NW	75	96	114	128	142	177	279	386	457	471	387	NW
August 24 and April 22	$I = 1.00$ $k_c = 1.00$ $k_r = 0.20$ $C = 0.00$	N	76	91	100	108	115	118	114	108	99	89	69	N
		NE	366	428	397	310	197	136	131	122	106	88	65	NE
		E	439	526	495	388	231	142	138	128	113	94	71	E
		SE	261	322	309	245	159	128	124	114	99	80	57	SE
		S	44	66	85	99	108	112	107	98	82	63	41	S
		SW	60	82	100	115	124	134	171	254	311	316	240	SW
		W	74	96	114	129	138	153	250	401	498	517	410	W
		NW	67	89	108	122	132	144	212	320	400	421	341	NW
September 22 and March 21	$I = 1.00$ $k_c = 1.00$ $k_r = 0.20$ $C = 0.00$	N	41	63	82	97	106	109	105	95	80	60	37	N
		NE	281	333	290	200	126	124	120	110	94	75	52	NE
		E	416	522	496	389	229	137	133	123	107	88	64	E
		SE	316	413	416	359	257	155	127	118	102	83	59	SE
		S	49	81	113	142	161	167	158	138	107	74	42	S
		SW	62	85	104	118	133	167	270	366	416	403	288	SW
		W	67	90	109	124	133	147	248	402	498	511	384	W
		NW	54	77	96	111	120	125	135	212	296	328	257	NW
October 23 and February 21	$I = 1.00$ $k_c = 1.00$ $k_r = 0.20$ $C = 0.00$	N	36	59	77	92	100	103	100	90	75	56	33	N
		NE	195	232	185	119	109	112	108	98	83	64	41	NE
		E	369	492	473	371	217	129	125	115	100	81	58	E
		SE	333	465	486	440	346	223	134	118	103	84	61	SE
		S	104	170	223	264	289	297	287	259	216	159	91	S
		SW	63	86	104	121	145	239	357	445	483	452	304	SW
		W	61	83	102	116	125	139	236	383	475	480	339	W
		NW	44	67	85	100	109	111	112	128	192	229	176	NW
November 21 and January 21	$I = 1.00$ $k_c = 1.00$ $k_r = 0.20$ $C = 0.00$	N	31	53	71	84	93	96	92	83	68	50	28	N
		NE	120	143	105	89	97	100	96	87	73	55	33	NE
		E	309	445	434	340	198	118	115	105	91	73	51	E
		SE	320	485	521	488	406	290	170	114	100	82	60	SE
		S	156	255	321	368	396	405	393	362	313	242	139	S
		SW	62	84	102	123	186	304	415	491	517	469	291	SW
		W	53	75	92	106	115	128	216	351	436	432	281	W
		NW	35	57	75	88	97	100	96	92	112	142	108	NW
December 21	$I = 1.00$ $k_c = 1.00$ $k_r = 0.20$ $C = 0.00$	N	29	51	68	81	90	92	89	80	66	48	26	N
		NE	95	112	84	84	93	95	92	83	69	51	29	NE
		E	283	423	416	325	189	113	110	101	87	69	47	E
		SE	308	485	528	500	423	311	190	115	98	81	59	SE
		S	169	281	352	400	429	438	427	395	343	267	151	S
		SW	61	83	101	125	206	324	431	502	523	468	279	SW
		W	49	71	88	101	110	122	206	336	417	410	256	W
		NW	32	54	71	84	92	95	91	86	89	112	84	NW

Correction factors for tabulated values

Type of glass	Single glazing		Double glazing with clear 6 mm glass inside		Single glazing and external light slatted blinds used intermittently	
	Lightweight	Heavyweight	Lightweight	Heavyweight	Lightweight	Heavyweight
Clear 6 mm	1.00	0.85	0.85	0.70	0.19	0.19
BTG 6 mm	0.70	0.60	0.53	0.45	0.16	0.16
BTG 10 mm	0.58	0.49	0.40	0.34	0.14	0.14
Reflecting	0.49	0.42	0.37	0.31	0.13	0.13
Strongly reflecting	0.25	0.21	0.16	0.14	0.09	0.10
Additional factor for air point control	0.76	0.73	0.76	0.73	0.76	0.73

Table A9.19 Cooling load due to solar gain through vertical glazing. (10 h plant operation)—W/m²

FOR CONSTANT DRY RESULTANT TEMPERATURE

LIGHTWEIGHT BUILDING — INTERMITTENT BLINDS — 10°N

Date	Climatic constants	Orientation	0800	0900	1000	1100	1200	1300	1400	1500	1600	1700	1800	Orientation
June 21	$I=1.00$ $k_c=1.00$ $k_r=0.20$ $C=0.00$	N	126	136	142	146	149	150	150	148	140	121	37	N
		NE	329	322	278	211	141	70	115	106	92	74	53	NE
		E	334	321	259	169	73	119	116	107	92	75	54	E
		SE	140	134	107	56	108	111	107	98	84	66	45	SE
		S	46	66	84	97	105	108	105	96	81	64	42	S
		SW	46	66	83	97	105	108	157	136	149	130	37	SW
		W	47	68	85	99	107	196	233	303	332	297	127	W
		NW	47	67	84	98	170	186	256	308	328	293	126	NW
July 23 and May 22	$I=1.00$ $k_c=1.00$ $k_r=0.20$ $C=0.00$	N	104	113	119	124	127	128	128	125	119	102	31	N
		NE	318	310	263	194	128	68	115	106	91	73	51	NE
		E	341	328	265	173	73	120	116	107	93	74	53	E
		SE	161	155	125	60	112	113	109	100	85	67	45	SE
		S	45	67	84	98	107	109	106	96	82	64	42	S
		SW	46	67	84	98	107	111	175	156	169	146	40	SW
		W	47	68	86	99	108	200	238	310	340	302	120	W
		NW	46	67	85	98	160	171	242	296	318	284	114	NW
August 24 and April 22	$I=1.00$ $k_c=1.00$ $k_r=0.20$ $C=0.00$	N	75	90	99	107	114	117	114	107	98	38	68	N
		NE	285	272	220	152	69	119	114	104	89	70	47	NE
		E	350	340	275	178	73	121	116	107	91	72	50	E
		SE	210	210	176	125	63	115	111	101	86	67	44	SE
		S	44	66	84	99	108	111	107	97	82	63	40	S
		SW	44	66	84	99	107	170	167	208	220	184	45	SW
		W	46	69	87	101	110	208	250	324	353	308	71	W
		NW	45	67	86	100	110	190	204	262	288	256	61	NW
September 22 and March 21	$I=1.00$ $k_c=1.00$ $k_r=0.20$ $C=0.00$	N	40	63	82	97	106	109	105	95	79	60	36	N
		NE	418	202	149	62	114	111	107	97	82	63	39	NE
		E	638	337	273	174	67	113	109	99	84	65	41	E
		SE	482	276	245	185	119	60	107	97	81	62	39	SE
		S	40	109	95	112	121	119	108	88	41	65	34	S
		SW	39	62	80	95	156	169	234	274	278	221	47	SW
		W	40	63	82	97	106	204	249	324	351	293	62	W
		NW	39	62	81	96	105	110	196	195	226	199	44	NW
October 23 and February 21	$I=1.00$ $k_c=1.00$ $k_r=0.20$ $C=0.00$	N	36	58	77	91	100	103	99	89	74	55	32	N
		NE	289	134	55	112	102	105	101	91	76	57	34	NE
		E	579	322	261	165	63	107	103	93	78	59	36	E
		SE	523	321	297	240	165	66	108	93	78	58	35	SE
		S	141	130	162	184	194	191	176	150	114	68	17	S
		SW	35	58	76	93	197	220	284	320	314	235	49	SW
		W	36	58	77	91	100	194	238	310	332	263	55	W
		NW	35	58	76	91	100	102	103	193	162	141	33	NW
November 21 and January 21	$I=1.00$ $k_c=1.00$ $k_r=0.20$ $C=0.00$	N	31	53	70	84	93	95	92	82	68	50	28	N
		NE	176	79	39	85	93	96	92	83	69	51	29	NE
		E	500	296	240	151	57	99	95	86	71	53	31	E
		SE	517	343	326	276	204	127	53	85	71	53	31	SE
		S	220	188	224	247	258	254	238	208	265	99	23	S
		SW	31	52	70	145	179	256	314	343	328	227	46	SW
		W	31	53	70	84	93	179	219	285	302	223	47	W
		NW	30	52	70	83	92	94	91	125	104	90	23	NW
December 21	$I=1.00$ $k_c=1.00$ $k_r=0.20$ $C=0.00$	N	29	51	68	81	89	92	88	79	65	48	26	N
		NE	138	36	82	82	90	93	89	80	66	49	27	NE
		E	464	283	230	145	55	95	91	82	68	51	29	E
		SE	505	347	333	286	216	139	55	85	68	51	29	SE
		S	242	207	244	267	278	275	258	227	181	107	25	S
		SW	29	50	69	157	192	267	322	348	329	219	45	SW
		W	29	50	68	81	89	172	210	274	288	206	43	W
		NW	29	50	67	81	89	92	88	82	131	73	20	NW

Correction factors for tabulated values

Type of glass (outside pane for double glazing)	Building weight	Single glazing — Light slatted blind Open	Single glazing — Light slatted blind Closed	Single glazing — Linen roller blind	Double glazing, internal shade — Light slatted blind Open	Double glazing, internal shade — Light slatted blind Closed	Double glazing, internal shade — Linen roller blind	Double glazing, mid-pane shade — Light slatted blind Open	Double glazing, mid-pane shade — Light slatted blind Closed	Double glazing, mid-pane shade — Linen roller blind
Clear 6mm	Light	1.00	0.77	0.66	0.95	0.74	0.65	0.58	0.39	0.42
	Heavy	0.97	0.77	0.63	0.94	0.76	0.64	0.56	0.40	0.40
BTG 6mm	Light	0.86	0.77	0.72	0.66	0.55	0.51	0.45	0.36	0.38
	Heavy	0.85	0.77	0.71	0.66	0.57	0.51	0.44	0.37	0.37
BTG 10mm	Light	0.78	0.73	0.70	0.54	0.47	0.45	0.38	0.34	0.36
	Heavy	0.77	0.73	0.70	0.53	0.48	0.45	0.37	0.34	0.34
Reflecting	Light	0.64	0.57	0.54	0.48	0.41	0.38	0.33	0.27	0.29
	Heavy	0.62	0.57	0.53	0.47	0.41	0.38	0.32	0.27	0.28
Strongly reflecting	Light	0.36	0.34	0.32	0.23	0.21	0.21	0.17	0.16	0.16
	Heavy	0.35	0.34	0.32	0.23	0.21	0.21	0.17	0.16	0.16
Additional factor for air point control	Light	0.91	0.91	0.91	0.91	0.91	0.91	0.80	0.80	0.80
	Heavy	0.83	0.83	0.83	0.90	0.90	0.90	0.78	0.78	0.78

Table A9.20 Cooling load due to solar gain through vertical glazing. (10 h plant operation)—W/m²
FOR CONSTANT DRY RESULTANT TEMPERATURE

LIGHTWEIGHT BUILDING UNPROTECTED 6mm CLEAR GLASS 20°N

Date	Climatic constants	Orientation	Sun Time											Orientation
			0800	0900	1000	1100	1200	1300	1400	1500	1600	1700	1800	
June 21	I = 1.00 k_c = 1.00 k_r = 0.20 C = 0.00	N	158	153	141	135	134	135	135	137	143	153	153	N
		NE	447	474	425	330	216	149	143	134	121	103	84	NE
		E	475	523	483	377	229	150	146	137	124	106	87	E
		SE	226	269	261	211	146	128	124	115	101	84	65	SE
		S	53	73	89	102	110	113	109	101	87	70	50	S
		SW	67	86	103	116	124	132	155	219	263	264	212	SW
		W	89	108	124	137	145	159	247	389	486	517	456	W
		NW	86	105	121	134	144	157	230	341	430	470	430	NW
July 23 and May 22	I = 1.00 k_c = 1.00 k_r = 0.20 C = 0.00	N	126	120	113	115	120	123	120	116	115	121	121	N
		NE	427	454	402	304	192	144	140	131	117	100	79	NE
		E	476	530	490	383	232	150	145	136	122	105	85	E
		SE	249	301	296	244	167	130	126	117	103	86	66	SE
		S	59	72	89	102	110	113	109	100	86	69	49	S
		SW	68	88	105	118	126	136	178	252	297	295	234	SW
		W	87	106	123	137	145	159	250	395	494	524	455	W
		NW	81	101	118	131	139	151	206	315	407	450	408	NW
August 24 and April 22	I = 1.00 k_c = 1.00 k_r = 0.20 C = 0.00	N	61	71	88	101	110	113	109	100	86	71	59	N
		NE	364	393	335	232	142	134	130	121	106	88	67	NE
		E	462	535	500	391	234	145	141	132	117	99	77	E
		SE	297	372	378	329	236	148	129	120	106	87	66	SE
		S	49	71	93	119	141	148	137	114	87	67	45	S
		SW	69	89	107	121	133	159	249	335	377	364	276	SW
		W	80	100	118	132	140	155	253	404	503	527	436	W
		NW	69	90	107	121	130	136	153	245	342	389	344	NW
September 22 and March 21	I = 1.00 k_c = 1.00 k_r = 0.20 C = 0.00	N	39	61	79	93	101	104	100	91	76	58	35	N
		NE	256	286	224	135	113	116	112	103	88	70	47	NE
		E	403	510	486	380	223	131	127	118	103	85	62	E
		SE	323	442	467	429	339	217	130	118	103	84	62	SE
		S	65	119	181	236	271	282	268	229	172	109	55	S
		SW	65	86	104	120	141	233	350	433	464	429	294	SW
		W	65	87	105	119	127	141	242	393	488	500	372	W
		NW	50	72	90	104	112	115	117	146	232	284	234	NW
October 23 and February 21	I = 1.00 k_c = 1.00 k_r = 0.20 C = 0.00	N	31	53	70	84	92	95	91	82	68	50	28	N
		NE	156	185	128	90	99	101	98	88	74	56	34	NE
		E	316	461	452	354	205	118	115	105	91	73	51	E
		SE	298	468	515	490	412	293	167	113	99	81	59	SE
		S	113	209	291	354	394	407	391	348	281	195	99	S
		SW	61	83	100	121	183	308	421	492	510	451	270	SW
		W	53	75	93	106	115	128	223	366	453	448	287	W
		NW	37	58	76	90	98	101	97	96	137	183	141	NW
November 21 and January 21	I = 1.00 k_c = 1.00 k_r = 0.20 C = 0.00	N	21	44	61	74	82	84	81	72	59	41	19	N
		NE	77	102	72	76	84	87	84	75	61	44	21	NE
		E	214	394	401	316	180	103	100	91	78	60	38	E
		SE	232	455	525	516	450	343	214	116	91	73	51	SE
		S	131	266	363	431	472	485	468	424	352	249	114	S
		SW	53	76	96	128	231	356	457	516	518	434	206	SW
		W	40	62	79	92	100	113	197	327	401	378	189	W
		NW	24	46	63	76	84	87	83	77	76	101	67	NW
December 21	I = 1.00 k_c = 1.00 k_r = 0.20 C = 0.00	N	18	40	57	70	77	80	77	68	55	37	16	N
		NE	53	76	60	71	79	81	78	70	57	39	17	NE
		E	172	363	378	299	169	97	93	85	72	54	32	E
		SE	199	440	521	518	458	356	232	124	87	69	48	SE
		S	126	278	381	451	492	505	489	444	369	259	110	S
		SW	49	72	93	137	247	368	464	518	513	418	173	SW
		W	34	57	74	86	94	106	186	309	377	346	149	W
		NW	19	42	59	71	79	81	78	70	63	75	46	NW

Correction factors for tabulated values

Type of glass	Single glazing		Double glazing with clear 6 mm glass inside		Single glazing and external light slatted blinds used intermittently	
	Lightweight	Heavyweight	Lightweight	Heavyweight	Lightweight	Heavyweight
Clear 6 mm	1.00	0.85	0.85	0.70	0.19	0.19
BTG 6 mm	0.70	0.60	0.53	0.45	0.16	0.16
BTG 10 mm	0.58	0.49	0.40	0.34	0.14	0.14
Reflecting	0.49	0.42	0.37	0.31	0.13	0.13
Strongly reflecting	0.25	0.21	0.16	0.14	0.09	0.10
Additional factor for air point control	0.76	0.73	0.76	0.73	0.76	0.73

Table A9.21 Cooling load due to solar gain through vertical glazing. (10 h plant operation)—W/m²

FOR CONSTANT DRY RESULTANT TEMPERATURE

LIGHTWEIGHT BUILDING INTERMITTENT BLINDS 20°N

Date	Climatic constants	Orientation	Sun Time 0800	0900	1000	1100	1200	1300	1400	1500	1600	1700	1800	Orientation
June 21	$I = 1.00$ $k_c = 1.00$ $k_r = 0.20$ $C = 0.00$	N	103	99	58	123	123	124	124	170	113	114	84	N
		NE	323	296	237	166	80	130	124	115	102	85	65	NE
		E	354	334	270	178	81	129	125	116	102	85	66	E
		SE	176	179	154	116	64	117	113	104	91	74	54	SE
		S	53	72	89	102	110	113	109	100	86	69	50	S
		SW	51	70	87	100	108	161	147	178	184	157	88	SW
		W	55	74	91	104	112	203	239	311	345	324	196	W
		NW	55	74	91	104	113	198	212	275	312	303	192	NW
July 23 and May 22	$I = 1.00$ $k_c = 1.00$ $k_r = 0.20$ $C = 0.00$	N	85	50	108	109	114	118	115	111	150	97	40	N
		NE	309	281	220	150	75	126	122	113	99	82	62	NE
		E	358	339	274	180	80	128	124	115	101	83	63	E
		SE	196	201	175	131	66	118	114	105	91	73	53	SE
		S	51	71	88	101	109	113	109	100	86	68	48	S
		SW	50	70	87	100	108	174	166	199	204	173	91	SW
		W	54	73	90	104	112	205	243	316	350	325	182	W
		NW	53	73	90	103	111	183	197	261	299	290	170	NW
August 24 and April 22	$I = 1.00$ $k_c = 1.00$ $k_r = 0.20$ $C = 0.00$	N	60	70	87	101	109	112	108	99	85	70	58	N
		NE	268	237	174	74	129	120	116	107	93	74	53	NE
		E	359	344	278	180	76	123	119	110	95	77	56	E
		SE	241	253	228	175	75	131	113	104	89	71	50	SE
		S	45	67	89	163	113	111	59	110	83	63	41	S
		SW	48	69	87	101	113	226	218	252	253	208	54	SW
		W	49	69	87	101	109	206	249	324	356	319	137	W
		NW	48	69	86	100	109	115	218	221	262	252	115	NW
September 22 and March 21	$I = 1.00$ $k_c = 1.00$ $k_r = 0.20$ $C = 0.00$	N	38	60	78	92	101	103	100	90	76	57	35	N
		NE	374	161	106	52	103	106	102	93	78	59	37	NE
		E	620	331	267	169	65	108	105	95	80	62	39	E
		SE	500	307	288	235	161	65	106	93	79	60	38	SE
		S	84	105	146	175	188	183	162	126	84	30	37	S
		SW	38	59	77	93	192	216	277	308	298	226	48	SW
		W	38	60	78	92	101	197	243	317	343	285	60	W
		NW	37	59	77	91	100	103	150	153	194	181	41	NW
October 23 and February 21	$I = 1.00$ $k_c = 1.00$ $k_r = 0.20$ $C = 0.00$	N	30	52	70	83	92	95	91	82	67	49	27	N
		NE	231	97	42	85	93	96	92	83	69	51	29	NE
		E	515	308	250	156	58	98	95	85	71	53	31	E
		SE	487	337	326	280	206	125	52	84	70	52	30	SE
		S	158	167	215	247	261	255	231	191	136	70	17	S
		SW	30	52	69	143	181	260	316	340	318	212	43	SW
		W	31	52	70	83	92	182	227	296	314	229	48	W
		NW	30	52	69	83	91	94	91	138	130	114	27	NW
November 21 and January 21	$I = 1.00$ $k_c = 1.00$ $k_r = 0.20$ $C = 0.00$	N	21	44	61	74	82	84	81	72	59	41	19	N
		NE	117	31	69	74	82	85	81	73	59	42	19	NE
		E	385	273	224	139	50	86	83	74	61	43	21	E
		SE	416	343	343	304	237	155	54	86	61	44	21	SE
		S	196	212	263	295	309	304	279	236	173	80	18	S
		SW	22	44	65	176	212	286	335	350	313	166	40	SW
		W	21	44	61	74	82	163	205	266	272	157	38	W
		NW	22	45	62	75	83	85	82	76	117	31	66	NW
December 21	$I = 1.00$ $k_c = 1.00$ $k_r = 0.20$ $C = 0.00$	N	18	40	57	69	77	80	76	68	55	37	15	N
		NE	82	25	59	70	78	80	77	68	55	38	16	NE
		E	331	257	212	131	46	81	78	70	56	39	17	E
		SE	375	339	344	308	245	164	90	37	57	39	17	SE
		S	198	225	277	310	324	319	294	249	182	45	70	S
		SW	18	40	97	138	220	291	337	348	304	142	35	SW
		W	18	40	57	70	77	155	194	251	252	129	33	W
		NW	18	41	58	70	78	80	77	69	92	24	45	NW

Correction factors for tabulated values

Type of glass (outside pane for double glazing)	Building weight	Single glazing Light slatted blind Open	Closed	Linen roller blind	Double glazing, internal shade Light slatted blind Open	Closed	Linen roller blind	Double glazing, mid-pane shade Light slatted blind Open	Closed	Linen roller blind
Clear 6mm	Light	1.00	0.77	0.66	0.95	0.74	0.65	0.58	0.39	0.42
	Heavy	0.97	0.77	0.63	0.94	0.76	0.64	0.56	0.40	0.40
BTG 6mm	Light	0.86	0.77	0.72	0.66	0.55	0.51	0.45	0.36	0.38
	Heavy	0.85	0.77	0.71	0.66	0.57	0.51	0.44	0.37	0.37
BTG 10mm	Light	0.78	0.73	0.70	0.54	0.47	0.45	0.38	0.34	0.36
	Heavy	0.77	0.73	0.70	0.53	0.48	0.45	0.37	0.34	0.34
Reflecting	Light	0.64	0.57	0.54	0.48	0.41	0.38	0.33	0.27	0.29
	Heavy	0.62	0.57	0.53	0.47	0.41	0.38	0.32	0.27	0.28
Strongly reflecting	Light	0.36	0.34	0.32	0.23	0.21	0.21	0.17	0.16	0.16
	Heavy	0.35	0.34	0.32	0.23	0.21	0.21	0.17	0.16	0.16
Additional factor for air point control	Light	0.91	0.91	0.91	0.91	0.91	0.91	0.80	0.80	0.80
	Heavy	0.83	0.83	0.83	0.90	0.90	0.90	0.78	0.78	0.78

Table A9.22 Cooling load due to solar gain through vertical glazing. (10 h plant operation)—W/m²

FOR CONSTANT DRY RESULTANT TEMPERATURE

LIGHTWEIGHT BUILDING
UNPROTECTED 6mm CLEAR GLASS 30°N

Date	Climatic constants	Orientation	0800	0900	1000	1100	1200	1300	1400	1500	1600	1700	1800	Orientation
June 21	I = 1.00 k_c = 1.00 k_r = 0.20 C = 0.00	N	129	105	103	115	122	125	121	114	105	110	130	N
		NE	448	439	364	252	159	147	143	135	123	107	89	NE
		E	507	538	491	382	234	154	151	143	130	114	96	E
		SE	273	329	336	296	217	144	131	123	110	95	76	SE
		S	59	77	94	112	131	138	127	107	90	75	57	S
		SW	78	96	112	123	134	154	228	302	336	323	259	SW
		W	98	115	131	143	150	163	252	395	495	534	491	W
		NW	90	108	123	135	143	149	169	265	372	439	437	NW
July 23 and May 22	I = 1.00 k_c = 1.00 k_r = 0.20 C = 0.00	N	101	87	97	110	117	120	116	108	97	90	101	N
		NE	424	417	340	226	145	142	139	131	118	102	83	NE
		E	503	542	496	387	235	152	149	141	128	112	93	E
		SE	294	358	369	330	247	158	132	124	111	95	77	SE
		S	58	77	97	128	155	165	151	120	91	74	56	S
		SW	79	97	112	125	137	169	258	335	368	350	278	SW
		W	95	113	128	141	148	162	253	399	500	537	486	W
		NW	85	103	119	131	138	143	154	240	348	417	412	NW
August 24 and April 22	I = 1.00 k_c = 1.00 k_r = 0.20 C = 0.00	N	53	69	85	98	106	108	105	97	83	68	52	N
		NE	353	350	270	163	126	129	125	117	104	87	67	NE
		E	475	536	498	388	232	143	140	131	118	101	82	E
		SE	329	417	439	406	322	207	133	124	110	94	74	SE
		S	60	88	142	202	244	257	240	194	131	79	55	S
		SW	76	95	112	125	143	222	333	410	437	407	309	SW
		W	84	103	119	131	139	153	251	401	501	529	453	W
		NW	69	89	105	117	125	128	132	176	279	351	337	NW
September 22 and March 21	I = 1.00 k_c = 1.00 k_r = 0.20 C = 0.00	N	36	56	73	86	94	96	93	84	71	54	33	N
		NE	228	240	162	98	103	106	102	93	80	63	42	NE
		E	381	490	469	366	212	122	119	110	97	80	59	E
		SE	321	459	504	483	408	288	161	115	101	84	63	SE
		S	82	163	254	330	379	395	375	322	242	149	70	S
		SW	66	86	103	122	176	303	416	485	499	444	292	SW
		W	61	81	98	111	118	132	231	378	471	479	350	W
		NW	45	65	82	94	102	105	103	105	173	240	209	NW
October 23 and February 21	I = 1.00 k_c = 1.00 k_r = 0.20 C = 0.00	N	23	45	61	73	81	84	80	72	59	42	21	N
		NE	114	141	87	78	85	88	85	76	63	47	25	NE
		E	246	418	420	331	187	104	101	93	80	63	41	E
		SE	243	450	523	518	455	346	210	110	91	75	53	SE
		S	109	230	337	420	470	486	466	411	325	213	94	S
		SW	55	77	95	122	227	359	462	519	515	430	217	SW
		W	43	65	81	93	101	114	205	342	420	402	220	W
		NW	27	49	65	77	85	88	84	80	94	140	101	NW
November 21 and January 21	I = 1.00 k_c = 1.00 k_r = 0.20 C = 0.00	N	12	33	50	61	68	71	68	60	47	30	10	N
		NE	34	67	51	62	70	72	69	61	48	31	11	NE
		E	99	320	355	284	158	85	82	74	61	44	24	E
		SE	119	388	500	515	467	372	246	125	78	60	40	SE
		S	86	245	371	459	512	528	508	450	357	224	72	S
		SW	41	63	85	140	261	383	472	513	489	362	97	SW
		W	25	47	63	75	82	94	174	293	352	299	79	W
		NW	13	34	50	62	69	72	69	61	54	65	27	NW
December 21	I = 1.00 k_c = 1.00 k_r = 0.20 C = 0.00	N	8	29	45	56	63	66	63	55	43	26	6	N
		NE	13	47	45	57	64	66	63	55	43	26	7	NE
		E	44	275	325	263	145	77	74	66	54	37	17	E
		SE	64	350	480	504	464	375	254	132	72	54	35	SE
		S	64	236	372	463	517	533	512	454	357	214	51	S
		SW	36	57	80	148	269	385	468	502	468	322	44	SW
		W	19	40	56	68	75	86	160	271	322	253	26	W
		NW	8	29	45	57	64	66	63	55	46	44	9	NW

Correction factors for tabulated values

Type of glass	Single glazing		Double glazing with clear 6 mm glass inside		Single glazing and external light slatted blinds used intermittently	
	Lightweight	Heavyweight	Lightweight	Heavyweight	Lightweight	Heavyweight
Clear 6 mm	1.00	0.85	0.85	0.70	0.19	0.19
BTG 6 mm	0.70	0.60	0.53	0.45	0.16	0.16
BTG 10 mm	0.58	0.49	0.40	0.34	0.14	0.14
Reflecting	0.49	0.42	0.37	0.31	0.13	0.13
Strongly reflecting	0.25	0.21	0.16	0.14	0.09	0.10
Additional factor for air point control	0.76	0.73	0.76	0.73	0.76	0.73

Table A9.23 Cooling load due to solar gain through vertical glazing. (10 h plant operation)—W/m²

FOR CONSTANT DRY RESULTANT TEMPERATURE

LIGHTWEIGHT BUILDING
INTERMITTENT BLINDS **30°N**

Date	Climatic constants	Orientation	Sun Time											Orientation
			0800	0900	1000	1100	1200	1300	1400	1500	1600	1700	1800	
June 21	$I=1.00$ $k_c=1.00$ $k_r=0.20$ $C=0.00$	N	47	99	97	109	116	118	115	107	99	150	97	N
		NE	307	262	192	87	144	132	128	120	108	92	74	NE
		E	367	342	276	183	85	133	129	121	109	93	75	E
		SE	215	227	208	164	75	129	116	108	96	80	62	SE
		S	58	75	92	110	175	65	125	105	89	73	55	S
		SW	57	75	90	102	112	210	197	224	222	187	117	SW
		W	61	79	94	106	113	204	241	315	353	342	251	W
		NW	61	79	94	106	114	120	230	235	287	301	240	NW
July 23 and May 22	$I=1.00$ $k_c=1.00$ $k_r=0.20$ $C=0.00$	N	40	82	93	105	112	115	112	103	93	120	78	N
		NE	291	245	175	81	131	128	125	117	104	88	69	NE
		E	369	345	278	184	84	130	127	119	106	90	71	E
		SE	232	246	228	182	125	68	115	107	94	78	60	SE
		S	54	73	93	176	124	120	62	116	87	69	51	S
		SW	54	72	88	100	159	163	216	243	239	200	120	SW
		W	59	77	92	105	112	204	244	318	356	341	236	W
		NW	58	76	92	104	112	116	207	220	273	286	216	NW
August 24 and April 22	$I=1.00$ $k_c=1.00$ $k_r=0.20$ $C=0.00$	N	52	69	85	98	105	108	105	96	83	67	51	N
		NE	245	198	130	65	115	117	114	106	92	76	56	NE
		E	362	344	278	180	77	121	118	109	96	79	60	E
		SE	268	291	276	228	158	70	111	102	89	72	53	SE
		S	46	121	128	161	175	169	144	105	43	66	41	S
		SW	48	67	83	96	185	206	262	288	279	226	110	SW
		W	51	70	86	99	106	201	245	321	355	326	171	W
		NW	49	69	85	97	105	108	165	179	232	241	141	NW
September 22 and March 21	$I=1.00$ $k_c=1.00$ $k_r=0.20$ $C=0.00$	N	36	56	72	85	93	96	92	84	70	53	32	N
		NE	327	123	48	90	96	98	95	86	73	56	35	NE
		E	591	320	258	161	60	100	97	88	75	58	37	E
		SE	503	328	321	277	204	121	53	86	73	56	35	SE
		S	109	144	200	239	256	249	219	169	108	33	43	S
		SW	35	55	72	140	179	257	311	332	310	224	46	SW
		W	36	56	73	85	93	186	233	306	331	270	57	W
		NW	35	56	72	85	93	95	93	160	164	161	37	NW
October 23 and February 21	$I=1.00$ $k_c=1.00$ $k_r=0.20$ $C=0.00$	N	23	45	61	73	81	83	80	72	59	42	20	N
		NE	173	38	84	75	82	85	82	73	60	43	22	NE
		E	428	287	234	144	51	86	83	74	62	45	23	E
		SE	423	340	345	308	240	153	53	80	62	45	23	SE
		S	159	195	255	295	313	305	275	222	150	39	58	S
		SW	23	45	63	167	213	289	337	348	308	173	39	SW
		W	23	45	61	74	81	166	213	278	287	179	43	W
		NW	23	45	61	73	81	84	80	76	152	86	22	NW
November 21 and January 21	$I=1.00$ $k_c=1.00$ $k_r=0.20$ $C=0.00$	N	11	33	49	61	68	71	68	60	47	30	10	N
		NE	33	66	51	62	69	71	68	61	48	31	10	NE
		E	240	240	202	123	41	71	68	60	48	41	10	E
		SE	271	322	343	316	256	174	91	32	48	31	11	SE
		S	143	216	282	324	342	334	302	245	161	36	33	S
		SW	13	35	96	148	233	301	341	339	273	60	69	SW
		W	13	34	51	63	70	144	186	240	227	52	67	W
		NW	12	34	50	62	69	72	69	61	53	65	27	NW
December 21	$I=1.00$ $k_c=1.00$ $k_r=0.20$ $C=0.00$	N	8	29	45	56	63	66	63	55	43	26	6	N
		NE	13	47	45	57	64	66	63	55	43	26	6	NE
		E	165	219	188	114	36	65	63	55	43	26	6	E
		SE	199	307	336	314	258	179	97	31	43	26	7	SE
		S	118	216	286	329	346	339	306	247	156	32	12	S
		SW	8	29	98	152	235	299	335	328	248	50	17	SW
		W	8	29	45	56	63	133	173	220	197	41	15	W
		NW	8	29	45	57	64	66	63	55	46	44	9	NW

Correction factors for tabulated values

Type of glass (outside pane for double glazing)	Building weight	Single glazing			Double glazing, internal shade			Double glazing, mid-pane shade		
		Light slatted blind		Linen roller blind	Light slatted blind		Linen roller blind	Light slatted blind		Linen roller blind
		Open	Closed		Open	Closed		Open	Closed	
Clear 6mm	Light	1.00	0.77	0.66	0.95	0.74	0.65	0.58	0.39	0.42
	Heavy	0.97	0.77	0.63	0.94	0.76	0.64	0.56	0.40	0.40
BTG 6mm	Light	0.86	0.77	0.72	0.66	0.55	0.51	0.45	0.36	0.38
	Heavy	0.85	0.77	0.71	0.66	0.57	0.51	0.44	0.37	0.37
BTG 10mm	Light	0.78	0.73	0.70	0.54	0.47	0.45	0.38	0.34	0.36
	Heavy	0.77	0.73	0.70	0.53	0.48	0.45	0.37	0.34	0.34
Reflecting	Light	0.64	0.57	0.54	0.48	0.41	0.38	0.33	0.27	0.29
	Heavy	0.62	0.57	0.53	0.47	0.41	0.38	0.32	0.27	0.28
Strongly reflecting	Light	0.36	0.34	0.32	0.23	0.21	0.21	0.17	0.16	0.16
	Heavy	0.35	0.34	0.32	0.21	0.21	0.21	0.17	0.16	0.16
Additional factor for air point control	Light	0.91	0.91	0.91	0.91	0.91	0.91	0.80	0.80	0.80
	Heavy	0.83	0.83	0.83	0.90	0.90	0.90	0.78	0.78	0.78

Table A9.24 Cooling load due to solar gain through vertical glazing. (10 h plant operation)—W/m²

FOR CONSTANT DRY RESULTANT TEMPERATURE

LIGHTWEIGHT BUILDING
UNPROTECTED 6mm CLEAR GLASS | 35°N

Date	Climatic constants	Orientation	Sun Time											Orientation
			0800	0900	1000	1100	1200	1300	1400	1500	1600	1700	1800	
June 21	$I = 1.00$ $k_c = 1.00$ $k_r = 0.20$ $C = 0.00$	N	116	94	104	115	122	125	122	114	104	98	119	N
		NE	445	420	333	217	147	147	144	137	125	110	93	NE
		E	521	545	495	386	237	157	154	147	135	120	103	E
		SE	297	360	374	340	261	168	134	127	115	100	83	SE
		S	64	82	103	140	173	184	168	132	96	78	61	S
		SW	85	101	116	127	140	181	272	344	372	352	284	SW
		W	104	120	135	146	153	166	255	398	500	541	507	W
		NW	94	111	126	137	144	147	155	231	342	422	437	NW
July 23 and May 22	$I = 1.00$ $k_c = 1.00$ $k_r = 0.20$ $C = 0.00$	N	88	82	96	108	115	117	114	106	94	84	91	N
		NE	418	395	306	191	138	140	137	129	117	102	84	NE
		E	513	544	497	386	235	152	149	141	129	114	96	E
		SE	315	385	403	371	291	187	134	127	114	99	82	SE
		S	63	84	116	167	206	219	202	158	106	78	60	S
		SW	83	101	115	127	142	201	301	375	401	377	300	SW
		W	97	115	129	141	148	161	253	399	501	540	497	W
		NW	86	103	118	129	136	139	144	205	316	397	409	NW
August 24 and April 22	$I = 1.00$ $k_c = 1.00$ $k_r = 0.20$ $C = 0.00$	N	51	68	84	96	103	105	102	94	82	66	50	N
		NE	344	328	237	138	123	125	122	114	101	86	67	NE
		E	478	533	494	384	229	141	138	130	117	102	83	E
		SE	344	436	466	440	362	245	143	125	112	96	78	SE
		S	67	105	179	252	302	317	297	243	167	94	60	S
		SW	80	98	113	128	155	260	372	443	463	426	324	SW
		W	85	103	118	130	137	151	248	397	497	527	458	W
		NW	69	87	102	114	122	124	126	149	148	330	331	NW
September 22 and March 21	$I = 1.00$ $k_c = 1.00$ $k_r = 0.20$ $C = 0.00$	N	34	54	69	81	89	91	88	80	67	51	31	N
		NE	212	217	136	90	97	99	96	88	76	59	39	NE
		E	366	476	457	356	204	116	113	105	92	76	56	E
		SE	316	462	516	503	434	319	182	112	99	83	63	SE
		S	89	182	285	370	424	441	419	361	272	167	77	S
		SW	66	85	101	121	200	333	442	504	510	447	287	SW
		W	58	78	93	105	113	126	223	368	459	466	336	W
		NW	42	61	77	89	96	99	96	96	147	218	195	NW
October 23 and February 21	$I = 1.00$ $k_c = 1.00$ $k_r = 0.20$ $C = 0.00$	N	19	40	56	68	75	77	74	66	54	37	17	N
		NE	92	121	72	71	78	80	77	70	57	41	20	NE
		E	205	389	400	316	177	96	93	85	73	56	36	E
		SE	208	429	517	523	468	364	228	113	86	70	49	SE
		S	102	232	350	440	495	512	491	431	336	214	88	S
		SW	51	72	91	127	245	376	474	522	508	408	183	SW
		W	37	58	74	86	93	105	194	326	400	372	181	W
		NW	22	43	59	71	78	80	77	72	77	120	81	NW
November 21 and January 21	$I = 1.00$ $k_c = 1.00$ $k_r = 0.20$ $C = 0.00$	N	7	27	43	54	61	63	61	53	41	25	6	N
		NE	12	52	44	55	62	64	61	54	42	25	6	NE
		E	37	271	325	264	144	75	72	64	53	36	17	E
		SE	56	336	472	501	463	375	252	127	69	53	34	SE
		S	59	220	360	457	515	533	511	448	345	198	47	S
		SW	35	55	78	143	267	385	468	499	460	309	37	SW
		W	18	38	54	65	72	83	160	272	321	249	20	W
		NW	7	28	44	55	62	64	61	53	45	49	7	NW
December 21	$I = 1.00$ $k_c = 1.00$ $k_r = 0.20$ $C = 0.00$	N	6	22	38	49	56	58	55	48	36	20	5	N
		NE	8	34	38	50	56	58	56	48	36	20	5	NE
		E	28	218	292	242	132	68	65	58	46	29	15	E
		SE	47	284	443	484	454	373	257	133	64	47	32	SE
		S	54	198	350	452	512	531	508	443	334	178	44	S
		SW	33	50	74	149	271	382	458	481	429	258	32	SW
		W	15	32	48	59	66	76	147	249	286	198	14	W
		NW	6	22	38	50	56	58	56	48	39	32	5	NW

Correction factors for tabulated values

Type of glass	Single glazing		Double glazing with clear 6 mm glass inside		Single glazing and external light slatted blinds used intermittently	
	Lightweight	Heavyweight	Lightweight	Heavyweight	Lightweight	Heavyweight
Clear 6 mm	1.00	0.85	0.85	0.70	0.19	0.19
BTG 6 mm	0.70	0.60	0.53	0.45	0.16	0.16
BTG 10 mm	0.58	0.49	0.40	0.34	0.14	0.14
Reflecting	0.49	0.42	0.37	0.31	0.13	0.13
Strongly reflecting	0.25	0.21	0.16	0.14	0.09	0.10
Additional factor for air point control	0.76	0.73	0.76	0.73	0.76	0.73

Table A9.25 Cooling load due to solar gain through vertical glazing. (10 h plant operation)—W/m²

FOR CONSTANT DRY RESULTANT TEMPERATURE

LIGHTWEIGHT BUILDING INTERMITTENT BLINDS 35°N

Date	Climatic constants	Orientation	0800	0900	1000	1100	1200	1300	1400	1500	1600	1700	1800	Orientation
June 21	$I = 1.00$ $k_c = 1.00$ $k_r = 0.20$ $C = 0.00$	N	45	87	97	109	115	118	115	107	97	130	99	N
		NE	295	241	169	82	130	131	128	120	108	93	76	NE
		E	371	343	276	183	86	132	129	122	110	95	78	E
		SE	232	248	233	189	132	68	115	108	96	81	64	SE
		S	57	75	140	122	135	129	109	54	89	71	54	S
		SW	59	76	91	102	166	172	222	247	240	202	131	SW
		W	66	83	97	109	115	205	243	317	357	350	274	W
		NW	66	82	97	108	115	119	199	216	275	299	257	NW
July 23 and May 22	$I = 1.00$ $k_c = 1.00$ $k_r = 0.20$ $C = 0.00$	N	85	78	93	105	112	114	111	103	91	80	126	N
		NE	279	225	153	76	125	127	124	116	104	89	72	NE
		E	372	346	279	184	84	130	127	119	107	92	74	E
		SE	249	268	254	209	146	70	115	107	95	80	62	SE
		S	54	75	164	141	155	149	125	57	97	69	51	S
		SW	56	73	88	100	174	188	240	264	256	214	133	SW
		W	60	77	92	104	111	202	242	318	357	346	255	W
		NW	60	77	91	103	110	112	181	199	258	281	230	NW
August 24 and April 22	$I = 1.00$ $k_c = 1.00$ $k_r = 0.20$ $C = 0.00$	N	50	68	83	95	102	105	102	94	81	66	50	N
		NE	232	178	112	63	113	115	112	104	91	76	57	NE
		E	362	343	276	178	76	119	116	108	96	80	61	E
		SE	281	308	297	253	182	75	119	101	89	73	54	SE
		S	49	149	156	195	212	204	174	126	48	76	42	S
		SW	49	67	82	97	212	229	283	305	291	235	121	SW
		W	51	69	85	97	104	197	242	318	353	328	187	W
		NW	50	68	83	95	102	105	147	158	216	234	152	NW
September 22 and March 21	$I = 1.00$ $k_c = 1.00$ $k_r = 0.20$ $C = 0.00$	N	34	53	69	81	88	91	87	79	67	51	31	N
		NE	302	106	42	83	90	93	90	81	69	53	33	NE
		E	570	313	252	156	57	95	92	84	71	55	35	E
		SE	498	336	334	294	223	135	52	82	70	54	34	SE
		S	121	162	223	266	284	277	243	188	119	35	46	S
		SW	33	53	68	150	196	274	325	340	312	221	45	SW
		W	34	53	69	81	89	178	227	299	322	260	54	W
		NW	33	53	68	80	88	90	87	139	148	150	35	NW
October 23 and February 21	$I = 1.00$ $k_c = 1.00$ $k_r = 0.20$ $C = 0.00$	N	19	40	56	67	75	77	74	66	54	37	17	N
		NE	143	32	69	68	76	78	75	67	55	38	18	NE
		E	375	273	225	137	46	79	76	68	56	40	19	E
		SE	379	336	348	316	251	164	53	83	56	40	19	SE
		S	152	201	268	312	331	323	289	230	151	38	50	S
		SW	20	41	60	183	225	298	342	347	297	149	36	SW
		W	20	40	56	68	75	156	204	265	269	150	38	W
		NW	19	40	56	67	75	77	74	69	127	70	18	NW
November 21 and January 21	$I = 1.00$ $k_c = 1.00$ $k_r = 0.20$ $C = 0.00$	N	7	27	43	54	61	63	61	53	41	25	6	N
		NE	12	52	44	55	62	64	61	53	42	25	6	NE
		E	157	219	189	114	35	63	60	53	41	25	5	E
		SE	184	301	334	314	259	179	94	29	42	25	6	SE
		S	106	208	282	328	347	339	303	240	146	30	8	S
		SW	8	28	94	151	235	300	333	323	239	47	10	SW
		W	7	27	43	54	61	131	173	220	195	40	9	W
		NW	7	28	44	55	62	64	61	53	45	49	7	NW
December 21	$I = 1.00$ $k_c = 1.00$ $k_r = 0.20$ $C = 0.00$	N	6	22	38	49	56	58	55	48	36	20	5	N
		NE	8	34	38	50	56	58	56	48	36	20	5	NE
		E	20	352	176	107	34	60	58	50	38	22	7	E
		SE	23	474	326	312	261	185	101	31	40	23	8	SE
		S	19	316	282	330	349	341	304	237	135	28	8	S
		SW	7	23	95	154	235	296	324	306	202	44	5	SW
		W	6	22	38	49	56	121	159	199	160	32	5	W
		NW	6	22	38	50	56	58	56	48	39	32	5	NW

Correction factors for tabulated values

Type of glass (outside pane for double glazing)	Building weight	Single glazing			Double glazing, internal shade			Double glazing, mid-pane shade		
		Light slatted blind		Linen roller blind	Light slatted blind		Linen roller blind	Light slatted blind		Linen roller blind
		Open	Closed		Open	Closed		Open	Closed	
Clear 6mm	Light	1.00	0.77	0.66	0.95	0.74	0.65	0.58	0.39	0.42
	Heavy	0.97	0.77	0.63	0.94	0.76	0.64	0.56	0.40	0.40
BTG 6mm	Light	0.86	0.77	0.72	0.66	0.55	0.51	0.45	0.36	0.38
	Heavy	0.85	0.77	0.71	0.66	0.57	0.51	0.44	0.37	0.37
BTG 10mm	Light	0.78	0.73	0.70	0.54	0.47	0.45	0.38	0.34	0.36
	Heavy	0.77	0.73	0.70	0.53	0.48	0.45	0.37	0.34	0.34
Reflecting	Light	0.64	0.57	0.54	0.48	0.41	0.38	0.33	0.27	0.29
	Heavy	0.62	0.57	0.53	0.47	0.41	0.38	0.32	0.27	0.28
Strongly reflecting	Light	0.36	0.34	0.32	0.23	0.21	0.21	0.17	0.16	0.16
	Heavy	0.35	0.34	0.32	0.23	0.21	0.21	0.17	0.16	0.16
Additional factor for air point control	Light	0.91	0.91	0.91	0.91	0.91	0.91	0.80	0.80	0.80
	Heavy	0.83	0.83	0.83	0.90	0.90	0.90	0.78	0.78	0.78

Table A9.26 Cooling load due to solar gain through vertical glazing. (10 h plant operation) —W/m²
FOR CONSTANT DRY RESULTANT TEMPERATURE

LIGHTWEIGHT BUILDING — UNPROTECTED 6mm CLEAR GLASS — 40°N

Date	Climatic constants	Orientation	0800	0900	1000	1100	1200	1300	1400	1500	1600	1700	1800	Orientation
June 21	I = 1.00; kc = 1.00; kr = 0.20; C = 0.00	N	103	92	105	116	122	124	121	114	103	94	108	N
		NE	440	399	302	187	146	148	145	138	127	113	97	NE
		E	533	550	498	387	239	159	157	150	139	125	109	E
		SE	322	389	409	381	306	201	138	130	119	105	89	SE
		S	70	89	126	183	227	242	223	174	115	83	67	S
		SW	91	106	120	131	146	216	316	385	407	381	308	SW
		W	109	125	139	149	156	168	257	400	503	647	521	W
		NW	98	114	128	138	145	147	151	200	312	403	434	NW
July 23 and May 22	I = 1.00; kc = 1.00; kr = 0.20; C = 0.00	N	80	83	97	107	114	116	113	106	95	84	84	N
		NE	412	374	274	165	138	140	137	130	118	104	88	NE
		E	523	548	498	381	236	153	151	143	132	118	102	E
		SE	337	412	436	410	334	224	140	130	118	104	88	SE
		S	70	93	147	215	264	280	259	206	135	84	66	S
		SW	89	105	119	131	150	239	344	413	433	403	322	SW
		W	103	119	132	143	150	163	254	399	502	544	509	W
		NW	89	105	119	130	136	138	142	177	286	377	405	NW
August 24 and April 22	I = 1.00; kc = 1.00; kr = 0.20; C = 0.00	N	50	67	81	92	99	101	99	91	79	65	50	N
		NE	334	304	205	119	119	121	118	110	99	84	67	NE
		E	479	529	488	379	225	138	135	128	116	101	84	E
		SE	357	453	490	470	398	282	161	125	113	98	81	SE
		S	73	127	217	301	356	374	351	291	204	113	65	S
		SW	83	100	114	131	175	297	407	472	486	443	337	SW
		W	85	102	116	128	135	148	244	391	492	523	460	W
		NW	69	85	100	111	118	120	119	128	218	308	323	NW
September 22 and March 21	I = 1.00; kc = 1.00; kr = 0.20; C = 0.00	N	32	50	65	76	83	85	82	75	63	48	29	N
		NE	196	194	113	84	91	93	90	82	71	56	37	NE
		E	348	460	443	345	196	110	107	99	87	72	54	E
		SE	307	460	522	517	455	345	204	110	97	82	63	SE
		S	96	198	311	402	460	479	456	393	297	182	82	S
		SW	65	83	99	121	222	358	462	518	516	445	280	SW
		W	56	74	88	99	106	119	214	357	445	449	319	W
		NW	39	57	72	83	90	92	89	88	123	196	180	NW
October 23 and February 21	I = 1.00; kc = 1.00; kr = 0.20; C = 0.00	N	15	35	50	61	68	70	67	60	48	33	13	N
		NE	70	101	59	64	71	73	70	63	51	35	16	NE
		E	161	354	377	299	165	87	84	77	65	49	30	E
		SE	169	401	503	519	472	375	242	117	80	64	45	SE
		S	92	226	353	450	510	529	506	441	339	207	78	S
		SW	47	66	86	132	258	386	478	518	493	378	146	SW
		W	32	52	67	78	84	96	182	309	375	336	139	W
		NW	18	38	53	64	70	72	70	64	64	100	61	NW
November 21 and January 21	I = 1.00; kc = 1.00; kr = 0.20; C = 0.00	N	6	21	36	47	54	56	53	46	34	19	5	N
		NE	9	38	37	48	54	56	53	46	35	19	5	NE
		E	27	213	290	232	131	66	63	56	44	28	14	E
		SE	45	271	433	478	451	370	253	127	61	45	31	SE
		S	52	184	337	444	507	527	502	434	320	164	43	S
		SW	32	47	70	143	267	380	454	474	418	246	31	SW
		W	1?	30	46	57	63	74	146	249	284	193	14	W
		NW	6	21	37	48	54	56	53	46	37	36	5	NW
December 21	I = 1.00; kc = 1.00; kr = 0.20; C = 0.00	N	5	15	31	42	48	50	48	41	29	13	4	N
		NE	6	22	31	42	44	50	48	41	29	13	4	NE
		E	21	152	250	218	118	58	56	49	37	21	12	E
		SE	39	204	390	452	434	361	250	130	56	38	29	SE
		S	47	150	313	428	493	514	488	417	295	131	40	S
		SW	29	41	65	145	264	369	436	447	373	182	29	SW
		W	13	23	39	50	56	66	131	223	242	135	12	W
		NW	5	15	31	42	48	50	48	41	30	20	4	NW

Correction factors for tabulated values

Type of glass	Single glazing Lightweight	Single glazing Heavyweight	Double glazing with clear 6 mm glass inside Lightweight	Double glazing with clear 6 mm glass inside Heavyweight	Single glazing and external light slatted blinds used intermittently Lightweight	Single glazing and external light slatted blinds used intermittently Heavyweight
Clear 6 mm	1.00	0.85	0.85	0.70	0.19	0.19
BTG 6 mm	0.70	0.60	0.53	0.45	0.16	0.16
BTG 10 mm	0.58	0.49	0.40	0.34	0.14	0.14
Reflecting	0.49	0.42	0.37	0.31	0.13	0.13
Strongly reflecting	0.25	0.21	0.16	0.14	0.09	0.10
Additional factor for air point control	0.76	0.73	0.76	0.73	0.76	0.73

Table A9.27 Cooling load due to solar gain through vertical glazing. (10 h plant operation)—W/m²

FOR CONSTANT DRY RESULTANT TEMPERATURE

LIGHTWEIGHT BUILDING
INTERMITTENT BLINDS **40°N**

Date	Climatic constants	Orien-tation	Sun Time											Orien-tation
			0800	0900	1000	1100	1200	1300	1400	1500	1600	1700	1800	
June 21	I = 1.00 k_c = 1.00 k_r = 0.20 C = 0.00	N NE E SE S SW W NW	45 285 378 251 59 62 69 68	86 224 348 271 79 78 84 84	99 151 280 260 179 92 98 97	110 82 187 218 154 103 109 108	116 131 90 155 170 184 115 114	118 133 135 73 163 197 203 116	116 130 132 116 135 248 242 177	109 123 125 109 61 269 317 195	98 112 114 98 105 259 359 259	120 98 100 84 73 217 356 293	101 82 84 68 57 146 292 269	N NE E SE S SW W NW
July 23 and May 22	I = 1.00 k_c = 1.00 k_r = 0.20 C = 0.00	N NE E SE S SW W NW	77 266 374 265 55 59 65 64	79 205 346 288 124 75 81 80	93 133 277 277 136 89 94 93	104 74 183 235 173 101 105 104	110 123 84 168 190 197 112 111	112 125 128 74 182 213 202 113	110 123 126 117 152 264 243 164	102 115 119 106 108 285 319 180	91 104 107 95 46 274 359 244	80 90 93 81 69 228 352 277	118 74 77 64 52 147 275 244	N NE E SE S SW W NW
August 24 and April 22	I = 1.00 k_c = 1.00 k_r = 0.20 C = 0.00	N NE E SE S SW W NW	50 219 360 291 86 48 51 50	67 159 340 322 123 65 68 67	81 66 273 316 183 79 83 81	92 111 176 275 226 142 94 93	99 110 75 204 244 174 101 100	101 112 117 125 236 250 192 102	98 110 114 62 202 301 238 101	91 102 106 98 148 320 314 189	79 90 94 87 86 301 350 201	64 76 80 72 31 242 327 227	49 58 62 55 42 130 201 163	N NE E SE S SW W NW
September 22 and March 21	I = 1.00 k_c = 1.00 k_r = 0.20 C = 0.00	N NE E SE S SW W NW	32 277 547 489 131 32 32 31	50 90 304 340 176 50 50 50	65 38 244 343 243 66 65 64	76 78 150 307 289 161 76 75	83 85 54 239 309 211 83 82	85 87 89 150 300 287 170 84	82 84 86 53 264 335 220 82	74 76 79 79 205 346 290 123	63 65 67 66 129 312 312 133	48 50 52 51 36 215 248 139	29 31 33 32 48 44 52 33	N NE E SE S SW W NW
October 23 and February 21	I = 1.00 k_c = 1.00 k_r = 0.20 C = 0.00	N NE E SE S SW W NW	15 113 317 326 139 16 16 17	35 27 257 325 203 36 36 36	50 57 213 345 275 90 51 52	61 62 129 319 323 143 62 63	68 69 42 258 343 232 68 69	70 71 72 172 334 302 146 71	67 68 69 86 297 341 193 68	60 61 62 32 234 339 251 63	48 49 50 50 148 279 247 107	33 33 34 34 35 121 120 27	13 14 15 15 40 30 32 60	N NE E SE S SW W NW
November 21 and January 21	I = 1.00 k_c = 1.00 k_r = 0.20 C = 0.00	N NE E SE S SW W NW	6 9 19 22 18 6 6 6	21 38 347 456 297 22 21 21	36 37 176 321 276 90 36 37	47 48 107 310 327 152 47 48	54 54 33 260 348 233 54 54	56 56 58 183 338 294 119 56	53 53 55 97 299 321 159 53	46 46 48 29 229 299 198 46	34 35 37 38 125 193 156 37	19 19 21 22 26 43 32 36	5 5 7 8 8 5 4 5	N NE E SE S SW W NW
December 21	I = 1.00 k_c = 1.00 k_r = 0.20 C = 0.00	N NE E SE S SW W NW	5 6 14 17 14 6 5 5	15 22 268 370 254 17 15 15	31 31 158 302 266 90 31 31	42 42 96 299 320 151 42 42	48 48 29 253 341 229 48 48	50 50 52 181 332 285 108 50	48 48 49 99 291 306 144 48	41 41 42 28 215 272 173 41	29 29 30 33 101 146 112 30	13 13 14 16 22 36<>27 20	4 4 5 7 7 5 4 4	N NE E SE S SW W NW

Correction factors for tabulated values											
Type of glass (outside pane for double glazing)	Building weight	Single glazing			Double glazing, internal shade			Double glazing, mid-pane shade		
		Light slatted blind		Linen roller blind	Light slatted blind		Linen roller blind	Light slatted blind		Linen roller blind
		Open	Closed		Open	Closed		Open	Closed	
Clear 6mm	Light	1.00	0.77	0.66	0.95	0.74	0.65	0.58	0.39	0.42
	Heavy	0.97	0.77	0.63	0.94	0.76	0.64	0.56	0.40	0.40
BTG 6mm	Light	0.86	0.77	0.72	0.66	0.55	0.51	0.45	0.36	0.38
	Heavy	0.85	0.77	0.71	0.66	0.57	0.51	0.44	0.37	0.37
BTG 10mm	Light	0.78	0.73	0.70	0.54	0.47	0.45	0.38	0.34	0.36
	Heavy	0.77	0.73	0.70	0.53	0.48	0.45	0.37	0.34	0.34
Reflecting	Light	0.64	0.57	0.54	0.48	0.41	0.38	0.33	0.27	0.29
	Heavy	0.62	0.57	0.53	0.47	0.41	0.38	0.32	0.27	0.28
Strongly reflecting	Light	0.36	0.34	0.32	0.23	0.21	0.21	0.17	0.16	0.16
	Heavy	0.35	0.34	0.32	0.23	0.21	0.21	0.17	0.16	0.16
Additional factor for air point control	Light	0.91	0.91	0.91	0.91	0.91	0.91	0.80	0.80	0.80
	Heavy	0.83	0.83	0.83	0.90	0.90	0.90	0.78	0.78	0.78

Table A9.28 Cooling load due to solar gain through vertical glazing. (10 h plant operation)—W/m²

FOR CONSTANT DRY RESULTANT TEMPERATURE

LIGHTWEIGHT BUILDING — UNPROTECTED 6mm CLEAR GLASS — 45°N

Date	Climatic constants	Orientation	0800	0900	1000	1100	1200	1300	1400	1500	1600	1700	1800	Orientation
June 21	$I = 1.00$ $k_c = 1.00$ $k_r = 0.20$ $C = 0.00$	N	93	93	105	115	121	123	120	114	103	94	99	N
		NE	432	377	269	163	145	147	145	138	128	115	101	NE
		E	542	554	499	388	240	161	158	152	141	128	114	E
		SE	346	417	443	420	349	240	148	133	123	110	95	SE
		S	77	99	160	234	286	303	281	224	147	90	73	S
		SW	97	111	124	136	159	255	358	423	440	409	332	SW
		W	114	129	141	151	157	169	258	400	504	551	532	W
		NW	101	116	128	138	144	146	149	175	282	382	428	NW
July 23 and May 22	$I = 1.00$ $k_c = 1.00$ $k_r = 0.20$ $C = 0.00$	N	74	84	96	106	112	114	112	105	95	83	78	N
		NE	404	351	243	145	137	139	136	129	119	106	91	NE
		E	531	549	497	386	236	154	151	145	134	121	106	E
		SE	359	437	466	445	375	263	156	132	121	108	93	SE
		S	78	108	155	266	322	339	317	257	172	97	72	S
		SW	94	109	122	136	169	278	384	448	463	428	344	SW
		W	107	122	134	144	151	163	254	398	502	546	519	W
		NW	92	107	119	129	136	137	139	155	256	357	400	NW
August 24 and April 22	$I = 1.00$ $k_c = 1.00$ $k_r = 0.20$ $C = 0.00$	N	50	65	78	88	95	97	94	87	77	63	49	N
		NE	322	280	176	108	114	116	113	106	95	82	66	NE
		E	478	522	481	372	220	134	131	124	114	100	84	E
		SE	368	467	509	495	429	316	183	124	113	100	84	SE
		S	80	150	254	345	404	423	399	335	240	134	71	S
		SW	85	101	114	132	199	330	437	497	505	456	349	SW
		W	85	101	114	124	131	143	238	384	485	517	461	W
		NW	68	83	96	106	113	115	113	116	189	285	314	NW
September 22 and March 21	$I = 1.00$ $k_c = 1.00$ $k_r = 0.20$ $C = 0.00$	N	30	47	61	71	77	79	76	69	59	45	27	N
		NE	180	172	94	77	84	86	83	76	65	51	34	NE
		E	327	441	427	332	187	102	100	93	82	68	50	E
		SE	296	454	523	525	470	364	224	112	93	79	62	SE
		S	100	210	330	427	488	507	483	418	316	194	86	S
		SW	64	81	97	125	242	377	476	525	516	438	269	SW
		W	52	69	83	93	99	112	205	343	428	430	300	W
		NW	36	53	67	77	83	85	82	80	103	175	165	NW
October 23 and February 21	$I = 1.00$ $k_c = 1.00$ $k_r = 0.20$ $C = 0.00$	N	12	30	45	55	61	63	60	53	43	28	10	N
		NE	48	82	49	56	63	64	62	55	45	30	12	NE
		E	114	313	349	279	152	77	75	68	57	42	24	E
		SE	126	362	480	506	468	377	249	119	73	58	40	SE
		S	78	212	348	450	514	534	509	440	332	193	66	S
		SW	41	60	80	135	264	388	472	504	469	338	106	SW
		W	26	44	59	69	75	86	169	288	346	294	94	W
		NW	13	32	46	56	62	64	62	56	53	81	40	NW
November 21 and January 21	$I = 1.00$ $k_c = 1.00$ $k_r = 0.20$ $C = 0.00$	N	4	14	29	40	46	48	45	39	27	12	4	N
		NE	6	24	29	40	46	48	45	39	27	12	4	NE
		E	20	147	246	216	117	56	53	47	35	20	12	E
		SE	37	193	376	442	426	355	244	122	52	37	28	SE
		S	46	138	298	415	484	505	479	404	280	121	39	S
		SW	29	39	61	137	258	363	429	436	359	172	28	SW
		W	12	22	37	48	54	63	130	221	238	130	12	W
		NW	5	14	29	40	46	48	45	39	29	23	4	NW
December 21	$I = 1.00$ $k_c = 1.00$ $k_r = 0.20$ $C = 0.00$	N	3	8	24	34	40	42	40	32	22	7	3	N
		NE	4	11	24	34	40	42	40	33	22	7	3	NE
		E	13	79	198	187	102	48	46	39	28	13	9	E
		SE	29	113	315	402	399	336	234	118	46	29	25	SE
		S	38	92	258	384	457	479	452	372	239	77	35	S
		SW	25	31	55	132	247	344	400	394	296	95	25	SW
		W	9	14	30	40	46	55	114	190	188	65	9	W
		NW	3	8	24	34	40	42	40	32	22	10	3	NW

Correction factors for tabulated values

Type of glass	Single glazing Lightweight	Single glazing Heavyweight	Double glazing with clear 6 mm glass inside Lightweight	Double glazing with clear 6 mm glass inside Heavyweight	Single glazing and external light slatted blinds used intermittently Lightweight	Single glazing and external light slatted blinds used intermittently Heavyweight
Clear 6 mm	1.00	0.85	0.85	0.70	0.19	0.19
BTG 6 mm	0.70	0.60	0.53	0.45	0.16	0.16
BTG 10 mm	0.58	0.49	0.40	0.34	0.14	0.14
Reflecting	0.49	0.42	0.37	0.31	0.13	0.13
Strongly reflecting	0.25	0.21	0.16	0.14	0.09	0.10
Additional factor for air point control	0.76	0.73	0.76	0.73	0.76	0.73

Table A9.29 Cooling load due to solar gain through vertical glazing. (10 h plant operation)—W/m²

FOR CONSTANT DRY RESULTANT TEMPERATURE

LIGHTWEIGHT BUILDING
INTERMITTENT BLINDS **45°N**

Date	Climatic constants	Orientation	0800	0900	1000	1100	1200	1300	1400	1500	1600	1700	1800	Orientation
June 21	I = 1.00 k_c = 1.00 k_r = 0.20 C = 0.00	N	88	87	100	109	115	117	115	108	98	89	142	N
		NE	274	207	135	83	132	134	132	125	115	102	87	NE
		E	383	351	282	189	93	137	134	128	118	105	90	E
		SE	270	293	285	245	180	79	124	110	99	86	72	SE
		S	61	134	148	187	204	196	164	116	49	74	58	S
		SW	65	80	92	105	211	223	272	290	277	233	160	SW
		W	72	86	99	108	114	201	241	317	360	361	308	W
		NW	71	85	98	108	114	115	161	175	244	286	278	NW
July 23 and May 22	I = 1.00 k_c = 1.00 k_r = 0.20 C = 0.00	N	71	80	93	103	109	111	109	102	91	80	112	N
		NE	256	188	83	133	125	127	124	118	107	94	79	NE
		E	378	348	279	184	87	130	127	120	110	97	82	E
		SE	282	308	300	261	194	81	131	106	96	83	68	SE
		S	59	152	166	208	226	218	184	131	51	78	54	S
		SW	61	76	89	103	230	238	287	305	290	241	161	SW
		W	66	81	91	104	110	198	240	316	359	355	290	W
		NW	66	80	93	103	109	111	112	218	229	270	253	NW
August 24 and April 22	I = 1.00 k_c = 1.00 k_r = 0.20 C = 0.00	N	49	65	78	88	94	96	94	87	76	63	49	N
		NE	205	141	61	100	106	108	105	98	88	74	58	NE
		E	357	336	269	172	74	113	110	103	93	79	63	E
		SE	300	335	332	294	225	140	63	96	85	72	56	SE
		S	97	144	209	255	275	266	229	170	100	33	43	S
		SW	48	64	77	152	193	269	317	332	311	248	140	SW
		W	51	67	80	90	96	185	233	308	345	326	213	W
		NW	50	65	79	89	95	97	95	163	185	218	170	NW
September 22 and March 21	I = 1.00 k_c = 1.00 k_r = 0.20 C = 0.00	N	30	47	60	70	77	79	76	69	58	44	27	N
		NE	251	76	34	72	78	80	78	71	60	46	29	NE
		E	518	294	236	143	50	83	80	73	62	48	31	E
		SE	474	340	349	317	251	162	54	81	62	48	31	SE
		S	138	188	259	307	328	319	281	217	136	37	50	S
		SW	30	47	63	175	223	298	342	348	309	207	42	SW
		W	30	47	61	71	77	160	211	280	299	234	49	W
		NW	29	46	60	70	76	78	75	107	119	127	30	NW
October 23 and February 21	I = 1.00 k_c = 1.00 k_r = 0.20 C = 0.00	N	11	30	45	55	61	63	60	53	43	28	10	N
		NE	83	22	47	55	61	63	60	54	43	28	10	NE
		E	252	238	200	119	37	64	61	54	44	29	11	E
		SE	265	308	338	318	261	177	88	29	44	29	11	SE
		S	120	199	276	327	348	339	299	232	140	31	28	S
		SW	12	31	89	147	235	302	336	327	255	91	23	SW
		W	12	30	45	55	61	134	181	234	221	89	23	W
		NW	12	31	45	55	61	63	61	55	89	21	39	NW
November 21 and January 21	I = 1.00 k_c = 1.00 k_r = 0.20 C = 0.00	N	4	14	29	40	46	48	45	39	27	12	4	N
		NE	6	24	29	40	46	48	45	39	27	12	4	NE
		E	14	262	157	95	28	49	47	40	29	14	5	E
		SE	16	353	295	294	250	177	94	26	31	15	6	SE
		S	13	236	258	314	337	327	283	205	93	20	7	S
		SW	5	15	84	147	226	281	300	264	138	34	5	SW
		W	4	14	29	40	46	106	143	170	108	27	4	W
		NW	5	14	29	40	46	48	45	39	29	23	4	NW
December 21	I = 1.00 k_c = 1.00 k_r = 0.20 C = 0.00	N	3	8	24	34	40	42	40	32	22	7	3	N
		NE	4	11	24	34	40	42	40	32	22	7	3	NE
		E	8	171	134	84	24	43	40	33	22	7	4	E
		SE	9	244	266	275	238	171	91	23	26	9	5	SE
		S	9	176	238	299	323	312	266	181	39	48	6	S
		SW	4	10	81	143	216	266	276	225	85	21	4	SW
		W	4	9	24	34	41	95	125	140	34	60	4	W
		NW	3	8	24	34	40	42	40	32	22	10	3	NW

Correction factors for tabulated values

Type of glass (outside pane for double glazing)	Building weight	Single glazing			Double glazing, internal shade			Double glazing, mid-pane shade		
		Light slatted blind		Linen roller blind	Light slatted blind		Linen roller blind	Light slatted blind		Linen roller blind
		Open	Closed		Open	Closed		Open	Closed	
Clear 6mm	Light	1.00	0.77	0.66	0.95	0.74	0.65	0.58	0.39	0.42
	Heavy	0.97	0.77	0.63	0.94	0.76	0.64	0.56	0.40	0.40
BTG 6mm	Light	0.86	0.77	0.72	0.66	0.55	0.51	0.45	0.36	0.38
	Heavy	0.85	0.77	0.71	0.66	0.57	0.51	0.44	0.37	0.37
BTG 10mm	Light	0.78	0.73	0.70	0.54	0.47	0.45	0.38	0.34	0.36
	Heavy	0.77	0.73	0.70	0.53	0.48	0.45	0.37	0.34	0.34
Reflecting	Light	0.64	0.57	0.54	0.48	0.41	0.38	0.33	0.27	0.29
	Heavy	0.62	0.57	0.53	0.47	0.41	0.38	0.32	0.27	0.28
Strongly reflecting	Light	0.36	0.34	0.32	0.23	0.21	0.21	0.17	0.16	0.16
	Heavy	0.35	0.34	0.32	0.23	0.21	0.21	0.17	0.16	0.16
Additional factor for air point control	Light	0.91	0.91	0.91	0.91	0.91	0.91	0.80	0.80	0.80
	Heavy	0.83	0.83	0.83	0.90	0.90	0.90	0.78	0.78	0.78

Table A9.30 Cooling load due to solar gain through vertical glazing. (10 h plant operation)—W/m²

FOR CONSTANT DRY RESULTANT TEMPERATURE

LIGHTWEIGHT BUILDING
UNPROTECTED 6mm CLEAR GLASS | **50°N**

Date	Climatic constants	Orientation	Sun Time 0800	0900	1000	1100	1200	1300	1400	1500	1600	1700	1800	Orientation
June 21	I = 1.00 k_C = 1.00 k_r = 0.20 C = 0.00	N NE E SE S SW W NW	87 422 550 369 85 102 119 105	94 353 556 444 117 115 132 118	105 239 498 473 200 127 144 129	114 147 387 455 285 141 152 138	119 145 240 389 343 181 158 143	121 146 161 280 361 294 170 145	119 144 159 167 338 397 257 145	113 138 153 136 276 457 399 157	104 129 144 126 186 470 503 252	94 117 132 115 105 435 554 361	92 104 119 101 80 356 541 421	N NE E SE S SW W NW
July 23 and May 22	I = 1.00 k_C = 1.00 k_r = 0.20 C = 0.00	N NE E SE S SW W NW	71 394 536 379 85 99 110 94	84 328 549 459 130 113 124 107	95 213 495 493 225 124 135 119	104 132 383 477 316 140 144 128	110 135 235 411 375 193 150 134	112 137 153 301 394 315 162 135	109 134 151 178 370 419 252 134	103 128 145 133 306 479 395 141	94 119 136 124 211 489 499 227	83 107 124 112 117 450 546 335	75 93 110 98 78 364 526 391	N NE E SE S SW W NW
August 24 and April 22	I = 1.00 k_C = 1.00 k_r = 0.20 C = 0.00	N NE E SE S SW W NW	49 309 474 377 88 87 85 66	63 256 513 478 173 101 99 80	75 150 471 524 287 113 111 92	84 102 364 515 383 132 120 101	90 108 214 454 445 224 126 107	91 110 129 345 465 358 138 109	89 108 127 207 440 461 232 107	83 101 120 122 374 516 376 108	73 92 111 113 273 519 475 163	61 79 98 100 156 467 508 263	48 65 84 86 77 359 459 303	N NE E SE S SW W NW
September 22 and March 21	I = 1.00 k_C = 1.00 k_r = 0.20 C = 0.00	N NE E SE S SW W NW	27 162 303 280 101 62 49 33	43 151 417 441 217 77 64 48	55 77 407 517 342 94 77 61	65 70 317 526 443 130 86 70	70 76 176 477 507 257 92 76	72 78 94 378 527 389 104 77	70 76 92 240 502 483 194 75	64 69 86 116 434 525 327 73	54 60 76 89 328 509 408 85	41 47 63 76 200 425 406 155	25 31 47 60 87 254 278 149	N NE E SE S SW W NW
October 23 and February 21	I = 1.00 k_C = 1.00 k_r = 0.20 C = 0.00	N NE E SE S SW W NW	8 26 64 80 63 36 20 9	25 65 264 312 190 53 37 26	38 40 314 444 330 72 50 39	48 49 256 483 438 134 59 49	53 54 138 453 504 263 65 54	55 56 67 370 525 380 76 56	53 54 65 248 499 457 153 54	46 47 58 118 428 480 264 48	36 37 48 64 314 432 310 43	23 24 35 51 171 288 245 63	6 8 18 35 52 63 48 20	N NE E SE S SW W NW
November 21 and January 21	I = 1.00 k_C = 1.00 k_r = 0.20 C = 0.00	N NE E SE S SW W NW	3 4 13 28 36 24 9 3	8 12 75 105 84 29 14 8	22 22 191 298 240 51 28 22	31 31 182 386 366 123 37 31	37 38 99 386 441 236 43 38	39 39 45 326 465 333 52 39	37 37 43 224 436 387 111 37	30 30 36 109 354 378 185 30	20 20 26 42 222 279 181 21	6 6 12 27 70 88 62 11	3 3 9 24 33 24 9 3	N NE E SE S SW W NW
December 21	I = 1.00 k_C = 1.00 k_r = 0.20 C = 0.00	N NE E SE S SW W NW	2 2 6 19 28 19 6 2	3 3 15 31 38 21 7 3	15 15 133 217 181 40 19 15	25 25 148 327 315 110 29 25	31 31 83 344 396 214 35 31	33 33 37 295 421 301 43 33	30 30 34 202 390 343 92 30	24 24 28 97 302 317 149 24	13 13 17 32 163 198 122 13	2 2 6 19 28 19 6 2	2 2 6 19 28 19 6 2	N NE E SE S SW W NW

Correction factors for tabulated values						
Type of glass	Single glazing		Double glazing with clear 6 mm glass inside		Single glazing and external light slatted blinds used intermittently	
	Lightweight	Heavyweight	Lightweight	Heavyweight	Lightweight	Heavyweight
Clear 6 mm	1.00	0.85	0.85	0.70	0.19	0.19
BTG 6 mm	0.70	0.60	0.53	0.45	0.16	0.16
BTG 10 mm	0.58	0.49	0.40	0.34	0.14	0.14
Reflecting	0.49	0.42	0.37	0.31	0.13	0.13
Strongly reflecting	0.25	0.21	0.16	0.14	0.09	0.10
Additional factor for air point control	0.76	0.73	0.76	0.73	0.76	0.73

Table A9.31 Cooling load due to solar gain through vertical glazing. (10 h plant operation)—W/m²

FOR CONSTANT DRY RESULTANT TEMPERATURE

LIGHTWEIGHT BUILDING INTERMITTENT BLINDS 50°N

Date	Climatic constants	Orientation	Sun Time											Orientation
			0800	0900	1000	1100	1200	1300	1400	1500	1600	1700	1800	
June 21	$I=1.00$	N	78	85	96	105	111	112	110	104	95	85	128	N
		NE	256	183	84	129	127	128	126	120	111	99	86	NE
	$k_c=1.00$	E	380	346	276	183	89	131	129	123	113	102	88	E
		SE	284	310	305	267	202	128	67	106	97	85	72	SE
	$k_r=0.20$	S	65	164	178	222	240	231	196	140	55	85	60	S
		SW	65	79	90	149	174	244	291	307	292	245	172	SW
	$C=0.00$	W	75	88	99	108	114	199	240	316	361	365	322	W
		NW	75	88	99	108	113	115	115	209	229	279	285	NW
July 23 and May 22	$I=1.00$	N	67	80	91	100	106	108	105	99	90	79	106	N
		NE	243	171	81	122	125	126	124	118	108	97	83	NE
	$k_c=1.00$	E	381	349	279	185	89	130	128	121	112	100	86	E
		SE	296	325	320	283	217	137	68	105	95	84	70	SE
	$k_r=0.20$	S	95	130	193	239	258	249	212	154	89	37	54	S
		SW	62	76	87	154	187	259	306	321	304	253	174	SW
	$C=0.00$	W	68	82	93	102	108	194	238	314	357	358	303	W
		NW	67	81	92	101	107	109	108	188	213	261	259	NW
August 24 and April 22	$I=1.00$	N	48	62	74	83	89	91	89	82	73	60	48	N
		NE	191	123	57	95	101	103	101	94	85	72	58	NE
	$k_c=1.00$	E	353	331	263	168	72	108	106	100	90	78	63	E
		SE	307	345	346	310	243	156	64	93	83	71	56	SE
	$k_r=0.20$	S	111	163	232	280	301	291	253	190	113	36	46	S
		SW	48	62	75	162	210	284	330	343	318	254	149	SW
	$C=0.00$	W	51	65	77	86	92	177	226	302	339	323	225	W
		NW	49	63	75	84	90	92	90	144	168	208	175	NW
September 22 and March 21	$I=1.00$	N	27	43	55	64	70	72	69	63	53	41	24	N
		NE	226	38	73	67	72	74	72	65	56	43	27	NE
	$k_c=1.00$	E	485	281	226	136	46	76	73	67	57	44	28	E
		SE	453	337	350	323	260	172	54	84	57	45	28	SE
	$k_r=0.20$	S	142	195	270	320	342	332	292	226	141	37	50	S
		SW	28	44	60	189	232	304	344	346	302	197	40	SW
	$C=0.00$	W	28	43	56	65	71	150	201	267	284	218	46	W
		NW	27	43	55	65	70	72	70	67	148	115	28	NW
October 23 and February 21	$I=1.00$	N	8	25	38	47	53	55	53	46	36	23	6	N
		NE	26	65	39	48	54	56	53	47	37	24	7	NE
	$k_c=1.00$	E	181	213	185	109	32	55	53	47	37	23	7	E
		SE	197	283	323	309	257	177	88	26	38	24	8	SE
	$k_r=0.20$	S	96	188	270	323	346	336	294	222	126	27	15	S
		SW	9	27	86	148	233	296	324	306	223	46	36	SW
	$C=0.00$	W	9	26	39	48	54	122	167	214	190	42	38	W
		NW	9	26	39	48	54	56	54	48	43	63	20	NW
November 21 and January 21	$I=1.00$	N	3	8	22	31	37	39	37	30	20	6	3	N
		NE	4	12	22	31	38	39	37	30	20	6	3	NE
	$k_c=1.00$	E	7	164	131	82	22	40	37	31	21	7	3	E
		SE	9	227	257	267	232	165	85	21	23	8	5	SE
	$k_r=0.20$	S	9	161	227	289	314	302	254	169	37	43	6	S
		SW	5	10	74	137	211	259	267	213	49	69	5	SW
	$C=0.00$	W	4	8	23	32	38	91	122	135	32	57	3	W
		NW	3	8	22	31	38	39	37	30	21	11	3	NW
December 21	$I=1.00$	N	2	3	15	25	31	33	30	24	13	2	2	N
		NE	2	3	15	25	31	33	30	24	13	2	2	NE
	$k_c=1.00$	E	4	12	204	70	19	34	32	25	14	4	4	E
		SE	5	17	365	240	213	153	79	19	18	5	5	SE
	$k_r=0.20$	S	6	16	309	261	288	276	224	130	29	6	6	S
		SW	3	5	64	125	192	233	229	154	38	3	3	SW
	$C=0.00$	W	2	3	15	25	31	76	100	96	20	2	2	W
		NW	2	3	15	25	31	33	30	24	13	2	2	NW

Correction factors for tabulated values											
Type of glass (outside pane for double glazing)	Building weight	Single glazing			Double glazing, internal shade			Double glazing, mid-pane shade		
		Light slatted blind		Linen roller blind	Light slatted blind		Linen roller blind	Light slatted blind		Linen roller blind
		Open	Closed		Open	Closed		Open	Closed	
Clear 6mm	Light	1.00	0.77	0.66	0.95	0.74	0.65	0.58	0.39	0.42
	Heavy	0.97	0.77	0.63	0.94	0.76	0.64	0.56	0.40	0.40
BTG 6mm	Light	0.86	0.77	0.72	0.66	0.55	0.51	0.45	0.36	0.38
	Heavy	0.85	0.77	0.71	0.66	0.57	0.51	0.44	0.37	0.37
BTG 10mm	Light	0.78	0.73	0.70	0.54	0.47	0.45	0.38	0.34	0.36
	Heavy	0.77	0.73	0.70	0.53	0.48	0.45	0.37	0.34	0.34
Reflecting	Light	0.64	0.57	0.54	0.48	0.41	0.38	0.33	0.27	0.29
	Heavy	0.62	0.57	0.53	0.47	0.41	0.38	0.32	0.27	0.28
Strongly reflecting	Light	0.36	0.34	0.32	0.23	0.21	0.21	0.17	0.16	0.16
	Heavy	0.35	0.34	0.32	0.23	0.21	0.21	0.17	0.16	0.16
Additional factor for air point control	Light	0.91	0.91	0.91	0.91	0.91	0.91	0.80	0.80	0.80
	Heavy	0.83	0.83	0.83	0.90	0.90	0.90	0.78	0.78	0.78

Table A9.32 Cooling load due to solar gain through vertical glazing. (10 h plant operation)—W/m²

FOR CONSTANT DRY RESULTANT TEMPERATURE

LIGHTWEIGHT BUILDING — UNPROTECTED 6 mm CLEAR GLASS — 55°N

Date	Climatic constants	Orientation	0800	0900	1000	1100	1200	1300	1400	1500	1600	1700	1800	Orientation
June 21	I = 1.00 k_c = 1.00 k_r = 0.20 C = 0.00	N	87	98	108	116	121	122	120	115	107	97	92	N
		NE	413	332	213	142	146	148	146	140	132	122	110	NE
		E	558	558	498	386	241	163	161	156	148	137	126	E
		SE	392	468	501	486	424	318	193	138	129	119	107	SE
		S	93	141	241	334	395	414	390	325	227	127	86	S
		SW	108	119	129	145	208	331	431	488	497	460	379	SW
		W	126	137	148	155	160	172	258	399	504	557	550	W
		NW	110	122	132	140	145	146	145	150	227	341	414	NW
July 23 and May 22	I = 1.00 k_c = 1.00 k_r = 0.20 C = 0.00	N	72	84	95	103	108	109	107	102	93	83	76	N
		NE	382	305	187	128	133	135	132	127	119	108	96	NE
		E	540	547	491	379	233	153	151	145	137	126	114	E
		SE	398	479	516	504	443	336	204	134	126	115	103	SE
		S	92	156	265	360	422	441	417	351	250	140	84	S
		SW	104	116	126	143	221	349	450	505	512	470	384	SW
		W	114	126	137	145	149	161	250	392	496	545	531	W
		NW	97	109	119	127	132	133	131	135	201	314	382	NW
August 24 and April 22	I = 1.00 k_c = 1.00 k_r = 0.20 C = 0.00	N	48	61	72	80	85	86	84	79	70	59	48	N
		NE	297	234	129	99	104	105	103	98	89	78	65	NE
		E	471	504	461	355	208	125	123	118	109	98	85	E
		SE	384	486	535	531	474	370	231	125	112	101	88	SE
		S	96	194	315	415	478	498	473	405	301	177	85	S
		SW	89	102	114	137	248	382	480	531	530	475	367	SW
		W	86	98	109	117	122	134	226	367	465	500	457	W
		NW	66	79	90	98	103	104	102	103	141	242	293	NW
September 22 and March 21	I = 1.00 k_c = 1.00 k_r = 0.20 C = 0.00	N	24	38	50	58	63	65	63	57	48	37	22	N
		NE	143	130	64	63	68	70	68	62	53	42	27	NE
		E	276	388	383	299	164	85	83	78	69	57	42	E
		SE	259	421	503	519	476	383	250	119	83	71	57	SE
		S	100	218	346	449	514	535	509	439	331	201	86	S
		SW	58	73	89	134	266	393	481	517	495	404	235	SW
		W	44	58	70	78	83	94	181	309	384	377	252	W
		NW	29	43	55	63	68	69	67	64	71	134	132	NW
October 23 and February 21	I = 1.00 k_c = 1.00 k_r = 0.20 C = 0.00	N	5	19	31	40	45	47	45	39	29	17	4	N
		NE	9	47	32	41	46	47	45	40	30	17	4	NE
		E	25	206	272	228	122	56	54	49	39	26	13	E
		SE	42	248	393	446	427	352	238	113	55	42	29	SE
		S	48	157	298	411	480	501	475	400	282	140	39	S
		SW	30	44	63	128	252	361	430	442	380	226	29	SW
		W	14	28	40	49	54	64	136	235	266	187	13	W
		NW	5	19	31	41	46	47	45	40	33	45	4	NW
November 21 and January 21	I = 1.00 k_c = 1.00 k_r = 0.20 C = 0.00	N	2	3	13	23	28	30	28	22	12	2	2	N
		NE	2	3	13	23	28	30	28	22	12	2	2	NE
		E	6	14	123	140	78	33	31	26	15	6	6	E
		SE	18	28	197	305	324	277	188	87	29	18	18	SE
		S	26	35	162	291	371	397	365	279	146	26	26	S
		SW	18	19	36	99	199	284	323	295	180	18	18	SW
		W	6	6	17	27	32	39	87	141	112	6	6	W
		NW	2	2	13	23	28	30	28	22	12	2	2	NW
December 21	I = 1.00 k_c = 1.00 k_r = 0.20 C = 0.00	N	1	2	6	16	22	23	21	15	5	1	1	N
		NE	1	2	6	16	22	23	21	15	5	1	1	NE
		E	4	7	60	99	60	26	24	17	8	4	4	E
		SE	14	18	102	225	263	231	155	67	19	14	14	SE
		S	19	24	89	219	304	331	297	205	77	19	19	S
		SW	14	14	24	78	165	236	261	214	89	14	14	SW
		W	4	4	9	18	24	30	67	97	52	4	4	W
		NW	1	2	6	16	22	23	21	15	5	1	1	NW

Correction factors for tabulated values

Type of glass	Single glazing		Double glazing with clear 6 mm glass inside		Single glazing and external light slatted blinds used intermittently	
	Lightweight	Heavyweight	Lightweight	Heavyweight	Lightweight	Heavyweight
Clear 6 mm	1.00	0.85	0.85	0.70	0.19	0.19
BTG 6 mm	0.70	0.60	0.53	0.45	0.16	0.16
BTG 10 mm	0.58	0.49	0.40	0.34	0.14	0.14
Reflecting	0.49	0.42	0.37	0.31	0.13	0.13
Strongly reflecting	0.25	0.21	0.16	0.14	0.09	0.10
Additional factor for air point control	0.76	0.73	0.76	0.73	0.76	0.73

Table A9.33 Cooling load due to solar gain through vertical glazing. (10 h plant operation)—W/m²

FOR CONSTANT DRY RESULTANT TEMPERATURE

LIGHTWEIGHT BUILDING INTERMITTENT BLINDS 55°N

Date	Climatic constants	Orien-tation	Sun Time 0800	0900	1000	1100	1200	1300	1400	1500	1600	1700	1800	Orien-tation
June 21	I = 1.00 k_c = 1.00 k_r = 0.20 C = 0.00	N	78	89	99	107	112	113	111	106	97	88	124	N
		NE	244	168	83	124	128	129	127	122	114	103	91	NE
		E	384	348	277	185	92	132	130	125	116	106	94	E
		SE	300	328	325	290	225	145	70	106	97	87	75	SE
		S	105	141	206	252	271	262	225	164	97	41	61	S
		SW	68	79	89	161	195	266	311	325	308	260	187	SW
		W	78	90	100	108	113	196	239	315	361	370	334	W
		NW	78	90	100	108	113	114	113	185	214	271	290	NW
July 23 and May 22	I = 1.00 k_c = 1.00 k_r = 0.20 C = 0.00	N	65	78	88	96	101	102	100	95	86	76	101	N
		NE	224	149	72	112	117	118	116	111	103	92	80	NE
		E	375	342	272	178	84	123	121	115	107	96	84	E
		SE	307	338	336	301	236	152	68	101	93	82	70	SE
		S	109	152	220	267	288	278	240	178	104	39	55	S
		SW	62	74	85	164	205	276	321	335	315	264	185	SW
		W	71	83	93	101	106	190	235	311	356	360	315	W
		NW	70	82	92	100	105	106	104	168	197	252	264	NW
August 24 and April 22	I = 1.00 k_c = 1.00 k_r = 0.20 C = 0.00	N	48	61	71	80	85	86	84	79	70	59	48	N
		NE	176	107	53	90	96	97	95	90	81	70	57	NE
		E	346	323	257	162	69	103	100	95	86	75	62	E
		SE	311	352	355	322	258	169	65	92	79	68	55	SE
		S	126	180	252	302	322	313	273	208	126	38	50	S
		SW	49	61	74	177	224	297	341	351	323	259	158	SW
		W	52	64	75	83	88	171	221	296	333	321	236	W
		NW	50	62	73	81	86	88	86	129	154	199	181	NW
September 22 and March 21	I = 1.00 k_c = 1.00 k_r = 0.20 C = 0.00	N	24	38	50	58	63	65	63	57	48	36	22	N
		NE	199	32	60	60	65	66	64	59	50	38	23	NE
		E	446	265	214	127	41	68	66	61	52	40	25	E
		SE	423	327	346	322	263	177	86	33	52	40	25	SE
		S	141	198	275	327	349	339	298	229	141	36	48	S
		SW	25	39	89	146	235	304	340	338	289	182	37	SW
		W	24	39	50	59	64	139	190	253	266	197	45	W
		NW	24	38	50	58	63	65	63	60	125	102	25	NW
October 23 and February 21	I = 1.00 k_c = 1.00 k_r = 0.20 C = 0.00	N	5	19	31	40	45	47	45	39	29	17	4	N
		NE	9	47	32	41	46	47	45	40	30	17	4	NE
		E	18	332	168	100	29	49	47	41	32	19	6	E
		SE	20	417	301	296	250	174	88	25	33	20	7	SE
		S	15	255	255	311	334	324	280	205	106	22	7	S
		SW	6	20	79	143	224	281	303	274	176	40	5	SW
		W	5	19	31	40	45	107	150	186	148	33	4	W
		NW	5	19	31	41	46	47	45	40	33	45	4	NW
November 21 and January 21	I = 1.00 k_c = 1.00 k_r = 0.20 C = 0.00	N	2	3	13	23	28	30	28	22	12	2	2	N
		NE	2	3	13	23	28	30	28	22	12	2	2	NE
		E	3	11	191	66	18	31	29	23	13	3	3	E
		SE	5	15	335	226	202	144	72	17	15	5	5	SE
		S	5	14	280	245	273	260	208	116	27	5	5	S
		SW	3	4	56	117	182	220	214	140	35	3	3	SW
		W	2	3	13	23	28	72	95	88	20	2	2	W
		NW	2	3	13	23	28	30	28	22	12	2	2	NW
December 21	I = 1.00 k_c = 1.00 k_r = 0.20 C = 0.00	N	1	2	6	16	22	23	21	15	5	1	1	N
		NE	1	2	6	16	22	23	21	15	5	1	1	NE
		E	3	6	109	22	59	24	22	16	7	3	3	E
		SE	4	9	200	187	170	121	30	57	9	4	4	SE
		S	4	9	175	204	230	216	157	40	62	4	4	S
		SW	3	4	14	142	154	182	159	81	21	3	3	SW
		W	3	3	8	17	23	29	115	20	51	3	3	W
		NW	1	2	6	16	22	23	21	15	5	1	1	NW

Correction factors for tabulated values

Type of glass (outside pane for double glazing)	Building weight	Single glazing Light slatted blind Open	Closed	Linen roller blind	Double glazing, internal shade Light slatted blind Open	Closed	Linen roller blind	Double glazing, mid-pane shade Light slatted blind Open	Closed	Linen roller blind
Clear 6mm	Light	1.00	0.77	0.66	0.95	0.74	0.65	0.58	0.39	0.42
	Heavy	0.97	0.77	0.63	0.94	0.76	0.64	0.56	0.40	0.40
BTG 6mm	Light	0.86	0.77	0.72	0.66	0.55	0.51	0.45	0.36	0.38
	Heavy	0.85	0.77	0.71	0.66	0.57	0.51	0.44	0.37	0.37
BTG 10mm	Light	0.78	0.73	0.70	0.54	0.47	0.45	0.38	0.34	0.36
	Heavy	0.77	0.73	0.70	0.53	0.48	0.45	0.37	0.34	0.34
Reflecting	Light	0.64	0.57	0.54	0.48	0.41	0.38	0.33	0.27	0.29
	Heavy	0.62	0.57	0.53	0.47	0.41	0.38	0.32	0.27	0.28
Strongly reflecting	Light	0.36	0.34	0.32	0.23	0.21	0.21	0.17	0.16	0.16
	Heavy	0.35	0.34	0.32	0.23	0.21	0.21	0.17	0.16	0.16
Additional factor for air point control	Light	0.91	0.91	0.91	0.91	0.91	0.91	0.80	0.80	0.80
	Heavy	0.83	0.83	0.83	0.90	0.90	0.90	0.78	0.78	0.78

Table A9.34 Cooling load due to solar gain through vertical glazing. (10 h plant operation)—W/m²

FOR CONSTANT DRY RESULTANT TEMPERATURE

LIGHTWEIGHT BUILDING — UNPROTECTED 6mm CLEAR GLASS — 60°N

Date	Climatic constants	Orientation	0800	0900	1000	1100	1200	1300	1400	1500	1600	1700	1800	Orientation
June 21	I = 1.00, k_c = 1.00, k_r = 0.20, C = 0.00	N	93	103	112	119	123	124	122	118	111	102	97	N
		NE	403	312	192	144	148	149	147	143	136	127	116	NE
		E	565	559	497	385	242	165	164	159	152	143	132	E
		SE	413	490	524	513	454	351	220	139	132	123	112	SE
		S	101	169	282	378	440	459	435	369	268	153	92	S
		SW	113	123	132	149	237	364	461	514	520	481	400	SW
		W	132	142	151	158	162	174	259	398	503	558	558	W
		NW	117	127	136	142	147	148	146	150	206	322	406	NW
July 23 and May 22	I = 1.00, k_c = 1.00, k_r = 0.20, C = 0.00	N	77	87	96	103	108	109	107	102	95	86	80	N
		NE	372	284	168	129	133	134	133	128	121	112	101	NE
		E	545	546	488	377	232	153	151	147	139	130	120	E
		SE	415	497	535	526	469	366	231	137	127	118	108	SE
		S	100	183	301	399	461	481	456	390	287	166	90	S
		SW	108	118	128	147	248	378	475	527	531	488	402	SW
		W	120	130	139	146	150	162	249	389	493	544	537	W
		NW	101	112	121	128	132	133	132	134	181	295	374	NW
August 24 and April 22	I = 1.00, k_c = 1.00, k_r = 0.20, C = 0.00	N	48	59	68	75	80	81	79	75	67	58	48	N
		NE	284	213	112	95	99	101	99	94	87	77	65	NE
		E	465	492	449	345	202	121	119	114	107	97	86	E
		SE	389	489	541	540	488	388	251	131	111	101	90	SE
		S	105	213	337	439	502	522	498	429	324	196	92	S
		SW	90	102	114	144	268	400	493	540	535	478	373	SW
		W	86	98	107	114	118	130	219	357	453	489	452	W
		NW	66	78	87	94	98	100	98	98	123	222	282	NW
September 22 and March 21	I = 1.00, k_c = 1.00, k_r = 0.20, C = 0.00	N	21	34	44	51	56	57	55	51	43	32	19	N
		NE	124	110	53	56	60	62	60	55	47	36	23	NE
		E	245	354	356	277	151	76	74	69	62	51	38	E
		SE	235	392	480	501	465	378	252	121	77	66	53	SE
		S	96	211	340	443	509	530	504	434	326	195	83	S
		SW	54	67	83	135	267	388	469	499	471	376	212	SW
		W	39	52	62	70	74	85	167	287	356	343	223	W
		NW	25	38	48	55	60	61	59	56	59	114	114	NW
October 23 and February 21	I = 1.00, k_c = 1.00, k_r = 0.20, C = 0.00	N	4	12	24	32	37	38	36	31	23	11	3	N
		NE	6	30	25	32	37	39	37	31	23	11	3	NE
		E	19	141	220	194	104	46	44	38	30	18	10	E
		SE	34	176	325	391	385	322	218	101	45	33	25	SE
		S	40	117	250	364	436	458	430	353	235	102	34	S
		SW	25	34	52	116	231	330	387	386	311	157	25	SW
		W	11	20	32	39	44	53	116	199	213	127	10	W
		NW	4	13	24	32	37	39	36	31	25	29	3	NW
November 21 and January 21	I = 1.00, k_c = 1.00, k_r = 0.20, C = 0.00	N	1	1	5	13	19	20	18	12	4	1	1	N
		NE	1	1	5	13	19	20	18	12	4	1	1	NE
		E	3	6	48	88	54	23	20	14	6	3	3	E
		SE	12	16	82	195	234	206	135	55	15	12	12	SE
		S	17	20	71	188	269	295	262	175	60	17	17	S
		SW	12	12	20	65	145	211	231	185	70	12	12	SW
		W	3	3	7	15	21	27	60	85	42	3	3	W
		NW	1	1	5	13	19	20	18	12	4	1	1	NW
December 21	I = 1.00, k_c = 1.00, k_r = 0.20, C = 0.00	N	1	1	1	6	11	12	10	5	1	1	1	N
		NE	1	1	1	6	11	12	10	5	1	1	1	NE
		E	1	1	5	42	33	13	11	6	1	1	1	E
		SE	7	7	12	99	152	141	88	29	7	7	7	SE
		S	10	10	15	97	176	202	169	87	10	10	10	S
		SW	7	7	9	35	95	144	148	87	7	7	7	SW
		W	1	1	2	7	12	16	35	39	1	1	1	W
		NW	1	1	1	6	11	12	10	5	1	1	1	NW

Correction factors for tabulated values

Type of glass	Single glazing		Double glazing with clear 6 mm glass inside		Single glazing and external light slatted blinds used intermittently	
	Lightweight	Heavyweight	Lightweight	Heavyweight	Lightweight	Heavyweight
Clear 6 mm	1.00	0.85	0.85	0.70	0.19	0.19
BTG 6 mm	0.70	0.60	0.53	0.45	0.16	0.16
BTG 10 mm	0.58	0.49	0.40	0.34	0.14	0.14
Reflecting	0.49	0.42	0.37	0.31	0.13	0.13
Strongly reflecting	0.25	0.21	0.16	0.14	0.09	0.10
Additional factor for air point control	0.76	0.73	0.76	0.73	0.76	0.73

Table A9.35 Cooling load due to solar gain through vertical glazing. (10 h plant operation)—W/m²

FOR CONSTANT DRY RESULTANT TEMPERATURE

LIGHTWEIGHT BUILDING INTERMITTENT BLINDS 60°N

Date	Climatic constants	Orientation	0800	0900	1000	1100	1200	1300	1400	1500	1600	1700	1800	Orientation
June 21	I = 1.00 k_c = 1.00 k_r = 0.20 C = 0.00	N	79	89	98	105	109	110	109	104	97	88	120	N
		NE	230	152	82	122	126	127	125	121	114	105	94	NE
		E	384	346	275	183	92	130	128	124	117	108	97	E
		SE	315	345	343	309	246	163	73	105	97	88	78	SE
		S	120	164	232	280	300	290	252	189	114	44	62	S
		SW	70	80	89	174	214	284	328	340	322	273	201	SW
		W	83	93	102	108	113	193	237	314	361	373	346	W
		NW	83	93	102	109	113	114	113	170	201	264	294	NW
July 23 and May 22	I = 1.00 k_c = 1.00 k_r = 0.20 C = 0.00	N	72	83	92	99	103	104	102	98	91	81	75	N
		NE	213	136	74	113	117	118	116	112	104	95	85	NE
		E	377	342	271	178	86	123	121	116	109	100	89	E
		SE	320	352	351	318	255	169	72	102	92	83	72	SE
		S	124	174	244	293	313	303	264	200	121	43	58	S
		SW	64	75	85	178	222	293	336	348	327	275	198	SW
		W	73	84	93	100	104	185	231	308	354	362	326	W
		NW	72	83	92	99	103	104	102	153	183	244	267	NW
August 24 and April 22	I = 1.00 k_c = 1.00 k_r = 0.20 C = 0.00	N	48	59	68	75	80	81	79	74	67	57	48	N
		NE	164	96	52	88	92	93	92	87	79	70	58	NE
		E	341	317	252	159	68	99	98	93	85	76	64	E
		SE	315	357	363	333	270	182	67	98	78	68	56	SE
		S	141	193	268	318	339	330	289	222	138	41	56	S
		SW	49	60	73	193	236	307	348	355	326	262	166	SW
		W	51	62	72	79	85	162	213	287	325	315	244	W
		NW	49	60	69	76	81	82	80	114	140	189	183	NW
September 22 and March 21	I = 1.00 k_c = 1.00 k_r = 0.20 C = 0.00	N	21	34	44	51	56	57	55	50	43	32	19	N
		NE	171	27	50	53	57	59	57	52	44	33	20	NE
		E	401	247	200	118	37	60	58	53	46	35	22	E
		SE	387	312	335	316	262	179	88	30	46	35	22	SE
		S	136	196	273	326	348	338	296	227	138	34	45	S
		SW	22	35	88	147	234	299	331	324	271	163	36	SW
		W	21	34	45	52	56	127	177	236	244	174	42	W
		NW	21	34	44	51	56	57	55	52	105	88	22	NW
October 23 and February 21	I = 1.00 k_c = 1.00 k_r = 0.20 C = 0.00	N	4	12	24	32	37	38	36	31	23	11	3	N
		NE	6	30	24	32	37	39	36	31	23	11	3	NE
		E	13	245	143	86	23	40	38	32	24	12	5	E
		SE	14	314	262	268	230	161	80	21	25	14	6	SE
		S	12	198	226	285	309	298	252	174	79	17	6	S
		SW	5	13	70	132	207	257	269	230	124	32	4	SW
		W	4	12	24	32	37	92	128	153	102	27	3	W
		NW	4	13	24	32	37	39	36	31	25	29	3	NW
November 21 and January 21	I = 1.00 k_c = 1.00 k_r = 0.20 C = 0.00	N	1	1	5	13	19	20	18	12	4	1	1	N
		NE	1	1	5	13	19	20	18	12	4	1	1	NE
		E	2	5	92	20	53	22	19	13	5	2	2	E
		SE	3	7	165	168	152	107	26	47	7	3	3	SE
		S	4	7	143	180	207	191	137	36	47	4	4	S
		SW	3	4	11	122	139	163	137	39	62	3	3	SW
		W	2	2	6	14	20	26	103	17	41	2	2	W
		NW	1	1	5	13	19	20	18	12	4	1	1	NW
December 21	I = 1.00 k_c = 1.00 k_r = 0.20 C = 0.00	N	1	1	1	6	11	12	10	5	1	1	1	N
		NE	1	1	1	6	11	12	10	5	1	1	1	NE
		E	1	1	5	42	33	13	11	6	1	1	1	E
		SE	2	2	8	168	109	74	17	25	2	2	2	SE
		S	3	3	8	172	144	130	79	20	3	3	3	S
		SW	1	1	4	75	95	105	75	21	1	1	1	SW
		W	1	1	2	7	12	16	35	39	1	1	1	W
		NW	1	1	1	6	11	12	10	5	1	1	1	NW

Correction factors for tabulated values

Type of glass (outside pane for double glazing)	Building weight	Single glazing			Double glazing, internal shade			Double glazing, mid-pane shade		
		Light slatted blind		Linen roller blind	Light slatted blind		Linen roller blind	Light slatted blind		Linen roller blind
		Open	Closed		Open	Closed		Open	Closed	
Clear 6mm	Light	1.00	0.77	0.66	0.95	0.74	0.65	0.58	0.39	0.42
	Heavy	0.97	0.77	0.63	0.94	0.76	0.64	0.56	0.40	0.40
BTG 6mm	Light	0.86	0.77	0.72	0.66	0.55	0.51	0.45	0.36	0.38
	Heavy	0.85	0.77	0.71	0.66	0.57	0.51	0.44	0.37	0.37
BTG 10mm	Light	0.78	0.73	0.70	0.54	0.47	0.45	0.38	0.34	0.36
	Heavy	0.77	0.73	0.70	0.53	0.48	0.45	0.37	0.34	0.34
Reflecting	Light	0.64	0.57	0.54	0.48	0.41	0.38	0.33	0.27	0.29
	Heavy	0.62	0.57	0.53	0.47	0.41	0.38	0.32	0.27	0.28
Strongly reflecting	Light	0.36	0.34	0.32	0.23	0.21	0.21	0.17	0.16	0.16
	Heavy	0.35	0.34	0.32	0.23	0.21	0.21	0.17	0.16	0.16
Additional factor for air point control	Light	0.91	0.91	0.91	0.91	0.91	0.91	0.80	0.80	0.80
	Heavy	0.83	0.83	0.83	0.90	0.90	0.90	0.78	0.78	0.78

CIBSE GUIDE—SECTION A9
ESTIMATION OF PLANT CAPACITY
Supplement A9/1

INTRODUCTION
General

Some designers have raised queries concerning the calculation procedures contained in Section A9 of the *Guide*. These notes have been prepared by a small Task Group to assist in the correct application of these methods. It should be appreciated that the need for extra care results from the improved accuracy of the current method, both in the assessment of heat losses and in the way that heat is introduced into the space by the different types of heat emitter. The sensible heating and cooling capacities determined by these calculation procedures do not incorporate safety margins except where specifically indicated and it is incumbent upon the designer to assess the plant margin required in particular circumstances.

Revisions to Other Guide Sections

Since the publication of the 1979 edition of Section A9, several closely related Sections have also been revised and particular attention is drawn to the following:

    Section A2 (1982) Weather and Solar Data
    Section A3 (1980) Thermal Properties of Building
                      Structures

Section A2 should be used to determine appropriate external design condition for both heating and cooling load calculations. Time lags and decrement factors are now tabulated in Section A3.

The example calculation for air conditioning plant (Appendix 2 in Section A9) has been revised to take account of these changes. See page 2 of this supplement.

Calculation Temperatures

The current edition of Section A9 shows how environmental temperature (t_{ei}) is used to determine the steady-state fabric heat requirement, and air temperature (t_{ai}) to determine the ventilation heat requirement (editions prior to 1970 used air temperatures only). The Section also shows how these temperatures may be related to dry resultant temperature by the use of factors F_1 and F_2. Since the occupants respond to both the radiant and air temperatures in the room Section A1 recommends the use of dry resultant temperature (t_c) as an index of thermal comfort. For practical purposes, dry resultant temperature is the average of the air and mean radiant temperatures. This combined temperature is used in the calculation of design loads. The plant capacity required to maintain a specified dry resultant temperature will depend upon the type of heating system chosen. Appendix 1, page A9.16, demonstrates how two different systems achieve and maintain a dry resultant temperature of 19°C. In summary:

	t_c/°C	t_{ei}/°C	t_{ai}/°C	Q_p/kW
Warm air system	19.0	18.0	22.4	15.5
Radiant Strip	19.0	20.2	15.6	14.6

It is important to note that, although the same dry resultant temperature is achieved, the air temperatures are

significantly different. As controllers and thermometers respond predominantly to air temperature, the designer must take care to specify which of these temperatures is to be maintained by the system. This has particular relevance in circumstances where a legal minimum temperature is prescribed, for example, where the Offices, Shops and Railway Premises Act 1963 requires a minimum temperature of 15.6°C to be achieved within one hour of the start of the occupied period.

HEATING
Steady State Heat Requirements

Because the type of heating system selected can have a significant effect on the calculated design load, it is essential that suitable values for F_1 and F_2 are employed in the calculation of the steady state heat requirement. It should be borne in mind that the radiative component of wall-mounted heat emitters will be considerably reduced if situated behind furniture. Similarly, the radiative component of floor warming systems will be reduced by carpets or other floor coverings. If these circumstances are likely to be encountered at any time during the life of the building, values appropriate to 100% convective heating may be more realistic, see Table A9.1.

Intermittent Heating

The above notes are concerned only with steady state heat loss and continuous operation. If intermittent operation is intended, some additional capacity will be required, both in central plant and individual emitters, to bring the building up to the desired temperature after a period of overnight or week-end cooling. In such cases, it is recommended that the total output under boosted intermittent operating conditions, Q_{pb}, be calculated using equation A9.18.

The values of F_3, given in Table A9.9 are based on early work by the Heating and Ventilating Research Association[1] (now BSRIA). The following formula is suggested as an alternative method by which F_3 may be calculated from the response factor, f_r, and the total hours of plant operation, n, including pre-heat, but neglecting the time for the system to reach its operating conditions:

$$F_3 = \zeta \left(\frac{(24 - n)(f_r - 1)}{24 + n(f_r - 1)} \right) + 1$$

The response factor is a measure of the thermal 'weight' of the building, see Table A9.9, Note 5 and is given by:

$$f_r = \frac{\Sigma(AY) + \frac{1}{3}NV}{\Sigma(AU) + \frac{1}{3}NV}$$

Values of thermal admittance, Y, for most constructions are tabulated in Section A3 of the Guide. The empirical factor ζ is included to ensure that the desired temperature is achieved nearer the start, rather than at the end of the occupied period, see Section A5, Fig. A5.12. For the time being, it is suggested that ζ be given the value 1.2.

If large values of F_3 are obtained, it may be preferable to extend the pre-heat period or operate continuously rather than greatly oversize the plant capacity. This decision is principally one of economics, based on considerations of capital and running costs. Attention is drawn to the notes concerning oversizing of heat emitters on page A9.8.

Example

Taking typical Y-values from Section A3 for the example given in Appendix 1, F_3 is calculated as follows:

Surface*	Area, A	U-value	(AU)	Y-value	(AY)
Floor	112.5	0.5	56.3	5.2	585.0
Roof	112.5	0.3	33.8	0.7	78.6
External walls	171.0	0.5	85.5	3.5	598.5
Glass	48.0	5.7	273.6	5.7	273.6
Doors	6.0	2.9	17.4	2.9	17.4
$\Sigma(A) = 450.0$		$\Sigma(AU) = 466.6$		$\Sigma(AY) = 1553.1$	

*Include internal partitions, if present.

Also:

$$\tfrac{1}{3}NV = \tfrac{1}{3} \times 1\tfrac{1}{2} \times 563$$

$$= 281.5 \ \text{W/m}^2\,\text{K}$$

Hence:

$$f_r = \frac{1553 + 282}{467 + 282} = 2.4$$

For eight hours plant operation, including one hour pre-heat:

$$F_3 = 1.2 \left(\frac{(24-8)(2.4-1)}{24 + 8(2.4-1)} \right) + 1 = 1.8$$

Thus, excluding distribution and back losses and neglecting internal heat gains, the calculated plant capacity is:

Warm air system: $Q_{pb} = 1.8 \times 15.5 = 27.9 \ \text{kW}$
Radiant strip   : $Q_{pb} = 1.8 \times 14.6 = 26.3 \ \text{kW}$

AIR CONDITIONING

Sensible Cooling Loads

Value of the climatic constants (I, k_c, k_r and C) are given in Tables A9.14 to 35 for information only and are not required for the calculation of cooling loads in the UK. Their derivation is discussed in detail in Section A2 (1982).

Cooling Loads due to Conduction

The factors F_u, F_y, F_v, F_{au}, and F_{ay} are determined as follows:

$$F_u = \frac{h_{ec}\,\Sigma(A)}{h_{ec}\Sigma(A) + \Sigma(AU)} \qquad \cdots \qquad \cdots \qquad \cdots \qquad \text{A5.19}$$

$$F_y = \frac{h_{ec}\,\Sigma(A)}{h_{ec}\,\Sigma(A) + \Sigma(AY)} \qquad \cdots \qquad \cdots \qquad \cdots \qquad \text{A5.36}$$

$$F_v = \frac{h_{ac}\,\Sigma(A)}{h_{ac}\,\Sigma(A) + \tfrac{1}{3}NV} \qquad \cdots \qquad \cdots \qquad \cdots \qquad \text{A5.18}$$

$$F_{au} = \frac{h_a\,\Sigma(A)}{h_a\Sigma(A) + \Sigma(AU)} \qquad \cdots \qquad \cdots \qquad \cdots \qquad \text{A5.22}$$

$$F_{ay} = \frac{h_a\,\Sigma(A)}{h_a\Sigma(A) + \Sigma(AY)} \qquad \cdots \qquad \cdots \qquad \cdots \qquad \text{A5.39}$$

The heat transfer coefficients take the following values:

$h_a = 4.5 \ \text{W/m}^2\,\text{K}$
$h_{ec} = 18 \ \text{W/m}^2\,\text{K}$
$h_{ac} = 6 \ \text{W/m}^2\,\text{K}$

Note that in early editions, equation A9.26 should be amended to read:

$$\tilde{Q}_{ua} = \frac{F_y}{F_v} AUf\tilde{t}_{eo(\theta-\varphi)} \qquad \cdots \qquad \cdots \qquad \cdots \qquad \text{A9.26}$$

Cooling Load due to Air Infiltration

Note that in early editions, equations A9.28 should be amended to read:

$$Q_v = \tfrac{1}{3}NVF_2(t_{ao}-t_c) \qquad \cdots \qquad \cdots \qquad \cdots \qquad \cdots \qquad \text{A9.28}$$

In the case of control on dry-resultant temperature and plant cooling at the air point, values of F_2 appropriate to 100% convective should be used, see Table A9.1. Alternatively, the following equation may be used:

$$F_2 = 1 + \frac{F_u\,\Sigma(AU)}{h_{ac}\,\Sigma(A)}$$

Fluctuations in Control Temperature

It should be noted that equations A9.29 and 30 (page A9.13) are approximate and are based on the assumption that the rise in temperature is sufficiently small for the 24 hour mean values to be unaffected. These expressions are *only* valid under these circumstances.

Air Conditioning Example (Appendix 2, page A9.17)

This example has been re-calculated, as follows, using U and Y values more representative of current practice. Orientation, location and dimensions: as given on page A9.17. Construction: see Section A3, as follows:

Surface	Area, A	U-value	(AU)	Y-value	(AY)	Decrement Factor, f	Time lag φ
External wall Table A3.17, 5(e)	8.0	0.49	3.9	4.3	34.4	0.2	9
Internal wall Table A3.20, 7(b)	42.0	0*	0	2.3	96.6	–	–
Roof Table A3.19, 7(b)	20.0	0.54	10.8	0.77	15.4	0.99	1
Internal floor Table A3.21, 2(b)	20.0	0*	0	3.2	64.0	–	–
Window Table A3.14	4.0	5.7	22.8	5.7	22.8	1	0
	$\Sigma(A) = 94.0$		$\Sigma(AU) = 37.5$		$\Sigma(AY) = 233.2$		

*No steady-stage heat flow through these surfaces, hence effective U-value is zero, see equation A5.16.

Solution (a)—Dry Resultant Temperature Control ($t_c = 21°C$)
Determine response factor, f_r, as follows:

Volume of room, $V = 60 \text{ m}^3$
Number of air changes, $N = 1 \text{ h}^{-1}$

Hence:

$$\tfrac{1}{3} NV = 20$$

$$f_r = \frac{233.2 + 20}{37.5 + 20} = 4.4 \text{ (Medium weight)}$$

Determine solar gain from Table A9.15 at mid-day (sun-time) in late September and apply correction factor for single clear 6 mm glazing with closed, light-slatted blind (interpolating for medium weight building, if necessary).

$$\text{Solar gain} = 333 \times 0.77 \times 4 = 1025.6 \text{ W}$$

Determine F_u from equation A5.19:

$$F_u = \frac{h_{ec} \Sigma(A)}{h_{ec} \Sigma(A) + \Sigma(AU)}$$

$$h_{ec} = 18 \text{ W/m}^2 \text{ K}$$

$$F_u = \frac{18 \times 94}{(18 \times 94) + 37.5} = \frac{1692}{1730} = 0.98$$

Determine F_v from equation A5.18:

$$F_v = \frac{h_{ac} \Sigma(A)}{h_{ac} \Sigma(A) + \tfrac{1}{3} NV}$$

$$h_{ac} = 6 \text{ W/m}^2 \text{ K}$$

$$F_v = \frac{6 \times 94}{(6 \times 94) + 20} = \frac{564}{584} = 0.97$$

Hence:

$$\frac{F_u}{F_v} = \frac{0.98}{0.97} = 1.01$$

Determine temperatures appropriate to light coloured, South facing wall and dark roof using Table A2.33(g):

$$\bar{t}_{eo} \text{ (wall)} = 20.5°C$$

$$\bar{t}_{eo} \text{ (roof)} = 20.0°C$$

$$\bar{t}_{ao} = 15.5°C$$

Hence, using equation A9.25, the mean conduction gains at the air point are:

Wall : $1.01 \times 8 \times 0.49 \times (20.5 - 21) = -2.0 \text{ W}$

Roof : $1.01 \times 20 \times 0.54 \times (20.0 - 21) = -10.9 \text{ W}$

Window: $1.01 \times 4 \times 5.7 \times (15.5 - 21) = -126.6 \text{ W}$

$$\text{Total Gain} = -139.5 \text{ W}$$

Cyclic loads are calculated as follows:

Determine F_y from equation A5.36:

$$F_y = \frac{h_{ec} \quad (A)}{h_{ec} \Sigma(A) + \Sigma(AY)}$$

$$h_{ec} = 18 \text{ W/m}^2 \text{ K}$$

$$F_y = \frac{18 \times 94}{(18 \times 94) + 233.2} = \frac{1692}{1925} = 0.88$$

Hence:

$$\frac{F_y}{F_v} = \frac{0.88}{0.97} = 0.91$$

Again, from Table A2.33(g):

$$\tilde{t}_{eo} \text{ (wall)} = 10.5 - 20.5 \text{ (at 0300 h)} = -10.0°C$$

$$\tilde{t}_{eo} \text{ (roof)} = 38.0 - 20.0 \text{ (at 1100 h)} = 18.0°C$$

$$\tilde{t}_{ao} = 18.5 - 15.5 \text{ (at 1200 h)} = 3.0°C$$

Hence, using equation A9.26, cyclic gains at the air point are:

Wall : $0.91 \times 8 \times 0.49 \times 0.2 \times (-10.0) = -7.1 \text{ W}$

Roof : $0.91 \times 20 \times 0.54 \times 0.99 \times (18.0) = 175.1 \text{ W}$

Window: $0.91 \times 4 \times 5.7 \times 1.0 \times (3.0) = 62.2 \text{ W}$

$$\text{Total Gain} = 230.2 \text{ W}$$

Cooling load due to internal gains $= 90 \text{ W}$

Cooling load due to infiltration is found using equation A9.28.

F_2 is obtained from Table A9.1, as follows:

$$\frac{NV}{3 \Sigma(A)} = \frac{60}{3 \times 94} = 0.2$$

$$\frac{\Sigma(AU)}{\Sigma(A)} = \frac{37.5}{94} = 0.4$$

Hence, $F_2 = 1.07$

Thus:

$$Q_v = \tfrac{1}{3} \times 1 \times 60 \times 1.07 (15.5 - 21) = -117.7 \text{ W}$$

Total sensible cooling load at the air point to hold the dry resultant temperature constant is the sum of the individual components:

$$1025.6 - 139.5 + 230.2 + 90 - 117.7 = 1088.6 \text{ W}$$

Solution (b)—Air Temperature Control ($t_{ai} = 21°C$)

The solar gain through the window has an additional air point correction obtained by interpolation for medium weight building, see bottom of Table A9.15.

$$\text{Solar gain} = 333 \times 0.77 \times 4 \times 0.87 = 892.3 \text{ W}$$

The 24 hour mean conductance loads at the air point, for air temperature control, require the evaluation of F_{au} from equation A5.22.

$$F_{au} = \frac{h_a \quad (A)}{h_a \Sigma(A) + \Sigma(AU)}$$

$$h_a = 4.5 \text{ W/m}^2 \text{ K}$$

$$F_{au} = \frac{4.5 \times 94}{(4.5 \times 94) + 37.5} = \frac{423}{461} = 0.92$$

The conductance loads are now:

Wall   : $0.92 \times 8 \times 0.49 \times (20.5 - 21) = -1.7$ W

Roof   : $0.92 \times 20 \times 0.54 \times (20.0 - 21) = -9.9$ W

Window : $0.92 \times 4 \times 5.7 \times (15.5 - 21) = -115.4$ W

$$\text{Total Gain} = -127.0 \text{ W}$$

The cyclic conduction loads are calculated using equation A9.26 substituting F_{ay} for F_y/F_v. F_{ay} is determined from equation A5.39, as follows:

$$F_{ay} = \frac{h_a \Sigma(A)}{h_a \Sigma(A) + \Sigma(AY)}$$

$$F_{ay} = \frac{4.5 \times 94}{(4.5 \times 94) + 233.2} = \frac{423}{656} = 0.64$$

Hence:

Wall   : $0.64 \times 8 \times 0.49 \times 0.2 \times (-10.0) = -5.0$ W

Roof   : $0.64 \times 20 \times 0.54 \times 0.99 \times (18.0) = 123.2$ W

Window : $0.64 \times 4 \times 5.7 \times 1.0 \times (3.0) = 43.8$ W

$$\text{Total Gain} = 162.0 \text{ W}$$

Cooling load due to internal gains = 90 W

Cooling load due to infiltration is found using equation A9.27:

$$Q_v = \frac{1}{3} \times 1 \times 60 (15.5 - 21) = -110 \text{ W}$$

Total sensible cooling load at the air point to hold the air temperature constant is:

$$892.3 - 127.0 + 162.0 + 90 - 110 = 907.3 \text{ W}$$

Reference

1. Intermittent Heating, HVRA Laboratory Report No. 26, 1964, Building Services Research and Information Association.

SECTION A10 MOISTURE TRANSFER AND CONDENSATION

Introduction ....*Page* A10–3

Notation A10–3

Hygroscopic Materials A10–3

Evaporation and Condensation at Plane Surfaces A10–4

Vapour Diffusion within Materials A10–5

Vapour Diffusion in Composite Structures A10–6

Prediction of Moisture Condensation A10–12

Sources of Moisture A10–14

Controlling and Eliminating Condensation A10–14

References A10–17

Appendix: Algorithm for Interstitial Condensation A10–18

This edition of Section A10 first published: 1986

SECTION A10 MOISTURE TRANSFER AND CONDENSATION

INTRODUCTION

Serious moisture problems can be caused by an inadequate understanding of the behaviour of water in buildings. Although calculations are not always straightforward, this Section of the *Guide* gives procedures for condensation prediction, control of moisture content and guidelines on how to avoid or minimise problems. Industrial drying and moisture conditioning are not included in this Section.

HYGROSCOPIC MATERIALS

Most materials will take up water when exposed to moist air, the equilibrium quantity depending on the nature of the material, its pore structure and the moisture saturation of the air. This phenomenon is of considerable importance in certain industries (eg. textiles, tobacco) and in assessing the thermal conductivity of building and insulating materials, see Section A3 of the *Guide*. Table A10.1 lists equilibrium moisture contents for various materials.

NOTATION

H	= specific enthalpy (sensible or latent) of room air (per kilogram of dry air)	kJ/kg
H_a	= specific enthalpy (sensible or latent) of supply air	kJ/kg
H_o	= initial specific enthalpy (sensible or latent) of room air	kJ/kg
H'	= specific enthalpy of room air, evaluated for sensible heat gain	kJ/kg
Nu	= Nusselt number	
Q_l	= rate of latent heat gain	W
G	= vapour resistance of element ..	N s/kg
G_i	= vapour resistance of inner element	N s/kg
G_o	= vapour resistance of outer element	N s/kg
G_t	= total vapour resistance of structure	N s/kg
G_s	= surface vapour resistance	N s/kg
$\mathscr{R}$	= gas constant	J/kg K
R_1	= thermal resistance of element 1, etc.	m² K/W
R_{si}	= inside surface thermal resistance	m² K/W
R_{so}	= outside surface thermal resistance	m² K/W
R_t	= total thermal resistance of structure	m² K/W
T	= absolute temperature	K
c_p	= specific heat capacity at constant pressure	J/kg K
d	= distance (or thickness)	m
g_a	= moisture content of supply air ..	kg/kg
g_{max}	= maximum moisture content of room air to avoid condensation	kg/kg
h_c	= convective heat transfer coefficient	W/m² K
h_m	= surface mass transfer coefficient	m/s
h_{m1}	= surface mass transfer coefficient at surface 1, etc.	m/s
l_e	= specific latent heat of evaporation	J/kg
m_v	= rate of vapour mass transfer per unit area	kg/m² s
m_{vi}	= rate of vapour mass transfer per unit area through inner element	kg/m² s
m_{vo}	= rate of vapour mass transfer per unit area through outer element	kg/m² s
n	= room air change rate	h⁻¹
p_s	= saturation vapour pressure at surface temperature	Pa
p_{v1}	= vapour pressure at surface 1, etc. of material	Pa
p_{va}	= vapour pressure in air	Pa
p_{vi}	= vapour pressure at inside surface	Pa
p_{vo}	= vapour pressure at outside surface	Pa
q	= rate of flow of heat per unit area	W/m²
r	= vapour resistivity	N s/kg m
t_d	= dry-bulb temperature	°C
t_{ai}	= inside air temperature	°C
t_{ao}	= outside air temperature	°C
t_1	= temperature at surface 1, etc. of material	°C
v	= volume flow rate of supply air ..	m³ /s
w	= condensation (or evaporation) rate	kg/m² s
w_1	= condensation (or evaporation) rate at surface 1, etc.	kg/m² s
Δ	= change in	
Σ	= sum of	
δ	= vapour permeability	kg m/N s
λ	= thermal conductivity	W/m K
μ	= diffusion resistance factor	
ρ_a	= density of air	kg/m³
θ	= time period	h

Table A10.1. Equilibrium moisture content of materials[1].

Material	Density / (kg/m³)	Moisture content at 50% saturation of ambient air/ (% by mass)
Brick	1600	0.5
Concrete	2300	1
Plaster		
Lime sand	1750	1
Cement sand	2000	1
Cork	95	1
Glasswool slab	120	0.5
Mineral wool	–	0
Slag wool	–	0
Strawboard	–	10
Woodwool/cement slab	360	10

Note:
For newly constructed buildings, moisture contents will be higher than that stated until 'drying out' is completed.

The moisture absorption is largely, though not solely, due to capillary forces. The vapour pressure over a concave surface is less than that over a plane surface, and water will condense upon any surface whose radius is such that the corresponding vapour pressure is less than that in the ambient air. If the radius is small enough, condensation will occur from unsaturated atmospheres. Table A10.2 shows the saturation of an air/water vapour mixture which is in equilibrium with a concave surface. If the saturation is greater than that given in Table A10.2, water will condense on the surface.

For example, a dry material containing pores of 2.1 nm radius will take up water from an atmosphere which is 60% saturated and these pores, and any smaller pores, will become filled with water. This process can contribute to the movement of water vapour through building materials. Thus, if the opposite face of the material is exposed to an atmosphere which is 40% saturated, moisture will evaporate from the pore menisci so that a state of dynamic equilibrium is set up; water condensing at one side, moving under capillary forces through the material to the other side and there evaporating.

Table A10.2. Pore radius for hygroscopic equilibrium.

Radius of curvature of pores/nm	Saturation of ambient air for equilibrium/%
2.1	60
5	80
10	90
100	99

EVAPORATION AND CONDENSATION AT PLANE SURFACES

Condensation of water occurs whenever moist air comes into contact with a surface whose temperature is below the dew-point temperature of the air. The dew-point (100% saturation) temperature can be found from the psychrometric data in Section C1 of the *Guide* while the surface temperature will be either measured or computed. Condensation cannot occur if the surface temperature is above the dew-point temperature and if the surface is wet under these conditions the moisture evaporates into the air.

For water vapour in air, the surface coefficient for mass transfer is related to the convective heat transfer coefficient by the Lewis relation:

$$h_m = \frac{h_c}{\rho_a c_p} \quad \dots \dots \dots \dots \dots \dots \dots \quad \text{A10.1}$$

where:

h_m = surface mass transfer coefficient ..   m/s
h_c = convective heat transfer coefficient   .. ..   W/m² K
ρ_a = density of air   .. ..   kg/m³
c_p = specific heat capacity at constant pressure   .. ..   J/kg K

At room temperature,

$$\rho_a \simeq 1.2 \text{ kg/m}^3 \text{ and } c_p = 1000 \text{ J/kg K}$$

Hence, equation A10.1 becomes:

$$h_m = (8.3 \times 10^{-4}) h_c \quad \dots \dots \dots \dots \quad \text{A10.2}$$

The total evaporation or condensation rate is given by:

$$w = \frac{h_m}{\mathscr{R}T} (p_{va} - p_s) \quad \dots \dots \dots \dots \dots \quad \text{A10.3}$$

where:

w = total rate of condensation (or evaporation) at surface ..   ..   ..   kg/m² s
$\mathscr{R}$ = gas constant   .. ..   J/kg K
T = absolute temperature at surface   K
p_{va} = vapour pressure in air   .. .. ..   Pa
p_s = saturation vapour pressure at surface temperature   .. .. ..   Pa

For water vapour, $\mathscr{R}$ is taken as 461 J/kg K and hence, at room temperatures;

$$\mathscr{R}T \simeq 135 \text{ kJ/kg}$$

A negative value of w denotes evaporation from the surface.

Section C3 of the *Guide* gives the derivation of values for convective heat transfer coefficients, but for common building surfaces the values in Table A10.3 should be used. Alternatively, data may be given in terms of Nusselt number:

$$Nu = \frac{h_c d}{\lambda} \quad \dots \dots \dots \dots \dots \dots \dots \quad \text{A10.4}$$

where:

Nu = Nusselt number (see Section C3)
d = distance .. .. m
λ = thermal conductivity .. .. .. W/m K

Evaporation or condensation is accompanied by the absorption or release of latent heat by the moisture, this being given by:

$$q = w\, l_e \quad .. \quad .. \quad .. \quad .. \quad .. \quad .. \quad \text{A10.5}$$

where:

q = rate of flow of heat per unit area W/m^2
l_e = specific latent heat of evaporation J/kg

Unless the surface can readily supply or dissipate this heat, the surface temperature will change with corresponding changes in the mass transfer. A negative value of q indicates that the moisture is absorbing heat from the surface, which may cause the surface temperature to fall.

Table A10.3. Values of convective heat transfer and surface mass transfer coefficients.

Heat flow direction	Convective heat transfer coefficient h_c/(W/m^2 K)	Surface mass transfer coefficient h_m/(m/s)
Downward	1.5	1.25×10^{-3}
Horizontal	3.0	2.5×10^{-3}
Upward	4.3	3.6×10^{-3}

Notes:
Airspeed at the surface is assumed to be not greater than 0.1 m/s.
For air, the following values are assumed;
$\rho_a = 1.2$ kg/m^3, $c_p = 1 \times 10^3$ J/kg K.

VAPOUR DIFFUSION WITHIN MATERIALS

Most solid materials permit the diffusion of water vapour to some extent and, whenever there is a difference in the vapour pressure across the material, a movement of water vapour takes place. This is analogous to the flow of heat through a material when subjected to a temperature difference and this similarity is exploited in the calculation methods described.

The rate of vapour mass transfer per unit area through an element of a given material is:

$$m_v = \frac{\Delta p_v}{G} \quad .. \quad .. \quad .. \quad .. \quad .. \quad .. \quad .. \quad \text{A10.6}$$

where:

m_v = rate of vapour mass transfer per unit area .. .. kg/m^2 s
Δp_v = vapour pressure difference across material .. .. Pa
G = vapour resistance of material .. N s/kg

Table A10.4. Vapour resistivities and thermal conductivities of materials.

Material	Density (kg/m^3)	Vapour Resistivity/ (GN s/kg m) Minimum	Vapour Resistivity/ (GN s/kg m) Typical	Thermal Conductivity/ (W/m K)
Brick				
common	1360	35	35	—
	1530	—	50	0.65
sand lime	900	—	50	—
	1530	—	85	—
	1770	—	110	—
perforated	1110	—	40	—
Brickwork	—	25	40	0.62 (inner leaf) 0.84 (outer leaf)
Concrete				
gravel	2130	30	200	1.5
pumice	650	30	40	0.22
	840	—	40	0.28
	1140	—	45	0.4
	1580	—	115	0.7
slag	1140	—	50	0.4
aerated	520	—	30	0.2
	750	—	45	0.25
	950	—	50	0.33
	1350	—	55	0.45
hollow blockwork	—	—	35	—
Mortar				
cement (1:3)	2000	—	100	—
lime	1800	—	50	—
Plaster	—	35	50	0.25
Plywood	—	150	520	0.14
Wood	—	—	50	0.14
Cork slab	128–230	—	40	0.045
	—	13	—	—
Glass wool	150	—	10	0.045
Foam glass	143	—	—	0.04
Mineral wool	—	5	6	0.04
bitumenised	210–440	5	10	—
Insulating fibreboard	—	13	20	0.057
Hardboard	—	410	520	0.13
Plasterboard	—	34	50	0.16
Strawboard	—	45	70	0.11
Woodwool/				
cement slab	300	—	15	—
	380	—	25	0.08
Foamed phenolic	70–100	21	80	0.036
Foamed urea formaldehyde	12	20	30	0.036
Foamed polyurethane				
open cell	30–35	—	30	0.026
closed cell	—	—	1000	—
Foamed polystyrene	30–35	—	500	—
	—	100	200	0.035

Note: Thermal conductivity values for other materials are given in Section A3.

Vapour Resistance

The vapour resistance of an element of a given material is defined thus:

$$G = r d \quad .. \quad .. \quad .. \quad .. \quad .. \quad .. \quad .. \quad \text{A10.7}$$

where:

r = vapour resistivity of material　.. 　N s/kg m
d = thickness of element　.. 　.. 　.. 　　　m

Vapour Resistivity

Values of vapour resistivity for common materials are given in Table A10.4 under two headings; "minimum" and "typical".

The "minimum" values are the smallest values found in relevant literature[2,3] and should not be used for general calculations. The "typical" values are taken from the middle of the range of values for each material and may be used for calculation in the absence of more specific data. However, it should be borne in mind that individual samples of material may exceed these typical values by a factor of two or more.

Table A10.5 gives an indication of the likely resistivities from fibrous and open-celled materials and may be used, with caution, in the absence of specific data. This table also gives a value for the vapour resistivity of air spaces within composite structures, i.e. 5 GN s/kg m.

Table A10.5. Approximate values of vapour resistivity for fibrous or open-celled materials.

Density/(kg/m³)	Vapour resistivity/(GN s/kg m)
1	5
600	20
800	30
1000	40
1500	100
2000	220
2500	520

Note: Vapour resistivity of air spaces = 5 GN s/kg m.

Table A10.6. Vapour resistances of films.

Material	Thickness /mm	Vapour resistance /(GN s/kg)
Polythene film	0.05	125
	0.1	200
	0.15	350
Mylar film	0.025	25
Gloss paint (average)	–	8
Interior paints	–	3
Varnishes (phenolic, epoxy, polyurethane)	0.05	5
Roofing felt	–	4 to 100
Kraft paper single	–	0.2
double	–	0.35
Building paper foiled backed	–	5
	–	> 4000
Aluminium foil	–	> 4000

It is impracticable to tabulate vapour resistivities of films and Table A10.6 gives approximate values of vapour resistance. It should be noted that these values apply to undamaged films only and the presence of any perforations may reduce the vapour resistance considerably.

Permeability and Diffusion Resistance Factor

Sometimes, vapour permeabilities or diffusion resistance factors are quoted rather than vapour resistivities. Although these quantities are not used in this Section, and their use is not recommended, their definitions are given, as follows:

$$\delta = \frac{1}{r} \quad .. \quad .. \quad .. \quad .. \quad .. \quad .. \quad \text{A10.8}$$

where:

δ = vapour permeability of material　kg m/N s
r = vapour resistivity of material　.. 　N s/kg m

$$\mu = \frac{\delta_a}{\delta} \quad .. \quad .. \quad .. \quad .. \quad .. \quad .. \quad \text{A10.9}$$

where:

μ = diffusion resistance factor
δ_a = vapour permeability of air　.. 　.. 　kg m/N s

The value of δ_a is approximately 200×10^{-12} kg m/N s.

Surface Vapour Resistance

In addition to the vapour resistance of the material itself, the transfer of moisture vapour from the air into the material will also depend upon a surface resistance, defined as follows:

$$G_s = \frac{\mathscr{R}T}{h_m} \quad .. \quad .. \quad .. \quad .. \quad .. \quad \text{A10.10}$$

where:

G_s = surface vapour resistance　.. 　.. 　N s/kg

However, these surface vapour resistances are generally small compared to the vapour resistance of the material and may be ignored without significant loss of accuracy.

VAPOUR DIFFUSION IN COMPOSITE STRUCTURES

Where a structure is composed of slabs of different materials in contact, the vapour resistance of the composite structure, G_t, is the sum of the resistances of the individual elements. Note that the total vapour resistance includes the vapour resistances of any air spaces within the structure, see Table A10.5, but the surface vapour resistances may usually be ignored.

Equation A10.6 may be rewritten for composite structures, thus:

$$m_v = \frac{p_{vi} - p_{vo}}{G_t} \quad .. \quad .. \quad .. \quad .. \quad .. \quad \text{A10.11}$$

where:

p_{vi} = inside vapour pressure .. .. ..   Pa
p_{vo} = outside vapour pressure.. .. ..   Pa
G_t = total vapour resistance .. .. ..   N s/kg

Example 1

Figure A10.1 shows a wall comprising two leaves of 110 mm brickwork separated by 50 mm of insulating fibreboard. It should be noted that this simple construction is for illustrative purposes only. The inside and outside conditions are as shown.

The rate of transfer of moisture through the structure may be calculated as follows.

Using either the tabulated data given in Section C1 of the *Guide* or the CIBSE Psychrometric Chart, the vapour pressures corresponding to the inside and outside conditions are:

Inside: p_{vi} = 1457 Pa
Outside: p_{vo} =   984 Pa

From Table A10.4, the vapour resistivities of the components of the structure are:

Brick: 35×10^9 N s/kg m
Fibreboard: 20×10^9 N s/kg m

Thus, using equation A10.11:

$$m_v = \frac{1457 - 984}{2(0.11 \times 35 \times 10^9) + (0.05 \times 20 \times 10^9)} \text{ kg/m}^2 \text{ s}$$

$$m_v = 54 \times 10^{-9} \text{ kg/m}^2 \text{ s}$$

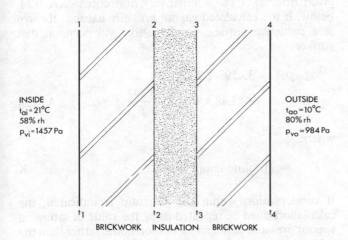

INSIDE
t_{ai}=21°C
58% rh
p_{vi}=1457 Pa

OUTSIDE
t_{ao}=10°C
80% rh
p_{vo}=984 Pa

BRICKWORK   INSULATION   BRICKWORK

Fig. A10.1. Wall construction for Example 1.

Condensation Within Structures

To determine whether condensation will occur within a structure, it is necessary to know the temperatures and corresponding vapour pressures at the inside, outside and internal surfaces.

The temperatures at the interfaces are calculated using the equation for steady-state heat flow through a structure. Strictly, this involves the inside environmental temperature, see Section A5[4]. However, for the purposes of this calculation, it may be assumed that the inside environmental and inside air temperatures are equal.

Therefore:

$$q = \frac{t_{ai} - t_{ao}}{R_t} \quad .. \quad .. \quad .. \quad .. \quad .. \quad \text{A10.12}$$

where:

q = rate of flow of heat per unit area   W/m^2
t_{ai} = inside air temperature .. .. ..   °C
t_{ao} = outside air temperature   .. ..   °C
R_t = total thermal resistance of structure .. ..   m^2 K/W

(cf: equation A10.11)

The total thermal resistance is given by;

$$R_t = R_{si} + R_1 + R_2 + \ldots + R_{so} \quad .. \quad .. \quad \text{A10.13}$$

where:

R_{si} = inside surface thermal resistance   m^2 K/W
R_1, R_2 = thermal resistance of element 1, 2 etc. .. ..   m^2 K/W
R_{so} = outside surface thermal resistance .. ..   m^2 K/W

The elements of the structure are numbered from inside to outside. Note that any air spaces present should be regarded as structural elements and numbered accordingly. The thermal resistances of such air spaces are given in Section A3[5].

Values of inside and outside surface thermal resistances are given in Tables A10.7 and A10.8. Further details are given in Section A3.

The thermal resistance of a given material is defined thus:

$$R = \frac{d}{\lambda} \quad .. \quad .. \quad .. \quad .. \quad .. \quad .. \quad .. \quad \text{A10.14}$$

where:

d = thickness of element   .. ..   m
λ = thermal conductivity of material   W/m K

Table A10.7 Inside surface thermal resistances, R_{si}.

Building element	Heat flow	Surface resistance / (m^2 K/W) High emissivity factor ($\frac{6}{5}E = 0.97$)	Low emissivity factor ($\frac{6}{5}E = 0.05$)
Walls	Horizontal	0·12	0·30
Ceilings or roofs, flat or pitched, floors	Upward	0·10	0·22
Ceilings and floors	Downward	0·14	0·55

Notes:
1. High emissivity factor assumes $\epsilon_1 = \epsilon_2 = 0.9$
   Low emissivity factor assumes $\epsilon_1 = 0.9, \epsilon_2 = 0.05$
2. Surface temperature is assumed to be 20°C
3. Air speed at the surface is assumed to be not greater than 0·1 m/s.

Table A10.8 Outside surface thermal resistances, R_{so}.

Building element	Emissivity of surface	Surface resistance for stated exposure / (m^2 K/W) Sheltered	Normal	Severe
Wall	High	0·08	0·06	0·03
	Low	0·11	0·07	0·03
Roof	High	0·07	0·04	0·02
	Low	0·09	0·05	0·02

Note: Form (shape) factor for radiative heat transfer is taken to be unity.

Using the notation of Example 1, in which the surfaces are numbered from 1 to 4 (inside to outside), the temperature and vapour pressure associated with surface 1 are denoted by t_1 and p_{v1} respectively. Note that t_1 and t_4 are surface temperatures which should *not* be taken to equal the inside and outside air temperatures.

The thermal resistances of the various elements of the structure are denoted by R_1, R_2 etc., where R_1 refers to the innermost element. Similarly, the vapour resistances are denoted by G_1, G_2 etc.

For surface 1, from equation A10.12;

$$q = \frac{t_{ai} - t_1}{R_{si}} \quad \dots \quad \dots \quad \dots \quad \text{A10.15}$$

Hence;

$$t_1 = t_{ai} - qR_{si} \quad \dots \quad \dots \quad \text{A10.16}$$

For surface 2:

$$q = \frac{t_{ai} - t_2}{R_{si} + R_1} \quad \dots \quad \dots \quad \text{A10.17}$$

where:

R_1 = thermal resistance of innermost element $\quad \dots \quad \dots$ m^2 K/W

Hence;

$$t_2 = t_{ai} - q(R_{si} + R_1) \quad \dots \quad \dots \quad \text{A10.18}$$

Similarly, for surface 3:

$$t_3 = t_{ai} - q(R_{si} + R_1 + R_2) \quad \dots \quad \text{A10.19}$$

Finally, for surface 4, if required:

$$t_4 = t_{ai} - q(R_{si} + R_1 + R_2 + R_3) \quad \dots \quad \text{A10.20}$$

The vapour pressures at the interfaces may be calculated using equation A10.11, having first determined the rate of vapour mass transfer through the structure, as described on page A10–5.

Therefore, for surface 2;

$$m_v = \frac{p_{v1} - p_{v2}}{G_1} \quad \dots \quad \dots \quad \dots \quad \text{A10.21}$$

where:

m_v = rate of vapour mass transfer per unit area $\quad \dots \quad \dots \quad$ kg/m^2 s

G_1 = vapour resistance of innermost element $\quad \dots \quad \dots \quad$ N s/kg

Hence;

$$p_{v2} = p_{v1} - m_v G_1 \quad \dots \quad \dots \quad \dots \quad \text{A10.22}$$

(The surface vapour resistances are neglected, hence p_{v1} may be regarded as equal to the vapour pressure corresponding to the inside conditions and p_{v4} equal to the vapour pressure corresponding to the outside conditions.)

Similarly, for surface 3;

$$p_{v3} = p_{v1} - m_v (G_1 + G_2) \quad \dots \quad \dots \quad \text{A10.23}$$

Knowing both the vapour pressure and temperature at each interface, the corresponding saturated vapour pressure (svp) may be determined from the tabulated data given in Section C1 or, alternatively, from equation A10.24, below. If the calculated vapour pressure exceeds the svp at a particular surface, condensation will occur at that surface.

$$\log_{10} p_s = 33.59 - 8.2 \log_{10} T + (2.48 \times 10^{-3})T - \frac{3\,142}{T} \quad \dots \quad \text{A10.24}$$

where:

T = absolute temperature $\quad \dots \quad \dots$ K

If condensation within the structure is indicated, the calculation must be repeated using the value of saturated vapour pressure at the condensation point, rather than the calculated vapour pressure. This is illustrated in the following examples.

Example 2

For the structure and conditions given in Example 1, the occurence of interstitial condensation may be predicted by the following method.

The thermal conductivities of the three elements are determined from Table A10.4. Hence, the heat flow through the structure is calculated using equations A10.13 and A10.15, as follows:

$$R_t = 0.12 + \frac{0.11}{0.62} + \frac{0.05}{0.057} + \frac{0.11}{0.84} + 0.06 \quad m^2\ K/W$$

$$R_t = 1.37\ m^2\ K/W$$

Therefore:

$$q = \frac{21-10}{1.37} = 8.0\ W/m^2$$

The temperature at surface 1 is given by equation A10.16, ie;

$$t_1 = 21 - (8 \times 0.12) = 20.0\ °C$$

Therefore, using equations A10.18 and A10.19, the temperatures at surfaces 2 and 3 are;

$$t_2 = 21 - 8\left(0.12 + \frac{0.11}{0.62}\right) = 18.6\ °C$$

$$t_3 = 21 - 8\left(0.12 + \frac{0.11}{0.62} + \frac{0.05}{0.057}\right) = 11.6\ °C$$

The rate of transfer of moisture was calculated in Example 1, ie;

$$m_v = 54 \times 10^{-9}\ kg/m^2\ s$$

The vapour pressures at surfaces 2 and 3 are given by equations A10.22 and A10.23, thus;

$$p_{v2} = 1457 - 54 \times 10^{-9}(0.11 \times 37 \times 10^9) = 1249\ Pa$$

$$p_{v3} = 1457 - 54 \times 10^{-9}(0.11 \times 37 \times 10^9 + 0.05 \times 20 \times 10^9) = 1195\ Pa$$

Using Section C1, the saturated vapour pressures corresponding to surface temperatures t_2 and t_3 are 2142 Pa and 1365 Pa, respectively. Therefore, there is no risk of condensation occuring at either of the internal surfaces.

Example 3

Consider the same structure but assume that the outside air temperature is 2 °C and the relative humidity is 84%.

From Section C1, the vapour pressure corresponding to the outside conditions is:

$$p_{vo} = 593\ Pa$$

Thus, from equation A10.11:

$$m_v = 94.5 \times 10^{-9}\ kg/m^2\ s$$

The heat flow is given by equation A10.12:

$$q = \frac{21-2}{1.37}$$

$$q = 13.9\ W/m^2$$

For surface 1, using equation A10.16;

$$t_1 = 19.3\ °C$$

Therefore, for surface 2, from equations A10.18 and A10.22;

$$t_2 = 16.9\ °C$$
$$p_{v2} = 1072\ Pa$$

The saturated vapour pressure corresponding to 16.9 °C is 1924 Pa. Hence condensation will not occur at surface 2.

For surface 3, using equations A10.19 and A10.23;

$$t_3 = 4.7\ °C$$
$$p_{v3} = 978\ Pa$$

The saturated vapour pressure corresponding to 4.7 °C is 854 Pa. Therefore in this case, the vapour pressure at surface 3 exceeds the saturated vapour pressure and condensation will occur.

The above example is shown diagramatically in Fig. A10.2. This suggests that the calculated vapour pressure line crosses the saturated vapour pressure (svp) line at two points. In reality, the vapour pressure cannot exceed the svp and the actual vapour pressure adjusts to the values indicated by the broken line, the excess moisture condensing out at surface 3, where the calculated vapour pressure exceeds the svp by the greatest amount.

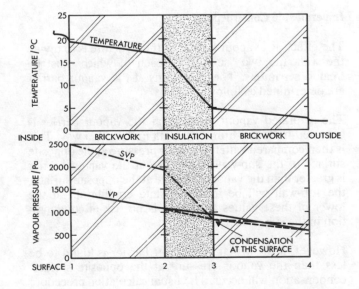

Fig. A10.2 Temperature, vapour pressure and saturation vapour pressures for construction and conditions given in Example 3.

The rate of vapour mass transfer into the structure must now be recalculated by substituting the svp for the calculated vapour pressure for the surface at which condensation is indicated. The rate of vapour mass transfer outwards from the point of condensation is calculated in a similar way. The difference between these rates gives the rate of condensation at the surface.

If a negative rate of condensation is obtained, this indicates that the value of vapour pressure for that surface was not the equilibrium value. Therefore the rates of vapour mass transfer should be recalculated using the equilibrium values.

When only positive rates remain, all the surfaces likely to suffer from interstitial condensation will have been identified.

Example 3 – Continued

Taking the inner elements, that is the inner brick leaf and the insulation, the rate of transfer of moisture is recalculated using equation A10.21, ie;

$$m_{vi} = \frac{1457 - 851}{(0.11 \times 35 \times 10^9) + (0.05 \times 20 \times 10^9)} \text{ kg/m}^2 \text{ s}$$

$$m_{vi} = 125 \times 10^{-9} \text{ kg/m}^2 \text{ s}$$

The rate of vapour mass transfer through the outer element alone is;

$$m_{vo} = \frac{851 - 593}{0.11 \times 35 \times 10^9} \text{ kg/m}^2 \text{ s}$$

$$m_{vo} = 67 \times 10^{-9} \text{ kg/m}^2 \text{ s}$$

Thus, rate of condensation at surface 2 is;

$$w_2 = 58 \times 10^{-9} \text{ kg/m}^2 \text{ s}$$

Impermeable Constructions

The effect of a vapour barrier in the structure is to divide the wall into two "sub-walls", each of which must be treated separately. The conditions at the vapour barrier are determined as follows.

The saturated vapour pressure at the vapour barrier is obtained from psychrometric data in the usual way. This is then compared with the vapour pressure at the opposite surface of the sub-wall. If the svp at the vapour barrier is greater than the vapour pressure at the opposite surface, the sub-wall will be in steady-state equilibrium at the lower of these values and there is no risk of condensation in the sub-wall.

However, if the svp at the vapour barrier is found to be less than the vapour pressure at the opposite surface, condensation will occur. The usual calculation procedure for condensation within structures should then be performed for the sub-wall, taking the svp as the prevailing condition at the vapour barrier.

Condensation Within Insulation Layer

The above method assumes that the saturated vapour pressure varies linearly with temperature. Although this is a satisfactory approximation over a small temperature range special care must be taken where large temperature differences are likely to be maintained over thick layers of insulation, such as in cold stores and refrigeration plants.

Therefore, although the usual calculation procedure may not indicate condensation within the overall structure, the non-linearity of the svp curve may result in the svp falling below the vapour pressure within the layer of insulation, giving rise to 'hidden' condensation. To assess the likelihood of this occurence, the svp should be determined at several intermediate points within the layer of insulation and compared with the vapour pressure line at these points.

Graphical Procedure

The Building Research Establishment has suggested a graphical procedure which may be more convenient for hand calculation. This is based on earlier work by Glaiser[6] and is summarised as follows.

(1) Determine the temperature at each interface using the method described on page A10–8.

(2) Determine the vapour resistance for each element and sum progressively to give the cumulative vapour resistance from inside to outside.

(3) Use the tabulated data given in Section C1 of the *Guide* to evaluate the saturated vapour pressure corresponding to the temperature at each surface.

(4) Plot the saturated vapour pressure against the cumulative vapour resistance of the structure.

(5) Plot the vapour pressures corresponding to the inside and outside conditions and join by a straight line. If this line **does not** cross the svp line there is no risk of interstitial condensation.

(6) If the lines cross, the vapour pressure line is replotted, starting from the inside, by reducing the calculated vapour pressure to equal the lowest svp value in the region of the crossover.

(7) If the revised vapour pressure line crosses the svp line elsewhere, step 6 must be repeated until all the crossovers are eliminated.

(8) At each point where the revised vapour pressure line touches the svp line, the rate of condensation should be determined by calculating the difference between the rate of vapour mass transfer from inside to the point of condensation and the rate of transfer from the point of condensation to the outside.

(9) The resulting figure is likely to be very small. Therefore, the Building Research Establishment

suggests that the conditions are assumed to exist for sixty days. Hence, to obtain the total condensation over this period in kg/m², the calculated rate of condensation should be multiplied by 5.184×10^6 seconds.

The following example shows how the method is applied to a typical composite structure.

Example 4

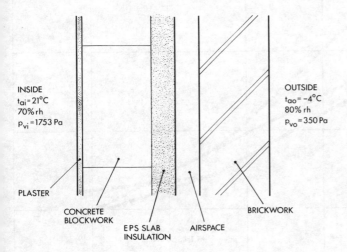

Fig. A10.3. Wall construction for Example 4.

Table A10.9. Materials specification for Example 4.

Element	Thickness /m	Thermal conductivity /(W/m K)	Vapour resistivity /(GN s/m kg)
Plaster	0.013	0.16	50
Concrete blockwork	0.100	0.51	50
EPS slab insulation	0.025	0.035	200
Air space	0.025	–	5
Brickwork	0.105	0.84	35

Table A10.10. Calculation Table for Example 4.

(1) Element	(2) $R/$ (m²K/W)	(3) $\Sigma R/$ (m²K/W)	(4) $G/$ (GN s/kg)	(5) $\Sigma G/$ (GN s/kg)	(6) $t/$ (°C)	(7) $p_s/$ (Pa)
Inside surface	0.12	0.12	*	0.0	19.0	2196
Plaster	0.08	0.20	0.7	0.7	17.6	2012
Concrete blockwork	0.2	0.40	5.0	5.7	14.2	1629
Insulation	0.71	1.11	5.0	10.7	2.1	716
Air space	0.18	1.29	0.1	10.8	-0.9	571
Brickwork	0.12	1.41	3.7	14.5	-3.0	480
Outside surface	0.06	1.47	*	14.5	-4.0	–
	$R_t = 1.47$		$G_t = 14.5$			

Note: For each element of the construction, the temperature given in column 6 refers to the outermost surface of the element.

* negligible

Step 1

The thermal resistance of each element is calculated using equation A10.14 (see column 2 in the Calculation Table). These values, along with the surface thermal resistances, are progressively summed to give the cumulative thermal resistance (col. 3).

The rate of flow of heat is determined using equation A10.12, thus:

$$q = \frac{21 - (-4)}{1.47} = 17.0 \text{ W/m}^2$$

Equations A10.15 etc are also used to calculate the temperature at each surface by using the appropriate value of ΣR, assuming that the rate of flow of heat is constant. (Note that the inside surface temperature is calculated in the same way.) The resulting values are entered in column 6.

Step 2

The vapour resistance is calculated for each element (including the air space) using equation A10.7 (col. 4). The surface vapour resistances are small and may be neglected. The cumulative vapour resistance is calculated by progressively summing these values (col. 5).

Step 3

Section C1 is used to determine the saturated vapour pressure, p_s, corresponding to the surface temperature at each interface (col. 7).

Step 4

The saturated vapour pressure is plotted (col. 7) against the cumulative vapour resistance (col. 5), see Fig. A10.4.

Step 5

The inside and outside vapour pressures are plotted and joined by a straight line.

Step 6

Vapour pressure line is then replotted to remove crossover.

Step 7

No further crossovers; condensation will occur at one location, indicated by the point of contact between the vapour pressure and svp lines.

Step 8

Rate of vapour mass transfer from inside to the condensation point is given by equation A10.11, thus:

$$m_{vi} = \frac{1753 - 571}{10.8 \times 10^9} = 109 \times 10^{-9} \text{ kg/m}^2 \text{ s.}$$

Rate of transfer from condensation point to outside:

$$m_{vo} = \frac{571 - 350}{(14.5 \times 10^9) - (10.8 \times 10^9)}$$

$$= 60 \times 10^{-9} \text{ kg/m}^2 \text{ s.}$$

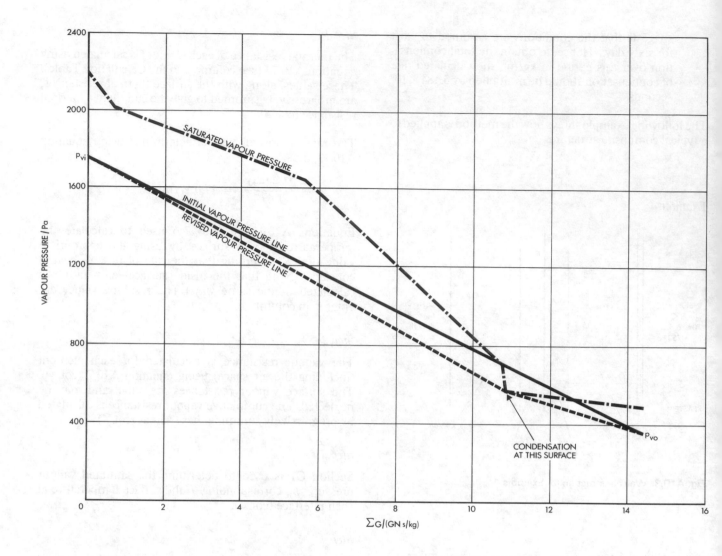

Fig. A10.4. Graphical representation – Example 4.

Therefore, rate of condensation:

$$w \quad = 49 \times 10^{-9} \text{ kg/m}^2 \text{ s}.$$

Step 9

Over a period of 60 days, total condensation is 0.25 kg/m².

PREDICTION OF MOISTURE CONDENSATION

General

The occurrence of condensation on surfaces such as walls, windows and in roofs can be predicted and consequently controlled. However, other forms of condensation have different causes and effects and therefore require different treatments. Table A10.11 summarises the properties of the various forms of condensation.

Table A10.11. Forms of condensation.

Nature	Type	Cause
Visible – prolonged	Permanent	Element surface temperature below the dew-point temperature. Normally occurs in winter through accumulation of moisture in space, poor thermal insulation of element, lack of heating.
Visible – spasmodic	Temporary	Element surface temperature below the dew-point temperature. Normally caused by build-up of excessive moisture in space such as kitchen or bathroom. Poor thermal insulation aggravates the precipitation of condensation. Can occasionally be caused by warm humid weather rapidly following a cold spell, the air coming into contact with cold building elements.
Invisible – if prolonged can become visible	Interstitial	Dew-point above temperature within element. Often caused by the mis-application of thermal insulation layer or vapour barrier. Interstitial condensation can appear on the surfaces of an element as a result of capillary penetration.

Interstitial Condensation

The previous methods enable the risks of interstitial condensation to be assessed if the inside and outside conditions are known. To predict the likelihood of condensation at the design stage suitable values of temperature and relative humidity must be assumed.

For this purpose, it is suggested that the following conditions be assumed to exist for a period of sixty days:

	Inside	Outside
Air temperature:	15 °C	5 °C
Relative humidity:	65%	95%

Surface Condensation

Some guidance on the prediction and control of surface condensation can be obtained from the flow chart, Fig. A10.5 which offers a rational approach by reducing the problem to one of finding dew-point and surface temperatures[7]. However, the case of interstitial condensation is not covered by the flow chart; this should be examined by the methods described earlier.

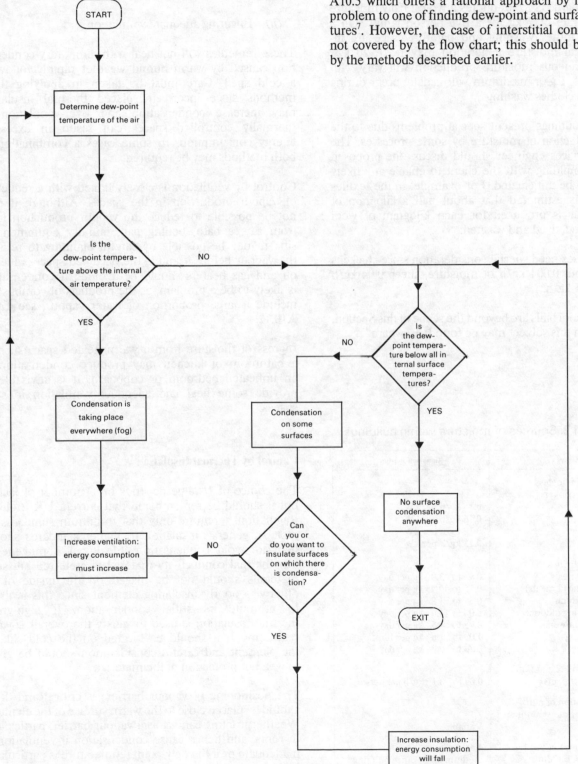

Fig. A10.5 Flow chart for prediction of surface condensation.

SOURCES OF MOISTURE

To undertake calculations on the risks of surface and interstitial condensation it is necessary to estimate the vapour pressure or moisture content of the air within the building. This will largely be determined by the sources of moisture associated with the occupants of the building. There is little information available on rates of moisture production but Table A10.12 gives estimates of the amount of moisture likely to be produced from various sources.

British Standard BS 5250[8] quotes a typical daily moisture production rate of 7 kg for a five person family. On a day when clothes washing and paraffin usage are included typical moisture generation may reach 20 kg[9]. The instantaneous moisture production will vary with the activities, e.g. a maximum will usually occur during cooking and clothes washing.

Industrial buildings present special problems due to the rate of production of moisture by some processes. The building services engineer should discuss the proposed use of the building with the client to enable any likely problems to be anticipated. For example, in the textiles industry it is estimated that about half a kilogram of water vapour is produced for each kilogram of wool that is scoured, dyed and washed.

Animal houses need special consideration since chickens produce about 0.004 kg/h of moisture, sheep 0.04 kg/h and pigs 0.15 kg/h.

Swimming pool halls are beyond the scope of this Section. Guidance on this subject may be found elsewhere[10].

Table A10.12. Sources of moisture within buildings.

Source	Amount of moisture
Combustion in flueless room heaters/cookers	
Paraffin	0.1 kg/h per kW
Natural gas	0.16 kg/h per kW
Butane	0.12 kg/h per kW
Propane	0.13 kg/h per kW
Household activities:	
Cooking (3 meals)	0.9 to 3.0 kg per day
Dish washing (3 meals)	0.15 to 0.45 kg per day
Clothes washing	0.5 to 1.8 kg per day
Clothes drying indoors	5.0 to 14.0 kg per day
Baths and showers	0.75 to 1.5 kg per day
Floor washing	1.0 to 1.5 kg per $10m^2$
Indoor plants	up to 0.8 kg per day
Perspiration and respiration of building occupants	0.04 to 0.1 kg/h per person
Direct penetration of rain, groundwater or moist ambient air	Variable
'Drying out' of water used in construction of building	4000 kg in one year for medium sized office building

CONTROLLING AND ELIMINATING CONDENSATION

It can be seen from Fig. A10.5 that if the desired room temperature and the rate of moisture production are constant, there are two methods for control of condensation:

(i) Ensuring that the temperature of any internal surface does not fall below the dew-point temperature of the air by the correct use of thermal insulation.

(ii) Ensuring adequate ventilation.

These remedies will not deal with temporary condensation caused by warm humid weather rapidly following a cold spell. Care must be taken in applying these methods since incorrectly placed thermal insulation may increase condensation and over-ventilation of thermally controlled spaces can result in excessive energy consumption. In some cases a combination of both methods may be required.

Control by ventilation is closely linked with a reduction of vapour production in the spaces. Although it may not be possible to reduce the vapour production itself from say, a bath, boiling pan, laundry equipment or sink it may be possible by careful planning to remove the vapour before it enters the occupied space. Flueless oil and gas heaters should be avoided if condensation is likely to be a problem, as the products of combustion include a large proportion of water vapour, see Table A10.12.

Ingress of moisture from a warm heated space such as a bathroom or kitchen may produce condensation in an unheated bedroom or cupboard. It is advisable to provide some heat and adequate ventilation in such spaces.

Control by Thermal Insulation

The choice of U-value depends on a number of factors but it should be remembered that current UK Building Regulations[11] require only that minimum standards be met. In general, insulation to higher standards should help to avoid condensation. Ideally, a homogeneous low thermal conductivity material is preferred but such materials should not be placed on the inside of an otherwise poorly insulating element since this is likely to promote interstitial condensation. If high-grade thermal insulation is used to satisfy the overall U-value requirement, it should be located on the cold side of the element and careful consideration should be given to weather protection of the material.

The positioning of vapour barriers is critical and these should be placed close to the warm surface of the element. Weatherproofing can act as a vapour barrier, particularly in roofs, and hence cause condensation if ventilation is inadequate or if the dew-point temperature is particularly high, such as occurs in swimming pool halls.

In special process applications such as cold stores[12] and refrigeration plants[13], the use of vapour barriers is essential to prevent moisture condensing inside the thermal insulation. These applications require careful design and a high level of site supervision during construction.

The introduction of cavities provides the benefits of increased thermal insulation with resistance to liquid water movement. However, cold bridges and corners require special attention.

The vapour pressure and saturation vapour pressure gradients should always be plotted for the construction to identify potential condensation problems. Figure A10.6 shows, in schematic form, the likely vapour pressure, saturation vapour pressure and temperature gradients for various configurations. Condensation is indicated if the vapour pressure and saturated vapour pressure lines touch at any point.

Control by Ventilation

The provision of adequate ventilation will ensure that moisture content and hence, vapour pressure, is kept under control[14]. In addition, ventilation prevents build-up of radon gas, phenols and other gaseous pollutants resulting from the materials used in the construction of the building. However, it is important not to over-ventilate as this may cause draughts, excessive heat loss and, consequently, increased fuel consumption.

Steady State Calculations

The ventilation required for situations where the moisture gains are known may be determined from the following equation for steady-state conditions:

$$v = \frac{Q_l}{(g_{max} - g_a)\, \rho_a l_e} \quad \ldots \ldots \ldots \ldots \quad \text{A10.25}$$

where:

v = flow rate of air $\ldots$ $\ldots$ $\ldots$ $\ldots$ m³/s
Q_l = rate of latent heat gain $\ldots$ $\ldots$ $\ldots$ W
g_{max} = maximum permissible moisture content of room air to avoid condensation $\ldots$ $\ldots$ $\ldots$ $\ldots$ $\ldots$ kg/kg
g_a = moisture content of supply air $\ldots$ kg/kg
ρ_a = density of air $\ldots$ $\ldots$ $\ldots$ $\ldots$ kg/m³
l_e = specific latent heat of evaporation of water $\ldots$ $\ldots$ $\ldots$ $\ldots$ $\ldots$ J/kg

Ventilation is difficult in the case of flat roofs and it is very important to place the thermal insulation on the outer side of the roof above the vapour barrier so that most of the roof construction, including the vapour barrier, is protected from cooling below the dew-point temperature.

Spaces protected by vapour barriers must be ventilated to prevent the build-up of moisture. A typical example is the case of a flat roof incorporating a vapour barrier, separated from the ceiling by a void which must be ventilated to the outside by waterproof vents.

Non-Steady State Calculations

If the moisture generation or ventilation is intermittent the steady state calculation will be inadequate and a non-steady state method must be used.

Equations may be written directly in terms of temperature or saturation, but these are complicated. It is simpler to write equations in terms of enthalpy and solve for either sensible or latent enthalpy. Dry-bulb temperature and moisture content (or saturation) may then be evaluated. A suitable enthalpy equation is given below. However, it is essential to evaluate the sensible heat gain (or loss) and the latent heat gain (or loss) from the space separately.

The specific enthalpy of the air in a ventilated space after a given time is:

$$H = (H_a + \Delta H)\,(1 - e^{-n\theta}) + H_o e^{-n\theta} \quad .. \quad \text{A10.26}$$

where:

H = specific enthalphy (sensible or latent) of room air per kilogram of dry air $\ldots$ $\ldots$ $\ldots$ $\ldots$ $\ldots$ $\ldots$ kJ/kg
H_a = specific enthalpy (sensible or latent) of supply air per kilogram of dry air $\ldots$ $\ldots$ $\ldots$ $\ldots$ $\ldots$ $\ldots$ kJ/kg
H_o = initial specific enthalpy (sensible or latent) of room air per kilogram of dry air $\ldots$ $\ldots$ $\ldots$ $\ldots$ $\ldots$ $\ldots$ kJ/kg
ΔH = change of specific enthalphy of room air over period θ (i.e. $\Delta H = (H - H_o)$) $\ldots$ $\ldots$ $\ldots$ kJ/kg
n = room air change rate $\ldots$ $\ldots$ $\ldots$ h⁻¹
θ = time period $\ldots$ $\ldots$ $\ldots$ $\ldots$ $\ldots$ h

Having obtained the specific enthalpy from equation A10.26, the following expression may be used to determine the dry-bulb temperature, provided that H is evaluated for sensible heat gain (or loss):

$$t_d = \frac{H' \times 10^3}{c_p} \quad \ldots \ldots \ldots \ldots \ldots \quad \text{A10.27}$$

where:

t_d = dry-bulb temperature $\ldots$ $\ldots$ $\ldots$ °C
H' = specific enthalpy of room air, evaluated for sensible heat gain $\ldots$ kJ/kg
c_p = specific heat capacity of air $\ldots$ $\ldots$ J/kg K

(c_p for moist air may be taken as 1025 J/kg K)

If it is required to find the moisture content and saturation, equation A10.27 may be used by inserting values appropriate to latent heat gain (or loss). Having obtained the enthalpy appropriate to latent heat gain/loss, the psychrometric data contained in Section C1 may be used to determine the moisture content and saturation at the calculated temperature.

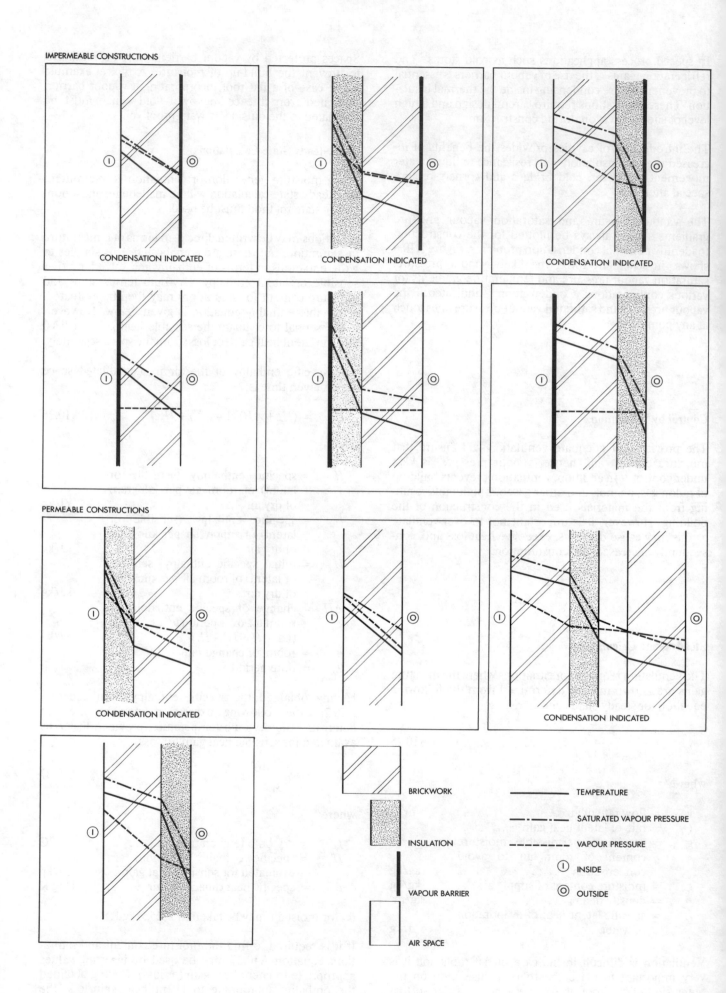

IMPERMEABLE CONSTRUCTIONS

CONDENSATION INDICATED   CONDENSATION INDICATED   CONDENSATION INDICATED

PERMEABLE CONSTRUCTIONS

CONDENSATION INDICATED   CONDENSATION INDICATED

BRICKWORK

INSULATION

VAPOUR BARRIER

AIR SPACE

TEMPERATURE

SATURATED VAPOUR PRESSURE

VAPOUR PRESSURE

INSIDE

OUTSIDE

Fig. A10.6. Behaviour of typical wall constructions.

Precautions with Intermittent Heating

For normally heated buildings with good ventilation, it is unlikely that condensation will occur in winter. However, for buildings with intermittent heating, the fall in temperature during periods without heating may cause condensation, particularly on surfaces that are poorly insulated or have low thermal capacity. Equations A10.26 and A10.27 apply during cooling. Further information on building behaviour and intermittent heating is given elsewhere[4, 15].

Precautions with Building Services Plant, Pipes, Ducts and Equipment

Condensation will occur on any surface in a building that is likely to be at a temperature below the dew-point.

Problems are likely to occur on:

(i) the surfaces of chilled water or chilled air networks with high risk points such as valves and spindles, pumps, fans, dampers and network supports.

(ii) the surfaces of networks not normally chilled, such as cold water storage tanks and cold water mains (where these mains pass through excessively heated or humid areas such as boiler houses, laundries, kitchens, swimming pools).

Thermal insulation with appropriately sealed vapour barriers is essential to avoid condensation in critical places.

The evaluation of conditions in difficult areas is relatively simple. Section C3 of the *Guide* includes equations which enable the prediction of surface temperatures of thermal plant and networks; these may be compared with the expected dew-point temperatures. British Standard BS 5422[13] provides further guidance.

REFERENCES

1 JOHANSSON, C. H., Moisture transmission and moisture distribution in building materials, *Technical Translation TT 189*, National Research Council, Ottawa, Canada.

2 PRANGNELL, R. D., The water vapour resistivity of building materials – a literature survey, *Materiaux et Constructions*, **4**, 24, November 1971.

3 Condensation, *BRE Digest 110*, Building Research Establishment, Watford, 1972.

4 Thermal response of buildings, CIBSE Guide Section A5, Chartered Institution of Building Services Engineers, London, 1979.

5 Thermal properties of building structures, CIBSE Guide Section A3, Chartered Institution of Building Services Engineers, London, 1980.

6 GLAISER, H., A graphical method for the investigation of diffusion processes, *Kaltetechnick*, **11**, 345, 1959.

7 FITZGERALD, D, Avoiding condensation in buildings, *Heating and Air Conditioning*, **55**, 10, October 1985.

8 BS 5250, Basic data for the design of buildings: the control of condensation in buildings, British Standards Institution, London 1975.

9 Surface condensation and mould growth in traditionally-built dwellings, *BRE Digest 297*, Building Research Establishment, Watford, 1985.

10 HOLT, J. S. C., Some aspects of swimming pool design, HVRA Technical Note No. 10, Building Services Research and Information Association, Bracknell, 1963.

11 The Building Regulations 1985, SI No. 1065, HMSO, London, 1985.

12 BS 2502, Specification for manufacture of sectional cold rooms (walk-in type), British Standards Institution, London, 1979.

13 BS 5422, Specification for the use of thermal insulating materials, British Standards Institution, London, 1977.

14 LOUDON, A. G., The effects of condensation and building design factors on the risk of condensation and mould growth in dwellings, *BRE Current Paper CP 31/71*, Building Research Establishment, Watford, 1971.

15 BILLINGTON, N. S., The cooling of rooms and surfaces, *Laboratory Report No. 82*, Building Services Research and Information Association, Bracknell, 1973.

APPENDIX

Algorithm for Interstitial Condensation

Enter the details of each layer of the wall (thickness, vapour resistivity, thermal conductivity) and the surface thermal and vapour resistances. Calculate the thermal and resistances of each layer, together with the cumulative resistances, starting from the inside.

DATA	Internal surface thermal resistance	RSIN
	Internal surface vapour resistance	GSIN
	Number of layers in wall	NLAY
QUANTITY	Cumulative thermal resistance at internal surface (interface 1) RCUM(1)=RSIN	RCUM(1)
	Cumulative vapour resistance at internal surface (interface 1) GCUM(1)=GSIN	GCUM(1)
DATA	Thickness of layer N	THIK(N)
	Thermal conductivity of layer N	COND(N)
	Vapour resistivity of layer N	DIFF(N)
QUANTITY	Thermal resistance of layer N RLAY(N)=THIK(N)/COND(N)	RLAY(N)
	Vapour resistance of layer N GLAY(N)=THIK(N) * DIFF(N)	GLAY(N)
	Cumulative thermal resistance up to and including layer N RCUM(N+1)=RCUM(N)+RLAY(N)	RCUM(N+1)
	Cumulative vapour resistance up to and including layer N GCUM(N+1)=GCUM(N)+GLAY(N)	GCUM(N+1)
DATA	Outside surface thermal resistance	ROUT
	Outside surface vapour resistance	GOUT
QUANTITY	Cumulative thermal resistance to outside air RCUM(NLAY+2)= RCUM(NLAY+1)+ROUT	RCUM(NLAY+2)
	Cumulative vapour resistance to outside air GCUM(NLAY+2)= GCUM(NLAY+1)+GOUT	GCUM(NLAY+2)

Enter the inside and outside design conditions (air temperatures and relative humidities) and calculate the inside and outside vapour pressures. Calculate the temperature distribution through the wall and the corresponding saturation vapour pressures at each interface. Check for surface condensation.

DATA	Inside air temperature	TIN
	Inside relative humidity	RHIN
	Outside air temperature	TOUT
	Outside relative humidity	RHOUT
QUANTITY	Inside vapour pressure VP(1)=SVPIN * RHIN/100	VP(1)
	Outside vapour pressure VP(NLAY+1)=SVPOUT * RHOUT/100	VP(NLAY+1)
	Heat flow through wall HEAT=(TIN-TOUT)/RCUM(NLAY+2)	HEAT
	Temperature at interface N TEMP(N)=TIN-RCUM(N) * HEAT	TEMP(N)
	Saturation vapour pressure at each interface	SVP(N)

IF TEMP(N)>=0 THEN SVP(N)=
  33.59051-8.2 * LOG10(273.15+TEMP(N))
  +(0.0024804 * (273.15+TEMP(N)))
  -3142.31/(273.158TEMP(N)))

IF TEMP(N)<0 THEN SVP(N)=
  12.5380997-(2663.91/(273.15+TEMP(N)))

Check for surface condensation.

IF VP(1)>=SVP(1) THEN
Surface condensation occurs

Enter the data appropriate to the inner and outer interfaces for the construction. Initially these will be 1 and NLAY+1. Starting from the inside, calculate the vapour pressure at each interface and compare this with the saturation vapour pressure. If the vapour pressure is not greater than the saturation vapour pressure, there is no condensation. If the vapour pressure is greater than the saturation vapour pressure than condensation occurs. In this case, the condition at the interface must be changed to the saturation vapour pressure and the wall, or section of wall, divided into two sections: from the inner interface to the condensation point and from the condensation point to the outer interface. Repeat the above procedure for each section.

Because the calculation can be repeated for a section of the wall before it has been completed for the whole wall, it provides an opportunity to use recursion if programmed in a language that permits this approach.

DATA	Inner interface	NIN
	Outer interface	NOUT
QUANTITY	Moisture flow between inner interface and outer interface WFLO=(VP(NIN)-VP(NOUT))/ (GCUM(NOUT)-GCUM(NIN))	WFLO
	Vapour pressure at interface N VP(N)=VP(NIN)-((GCUM(N)- GCUM(NIN)) * WFLO	VP(N)

IF VP(N)<=SVP(N) THEN
Carry on to next interface

IF VP(N)>SVP(N) THEN
VP(N)=SVP(N)

Repeat calculation for sub-sections of wall.

Calculate the condensation at each interface by taking the difference between the moisture flow to and from each interface. Ignore inner surface when doing this.

QUANTITY	Flow to interface N FLO1=(VP(N-1)-VP(N))/ (GCUM(N)-GCUM(N-1))	FLO1
	Flow from interface N FLO2=(VP(N)-VP(N+1))/ (GCUM(N+1)-GCUM(N))	FLO2
	Condensation at interface N DRIP(N)=FLO1-FLO2	DRIP(N)

END

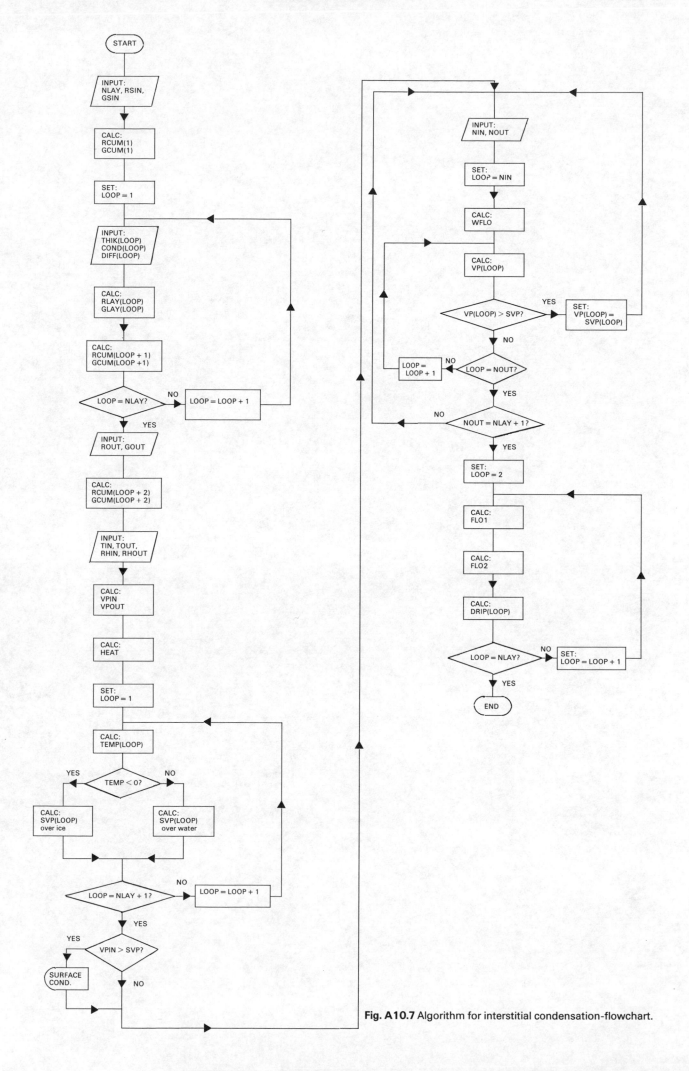

Fig. A10.7 Algorithm for interstitial condensation-flowchart.

INDEX to VOLUME A

'A' scale for sound meter .... A1–15 to 17
Active occupations and comfort A1–6
Admittance (Y value) A3–21; A8–5, 13
Admittances and decrement factors A3–23 to 30; A5–11
Air change rate A1–9
Air conditioning plant sizing, ... A5–9
    central plant A9–13
    continuous operation,
        to maintain dry resultant temperature A5–9
        at constant air temperature A5–10
    design conditions A9–12
    fluctuations in control temperature A5–10
    intermittent operation A5–10; A9–13
    reliability assessment .... A9–13 to 15
    sensible heat load A5–9; A9–12
    summertime temperatures A5–10
Air cooling load .... A9–20 to 41
Airflow,
    internal resistance to A4–10
    rates of A4–4, 8
Air handling type, luminaires A7–4
Air infiltration,
    and natural ventilation .... A4–3 to 15
    and stack effect A4–5
    and wind A4–5
    basic rates A4–3, 10, 11
    calculation of A4–4
    chart A4–8
    correction factors in, chart A4–9, 10
    empirical values for A4–13, 14
    in factories A4–15
    internal resistance to air flow A4–10
    pressures on building A4–5
    rates of flow,
        for design purposes A4–8
        through cracks A4–4
    representative areas for A4–12
    room A4–3, 11
    through windows A4–9
    total .... A4–11 to 13
    variation with exposure A4–13
Air movement, effect on comfort A1–6
Air space per person and fresh air supply A1–9
Air spaces, thermal resistances A3–7, 8
    standard values A3–16
Air temperature, outdoor .... A8–6 to 9, 10
Air-to-air heat gain A8–12
Algorithm for interstitial condensation A10–18
Allowance, for height of space, heat loss A9–6
    for intermittent heating A9–5
Alternating solar gain A8–5
Alternating solar gain factor A8–11
Altitude corrections for,
    external summer temperatures A2–18
    external winter temperatures A2–4
    seasonal mean dry bulb isotherms A2–7
    solar radiation A2–61
    wind speed A2–31
Alumina, thermal properties and density A3–31
Amplitude, noise A1–17
Animal bodies, heat emission from A7–4
Annual weather data, UK A2–21
Areal reduction factor, rainfall A2–36
Areas, representative, for air infiltration A4–11, 12

Art galleries, design temperatures A1–5
Artificial lighting, ... A1–10 to 15
    heat gains A1–7, 8; A7–4
Asbestos, thermal properties and density A3–31, 32
Ash, thermal properties and density A3–32
Asphalt roof A3–29
Asphalt, thermal properties and density A3–32
Asymmetric radiation A1–7
Atmospheric pollution A2–38

'B' scale for sound meter A1–15
Background noise A1–16, 17
Ballast, power dissipation of A7–4
Banded weather data, ... A2–21
    based on dry bulb temperature A2–25
    based on global solar radiation A2–22
    based on solar irradiance simulation A2–66
Basal metabolic rate A7–4
Basic infiltration rate A4–3, 10, 11
Beaufort scale of winds and pressures A2–35
Bitumen, thermal properties and density A3–32
Blanket, thermal properties and density A3–32
Block storage heaters A9–9, 10
Blockwork .... A3–8 to 16; A3–23 to 28
Body heat A1–9; A7–3
Boilers,
    control A9–11
    lagging A3–32
    load curves A9–11
    low load operation A9–11
    multiple installations A9–10, 11
    size ratios A9–11
Buoyancy forces (stack effect) A4–11
Bricks and blocks, U values & thermal properties .. A3–8
                      to 16; A10–5
    external walls, single leaf A3–23, 24
    cavity .... A3–25 to 28
Brickwork,
    density A3–22
    standard moisture content A3–6
    thermal properties A3–23, 25
    U values A3–23, 25
    vapour resistivity A10–5
Broadband noise A1–16
Building classification and response factors A8–11;
                          A9–9
Building Regulations and thermal insulation A3–4;
                        A10–14
Building structures, thermal properties ...... A3–3 to 46
    thermal response of .... A5–2 to 8
Bulk density of miscellaneous materials .... A3–31 to 42

'C' scale for sound meter A1–15
Calcium silicate, thermal properties and density .. A3–32
Calculation,
    cooling load .... A9–11 to 13
    heat requirements .... A9–4 to 10
    example, air conditioning A9–17
        heating A9–16

U values for wall, bridged inner leaf A3–10
thermal resistance of slotted block A3–14
thermal resistance of foam filled block A3–15
U values for solid & suspended floors A3–19
Cardboard, thermal properties and density A3–32
Carpeting, thermal properties and density A3–32
Casual gains A7–3; A8–10, 14
Casual gains, instantaneous A8–10
Casual heat gain, ... A8–5, 12
mean A8–10
Cavity construction, external walls, thermal properties ..
A3–25 to 28
Ceiling, panels, maximum vector radiant temperature ...
A1–7
Ceilings,
admittances and decrement factors A8–13
surface resistance A3–7
Cement, thermal properties and density A3–32
Central cooling plant size A9–13
Central plant, size A9–10
Chalk, thermal properties and density A3–33
Charcoal, thermal properties and density A3–33
Churches, intermittent heating A9–9
Cinema, typical occupancy A7–3
Clothing, body insulation A1–3
Cloudiness A2–65
Coal, thermal properties and density A3–33
Cold bridges .... A3–8 to 16
Cold weather data, UK .... A2–4 to 12
Combined method (U value) A3–11
Comfort,
active occupations A1–6
air speed A1–6
design conditions A1–5
humidity A1–9
indices A1–4
requirements A1–5
thermal .... A1–3 to 17
thermal indices A1–4
Comfort zone .... A1–4 to 5
Composite structure, vapour diffusion A10–6
Concrete,
densities and conductivities A3–5, 22
internal floors, U values A3–30
roofs, U values & thermal properties A3–29
solid and suspended floors, U values A3–17
standard moisture content A3–5
walls, U values & thermal properties,
external walls, cavity .... A3–25 to 28
external walls, single leaf A3–23, 24
internal A3–30
Condensation,
control of .... A10–14 to 15
forms of A10–12
interstitial A10–13, 14
local A10–17
permanent A10–12
rate of A10–10
surface A10–13
temporary A10–12, 14
Condensation within structures A10–7, 8
Conductance, hypothetical, derivation of A5–12
Conduction,
masonry, homogeneous A3–5
miscellaneous materials .... A3–31 to 42
testing A3–44
values used in calculating U & Y values ... A3–22
Constant of proportionality, cooling load A9–21
Convection,
coefficients A3–6

loss from humans A1–3
Convective heat transfer coefficient A3–6; A10–4, 5
Convective heating,
height allowance A9–6
load calculations, ... A9–6
air & environmental temperatures ... A5–4 to 9
Cooling data, UK, ... A9–20, 21
all latitudes .... A9–22 to 41
Cooling load A7–3
Cooling load calculation .... A9–11 to 13
Cooling load due to,
air infiltration A9–12
internal gains A9–12
conduction A9–12
outdoor air supply A9–12
solar window gains A9–12
Cooling load, reduction of peak A9–13
tables .... A9–20 to 41
plant size A9–13
Cooling plant capacity .... A9–11 to 41
Cork, thermal properties and density A3–33
Correction to NR criteria A1–16
Colour Rendering Index (CRI) A1–13
Critical speed, vibration A1–18
Cross ventilation A4–7
Cyclic conditions A5–6
energy balance with respect to,
air temperature A5–7
dry resultant temperature A5–7
fabric transfers due to,
external fluctuations A5–6
fluctuations of inside temperature A5–6
ventilation transfers A5–6

Daily swings in indoor temperature A5–10
Damage to hearing by noise A1–15
Damage to structures by vibration A1–18
Dance halls,
outdoor air supply rate A1–9
typical occupancy A7–3
Data processing equipment, heat gains from A7–7
Daylight,
availability A2–36
factor A1–11
Daytime and night-time temperatures A2–4, 6
dBA rating A1–15
Decibels A1–15
Decrement factor (f) A3–21; A8–12, 13
Degree days A2–11
Density,
brickwork A3–22
concrete A3–22
masonry A3–5
miscellaneous .... A3–21 to 42
Department store, design temperatures A1–5
outdoor air supply rate A1–9
typical occupancy A7–3
Derivation of admittance, decrement factor and
surface factor A3–45, 46
Design,
intensities of solar radiation, UK A2–63, 64;
A2–76 to 79
worldwide .... A2–79 to 92
Design conditions A1–5
outside, for summer .... A2–39 to 53
outside, for winter .... A2–39 to 53
Design thermal transmittance A3–4
Design U & Y value tables .... A3–22 to 30

Dew-point temperature, see Temperature, dew-point
Diatomaceous,
      earth A3–33
      insulating powder A3–33
Diffusion resistance factor A10–6
Discharge coefficient, flow through opening A4–4
Displacement & vibration A1–17
Diversity factors,
      central plant, continuous heating A9–10
Double glazing, U values A3–20
Draughts A1–6
Dry resultant temperature, ... A1–5
      variation with air-speed A1–6
Dry resultant temperature at centre of room A5–4; A9–3

Ear damage A1–15
Ear's response to sound A1–15
Effective area of openings A4–7
Effective heat input A8–12
Effective solar heat input A8–11
Effective temperature A1–4
Effects of sounds on man A1–15, 16
Effects of vibration A1–18
Efficiencies, average, of motors and drives A7–6
Electric heaters,
      thermal storage A9–9
Electric motors,
      efficiencies A7–6
      heat gain A7–6
Electrical appliances domestic, heat gain A7–7
Electronic data processing equipment,
      heat gains from A7–6, 7
Emissivity factor A3–6
Energy,
      availability, solar A2–74
      wind A2–30
      balance triangle A5–5
      consumption calculation A2–7
      dissipation in lamps A7–4
      distribution for fluorescent fittings A7–5
Energy inputs, ... A5–7
      radiant energy,
           back losses A5–8
           from which occupants are screened A5–7
           solar gains through windows A5–8
           which fall on room occupants A5–7
Enthalpy, ... A10–15
      specific A10–15
Environmental criteria for design .... A1–3 to 20
Environmental temperature, ... A5–4
      and radiant temperature A5–4
      derivation A5–11
      inside A9–3
      internal A8–5, 14
      mean internal A8–10, 13
      peak internal .... A8–13 to 14
Equal loudness contours A1–15
Equilibrium moisture content A10–4
Equipment, heat gains from .... A7–6 to 9
Equivalent temperatures A1–4
Estimation of cooling requirements,
      notation A9–2, 3
      plant capacity .... A9–2 to 41
Evaporation,
      from humans A1–3
      latent heat of A10–5
      rates A10–4

Exposure, effect on air infiltration A4–13
      permissible to noise A1–16
External,
      design temperature,
           summer .... A2–39 to 53
           winter .... A2–39 to 53
      masonry walls, density & conductivity A3–5
      walls, thermal properties,
           cavity construction .... A3–25 to 28
           single leaf construction A3–23, 24

Fabric losses A8–14; A9–4
Factories,
      air infiltration in A4–15
      design temperatures A1–5
      outdoor air supply rate A1–9
      typical occupancy A7–3
Factors for solar gain .... A9–20 to 41
Felt, thermal properties and density A3–34
Fibreboard, thermal properties and density A3–34
Fibrous materials, vapour resistivity A10–6
Films, vapour resistance of A10–6
Flat roofs,
      U values and thermal properties A3–29
Floor,
      admittances and surface factors ... A3–30; A8–13
      calculation of U values A3–19
      correction to U values A3–18
      covering, thermal properties and density .. A3–34
      internal, U values A3–30
      solid, U values A3–17
      surface resistance A3–7
      suspended ground, thermal resistance A3–17
      suspended, ground A3–18, 19
      suspended, U values A3–17
      thermal properties and density of flooring . A3–34
Flow chart, surface condensation A10–13
Fluorescent fittings, energy distribution for A7–5
Frequency, sound and vibration .... A1–15 to 18

Gas heated appliances, heat gains from A7–8
Gases, thermal properties and density A3–34
Gasket materials, thermal properties and density   A3–34
Glare,
      disability A1–13
      discomfort A1–14
Glass, solar gains .... A9–20 to 41
      thermal properties and density A3–35
      U values for glazing A3–20
Glass fibre, thermal properties and density A3–35
Globe temperature A1–4
Gradient, temperature, vertical air A9–8
Granolithic, thermal properties and density A3–35
Graphical method, interstitial condensation A10–10
Graphite, thermal properties and density A3–35
Gravel, thermal properties and density A3–35
Grease, lubricating, thermal properties and
      density A3–24
Greenwich Mean Time (GMT) A2–3
Ground reflection factors A2–67
Gypsum, thermal properties and density A3–35

Hardboard, thermal properties and density A3–35
Hearing damage A1–15

Heat bridging of construction .... A3–8 to 16
Heat dissipation from,
    animals A7–4
    electric lights and motors A7–5, 6
    electronic data processing units A7–7
    human body A1–4; A7–3
    gas appliances A7–8
Heat emission from human bodies A1–4, A7–3
Heat emission, latent .... A7–3 to 4, A7–7 to 9
    sensible .... A7–3 to 4, A7–7 to 9
Heat from artificial lighting A1–7
Heat gains,
    air to air A8–12
    casual .... A7–3 to 9; A8–5, 12
    from electric appliances A7–7
    from gas appliances A7–8
    from human and animal bodies ... A1–3, 4; A7–3
    from lights and motors A7–5, 6
    internal .... A7–3 to 9
    latent A7–3
    mean, ... A8–5, 13
        casual A8–10
        solar A8–5
    sensible A7–3
    solar, cooling loads .... A9–20 to 41
    structural A8–12
    swing, mean to peak A8–10
    total mean A8–10
Heat input, effective A8–12
    effective solar A8–11
Heating,
    allowance for intermittent A9–9
    application, to maintain dry resultant
    temperature A5–9
    boiler size ratios, ... A9–11
        central plant size A9–10
        diversity factors for central plant A9–10
    highly intermittent A9–9
    intermittent A9–8
    multiple boiler installations A9–10
    optimum boiler control A9–11
    radiant A9–9
    selective systems A9–10
    steady state requirements A9–4
    storage systems A9–9
Heating temperatures,
    external design, UK A2–4
    external design, worldwide .... A2–39 to 53
Heat island effect A2–12
Heat load calculations .... A9–11 to 13
Heat loss,
    intermittent heating A9–8
    temperature gradient in space A9–8
Height,
    allowance, heat loss A9–6
    correction for external design temperature,
        summer A2–18
        winter A2–4
    corrections,
        seasonal mean dry bulb isotherms A2–7
        solar irradiances A2–61
        wind speed A2–31
    walls and exposure A3–7
Heights above sea level, UK A2–5, 6
    worldwide .... A2–40 to 53
Highly intermittent systems A9–9
High temperature radiant systems A9–9
Hollow bricks and blocks, thermal transmittance .. A3–8
        to 16
Homogeneous masonry materials A3–5

Honeycomb paper board,
    thermal properties and density A3–35
Hospitals, design temperatures A1–5
Human,
    body, heat emission from A1–3, 4; A7–3
    ears, response to sound A1–15
    metabolic rate A1–3, 4; A7–3
    reaction to vibration A1–18
Humidity, and comfort A1–9
Hygroscopic materials A10–3

Ice, thermal properties and density A3–35
Illuminance, daylight A2–36
Illumination .... A1–10 to 15
Illumination levels for various tasks, ... A1–10 to 15
    performance A1–11
    pleasantness A1–13
    safety A1–10
Indices, for thermal comfort A1–4
Indoor temperature, peak A8–10
Inside air temperature A5–4, 9–3
Inside design temperature .... A5–4 to 6
Inside environmental temperature A5–4; A9–3
Inside surface resistance A3–7
Installed power for lighting installations A7–5
Instantaneous casual gains A8–10
Intermediate floors, U and Y values A3–30
Intermittent heating, ... A9–8; A10–17
    allowance A9–9
    highly (intermittent) systems A9–9
Intermittent operation A5–17
Internal constructions, thermal properties A3–21
Internal environmental temperature, ... A8–12, 13
    mean A8–10, 13
    peak .... A8–5, 13 to 14
    swing A8–12
Internal floors/ceilings, thermal properties A3–30
Internal heat gains .... A7–3 to 9
Internal resistance to air flow A4–10
Internal walls/partitions, thermal properties ... A3–30
Interstitial condensation A10–9, 12, 13
Ionisation of air A1–9
Irradiance, mean solar A8–5
    solar A8–5, 10, 11
    total solar A8–4
Isolation, from vibration A1–18
Isopleths,
    global solar radiation, UK A2–76
    hourly mean wind speed, UK ... A2–30; A4–10
    maximum 3-second gust speed, UK A2–31
    seasonal degree days, UK A2–12
    wind energy, UK A2–31
Isotherms,
    dry bulb temperature, frequency, UK ... A2–19
    dry bulb temperature, seasonal means, UK
        A2–7
    wet bulb temperature, frequency, UK ... A2–19

Lamp data A1–8
Lamps, ... A1–14
    energy dissipation from A7–4
Lantern light, U value A3–20
Latent heat,
    from appliances A7–7, 9
    from humans and animals A7–3, 4

from miscellaneous appliances ...... A7–7 to 9
gain .... A7–3 to 9
of evaporation A10–5
Laylight, U value A3–20
Level of illuminance A1–12
Lewis relation A10–4
Lighting, ... A1–10 to 15
artificial, hours of use A2–36
for performance A1–13
for pleasantness A1–11
for safety A1–10
heat gains from .... A7–4 to 5
levels .... A1–10 to 13
Lightweight structure,
solar gain factors .... A9–20 to 41
Liquids, thermal properties and density A3–36
Load, cooling plant .... A9–11 to 13; A9–17
Local Apparent Time (sun time) A2–53
Local condensation A10–17
Long wave radiation loss A2–69
Low load operation of boilers A9–11
Luminaires, air handling type A7–4
fluorescent A7–5
recessed A7–5
tungsten A7–4
Luminaires, energy dissipation from .... A7–4 to 5

Materials, fibrous, vapour resistivities A10–6
hygroscopic A10–3
properties and density .... A3–31 to 42
vapour resistivities A10–5
Mean casual heat gain A8–10
Mean internal environmental temperature A5–4;
A8–10, 13
Mean solar gain, ... A8–5, 13
factor A8–5
Mean total solar irradiance A8–4, 5
Metabolic rate,
of human and animal bodies .. A1–3, 4; A7–3, 4
Metals, thermal properties and density A3–36
Meteorological Office A2–3
Mineral wool, thermal properties and density .. A3–36
vapour resistivity A10–5
Miscellaneous,
electrical appliances, heat gains A7–7
gas appliances, heat gains A7–9
Moisture, in building materials A3–6; A10–3
comfort A1–9
loss from humans A1–4
production rates A10–14
sources of A10–14
Moisture content, ... A10–4, 14, 15
of masonry materials .... A3–5 to 6, 43
Motors and drives
efficiencies A7–6
heat gains from A7–6
Multiple boiler installations A9–10

Natural ventilation,
and infiltration rates A4–3, 6
calculation of A4–4
Noise, ... A1–15 to 18
background conditions A1–16, 17
criterion curves A1–16, 17
ratings recommended A1–17
Noise criteria (NC) curves A1–16

Noise rating (NR) curves A1–16
corrections A1–16
levels recommended A1–17
Non-steady state moisture generation A10–15
Non-steady state thermal characteristics ... A3–20, 21
Normal wind exposure A3–7
Nusselt number A10–4

Occupancy, typical, in buildings A7–3
Octave bands A1–16
Odour dilution, by outdoor air A1–9
Offices, design temperatures A1–5
typical occupancy A7–3
Openings, rates of flow through A4–4
Outdoor air supply rates A1–9
Outdoor temperature, mean A8–5
peak A8–5
Outside,
air requirements A1–9
air temperatures .... A5–4; A8–6 to 9, A9–3
design temperature A2–6; A5–4
surface resistance A3–7
Overall thermal performance A3–21
Overheating design, temperate localities A2–65
tropical localities A2–65
Overload capacity, winter design dry bulb
temperatures A2–5

Paints, thermal properties and density A3–37
vapour resistance A10–6
Panel, radiant, design chart A1–7
Paper, thermal properties and density A3–37
Peak indoor temperature A8–10
Peak internal environmental temperature .. A8–5, 13,
14
Peak outdoor temperature A8–5
Perceptible vibrations A1–18
Permanent condensation A10–12
Permeability, vapour A10–6
Permissible exposure to noise A1–16
Perspiration, evaporation of A1–3
Phon A1–15
Pitched roofs, U values and thermal properties A3–29
Plant, capacity .... A2–4; A9–2 to 41
Plastics,
cellular, thermal properties and density A3–37,
38
solid sheet, thermal properties and density .....
A3–38
Plaster, thermal properties and density A3–37
Plasterboard, thermal properties and density .. A3–37
Plastering, thermal properties and density A3–37
Pollution, atmospheric A2–38
Powders, thermal properties and density A3–38
Precipitation, ... A2–35
monthly and annual totals, UK A2–35
monthly and annual totals, worldwide A2–40 to
53
rainfall areal reduction factor A2–36
rainfall duration and frequency A2–36
Preheating time A9–8
Preliminary load assessment A7–5
Pressure coefficient A4–3, 5, 8
Pressure differences, due to stack effect A4–5, 6
due to wind effect A4–5
Prevailing winds, ... A2–32
duration and frequency, UK A2–33

Properties, materials .... A3–31 to 42
Proportional area method (discrete bridges) A3–9

Radiant heat gains A7–4
Radiant heating A9–9
Radiant panel heaters A1–7
Radiant temperature .... A1–6, 19 to 20
Radiation, ... A7–4
    asymmetric and discomfort A1–7
    for comfort .... A1–6 to 8
    from humans A1–3
    short wave A1–8
Radiation factors, ... A2–61
    and banded weather data A2–22
    and overheating design A2–65
    and simulation of solar irradiance A2–65
    direct and diffuse A2–61
    direct (sky clarity), correction A2–65
    overall, correction A2–65
Radiative heat transfer coefficients A3–6
Rates, basic, of air infiltration A4–3, 10, 11
    of air flow through cracks A4–4
    of infiltration for design purposes A4–8
    of natural ventilation A4–6
Recessed luminaires, energy distribution A7–5
Recommended NR levels A1–16
Rectal temperature of animals A7–4
Reflective insulation and airspaces A3–7, 8
Refractory brick, thermal properties and density .....
                                        A3–38, 39
Refractory insulating concrete, thermal properties
    and density A3–39
Refrigeration, plant capacity A9–13
Relative humidity,
    animal rooms A1–9
    comfort A1–9
Reliability, assessment .... A9–13 to 15
Representative areas for infiltration A4–11. 12
Resistance of airspace, thermal .... A3–7 to 8
    vapour A10–5
Resistance, surface A3–7
    thermal A3–5
    to air flow by infiltration A4–10
Resistivities of miscellaneous materials .. A3–31 to 42
Response, to lighting .... A1–10 to 14
    of human ear to sound A1–14
    of humans to vibration A1–18
Response factor of rooms A8–11, 14
Restaurants, design temperatures A1–5
    outdoor air supply rate A1–9
    typical occupancy A7–3
Resultant temperature A1–4; A9–3
Requirements for comfort .... A1–3 to 18
Roof,
    heat loss due to temperature gradient A9–6
    flat and pitched, U values A3–29
    surface resistance A3–7
    vapour barriers in A10–14
Roofing, thermal properties and density A3–39
Roofing felt, thermal properties and density ... A3–39
Roofs, thermal properties, ... A3–29
Room infiltration A4–3, 11

Salt, thermal properties and density A3–39
Sand, thermal properties and density A3–39
Sarking felt, thermal properties and density ... A3–39

Saturation vapour pressure A10–10, 17
Sawdust, thermal properties and density A3–39
Scale of frequencies A1–16
Sealing compound, thermal properties and density ...
                                        A3–39
Sedentary comfort zone A1–4
Sedentary occupations, criteria for A1–4
Sensible heat emissions .... A7–7 to 9
Sensible heat gain A7–3; A10–15
Sensitivity of, human ears A1–15
    human eyes .... A1–10 to 15
    humans to vibration A1–18
Shading coefficients A5–15
Shading factors for solar gain .... A9–20 to 41
Shadow angle, horizontal and vertical A2–57
Single glazing,
    factors for solar gain .... A9–20 to 41
    U values A3–20
Single–sided ventilation A4–7
Sizing,
    cooling plant A9–13
    heating plant A9–10
Skylight, U values A3–20
Smoking, fresh air supply A1–9
Snow, thermal properties and density A3–40
Soil, thermal properties and density A3–40
Sol-air increments, derivation of A5–12
Sol-air temperature, .. A2–69; A5–4; A8–6 to 9; A9–3
    derivation A5–12
    excess temperature difference A9–3
Solar,
    altitude, definition A2–53
        tables A2–54
    azimuth, definition A2–53
        tables A2–54
    cooling loads, ... A2–65
        all latitudes, dry resultant temperature ......
                                    A9–20 to 41
    data A2–53
    energy availability A2–74
    gain, alternating A8–5
    gain factor, alternating mean A8–5
    gains through glass/blind combinations .. A5–14
Solar irradiance, ... A8–5, 10, 11
    basic values, SE England A2–60
    basic values, worldwide .... A2–80 to 92
    calculation of basic values A2–59
    calculation of design values A2–61
    design "maxima", SE England A2–63
    design values, horizontal and vertical
        surfaces A2–66
    design values, sloping surfaces A2–67
    diurnal radiation, SE England A2–64
    height correction factor A2–61
    mean A8–5
    radiation factors A2–61
    total A8–4
Solar irradiation, banded weather data A2–21
    monthly means, isopleths UK ..... A2–76 to 78
    monthly means, SE England A2–75
Solar protection A8–5
Solar radiation A8–11
Solid floors, U values A3–17
Sound, ... A1–15 to 18
    annoyance A1–15
    background condition A1–16
    equal loudness contours A1–15
    exposure times A1–16
    hearing damage A1–15
    human ear, response of A1–15

levels, recommended noise ratings A1–17
magnitude A1–15, 16
spectrum A1–15, 16
speech intelligibility A1–17
waves, effect on man A1–15
Sources of moisture A10–14
Space, per person and fresh air supply A1–8
Specific enthalpy A10–15
Speech intelligibility A1–17
Speech interference level A1–16, 17
Speech levels for telephone conversation A1–17
Stack effect, ... A4–3, 5, 7
    pressure differences due to A4–5
Standard air space resistances A3–8, 16
Standard moisture content for masonry A3–6
Standard octave bands A1–16
Steady state moisture generation A10–15
Steady state thermal characteristics, ... A3–4; A5–13
    energy balances A5–4
Stone, thermal properties and density A3–40
Stoneware, thermal properties and density A3–40
Storage systems A9–9, 10
Structural heat gain A8–12, 14
Structural noise, vibration A1–18
Structure, heavyweight .... A8–11 to 12; A9–9
    lightweight .... A8–11 to 12; A9–9
Summer comfort A1–5
Summertime temperatures in buildings ... A8–3 to 15
Sunpath diagrams A2–57
Sunshine,
    average annual duration, worldwide A2–40
    durations, banded weather data A2–22
Sun time (Local Apparent Time) A2–53
Surface condensation, ... A10–13
    flowchart A10–13
Surface emissivity A3–6
Surface factor(F) A3–21
Surface mass transfer coefficient A10–4, 5
Surface thermal resistances A3–6, 7; A10–8
Surface vapour resistances A10–6
Suspended floors, U values A3–18, 19
Suspended timber ground floors, U values A3–19
Sweating (evaporation) A1–3
Swing, mean to peak, in heat gain A8–10
    in internal environmental temperature .. A8–12

Temperature,
    air and environmental A5–4
    dew point, ... A10–4
      typical winter weather situations A2–7
      warm weather records A2–14
    dry bulb,
      average diurnal range, worldwide A2–40
      banded weather data A2–22
      coincidence of wind speed and low
        temperature, London A2–10
      coincidence with design "maximum"
        solar irradiance A2–62
      coincidence with wet bulb temperature ......
        A2–14
      frequency of mean values, UK A2–5
      height corrections, seasonal mean
        isotherms A2–7
      height corrections, summer design values ....
        A2–18
        winter design values A2–4
      isotherms, frequency, UK A2–19

seasonal means, UK A2–7
simulation of hourly values A2–21
summer design values, derivation A2–18
    worldwide A2–40
town climate A2–12
winter design values, derivation A2–4
    worldwide A2–40
dry resultant A1–5, 6; A5–4; A9–3
effective A1–4
environmental, inside A5–4
equivalent A1–4
globe A1–4
internal environmental A8–12, 13
    mean A8–10, 13
    peak A8–5, 13, 14
interrelation, environmental, air and mean
    radiant A5–4
mean radiant A1–6; A5–4
mean surface A5–4
of animals A7–4
of buildings in summer .... A8–3 to 15
of radiant panels A1–6, 7
outdoor, mean A8–5
    peak A8–5
outside air temperature A5–4, A8–6 to 9; A9–3
ratios, F1 & F2 .... A5–16
resultant, dry A1–5, 6; A5–4; A9–3
sol-air, ... A5–4
    derivation A2–69
    values, SE England .. A2–70 to 74; A8–6 to 9
wet bulb,
    average diurnal range worldwide A2–40
    banded weather data A2–22
    coincidence with dry bulb temperature A2–14
    height correction, summer design
      values A2–18
    isotherms, frequency UK A2–19
    simulation of hourly values A2–21
    summer design values, derivation A2–18
    worldwide A2–40
Temporary condensation A10–12
Terrazzo, thermal properties and density A3–41
Theatre, typical occupancy A7–3
    outdoor air supply rate A1–9
Thermal and other properties of building
    structures .... A3–3 to 42
Thermal admittance (Y value) A3–21; A8–5, 13
Thermal bridges (dynamic conditions) A3–21
Thermal comfort A1–3
Thermal comfort indices A1–4
Thermal conductivity, ... A3–3 to 46; A10–5
    of masonry materials A3–5
    of miscellaneous materials .... A3–31 to 42
Thermal conductivity and conductance testing . A3–44
Thermal environment .... A1–3 to 8
Thermal indices A1–4
Thermal insulation, ... A10–14, 17
    Building Regulations A3–4
    control of condensation by A10–14
Thermal properties of building structures . A3–3 to 46
Thermal properties of miscellaneous materials A3–31
    to 42
Thermal radiation .... A1–6 to 8
Thermal resistance, ... A3–3 to 46
    definition A3–5
    of airspaces .... A3–8 to 16
    of airspaces, standard .... A3–8 to 16
    of clothing A1–3
    of homogeneous materials A3–5
    surface A3–7; A10–8

Thermal resistivity,
    of miscellaneous materials .... A3–31 to 42
Thermal response of buildings, ... A5–2 to 18
    notation A5–2, 3
Thermal transmittance (U value) A3–4; A8–5, 13
Tiles, thermal properties and density A3–41
Timber, thermal properties and density A3–41
Town climate A2–12
Transmittance, thermal A3–4; A8–5, 13
Tungsten luminaires A7–4

U values, ... A3–4; A8–5, 13
    external walls,
        cavity construction .... A3–22 to 24
        single leaf construction .... A3–25 to 28
    floors,
        internal A3–30
        solid and suspended A3–17
    glazing A3–20
    non-homogeneous & heat bridged
        constructions .... A3–8 to 16
    roofs,
        flat A3–29
        pitched A3–29
    simple construction A3–8
    walls,
        internal A3–30
    windows A3–20

Values used in calculating U & Y values A3–22
Vapour, barriers A10–14, 15
    diffusion A10–5, 6
    mass transfer, rate of A10–5, 6, 9
    pressure A10–9, 14
    production A10–14
    resistance A10–5, 6
    resistivity A10–5
Venetian blind factors for solar gain A8–5, 11
Ventilated airspace and thermal resistance A3–16
Ventilation, ... A1–8 & 9
    allowance A4–15; A8–10
    and infiltration .... A4–3 to 15
    cross A4–7
    cyclic transfers A5–6
    for comfort .... A1–8 & 9
    openings A4–8
    physiological considerations A1–8
    rate, minimum A1–9
    rates, ... A4–6; A8–5, 10
        calculation of A4–12
    single-sided A4–7
Vibration, ... A1–17, 18
    damage to structures A1–18
    isolation A1–18
    sensitivity of humans to A1–18
Volume flow rate A4–3, 4

Wall and ceiling boards, thermal properties and
    density A3–41
Wall azimuth A2–53
Wall cavity and airspace resistance A3–8, 16

Wall solar azimuth A2–53
Walls, see also U values .... A3–25 to 28
    admittances and decrement factors A8–13
    exposure and height A3–7
    surface resistance A3–7
Water, thermal properties and density A3–41
Weather data .... A2–3 to 95
Weather,
    annual, UK A2–21
    data, cold, UK A2–4
    data, warm, UK A2–12
    data, worldwide A2–39
    Example Year, UK A2–29
    typical winter situations, UK A2–7
    warm, records, UK A2–12
Wind, ... A2–30
    and infiltration A4–5
    Beaufort scale A2–35
    daily mean speed, banded weather data . A2–22
    effect, pressure differences due to A4–5
    energy isopleths A2–31
    energy variation with height and
        terrain A2–32
    exposure, normal A3–7
    hourly mean speed isopleths A2–30
    maximum 3-second gust speed isopleths,
        UK A2–31
    prevailing, UK A2–32
    prevailing direction and frequency, UK .. A2–33
    speed and coincidence with low temperatures,
        London A2–10
    speed, variation with height and terrain   A2–31;
                                    A4–5
Wind speed and exposure A3–7
Windows,
    air infiltration through A4–9
    infiltration coefficient A4–9
    surfaces factors and admittances A8–13
    U values A3–20
Winter external design temperature,
    UK A2–4
    worldwide .... A3–40 to 53
Wood intermediate floors, U values A3–30
Wood waste board, thermal properties and
    density A3–42
Wood wool building slabs, thermal properties
    and density A3–42
World weather data, ... A2–39 to 53
    basic solar irradiances A2–80
    dry bulb temperatures,
        average diurnal range A2–40
        summer design values A2–40
        winter design values A2–40
    external design temperatures A2–18
    heights above sea level .... A2–40 to 53
    precipitation, monthly and annual totals   A2–40
                                     to 53
    sunshine, average annual duration   A2–40 to 53
    wet bulb temperatures, summer design
        values .... A2–40 to 53

Y values A3–21; A8–5, 11

Zone, comfort A1–4